Lecture Notes in Computer Science 11788

More information about this series at http://www.springer.com/series/7409

Alberto H. F. Laender · Barbara Pernici ·
Ee-Peng Lim · José Palazzo M. de Oliveira (Eds.)

Conceptual Modeling

38th International Conference, ER 2019
Salvador, Brazil, November 4–7, 2019
Proceedings

 Springer

Editors
Alberto H. F. Laender (iD)
Universidade Federal de Minas Gerais
Belo Horizonte, Brazil

Barbara Pernici
Politecnico di Milano
Milan, Italy

Ee-Peng Lim
Singapore Management University
Singapore, Singapore

José Palazzo M. de Oliveira
Univ Federal do Rio Grande do Sul
Porto Alegre, Brazil

ISSN 0302-9743 ISSN 1611-3349 (electronic)
Lecture Notes in Computer Science
ISBN 978-3-030-33222-8 ISBN 978-3-030-33223-5 (eBook)
https://doi.org/10.1007/978-3-030-33223-5

LNCS Sublibrary: SL3 – Information Systems and Applications, incl. Internet/Web, and HCI

This Springer imprint is published by the registered company Springer Nature Switzerland AG
The registered company address is: Gewerbestrasse 11, 6330 Cham, Switzerland

Preface

We are proud to present the proceedings of the 38th International Conference on Conceptual Modeling (ER 2019), held in Salvador, Brazil, during November 4–7, 2019. The ER conference series is an annual premier forum featuring the latest research breakthroughs in theories, models, methods, and tools for developing, communicating, and applying conceptual models.

This year, we are very delighted to celebrate 40 years of ER and to bring the conference back to Brazil after 10 years. We have put together a strong scientific program consisting of keynote talks by four distinguished speakers, oral presentations of accepted main conference papers, a doctoral consortium, seven workshops, and four tutorials. For the keynote talks, we were extremely honored to have Veda C. Storey, the winner of Peter Chen Award 2018 and Full Professor of Computer Information Systems and Professor of Computer Science at the Georgia State University (USA), Marco A. Casanova, Professor of Computer Science at the Pontifical Catholic University of Rio de Janeiro (Brazil), Barbara Weber, Professor for Software Systems Programming and Development at the University of St. Gallen (Switzerland), and Paul D. Nielsen, Director and CEO of the Software Engineering Institute (USA), sharing their research and practice insights. The industrial keynote talk was delivered by C. Mohan, an outstanding researcher from IBM Research, an IBM fellow, and a database community leader bestowed with many awards and honors.

For the main conference, we received 142 paper submissions of which 22 were accepted as full papers and another 22 were accepted as short papers. The overall acceptance rate was about 31%. In our review process, each paper was reviewed by three PC members and one senior PC member to ensure that all accepted papers were carefully selected. All the accepted papers were given presentation timeslots distributed into 12 paper sessions. In addition, ER 2019 hosted a Doctoral Consortium for PhD students and academics to share their research ideas, to seek advice, and to explore collaboration in conceptual modeling research. The conference also included an ER Forum to cover emerging and early stage research, as well as poster and demo sessions to increase opportunities for interaction.

Finally, we would like to thank all participants, authors, reviewers, and organizers of the conference for their contribution to making ER 2019 a successful event. We thank Springer for their proceedings support and EasyChair for its wonderful conference management system. Special thanks to our many sponsors and to the ER Steering Committee for their support and advice.

November 2019

Alberto H. F. Laender
Barbara Pernici
Ee-Peng Lim
José Palazzo M. de Oliveira

Organization

Conference General Co-chairs

José Palazzo M. de Oliveira — Universidade Federal do Rio Grande do Sul, Brazil
Vaninha Vieira dos Santos — Universidade Federal da Bahia, Brazil

Program Committee Co-chairs

Alberto H. F. Laender — Universidade Federal de Minas Gerais, Brazil
Barbara Pernici — Politecnico di Milano, Italy
Ee-Peng Lim — Singapore Management University, Singapore

Industrial Chair

Ana Carolina Salgado — Universidade Federal de Pernambuco, Brazil

Workshop Co-chairs

Giancarlo Guizzardi — Free University of Bolzano-Bozen, Italy
Frederik Gailly — Ghent University, Belgium
Rita Suzana Pitangueira Maciel — Universidade Federal da Bahia, Brazil

Poster and Tools Demonstration Co-chairs

Renata Guizzardi — Universidade Federal do Espírito Santo, Brazil
Daniela Barreiro Claro — Universidade Federal da Bahia, Brazil

Tutorial Co-chairs

Mirella M. Moro — Universidade Federal de Minas Gerais, Brazil
Jolita Ralyté — University of Geneva, Switzerland

Doctoral Symposium Chairs

Samira Si-Said Cherfi — Conservatoire National des Arts et Métiers, France
Vanessa Braganholo — Universidade Federal Fluminense, Brazil

Forum Chair

Ignacio Panach Navarrete — Universitat de València, Spain

Publicity Chair

José Palazzo M. de Oliveira   Universidade Federal do Rio Grande do Sul, Brazil

Local Arrangements Chairs

Daniela Barreiro Claro   Universidade Federal da Bahia, Brazil
Fabiola Greve   Universidade Federal da Bahia, Brazil
Rita Suzana Pitangueira   Universidade Federal da Bahia, Brazil
Maciel

Web Master

Gabriel Machado Lunardi   Universidade Federal do Rio Grande do Sul, Brazil

Treasurer

Stephen W. Liddle   Brigham Young University, USA

ER Steering Committee Liaison

Sudha Ram   University of Arizona, USA

Program Committee

Jacky Akoka   Conservatoire National des Arts et Métiers, France
João Paulo Almeida   Universidade Federal do Espírito Santo, Brazil
Yuan An   Drexel University, USA
João Araújo   Universidade NOVA de Lisboa, Portugal
Paolo Atzeni   Università degli Studi Roma Tre, Italy
Claudia P. Ayala   Universitat Politècnica de Catalunya, Spain
Fatma Başak Aydemir   Boğaziçi University, Turkey
Wolf-Tilo Balke   Technische Universität Braunschweig, Germany
Zhifeng Bao   RMIT University, Australia
Ladjel Bellatreche   LIAS, ENSMA, France
Sourav S. Bhowmick   Nanyang Technological University, Singapore
Sandro Bimonte   IRSTEA, France
José Borbinha   Universidade de Lisboa, Portugal
Mokrane Bouzeghoub   UVSQ, CNRS, France
Shawn Bowers   Gonzaga University, USA
Stephane Bressan   National University of Singapore, Singapore
Robert Andrei Buchmann   Babeş-Bolyai University of Cluj-Napoca, Romania
Cristina Cabanillas   Vienna University of Economics and Business, Austria
Diego Calvanese   Free University of Bozen-Bolzano, Italy
Maria Luiza Campos   Universidade Federal do Rio de Janeiro, Brazil
Cinzia Cappiello   Politecnico di Milano, Italy

Silvana Castano	Università degli Studi di Milano, Italy
Stefano Ceri	Politecnico di Milano, Italy
Luca Cernuzzi	Universidad Católica, Paraguay
Reynold Cheng	The University of Hong Kong, China
Samira Si-Said Cherfi	Conservatoire National des Arts et Métiers, France
Meng-Fen Chiang	Singapore Management University, Singapore
Roger Chiang	University of Cincinnati, USA
Isabelle Comyn-Wattiau	ESSEC Business School, France
Dolors Costal	Universitat Politècnica de Catalunya, Spain
Altigran S. da Silva	Universidade Federal do Amazonas, Brazil
Fabiano Dalpiaz	Utrecht University, The Netherlands
Valeria De Antonellis	Università degli Studi di Brescia, Italy
Sergio De Cesare	University of Westminster, UK
Gill Dobbie	The University of Auckland, New Zealand
Marlon Dumas	University of Tartu, Estonia
Johann Eder	Alpen-Adria-Universität Klagenfurt, Austria
Vadim Ermolayev	Zaporizhzhia National University, Ukraine
Sergio España	Utrecht University, The Netherlands
Ricardo A. Falbo	Universidade Federal do Espírito Santo, Brazil
Hans-Georg Fill	University of Fribourg, Switzerland
Xavier Franch	Universitat Politècnica de Catalunya, Spain
Ulrich Frank	Universität Duisburg-Essen, Germany
Frederik Gailly	Ghent University, Belgium
Hong Gao	Harbin Institute of Technology, China
Ming Gao	East China Normal University, China
Faiez Gargouri	Institut Supérieur d'Informatique et de Multimédia de Sfax, Tunisia
Marcela Genero	Universidad de Castilla-La Mancha, Spain
Aurona Gerber	University of Pretoria, South Africa
Mohamed Gharzouli	Constantine 2 University, Algeria
Aditya Ghose	University of Wollongong, Australia
Paolo Giorgini	Università di Trento, Italy
Matteo Golfarelli	Università degli Studi di Bologna, Italy
Cesar Gonzalez-Perez	Incipit, CSIC, Spain
Georg Grossmann	University of South Australia, Australia
Nicola Guarino	ISTC, CNR, Italy
Esther Guerra	Universidad Autónoma de Madrid, Spain
Giancarlo Guizzardi	Free University of Bolzano-Bozen, Italy
Renata Guizzardi	Universidade Federal do Espírito Santo, Brazil
Claudio Gutierrez	Universidad de Chile, Chile
Sven Hartmann	Clausthal University of Technology, Denmark
Martin Henkel	Stockholm University, Sweden
Jennifer Horkoff	University of Gothenburg and Chalmers University of Technology, Sweden
Hao Huang	Wuhan University, China
Chih-Chieh Hung	Tamkang University, Taiwan

Shareeful Islam	University of East London, UK
Matthias Jarke	RWTH Aachen University, Germany
Manfred Jeusfeld	University of Skövde, Sweden
Paul Johannesson	Royal Institute of Technology, Sweden
Ivan Jureta	University of Namur, Belgium
Hung-Yu Kao	National Cheng Kung University, Taiwan
Gerti Kappel	Vienna University of Technology, Austria
Dimitris Karagiannis	University of Vienna, Austria
Agnes Koschmider	Karlsruhe Institute of Technology, Germany
John Krogstie	Norwegian University of Science and Technology, Norway
Dongwon Lee	The Pennsylvania State University, USA
Mong Li Lee	National University of Singapore, Singapore
Julio Cesar Leite	Pontifícia Universidade Católica do Rio de Janeiro, Brazil
Stephen Liddle	Brigham Young University, USA
Tok Wang Ling	National University of Singapore, Singapore
Sebastian Link	The University of Auckland, New Zealand
Jiaheng Lu	University of Helsinki, Finland
Bernadette Farias Lóscio	Universidade Federal de Pernambuco, Brazil
Hui Ma	Victoria University of Wellington, New Zealand
Wolfgang Maass	Saarland University, Germany
Heinrich C. Mayr	Alpen-Adria-Universität Klagenfurt, Austria
Claudia Bauzer Medeiros	Universidade de Campinas, Brazil
Lourdes Moreno	Universidad Carlos III de Madrid, Spain
Regina Motz	Universidad de la República, Uruguay
Haralambos Mouratidis	University of Brighton, UK
John Mylopoulos	University of Toronto, Canada
Wilfred Ng	The Hong Kong University of Science and Technology, China
Quoc Viet Hung Nguyen	Griffith University, Australia
Selmin Nurcan	Université Paris 1 Panthéon-Sorbonne, France
Antoni Olivé	Universitat Politècnica de Catalunya, Spain
Andreas L. Opdahl	University of Bergen, Norway
Jinsoo Park	Seoul National University, South Korea
Jeffrey Parsons	Memorial University of Newfoundland, Canada
Oscar Pastor	Universitat Politècnica de Valencia, Spain
Zhiyong Peng	State Key Laboratory of Software Engineering, China
Fabio Porto	National Laboratory of Scientific Computation, Brazil
Henderik Proper	Public Research Centre Henri Tudor, Luxembourg
Christoph Quix	Fraunhofer, Germany
Jolita Ralyté	University of Geneva, Switzerland
Sudha Ram	University of Arizona, USA
Manfred Reichert	University of Ulm, Germany
Hajo A. Reijers	Utrecht University, The Netherlands
Iris Reinhartz-Berger	University of Haifa, Israel

Manuel Resinas	Universidad de Sevilla, Spain
Daniel Riesco	Universidad Nacional de San Luis, Argentina
Colette Rolland	Université Paris 1 Panthéon-Sorbonne, France
Marcela Ruiz	Utrecht University, The Netherlands
Antonio Ruiz-Cortés	Universidad de Sevilla, Spain
Motoshi Saeki	Tokyo Institute of Technology, Japan
Melike Sah	Near East University, Cyprus
Klaus-Dieter Schewe	Software Competence Center Hagenberger, Germany
Jie Shao	University of Science and Technology of China, China
Peretz Shoval	Ben-Gurion University, Israel
Pnina Soffer	University of Haifa, Israel
Il-Yeol Song	Drexel University, USA
Veda C. Storey	Georgia State University, USA
Stefan Strecker	University of Hagen, Germany
Arnon Sturm	Ben-Gurion University, Israel
David Taniar	Monash University, Australia
Ernest Teniente	Universitat Politècnica de Catalunya, Spain
Bernhard Thalheim	Christian-Albrechts-Universität zu Kiel, Germany
Juan-Carlos Trujillo	Universidad de Alicante, Spain
Panos Vassiliadis	University of Ioannina, Greece
Gottfried Vossen	ERCIS Muenster, Germany
Chaokun Wang	Tsinghua University, China
Hongzhi Wang	Harbin Institute of Technology, China
Xianzhi Wang	University of Technology Sydney, Australia
Xiaoli Wang	Xiamen University, China
Mathias Weske	University of Potsdam, Germany
Manuel Wimmer	Johannes Kepler Universität Linz, Austria
Carson Woo	The University of British Columbia, Canada
Robert Wrembel	Poznan University of Technology, Poland
Shuichiro Yamamoto	Nagoya University, Japan
Eric Yu	University of Toronto, Canada
Apostolos Zarras	University of Ioannina, Greece
Jelena Zdravkovic	Stockholm University, Sweden
Wenjie Zhang	The University of New South Wales, Australia
Xiangmin Zhou	RMIT University, Australia
Xuan Zhou	Renmin University of China, China

External Reviewers

Kevin Andrews
Kimon Batoulis
Iris Beerepoot
Mario Marcelo Beron
Robert Bill
Dominik Bork
Tsz Nam Chan
Yuxing Chen
Kelli de Faria Cordeiro
Sybren De Kinderen
Juan de Lara
Victoria Döller
Irene Bedilia Estrada Torres
Marco Franceschetti
Fáber Danilo Giraldo Velásques
Israel Gonzalez-Carrasco
Tobias Grubenmann
Wided Guédria
Stephan Haarmann
Fayçal Hamdi
Anasthasia Haryanto
Chengkun He
Leschek Homann
Klaus Kammerer
Jelmer Koorn

Robin Kraft
Vimal Kunnummel
Julius Köpke
Jens Lechtenbörger
Xiaodong Li
Xixi Lu
José Luis López-Cuadrado
Xavier Oriol
Cristhian Parra
Daniel Ramos da Silva
Simon Remy
Alejandro Sanchez
Michael Stach
Jihae Suh
Pablo Trinidad
Jan Martijn Van Der Werf
Bernhard Wally
Zhuo Wang
Sabine Wolny
Pengfei Xu
Qian Yan
Gongsheng Yuan
Chao Zhang
Zichen Zhu

Organized By

Instituto de Informática, Universidade Federal do Rio Grande do Sul, Brazil
Departamento de Ciência da Computação, Universidade Federal da Bahia, Brazil

Sponsored By

The ER Institute
Sociedade Brasileira de Computação (Brazilian Computer Society)

Invited Talks

Next Generation Modeling Environments

Barbara Weber[1,2]

[1] Institute of Computer Science, University of St. Gallen, 9000 St. Gallen,
Switzerland
barbara.weber@unisg.ch
[2] Software and Process Engineering, Technical University of Denmark, 2800 Kgs.
Lyngby, Denmark

Abstract. Conceptual models play an important role in many organizations. They serve as tools for communication and documentation, are often a central part in process improvement initiatives, and are key to the development and evolution of information systems. Existing modeling tools typically support end users in a rather generic and non-personalized manner. However, users not only differ in their modeling expertise and the challenges they encounter while modeling, but also in their preferences. Therefore, they would benefit from a new generation of modeling environments that are highly personalized and adapt themselves to users' needs. This keynote presents a vision of such modeling environments with a focus on process modeling. Next generation process modeling environments are not limited to graphical user interfaces, but allow end users to interact with them in their preferred modality (e.g., natural language user interfaces like chatbots and conversational agents). For example, recent research by [4] shows how a process model can be transformed into a conversational agent to guide process actors through the process steps. Another key characteristic of next generation process modeling environments is the continuous collection of multi-modal data. Amongst others data collection may include behavioral data (e.g., user interactions), data on how the model and its properties change over time, and (neuro-)physiological data of the modeler collected with biosensors. Next generation modeling environments analyze the collected data while the system is being used to obtain insights and continuously adapt themselves in response to the obtained insights. For example, data about the model and how it has evolved over time can be used to predict the expertise level of a modeler [3]. Behavioral data can be exploited not only to derive behavioral patterns or modeling styles [1, 5], but also to automatically detect the modeling activity a user is currently engaged in [2]. Neuro-physiological data, in turn, can be used in a learning setting to assess the cognitive state of a user (e.g., identify states of high cognitive load) and to adapt the difficulty of the materials provided accordingly [7]. With inherent data collection and analysis capabilities, the boundaries between development and evaluation will increasingly blur and continuous experimentation will become an integral part of system development. Our work on Cheetah Experimental Platform is a first step towards this direction [6]. The keynote highlights this potential with several examples from our research and touches upon challenges that come with the development of next generation modeling environments.

References

1. Abbad Andaloussi, A., Burattin, A., Slaats, T., Petersen, A.C.M., Hildebrandt, T.T., Weber, B.: Exploring the understandability of a hybrid process design artifact based on DCR graphs. In: Reinhartz-Berger, I., Zdravkovic, J., Gulden, J., Schmidt, R. (eds.) BPMDS/EMMSAD -2019. LNBIP, vol. 352, pp. 69–84. Springer, Cham (2019). https://doi.org/10.1007/978-3-030-20618-5_5

2. Burattin, A., Kaiser, M., Neurauter, M., Weber, B.: Learning process modeling phases from modeling interactions and eye tracking data. Data Knowl. Eng. **121**, 1–17 (2019)

3. Burattin, A., et al.: Who is behind the model? classifying modelers based on pragmatic model features. In: Weske, M., Montali, M., Weber, I., vom Brocke, J. (eds.) BPM 2018. LNCS, vol. 11080, pp. 322–338. Springer, Cham (2018). https://doi.org/10.1007/978-3-319-98648-7_19

4. López, A., Sànchez-Ferreres, J., Carmona, J., Padró, L.: From process models to chatbots. In: Giorgini, P., Weber, B. (eds.) CAiSE 2019. LNCS, vol. 11483, pp. 383–398. Springer, Cham (2019). https://doi.org/10.1007/978-3-030-21290-2_24

5. Pinggera, J., et al.: Styles in business process modeling: an exploration and a model. Softw. Syst. Model. **14**(3), 1055–1080 (2015)

6. Pinggera, J., Zugal, S., Weber, B.: Investigating the process of process modeling with cheetah experimental platform. In: Mutschler, B., Recker, J., Wieringa, R.J., Ralyté, J., Plebani, P., (eds.) Proceedings of the 1st International Workshop on Empirical Research in Process-Oriented Information Systems, in conjunction with the CAISE 2010, ER-POIS@CAiSE 2010, CEUR Workshop Proceedings, Hammamet, Tunisia, 8 June 2010, vol. 603, pp. 13–18. CEUR-WS.org (2010)

7. Weber, B., et al.: Fixation patterns during process model creation: initial steps toward neuro-adaptive process modeling environments. In: Bui, T.X., Jr., Sprague, R.H. (eds.) 49th Hawaii International Conference on System Sciences, HICSS 2016, Koloa, HI, USA, 5–8 January 2016, pp. 600–609. IEEE Computer Society (2016)

State of Permissionless and Permissioned Blockchains: Myths and Reality

C. Mohan

IBM Almaden Research Center, San Jose, CA 95120, USA
cmohan@us.ibm.com @seemohan

Abstract. It has been a decade since the concept of blockchain was invented as the underlying core data structure of the permissionless or public Bitcoin cryptocurrency network. Since then, several cryptocurrencies, and associated concepts like tokens and ICOs have emerged. After much speculation and hype, significant number of them have become problematic or worthless, even though some countries have embraced them! The permissionless blockchain system Ethereum emerged by generalizing the use of blockchains to manage any kind of asset, be it physical or purely digital, with the introduction of the concept of Smart Contracts. Over the years, numerous myths have developed with respect to the purported utility and the need for permissionless blockchains. The adoption and further adaptation of blockchains and smart contracts for use in the permissioned or private environments is what I consider to be useful and of practical consequence. Hence, the technical aspects of only private blockchain systems will be the focus of my ER 2019 keynote. Along the way, I will bust many myths associated with permissionless blockchains. I will also compare traditional database technologies with blockchain systems' features and identify desirable future research topics.

Keywords: Bitcoin · Smart contracts · Private blockchains · Hyperledger fabric · Enterprise ethereum alliance · Quorum · R3 corda · Sawtooth · Cryptocurrencies · Byzantine faults · Consensus

Bibliography

1. Alibaba: Blockchain as a Service. https://www.alibabacloud.com/help/product/84950.htm
2. Alibaba Group: Alibaba Cloud Launches Global Blockchain as a Service, October 2018. https://www.alibabagroup.com/en/news/press_pdf/p181024.pdf
3. AWS: Amazon Managed Blockchain. https://aws.amazon.com/managed-blockchain/
4. AWS: Amazon Quantum Ledger Database (QLDB). https://aws.amazon.com/qldb/
5. Androulaki, E., et al.: Hyperledger fabric: a distributed operating system for permissioned blockchains. In: Proceedings of 13th EuroSys Conference, Porto, Portugal, April 2018. https://arxiv.org/pdf/1801.10228

6. Androulaki, E., Cachin, C., De Caro, A., Kokoris-Kogias, E.: Channels: horizontal scaling and confidentiality on permissioned blockchains. In: Proceedings of European Symposium on Research in Computer Security, Barcelona, Spain, September 2018

7. Baidu: Blockchain Solution. https://cloud.baidu.com/solution/blockchain.html

8. Baidu: Super Chain – XuperChain. https://xchain.baidu.com/

9. Bakshi, S., Yarmosh, Y., Zhang, L., Freund, A.: Enterprise Ethereum Alliance Off-Chain Trusted Compute Specification V0.5, October 2018. https://entethalliance.org/wp-content/uploads/2018/11/EEA_Off_Chain_Trusted_Compute_Specification_V0_5-1.pdf

10. BigchainDB: BigchainDB 2.0 – The Blockchain Database, May 2018. https://www.bigchaindb.com/whitepaper/bigchaindb-whitepaper.pdf

11. Brandenburger, M., Cachin, C., Kapitza, R., Sorniotti, A.: Blockchain and Trusted Computing: Problems, Pitfalls, and Solution for Hyperledger Fabric, May 2018. https://arxiv.org/pdf/1805.08541

12. Brown, R.: The Corda Platform: An Introduction, May 2018. https://www.corda.net/content/corda-platform-whitepaper.pdf

13. Burnett, D., Coote, R., Nevile, C., Noble, G. (eds.) Enterprise Ethereum Alliance – Enterprise Ethereum Client Specification V2, October 2018. https://entethalliance.org/wp-content/uploads/2018/11/EEA_Enterprise_Ethereum_Client_Specification_V2.pdf

14. Buterin, V.: Ethereum: The Ultimate Smart Contract and Autonomous Corporation Platform on the Blockchain, December 2013. https://web.archive.org/web/20131219030753/vitalik.ca/ethereum.html

15. Dinh, A., Wang, J., Chen, G., Liu, R., Ooi, B.C., Tan, K.-L.: Blockbench: a framework for analyzing private blockchains. In: Proceedings of ACM SIGMOD International Conference on Management of Data, Chicago, USA, June 2017. http://www.comp.nus.edu.sg/~ooibc/blockbench.pdf

16. Dinh, A., Zhang, M., Ooi, B.C., Chen, G.: Untangling blockchain: a data processing view of blockchain systems. IEEE Trans. Knowl. Data Eng. **30**(7), 1366–1385 (2018)

17. Ethereum: A Next-Generation Smart Contract and Decentralized Application Platform, March 2019. https://github.com/ethereum/wiki/wiki/White-Paper

18. FISCO BCOS: FISCO BCOS Featured Cases, September 2018. https://www.fisco-bcos.org/assets/docs/FISCO%20BCOS%20-%20Featured%20Cases.pdf

19. FISCO BCOS: The Building Block of Open Consortium Chain. https://www.fisco-bcos.org/

20. Gorenflo, C., Lee, S., Golab, L., Keshav, S.: FastFabric: Scaling Hyperledger Fabric to 20,000 Transactions per Second, March 2019. https://arxiv.org/pdf/1901.00910.pdf

21. Greenspan, G.: The Blockchain Immutability Myth, May 2017. https://www.coindesk.com/blockchain-immutability-myth

22. Greenspan, G.: Three (non-pointless) permissioned blockchains in production, November 2017. https://www.multichain.com/blog/2017/11/three-non-pointless-blockchains-production/

23. Greenspan, G.: R3 Corda: Deep Dive and Technical Review - A Detailed Look at the Non-Blockchain Blockchain, May 2018. https://www.multichain.com/blog/2018/05/r3-corda-deep-dive-and-technical-review/
24. Greenspan, G.: Smart Contract Showdown: Hyperledger Fabric vs MultiChain vs Ethereum vs Corda - There's More than One Way to Put Code on a Blockchain, December 2018. https://www.multichain.com/blog/2018/12/smart-contract-showdown/
25. Greenspan, G.: Multichain 2.0 Beta Released, December 2018. https://www.multichain.com/blog/2018/12/multichain-2-0-beta-released/
26. Hearn, M.: Corda: A Distributed Ledger, November 2016. https://www.corda.net/content/corda-technical-whitepaper.pdf
27. Hileman, G., Rauchs, M.: Global Blockchain Benchmarking Study, The Cambridge Center for Alternative Finance, September 2017. https://www.jbs.cam.ac.uk/fileadmin/user_upload/research/centres/alternative-finance/downloads/2017-09-27-ccaf-globalbchain.pdf
28. Huawei: Huawei Blockchain Whitepaper - Toward a Trusted Digital World, April 2018. https://static.huaweicloud.com/upload/files/pdf/20180416/20180416142450_61761.pdf
29. Hyperledger: Five Hyperledger Blockchain Projects Now in Production, November 2018. https://www.hyperledger.org/blog/2018/11/30/six-hyperledger-blockchain-projects-now-in-production
30. Hyperledger: Case Study: How Walmart Brought Unprecedented Transparency to the Food Supply Chain with Hyperledger Fabric, February 2019. https://www.hyperledger.org/wp-content/uploads/2019/02/Hyperledger_CaseStudy_Walmart_Printable_V4.pdf
31. Hyperledger Caliper: Getting Started. https://hyperledger.github.io/caliper/docs/1_Getting_Started.html
32. IBM: IBM Blockchain Platform – Technical Overview, February 2019. https://www-01.ibm.com/common/ssi/cgi-bin/ssialias?htmlfid=KUW12555USEN&
33. IBM: Maersk. TradeLens Documentation. https://docs.tradelens.com/
34. IEEE: IEEE Blockchain Standards. https://blockchain.ieee.org/standards
35. Intel: Intel Select Solution for Blockchain: Hyperledger Fabric, February 2019. https://www.intel.com/content/dam/www/public/us/en/documents/solution-briefs/select-block-chain-hyperledger-fabric-sb-final.pdf
36. ISO: ISO/TC 307 Blockchain and Distributed Ledger Technologies. https://www.iso.org/committee/6266604.html
37. JD.com: JD Launches Blockchain Open Platform, August 2018. https://jdcorporateblog.com/jd-launches-blockchain-open-platform/
38. JP Morgan: Quorum: Ethereum for Enterprise Applications, October 2017. https://github.com/jpmorganchase/quorum-docs/blob/master/Quorum_Architecture_20171016.pdf
39. JP Morgan: Quorum Whitepaper v0.2, September 2018. https://github.com/jpmorganchase/quorum-docs/blob/master/Quorum%20Whitepaper%20v0.2.pdf
40. Microsoft: Azure Blockchain Workbench Documentation. https://docs.microsoft.com/en-us/azure/blockchain/workbench/

41. Mohan, C.: State of public and private blockchains: myths and reality. In: Proceedings of ACM SIGMOD International Conference on Management of Data, Amsterdam, The Netherlands, July 2019. http://bit.ly/sigBcP

42. Mohan, C.: Permissioned/Private Blockchains and Databases. http://bit.ly/CMbcDB

43. Murthy, C.: Blockchain DB-unked, August 2016. https://ripple.com/files/db-unked.pdf

44. Nakamoto, S.: Bitcoin: A Peer-to-Peer Electronic Cash System, 2008. https://bitcoin.org/bitcoin.pdf

45. Narayanan, A., Clark, J.: Bitcoin's academic pedigree. In: ACM Queue, vol. 15, no. 4, August 2017. https://queue.acm.org/detail.cfm?id=3136559

46. Nasir, Q., Qasse, I., Talib, M.A., Nassif, A.B.: Performance analysis of hyperledger fabric platforms. Secur. Commun. Netw. **2018**, 14 (2018). Article ID 3976093. http://downloads.hindawi.com/journals/scn/2018/3976093.pdf

47. Natoli, C., Gramoli, V.: The blockchain anomaly. In: Proceedings of IEEE 15th International Symposium on Network Computing and Applications, Cambridge, USA, November 2016. https://arxiv.org/pdf/1605.05438

48. Natoli, C., Gramoli, V.: The balance attack or why forkable blockchains are ill-suited for consortium. In: Proceedings of 47th Annual IEEE/IFIP International Conference on Dependable Systems and Networks, Denver, USA, June 2017. https://research.csiro.au/data61/wp-content/uploads/sites/85/2016/08/balance_attack.pdf

49. Oracle: Oracle Cloud - Using Oracle Blockchain Platform, Release 19.1.3, March 2019. https://docs.oracle.com/en/cloud/paas/blockchain-cloud/user/using-oracle-blockchain-platform.pdf

50. Rauchs, M. et al.: Distributed Ledger Technology Systems – A Conceptual Framework, The Cambridge Center for Alternative Finance, August 2018. https://www.jbs.cam.ac.uk/fileadmin/user_upload/research/centres/alternative-finance/downloads/2018-10-26-conceptualising-dlt-systems.pdf

51. Rauchs, M. et al.: 2nd Global Cryptoasset Benchmarking Study, The Cambridge Center for Alternative Finance, December 2018. https://www.jbs.cam.ac.uk/fileadmin/user_upload/research/centres/alternative-finance/downloads/2019-01-ccaf-2nd-global-cryptoasset-benchmarking.pdf

52. Ripple: Product Overview, October 2017. https://ripple.com/files/ripple_product_overview.pdf

53. SAP: Blockchain Application Enablement. https://help.sap.com/viewer/product/BLOCKCHAIN_APPLICATION_ENABLEMENT/BLOCKCHAIN/en-US

54. SAP: Hyperledger Fabric on SAP Cloud Platform. https://help.sap.com/viewer/product/HYPERLEDGER_FABRIC/BLOCKCHAIN/en-US

55. Sawtooth: Hyperledger Sawtooth Documentation, V1.1.4. https://sawtooth.hyperledger.org/docs/core/releases/latest/

56. Schuster, B.: The Ripple Currency Problem: Why Permissioned Blockchains Will Devalue XRP, December 2017. https://hackernoon.com/the-ripple-currency-problem-why-permissioned-blockchains-will-devalue-xrp-d79aef84c074

57. Tencent: TBaas. https://cloud.tencent.com/document/product/663

58. Thakker, P., Senthil Nathan, N., Viswanathan, B.: Performance benchmarking and optimizing hyperledger fabric blockchain platform. In: Proceeding of 26th IEEE International Symposium on the Modeling, Analysis, and Simulation of Computer and Telecommunication Systems, Milwaukee, USA, September 2018. https://arxiv.org/pdf/1805.11390.pdf

59. Walch, A.: Open source operational risk: should public blockchains serve as financial market infrastructure? In: Lee, D., Chuen, K., Deng, R. (eds.) Handbook of Digital Banking and Internet Finance, vol. 2. Elsevier (2017). https://ssrn.com/abstract=2879239

60. Walch, A.: Deconstructing 'Decentralization': exploring the core claim of crypto systems. In: Crypto Assets: Legal and Monetary Perspectives January 2019. (to appear). https://ssrn.com/abstract=3326244

61. Wang, S., et al.: An efficient storage engine for blockchain and forkable applications. In: Proceedings of International Conference on Very Large Data Bases, Rio de Janeiro, Brazil, August 2018. http://www.vldb.org/pvldb/vol11/p1137-wang.pdf

62. Wikipedia: Blockchain (database). https://en.wikipedia.org/wiki/Blockchain_(database)

Contents

Domain Specific Models I

Domain Specific Models II

Decision Making

Requirements Modeling

Invited Talks

Data Management in the Era of Digitalization

Veda C. Storey[✉]

Computer Information Systems, J. Mack Robinson College of Business,
Georgia State University, Atlanta, GA 30302-4015, USA
VStorey@gsu.edu

Abstract. In an increasingly digital world, the modeling and management of data is more important than ever as we move from the traditional management of data through the era of big data and now to an era of digitalization. Many of the traditional data challenges remain, which can be presented and understood in terms of data semantics, structure, syntax, and situation. Implications are provided for continued work on these well-known challenges with respect to an emerging technology.

Keywords: Data management · Digitalization · Data challenges · Data representation · Syntax · Structure · Situation · Semantics · Big data · Blockchain

1 Introduction

Research on conceptual modeling has focused on ways to model real world applications and represent them in a form that users and developers can understand [4, 13, 15]. Over time, systems are increasingly being developed for more and more complex applications. Our society now functions in an ever-expanding digital world, with many human activities mediated or shaped by digital information [10]. We live in an era of digitalization, where most functions of business and society are critically dependent on data of many different forms. As the digital revolution continues, the digitalization of human activities generates large amounts of data, having the potential to be both disruptive and transformative [8]. Thus, the success of digitalization is based on the ability to manage data, whether it be traditional or big, newly generated or repurposed, structured or unstructured data, or numeric or text data.

There are, obviously, many challenges associated with managing data of all types. Besides dealing with the sheer volume of big data, for example, there is a need to discover and interpret patterns. Traditional data management has always been concerned with the need to capture an accurate representation of business operations. The surge of social media and the need for its interpretation and use for customer management has led to much research on sentiment, and other types of, analysis involving user-generated online content.

Data management has progressed from developing tools and techniques for traditional, structured data, to managing big data and creating opportunities for novel uses of data from new, and emerging, technologies. Proper management of data is critical, as is archiving data for future use [14]. This paper proposes that data management in the

© Springer Nature Switzerland AG 2019
A. H. F. Laender et al. (Eds.): ER 2019, LNCS 11788, pp. 3–6, 2019.
https://doi.org/10.1007/978-3-030-33223-5_1

era of digitalization faces many of the problems of traditional and big data management which can be expressed in terms of data semantics, structure, syntax and situation.

2 Traditional Data Management

Data has long been used to support decision making, as reflected by early work in decision support systems and business intelligence. Business intelligence existed before the era of big data, with data being used for both descriptive and predictive purposes. The role of data in decision-making is further reflected in the movement towards data-driven decision making. Accurate and timely data is essential for good decision making. Responsible and insightful decision making, in turn, is the key to organizational survival in a competitive, global environment. The availability of data is even one of the three traditional components of information security. As the management of data has progressed, the potential of its contribution has also increased.

Traditional challenges of data management are data semantics, structure, syntax, and situation. Fundamentally, the data must be correct and represented properly (syntax and structure) and reflect the real-world application being modeled (semantics for a given situation or application domain). Application programs are needed to summarize, classify, abstract, and present the data. The user, or decision maker, ultimately, decides how to use the data to make decisions and inferences.

3 Big Data Management

Business intelligence and data analytics initiatives are found in all industries [2, 7]. The big data era shepherded in a wave of creative capture and uses of data. Access to large data sets and powerful processing capabilities, combined with situation or context-dependent methodologies and automation of large-scale network analysis, facilitate assessments and prediction capabilities [6]. At the heart of all this activity is data.

Big data has claims of, and experiences with, transformative decision-making support, real-time information, and text mining advances. Big data has generally been described by the three Vs of volume, velocity, and variety. The two best-known "additional Vs" are veracity (accuracy) and value. Well-recognized challenges arise from these characteristics. The volume (scale) may be so large that it is difficult for human decision makers to understanding it, and requires advances in processing capabilities. The velocity is practically, too fast [5]. Perhaps, most importantly, the value is difficult to ascertain [11]. Modeling and representing big data are not straightforward activities for specific applications. Semantic integration is required.

Many challenges of big data remain the same as traditional data management and do not simply go away simply because the data is 'big'. These challenges have remained unsolved for many years, despite advances, which have continued into the big data era. For example, when data is centralized, as in traditional data, it may be too structured. When data is overly structured, it can be very difficult to realize its potential value. The syntax must be correct. There is some understanding of data semantics, but it remains both difficult [12] and dependent on the application domain (situation). The

traditional characteristics of big data, represented by the "Vs" of big data, can be extended to include the data management challenges of big data, as characterized by four "Ss" of syntax, structure, semantics and situation.

4 Blockchain Technology Data Management

The era of digitalization is a result of open environments [9] from which block chain technology has emerged. Blockchain is a distributed network of peer to peer, encrypted public and private ledgers, composed of data records in blocks linked into an immutable chain that is verified and managed using smart contracts to execute transactions [1]. Blockchain's architecture is intended to support immutable trust worthy records without a trusted third party.

Blockchain is just a technology with implementation challenges, including how to manage data effectively. Blockchain can generate large amounts of data in a short period of time, displaying many of the characteristics and challenges of big data, even though the data may be more structured. Data is captured from transactions recorded in a distributed ledger. These transactions have a mixture of traditional and big data. With digitalization, data becomes increasingly ubiquitous and its management might require work that falls somewhere between traditional and big data management.

There are two types of semantics in blockchain: the semantics of the data; and the semantics of the transaction. Suppose one were to draw an entity relationship diagram [3] for the semantics of the data and data flow diagrams [16] for the semantics of the transactions, including their associated smart contracts. This might currently be the best effort that can be made to represent semantics. However, the semantics are still inherent in the "labels" assigned, which is a syntactical solution.

The best way to implement blockchain applications may be by object-oriented technology because the database is distributed, and the "trust", decentralized. Blockchain can make the integration (of schemas) a great deal easier, because there are no longer silos. From a traditional data perspective, there are distributed databases. To implement the distributed trust environment, the semantics of trust must be documented. Even if the domain is known, the transaction should also provide context (situation). It should be related to structure (e.g., the part of the workflow the transaction is executing). Finally, the identification of the person who is responsible for a transaction must be recorded.

5 Conclusion

In an increasing digital world, information systems deal with complex and diverse data with many associated challenges for modeling, accessing, and manipulating data. This paper has identified four characteristics of traditional data management that continue to exist in today's world that heavily emphasizes the digitalization of business processes and societal operations. The results of traditional research should not be overlooked when dealing with increasingly complex challenges, as we progress from traditional

data management, to the era of big data, and now to an era where the digitalization of applications and processes are having a profound impact on our world.

Acknowledgements. This research was supported by the J. Mack Robinson College of Business, Georgia State University. Thanks to Carson Woo for his helpful comments and insights on this paper. Special thanks to the *International Conference on Conceptual Modeling* for the honour of presenting my work as a recipient of the 2018 Peter P. Chen Award.

References

1. Beck, R., Avital, M., Rossi, M., Thatcher, J.B.: Blockchain technology in business and information systems research. Bus. Inf. Syst. Eng. **59**(6), 381–384 (2017). https://doi.org/10.1007/s12599-017-0505-1
2. Chen, H., Chiang, R.H., Storey, V.C.: Business intelligence and analytics: from big data to big impact. MIS Q. **36**(4), 1165–1188 (2012)
3. Chen, P.P.S.: The entity-relationship model—toward a unified view of data. ACM Trans. Database Syst. (TODS) **1**(1), 9–36 (1976)
4. Delcambre, L.M.L., Liddle, S.W., Pastor, O., Storey, V.C.: A reference framework for conceptual modeling. In: Trujillo, J.C., et al. (eds.) ER 2018. LNCS, vol. 11157, pp. 27–42. Springer, Cham (2018). https://doi.org/10.1007/978-3-030-00847-5_4
5. Embley, D.W., Liddle, S.W.: Big data—conceptual modeling to the rescue. In: Ng, W., Storey, V.C., Trujillo, J.C. (eds.) ER 2013. LNCS, vol. 8217, pp. 1–8. Springer, Heidelberg (2013). https://doi.org/10.1007/978-3-642-41924-9_1
6. Goes, P.B.: Editor's comments: big data and IS research. MIS Q. **38**(3), iii–viii (2014)
7. Gupta, M., George, J.F.: Toward the development of a big data analytics capability. Inf. Manage. **53**(8), 1049–1064 (2016)
8. Larsen, H.: The crisis of public service broadcasting reconsidered: commercialization and digitalization in Scandinavia. Crisis Journal. Reconsidered: Democ. Cult. Prof. Codes, Digital Future 43–58 (2016)
9. Parsons, J., Wand, Y.: A foundation for open information environments. In: Proceedings of the European Conference on Information Systems (ECIS), Tel Aviv, Israel (2014)
10. Pentland, B., Recker, J., Kim, I.: Capturing reality in flight? empirical tools for strong process theory. In Proceedings of the International Conference on Information Systems 2017, Seoul, South Korea, pp. 1–12 (2017)
11. Storey, V.C., Song, I.Y.: Big data technologies and management: what conceptual modeling can do. Data Knowl. Eng. **108**, 50–67 (2017)
12. Storey, V.C., Thalheim, B.: Conceptual modeling: enhancement through semiotics. In: Mayr, H.C., Guizzardi, G., Ma, H., Pastor, O. (eds.) ER 2017. LNCS, vol. 10650, pp. 182–190. Springer, Cham (2017). https://doi.org/10.1007/978-3-319-69904-2_15
13. Storey, V.C., Trujillo, J.C., Liddle, S.W.: Research on conceptual modeling: themes, topics, and introduction to the special issue. Data Knowl. Eng. **98**, 1–7 (2015)
14. Storey, V.C., Woo, C.: Data challenges in the digitalization era. In: Proceedings of the 28th Workshop on Information Technologies and Systems, Santa Clara, California (2018)
15. Thalheim, B.: Conceptual model notions – a matter of controversy: conceptual modelling and its lacunas. Enterp. Model. Inf. Syst. Archit. (EMISAJ) **13**, 9–27 (2018)
16. Valacich, J., George, J., Hoffer, J.: Essentials of Systems Analysis and Design, 8th edn. Prentice Hall Press, Upper Saddle River (2016)

Keyword Search over RDF Datasets

(Extended Abstract)

Marco A. Casanova$^{(\boxtimes)}$ ⓘ

Department of Informatics, PUC-Rio, Rio de Janeiro, RJ, Brazil
casanova@inf.puc-rio.br

Abstract. This extended abstract first introduces the problem of keyword search overRDF datasets. Then, it expands the discussion to cover the question of serendipitous search as a strategy to diversify answers. Finally, it briefly presents the entity relatedness problem, which refers to the problem of exploring an RDF dataset to discover and understand how two entities are connected.

Keywords: Keyword search · Serendipity · Entity relatedness · RDF · SPARQL

1 Introduction

Keyword search is typically associated with information retrieval systems, especially those designed for the Web. The user just specifies a few terms, called *keywords*, and the system must retrieve the documents, such as Web pages, that best match the list of keywords. Keyword search over relational databases, as well as over RDF datasets, has also been studied for some time. In particular, the adoption of RDF as the underlying data model adds flexibility and imposes no strict distinction between data and metadata, that is, a keyword may match the name or description of a class or of a property in the same way that it may match a data value. An RDF management system may also offer an inference layer so that one may expand the stored RDF data with derived data in ways that surpass (relational) views. Thus, a keyword may match derived data as much as stored data. Lastly, an RDF dataset is equivalent to a labeled graph, called an RDF graph, which allows the use of graph concepts and algorithms for keyword search.

Keyword search over RDF datasets imposes distinct challenges when compared with traditional keyword search. Indeed, in the latter case, an answer for a keyword query is a document that matches as many keywords as possible, and the various answers (documents) are ranked using well-known measures. By contrast, in the former case, keywords select nodes and edges from an RDF graph, and it is up to the system to find a connected subgraph of the RDF graph that covers these nodes and edges to create an answer for the keyword query. Since there might be more than one such subgraph, the system must rank them according to some reasonable measure.

This extended abstract first discusses the problem of keyword search for RDF datasets. Then, it expands the discussion to serendipitous search as a strategy to diversify answers. Finally, it briefly presents the entity relatedness problem, which refers to the problem of exploring an RDF graph to discover how two entities are connected.

A. H. F. Laender et al. (Eds.): ER 2019, LNCS 11788, pp. 7–10, 2019.
https://doi.org/10.1007/978-3-030-33223-5_2

2   Classic Keyword Search Over RDF Datasets

An *Internationalized Resource Identifier* (IRI) is a global identifier that denotes a resource. A *blank node* identifier is a local identifier. RDF [3] describes data as triples of the form (s,p,o), where s is the *subject*, p is the *predicate* (or *property*) and o is the *object* of the triple. The subject of a triple is an IRI or a blank node, the predicate is an IRI, and the object is an IRI, a blank node or a *literal*. An RDF dataset is a set T of RDF triples and is equivalent to a labeled graph G_T whose nodes are the RDF terms that occur as subject or object of the triples in T and there is an edge (s,o) in G_T labeled with p iff $(s,p,o) \in T$. We will use the terms RDF dataset and RDF graph interchangeably.

RDF *Schema* [2] is a specific vocabulary that permits defining classes and properties, and hierarchies thereof, among other constructs. It should be noted that an RDF dataset may not have an RDF schema. SPARQL 1.1 [6] is a query language to access RDF datasets. The WHERE clause of a SPARQL query is a set of *triple patterns*, defined like RDF triples, except that the subject, predicate or object can be a variable.

A *keyword query* is simply a set of literals, or *keywords*, $K = \{K_1,...,K_n\}$. A keyword K_i *matches* a triple (s,p,o) iff o is a literal and K_i and o are considered similar (according to some criterion). An *answer* for K over an RDF dataset T is a subset A of T such that there are triples in A that match some of the keywords in K. Note that this notion of answer allows keywords to remain unmatched and permits the RDF graph induced by A to be disconnected. However, answers that induce minimal, connected graphs that match as many keywords as possible should be preferred. Also, note that a keyword may match the label or the description of a class or property, which alters the interpretation of a keyword query. For example, if C is a class with a property rdfs:label whose value is the literal "city", then the keyword query $K = \{city, Princeton\}$ can be interpreted as requesting an instance c of class C such that c has a property whose value matches "*Princeton*". The problem of keyword search over RDF datasets is then defined as: *"Given an RDF dataset T and a keyword query K, find a minimally connected answer for K over T that matches as many keywords as possible"*.

Given a keyword query K, an RDF keyword query processing tool first matches the keywords in K with literals that occur in the RDF graph and then either directly crawls the RDF graph to find answers for K or compiles a SPARQL query that returns answers for K. Variations of this basic process may adopt an ontology to expand the keyword matching process, and may introduce ranking strategies to order the keyword matches, to improve the crawling or compilation processes, and to order the answers [11].

The tools also differ on the strategy adopted to compile the SPARQL query. *Schema-based* tools [5] explore the RDF schema to compile a SPARQL query with a minimal set of join clauses – and this is a key idea. In fact, the tool described in [9] supports keyword query processing for both relational databases and RDF datasets with schemas. To circumvent the lack of an RDF schema, *graph-based* tools may compile a SPARQL query based on elementary query graph building blocks, such as entity/class nodes and predicate edges, or graph summarizations. We also find a strategy [10] that estimates set similarity measures using KMV-synopses [1], which in turn drive the SPARQL query compilation process, and a strategy based on tensor calculus.

3 Beyond the Basics: Serendipitous Search

Serendipity is defined as "the art of making an unsought finding". In a seminal work, Van Andel [12] defined a list of seventeen serendipity patterns, each one representing a different form of serendipity. The problem of *RDF serendipitous search* can then be intuitively defined as: *"Given an RDF dataset T and a query Q, find additional answers related to the original answers for Q by some serendipity pattern"*.

A strategy to incorporate serendipity into query processing would then be to mimic Van Andel's patterns. This strategy was implemented in [4] for four patterns: *analogy, surprising observation, disturbance,* and *inversion*. To capture the first two patterns, the process explores the answers for a query to invoke secondary queries with the recently acquired data. To capture the disturbance pattern, the process changes the order of the answer list to expose items that the user would normally neglect. To capture the inversion pattern, the process also formulates alternative queries.

When combined with keyword search, which allows considerable latitude in constructing answers, serendipitous search may produce interesting results that enrich the user's experience. For example, when processing the keyword query {*Einstein, Gödel, Princeton*}, the system may return that Einstein and Gödel were neighbors at Princeton, they died in that city and worked at the Institute for Advanced Study (IAS) at Princeton University (which are the expected answers). But the system may expand these answers to include that Gödel won the first Einstein Award in 1951, created by IAS to honor Einstein, and that Gödel's favorite movie was "Snow White" (trivia about the foremost mathematical logician of the twentieth century).

4 An Interesting Special Case: Entity Relatedness

When a keyword query K simply selects two nodes, N_1 and N_2, of the RDF graph, an answer for K reduces to a path between N_1 and N_2, called a *relationship path*. The *entity relatedness problem* is then defined as: *"Given an RDF graph G_T and two entities, represented by two nodes N_1 and N_2 of G_T, compute the relationship paths that better describe the connectivity between the given entities"*. For example, DBpedia has more than 10,000 paths between the entries for Einstein and Gödel, that is, the keyword query {*Einstein, Gödel*} has, in this not infrequent case, the patently unwieldy total of more than 10,000 answers over DBpedia, and this is a problem.

There are two basic approaches to address this problem. First, one may try to abstract out the (large) set of relationship paths into a description meaningful to the users [7], or one may rank the relationship paths in an order that reflects their relevance [8], which raises additional questions. The relevance of a path π may have to do with its coherence, measured by how similar neighboring entities (nodes) in π are, or the relevance may be measured by how informative the labels of the edges are, similarly to information retrieval, or by a combination of both. The work in [8] reports an extensive comparison between different combinations of similarity and path ranking measures.

5 Final Remarks: What Else?

RDF Keyword search is tightly related to the exploration of knowledge bases, as a goal in itself or to complement traditional information retrieval. In this context, immediate challenges include to implement keyword search with sub-second response time for large RDF knowledge bases, and to fully incorporate such technology into mainstream search engines and question-and-answer tools to enhance the overall user experience.

Acknowledgments. This work was partly funded by grants CAPES/88881.134081/2016-01, CNPq/302303/2017-0, and FAPERJ/E-26-202.818/2017. The author gratefully acknowledges Altigran Silva, for his inspiring work, and the contributions to the research reported here of Bernardo Nunes, Luiz André Paes Leme, Antonio Furtado, Grettel García, Yenier Izquierdo, Elisa Menendez, José Herrera, Jerônimo Eichler, and Ângelo Neves.

References

1. Beyer, K. et al.: On synopses for distinct-value estimation under multiset operations. In: Proceedings 2007 ACM SIGMOD, Beijing, China, pp. 199–210 (2007)
2. Brickley, D., Guha, R.V. (eds): RDF Schema 1.1. W3C Recommendation, 25 February 2014
3. Cyganiak, R., Wood, D., Lanthaler, M. (eds.): RDF 1.1 Concepts and Abstract Syntax. W3C Recommendation, 25 February 2014
4. Eichler, J.S.A., et al.: Searching linked data with a twist of serendipity. In: Dubois, E., Pohl, K. (eds.) CAiSE 2017. LNCS, vol. 10253, pp. 495–510. Springer, Cham (2017). https://doi.org/10.1007/978-3-319-59536-8_31
5. García, G.M., Izquierdo, Y.T., Menendez, E., Dartayre, F., Casanova, M.A.: RDF keyword-based query technology meets a real-world dataset. In: Proceedings of 20th International Conference on Extending Database Technology, Venice, Italy (2017)
6. Harris, S., Seaborne, A.: SPARQL 1.1 Query Language. W3C Recommendation, 21 March 2013
7. Herrera, J.E.T., Casanova, M.A., Nunes, B.P., Lopes, G.R., Leme, L.A.P.P.: DBpedia profiler tool: profiling the connectivity of entity Pairs in DBpedia. In: Proceedings of Intelligent Exploration of Semantic Data - IESD, A Workshop at ISWC 2016, Kobe, Japan (2016)
8. Herrera, J.E.T., Casanova, M.A., Nunes, B.P., Leme, L.A.P.P., Lopes, G.R.: An entity relatedness test dataset. In: d'Amato, C., et al. (eds.) ISWC 2017. LNCS, vol. 10588, pp. 193–201. Springer, Cham (2017). https://doi.org/10.1007/978-3-319-68204-4_20
9. Izquierdo, Y.T., García, G.M., Menendez, E.S., Casanova, M.A., Dartayre, F., Levy, C.H.: QUIOW: a keyword-based query processing tool for RDF datasets and relational databases. In: Hartmann, S., Ma, H., Hameurlain, A., Pernul, G., Wagner, R.R. (eds.) DEXA 2018. LNCS, vol. 11030, pp. 259–269. Springer, Cham (2018). https://doi.org/10.1007/978-3-319-98812-2_22
10. Izquierdo, Y.T., et al.: Keyword Search over Schema-less RDF Datasets by SPARQL Query Compilation (Submitted for publication)
11. Menendez, E.S., Casanova, M.A., Paes Leme, L.A.P, Boughanem, M.: Novel Node Importance Measures to Improve Keyword Search over RDF Graphs. (to appear DEXA 2019)
12. Van Andel, P.: Anatomy of the unsought finding serendipity: origin, history, domains, traditions, appearances, patterns and programmability. Br. J. Philos. Sci. **45**(2), 631–648 (1994)

Conceptual Modeling

OOC-O: A Reference Ontology on Object-Oriented Code

Camila Zacché de Aguiar$^{(\boxtimes)}$, Ricardo de Almeida Falbo$^{(\boxtimes)}$, and Vítor E. Silva Souza$^{(\boxtimes)}$

Ontology & Conceptual Modeling Research Group (NEMO),
Federal University of Espírito Santo, Vitoria, Brazil
camila.zacche.aguiar@gmail.com, {falbo,vitorsouza}@inf.ufes.br
http://nemo.inf.ufes.br/

Abstract. With the rise of polyglot programming, different programming languages with different constructs have been combined in the same software development projects. However, to our knowledge, no axiomatization demonstrating the existential commitments of a language have been presented, nor is there effort to adopt a consensual conceptualization between languages, in particular object-oriented ones. In this paper, we propose OOC-O, a reference ontology on Object-Oriented Code whose purpose is to identify and represent the fundamental concepts present in OO source code. The ontology is based on UFO, was developed according to the SABiO method, verified according to its competency questions and validated by instantiation of concepts in OO code form and a process of harmonization among popular object-oriented languages.

Keywords: Object-Oriented Ontology · Polyglot programming · Object-Oriented Programming Language

1 Introduction

A Programming Language is defined by a formal grammar, however there must also be a meaning for each construct of the language. Programs have their meanings given by the semantics of their constructs which, generally, must be preserved across programs. Without the semantics of constructs, it would be difficult to verify if the code represents what it was designed to do. In general, a programming language is presented through its syntax containing some informal explanation of its semantics [27]. To the best of our knowledge, no axiomatization demonstrating the existential commitments of object-oriented (OO) constructs of a language have been presented, nor is there effort to adopt a consensual conceptualization of object-oriented constructs between languages.

Thus, in this paper we propose OOC-O, a reference ontology on Object-Oriented Code whose purpose is to identify and represent the fundamental concepts present in OO source code. This reference ontology is based on UFO [14]

© Springer Nature Switzerland AG 2019
A. H. F. Laender et al. (Eds.): ER 2019, LNCS 11788, pp. 13–27, 2019.
https://doi.org/10.1007/978-3-030-33223-5_3

and was developed according to the SABiO method [11], in a modular way to foster its reuse. Ontology verification was guided by competency questions, whereas its validation consisted of both instantiating its concepts in OO code form and by harmonizing popular OO languages using the ontology as interlanguage. The latter resulted from the ontology capture process, whose objective was to reduce semantic and syntactic conflicts between languages.

Although OOC-O is applicable in several contexts, it is being built in the context of polyglot programming, i.e., different programming languages with different constructs combined in the same software development project. If on the one hand the combination of different programming languages with specific responsibilities can reduce the effort to implement solutions [12], on the other hand, the effort to implement an algorithm may differ between programming languages depending on its constructs [24]. In this context, OOC-O has been used as support for both programmers to understand different syntaxes and semantics of object-oriented constructs, as well as for integrated development tools to interoperate different languages. The ontology has already been used to migrate classes with object/relational mappings from one language to another [30] and is currently being used in an effort to produce a unified solution for identifying smells in OO source code. Furthermore, OOC-O is part of a larger effort of creating an ontology network on software development frameworks.[1]

The remainder of this paper is organized as follows. Section 2 discusses briefly the main concepts found in most OO programming languages as well as the ontological foundations used for developing OOC-O. Section 3 presents OOC-O. Section 4 addresses ontology verification and validation. Section 5 discusses related works. Finally, Sect. 6 concludes the paper.

2   Baseline

Object-oriented (OO) programming is defined as a software implementation method in which programs are organized as cooperative collections of **objects**, each of which representing an instance of some **class**, and whose classes are members of a hierarchy of classes linked by **inheritance relationships**. A class serves as a template from which objects can be created. It is a defined type that determines the data structures (**attributes**) and **methods** associated with that type. In order for the attributes and methods of a class to be used in defining a new class, **inheritance** is applied as a means of creating abstractions.

Abstraction is the mechanism of representing only the essential characteristics, ignoring the irrelevant details as a way of hiding implementation. To hide data, *encapsulation* applies a packaging of methods and attributes accessible or modifiable only via the interface. Moreover, abstraction can be defined by *polymorphism*, attributing the ability to take on many forms and by *genericity*, attributing the ability to take several types independently of the structure.

Abstraction, encapsulation, inheritance and polymorphism are the main principles of object orientation [7]. In other words, if any of these elements is missing,

---

[1] https://nemo.inf.ufes.br/projects/sfwon/.

you have something less than an OO language [5]. Thus, we consider an OO programming language as a tool that supports these four fundamental principles: *Abstraction* is realized in a OO code by means of **classes** containing attributes and methods; *Encapsulation* is implemented by **accessor methods** hiding internal information of the class, avoiding direct access to its attributes, and by **element visibility** avoiding unwanted access to these elements; *Inheritance* is directly represented as a relation between a **subclass** that inherits characteristics from a **superclass**; and, finally, *Polymorphism* takes place via the concepts of **method override**, in which a method declaration in the subclass modifies the method declared in the superclass, **abstract class**, whose abstract methods are implemented according to the subclass that inherits them, and **generic class/method**, whose definition can be used by different data types.

Considering the range of existing languages, we selected languages that provide constructs for the basic OO principles discussed above in order to form the baseline of our research, namely: Smalltalk, Eiffel, C++, Java and Python. The selection took into account the first two OO programming languages ever proposed and the three currently most popular OO languages according to the TIOBE[2] IEEE Spectrum[3] and Redmonk[4] indexes.

In order to build an ontology on OO source code, we followed a systematic approach for building ontologies named SABiO [11], a method that considers activities for the development of reference ontologies and to its implementation as operational ontologies. In this paper, we developed only the reference ontology and, therefore, only the early stages of SABiO were performed. In Purpose Identification and Requirements Elicitation, we identify the purpose and intended uses of the ontology, define its functional requirements, by means of Competency Questions, and also non-functional ones (NFRs), and decompose the ontology into appropriate modules. Ontology Capture and Formalization phase follows, aiming at objectively recording the domain conceptualization based on an ontological analysis using a foundation ontology and representing it in a graphic model.

In addition, SABiO suggests five support processes, applied as follows: Knowledge Acquisition, to gather domain knowledge reliably through specialists and bibliographic material; Reuse, to take advantage of conceptualizations already established for the domain; Documentation, to record the results of the development process by means of a Reference Ontology Specification; Configuration Management, to control changes, versions, and delivery by means of a repository; and Evaluation, to evaluate the suitability of the ontology by means of verification, ensuring that the ontology satisfies its requirements, and validation, ensuring that the ontology is able to represent real world situations.

For building our conceptual models, we used the OntoUML modeling language, which is based on the UML 2.0 class diagram and incorporates important foundational distinctions made by the Unified Foundational Ontology

---

[2] tiobe.com, January 2019.

[3] spectrum.ieee.org/at-work/innovation/the-2018-top-programming-languages, July 2018.

[4] redmonk.com/sogrady/2019/03/20/language-rankings-1-19/, January 2019.

(UFO) [14]. Such distinctions are made explicit in the model by means of UML class stereotypes, summarized as follows: ≪category≫, a rigid type whose instances share common intrinsic properties but obey different principles of identity (non-sortal, rigid entities); ≪kind≫, a rigid sortal type that is formed by distinct parts (functional complex) and supplies an identity principle for its instances; ≪subkind≫, a rigid sortal type whose instances inherit an identity principle from a kind; ≪role≫, an anti-rigid sortal type whose specialization condition is given by extrinsic (relational) properties; ≪relator≫, a concept connecting other concepts, and thus existentially dependent on them; and ≪quality≫, a type whose instances represent intrinsic properties of an individual associated with a quality structure. This choice is motivated by UFO having a modeling language with stereotypes covering the domain studied and the availability of an ontology network on software engineering represented in such language, facilitating integration and reuse.

3   Object-Oriented Code Ontology (OOC-O)

The Object-Oriented Code Ontology (OOC-O) aims to identify and represent the semantics of the entities present at compile time in object-oriented (OO) code. Given such scope, even though objects are the fundamental constructs in OO programming and messages are responsible for exchanges between objects, they are not covered by OOC-O, since they exist only at runtime. The intention is to use the ontology to assist the understanding of different programming languages and to support the development of tools that work with these languages, in the context of polyglot programming and object-oriented frameworks.

We elicited the following non-functional requirements for OOC-O: NFR1 – be modular or embedded in a modular framework to facilitate reuse of other ontologies and, consequently, its own reuse by other ontologies; and NFR2 – be based on well-known sources from the literature. In response to **NFR1** and to facilitate viewing, we decomposed the ontology into three modules, namely: OOC-O Core (an overview of the main concepts), OOC-O Class (detailing concepts derived from Class) and OOC-O Class Members (detailing concepts derived from Class Members, i.e., Methods and Attributes). Moreover, we integrated OOC-O into the Software Engineering Ontology Network (SEON) [23], to reuse relevant concepts, as well as SEON's grounding in UFO. Two ontologies from SEON were reused: the Software Process Ontology (SPO) [19] and the Software Ontology (SwO) [8]. Along the paper, fragments of these reused ontologies in OOC-O are preceded by the corresponding acronyms (SPO:: and SwO::, respectively) and highlighted using different colors. Regarding **NFR2**, ontology capture was supported by a process of knowledge acquisition that used consolidated sources of knowledge referring to the five programming languages selected in this research, including books [15,17,18,22,25,28] and standards [9,13].

For functional requirements, we have iteratively defined twenty five competency questions (CQs) detailed in OOC-O's Reference Ontology Specification document [2], for instance: **CQ1:** What makes up an OO source code? **CQ2:** What is the visibility of an element present in an OO source code? **CQ3:** How

are classes logically organized in an OO source code? **CQ4:** What elements compose a class? **CQ5:** Which are the parent classes of a class? **CQ6:** What is a root class? **CQ7:** What are the variables of a method? **CQ8:** What is the mutability of a variable? **CQ9:** What types of classes are present in an OO source code? **CQ10:** What types of methods are present in an OO source code?

During ontology capture and formalization, we performed ontological analysis based on UFO, representing OOC-O in OntoUML. Such process was conducted iteratively, in order to address different aspects/refinements at each iteration, and interactively, so domain experts and ontology engineers could discuss the conceptualization of the domain in OntoUML. Finally, to ensure consensual understanding of the domain, the concepts were defined in a dictionary of terms and mapped to the concepts of each selected programming language, detailed in a technical report [1]. In what follows, we present the three modules of OOC-O. More details of the ontology can be found in its specification document [2].

3.1 OOC-O Core Module

Figure 1 shows the core concepts of OOC-O and how they integrate with SEON through the SPO and SwO ontologies.

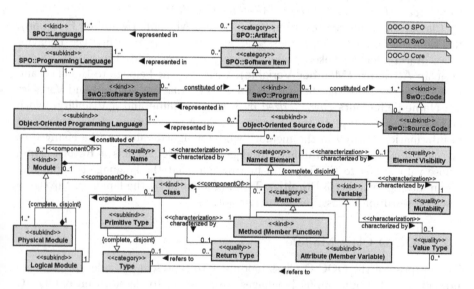

Fig. 1. Object-Oriented Code Ontology: core module

SPO establishes a common conceptualization on the software process domain (processes, activities, resources, people, artifacts, procedures, etc.). We reuse the concept of software **Artifact**, object consumed or produced during the software process, which is *represented in* a **Language**, a set of symbols used for encoding

and decoding information. A software artifact can be, among other things, a **Software Item** such as a piece of software produced during the software process.

SwO further specializes this concept: a **Software System** is a Software Item that aims at satisfying a system specification. It is *constituted of* **Programs**, which are Software Items that aim at producing a certain result through execution on a computer, in a particular way, given by a program specification. In turn, Programs are *constituted of* **Code**, a Software Item representing a set of computer instructions and data definitions which are *represented in* a **Programming Language** as a **Source Code**.

OOC-O is anchored in the concept of **Object-Oriented Source Code**, a Source Code specialization *represented in* an **Object-Oriented Programming Language**. Such code is *constituted of* **Physical Modules**, i.e., physical units in which the physical files (ex: .java) are stored (e.g., a directory in the file system). Physical Modules are *composed of* **Classes** *organized in* **Logical Modules**, i.e., packages or namespaces that group classes and allow programmers to control dependencies, visibility, etc. Both **Modules** (Physical or Logical) can be *decomposed in* their respective sub-Modules. However, decomposition can only take place among modules of the same type, i.e., $\forall m_1, m_2 : Module, PhysicalModule(m_1) \wedge componentOf(m_1, m_2) \rightarrow PhysicalModule(m_2)$ (**A1**) and $\forall m_1, m_2 : Module, LogicalModule(m_1) \wedge componentOf(m_1, m_2) \rightarrow LogicalModule(m_2)$ (**A2**).

Classes are *composed of* **Members**, be it a **Method (Member Function)**, function that belongs to the class and provides a way to define the behavior of an object, being invoked when a message is received by the object [18]; or be it an **Attribute (Member Variable)**, variable that belongs to the class and provides a way to define the state of its objects. Classes, Methods and Variables are **Named Elements** *characterized by* a unique **Name** and a **Visibility**, which defines the access type to the element. Attribute is a subtype of **Variable**, item of information located in the memory whose assigned value can be changed or not according to its **Mutability**. Analogously, a Method has a **Return Type**, whose values *refer to* the **Types** of information that the language is capable of manipulating, whether a **Primitive Type**, predefined by the language through a reserved word; or a Class, predefined or not.

3.2   OOC-O Class Module

The purpose of the OOC-O Class module is to represent the relevant concepts present in OO programming languages with respect to classes. Hence, OOC-O Class module, shown in Fig. 2, is centered on the Class concept already presented in OOC-O Core earlier.

Every Class must either be a **Concrete Class**, implemented class that can and intends to have instances, or an **Abstract Class**, incompletely implemented class whose descendants will use as a basis for further refinement [9]. Abstract class, in contrast to Concrete Class, should not have instances and should be an Extendable Class. Further, every class must be either an **Extendable Class**,

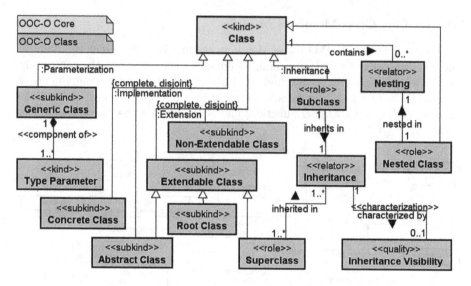

Fig. 2. Object-Oriented Code Ontology: class module

class available to be extended through Inheritance, or **Non-Extendable Class**, the opposite.

An Extendable Class can assume the **Superclass** role when relating to a Class that assumes the **Subclass** role in an **Inheritance** relationship: $\forall c_1, c_2 : Class, i : Inheritance, inheritsIn(c_1, i) \land inheritedFrom(c_2, i) \rightarrow subClassOf(c_1, c_2)$ (**A3**). The relationship between a Superclass and a Subclass is established mainly by the existence of a "is-a" relation between them [26].

In this context, **Inheritance Visibility** can be set to limit the Subclass permission on the members of the Superclass. The Extendable Class inherited by all classes directly or indirectly in an OO code is known as **Root Class** [9] and introduces several general-purpose resources. When present, the Root Class is a common ancestor for all other existing classes, i.e., $\forall c : Class, r : RootClass, c \neq r \rightarrow descendantOf(c, r)$ (**A4**), where $descendantOf$ is defined in terms of the $subClassOf$ predicate introduced above, according to the following axioms: $\forall c_1, c_2 : Class, subclassOf(c_1, c_2) \rightarrow descendantOf(c_1, c_2)$ (**A5**) and $\forall c_1, c_2, c_3 : Class, subclassOf(c_1, c_2) \land descendantOf(c_2, c_3) \rightarrow descendantOf(c_1, c_3)$ (**A6**).

Finally, a Class can also assume the **Nested Class** role when relating to another Class by means of its declaration being within the body of that Class [13] (we refer to this as **Nesting**). Furthermore, a Class can be a **Generic Class**, when it describes a template for a possible set of types [9]. A Generic Class is *composed of* **Type Parameters**, which are identifiers that specify generic type names whose instances must define recognized types that will replace the Type Parameter at runtime.

3.3 OOC-O Class Members Module

The purpose of the OOC-O Class Members module is to represent the relevant concepts present in OO programming languages with respect to the component members of the classes. As methods and attributes are the key components of a class, OOC-O Class Members module, shown in Fig. 3, is centered on the concepts of Method (Member Function) and Attribute (Member Variable) already presented in OOC-O Core.

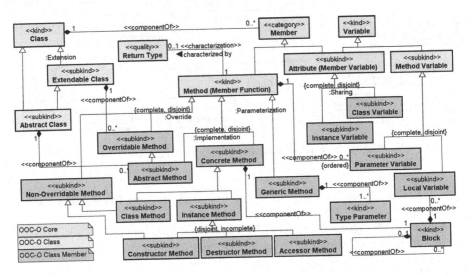

Fig. 3. Object-Oriented Code Ontology: class members

Every Method of a Class must be either a **Concrete Method**, implemented in its own (concrete or abstract) Class by means of Blocks; or an **Abstract Method**, belonging to an Abstract Class and implemented (or "made concrete") only in its Subclasses. A Concrete Method can be specialized according to its execution context, either in the context of the class, invoked by the class in a **Class Method**, or in the context of the object, invoked by the object in an **Instance Method**. An Instance Method can be specialized in **Accessor Method**, which provides an interface between the internal data of the object and the external world [15], in **Constructor Method**, which specifies how an object should be created and initialized, or in **Destructor Method**, which is responsible for cleaning unusable objects. Return Type cannot characterize neither a Constructor nor a Destructor Method: $\forall rt : ReturnType, m : Method, characterization(rt, m) \rightarrow \neg ConstructorMethod(m) \land \neg DestructorMethod(m)$ (**A7**).

Further, every Method must be either an **Overridable Method**, method belonging to an Extendable Class that can be overwritten in descendant classes [25], such as an Abstract Method declared in an Abstract Class to be implemented by Subclasses; or a **Non-Overridable Method**, method that can be inherited but is not allowed to be overwritten in descendant classes, such

as Class Methods and Constructor Methods. A Method can also be a **Generic Method** when describing a template for a possible set of methods *composed of* one or more **Type Parameters**.

Variables, in turn, can be associated with methods, i.e., be a **Method Variable**, or classes, i.e., an **Attribute (Member Variable)**. In an indirect way, Method Variable is member of a Class, since a Class is *composed of* Methods. Method Variable can be a **Parameter Variable** declared within the signature of a Method or **Local Variable** declared within a Block. Part-of relations among Methods, Blocks and Local Variables are transitive in the following ways: $\forall v : LocalVariable, b_1, b_2 : Block, componentOf(v, b_1) \wedge componentOf(b_1, b_2) \to componentOf(v, b_2)$ (**A8**) and $\forall v : LocalVariable, b : Block, m : ConcreteMethod, componentOf(v, b) \wedge componentOf(b, m) \to componentOf(v, m)$ (**A9**). An Attribute can be a **Class Variable** when shared by all objects of the Class or an **Instance Variable** when it represents the particular state of each object.

4 Evaluation

The evaluation of a reference ontology comprises activities of verification and validation. For ontology **verification**, SABiO suggests identifying whether the elements that make up the ontology are able to answer the competency questions raised. Table 1 presents the results for some of the raised CQs (cf. Sect. 3), showing which concepts and relations are used to answer a CQ.

Table 1. Results for OOC-O verification.

ID	Competency question	Axiom
CQ1	Object-Oriented Source Code *constituted of* Physical Module; Class *component of* Physical Module	
CQ2	Named Element *characterized by* Element Visibility	
CQ3	Class *organized in* Logical Module	
CQ4	Member *component of* Class; Attribute (Member Variable) and Method (Member Function) *subtype of* Member	
CQ5	Subclass *subtype of* Class; Subclass *inherits in* Inheritance; Superclass *inherited in* Inheritance	A3, A5, A6
CQ6	Extendable Class *subtype of* Class; Root Class *subtype of* Extendable Class; Subclass *subtype of* Class; Subclass *inherits in* Inheritance; Superclass *inherited in* Inheritance.	A3, A4, A5, A6
CQ7	Parameter Variable *component of* Method; Local Variable *component of* Block; Block *component of* Block; Block *component of* Concrete Method; Concrete Method *subtype of* Method	A8, A9
CQ8	Variable *characterized by* Mutability	
CQ9	Generic Class *subtype of* Class; Concrete Class *subtype of* Class; Abstract Class *subtype of* Class; Non-Extendable Class *subtype of* Class; Extendable Class *subtype of* Class	
CQ10	Generic Method *subtype of* Method; Concrete Method *subtype of* Method; Abstract Method *subtype of* Method; Overridable Method *subtype of* Method; Non-Overridable Method *subtype of* Method	

For ontology **validation**, the ontology should be instantiated to check if it is able to represent real world situations. For this, we use the same OO code fragment written in the selected languages to instantiate the concepts of the ontology. Table 2 shows some results of the OOC-O instantiation. It is worthy to say that since there are orthogonal generalization sets that are disjoint and complete (e.g., *:Implementation* and *:Extension* in Class concept), each concept instance (e.g., the Polygon class) is classified in at least each of these generalization sets (e.g., Concrete Class or Abstract Class, and Extendable Class or Non-Extendable Class). The complete table is available in a technical report [1].

Table 2. Results for OOC-O instantiation.

Language Code	OOC-O Instance

Smalltalk Code
`Object subclass: #Polygon`
`    instanceVariableNames: 'side'`
`    perimeter ...`
	Polygon = Concrete Class & Extendable Class & Subclass
	Object = Superclass & Root Class
	side = Instance Variable
	perimeter = Instance Method & Overridable Method

Eiffel Code
`class Polygon`
`feature{ANY}`
`    perimeter() is    do ... end`
`feature{NONE}`
`    side : INTEGER`
`end`
	Polygon = Concrete Class & Extendable Class & Subclass
	side = Instance Variable
	INTEGER = Value Type
	perimeter = Instance Method & Non-Overridable Method
	NONE and ANY = Element Visibility

C++ Code
`class Polygon{`
`    private: int side;`
`    public: void perimeter(){};`
`};`
	Polygon = Concrete Class & Extendable Class
	side = Instance Variable
	perimeter = Instance Method
	private and public = Element Visibility
	void and int = Value Type

Java Code
`public class Polygon{`
`    private int side;`
`    public void perimeter(){};`
`}`
	Polygon = Concrete Class & Extendable Class & Subclass
	side = Instance Variable & Overridable Method
	perimeter = Instance Method
	private and public = Element Visibility
	void and int = Value Type

Python Code
`class Polygon:`
`    side = None`
`    def perimeter(): ...`
	Polygon = Concrete Class & Extendable Class & Subclass
	side = Instance Variable
	None = Initial Variable Value
	perimeter = Concrete Method & Overridable Method

From OOC-O's instantiation we can see that the code relative to class definition incorporates the semantics of **concrete** and **extendable** class in the ontology. Most languages, explicitly (Smalltalk) or implicitly (Eiffel, Java and Python), incorporates **subclass** semantics, since all classes are subclasses of the **root** class of these languages such as the Object class in Smalltalk, Java and Python, and the Any class in Eiffel (C++ does not have a root class). Code relative to method definition in different languages incorporates a highly variable semantics, including the semantics of **instance, concrete, overridable** and **non-overridable** methods in the ontology. The **element visibility**

is either explicitly defined with keywords (`private` and `public` in Java and C++, and `none` and `any` in Eiffel) or is private by default (Smalltalk) or is public by default (Python). The **value type** is explicitly defined in some languages (Eiffel, C++, Java) and defined by the assigned value (Python) or defined as an object (Smalltalk) in others.

We also performed a harmonization between the elements of the selected languages and the concepts of OOC-O, applying equivalence relations. Table 3 shows some of these matches and the complete table is available in a technical report [1]. Although the OO principles are well established, the way they are handled in the programming languages is not uniform. Each language adopts different syntax and semantics for their constructs, resulting in different levels in which those principles are addressed. In this context, OOC-O can be used to support interoperability among them.

Therefore, **Abstraction** is represented by the class concept in the languages, being composed by members such as method in Smalltalk, Java and Python, or routine in Eiffel, or member function in C++, and by attribute in Eiffel, or data attribute in Python, or instance variable in Smalltalk, C++ and Java. **Inheritance** is represented by subclass in Smalltalk, Eiffel, Java and Python, or derived class in C++, and by superclass in Smalltalk, Eiffel, Java and Python, or base class in C++. **Encapsulation** is represented by access in Smalltalk and Eiffel, or access modifier in C++ and Java, and by the public visibility in Python. Encapsulation is represented also by accessor method in Smalltalk, however, the accessor method concept in Eiffel, C++, Java and Python is not equivalent to accessor method in the ontology because in these languages there is only a convention for treating an instance method as an accessor method. **Polymorphism** is represented by routine redefinition in Eiffel or virtual function in C++. Smalltalk, Java and Python incorporate the semantics of overridable method to the method concept. Polymorphism is represented also by generic class/method in Eiffel, Java and Python, or template in Smalltalk and C++. Polymorphism is represented also by abstract class in Smalltalk, C++, Java and Python, or deferred class in Eiffel.

Finally, in a separate research effort [30], the OOC-O reference ontology presented in this paper was implemented in OWL, giving rise to its operational version OOC-OWL (also available in the aforementioned website). OOC-OWL was then used by ORM-OWL (Object/Relational Mapping Ontology) to instantiate source code with ORM annotations and migrate it from one language/framework to another using the ontology as an interlingua.

5 Related Works

Concepts that were originally developed by OO programming languages have appeared in many other areas such as database [3], development methodology [21], data analysis [6], and others. Therefore, there are several works that discuss and formalize fundamentals of programming language, discussing semantic theories to be applied in the definition of programming languages ontologies [27],

Table 3. Equivalence between selected OO programming languages and OOC-O.

Lang.	Language concept	OOC-O concept
Smalltalk	Class	Concrete Class & Extendable Class
	Abstract Class	Abstract Class
	Template	Generic Class
	Method	Concrete Method & Overridable Method
	Accessor Method	Accessor Method
	Instance Variable	Instance Variable
	Access	Element Visibility
Eiffel	Class	Concrete Class & Extendable Class
	Deferred Class	Abstract Class
	Frozen Class	Non-Extendable Class
	Generic Class	Generic Class
	Routine	Instance Method & Non-Overridable Method
	Routine Redefinition	Overridable Method
	Accessor Routine	Instance Method
	Attribute	Instance Variable
	Access	Element Visibility
C++	Class	Concrete Class & Extendable Class
	Abstract Class	Abstract Class
	Final Class	Non-Extendable Class
	Template	Generic Class
	Member Function	Instance Method
	Final Member Function	Non-Overridable Method
	Virtual Member Function	Overridable Method
	Accessor Member Function	Instance Method
	Instance Variable	Instance Variable
	Access Modifier	Element Visibility
Java	Class	Concrete Class & Extendable Class
	Abstract Class	Abstract Class
	Final Class	Non-Extendable Class
	Generic Class	Generic Class
	Method	Instance Method & Overridable Method
	Abstract Method	Abstract Method
	Final Method	Non-Overridable Method
	Accessor Method	Instance Method
	Instance Variable	Instance Variable
	Access Modifier	Element Visibility
Python	Class	Concrete Class & Extendable Class
	Abstract Class	Abstract Class
	Generic Class	Generic Class
	Method	Concrete Method & Overridable Method
	Accessor Method	Instance Method
	Data Attribute	Instance Variable

or of the object orientation, using the ontological view to define the formal basis of the object notion [29] or introducing a new view on the roles in OO programming languages, such in the powerJava language extended from Java [4]. However, this research is interested in identifying and formalizing the relevant concepts in OO programming languages, little explored as far as we know.

Evermann & Wand [10] apply semantic mapping between ontological concepts of the BWW ontology and OO programming language constructs to assign semantics and rules in the context of software modeling. The BWW concepts (thing, property and functional schema) are mapped to UML concepts (object, class, attribute, attribute of 'ordinary' class and attribute of association class). Although the research has applied an ontological analysis to map object-oriented constructs, it covers only a small portion of that domain.

Kouneli et al. [16] apply an operational ontology of programming language for representing the knowledge delivered by a distance learning course on computer programming. Although the ontology is built following a methodology and sources of information of the Java language, it is not based on any foundation ontology. The concepts of the ontology are anchored in the Thing concept and hierarchically organized from Java Element (Class, Constructor, Data Type, Exception, Interface, Method (AbstractMethod, FinalMethod, ClassMethod and InstanceMethod), Object, Operator, Package, Statement, Thread and Variable (ClassVariable, InstanceVariable, LocalVariable and Parameter)), Keyword and Literal Value. Unlike OOC-O, this ontology only represents the Java programming language domain and incorporates non-object-oriented concepts such as exception, operator, statement, and thread.

Pastor et al. [20] elaborate the O3 reference ontology, inspired by BWW and the FRISCO framework to semantically map the concepts of the OO programming paradigm. The concepts of BWW (thing, property, substantial and relation) are specialized for the concepts of the OO paradigm (class (generalization, specialization), domain (primitive type)), attribute (variable, constant), interface). Although the research has applied an ontological analysis to map object-orientation concepts, it covers only a small portion of that domain and incorporates non-object-oriented concepts such as constraint, service, relation, agent, server and others.

6   Final Considerations

This paper presents a reference ontology about the concepts of object-oriented programming code based on a foundation ontology. The OOC-O ontology is built according to an ontology engineering method and based on well-known data sources. Verification and validation activities were successfully accomplished, by answering competency questions, instantiating the ontology in fragments of OO code, harmonizing between object-oriented languages (Smalltalk, Eiffel, C++, Java and Python) and checking the coverage of the fundamental OO concepts.

The OOC-O ontology is not intended to represent principles or philosophies of object orientation, but rather the semantic representation of OO programming

language code. To the best of our knowledge, we have not found any related work that covers the proposed domain in depth. Finally, in future work, we intend to use the ontology at the foundation of tools in a polyglot programming development environment and in the context of semantic interoperability among different object-oriented frameworks.

References

1. Aguiar, C.Z.: Object-Oriented Code Ontology – Harmonization Document of Object-Oriented Programming Language. Techical report, Federal University of Espírito Santo (2019).http://nemo.inf.ufes.br/projects/sfwon/
2. Aguiar, C.Z.: Object-Oriented Code Ontology – Reference Ontology Specification Document. Technical report, Federal University of Espírito Santo (2019). http://nemo.inf.ufes.br/projects/sfwon/
3. Atkinson, M., Dewitt, D., Maier, D., Bancilhon, F., Dittrich, K., Zdonik, S.: The object-oriented database system manifesto. In: Deductive and Object-Oriented Databases, pp. 223–240. Elsevier (1990)
4. Baldoni, M., Boella, G., Van Der Torre, L.: powerjava: ontologically founded roles in object oriented programming languages. In: Proceedings of the 2006 ACM Symposium on Applied Computing, pp. 1414–1418. ACM (2006)
5. Booch, G.: Coming of age in an object-oriented world. IEEE Softw. **11**(6), 33–41 (1994)
6. Brun, R., Rademakers, F.: Root-an object oriented data analysis framework. Nucl. Instrum. Methods Phys. Res. Sect. A: Accel. Spect. Detect. Assoc. Equip. **389**(1–2), 81–86 (1997)
7. Conaway, C.F., Page-Jones, M., Constantine, L.L.: Fundamentals of Object-Oriented Design in UML. Addison-Wesley, Boston (2000)
8. Duarte, B.B., Leal, A.L.C., Falbo, R.D.A., Guizzardi, G., Guizzardi, R.S., Souza, V.E.S.: Ontological foundations for software requirements with a focus on requirements at runtime. Appl. Ontol. **13**(2), 73–105 (2018). https://doi.org/10.3233/AO-180197
9. Eiffel, E.: Eiffel: analysis, design and programming language. In: ECMA Standard ECMA-367. ECMA (2006)
10. Evermann, J., Wand, Y.: Ontology based object-oriented domain modelling: fundamental concepts. Requir. Eng. **10**(2), 146–160 (2005)
11. Falbo, R.A.: Sabio: Systematic approach for building ontologies. In: ONTO. COM/ODISE@ FOIS (2014)
12. Fjeldberg, H.C.: Polyglot programming. Ph.D. thesis, Master thesis, Norwegian University of Science and Technology, Trondheim/Norway (2008)
13. Gosling, J., Joy, B., Steele, G., Bracha, G., Buckley, A., Smith, D.: The Java Language Specification: Java SE, 10 edn., 20 February 2018 (2018)
14. Guizzardi, G., Wagner, G.: A unified foundational ontology and some applications of it in business modeling. In: CAiSE Workshops, no. 3, pp. 129–143 (2004)
15. Hunt, J.: Java and Object Orientation: An Introduction. Springer, Heidelberg (2002). https://doi.org/10.1007/978-1-4471-0125-3
16. Kouneli, A., Solomou, G., Pierrakeas, C., Kameas, A.: Modeling the knowledge domain of the java programming language as an ontology. In: Popescu, E., Li, Q., Klamma, R., Leung, H., Specht, M. (eds.) ICWL 2012. LNCS, vol. 7558, pp. 152–159. Springer, Heidelberg (2012). https://doi.org/10.1007/978-3-642-33642-3_16

17. Lafore, R.: Object-Oriented Programming in C++. Pearson Education, Prentice Hall (1997)
18. LaLonde, W.R., Pugh, J.R.: Inside Smalltalk, vol. 2. Prentice Hall, London (1990)
19. de Oliveira Bringuente, A.C., de Almeida Falbo, R., Guizzardi, G.: Using a foundational ontology for reengineering a software process ontology. J. Inf. Data Manage. **2**(3), 511 (2011)
20. Pastor, O.: Diseño y Desarrollo de un Entorno de Producción Automática de Software basado en el modelo orientado a Objetos. Ph.D. thesis, Tesis doctoral dirigida por Isidro Ramos, DSIC, Universitat Politècnica de... (1992)
21. Pastor, O., Insfrán, E., Pelechano, V., Ramirez, S.: Linking object-oriented conceptual modeling with object-oriented implementation in Java. In: Proceedings of Database and Expert Systems Applications, 8th International Conference, DEXA 1997, Toulouse, France, 1–5 September 1997, pp. 132–141 (1997)
22. Phillips, D.: Python 3 Object-Oriented Programming. Packt Publishing Ltd., Birmingham (2015)
23. Borges Ruy, F., de Almeida Falbo, R., Perini Barcellos, M., Dornelas Costa, S., Guizzardi, G.: SEON: a software engineering ontology network. In: Blomqvist, E., Ciancarini, P., Poggi, F., Vitali, F. (eds.) EKAW 2016. LNCS (LNAI), vol. 10024, pp. 527–542. Springer, Cham (2016). https://doi.org/10.1007/978-3-319-49004-5_34
24. Schink, H., Broneske, D., Schröter, R., Fenske, W.: A tree-based approach to support refactoring in multi-language software applications. In: Proceedings of the 2nd International Conference on Advances and Trends in Software Engineering, Lisbon, Portugal, pp. 3–6 (2016)
25. Sebesta, R.W.: Concepts of Programming Languages. Pearson, Boston (2012)
26. Tucker, A.B.: Programming Languages: Principles and Paradigmas. Tata McGraw-Hill Education, New York (2007)
27. Turner, R., Eden, A.H.: Towards a programming language ontology. Citeseer (2007)
28. Tyrrell, A.J.: Eiffel Object-oriented Programming. Springer, Heidelberg (1995). https://doi.org/10.1007/978-1-349-13875-3
29. Wand, Y.: A proposal for a formal model of objects. In: Object-Oriented Concepts, Databases, and Applications, pp. 537–559. ACM (1989)
30. Zanetti, F., Aguiar, C.Z., Souza, V.E.S.: Representacao ontologica de frameworks de mapeamento objeto/relacional. In: 12th Seminar on Ontology Research in Brazil (ONTOBRAS) (2019). (to appear)

Relations in Ontology-Driven Conceptual Modeling

Claudenir M. Fonseca[1(✉)], Daniele Porello[2], Giancarlo Guizzardi[1,3],
João Paulo A. Almeida[3], and Nicola Guarino[2]

[1] Conceptual and Cognitive Modeling Research Group (CORE),
Free University of Bozen-Bolzano, Bolzano, Italy
{cmoraisfonseca,giancarlo.guizzardi}@unibz.it
[2] ISTC-CNR Laboratory for Applied Ontology, Trento, Italy
{daniele.porello,nicola.guarino}@cnr.it
[3] NEMO, Federal University of Espírito Santo, Vitoria, Brazil
jpalmeida@ieee.org

Abstract. For over a decade now, a community of researchers has contributed
to the ontological foundations of Conceptual Modeling by participating to the
development of the Unified Foundational Ontology (UFO) and the UFO-based
modeling language OntoUML, which have been successfully employed in a number of different sectors. The empirical feedback from these experiences led us to
reconsider UFO's *theory of relations*, proposing a new theory that has already
been applied to model subtle notions in the business domain, such as value, risk,
service, and contract. In this paper, we advance a first formal characterization of
this new theory, which is then used to design a new metamodel for OntoUML.

Keywords: Relations · Relationships · Ontology-driven conceptual modeling ·
OntoUML · UFO

1 Introduction

Applied philosophical theories have gained an increasing importance in conceptual
modeling in the past decades, supporting different modeling approaches. More specifically, the notion of foundational ontologies emerged in the form of comprehensive
theories seeking to consistently define fundamental concepts in the field, e.g., *types and
taxonomic structures, roles and relational properties, part-whole relations, multi-level
structures*, etc. An ontology developed with the goal of providing foundations for all
these major conceptual modeling constructs is UFO (Unified Foundational Ontology)
[10, 14]. Over the years, UFO has been employed for the evaluation and (re)design of
conceptual modeling languages and reference models in a variety of domains [12]. One
of the main applications of UFO has been the design of a general-purpose language
for *ontology-driven conceptual modeling* (ODCM) OntoUML. Following a systematic
language engineering process [10], OntoUML has been created as a revised version
of UML such that: (i) its modeling primitives reflect the ontological distinctions put
forth by UFO; (ii) its metamodel includes semantically-motivated syntactic constraints

that reflect the axiomatization of UFO. Research shows that UFO and OntoUML are among the most used foundational ontology and modeling language in the ODCM literature, respectively [24]. Moreover, empirical evidence shows that OntoUML significantly contributes to improving the quality of conceptual models without requiring an additional effort to produce them. For instance, Verdonck's work [23] reports on a modeling experiment conducted with 100 participants in two countries showing the advantages of OntoUML when compared to a classical conceptual modeling language (EER).

The observations of the way OntoUML was applied over the years, conducted by several groups in a variety of domains, are a fruitful empirical source of knowledge on the language and its foundations [12]. In particular, we observed a number of different ways in which people did slightly subvert the syntax of the language, ultimately creating what we called *systematic subversions* [10]. These "subversions" did (purposefully) produce models that were grammatically incorrect, but which were needed to express intended meanings that could not be expressed otherwise. We labeled them as "systematic" because they were recurring in the works of different authors that, independently of each other, were subverting the language in the same manner and with the same modeling intention. One of these "subversions" led us to reconsider UFO's *theory of relations* [6,7], proposing a new theory that has been applied to model a number of different notions, including *value, risk, preference, service* and *contract* [5,17,21], whose (preliminary) formal characterization will be presented here for the first time.

Relations are fundamental for conceptual modeling, and, for many years, researchers have been looking at ontological theories to account for relevant distinctions among them, and provide ways to *talk* of them by means of *reification* mechanisms [1,3,11,25]. In this paper, leveraging on previous revisitations of UFO's notion of *relator* [6,7,9], we present UFO's new theory of relations as well as its OntoUML counterpart (a suitable fragment of OntoUML 2.0 [13]). As we demonstrate, this new theory is much richer than the existing proposals in the literature, with important consequences for conceptual modeling practice.

The contributions of this paper are three-fold. First, we present a first formal characterization for this new theory of relations. Second, following the same ontology-based language engineering approach that was used to create the original version of OntoUML [10], we employ this new formalized version of the theory to propose an enhanced metamodel for OntoUML 2.0. Finally, we employ this metamodel to implement a model construction and verification tool for OntoUML 2.0. The remainder of this paper is organized as follows: Sect. 2 provides the background for the paper briefly reviewing OntoUML and UFO, including its new ontological theory of relations. The section also briefly analyzes the limitations of the original version of OntoUML and its underlying theory with respect to the conceptual modeling of relations; Sect. 3 presents a rich formalization of the new theory, accounting for relators and for different kinds of relations; Sect. 4 presents the OntoUML 2.0 relations metamodel and the modeling patterns [9] for the various kinds of relations, incorporated into the language; Sect. 5 briefly discusses related work and presents our final considerations.

2   Background: UFO, OntoUML and a New Theory of Relations

OntoUML was originally designed to represent invariant structures of endurants (object-like entities) and their relations, reflecting the ontological distinctions in UFO. In this foundational ontology, endurants are partitioned into *substantials* and *moments*. Substantials are existentially independent individuals, e.g., a car, a person, or an organization. In contrast, moments are specific *aspects* of individuals that are existentially dependent on them, such as (a) a flower's color or (b) Bob's headache, and may be also existentially dependent on other individuals, as in the case of (c) John's love for Mary or (d) the marriage between John and Mary. The specific sort of existential dependence connecting moments to their *bearers* is termed *inherence*. Each of these examples of moments reflects a different category within UFO (Fig. 2)[1]: (a) is an example of a *quality*, a particular aspect of an individual that may be useful to compare it with other individuals, on the basis of the value it takes in a certain quality space (for instance, a position within the RGB spectrum) [10]; (b) and (c) are examples of *modes*, i.e., aspects that can have their own qualities; in particular, (b) is an *intrinsic mode*, since it only depends on its bearer, while (c) is an example of *extrinsic mode*, also called *externally dependent mode* since, besides inhering in John, it is also existentially dependent on Mary, accounting for a one-sided relationship between John and Mary; finally, (d) may be seen as a sum of externally dependent modes accounting for reciprocal one-sided relationships (such as John's love for Mary, John's obligations towards Mary, and the reciprocal relationships on Mary's side), which form altogether a complex two-sided relationship. Qualities and intrinsic modes are collectively called *intrinsic moments*, as they are intrinsic to their bearers. *Extrinsic modes* include externally dependent modes and mereological sums of two or more externally dependent modes, which are collectively called *relators*.

In OntoUML, an association stereotyped as *«characterization»* represents (at the type-level) the existence of an *inherence* relation connecting the instances of those types, i.e., connecting intrinsic moments and their bearers. Analogously, associations stereotyped as *«mediation»* are used to connect relators to their relata.[2] Both *«characterization»* and *«mediation»* are special cases of *existential dependence* [10].

The original version of UFO made a fundamental distinction between *formal* and *material* relations. Intuitively, the former were assumed to hold "directly without any further intervening individual", while the latter required the existence of an intervening individual. Formally, material relations where defined as presupposing the existence of a *relator* composed of externally dependent modes (each inhering in one relatum and externally dependent on the other) all historically dependent on a common external *foundation event*. Formal relations where defined as relations that are not material. Typical examples of material relations where *married-with* or *employed-by*, while formal relations included inherence, mediation and parthood, as well as *comparative relations* such as *heavier-than*.

---

[1] The taxonomy we are describing, depicted in Fig. 2, has been slightly changed with respect to UFO's original one.

[2] We stick to the term 'mediation' just for reasons of compatibility with previous papers. In the past we also used 'involvement', which is perhaps a better terminological alternative.

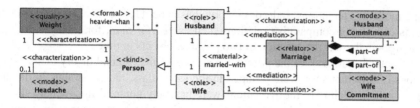

Fig. 1. Example of relations in the current version of OntoUML.

Figure 1 illustrates how these relations appear in OntoUML in its current version. Stereotypes are used to distinguish «formal» and «material» relations, as well as to identify «characterization» and «mediation». Moreover, the *derivation* relation is represented by a dashed line connecting the relator type Marriage and the relation marriedwith, such that we have that the tuple $\langle John, Mary \rangle$ instantiates the latter iff it is mediated by an instance of the former, i.e., by a particular instance of Marriage.

2.1 Limitations of UFO/OntoUML 1.0 Regarding the Modeling of Relations

In the original version of UFO, the distinction between formal and material was exhaustive, i.e., all relations that were not consider material (i.e., mediated by an external entity) were automatically classified as formal. Take, for example, the ternary relation of *Economic Preference* [18], defined between an agent and two resources. This relation is completely grounded on two modes of the agent, namely, two *value ascriptions* made by that agent with respect to those resources. However, in this case, there is no property that is acquired by these resources in virtue of being preferred (or deprecated) by that agent! The only entity that has relational properties grounding that relation is that agent. Now, since in UFO relators are aggregations of externally dependent modes of all relata, the sum of the valuations of this agent is not a relator and, hence, *preference* cannot be considered a *material* relation. As a consequence, it must be considered a formal relation and, hence, classified together with relations as diverse as *being-older* than and *existential dependence*.

So, the original UFO theory of relations was too restrictive (w.r.t. *material relations*), proscribing the existence of *single-side relational moments*. On the other hand, the theory was too permissive (w.r.t. *formal relations*), including in the same class, for example, relations holding directly as soon as their relata exist (e.g., existential dependence, inherence, instantiation) and relations reducible to intrinsic properties of the relata (e.g., *comparative relations* such as *older-than*), as well as the so-called *mere Cambridge relations* [7], e.g., economic preference or value ascription.

A practical drawback of the aforementioned *restrictive* aspect is the difficulty in modeling relations based on single-side relational qualities, which abound in practice. For example, this shortcoming of the language has caused several experienced researchers to radically diverge regarding the modeling of standard relations in the ISO REA framework [8]. Moreover, since *relationship reification* was restricted to material relations, the modeling benefits of reifying other types of relationships would often

escape modeler's attentions. Indeed, in a previous paper [12] some of us discussed the benefits of reifying comparative relations such as *heavier-than*, for example, to track the changes in the weight variation of two physical objects in time.

A practical drawback of the *permissive* aspects of the original theory is that, since relations of different sorts were grouped in the same class, the constraints in the language for the modeling of these relations were basically non-existing, namely, the use of standard associations with a stereotype «formal». As a consequence, for example, when modeling *comparative relations*, there was nothing in the language forcing the modeler to pay attention to the existence of particular qualities in the relata that would ground that relation (e.g., in the way that *heavier-than* should be grounded in the individual weights of the relata). Furthermore, as demonstrated by [20], after analyzing a repository of dozens of OntoUML models, a frequent anti-pattern in ontology-driven conceptual modeling is the use of the «formal» stereotype to model relations neglecting a deeper analysis of their nature, exactly because of the lack of additional constraints associated with that stereotype.

As a final limitation, we highlight that although the original OntoUML metamodel explicitly represents different forms of existential dependence (e.g., inherence, mediation), it does not provide any native support for other forms of *specific dependence*, which recurrently appeared in practical domains. The most prominent of these being *external dependence* (for example, in the domains of Service [5] and Risk [21]) and *historical dependence* (for an example, in many *ontologies of artifacts* [26]).

2.2   Extending UFO's Original Theory of Relations

In a recent series of papers [6,7,9], Guarino and Guizzardi revisited the ontological nature of relations and relationships by focusing on the following question: if a relation R holds for relata x and y, what is there in the world that is the *truthmaker* of this relational sentence, i.e., what is responsible for its truth? What is the nature of such truthmaker? By relying on distinctions with respect to different types of truthmakers, the authors proposed a *typology of relation types* that goes beyond the original distinction between *formal* and *material*, relying on two orthogonal distinctions: *internal/external* and *descriptive/non-descriptive*.

So far, we kept refining our own understanding of these two distinctions in an informal way, resulting in changes in the way some relations where classified. Indeed, as discussed in [9], the philosophical terms used for such distinctions are often used in different ways, so that it is difficult to draw an accurate picture. This is the reason why, in this paper, we decided to aim at a rigorous axiomatic characterization, both to clarify the ontological assumptions behind these distinctions and to allow us to formally derive the constraints to be implemented in the new version of OntoUML (OntoUML 2.0) in order to enforce ontologically well-founded modeling patterns (Table 1).

According to a definition originally due to Russell [19], **internal relations** are relations derivable in terms of the intrinsic properties of their relata. A classic example are comparative relations. They may hold either in virtue of intrinsic moments of the relata (e.g., John is taller than Mary because of their intrinsic height qualities) or just in virtue of the way the relata intrinsically are, without involving their qualities (e.g., John's height is greater than Mary's height). **External relations**, in contrast, cannot be

just defined in terms of intrinsic properties of their relata. This means that they either: (i) rely on at least one property of a relatum that depends on something else (typically, the other relatum). The classic example is the marriage relation, whose truthmaker is composed of the mutual commitments and obligations of the partners, which are modes inhering in each of them and externally dependent on the other one; (ii) are primitive non-analyzable relations (e.g., existential dependence and its specializations such as *inherence* and *mediation*). In summary, in the case of an external relation connecting *x* and *y*, there is something about *x* that requires the existence of *y*. This externally dependent entity is either a moment of *x* or *x* itself.

In an orthogonal dimension, **descriptive relations** hold in virtue of some *moment* (aspect) of the relata. For example, both *in love with* and *heavier than* between people hold because of specific moments of their relata (a love mode in the first case; weight qualities in the second case). In contrast, **non-descriptive relations** hold because of the entity as a whole (e.g., *greater than* between two qualities, such as weight or height). Each combination of the two distinctions (i.e., *internal/external* and *descriptive/non-descriptive*) corresponds to an interesting class of relations. For example, in this account of descriptiveness, a *historical dependence* relation such as *born in* turns out to be non-descriptive (since it does not involve an intrinsic quality of its relata) and external, since what makes it true is something external to both individuals. Unlike the cases we have been discussing so far, such external entity is not an endurant (quality, mode, relator) but an *event*, namely, a person's birth. Moreover, comparative relations among objects are examples of internal and descriptive and relations similar to *married-with* are examples of external descriptive ones.

As discussed in depth in [6], there are important benefits, from a conceptual modeling point of view, in explicitly representing truthmakers via *relationships reification*, ranging from addressing ambiguity in *single-tuple* versus *multiple-tuple* cardinality constraints, clarifying the semantics of relations involving relations (e.g., relation subsetting, relation specialization, relation redefinition), modeling n-adic relations, etc. Guarino, Sales and Guizzardi [9], use these combinations devise a set of *truthmaking patterns* designed to properly represent truthmakers in all the cases where the relation merits reification, namely, all descriptive relations and some external non-descriptive ones. We explore these patterns in Sect. 4 incorporating them into the language as means to support ontology-driven conceptual modeling.

3   A Formal Theory of Relations

We present the first formalization of the aspects previously discussed. This formalization builds upon but significantly extends UFO's formalization for endurant types in [13][3] and serves as the foundational layer for Sect. 4.

Our formal theory is expressed in first-order modal logic QS5 with fixed domain of interpretation [4]. We omit the outermost necessity operator and universal quantifier, in case their scope takes the full formula. Assuming a fixed domain of interpretation, the elements of the domains are construed as *possibilia*, i.e., entities that exist at least in a

---

[3] We only present an excerpt of the formalization here. The complete formalization is available at https://github.com/diporello/UFO-Ontology-of-Relations/.

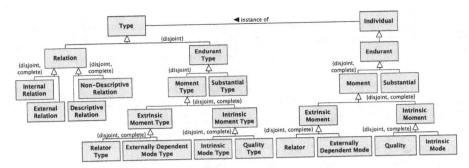

Fig. 2. Taxonomy of UFO types.

possible world. UFO introduces then a non-logical *existence predicate* (ex) defined on the possible entities at issue (here Thing) (a1). By means of ex, we define the relation of *existential dependence* between two entities, ed(x,y) (a2), and of existential independence, ind(x,y), (a3). These axioms serve also the formalization of the *inherence* relation (a4)–(a7). A moment can be defined as an endurant that inheres in some endurant, which is the *bearer* of the moment (a10) (e.g. John's courage). Moreover, a moment cannot inhere in two separate individuals, (a8). By axiom (a10), the bearer of a moment always exists and, by (a8), it is unique, thus the dependence is functional and we can introduce the function symbol $\beta(x)$ to indicate the unique *bearer* of a moment (d1). Moments are then partitioned into *intrinsic moments*, which existentially depend only on their bearer, and *extrinsic moments*, which depend on entities that are distinguished from the bearers (a11). Intrinsic moments are then divided into *qualities* (e.g. weight, length, color) in case the moment is measurable by a certain quality space (cf. [10]), and *intrinsic modes* (e.g. courage), which may not be measurable. *Extrinsic moments* are divided into *externally dependent modes* (edm) and *relators*. The former are moments that inhere in one entity and depends on another. We shall approach relators in the next paragraphs. Extrinsic moments do play a relational role between the entities on which they depend, cf. [10]. E.g. John's love for Mary inheres in John and existentially depends on Mary. We introduce the relation of external dependence, (a12).

a1 $\mathrm{ex}(x) \rightarrow \mathrm{Thing}(x)$

a2 $\mathrm{ed}(x,y) \leftrightarrow \Box(\mathrm{ex}(x) \rightarrow \mathrm{ex}(y))$

a3 $\mathrm{ind}(x,y) \leftrightarrow \neg\mathrm{ed}(x,y) \wedge \neg\mathrm{ed}(y,x)$

a4 $\mathrm{inheresIn}(x,y) \rightarrow \mathrm{Moment}(x) \wedge \mathrm{Endurant}(y)$

a5 $\mathrm{inheresIn}(x,y) \rightarrow \mathrm{ed}(x,y)$

a6 $\neg\mathrm{inheresIn}(x,x)$

a7 $\mathrm{inheresIn}(x,y) \wedge \mathrm{inheresIn}(y,z) \rightarrow \neg\mathrm{inheresIn}(x,z)$

a8 $\mathrm{inheresIn}(x,y) \wedge \mathrm{inheresIn}(x,z) \rightarrow y = z$

d1 $\beta(x) =_{def} \iota y.\, \mathrm{inheresIn}(x,y)$

a9 $\mathrm{inheresIn}(x,y) \rightarrow \neg\mathrm{inheresIn}(y,x)$

a10 $\mathrm{Moment}(x) \leftrightarrow \mathrm{Endurant}(x) \wedge \exists y\, \mathrm{inheresIn}(x,y)$

a11 $\mathrm{ExtrinsicMoment}(x) \leftrightarrow \mathrm{Moment}(x) \wedge \mathrm{ed}(x,y) \wedge \exists y.(\mathrm{ind}(y,\beta(x)))$

a12 $\mathrm{externallyDepends}(x,y) \leftrightarrow \mathrm{Moment}(x) \wedge \mathrm{ed}(x,y) \wedge \mathrm{ind}(y,\beta(x)))$

Finally, we assume a classical extensional mereology. For reason of space, we do not present the related axioms, relying on [15,22]. We denote by Pxy and $PPxy$ the relation of *part* and *proper part* (respectively).

We present now the theory of relations. We write $\langle x_1, \ldots, x_n \rangle :: r$ for the instantiation of an *n*-ary relation r by $x_1, \ldots, x_n$, cf. [16]. We limit ourselves to binary relations, the case of *n*-ary relations is a simple generalization. Hence, we can introduce a taxonomy of *n*-ary universals (i.e. relations), cf. Fig. 2. The taxonomy of relations is motivated by the specific truthmaking patterns, which are explicit in the right-hand part of axioms (a15) and (a16). This patterns indicate a necessary condition about the properties of the entities that are relevant to assess the relational statement at issue. By presenting the necessary conditions for the relational to hold (i.e. by $\rightarrow$), we are not committing to a characterization of the relational statement. For example, for an internal relation such as r = *heavier-than*, it is *necessary* for classifying $\langle x, y \rangle :: r$ that two qualities of these relata exists, namely, their weights. However, this is may not suffice, as we also need that the weight of x *is greater than* the weight of y. We approach this point in Sect. 4, where we characterize a particular subtype of internal relations.

To associate a relation (or, as we shall see, also a type) to the correct relevant properties, we assume a primitive relation of *derivation*, $\mathtt{der}(x, y)$. For instance, $\mathtt{der}$ associates a comparative relation such as r = *heavier-than* the *weight* qualities of the relata (and not e.g. the *colour* qualities).

An **internal relation**, (a15), holds *in virtue of intrinsic property* of the relata (e.g. *heavier-than* holds because of the weights of the relata). Defining the intrinsic properties of an entity is of course a difficult endeavour, cf. [9]. Here, we approximate, by assuming that intrinsic properties include types of intrinsic moments. Axiom (a13) does not exclude that we may list further intrinsic properties. Notice that the constraint about $\mathtt{der}$ is also required to define the relevant moment type that defines the intrinsic property. **External relations** are the non-internal ones, i.e. they are not reducible to relevant properties of the relata. As we shall discuss in the sequel, primitive relations are also construed here as external relations.

Descriptive relations are here restricted to mention moments of the relata, i.e. to simplify the presentation, we do not discuss moments that inhere the sum of the relata, cf. [9]. By (a16), descriptive relational statements may hold in two cases: (*i*) in virtue of a pertinent extrinsic moment m that inheres in one of the relata and depends on the other (for external descriptive relations, e.g. *John admires Mary*) *or* (*ii*) in virtue of the existence of pertinent intrinsic moments of the relata (for internal descriptive ones, e.g., John is *taller-than* Mary). Theorem (t1) indeed shows that, if r is descriptive and external, then there exists an extrinsic moment of one relatum that depends on the other.

a13 $\mathtt{Type}(p) \wedge \Box(x :: p \leftrightarrow \exists m, t(\mathtt{IntrinsicMoment}(m) \wedge \mathtt{IntrinsicMomentType}(t) \wedge$
$m :: t \wedge \mathtt{inheresIn}(m, x)) \rightarrow \mathtt{IntrinsicProperty}(p)$

a14 $\mathtt{der}(x, y) \rightarrow (\mathtt{Relation}(x) \vee \mathtt{Type}(x)) \wedge (\mathtt{Relation}(y) \vee \mathtt{Type}(y))$

a15 $\mathtt{Internal}(r) \leftrightarrow \forall xy.(\Diamond\langle x, y \rangle :: r \rightarrow \exists pp'.(\mathtt{IntrinsicProperty}(p) \wedge$
$\mathtt{IntrinsicProperty}(p') \wedge \mathtt{der}(r, p) \wedge \mathtt{der}(r, p') \wedge x :: p \wedge y :: p'))$

a16 $\mathtt{Descriptive}(r) \leftrightarrow \forall x_1 x_2.(\Diamond\langle x_1, x_2 \rangle :: r \rightarrow \exists z.(\mathtt{MomentType}(z) \wedge \mathtt{der}(r, z)$
$\wedge \exists m.(\mathtt{ExtrinsicMoment}(m) \wedge m :: z \wedge \bigvee_{i,j\in\{1,2\}}^{i\neq j}(\mathtt{inheresIn}(m, x_i) \wedge$

$$\text{ed}(m, x_j)))$$
$$\vee \exists m_1 m_2.((\bigwedge_{i \in \{1,2\}}(\text{IntrinsicMoment}(m_i) \wedge m_i :: z \wedge \text{inheresIn}(m_i, x_i))))))$$

t1 $\text{Descriptive}(r) \wedge \text{External}(r) \wedge \Diamond\langle x_1, x_2\rangle :: r \rightarrow \exists x m.(\text{MomentType}(x) \wedge$
$\text{ExtrinsicMoment}(m) \wedge \text{der}(r, x) \wedge m :: x \wedge \bigvee_{i,j \in \{1,2\}}^{i \neq j}(\text{inheresIn}(m, x_i) \wedge$
$\text{ed}(m, x_j))$

For internal relations, we have two cases of truthmaking. If they are also descriptive, we look for moments of the relata, e.g. the weight quality of the relata in a comparative statement between objects such as *John is heavier than Paul*. If they are not descriptive, we search for intrinsic properties of the relata that are not moments. One example is the value of the weight quality in comparative statements between qualities as in *The weight of John is greater than the weight of Paul*, which is here understood as an intrinsic property of the relata but not a quality (a moment) of the relata.

For external non-descriptive relations, we have that there is no moment of the relata that is relevant to the truthmaking and also that there is no intrinsic properties of the relata to which we can reduce the relational statement. For this reason, external non-descriptive relations categorize our primitive undefined relations. For external descriptive relations, we have two cases of truthmaking. For *one-sided relations* (e.g. *John admires Mary*), the existence of the pertinent externally dependent mode suffices. For *double-sided relations* (*John is married to Mary*), a single externally dependent mode is not enough, we need the two modes inhering in both relata. That is, we need to introduce relators. *Relators* are formalized as mereological sums of externally dependent modes such that: they share the same foundation; they inhere in some entity; and, they existentially depend on another relatum, cf. [10]. We start by defining the *foundation* of an extrinsic moment as an event and we assume that the foundation is unique, cf. (a17) and (a18). For reasons of space, we cannot fully discuss here the theory of events [7]. Axiom (a19) defines relators as objects that have at least two parts (cf. Pmx and Pnx in (a19)), which indeed are externally dependent modes that inhere some individual, share the same foundation, and depend on another individual.

a17 $\text{foundedBy}(x, y) \rightarrow (\text{ExtrinsicMoment}(x) \wedge \text{Event}(y))$

a18 $\text{ExtrinsicMoment}(x) \rightarrow \exists! y\, \text{foundedBy}(x, y)$

a19 $\text{Relator}(x) \leftrightarrow \exists mnyze.(\text{Edm}(m) \wedge \text{inheresIn}(m, y) \wedge \text{Edm}(n) \wedge \text{inheresIn}(n, z) \wedge$
$\text{P}mx \wedge \text{P}nx \wedge m \neq n \wedge y \neq z \wedge \text{foundedBy}(m, e) \wedge \text{foundedBy}(n, e) \wedge \text{ed}(m, z) \wedge$
$\text{ed}(n, y))$

a20 $\text{mediates}(x, y) \leftrightarrow \text{Relator}(x) \wedge \text{Endurant}(y) \wedge \exists z.(\text{Edm}(z) \wedge \text{inheresIn}(z, y) \wedge$
$\text{P}zx)$

t2 $\text{Relator}(x) \rightarrow \exists yz.(\text{mediates}(x, y) \wedge \text{mediates}(x, z) \wedge y \neq z)$

Mediation links a relator x and an individual y that the relator connects (a20). A relator is a particular type of moment, hence it has a unique bearer, which can be defined as the mereological sum of all the individuals mediated by the relator, cf. [15,22]. By (a19) and (a20), a relator must connect at least two individuals (t2).

4   Towards a New UML Profile for Modeling Relations

OntoUML is an ODCM language that extends UML class diagrams by defining stereo-types that reflect UFO ontological distinctions into language constructs (e.g., classes and associations). As discussed previously, constructs decorated with OntoUML stereo-types carry a precise semantics grounded by UFO, and enriched by a set of *semantically motivated syntactical constraints* [2], reflecting UFO's axiomatization. In addition to ensuring ontological model consistency, the stereotyped constructs and constraints guide the modeler into addressing ontological issues concerning the subject domain. In particular, the OntoUML constructs for relations guide the modeler concerning the inclusion of truthmakers of domain relations in a model.

The specification of OntoUML is presented as a UML profile (a *lightweight extension*) in Fig. 3. All relation types are represented as stereotypes of UML associations. Stereotypes in gray are concrete, and, hence, are the only ones that appear in models. These stereotypes are discussed throughout this section, which concludes with a summary of the constraints governing their use (Table 1, reflecting the formalization). The stereotypes introduced here capture different types of domain relations that may hold between types of endurants. We shall recall the semantics for each of the stereotypes for endurant types used here, namely, «kind», «relatorKind», «modeKind», «qualityKind» and «role»[4]. The first four stereotypes in the list identify the ontological nature of the decorated type's instances and serve to mark the basic ontological categories instantiated by their instances. Types decorated by «kind» have object-like individuals (sub-stantials) as instances (e.g., *Person*, *Car* or *Organization*); types decorated by «quality-Kind» have qualities as instances(e.g., *Weight* or *Color*). Types decorated by «mod-eKind» have modes as instances (e.g., *Headache* or *Commitment*), including externally dependent modes. Types decorated by «relatorKind» have relators as instances (e.g., *Marriage* or *Enrollment*). These stereotypes are used to represent the *kinds* of entities in the domain, and capture *essential* properties of these entities, classifying them *necessarily*. For example, a *Person* is essentially so, although she can contingently be a *Student*, a *Wife*, a *Client*, an *Employee*, etc. Analogously, an *Enrollment* is essentially so, although it can contingently be a *suspended enrollment*, an *insured enrollment*, *grounds for visa application*, etc. The stereotype «role» decorates types that classify endurants of a given kind dynamically according to some relational property, e.g., the case for *Husband* and *Wife*, whose instances are instances of *Person* involved in a *married-with* relation (see Fig. 4). Types stereotyped as «role» can specialize types decorated with any of the other mentioned class stereotypes.

The following OntoUML stereotypes for domains relations are defined: «characterization», «mediation», «external dependence», «comparative», «material», and «historical». Their usage is exemplified in Fig. 4. The «characterization», «mediation» and «external dependence» stereotypes decorate associations representing different sorts of existential dependencies, all external and non-descriptive. An association stereotyped with «characterization» connects a moment type (either a quality or a mode type) to the endurant type in which its instances *inhere*. An association stereotyped with «media-

---

[4] The set of stereotypes for endurant types presented here is partial, but suffices for the interpretation of the discussed relations and examples. The complete list is drawn from [13].

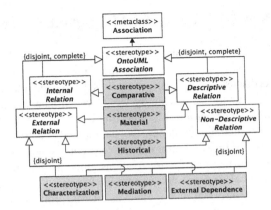

Fig. 3. OntoUML profile for relations.

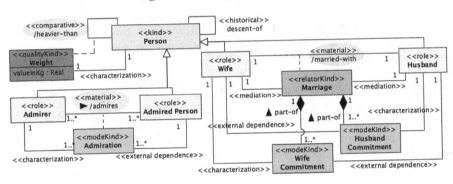

Fig. 4. OntoUML patterns for the reification of relations.

tion» binds a relator type to each endurant type mediated by it. Finally, an association stereotyped with «external dependence» binds an externally dependent mode type to some endurant type on which its instances depend.

The «comparative» stereotype decorates associations representing comparative relations holding between endurant types. Comparative relations, such as *heavier-than*, are descriptive and internal, requiring the usage of a reification pattern to reveal their truthmakers. The truthmaker of a comparative relation is an equivalent relation holding between common qualities of the relata. For example, *heavier-than* holds between instances of *Person* whenever their qualities of *Weight* are related by a special relations (e.g., *greater-than* relation), i.e., the *heavier-than* relation is derived from a pair of weight qualities of the relata, which, in turn, are related by a *greater-than* relation (a internal and non-descriptive relation). Comparative relations are captured in the models by: (a) adding a derivation association (the dashed line in the model) connecting the comparative relation to the quality type of their truthmakers; (b) including a *derivation rule* in the model that strengthens axiom (**a15**) by including a condition representing the internal relation between the values of the appropriate qualities. In general, we have the following general *derivation pattern*: if a comparative relation C_R is derived from

the quality type Q then $\langle x, y \rangle :: C_R \leftrightarrow (\exists q_x, q_y, r. \ (q_x :: Q \wedge q_y :: Q \wedge \texttt{inheresIn}(q_x, x) \wedge$ $\texttt{inheresIn}(q_y, y) \wedge \texttt{Internal}(r) \wedge \neg\texttt{Descriptive}(r) \wedge \langle q_x, q_y \rangle :: r))$. In the example of Fig. 4, this general pattern can take the following OCL form:

```
context Person::heavier-than: Set(Person)
derive: Person.allInstances()->select( p : Person |
                self.weight.valueInKg > p.weight.valueInKg)
```

This pattern reveals not only the quality used as basis for the comparative relation, but also the way they relate to one another that makes true the comparison. With the addition of «comparative» and this general *derivation rule pattern*, we deprecate the former «formal» stereotype.

The «material» stereotype decorates associations representing external descriptive relations, i.e., relations that hold *in virtue of* some relational endurant that is bound to the relata. The first kind of material relations acknowledged in OntoUML are those which truthmakers are relators, in which case the relator mediates all the relata and a derivation relation connects the material one to the relator, as it is for *married-with* and *Marriage*. In addition to relators, externally dependent modes can play the role of relational properties and truthmakers for one-sided material relations, in which case a mode type is connected through derivation to the relation and it inheres in one relatum (through *characterization*) and *externally depends* on the other, as it is for *admires* and *Admiration*. Externally dependent modes may also compose relators, requiring that they *inhere in* and *externally depend* on endurants mediated by the relator they are part of. Modes and relators capture the "life" of the relations derived by them, accounting for identity and properties of the relation that belongs not to the relata but to relation itself.

Lastly, the «historical» stereotype decorates associations representing historical relations. Historical relations are external and non-descriptive and, even though they may hold between endurants, their truthmakers are not endurants, but events (or compositions of events) responsible for the truth of the relation. This can be the case of *descent-of*, captured here as the relation holding between a person and each of his/her ancestors, all of whom participate in a chain of reproduction events. At this point, OntoUML does not officially account for the representation of events, thus, we include historical relations without a reification pattern for the inclusion of events as truthmakers. This is feature of our proposal to be revisited as soon as OntoUML incorporates primitives for the representation of events and event relations.

In addition to the rules presented throughout this section regarding the semantics of relations, their possible relata and truthmaking patterns, Table 1 collects additional constraints that emerge from our formalization. These constraints ensure the adherence to the truthmaking patterns discussed above. This profile is implemented as an extension for a UML CASE tool that incorporates the stereotypes for OntoUML 2.0 and syntactically verifies models for the language's constraints, informing the modeler of any violations or model incompleteness[5].

---

[5] https://github.com/nemo-ufes/OntoUML-2.0-for-Visual-Paradigm.

Table 1. OntoUML constraints on external descriptive relations.

Constraints
From (a16) and (a19), associations decorated as «material» must have a derivation association towards a class decorated as «modeKind», for one-sided relations, and «relatorKind», for others.
From (a16) and (t1), classes decorated as «modeKind» and connected, through derivation, to some «material» relation must have a «characterization» relation towards one of the relata and an «external dependence» relation towards the other.
From (a19) and (t2), classes decorated as «relatorKind» and connected, through derivation, to some «material» relation must have a «mediation» relation towards each relata.
From (a19) and (a20), classes decorated «modeKind» and connected, through *part-of* relation, to some «relatorKind» must have a «characterization» relation towards one of the classes mediated (i.e., «mediation») by the relator.
From (a19), classes decorated «modeKind» and connected, through *part-of* relation, to some «relatorKind» must have a «external dependence» relation towards at least one of the classes mediated (i.e., «mediation») by the relator.
From (a15) and (a16), associations decorated as «comparative» must have a derivation association towards a class decorated as «quality».
From (a15) and (a16), classes decorated as «qualityKind» and connected, through derivation, to some «comparative» relation must have a «characterization» relation towards a class specialized by the relata or the relata themselves.

5   Final Considerations

We contributed to the ontological foundations of conceptual modeling by proposing a formal *ontological theory of relations*. We believe this theory makes an important contribution advancing the state of art in the field. Relations are one of conceptual modeling's most fundamental constructs. However, most existing foundational theories for conceptual modeling only recognize the most basic distinctions among the fundamental categories of relations. For example, the BWW ontology [25], which is the most used foundational ontology in ODCM [23], only countenances two types of properties, namely, *intrinsic and mutual properties*, and two types of relations, namely, *coupling and non-coupling relations*. As discussed in [11], the former distinction is analogous to our distinction between *intrinsic and extrinsic (i.e., externally dependent) moments*. Nevertheless, in our approach properties are instantiated, with several advantages (see in depth discussion in [10,11]). Moreover, the BWW notion of mutual properties seems to conflate the (type-level counterpart of) our notions of externally dependent modes and relators. The latter distinction, as discussed in [10], is similar to the former UFO/OntoUML distinction between formal and material relations, which, as argued here, is insufficient to address subtle modeling requirements.

Our theory was developed to address a number of empirically elicited requirements, collected from observing the practice of the OntoUML community while using these notions to model a variety of domains (*claim to relevance*). Despite the empirical origin of these requirements, they are very much in line with the philosophical literature (*claim to ontological adequacy*). Additionally, following the same strategy as in [13], our formalization has been checked for its consistency using automated theorem provers

(*claim to consistency*). Besides these foundations, we make a contribution to the practice of conceptual modeling by (re)designing a modeling profile based on this theory (following a well-tested approach to ontology-based language engineering [10]), and by providing a computational tool for model creation and verification according to this profile (*claim to realizability*). More broadly, the work presented here is part of a research program aimed at addressing a fuller evolution of UFO and OntoUML [13].

References

1. Bera, P., Evermann, J.: Guidelines for using UML association classes and their effect on domain understanding in requirements engineering. Requirements Eng. **19**(1), 63–80 (2014)
2. de Carvalho, V.A., Almeida, J.P.A., Guizzardi, G.: Using reference domain ontologies to define the real-world semantics of domain-specific languages. In: Jarke, M., et al. (eds.) CAiSE 2014. LNCS, vol. 8484, pp. 488–502. Springer, Cham (2014). https://doi.org/10.1007/978-3-319-07881-6_33
3. Evermann, J.: The association construct in conceptual modelling – an analysis using the bunge ontological model. In: Pastor, O., Falcão e Cunha, J. (eds.) CAiSE 2005. LNCS, vol. 3520, pp. 33–47. Springer, Heidelberg (2005). https://doi.org/10.1007/11431855_4
4. Fitting, M., Mendelsohn, R.L.: First-Order Modal Logic, vol. 277. Springer, Heidelberg (2012)
5. Griffo, C., et al.: From an ontology of service contracts to contract modeling in enterprise architecture. In: Proceedings of 21st EDOC (2017)
6. Guarino, N., Guizzardi, G.: "We need to discuss the *Relationship*": revisiting relationships as modeling constructs. In: Zdravkovic, J., Kirikova, M., Johannesson, P. (eds.) CAiSE 2015. LNCS, vol. 9097, pp. 279–294. Springer, Cham (2015). https://doi.org/10.1007/978-3-319-19069-3_18
7. Guarino, N., Guizzardi, G.: Relationships and events: towards a general theory of reification and truthmaking. In: Adorni, G., Cagnoni, S., Gori, M., Maratea, M. (eds.) AI*IA 2016. LNCS, vol. 10037, pp. 237–249. Springer, Cham (2016). https://doi.org/10.1007/978-3-319-49130-1_18
8. Guarino, N., et al.: On the ontological nature of REA core relations. In: Proceedings of 12th VMBO (2018)
9. Guarino, N., Sales, T.P., Guizzardi, G.: Reification and truthmaking patterns. In: Trujillo, J.C., et al. (eds.) ER 2018. LNCS, vol. 11157, pp. 151–165. Springer, Cham (2018). https://doi.org/10.1007/978-3-030-00847-5_13
10. Guizzardi, G.: Ontological foundations for structural conceptual models. Telematica Instituut/CTIT (2005)
11. Guizzardi, G., Wagner, G.: What's in a relationship: an ontological analysis. In: Li, Q., Spaccapietra, S., Yu, E., Olivé, A. (eds.) ER 2008. LNCS, vol. 5231, pp. 83–97. Springer, Heidelberg (2008). https://doi.org/10.1007/978-3-540-87877-3_8
12. Guizzardi, G., et al.: Towards ontological foundations for conceptual modeling: the unified foundational ontology (UFO) story. Appl. Ontol. **10**(3–4), 259–271 (2015)
13. Guizzardi, G., Fonseca, C.M., Benevides, A.B., Almeida, J.P.A., Porello, D., Sales, T.P.: Endurant types in ontology-driven conceptual modeling: towards OntoUML 2.0. In: Trujillo, J.C., et al. (eds.) ER 2018. LNCS, vol. 11157, pp. 136–150. Springer, Cham (2018). https://doi.org/10.1007/978-3-030-00847-5_12
14. Guizzardi, G., Wagner, G., de Almeida Falbo, R., Guizzardi, R.S.S., Almeida, J.P.A.: Towards ontological foundations for the conceptual modeling of events. In: Ng, W., Storey, V.C., Trujillo, J.C. (eds.) ER 2013. LNCS, vol. 8217, pp. 327–341. Springer, Heidelberg (2013). https://doi.org/10.1007/978-3-642-41924-9_27

15. Hovda, P.: What is classical mereology? J. Philos. Log. **38**(1), 55–82 (2009)
16. Olivé, A.: Conceptual Modeling of Information Systems. Springer, Heidelberg (2007). https://doi.org/10.1007/978-3-540-39390-0
17. Porello, D., Guizzardi, G.: Towards a cognitive semantics of types. In: Esposito, F., Basili, R., Ferilli, S., Lisi, F. (eds.) AI*IA 2017. LNCS, vol. 10640, pp. 428–440. Springer, Cham (2017). https://doi.org/10.1007/978-3-319-70169-1_32
18. Porello, D., Guizzardi, G.: Towards an ontological modelling of preference relations. In: Ghidini, C., Magnini, B., Passerini, A., Traverso, P. (eds.) AI*IA 2018. LNCS, vol. 11298, pp. 152–165. Springer, Cham (2018). https://doi.org/10.1007/978-3-030-03840-3_12
19. Russell, B.: Philosophical Essays. Routledge, Abingdon (2009)
20. Sales, T.P.: Ontology validation for managers. Master's thesis, UFES (2014)
21. Sales, T.P., Baião, F., Guizzardi, G., Almeida, J.P.A., Guarino, N., Mylopoulos, J.: The common ontology of value and risk. In: Trujillo, J.C., et al. (eds.) ER 2018. LNCS, vol. 11157, pp. 121–135. Springer, Cham (2018). https://doi.org/10.1007/978-3-030-00847-5_11
22. Varzi, A.: Mereology. In: Zalta, E.N. (ed.) The Stanford Encyclopedia of Philosophy, Winter 2016 edn. Metaphysics Research Lab, Stanford University (2016)
23. Verdock, M., et al.: Comparing traditional conceptual modeling with ontology-driven conceptual modeling: an empirical study. Inf. Syst. **81**, 92–103 (2019)
24. Verdonck, M., Gailly, F.: Insights on the use and application of ontology and conceptual modeling languages in ontology-driven conceptual modeling. In: Comyn-Wattiau, I., Tanaka, K., Song, I.-Y., Yamamoto, S., Saeki, M. (eds.) ER 2016. LNCS, vol. 9974, pp. 83–97. Springer, Cham (2016). https://doi.org/10.1007/978-3-319-46397-1_7
25. Wand, Y., et al.: An ontological analysis of the relationship construct in conceptual modeling. ACM Trans. Database Syst. (TODS) **24**(4), 494–528 (1999)
26. Wang, X., et al.: Towards an ontology of software: a requirements engineering perspective. In: Proceedings of the 8th International Conference on Formal Ontology in Information Systems (FOIS), Rio de Janeiro (2014)

Capturing Multi-level Models in a Two-Level Formal Modeling Technique

João Paulo A. Almeida[1], Fernando A. Musso[1], Victorio A. Carvalho[2],
Claudenir M. Fonseca[3(✉)], and Giancarlo Guizzardi[1,3]

[1] Ontology and Conceptual Modeling Research Group (NEMO),
Federal University of Espírito Santo (UFES), Vitória, Brazil
jpalmeida@ieee.org, fernandomusso14@gmail.com
[2] Federal Institute of Espírito Santo (IFES), Colatina, Brazil
victorio@ifes.edu.br
[3] Conceptual and Cognitive Modeling Research Group (CORE),
Free University of Bozen-Bolzano, Bolzano, Italy
{cmoraisfonseca,giancarlo.guizzardi}@unibz.it

Abstract. Conceptual models are often built with techniques that propose a strict stratification of entities into two classification levels: a level of types (or classes) and a level of instances. Multi-level conceptual modeling extends the conventional two-level scheme by admitting that types can be instances of other types, giving rise to multiple levels of classification. Nevertheless, the vast majority of tools and techniques are still confined to the two-level scheme, and hence cannot be used for multi-level models directly. We show here how a multi-level model in ML2 can be transformed into a two-level specification in the formal modeling technique Alloy, thereby leveraging the Alloy analyzer to multi-level models.

Keywords: Multi-level modeling · Model transformation

1 Introduction

Conceptual modeling is usually undertaken by capturing invariant aspects of the entities in a subject domain, which is supported in most conceptual modeling approaches through constructs such as "classes" and "types", reflecting the use of "kinds", "categories" and "sorts" in accounts of a subject domain by subject matter experts. In the conventional two-level representation scheme, a conceptual model is stratified into two levels of entities: a level of types (or classes) and a level of instances (or individuals). The level of types captures invariants that apply exclusively to the level of instances. In this scheme, the subject matter can be understood as consisting of individuals, and the purpose of the conceptual model is to establish which structures of individuals are admissible according to some (shared) conceptualization of the world [16].

The two-level scheme, however, reveals its limitations whenever we are interested in invariants about categories themselves [8], i.e., whenever categories of categories are part of the domain of inquiry. For example, in the biological taxonomy domain [2,6], living beings are classified according to biological taxa (such as, e.g., Animal, Mammal,

© Springer Nature Switzerland AG 2019
A. H. F. Laender et al. (Eds.): ER 2019, LNCS 11788, pp. 43–51, 2019.
https://doi.org/10.1007/978-3-030-33223-5_5

Carnivoran, Lion), each of which is classified by a biological taxonomic rank (e.g., Kingdom, Class, Order, Species) [22]. Cecil (the lion killed in the Hwange National Park in Zimbabwe in 2015) is an instance of Lion, which is an instance of Species. Species, in its turn, is an instance of Taxonomic Rank. Thus, to describe the conceptualization in this domain, one needs to represent entities of different (yet related) classification levels, such as specific living beings (Cecil), types of living beings (Lion), types of types of living beings (Species, Animal Species). In fact, classification levels can be added as required, e.g., Taxonomic Rank classifies the types of types of living beings. Other examples of multiple classification levels can be found in organizational roles, software engineering [15] and product types [23].

The need to represent entities in such domains led to what is currently termed "multi-level modeling" [4,23]. Techniques for multi-level modeling must provide modeling concepts to deal with types in various classification levels and address the relations that may occur between those types. Moreover, they must account for types behaving as instances and, as such, respecting invariants and holding values for properties they exemplify (in other words, types in a multi-level model have two facets: a "class" or type facet, and an "object" or instance facet [4]).

Despite the benefits of multi-level modeling, multi-level mechanisms pose a challenge to the reuse of existing two-level techniques and tools. In this paper, we demonstrate how multi-level models can be accommodated in a conventional two-level language. We propose a systematic transformation of multi-level models represented in the ML2 Multi-Level Modeling Language [13] into conventional Alloy [17] specifications, following a transformation pattern that is based on the reification of the instance facet of a type and its systematic linking with the type facet. This allows us to leverage model simulation and verification support originally designed with a conventional two-level scheme to multi-level conceptual models.

The remainder of this paper is organized as follows: Sect. 2 discusses a classical workaround employed when we are confined to two levels of classification, namely, the powertype pattern. Section 3 briefly presents the multi-level modeling language we adopt here (ML2). Section 4 discusses how multi-level models are represented in a corresponding two-level specification in Alloy. Section 5 presents some conclusions.

2 The Classical Two-Level Workaround – The Powertype Pattern

Let us consider the biological taxonomy domain as a paradigmatic example of a multi-level domain [2,6]. We are interested in this domain not only in capturing features of certain organisms (e.g., its weight), but also features of types of organisms and their properties. For example, a Species (like other taxa) is named by a Person (the Lion species was named by Carl Linnaeus) and can be attributed a conservation status. Further, being a member of a certain species, an organism has certain features in virtue of being a member of the species. For example, all lions are warm blooded, while all frogs are cold blooded.

In the conventional two-level approach, entities in the domain have to be classified either as classes (or types) or as instances. Strictly speaking, there is no room for meta-types such as Species or meta-meta-types such as Taxonomic Rank. Workarounds are

available as discussed in [19, 20], but these often introduce accidental complexity. For example, an early approach that has aimed to accommodate multiple domain levels within two modeling levels is the powertype pattern proposed by [24]. In this pattern, all types are treated as regular classes, and a "base type" (such as Organism, Taxon) is related to a "powertype" (such as Species, Taxonomic Rank), through a user-defined (and regular) association (such as classified by, ranked in). See Fig. 1 for a model capturing this scenario using UML's support for powertypes.

This workaround creates a number of difficulties, some of which are discussed in [19,20]. First of all, a modeler needs to handle explicitly two notions of instantiation, a native one provided by the modeling technique (and thus between classes and instances) and another that corresponds to the user-defined association (classified by, ranked in). In the case of the latter, since it is a regular user-defined association, no support for its instantiation semantics is provided by the modeling technique, and hence, instantiation semantics needs to be *emulated* manually by the modeler. The pattern is based on the duplication of the instances of the powertype: this is because they must be admitted both at the instance level (e.g., Lion as an instance of Species, carrying values for taxonAuthor, conservation status, warmblooded) and at the same time at the class level (e.g., Lion as a specialization of Organism). The management of the duplicated entities—although key to the pattern—is left to the model user.

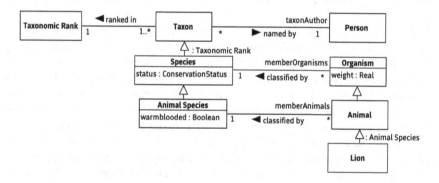

Fig. 1. The powertype pattern with a regular user-defined association

3   The ML2 Multi-level Modeling Language

The root of the problem discussed in the previous section is that two-level languages fail to recognize classes as instances of other (meta)classes [3, 14]. This has motivated some of us in the past to propose a Multi-Level Modeling Language (ML2) [13], following work on theoretical foundations for Multi-Level Modeling (MLT [8, 10] and MLT* [1]).

The language provides support to the specification of properties of individuals, their types (the so-called first-order types), second-order types (whose types are first-order

types) and so on. Further, the language incorporates notions of powertype in the literature (including Odell's [24] and Cardelli's powertypes [7]). The language supports a number of features typical of multi-level modeling techniques, some of which are exemplified here; we refer the reader to [12,13] for further details.

In Listing 1.1, we employ ML2 to revisit the example from Fig. 1 presenting how a language that is not limited to the two-level scheme captures the multi-level notions.

```
1   order 2 class AnimalSpecies categorizes Animal {
2     regularity instancesAreWarmBlooded: Boolean
3     determinesValue isWarmBlooded
4     ref taxonAuthor : Person };
5   class Organism { weight : Number};
6   class Animal specializes Organism { isWarmBlooded :Boolean };
7   class Lion : AnimalSpecies specializes Animal {
8     ref taxonAuthor = CLinnaeus
9     instancesAreWarmBlooded = true };
10  class Person { name : String };
11  individual CLinnaeus : Person { name = 'Carl Linnaeus' };
12  individual Cecil : Lion { isWarmBlooded = true };
```

Individuals (entities that are not classes) are marked individual. Simple class declarations capture first-order classes (e.g., Animal, Lion and Person), whose instances are individuals (e.g., Cecil and CLinnaeus). Higher-order classes are declared by using a order modifier (e.g., AnimalSpecies in Line 1 is a second-order class).

Differently from the conventional powertype approach, rather than relying on domain relations with no specialized semantics (such as ranked in or classified by in Fig. 1), ML2 enables the expression of instantiation between classes, which is represented by a colon. Given the specialized semantics, constraints enforce that high-order classes can only have as instances classes at the order immediately below. Standard modeling features of specialization, attributes and references are also present in the language, and both attributes and references may have values assigned for their instances. For example, 'Carl Linnaeus' is the name of CLinnaeus (an individual Person) and CLinnaeus is the taxonAuthor of Lion. In addition, regularity features are used to represent *deep instantiation* [2], when the attributes of a higher-order type affect entities at lower levels. By assigning instancesAreWarmBlooded=true in the declaration of Lion (Line 7), the value of isWarmBlooded is regulated for all its instances, including Cecil. The determinesValue keyword (Line 3) specifies the sort of regulation and the regulated feature. (See [12,13] for other kinds of regulation supported in ML2.)

The powertype pattern semantics is supported with the so-called categorization relations between classes. All instances of a class that categorizes another (in an adjacent lower order) are (direct or indirect) specializations of the categorized class. Thus, by declaring that AnimalSpecies categorizes Animal (Line 1), all instances of AnimalSpecies (such as Lion) specialize Animal (a constraint enforced by ML2).

4   A Systematic Two-Level Solution and Its Alloy Implementation

Similarly to the powertype pattern discussed in Sect. 2, we reify the instance facet of a type in our two-level representation scheme. However, differently from the powertype pattern, the instance and type facets are systematically linked to each other. The result is that the expression of multi-level constraints becomes possible, and, at the same time, the technique-native support for instantiation, attribute assignment and specialization is preserved. We establish the following *representation rules* for a two-level scheme: (i) each ML2 class is represented as a regular class (capturing its type facet); (ii) each ML2 class (at any order) is reified at the instance level (capturing its instance facet); (iii) native instantiation of a class is reflected in explicit instantiation links between a class instance and the reified class being instantiated; (iv) in addition to instantiation, specialization is reified as links between the reified classes. In order to ensure that the multi-level semantics is preserved, (v) all classes specialize classes in a top-level library corresponding to ML2 notions (Type, its ordered specializations, Individual).

The established correspondence results in the representation schema shown in Fig. 2. The topmost layer that corresponds to ML2 notions is represented in white. It is extended by introducing Taxonomic Rank, Animal Species, Animal and Lion corresponding to the classes in Listing 1.1 (Person was omitted due to space constraints). The figure also shows a possible instance level. As required, it includes reified instances of Type (e.g., lionReified) that correspond to the various classes on the left-hand side of the figure (e.g., lionReified corresponds to the Lion class). It also shows a possible instance of Lion, called cecil. The object level shows cecil linked to lionReified through the instance of association. As discussed in Sect. 2, there is a purposeful duplication of the Lion entity in order to reveal its instance facet at the object level through lionReified.

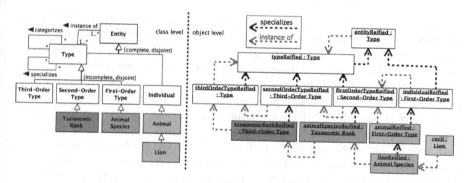

Fig. 2. Reification example.

We employ this principled approach to implement a transformation from ML2 into a conventional two-level language dubbed Alloy [17]. Alloy is a formal two-level language designed to support lightweight formal techniques for simulation and verification of model specifications. For the implemented transformation, an Alloy specification of

the top-level ML2 layer (in fact, MLT* [9]) is imported in all of the generated Alloy specifications, serving as the topmost layer for our transformation. We shall explore how each representation rule discussed above is applied in the ML2 to Alloy transformation. In order to illustrate the application of the transformation, we use the example discussed in Listing 1.1 and the corresponding Alloy fragment in Listing 1.2.

```
1   sig Animal in Organism { isWarmblooded: Boolean }
2   one sig AnimalReified in Species {}
3   fact AnimalReifiedDefinition {
4     all e: Entity | e in AnimalReified iff
5       (all e': Entity | iof[e',e] iff e' in Animal) }
6   sig Lion in Animal {}
7   one sig LionReified in AnimalSpecies {} {
8     taxonAuthor = CarlLinnaeus
9     instancesAreWarmBlooded = true }
10  fact LionReifiedDefinition {
11    all e: Entity | e in LionReified iff
12      (all e': Entity | iof[e',e] iff e' in Lion) }
13  one sig Cecil in Lion {}
14  one sig CarlLinnaeus in Person {} { name = "Carl_Linnaeus" }
15  sig AnimalSpecies in Species {
16    instancesAreWarmBlooded: Boolean }
17  one sig AnimalSpeciesReified in Order2Type {}
18  fact AnimalSpeciesReifiedDefinition {
19    all e: Entity | e in AnimalSpeciesReified iff
20      (all e': Entity | iof[e',e] iff e' in AnimalSpecies) }
21  fact AnimalSpeciesCategorizesAnimal {
22    categorizes[AnimalSpeciesReified,AnimalReified] }
23  fact instancesAreWarmbloodedRegulatesisWarmblooded {
24    all x:Animal |
25      x.isWarmblooded = (x.iof).instancesAreWarmblooded }
```

Concerning rule (i), class declarations, native specialization, typing of relations and attributes, are all supported by Alloy directly. This allows for a direct representation of classes, e.g., in lines 1, 6 and 15 (Animal, Lion and AnimalSpecies) and respective specializations (Species, Organism and Person were omitted due to space constraints). Attribute and reference declarations are supported directly (see isWarmBlooded in line 1 and instancesAreWarmBlooded in line 16).

Concerning rule (ii), we include the instance facet of classes into the specification. Due to the absence of native support for instance declaration in Alloy, we make use of singletons, see lines 2, 7 and 17 (AnimalReified, LionReified, AnimalSpeciesReified), a solution we also employ for the representation of individuals in lines 13 and 14 (Cecil and CarlLinnaeus). These instance facets (for classes and individuals alike) are the holders of any assignments and are used to declare categorizations (see lines 21 and 22 for AnimalSpecies categorizing Animal).

Concerning rule (iii), instantiation is reified through the iof predicate that is defined in the top-level library for MLT* imported in all specifications. This rule further binds

the different facets of classes by enforcing that, whenever an entity natively instantiates a class (as denoted with the keyword in) it also has an explicit instantiation link with the reified class (and vice-versa). See lines 3–5, 10–12 and 18–20 which respectively bind Animal and AnimalReified, Lion and LionReified, and AnimalSpecies and AnimalSpeciesReified, following the same transformation pattern.

Specialization links between reified classes (iv) do not have to be declared explicitly, as they are a logical consequence of rule (iii) and the definition of specialization in the top-level library. Rule (v) results in declaration of specializations towards the library classes (Order1Type, Order2Type). Finally, regularity attributes result in the declaration of a regulation fact (lines 23–25). In this case, all animals of a certain species are warmblooded (or not) as defined by the species instancesAreWarmBlooded attribute.

The transformation was implemented on top of the Eclipse-based ML2 editor https://github.com/nemo-ufes/ML2-Editor. The full implementation of the transformation and the listing of the original ML2 model and corresponding Alloy specification can be found in https://github.com/nemo-ufes/ml2-to-alloy.

5   Final Considerations

In this paper, we have shown how to capture ML2 multi-level models in a two-level representation scheme in Alloy. The approach builds up on the powertype pattern, by reifying the instance facet of types. Differently from the powertype pattern, we systematically link type and instance facets. As a result, a two-level technique such as Alloy can be directly used in the simulation and verification of multi-level models. By incorporating a formally defined (MLT*-based) top-level library, we can enforce consistent usage of ML2 notions, from instantiation and order stratification to regularity features.

The literature presents a number of approaches for dealing with multi-level domains within the limitation of two-level schemes. We observe among these three typical cases: (i) the application of the powertype pattern that captures relations between classes of different orders [15]; (ii) the reification of classes as entities that capture their instance facets [18]; (iii) and the application of metamodeling strategies consisting on stacking two-level models to represent higher-order classes as metaclasses [21]. Each of these approaches exhibit some limitations in the representation of multi-level domains: (i) powertype-based approaches fail to link instance and type facets and do not capture the specialized instantiation semantics underlying categorization relations, (ii) simple reification approaches fail to provide level structuring mechanisms which are require to rule out unsound models [5]; and (iii) the stacking (or cascading) approach places corresponding entities in distinct two-level models preventing the expression of cross-level relations (such as named by between Species and Person).

We expect the transformation approach we discuss here to be applicable to other two-level representation languages with minor effort. We are working on a first-order logic formalization of the approach, in order to generalize it to other techniques beyond Alloy. It is part of our present research agenda to explore the implications of our approach to the representation of multi-level models in OWL-DL and UML, following the work reported in [6, 11].

Acknowledgments. This work has been partially supported by CNPq (407235/2017-5, 312123/2017-5), CAPES (23038.028816/2016-41), FAPES (69382549) and FUB (OCEAN Project).

References

1. Almeida, J.P.A., Fonseca, C.M., Carvalho, V.A.: A comprehensive formal theory for multi-level conceptual modeling. In: Mayr, H.C., Guizzardi, G., Ma, H., Pastor, O. (eds.) ER 2017. LNCS, vol. 10650, pp. 280–294. Springer, Cham (2017). https://doi.org/10.1007/978-3-319-69904-2_23
2. Atkinson, C., Kühne, T.: Model-driven development: a metamodeling foundation. IEEE Softw. **20**(5), 36–41 (2003)
3. Atkinson, C., Kühne, T.: Meta-level independent modelling. In: Proceedings of the 14th ECOOP (2000)
4. Atkinson, C., Kühne, T.: The essence of multilevel metamodeling. In: Gogolla, M., Kobryn, C. (eds.) UML 2001. LNCS, vol. 2185, pp. 19–33. Springer, Heidelberg (2001). https://doi.org/10.1007/3-540-45441-1_3
5. Brasileiro, F., Almeida, J.P.A., Carvalho, V.A., Guizzardi, G.: Applying a multi-level modeling theory to assess taxonomic hierarchies in Wikidata. In: Proceedings of the 25th WWW (2016)
6. Brasileiro, F., Almeida, J.P.A., Carvalho, V.A., Guizzardi, G.: Expressive multi-level modeling for the semantic web. In: Groth, P., et al. (eds.) ISWC 2016. LNCS, vol. 9981, pp. 53–69. Springer, Cham (2016). https://doi.org/10.1007/978-3-319-46523-4_4
7. Cardelli, L.: Structural subtyping and the notion of power type. In: Proceedings of the 15th POPL (1988)
8. Carvalho, V.A., Almeida, J.P.A.: Toward a well-founded theory for multi-level conceptual modeling. Softw. Syst. Model. **17**, 205–231 (2018)
9. Carvalho, V.A., Almeida, J.P.A., Fonseca, C.M., Guizzardi, G.: Extending the foundations of ontology-based conceptual modeling with a multi-level theory. In: Johannesson, P., Lee, M.L., Liddle, S.W., Opdahl, A.L., López, Ó.P. (eds.) ER 2015. LNCS, vol. 9381, pp. 119–133. Springer, Cham (2015). https://doi.org/10.1007/978-3-319-25264-3_9
10. Carvalho, V.A., Almeida, J.P.A., Fonseca, C.M., Guizzardi, G.: Multi-level ontology-based conceptual modeling. Data Knowl. Eng. **109**(C), 3–24 (2017)
11. Carvalho, V.A., Almeida, J.P.A., Guizzardi, G.: Using a well-founded multi-level theory to support the analysis and representation of the powertype pattern in conceptual modeling. In: Nurcan, S., Soffer, P., Bajec, M., Eder, J. (eds.) CAiSE 2016. LNCS, vol. 9694, pp. 309–324. Springer, Cham (2016). https://doi.org/10.1007/978-3-319-39696-5_19
12. Fonseca, C.M.: ML2: an expressive multi-level conceptual modeling language. Master's thesis. Federal University of Espírito Santo (2017)
13. Fonseca, C.M., Almeida, J.P.A., Guizzardi, G., Carvalho, V.A.: Multi-level conceptual modeling: from a formal theory to a well-founded language. In: Trujillo, J.C., et al. (eds.) ER 2018. LNCS, vol. 11157, pp. 409–423. Springer, Cham (2018). https://doi.org/10.1007/978-3-030-00847-5_29
14. Foxvog, D.: Instances of instances modeled via higher-order classes. In: FOnt 2005 Workshop, Proceedings of the 28th KI (2005)
15. Gonzalez-Perez, C., Henderson-Sellers, B.: A powertype-based metamodelling framework. Softw. Syst. Model. **5**, 72–90 (2006)
16. Guizzardi, G.: On ontology, ontologies, conceptualizations, modeling languages, and (meta)models. Front. Artif. Intell. Appl. **155**, 18 (2007)

17. Jackson, D.: Software Abstractions: Logic, Language, and Analysis. MIT Press, Cambridge (2012)

18. Kimura, K., et al.: Practical multi-level modeling on MOF-compliant modeling frameworks. In: Proceedings of the 2nd MULTI Workshop (2015)

19. Kühne, T., Schreiber, D.: Can programming be liberated from the two-level style: multi-level programming with DeepJava. In: Proceedings of the 22nd OOPSLA (2007)

20. Lara, J.D., Guerra, E., Cuadrado, J.S.: When and how to use multilevel modelling. ACM Trans. Softw. Eng. Methodol. (TOSEM) **24**, 12 (2014)

21. Macías, F., Rutle, A., Stolz, V.: MultEcore: combining the best of fixed-level and multilevel metamodelling. In: Proceedings of the 3rd MULTI Workshop (2016)

22. Mayr, E.: The Growth of Biological Thought: Diversity, Evolution, and Inheritance. Harvard University Press, Cambridge (1982)

23. Neumayr, B., Grün, K., Schrefl, M.: Multi-level domain modeling with m-objects and m-relationships. In: Proceedings of the 6th APCCM (2009)

24. Odell, J.: Power types. J. OO Program. **7**, 8–12 (1994)

An SQL^o Front-End for Non-monotonic Inheritance and De-referencing

Joel Oduro-Afriyie(ID) and Hasan M. Jamil$^{(\boxtimes)}$(ID)

Department of Computer Science, University of Idaho, Moscow, ID, USA
odur8117@vandals.uidaho.edu, jamil@uidaho.edu

Abstract. We revisit the issues of non-monotonic inheritance and structure traversal in object-relational databases with new insights to propose OO extensions of SQL and demonstrate that they are sufficient and powerful enough for modeling classes, non-monotonic inheritance and de-referencing. In particular, we show that simple tweaking of SQL with *tuple ID* helps capture these OO features cleanly and empowers application developers with a powerful knowledge modeling tool.

Keywords: Object-oriented modeling · Abstract relations · Object-relational query language · Translational semantics · Inheritance and overriding

1 Introduction

Numerous applications can benefit from the simple software engineering idea of inheritance and overriding. Despite significant interests in modeling these convenient features in database query languages, a fully functional object-oriented (OO) [2] or object-relational (OR) database [4] did not materialize mainly because it was extremely difficult to combine the simplicity and declarativity of SQL-like languages with the power of full object-orientation in a single platform. Serious efforts to craft an OO SQL date back to early to late 90s [5,7], and no similar efforts can be seen since then. Even in those early efforts, researchers were mainly focused on supporting abstract data types (ADTs). The community then was eager to find a query language that looks and feels like C++. Not surprisingly, the CQL++ [3], or SQL/XNF [7] type database languages basically attest to the reality, although a limited number of research focused on features such as inheritance without much success [5]. The OQL [1] or O₂ [2] languages are complex to say the least, and this explains why they did not become popular.

In this paper, we propose a novel approach to class hierarchy and inheritance modeling with overriding, and object de-referencing, in classical relational database systems without the need for a new algebra based on the conviction that minimally extending SQL to support the urgently needed OO features is prudent. In the remainder of the paper, we mainly use an illustrative example to expose the modeling and query mapping technique we propose without much

© Springer Nature Switzerland AG 2019
A. H. F. Laender et al. (Eds.): ER 2019, LNCS 11788, pp. 52–60, 2019.
https://doi.org/10.1007/978-3-030-33223-5_6

details for the sake of brevity and for expository purposes. A complete technical discussion on the model, language and query transformation is deferred to a full article we plan to publish elsewhere.

2 The OR Model

The *object relational model*, or the OR data model, we propose, has two types of tables – *traditional* tables (called simply tables) and *abstract* tables. Tables are defined in standard ways using create table statements. For example, the instance *Professors* in Fig. 1(a) is declared by the statement

c_1: create table *Professors* (
　　PiD tupleID(3) primary key,
　　Name string(10),
　　Rank string(10)
　　Dept string(10));

q_1: select *
　　from *Professors*;

Professors is a first normal form traditional table declaration, and thus all standard SQL statements can be used on it and query q_1 above returns the entire table in Fig. 1(a). In this statement, tupleID is a special string data type discussed in the context of objects and classes below in more detail.

PiD	Name	Rank	Dept
p-1	Sharon	Assoc	CS
p-2	Pierre	Full	$\perp$
p-3	Tanaka	$\perp$	Econ
p-4	Alfredo	Full	CS

(a) Table *Professors*

PiD	Dept	Salary
p-1	e-7	110K
p-4	e-7	$\perp$
p-3	e-8	105K

(b) Table *Works*

TiD	Name	State
t-a	$\perp$	DC
t-b	Pria	$\perp$
t-c	Aphrodite	TX

(c) Abstract table *People*

TiD	Name	State
t-a	$\perp$	$\perp$
t-b	Pria	DC
t-c	Aphrodite	TX

(d) View of table *People*

TiD	Name	State	SiD	Par
n-a	$\perp$	ID	s-1	t-4
n-b	Clint	$\perp$	s-2	t-5
n-c	Moira	TX	s-3	t-3
n-d	Alex	PA	s-4	$\perp$

(e) Abstract table *Students*

TiD	Name	State	SiD	Par
n-a	$\perp$	$\perp$	$\perp$	$\perp$
n-b	Clint	ID	s-2	t-5
n-c	Moira	TX	s-3	t-3
n-d	Alex	PA	s-4	$\perp$

(f) View of table *Students*

TiD	DiD	Name	Chair
e-6	d-0	CS	p-1
e-7	d-1	$\perp$	p-4
e-8	d-2	Math	p-1
e-9	d-3	Econ	p-3

(g) Abstract table *Departments*

TiD	Name	State	SSN	Income
t-2	$\perp$	$\perp$	000	45K
t-3	Joe	WA	001	$\perp$
t-4	$\perp$	OH	014	90k
t-5	Maria	$\perp$	207	$\perp$

(h) Abstract table *Parents*

TiD	Name	State	SSN	Income
t-2	$\perp$	$\perp$	$\perp$	$\perp$
t-3	Joe	WA	001	45K
t-4	$\perp$	OH	014	90k
t-5	Maria	DC	207	45K

(i) View of table *Parents*

TiD	DiD	Name	Chair
e-6	$\perp$	$\perp$	$\perp$
e-7	d-1	CS	p-4
e-8	d-2	Math	p-1
e-9	d-3	Econ	p-3

(j) View of table *Departments*

TiD	Name	State	SiD	Par	Major
u-e	$\perp$	$\perp$	s-5	$\perp$	$\perp$
u-f	Ovro	MI	s-6	$\perp$	e-7
u-g	Abebi	ID	s-7	t-5	e-9
u-h	Odelia	$\perp$	s-8	t-4	e-8

(k) Abstract table *UnderGrads*

TiD	Name	State	SiD	Par	Major
u-e	$\perp$	$\perp$	$\perp$	$\perp$	$\perp$
u-f	Ovro	MI	s-6	t-4	e-7
u-g	Abebi	ID	s-7	t-5	e-9
u-h	Odelia	ID	s-8	t-4	e-8

(l) View of table *UnderGrads*

Name	CName
Sharon	Alfredo

(m) Aggregation query

Fig. 1. OR model tables: traditional and abstract relations in class hierarchy.

Objects, Classes and Instances. In contrast, the abstract table *People* models a class object of type *People* and a set of instance objects of the same type through the create abstract table declaration below.

c_2: create abstract table *People* (
    TiD tupleID(3) auto,
    Name string(10),
    State string(2),
    default values (($\bot$, $\bot$, "*DC*")));

q_2: select *
    from *People*;

This create abstract table statement specifies an extended first normal form table under the scheme *People (TiD, Name, State)* with several unique properties. First, the scheme includes a distinguished attribute named *TiD*. This attribute represents a domain of unique object IDs mandated by the concepts of OO database models. In our model, all objects have an immutable ID, called the *OID*, and these IDs in OR model are synonymous to the concept of tuple IDs (denoted *TiDs*) first introduced by Sieg and Sciore [8]. These tuple IDs can be created in several ways. The keywords tupleID(3) auto states that *TiD* is an automatically generated string type object ID of length three. In OR model, tupleID has a string domain that can have system generated values. Thus, it requires a type declarations and optionally a method for generating it (e.g., auto). In contrast, the declaration

TiD tupleID compose(string(2)+"-"+integer(2))

says the tuple ID is a five character long string supplied by the user which has the format first two characters, followed by a hyphen and then finally has a two digit integer, resulting in a five character unique tuple ID. In this case too, database wise uniqueness is preserved. Furthermore, since these IDs in *TiD* columns are unique database wide in all abstract and traditional tables, they are candidate keys by default. We call them *object keys*. However, *tupleID*, *auto* and *compose* features can be used to type any attribute. But the uniqueness is enforced only for the distinguished attribute *TiD* in ways consistent with the TiD algebra [8].

Figure 1(c) shows an instance of the abstract table *People*. In our model, all abstract tables have the column *TiD* (but unlike TiD algebra, not all tables have *TiD* columns), and thus all tuples in every abstract table have a unique object ID. Observe also that the instance has two partitions. In the top partition, we have the tuple $\langle$t-a, $\bot$, DC$\rangle$, and in the bottom partition we have tuples {$\langle$t-b, *Pria*, $\bot\rangle$, $\langle$t-c, Aphrodite, TX$\rangle$}. The lone tuple with *TiD* t-a in the top partition is the default value of the class object *People* as stated in the default values clause in the create abstract table statement. In this tuple, the first $\bot$ corresponding to the *TiD* column is replaced by the system generated object ID *t-a*. This tuple contains the class default values for each column, e.g., *State* has default class value *DC*, but *Name* does not. Finally, the bottom partition contains the instance objects, each of which also has an object ID, e.g., *t-b* and *t-c*.

Inheritance and Overriding. The consequence of having a class default value is interesting and far reaching. For example, the query q_2 above now returns the abstract table "view" in Fig. 1(d). We make several important observations. First, this table does not have a class default value tuple, i.e., all the values are null ($\perp$) because we have closed the inheritance and the default values are no longer useful. Also note that tuple $t\text{-}b$ inherited the default *State* value DC and replaced the null value. However, since the tuple $t\text{-}c$ already has a local value TX, it overrode the value DC and not inherited. This is in the spirit of dynamic inheritance with overriding in OO systems, called *non-monotonic inheritance*.

Relationships and Aggregation. Being a superset of the relational data model and SQL, the OR model and its query language SQL° supports relationships by respecting foreign keys. In the create table declaration below, the references clause declares a foreign key in *Works* that references the primary key of *Departments*, indicating *Dept* can accept null values. In contrast, the aggregates clause (in the sense of SDM [6]), though similar to references, cannot accept null values. Here too, the *PiD* column references a column in another table, but not necessarily a primary key. Instead, it is an OID or tuple ID column. Note that *PiD* is not a distinguished column name though it has the tuple ID domain. Thus uniqueness is not maintained by default, but declaring it the primary key enforces uniqueness in traditional sense, not in OO sense.

c_3: create table *Works* (
    PiD tupleID(3) primary key references *Professors(PiD)*,
    Dept tupleID(3) aggregates *Departments(TiD)*,
    Salary integer(7));

The instance table in Fig. 1(b) over the scheme *Works(PiD, Dept, Salary)* is essentially a relationship between *Professors* and *Department* in ER sense. The fundamental difference between aggregates and references is that the objects in the former referenced tables need not be explicitly joined to access their columns as is the case for latter reference types. The query below clarifies this distinction.

q_3: select $P_1 \rightarrow Name$, $Chair \rightarrow Name$ as $CName$
    from *Works* W_1, *Professors* P_1, *Professors* P_2
    where $W_1.PiD = {}_P1.PiD$ and $Salary > 109K$ and $W_1.Dept \rightarrow Chair =$
    $P_2.PiD$ and $W_1.Dept \rightarrow Name = P_2.Dept$;

This query returns names of all professors and their chair's who earn more than \$109K with their chair also from the same department. This query will return the table in Fig. 1(m). Had the *Professors* table been declared as an abstract table, we could have written this query in a much simpler way using OO de-referencing features. Also note that the *Department* table is not referenced in the where clause yet became accessible via de-referencing.

Class Hierarchies. Similar to classes in OO systems, abstract tables can be organized in table hierarchies. While classes or abstract tables[1] can have multiple subclasses, they can only have unique superclasses. Subclasses in OR model inherit properties and their default values, and all key and other integrity constraints, from their superclasses. While integrity constraints and the scheme of a class are inherited monotonically, their class default values are inherited non-monotonically in an overriding fashion based on specificity preference principle.

For example, consider an instance object s-1 in *Students* class in Fig. 1(e), where *Students* is a subclass of *People* in Fig. 1(c). The following create abstract table statement defines the subclass relationship between these two tables.

c_4: create abstract table *Students* inherits *People* (
    SiD string(3) primary key,
    Par tupleID(3) aggregates *Parents*,
    default values $((\perp, \perp, "ID", "s\text{-}0", \perp))$);

Being a subclass of *People*, not only does *Students* inherit the scheme of *People* and the object key, it also introduces two new attributes {*SiD, Parent*}, a new primary key *SiD*, and a new default value *ID* for the inherited attribute *State*. In this case, all instances of *Students* (as well as all its subclasses) will inherit, when appropriate, the default value *ID* for *State*, and not *DC* since the local or specific value *ID* at *Students* overrides the inherited value for *State* in *People*.

Null Closure. In a select query, the relation list in the from clause can be both traditional and abstract tables. Since abstract tables can be subclass of another class table, a long chain of inheritance becomes complicated. Each abstract table has the potential to have inherited values from superclasses at arbitrary height. Since updates in all tables are allowed, a static inheritance of all default values to lower subclasses and instances is not a prudent choice though the approach could make query processing substantially cheaper. But updates in class default values have the potential to invalidate statically inherited values before the update and leave the recovery from the state of erroneous inheritance at jeopardy. We use a process called *null closure* to dynamically inherit the class default values down to all subclasses and instances in an overriding manner.

3   Mapping SQL^O to SQL

Implementation of the SQL^O language is based on a translational semantics of SQL^O programs to SQL, so that we can understand the semantics in terms of the well known meaning of SQL, and obviate the need for a native SQL^O implementation, saving effort and cost. The correctness of SQL^O is then established based on the soundness and completeness properties of SQL relative to the OR data model and its intended semantics. We argue that SQL^O is sound and complete

---

[1] In this article, we use the terms sub and superclasses interchangeably with sub and supertables for convenience.

too by showing that the translation outlined preserves the intended semantics of SQL^O. In the following sections, we only discuss translation of the SQL^O specific statements not available in SQL by way of examples.

3.1 Creating Class Tables

The *People* class table declaration in Sect. 2 is translated as follows. We create two separate tables in SQL for each create abstract table statement to implement class and instance objects in two partitions. The class tables are annotated with subscript c and instance tables with i as follows.

c_5: create table *People$_c$* (
   TiD varchar(3) auto unique,
   Name varchar(10),
   State varchar(2));

u_1: insert into *People$_c$(TiD, Name, State)*
   values (*$AutoKey, NULL, 'DC'*);

c_6: create table *People$_i$* (
   TiD varchar(3) auto unique,
   Name varchar(10),
   State varchar(2));

In the above statements auto is a directive to create a random key that will never be assigned to another *TiD* column of any tuple. Major database systems like Oracle support similar unique primary key generation. In the insert statement we use the *$AutoKey* keyword to call a function to generate the OID or the tuple ID, and insert this tuple into *People$_c$* as the class default value. The unique declaration makes *TiD* a candidate key, but not the primary key of the table. The uniqueness of *TiD* is ensured by checking a unary system table called *UniqueKeys* we maintain which logs all *TiD* values ever assigned and in use in our databases. Note that the statement u_1 above, implements the semantics of the default values declaration in statement c_2 in Sect. 2.

The subclass table *Students* in Sect. 2 is accomplished by creating the SQL statements below. Note that for aggregation, we required that the *Parent* cannot have null values, and the referenced *Parents* object cannot be deleted without deleting the *Students* object.

c_7: create table *Students$_c$* (
   TiD varchar(3) unique,
   Name varchar(10),
   State varchar(2),
   SiD varchar(3) primary key,
   Par varchar(3) not null
      foreign key references *Parents$_i$ (TiD)*
      on update cascade
      on delete restrict);

u_2: insert into *Students$_c$ (TiD, Name, State,*
   SiD, Par)
   values (*$AutoKey, NULL, 'ID', 's-0', NULL*);

c_8: create table *Students$_i$* (
   TiD varchar(3) unique,
   Name varchar(10),
   State varchar(2),
   SiD varchar(3) primary key,
   Par varchar(3) not null foreign key
      references *Parents$_i$ (TiD)*
      on update cascade
      on delete restrict);

u_3: insert into *ClassHierarchy(SubClass,*
   SuperClass)
   values (*'Students', 'People'*);

We do not separately discuss the statements such as insert, delete and update, which can be handled trivially. Finally, we enter the subtable relationship specified in the inherits keyword into the system table *ClassHierarchy* as a pair

⟨'*Students*', '*People*'⟩ to be able to create the class hierarchy for null closure discussed next. The inherits keyword also prompts the inclusion of the attributes in the superclass *People* into the current table *Students*.

3.2 Computing Null Closure and Table View

Prior to processing queries, we first process null closure discussed in Sect. 2 for all directly or implicitly referred abstract tables to ground the tables with inherited values in real time. On analysis of the query in terms of the tables included in the from clauses, and the cross referencing of the de-reference operators with the schemes, a list of abstract tables is created that potentially warrant null closures. A precedence graph of subclass-superclass relationship for each of these tables is constructed using the *ClassHierarchy* system table and for every table, a maximal scheme is created to list the attributes that all clauses will need. We then proceed to create two sets of views – one for the class tables and one for the instance tables, and we then use only the views corresponding to each instance table in the rewritten queries as follows.

Let us explain the process of using the query that asks *list the names of all undergraduate non computer science majors resident in Idaho and their parents' income such that their parents earn more than $75K and their department chairs are computer science professors*. This query can be posed in SQL^O as the following expression.

q_4: select *Name, Par→Income*
    from *UnderGrads, Professors*
    where *State = 'ID'* and *Par→Income > 75K* and *Major→Name ≠ 'CS'*
    and *Major→Chair = PiD* and *Dept ='CS'*;

This query assumes that the following DDL statement has already been defined.

c_{10}: create abstract table *UnderGrads* inherits *Students* (
    Major tupleID(3) aggregates *Departments(TiD)*);

In this query three abstract tables *UnderGrads, Departments* and *Parents*, and a traditional table *Professors* are involved. This information is derived from the database schema definitions, i.e., *Major* in *UnderGrads* aggregates *Departments* where student majors are found. Similarly, *Parent* aggregates *Parents* where their *Income* is listed. The de-reference operators in the query actually give away this information. Finally, *Chair* in *Departments* aggregates *Professors* where we find their department. While *UnderGrads* and *Persons* participate in a class hierarchy and require null closure as shown below, *Departments* does not.

c_{11}: create view *People$_{cv}$(TiD, Name, State)* as
    select *TiD, Name, State*
    from *People$_c$*;

c_{12}: create view *Students$_{cv}$(TiD, Name, State, SiD, Par)* as
    select *V.TiD,*

case when $V.Name=NULL$ then $U.Name$ else $V.Name$,
case when $V.State=NULL$ then $U.State$ else $V.State$,
case when $V.Par=NULL$ then $U.Par$ else $V.Par$
from $People_{cv}$ as U, $Students_c$ as V;

c_{13}: create view $UnderGrads_{cv}(TiD,\ Name,\ State,\ Par,\ Major)$ as
  select $V.TiD$,
    case when $V.Name=NULL$ then $U.Name$ else $V.Name$,
    case when $V.State=NULL$ then $U.State$ else $V.State$,
    case when $V.Par=NULL$ then $U.Par$ else $V.Par$,
    case when $V.Major=NULL$ then $U.Major$ else $V.Major$
  from $Students_{cv}$ as U, $UnderGrads_c$ as V;

c_{14}: create view $Parents_{cv}(TiD,\ Income)$ as
  select $V.TiD$,
    case when $V.Income=NULL$ then $U.Income$ else $V.Income$,
  from $People_{cv}$ as U, $Parents_c$ as V;

The above statements only close the nulls in class tables. To truly inherit the default values, we now close the inheritance in all three instance tables as follows.

c_{15}: create view $UnderGrads_{iv}(TiD,\ Name,\ State,\ Par,\ Major)$ as
  select $V.TiD$,
    case when $V.Name=NULL$ then $U.Name$ else $V.Name$,
    case when $V.State=NULL$ then $U.State$ else $V.State$,
    case when $V.Par=NULL$ then $U.Par$ else $V.Par$,
    case when $V.Major=NULL$ then $U.Major$ else $V.Major$
  from $UnderGrads_{cv}$ as U, $UnderGrads_i$ as V;

c_{16}: create view $Parents_{iv}(TiD,\ Income)$ as
  select $V.TiD$,
    case when $V.Income=NULL$ then $U.Income$ else $V.Income$,
  from $Parents_{cv}$ as U, $Parents_i$ as V;

c_{17}: create view $Departments_{iv}(TiD,\ Name,\ Chair)$ as
  select $V.TiD$,
    case when $V.Name=NULL$ then $U.Name$ else $V.Name$,
    case when $V.Chair=NULL$ then $U.Chair$ else $V.Chair$
  from $Departments_c$ as U, $Departments_i$ as V;

The script above completes the steps for computing the null closures and generates three view tables for our query – i.e., $UnderGrads_{iv}$, $Parents_{iv}$ and $Departments_{iv}$.

3.3 Inheritance and Object Traversal in SQL Using Query Rewriting

As a final step, we rewrite the SQL^O query in Sect. 3.2 as a large join query to accommodate object traversals anticipated by the de-reference operators over the three null closed instance views we have generated and the traditional table:

q_6: select $U.Name,\ V.Income$
  from $UnderGrads_{iv}$ as $U,\ Parents_{iv}$ as $V,\ Departments_{iv}$ as $W,$
  $Professors$ as X
  where $U.State\ =\ 'ID'$ and $U.Par=V.TiD$ and $V.Income\ >\ 75K$
    and $U.Major=W.TiD$ and $W.Name\ \neq\ 'CS'$ and $W.Chair=X.PiD$
    and $X.Dept\ =\ 'CS'$;

In our example database, there are two potential Idaho resident undergraduate students, *Abebi* and *Odelia*. However, *Abebi*'s parent *Maria*'s income is less than \$75K, and her department chair *Tanaka* is not a computer science professor, and thus does not qualify to be in our response. However, *Odelia* is a Math major, and her department chair *Sharon* is a computer science professor and her parent also has income higher than \$75K although the parent name is missing. So, SQL^O appropriately returns the tuple $\langle Odelia,\ 90K \rangle$ as a response.

4   Conclusion

Our goal in this paper was to show that complex objects, class hierarchies, inheritance, overriding and structure traversal can be modeled as a simple extension of SQL. While we did not discuss a complete translation algorithm for brevity, we have presented the overall idea behind the translation of an SQL^O database and queries to a semantically equivalent SQL database. We have shown that the two most coveted OO features, namely inheritance with overriding and object traversal, can be captured within relational model based on a translational semantics without the need for an entirely new language or a formal foundation.

References

1. Alashqur, A.M., Su, S.Y.W., Lam, H.: OQL: A query language for manipulating object-oriented databases. In: VLDB, pp. 433–442 (1989)
2. Bancilhon, F., Delobel, C., Kanellakis, P.C. (eds.): Building an Object-Oriented Database System, The Story of O2. Morgan Kaufmann, Burlington (1992)
3. Dar, S., Gehani, N.H., Jagadish, H.V.: CQL++: a SQL for the Ode object-oriented DBMS. In: Pirotte, A., Delobel, C., Gottlob, G. (eds.) EDBT 1992. LNCS, vol. 580, pp. 201–216. Springer, Heidelberg (1992). https://doi.org/10.1007/BFb0032432
4. Feuerlicht, G., Pokorný, J., Richta, K.: Object-relational database design: can your application benefit from SQL: 2003? In: Barry, C., Lang, M., Wojtkowski, W., Conboy, K., Wojtkowski, G. (eds.) ISD, Challenges in Practice, Theory, and Education, vol. 2, pp. 975–987. Springer, Boston (2007). https://doi.org/10.1007/978-0-387-78578-3_30
5. Fuh, Y., et al.: Implementation of SQL3 structured types with inheritance and value substitutability. In: VLDB, pp. 565–574 (1999)
6. Hammer, M., McLeod, D.: Database description with SDM: a semantic database model. ACM Trans. Database Syst. **6**(3), 351–386 (1981)
7. Mitschang, B., Pirahesh, H., Pistor, P., Lindsay, B.G., Südkamp, N.: SQL/XNF - processing composite objects as abstractions over relational data. In: ICDE, pp. 272–282 (1993)
8. Sieg Jr., J., Sciore, E.: Extended relations. In: ICDE, pp. 488–494 (1990)

Big Data Technology I

Modeling Data Lakes with Data Vault: Practical Experiences, Assessment, and Lessons Learned

Corinna Giebler[1]([⊠])[ID], Christoph Gröger[2][ID], Eva Hoos[2],
Holger Schwarz[1], and Bernhard Mitschang[1]

[1] University of Stuttgart, Universitätsstraße 38, 70569 Stuttgart, Germany
{Corinna.Giebler,Holger.Schwarz,
Bernhard.Mitschang}@ipvs.uni-stuttgart.de
[2] Robert Bosch GmbH, Borsigstraße 4, 70469 Stuttgart, Germany
{Christoph.Groeger,Eva.Hoos}@de.bosch.com

Abstract. Data lakes have become popular to enable organization-wide analytics on heterogeneous data from multiple sources. Data lakes store data in their raw format and are often characterized as schema-free. Nevertheless, it turned out that data still need to be modeled, as neglecting data modeling may lead to issues concerning e.g., quality and integration. In current research literature and industry practice, Data Vault is a popular modeling technique for structured data in data lakes. It promises a flexible, extensible data model that preserves data in their raw format. However, hardly any research or assessment exist on the practical usage of Data Vault for modeling data lakes. In this paper, we assess the Data Vault model's suitability for the data lake context, present lessons learned, and investigate success factors for the use of Data Vault. Our discussion is based on the practical usage of Data Vault in a large, global manufacturer's data lake and the insights gained in real-world analytics projects.

Keywords: Data lakes · Data Vault · Data modeling · Industry experience · Assessment · Lessons learned

1 Introduction

The advance of digitalization leads to large amounts of heterogeneous data. Businesses that apply data analytics on these data can gain a large competitive advantage [1]. Data lakes [2] are highly popular, since they enable the integration and explorative analysis of heterogeneous data. Typically, data lakes are built using a *schema-on-read approach* [2, 3] to allow the flexible usage beyond predefined use cases—so called use-case-independence. Technology-wise, data lakes are heavily associated with the Hadoop Distributed File System [2]. Even though data of any format may be stored in the data lake, most data lakes in industry practice nowadays mainly contain structured data [4].

However, when managing data with the schema-on-read approach, data modeling must not be neglected [5, 6]. It turned out that a lack of meaningful structure for data may lead to quality issues, integration issues, performance issues and deviations from enterprise goals [6]. Standardizing data modeling in data lakes has two advantages for

© Springer Nature Switzerland AG 2019
A. H. F. Laender et al. (Eds.): ER 2019, LNCS 11788, pp. 63–77, 2019.
https://doi.org/10.1007/978-3-030-33223-5_7

organizations: Technical and organizational processes (e.g., for ETL and project management) can be reused, and data from different contexts can easily be combined. One candidate for modeling data in data lakes is *Data Vault* [7, 8]. It is used to model data lakes in both research and industry practice. Data Vault is a combination of dimensional modeling and third normal form [7] and supports agile project management and use-case-independent modeling [8, 9]. Because it is a simple and flexible modeling technique, Data Vault qualifies for data modeling in data lakes [5].

Currently, there is little conceptual work on Data Vault available in both industry and research. Aside from the reference books of its inventor [7, 8], there are some rudimentary comparisons between Data Vault and other modeling techniques [9, 10]. Research also deals with the creation of a conceptual Data Vault model [11], the automated physical design of Data Vault [12], or the direct transformation from JSON to a Data Vault schema [13]. However, there are neither insights on practical experiences nor detailed assessments for Data Vault, especially not in the context of data lakes.

In this paper, we close this gap by providing guidance on the usage of Data Vault in data lakes. Our contributions include the following:

- We investigate exemplary real-world analytics projects from three different core business domains at a large, globally active manufacturer and provide insights into the practical experiences made.
- We identify the shortcomings of Data Vault and demonstrate possible solutions.
- We present lessons learned and derive general success factors for the use of Data Vault in data lakes.
- We assess Data Vault as data modeling technique for structured data in data lakes.

The remainder of this paper is structured as follows: Sect. 2 describes the Data Vault model and its characteristics in detail. Section 3 discusses the exemplary analytics projects, the difficulties that arose, and possible solutions. Section 4 assesses Data Vault based on the experiences made, presents the lessons learned, and derives success factors for Data Vault modeling. Section 5 gives an overview and comparative evaluation concerning modeling alternatives. Finally, Sect. 6 concludes the paper.

2 Data Vault Basics

After a first version of Data Vault was published in 2012 [7], the current Data Vault model 2.0 extended and adapted the modeling technique further for enhanced performance [8]. Subsection 2.1 describes the Data Vault model's components and modeling guidelines. Subsection 2.2 details the key characteristics of Data Vault.

2.1 The Data Vault Model

This paper deals with Data Vault 2.0 as described in the reference book [8]. The Data Vault model is a conceptual and logical data model using table structures. Data Vault represents entities, relationships between entities, and additional context data in three different table types: *hubs*, *links*, and *satellites*.

Hubs represent business objects. Two example hubs are depicted in white in Fig. 1. A hub contains the business key of the business object it represents, *WPKey* or *MKey* in the example, and a unique surrogate key *WPHashKey* or *MHashKey*, hashed from this business key. Besides those two keys, a hub contains a load date, and a record source. The load date specifies when an entry was first added to the hub. The record source identifies the source system the entry was loaded from.

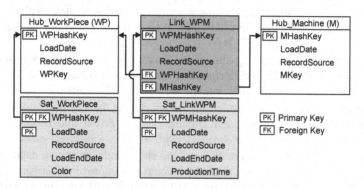

Fig. 1. The Data Vault model consists of three different table types: hubs, links, and satellites. Hubs represent business objects (e.g., work pieces or machines), while links connect hubs. Satellites contain descriptive attributes, such as *Color* or *ProductionTime* [8].

Links represent associations or hierarchies between hubs. They refer to the connected hubs via their surrogate keys. The primary key of each link is a hash of the business keys it connects. In the exemplary link in Fig. 1 (dark grey), the *WPMHashKey* is compound of the *WPKey* and the *MKey*. Like the hub, the link contains a load date and a record source. All links express many-to-many relationships. This adds flexibility to the model: If solely the cardinalities of a relationship in the source system change, this has no effect on the links in the Data Vault model. New entities can be added to the model without changing existing hubs, adding more flexibility. Instead, a new link is created or existing links are updated. There exist multiple types of links, e.g., *SAME-AS-links* indicate that entries of two hubs refer to the same business object.

Satellites add additional information to hubs and links. In the example in Fig. 1, the satellites (light grey) contain the color of a work piece or the production time associated with the combination of a work piece and a machine. One hub or link may have multiple satellites holding all attributes that are not covered by the hubs and links themselves. Satellites contain the surrogate key of the hub or link they belong to as both primary key and foreign key. One satellite can hold multiple entries for the same hub or link entry for historization. Thus, the load date is the second part of the primary key, to create a unique identifier. In addition, each satellite entry contains the record source and a load end date. This load end date indicates when the entry's validity expired. Whenever data changes in the source system, a new entry is added to the satellite and the load end date of the old entry is updated. In this way, a historization according to Kimball's slowly changing dimensions type 2 [14] is achieved. Just like

for links, there exist different types for satellites as well, such as *multi-active satellites*, which store multiple entries for one parent key (e.g., multiple phone numbers for one customer).

Not all additional information on a hub or link should be kept in one single satellite, as this might lead to huge satellites. Instead, the reference proposes two splitting techniques: First, we may split satellites by source system. This eases the process of adding new source systems, as this only requires an additional satellite. Second, we may split satellites by the change frequency of contained attributes. With this, static attributes do not need to be updated every time a frequently changing attribute is changed.

In addition to these modeling structures, Data Vault comes with a *schema architecture* shown in Fig. 2. This architecture consists of the *Raw Vault*, the *Business Vault*, and *Data Marts*. Data first is loaded into the *Raw Vault*. Here, only *hard business rules* [9, 16] are applied, i.e., technical rules that do not change the meaning of data, such as the distribution into hubs, links, and satellites, or conversion into Unicode. Further transformations are applied in the *Business Vault*. Here, *soft business rules* [9, 16] are applied, which add business logic to the data. They might aggregate data, calculate KPIs, and much more. They may also add structures to improve performance, such as *bridge tables* containing frequently queried relationships. The Business Vault is an optional modeling layer based on top of a Raw Vault. It is not necessary to add all data from the Raw Vault to the Business Vault in the same level of detail. Finally the use-case-specific *Data Marts*, derived from Raw Vault or Business Vault, may be in any format, e.g., star schema or flat tables.

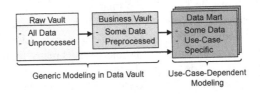

Fig. 2. Data Vault comprises three parts: Raw Vault, Business Vault, and Data Marts. The Raw Vault contains all data, while the Business Vault adds additional information to some data to increase performance. The use-case-specific Data Marts can be derived from either Vault [8].

2.2 Key Characteristics of Data Vault

The popularity of the Data Vault model is based on three key characteristics that result from its table structure: *flexibility*, *loading efficiency*, and *auditability* [7, 8].

Flexibility covers two aspects: (I) data are not changed in their meaning when saved in the Raw Vault. Instead, they are transferred into new tables and only hard business rules are applied. This means that they can be used for any desired use case. (II) the Data Vault model is easily adaptable and extendible. Changes in the source systems can easily be reflected in the Data Vault model with no or only little updates to existing tables [8]. Links are only updated if a new hub is added to the relationship. The addition of an attribute may be realized by updating a satellite, or by adding an entirely

new satellite. In all other cases, such as adding a new entity or relationship, or even an entire source system, it is sufficient to add new tables to the Data Vault model. This supports an agile approach in which one use case is implemented after the other and new business objects, relationships, and attributes are added on purpose. Data Vault 2.0 provides a project management methodology taking advantage of this characteristic [8].

The Data Vault model enables high *loading efficiency*. In Data Vault 1.0, tables of the same type could be loaded in parallel. However, the dependencies between tables enforce a certain order: first hubs, then links and finally satellites. Data Vault 2.0 addresses this issue, allowing all tables to be loaded in parallel. The Data Vault model also provides *auditability*, as all changes made to a source system entry are stored in the satellites. For this, each change to the data is stored as a separate record with a timestamp that indicates its expiration date.

3 Data Vault Modeling for Data Lakes in Practice

Based on the key characteristics presented in Subsect. 2.2, research literature suggests to use Data Vault for modeling data in data lakes [5]. To assess the suitability of this approach, we examined the usage of Data Vault in a real-world enterprise-wide data lake. This data lake is part of the industry 4.0 initiative of a large, global manufacturer, producing goods for various sectors, e.g., mobility or industry. Its data sources range from Enterprise Resource Planning (ERP) systems and Manufacturing Execution Systems (MES) to internet of things (IoT) devices.

We investigated the use of Data Vault in analytical projects from various business domains in the manufacturer's enterprise. In the following subsections, we detail three of them that provide significant insights into Data Vault modeling for data lakes. These business domains are *manufacturing* (Subsect. 3.1), *finance* (Subsect. 3.2), and *customer service* (Subsect. 3.3). We identify ways in which the domains benefit from Data Vault, and present issues that arose and their possible solutions. Table 1 summarizes the characteristics of those domains. For the used data, we distinguish two data categories: (I) *Transactional enterprise data* that refer to business transactions and business objects, and (II) *non-transactional enterprise data* that originate from novel data sources (e.g., sensors or user generated content) and describe certain aspects of a business activity in detail. Other aspects of interest are the source systems involved, the process type [16], involved users, and addressed analytic capabilities.

3.1 Manufacturing Domain

In the manufacturing business domain, the goal of projects is to enable data-driven manufacturing [17]. The captured data are used for, e.g., process performance reporting and predictive maintenance. All projects are managed in an agile manner.

The focus of the analytics projects in this domain mainly lies on the analysis of *non-transactional data*. Data originate from numerous *MES* and are captured by sensors during manufacturing. *Transactional data*, such as master data, data from *ERP systems*, and *manually added data*, e.g., defect codes added by domain experts, are used as additional source of information. Since goods for sale are produced in this

Table 1. Overview over characteristics of the investigated domains.

	Manufacturing domain	Finance domain	Customer service domain
Used data	Transactional, Non-transactional	Transactional	Transactional, Non-transactional
Kinds of source systems	ERP systems, Master data, MES, Manually added	ERP systems	ERP systems, IoT devices, Master data, Simulations
Process type	Primary	Support	Primary
Involved users	Business user, Domain experts, Data scientists	Business user, Domain experts, Data scientists	Domain experts
Analytic capabilities	Descriptive, Diagnostic, Predictive	Descriptive, Predictive	Descriptive

domain, the processes are *primary processes*. All kinds of users are equally involved in this analytics project. *Business users* create reports on different aspects of the process, such as factory efficiency (*descriptive* use cases). *Domain experts* use the data for *diagnostic* use cases, e.g., to analyze test results and optimize processes. *Data scientists* finally enable *predictive* use cases, such as predictive maintenance and quality assessment.

Experiences with Data Vault. The analytics projects in this domain benefit from the Data Vault characteristics in three ways: (I) the flexibility of Data Vault allows use-case-independent modeling, (II) facilitates the agile development, and (III) allows the incremental integration of numerous source systems, which is necessary due to the large number of different source systems involved in this domain.

One major issue arose during the usage of Data Vault in this business domain: Due to the integration of a large number of source systems the hash key generation became quite complex. Across all the different source systems, the same business key is often used for different business objects. In such a case, the Data Vault modeling reference suggests to either extend the business key with the source system, or to create one separate hub per source system. However, in the first approach, source systems are not properly integrated. The second approach would quickly result in a large and overly complex data model due to the large number of source systems involved in this domain (over 600). Thus, two different approaches to solve this issue were developed. In the first approach, the business key was extended using additional attributes to create a unique composed key. However, deciding which attributes to add is complex, especially when schemata or business logic change in the source systems, or when many business objects share the same values for a majority of their attributes. Therefore, a second solution was developed. In this approach, a satellite is added for each involved source system. If a business key is available in more than one source system, entries in all affected satellites are added. To retrieve the information on one certain object, both business key and source system have to be provided in the query. Figure 3 shows an

example hub with two associated source system satellites. This solution is similar to the proposed extension of the business key, but also integrates the different source systems.

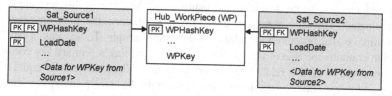

Fig. 3. If the same business key refers to different business objects in different source systems, one satellite per source system is added to the business key.

Overall, even though the Data Vault reference did not sufficiently cover the issue of ambiguous business keys and thus had to be extended, Data Vault provides the significant benefits of flexibility and simple integration of new source systems. Especially regarding the large number of MES, this is an essential feature in this domain.

3.2 Finance Domain

The second business domain under consideration concerns finance and controlling. Data are used, for instance, to generate reports on wins and losses or to predict future revenue. Multiple teams work agilely and in parallel on independent projects in this domain. For example, one team is responsible for all use cases related to key performance indicator (KPI) calculation, while another team deals with prediction use cases.

Only *transactional data* from *ERP systems* are used in this domain. The goal is to organize and coordinate other processes in the company, making this domain's processes *support processes*. Mainly *business users* are involved in this domain. They carry out *descriptive* use cases. However, *domain experts* and *data scientists* are also involved, focusing on *predictive use cases*, such as resource planning and revenue forecasts.

Experiences with Data Vault. In this business domain, the Data Vault characteristics benefit analytics projects in four ways: (I) Data Vault's flexibility allows use-case-independent modeling and (II) supports multiple teams working in parallel. (III) Data Vault's high loading efficiency makes source data quickly available for analysis, which is especially important for generating reports including recent data updates. (IV) Data Vault's auditability allows to detect tampering with sensitive data.

However, during the project iterations already carried out, the analytics project team encountered three difficulties affecting the Data Vault model and the modeling process:

A major issue was the *application of business logic*. The necessary business logic is split across the different layers of Data Vault (see Fig. 2): hard business rules are applied in the Raw Vault, while soft business rules are applied in the Business Vault. However, some business rules, e.g., currency conversion or resolving factorization, can not be clearly classified as hard or soft. For these rules, it is debatable whether the meaning of the data remains the same. Therefore, the project team extended the Data Vault reference to apply all these non-classifiable rules in the Raw Vault.

Modeling roles, i.e., the function an entity has in a relationship, in the Data Vault model is not covered by the Data Vault reference. However, roles are important in many use cases. For example, an order might have both a billing address and a shipping address, which have to be differentiated using roles. Again, two different approaches were evaluated. The first approach uses one link between the hubs involved in a relationship, i.e., the order and the address hub in the example. To this link, a satellite is added that contains the role of the relation. However, the link's primary key consists of the business keys of the related hub entries. If the billing address is equal to the shipping address for one certain order, two entries with the same primary key are added to the link table. The second and preferred approach therefore uses one link per role, as shown in Fig. 4.

Fig. 4. Modeling roles in relationships in Data Vault should be done using one link per role.

To *save analytical results* for future use, e.g., to compare predictions to reality, an adaption of the Data Vault model is required. However, it is unclear how these results can be integrated into Data Vault, as this use case is not described in the Data Vault modeling reference. As a solution, a new hub was introduced that represents the analysis itself. It is linked to all hubs used in the analysis. Its satellites contain the analysis results. This way, source system data is clearly separated from processed data.

In summary, various issues arose in this domain that could not be solved using the standard Data Vault modeling reference. Instead, Data Vault had to be adapted or extended. However, the domain also greatly benefits from the key characteristics of Data Vault such as the flexibility for agile project management and parallel developer teams.

3.3   Customer Service Domain

The last domain to detail is the domain of customer service. Here, field data captured by IoT devices are used for, e.g., maintenance and product lifecycle management. For this purpose, a product is equipped with sensors that continuously capture data on its behavior. This field data then is compared to previously calculated simulation results.

The majority of data used are *non-transactional* field data captured by sensors and *simulation data. Transactional data*, in particular *master data* and data from *ERP systems*, are used to add additional information, such as product information. Since the data are used to improve the product and add value to the customer, the processes in this domain are *primary processes*. The only involved *user group* are *domain experts*, who execute *descriptive analysis* on the data, such as comparing field data to simulation data. Analytics projects in this domain are executed agilely.

Experiences with Data Vault. Data Vault provides two major benefits to analytics projects in this domain through its flexibility, which (I) allows use-case-independent modeling and (II) supports agile project management.

The major issue encountered in this domain concerns the management of IoT data in Data Vault. Once captured, IoT data do not change. Thus, the Data Vault modeling reference suggests using *nonhistorized links* to store sensor data [8] (see Fig. 5). In such a link, the load end date is omitted. However, this quickly results in satellites with a large amount of entries due to the periodic capture of IoT data. Another idea developed in this domain was to store IoT data in an external system providing cheap storage for large amounts of data, e.g., HDFS. A link to these systems is stored in a satellite, similarly to link-based integration [18]. Using multi-active satellites [8], it is even possible to link multiple files to the same link or hub entry. However, this approach may lead to longer execution times, as the IoT data have to be retrieved from this external system.

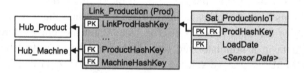

Fig. 5. To store sensor data, a nonhistorized link is suggested by the Data Vault modeling reference [8]. The associated satellite contains no load end date.

Up until now, the project team has not yet found out which solution to prefer. Both approaches still have to be balanced against each other. However, it is clear that there are ways to manage even IoT data in the Data Vault model.

4 Lessons Learned and Overall Assessment

After examining the issues that arise in different business domains when using Data Vault in data lakes, this section deduces the lessons learned. To this end, we discuss and classify the issues encountered with Data Vault and highlight the solutions developed in the examined domains (Subsect. 4.1). Based on these insights, we assess the adequacy of Data Vault for structured data in data lakes and derive generally valid success factors for Data Vault modeling (Subsect. 4.2).

4.1 Lessons Learned and Classification of Issues

The issues that arose during the practical usage of Data Vault can be assigned to one of two classes (see Fig. 6): (I) issues only insufficiently covered by the modeling reference, and (II) issues not covered by the modeling reference at all.

Data Vault reference insufficient	Not covered by Data Vault reference
• Ambiguous Business Keys • Application of Business Logic • IoT Data	• Roles • Saving Analysis Results

Fig. 6. Different issues arose when using Data Vault in data lakes, which the Data Vault modeling reference either only insufficiently covered or not covered at all.

(I) Insufficiently Covered

- The *management of ambiguous business keys*. In this issue, the same business key refers to different business objects in various source systems (Sect. 3.1). The Data Vault modeling reference suggests two different approaches to model ambiguous business keys, which both have their drawbacks. Instead, one hub was created and separate satellites for the different source systems were added.
- The *application of business logic* (Sect. 3.2). In the finance domain, not all rules could clearly be classified as hard or soft. In the domain, the developers classified these ambiguous business rules as hard rules and applied them in the Raw Vault.
- The *handling of IoT data* (Sect. 3.3). The Data Vault modeling reference suggests storing IoT data in a nonhistorized link. However, the satellite tables containing these data would become very large. Alternatively, IoT data can be stored in an external low-cost system. So far, there is no evidence on which approach is preferable.

(II) Not Covered

- The *modeling of roles in relationships* (Sect. 3.2). To solve this issue, one link per role was added between the affected hubs.
- The *saving of analysis results* (Sect. 3.2). In this case, an additional hub was added to the model to represent the analysis itself and to contain the results.

Both of these uncovered issues are not specific for the analyzed domains. Roles in relationships occur in multiple business divisions, e.g., in human resources to differentiate the roles of people working on a certain project. Storing analysis results or transformed data back into the data lake is also a reoccurring use case [19, 20]. The solutions developed for these issues comply with Data Vault modeling by using only existing modeling structures (links and satellites). However, an extension to the Data Vault model to directly cover these issues would be worthwhile to have.

4.2   Assessment and Success Factors for Data Vault in Data Lakes

Overall, analytics projects in each of the three examined business domains profited from the key characteristics of Data Vault mentioned in Sect. 2.2. Especially Data Vault's flexibility was beneficial in all domains, due to agile project management, integration of multiple source systems, and support of parallel development. The business domains also benefitted from high loading efficiency and auditability. However, various issues arose during modeling. From the experience gained with these issues, we derive three generally valid success factors for Data Vault modeling in data lakes:

(I) Identify shortcomings of the Data Vault modeling reference. As shown above, not all issues encountered in the projects are sufficiently covered by the Data Vault reference, requiring an extension or adaption of the reference.

(II) Define a data architecture for data lakes. While for data warehouses, the Data Vault reference proposes a schema architecture (see Fig. 2) [8], such an architecture does not exist for data lakes. It is unclear whether the given architecture is applicable in the data lake context. However, defining the Data Vault layers and the applied business rules is of great importance and thus could be the basis of a data lake architecture.

(III) Identify inconsistencies in source systems. These issues, such as ambiguous business keys, may lead to severe problems in integration and analysis. Therefore, they have to be addressed during data integration.

These success factors necessitate an enterprise-wide set of data modeling guidelines that contain both modeling specifications and best practices for data modeling. Thereby, these guidelines extend or even change the Data Vault modeling reference to fit the context. They also should be communicated across domains to ensure consistent data modeling across the data lake. We conclude that combined with such guidelines, Data Vault is well suited to model structured data in data lakes.

5 Related Work and Comparative Evaluation

While we discussed Data Vault for data lake modeling, there are other alternatives from both the data warehouse and the data lake context. Subsection 5.1 presents these alternate modeling techniques. Subsection 5.2 compares Data Vault to some of these alternatives using criteria relevant in the studied domains and data lakes in general.

5.1 Related Work

Representing the real world as accurately as possible is the aim of the well-known entity-relationship model (ER model) [21]. Here, business objects are modeled as entities with relationships between them. However, the ER model is only a conceptual model and other techniques are used for logical and physical modeling.

For the data warehousing context, dimensional modeling was developed as conceptual and logical model [14]. Data is stored in either fact tables or dimension tables. Fact tables contain the metrics and measurements of interest for the business, e.g., sales figures. Dimension tables allow to aggregate these so-called facts, e.g. along a time axis.

Another approach to data warehouse modeling is normalization [22]. Especially the third normal form was used for logical modeling. To allow historization, the third normal form can be alternated into so called head-version tables [9]. Here, attributes are divided into static attributes and attributes that should be historized. Static attributes are stored in a so-called head table together with the business key. Attributes to be historized are stored in one or more version tables linking to the respective head table.

As a next step, Data Vault emerged as combination of dimensional modeling and third normal form [7]. It is a conceptual and logical modeling technique.

The digitalization poses new challenges on data analytics and data management, which are addressed in data lakes [2, 3]. For this context, additional modeling techniques were recently proposed. Data droplets, for example, model the entire data lake as a composition of small RDF graphs [23]. In another modeling technique [24], each data entry is modeled as a small graph of four nodes, containing different information on the entry, e.g., the data itself or its metadata. These four-tuples then are connected to each other via their metadata nodes. To our knowledge, there exists no practical experience report on the adequacy of these modeling techniques for data lakes.

5.2   Comparative Evaluation

As shown in the course of this paper, different domains with different requirements benefitted from the use of Data Vault for data lake modeling. Nevertheless, Data Vault also revealed some weaknesses in the form of insufficiently addressed modeling issues. We thus compare Data Vault to dimensional modeling [14] and head-version tables [9] (as an alternation of third normal form) to evaluate whether these alternatives are more suitable for data lake modeling, using criteria relevant in the domains and data lakes in general. We will not investigate ER modeling, as it is only conceptual, nor first modeling approaches developed for data lakes specifically (such as data droplets [23]), as these modeling approaches are still immature and not widespread in practice.

Table 2 depicts the result of this qualitative comparison. *Use-Case-Independence*, as is necessary in data lakes, is achieved by all techniques but dimensional modeling, where the analytic goals define the model. *Support of agile project management* (see investigated domains) is only provided by Data Vault. In case of the other modeling techniques, the schema of already existing tables has to be changed, e.g., to add a new attribute. Similarly, *Source Schema Changes*, which happen in especially agile projects, result in many changes for dimensional modeling and head-version tables but not for Data Vault. *High Loading Efficiency*, as needed in the domains, is provided by Data Vault and partially by dimensional modeling, where dimension tables can be loaded in parallel. In head-version tables, too many dependencies between tables make parallel loading very complex. *Auditability* is achieved in all techniques using e.g., slowly changing dimensions for dimensional modeling [14]. The *Number of Tables* is small for dimensional modeling, where one fact table and only few tables for dimensions are needed. Data Vault typically has an even higher number of tables than the head-version model, especially in cases, where many one-to-one relationships are involved. While head-version tables represent these relationships without additional tables, Data Vault creates a link table for each of them. The *Query Performance* is directly dependent of the number of tables, which is why dimensional modeling typically needs fewer JOINS than Data Vault. However, this issue can be addressed by providing pre-joined tables in Business Vault and Data Marts. The *Understandability*, which plays a role whenever non-data scientists use the data, is affected by the number of tables as well, but also by the overall complexity of the model. Here, dimensional modeling is easiest to understand due to its simple structure. The *Integration of Multiple Source Systems*, as needed

in the domains, finally is simple in Data Vault and can be solved using satellites. In the other techniques however, more complex integration techniques are necessary.

Table 2. Comparative evaluation of modeling techniques

	Data vault	Dim. modeling	Head-version tables
Use-case-independence	Yes	No	Yes
Support of agile project management	Yes	No, many changes necessary	Often, adaption is necessary
Source schema changes	Few changes necessary	Mostly big changes necessary	Mostly big changes necessary
High loading efficiency	Yes	Parallel loading of dimensions possible	No
Auditability	Yes	Yes	Yes
Number of tables	Very large	Small	Large
Query performance	Many JOINS	Few JOINS	Depends
Understandability	Medium	Very high	Medium
Integration of multiple source systems	Very simple using satellites	Complex	Complex

Overall, Data Vault addresses most criteria very well. However, especially dimensional modeling has its strengths were Data Vault has its weaknesses (number of tables, performance, and understandability). Thus, in cases where these criteria are of great importance, e.g., for KPI-focused or aggregation-focused use cases, we propose to use dimensional data marts on top of Data Vault, as already indicated in Fig. 2.

6 Conclusion

Data lakes recently emerged to enable the use-case-independent use of data. However, even data in a data lake have to be modeled. Without data modeling, data are prone to quality and integration issues. Research literature suggests Data Vault for this purpose. To determine the adequacy of Data Vault for data lake modeling, we examined real-world business domains at a large, globally active manufacturer. We provided insights into three domains and discussed the experiences made with the practical application of Data Vault for data lakes. It turned out that even though some of the projects used data rather untypical for Data Vault (e.g., IoT data), it was successfully applied in all projects. However, multiple issues arose when using Data Vault, some that were only insufficiently covered by the Data Vault modeling reference, some that were not covered at all. To successfully use Data Vault in data lakes, a set of enterprise-wide modeling guidelines is necessary, which extend the available Data Vault modeling reference and contain solution approaches and best practices.

References

1. Margulies, J.C.: Data as competitive advantage. Winterberry Gr., October, pp. 1–28 (2015)
2. Mathis, C.: Data lakes. Datenbank-Spektrum **17**(3), 289–293 (2017)
3. Fang, H.: Managing data lakes in big data era: what's a data lake and why has it became popular in data management ecosystem. In: Proceedings of the 2015 IEEE International Conference on Cyber Technology in Automation, Control, and Intelligent Systems (CYBER) (2015)
4. Russom, P.: Data lakes - purposes, practices, patterns, and platforms. TDWI (2017)
5. Topchyan, A.R.: Enabling data driven projects for a modern enterprise. In: Proceedings of the Institute for System Programming of the RAS (ISP RAS 2016), vol. 28, no. 3, pp. 209–230 (2016)
6. Stiglich, P.: Data modeling in the age of big data. Bus. Intell. J. **19**(4), 17–22 (2014)
7. Linstedt, D.: Super Charge Your Data Warehouse: Invaluable Data Modeling Rules to Implement Your Data Vault (2012)
8. Linstedt, D., Olschimke, M.: Building a Scalable Data Warehouse with Data Vault 2.0. Elsevier Ltd., Amsterdam (2015)
9. Schnider, D., Martino, A., Eschermann, M.: Comparison of data modeling methods for a core data warehouse. Trivadis (2014)
10. Yessad, L., Labiod, A.: Comparative study of data warehouses modeling approaches: Inmon, Kimball and Data Vault. In: 2016 International Conference on System Reliability and Science (ICSRS) (2016)
11. Jovanovic, V., Bojicic, I.: Conceptual data vault model. In: Proceedings of the 15th Southern Association for Information Systems Conference (SAIS) (2012)
12. Krneta, D., Jovanovic, V., Marjanovic, Z.: A direct approach to physical data vault design. Comput. Sci. Inf. Syst. **11**(2), 569–599 (2014)
13. Cernjeka, K., Jaksic, D., Jovanovic, V.: NoSQL document store translation to data vault based EDW. In: 2018 41st International Convention on Information and Communication Technology, Electronics and Microelectronics (MIPRO) (2018)
14. Kimball, R., Ross, M.: The Data Warehouse Toolkit: The Definitive Guide to Dimensional Modeling. Wiley, Hoboken (2013)
15. Inmon, W.H., Linstedt, D.: Data Architecture: A Primer for the Data Scientist - Big Data, Data Warehouse and Data Vault. Elsevier Ltd., Amsterdam (2014)
16. Porter, M.E.: Competitive Advantage: Creating and Sustaining Superior Performance. Free Press, New York (1985)
17. Gröger, C.: Building an Industry 4.0 analytics platform. Datenbank-Spektrum **18**(1), 5–14 (2018)
18. Gröger, C., Schwarz, H., Mitschang, B.: The deep data warehouse: link-based integration and enrichment of warehouse data and unstructured content. In: Proceedings of the 2014 IEEE 18th International Enterprise Distributed Object Computing Conference (EDOC) (2014)
19. IBM Analytics: The governed data lake approach. IBM (2016)
20. Terrizzano, I., Schwarz, P., Roth, M., Colino, J.E.: Data wrangling: the challenging journey from the wild to the lake. In: Proceedings of the 7th Biennial Conference on Innovative Data Systems Research (CIDR) (2015)
21. Chen, P.P.-S.: The entity-relationship model-toward a unified view of data. ACM Trans. Database Syst. **1**(1), 9–36 (1976)

22. Inmon, W.H.: Building the Data Warehouse. Wiley, Hoboken (2005)
23. Houle, P.: Data Lakes, Data Ponds, and Data Droplets (2017). http://ontology2.com/the-book/data-lakes-ponds-and-droplets.html
24. Walker, C., Alrehamy, H.: Personal data lake with data gravity pull. In: Proceedings of the 2015 IEEE Fifth International Conference on Big Data and Cloud Computing (BDCloud) (2015)

Requirements-Driven Visualizations for Big Data Analytics: A Model-Driven Approach

Ana Lavalle[1,2]([envelope]), Alejandro Maté[1,2], and Juan Trujillo[1,2]

[1] Lucentia (DLSI), University of Alicante, Carretera San Vicente del Raspeig s/n, San Vicente del Raspeig, 03690 Alicante, Spain
{alavalle,amate,jtrujillo}@dlsi.ua.es
[2] Lucentia Lab, C/Pintor Pérez Gil, N-16, Alicante, Spain

Abstract. Choosing the right Visualization techniques is critical in Big Data Analytics. However, decision makers are not experts on visualization and they face up with enormous difficulties in doing so. There are currently many different (i) Big Data sources and also (ii) many different visual analytics to be chosen. Every visualization technique is not valid for every Big Data source and is not adequate for every context. In order to tackle this problem, we propose an approach, based on the Model Driven Architecture (MDA) to facilitate the selection of the right visual analytics to non-expert users. The approach is based on three different models: (i) a requirements model based on goal-oriented modeling for representing information requirements, (ii) a data representation model for representing data which will be connected to visualizations and, (iii) a visualization model for representing visualization details regardless of their implementation technology. Together with these models, a set of transformations allow us to semi-automatically obtain the corresponding implementation avoiding the intervention of the non-expert users. In this way, the great advantage of our proposal is that users no longer need to focus on the characteristics of the visualization, but rather, they focus on their information requirements and obtain the visualization that is better suited for their needs. We show the applicability of our proposal through a case study focused on a tax collection organization from a real project developed by the Spin-off company Lucentia Lab.

Keywords: Data visualization · Big Data Analytics · Model Driven Architecture · User requirements

1 Introduction

Data is continuously growing, specially since the last decade. With ever larger amounts of data that need to be interpreted and analyzed, using the right visualizations is crucial to help decision makers to properly analyze the data and guide them to take better informed decisions.

© Springer Nature Switzerland AG 2019
A. H. F. Laender et al. (Eds.): ER 2019, LNCS 11788, pp. 78–92, 2019.
https://doi.org/10.1007/978-3-030-33223-5_8

In this new era of Big Data Analytics, there has been an increasing interest from both the academic and industry worlds in different phases of the data life cycle: from the storage to the analysis, cleaning or integration and, of course, the visualization. Data and Information Visualization are becoming strategic for the exploration and explanation of large data sets due to the great impact that data have from a human perspective. An effective, efficient and intuitive representation of the analyzed data may result as important as the analytic process itself [6]. However, larger data sets and their complexity in terms of heterogeneity contribute to make the representation of data more complex [5].

In this context, defining and implementing the right visualization for a given data set is a complex task for companies, specially in the age of Big Data where heterogeneous and external data sources require knowledge of the underlying data to create an adequate visualization. As such, choosing the wrong visualizations and misunderstanding the data leads to wrong decisions and considerable losses. One of the key difficulties for defining the right visualization technique is the lack of expertise in information visualization of decision makers. Another critical aspect is that, apparently, a large set of visualizations may be equally valid for any given data sets, which has been proven to be absolutely wrong [21], each data set and each analysis has its particular characteristics and not always all the types of visualization are valid to represent them.

In order to tackle the above-presented problems, we propose an approach, based on the Model Driven Architecture (MDA) [16] proposed by the Object Management Group (OMG).

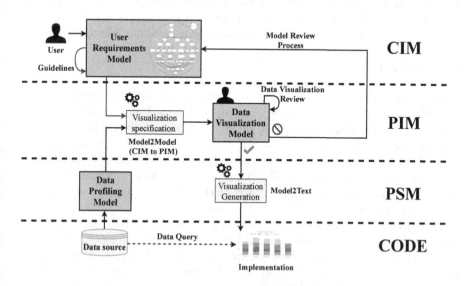

Fig. 1. Overall view of the process proposed.

Figure 1 summarizes the process followed in our proposal, aligned with MDA. Firstly, a sequence of questions guides users in creating a Goal-Oriented [12]

model that captures their needs. This model (CIM layer) enables them to capture all the visualizations that are needed to tackle their information needs. The user requirements together with the data profiling information coming through the Data Profiling Model (at PSM layer) are used as a visualization specification that is input to a model to model transformation. This transformation generates the Data Visualization Model (PIM layer). This model allows users to specify exactly how they need to visualize the data. It also allows them to determine if the proposed visualization is adequate to satisfy the essential requirements for which it was created. The validation process is performed through a questionnaire according to user goals model. If the proposed visualization passes the validation. Otherwise, an unsuccessful validation points out to the existence of missing or wrongly defined requirements that must be reviewed. This process is repeated until all user requirements are fulfilled. Finally, a model to text transformation generates the implementation of the visualization using the data visualization model as input.

The great advantage of our proposal is that users no longer focus on the underlying technical aspects or finding the most adequate visualization technique to be used in every different data analytic process. By following our approach, decision makers obtain the visualization technique that is better suited to their information needs and the characteristics of the data at hand in a semi-automatic way. This is achieved thanks to our alignment with MDA, enabling us to incrementally refine the visualization until its implementation is obtained.

The rest of the paper is structured as follows. Section 2 presents the related work in this area. Section 3 presents the different proposed models of the approach based on the MDA. Section 4 discusses a real case study in the fiscal domain. Finally, Sect. 5 summarizes the conclusions and our future work.

2   Related Work

Several works have focused on proposing different ways to find the best visualization. [2] surveys the main classifications proposed in the literature and integrates them into a single framework based on six visualization requirements. In [11], authors propose a framework for choosing the best visualization where the main types of charts are related to users goals and to data dimensionality, cardinality, and data type they support. Finally, [9] proposes a model to automate the translation of visualization objectives specified by the user into a suitable visualization type based on seven visualization requirements.

Additionally, several approaches are focused on the analysis of visualization representations. [15] describes an information visualization taxonomy. [18] make a revision of visualization techniques for Big Data to determine which are the most optimistic when analyzing Big Data. [4] propose a metamodel to represent tree and graph views by modeling nodes and edges. Similarly, [7] uses nodes and edges to draw basic shapes like lines and circles.

Other works are focus on visual analytics recommendation systems. [20] detail the key requirements and design considerations for a visualization recommendation system and identify a number of challenges in realizing this vision

and describe some approaches to address them. [8] propose EventAction, a prescriptive analytics interface designed to present and explain recommendations of temporal event sequences. Additionally, [21] propose SEEDB, a visualization recommendation engine to facilitate fast visual analysis, SEEDB explores the space of visualizations, evaluates promising visualizations for trends, and recommends those it deems most "useful" or "interesting". In [14] authors propose a new language VizDSL for creating interactive visualizations that facilitate the understanding of complex data and information structures for enterprise systems interoperability.

To the best of our knowledge, the only approaches that follow the MDA philosophy in the Big Data Context are presented within the TOREADOR project. In [1], the authors propose a Model-driven approach that aims to lower the amount of competences needed in the management of a Big Data pipeline. [10] illustrates a use case exploiting the Model-driven capabilities of the TOREADOR platform as a way to fast track the uptake of business-driven Big Data models. [13] provides a layered model that represents tools and applications following the Dataflow paradigm.

Despite all the work presented so far, none of the approaches provide a way to easily translate user requirements into visual analytics implementations. Furthermore, there is an absence of a methodology that guides users in obtaining the most adequate visualization, allowing them to focus on their own needs rather than on the characteristics of the visualization.

3   A MDA Approach for Visual Analytics

As previously introduced in the paper, specifying the right visualization for a user is a challenging task. User has not only to take into account her needs, which are on a completely different abstraction level, but also consider characteristics of the data that make inadequate the use of certain visualizations. In order to let the user focus on her information needs, we aim to bridge the gap between the user requirements and their visualization implementation.

To this aim, we propose a development approach Fig. 1 in the context of the Model Driven Architecture [16]. Our main goal is to help users to generate the visualizations that are better suited to meet their information needs. Following the basic principles of MDA, our proposal builds on three types of models:

- **User Requirements Model (CIM layer):** Allows users to capture their information needs and certain visualization aspects that are needed to tackle them.
- **Data Visualization Model (PIM layer):** Enables users to specify the characteristics of their visualizations before obtaining their implementation.
- **Data Profiling Model (PSM layer):** Abstracts the required information from the data sources to (i) aid in determining the most adequate visualization and (ii) take certain aspects of data into account for their representation (such as whether they are numeric or categorical).

The process starts by capturing information needs at the CIM level. Then, a data profiling process is run to generate a data profiling model at the PSM level that contains the relevant data characteristics for the process. Once both models have been obtained, they are processed through a model to model transformation that generates a data visualization model at the PIM level. This model provides the user with the better suited visualization for her needs and the data available, and allows her to modify different aspects of the visualization such as the axis where each attribute should be positioned, the orientation, or the color range among others. Once the model refinement process is finished, a model to text transformation generates the implementation using a visualization library, such as D3.js in our case.

3.1   User Requirements Model

Our approach starts from a goal-oriented requirements model that allows us to capture information needs. To describe the coordinates required to build a visualization context (*Goal, Interaction, User, Dimensionality, Cardinality, Independent Type, and Dependent Type*) we follows the specification to automate data visualization in Big Data Analytics given in [9], in this way we make sure that the visualization specification is addressed in terms of Big Data. Due to paper constraints, we cover only the main aspects of our requirements model.

Our metamodel shown in Fig. 2 is an extension of i* and the *i* for Data Warehouses* extension [12]. Existing elements in the i* core are represented in blue (light grey), whereas those in i* for Data Warehouses are represented in red (dark grey). The new concepts added by our proposal are represented in white.

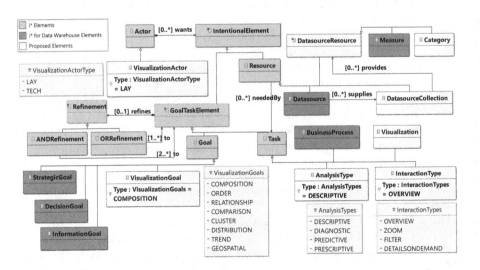

Fig. 2. User requirements metamodel. (Color figure online)

The first element is the *VisualizationActor*, which models the user of the system. There are two types of Visualization Actors: Lay, if she has no knowledge of complex visualizations, and Tech, if she has previous experience and is accustomed to Big Data Analytics. Next is the *BusinessProcess* on which users will focus their analysis. The business process will serve as the guideline for the definition of *Goals*.

The *AnalysisType* allows users to express which kind of analysis they wish to perform. The type of analysis can be determined by selecting which question from the following ones [19] is to be answered: How to act? (Prescriptive), Why has it happened? (Diagnostic), What is going to happen? (Predictive) or What to do to make it happen? (Descriptive).

Next, a Visualization represents a specific visualization that will be implemented to satisfy one or more *VisualizationGoals*. Each *VisualizationGoal* describes an aspect of the data that the visualization should reflect. These goals can be Composition, Order, Relationship, Comparison, Cluster, Distribution, Trend, or Geospatial, as considered in [9].

Along with *VisualizationGoals*, Visualizations have one or more *InteractionTypes*, that capture how the user will interact with the visualization. The different kinds of interaction are Overview, Zoom, Filter, or Details on Demand as [9] consider to data visualization in Big Data Analytics. Finally, a Visualization makes use of one or more *DatasourceResource* elements which feed the data to the visualization.

Using these concepts we allow users to define their needs instead of focusing on technical details that are not relevant at this level.

3.2 Data Profiling Model

Our second model is the Data Profiling Model. This model captures the data characteristics that are relevant to the visualization and is generated through a data profiling process. Firstly, users will select the data sources that they want to be represented in the visualization. Consequently, the data analyst will analyze the data sources extract the values of the coordinates by analyzing the features of the data sources. In this way, users do not need to manually inspect the data or have a deep understanding.

To know how to delimit the values for each coordinate we have use the values proposed in [9] to Big Data Analytics. In this way we classify the Dimensionality, Cardinality, and Dependent/Independent Type as follows:

Cardinality represents the cardinality of the data. It can either be *Low* or *High*, depending of the numbers of items to represent. *Low* cardinality considers a few items to a few dozens of items while *High* cardinality is set if there are some dozens of items or more.

Dimensionality is used to declare the number of variables to be visualized. Specifically, it can be *1-dimensional* when the data to represent is a single numerical value or string, *2-dimensional* when one variable depends on other, *n-dimensional* when a data object is a point in an n-dimensional space, *Tree*

when a collection of items have a link to one other parent item, or *Graph* when a collection of items are linked to arbitrary number of other items.

Type of Data: is used to declare the type of each variable. It can be *Nominal* when each variable is assigned to one category, *Ordinal* when it is qualitative and categories can be sorted, *Interval* when it is quantitative and equality of intervals can be determined, or *Ratio* when it is quantitative with a unique and non-arbitrary zero point.

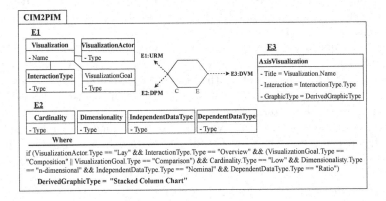

Fig. 3. Generation of axis based visualizations from user requirements.

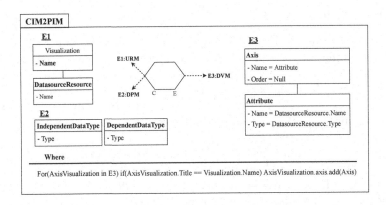

Fig. 4. Generation of axes for axis based visualizations from user requirements.

3.3   Visualization Specification Transformation - (Model to Model)

Information coming from User Requirements Model and the Data Profiling Model form the Visualization Specification. This specification is transformed

into a data visualization model using a set of model to model transformations, presented in Figs. 3 and 4 by the OMG standard language QVT [17]. According to the nature of the visualization to be derived, there are two types of transformations. On the one hand, we can have axis-based visualizations, such as column chart, line chart, bubble chart, etc. On the other hand, some visualizations such as dendrogram, chord or graphs require graph-based visualizations, which make use of nodes and edges instead of axis.

Due to space constraints, we will focus on how axis-based visualizations are derived. Our first transformation (Fig. 3), generates the visualization element, an AxisVisualization in this case. An AxisVisualization is derived according to the graphic type established by the transformation. This value is derived using the imperative part of the transformation (Where clause) according to the specific criteria established by [9] for the each graphic type. The values Cardinality, Dimensionality, IndependentDataType and DependentDataType are obtained from the data profiling. Finally, the visualization name and interaction type defined in the User Requirements Model are used to establish the title and interaction of the Axisvisualization.

Next, as Fig. 4 shows, each of the axes is generated individually. An axis is generated for each measure or category (abstracted by the DatasourceResource element) in the User Requirements Model. Afterwards, each axis is assigned their corresponding visualization by iterating over the data visualization model, completing the derivation of the visualization.

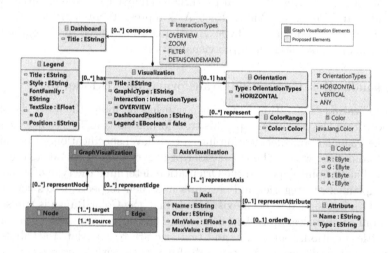

Fig. 5. Data visualization metamodel. (Color figure online)

3.4 Data Visualization Model

In order to verify if the recommended visualization is adequate to satisfy the information needs of the user and allow her to customize each visualization, we

require an abstraction of the visualization to be generated. Despite our best efforts, there is no metamodel proposed so far to model visual analytics. Thus, to support our process, we have defined a novel visualization metamodel.

Our metamodel shown in Fig. 5 is composed of elements extracted from [4] to define tree and graph visualizations, represented in blue (grey) color, while new concepts added by our proposal to detail the specification of visualizations represented in white. In the following, we describe the concepts included in the proposed metamodel.

The main element is *Visualization*, this element collects all the visualization requirements that should be met. It contains a visualization Title; a Legend, that may be shown or not; a Graphic Type that determines the type of visualization; a set of interactions that contain the type of interaction that must be supported (Overview, Zoom, Filter or Details-on-demand); and a Dashboard Position, in the event that the visualization will be part of a *Dashboard*.

In order to define the representation of a visualization, other elements are necessary. A visualization has and *Orientation*, either Horizontal, Vertical, or Any (when the graphic type does not have orientation). Moreover, a visualization has a *ColorRange*, that represents the range of colours that will be used by the visualization, an aspect of special importance for color-blind users.

A visualization will be instanced as either a *Graph Visualization* or an *Axis Visualization* depending on the type of visualization. A *Graph Visualization* may contain several *Nodes* and *Edges* [4]. Meanwhile, an *Axis Visualization* constaints a series of axes that represent the data. An *Axis* is may have a Name, Order, Minimum Value and Maximum Value. Each Axis represents an Attribute at most. An *Attribute* has a Name and a Type. Attributes can be used to be represented or to set the order of the data in the visualization.

3.5   Visualization Generation Transformation - (Model to Text)

The Visualization Generation Transformation has as input the data visualization model from the previous step. This transformation transforms each element within the visualization specification into a code level specification for a graphic library. In our case, we use the D3 JavaScript library [3] for generating the visualization. The GraphicType and the Orientation determine the type of visualization to implement. Categories and measures and their respective axes determine how the data is assigned to each axis. Meanwhile, the Color Range is translated into custom color scales. Moreover, if a Legend has been defined, the type of the legend, title, position, font family and text size are be translated attributes in the corresponding d3.legend function call. Finally, the title is used to provide a name to the visualization created, and the dashboard position is used to assign a position to the visualization.

4   Case Study

In order to evaluate the validity of our approach we have applied it to a real case study, based on a tax collection organization. Due to space constraints, we

provide a reduced example including enough data in order to allow readers to completely understand the approach. Therefore, the example is constrained to a Tax Region Area covering only three provinces. The organization requires a set of visualizations to analyze their data in order to help them detect underlying patterns in their unpaid bills and tax collection distribution. Due to the sensitivity of their data, we are not allowed to show the real values.

4.1 Specifying User Requirements

Through the application of our User Requirements Model to a tax collection organization, the Fig. 6 has been generated. A tax collector user wants to analyze the unpaid debts. Therefore, the analysis will focus on the *"Tax collection"* business process. Defining a business process helps determining the scope of the analysis and the goals pursued. The user is not a specialist in Big Data Analytics but rather an expert in tax management, thus she is defined as *"Lay user"*.

Next, the main objectives of the business process are defined as shown in Fig. 6. Specifically, the user defined her strategic goal as *"Reduce the unpaid bills"*. Strategic goals are achieved by means of analyses that support the decision-making process. The analysis type allows users to express what kind of analysis they wish to perform. In this case, the user wishes to know why bills are unpaid. Thus, the user decides to perform a *"Diagnostic analysis"*.

The diagnostic analysis is decomposed into decision goals. The user defined her decisions goals as: *"Identify unpaid bills"*, *"Identify the quantities unpaid"*, and *"Analyze the evolution"*. Decisions goals communicate the rationale followed by the decision-making process; however, by themselves they do not provide the necessary details about the data to be visualized. Therefore, for each decision goal we specify one or more information goals.

From each of the decision goals the user refined the following information goals: *"Identify places with more unpaid bills"*, *"Identify the type of unpaid bills"*, *"Identify who has unpaid bills"*, and *"Evolution of unpaid bills"*. Information goals represent the lowest level of goal abstraction. And for each information goal, we will have one visualization to achieve it. A visualization is characterized by one or more visualization goals which describe what aspects of the data the visualization is trying to reflect, and one or more kinds of interaction that they will like to have with the visualization. Moreover, a visualization will make use of one or more data source elements to get the relevant data from the database. In this case, the user defines the interactions she want to have with each visualization and her visualization goals following user guidelines. *"Overview"*, *"Zoom"* and *"Details-on-demand"* have been defined as interactions and *"Geospatial"*, *"Composition"*, *"Comparison"*, *"Order"*, and *"Trend"* as visualization goals. Finally, the user specifies the data source where the analysis will be performed and selects the Categories and Measures that will populate the visualizations.

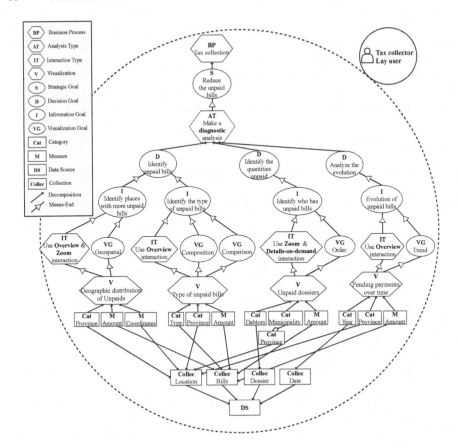

Fig. 6. Application of our user requirements metamodel to the case study.

4.2   Profiling Data Sources

Once user have defined the data sources and collections from where the data will be extracted, it is possible to profile data sources to determine Dimensionality, Cardinality and Dependent/Independent Type.

We focus on the **"Identify the type of unpaid bills"** Information Goal from our Goal-Oriented model, which requires information about categories *"Type"* and *"Province"* and measures *"Amount"*. Firstly, by the Data Profiling Model, are classified the independent variables *"Type"* and *"Province"* as **Nominal** and the dependent variable *"Amount"* as **Ratio**. Dimensionality is set to **n-dimensional**, because the user has defined 3 variables to visualize. Finally, the Cardinality is defined as **Low** Cardinality because the data contains a few items to represent 3 provinces to represent and there are 6 types of bills.

Overall, the visualization specification obtained through User Requirements Model and Data Profiling Model are:

- **Visualization Goal:** Composition & Comparison
- **Interaction:** Overview
- **User:** Lay
- **Dimensionality:** n-dimensional
- **Cardinality:** Low
- **Independent Type:** Nominal
- **Dependent Type:** Ratio

With the definition of this visualization specification, by applying our visualization specification transformation, the visualization type generated is "Stacked Column Chart".

4.3   Specifying Data Visualizations Requirements

The visualization specification is used as input of the Data Visualization Model. A visualization tool will be generated as Fig. 7 shows using the information collected in the process.

The tool shows the most suitable visualization type, the integration type defined by the user and a representation of the visualization. It also shows the selected elements to be represented in the visualization. The user will have to choose in which **axes** she want to see each element represented. In this case, we have *"Province"* in X axis, *"Amount"* in Y axis and *"Type"* as Color. The user also has to select the element that determines the **order** in the visualization. Other element to specify is the **orientation** of the visualization, this can be defined as horizontal, vertical or any if the visualizations have no orientation. In this case the user has decide to user a horizontal orientation. Next element is the **legend**, which can be shown or not. A legend may have a title, a type (in this case the user has decide to represent it like a list), a position on the visualization, a font family, and a text size. The **range of colours** used to represent the visualization also has to be choose, the user can choose one of the color ranges proposed or personalize a range. Finally, the user can give a dashboard position to the visualization and a title.

The user will review the data visualization model until she achieves her visualization requirements. Once all the elements have been customized, the user has to validate if the visualization obtained does contribute to answer her informational goal, in this case *"Identify the type of unpaid bills"*. If the visualization is validated, it will be generated making a call to the D3 JavaScript library [3], obtaining the visualization shown in Fig. 8. Otherwise, an unsuccessful validation would generated a review of the existing user requirements model, to start a new iteration and generating in turn an updated model.

This visualization, combined with those generated for the others information goals, will be grouped into a dashboard, aimed at satisfying the analytic requirements of our tax collector user with the most adequate visualizations and covering all the data required by the analysis.

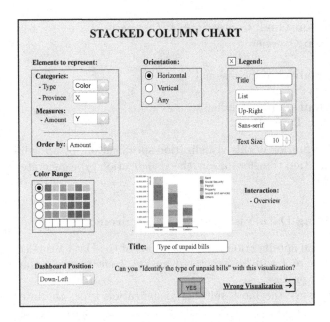

Fig. 7. Application of our data visualization metamodel to the case study.

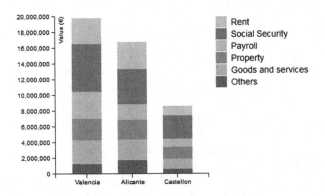

Fig. 8. Visualization rendered in D3.js.

5 Conclusions and Future Work

In this paper, we have presented an approach in the context of the Model Driven Architecture (MDA) standard in order to help users derive the most adequate visualizations. Our approach envisages three different models, (i) a requirements model based on goal-oriented modeling for representing information require-ments; (ii) a data profiling model that abstracts the required information from

the data sources; and, (iii) a visualization model for capturing visualization details regardless of their implementation technology. Together with these models, we have proposed a series of transformations that allow us to bridge the gap between information requirements and the actual implementation. The great advantage of our proposal is that users can focus on their information needs and obtain the visualization that is better suited for their particular case, without requiring visualization expertise. In order to check the validity of our approach, we have applied our approach to a real use case focused on a tax collection organization. The results obtained, as well as a currently ongoing family of experiments, support the approach presented.

As part of our future work, we are working on the definition and generation of dashboards as a whole. In this way, we will simplify and reduce the resources required to obtain visual analytics, which is of special interest for small and medium companies who cannot afford hiring several analysts in order to cover data, visualization, and business expertise required for Big Data analytics.

Acknowledgments. This work has been co-funded by the ECLIPSE-UA (RTI2018-094283-B-C32) project funded by Spanish Ministry of Science, Innovation, and Universities. Ana Lavalle holds an Industrial PhD Grant (I-PI 03-18) co-funded by the University of Alicante and the Lucentia Lab Spin-off Company.

References

1. Ardagna, C.A., Bellandi, V., Ceravolo, P., Damiani, E., Bezzi, M., Hébert, C.: A model-driven methodology for big data analytics-as-a-service. In: International Conference on Big Data, pp. 105–112. IEEE (2017)
2. Börner, K.: Atlas of Knowledge. MIT Press, Cambridge (2014)
3. Bostock, M.: Data-driven documents (2019). https://d3js.org/
4. Bull, R.I., Favre, J.: Visualization in the context of model driven engineering. In: MDDAUI, vol. 159 (2005)
5. Caldarola, E.G., Rinaldi, A.M.: Improving the visualization of wordnet large lexical database through semantic tag clouds. In: International Congress on Big Data, pp. 34–41. IEEE (2016)
6. Caldarola, E.G., Rinaldi, A.M.: Big data visualization tools: a survey - the new paradigms, methodologies and tools for large data sets visualization. In: Proceedings of the 6th International Conference on Data Science, Technology and Applications, DATA. INSTICC, SciTePress (2017)
7. Domokos, P., Varró, D.: An open visualization framework for metamodel-based modeling languages. Electr. Notes Theor. Comput. Sci. **72**(2), 69–78 (2002)
8. Du, F., Plaisant, C., Spring, N., Shneiderman, B.: Eventaction: visual analytics for temporal event sequence recommendation. In: 2016 IEEE Conference on Visual Analytics Science and Technology (VAST), pp. 61–70. IEEE (2016)
9. Golfarelli, M., Rizzi, S.: A model-driven approach to automate data visualization in big data analytics. Inf. Vis. (2019, to appear)
10. Leida, M., Ruiz, C., Ceravolo, P.: Facing big data variety in a model driven approach. In: RTSI, pp. 1–6. IEEE (2016)
11. Madhu Sudhan, S., Chandra, J.: IBA graph selector algorithm for big data visualization using defense data set. Int. J. Sci. Eng. Res. (IJSER) **4**(3), 1–7 (2013). ISSN: 2229-5518

12. Maté, A., Trujillo, J., Franch, X.: Adding semantic modules to improve goal-oriented analysis of data warehouses using I-star. J. Syst. Softw. **88**, 102–111 (2014)
13. Misale, C., Drocco, M., Aldinucci, M., Tremblay, G.: A comparison of big data frameworks on a layered dataflow model. Parallel Process. Lett. **27**, 1740003 (2017)
14. Morgan, R., Grossmann, G., Stumptner, M.: VizDSL: towards a graphical visualisation language for enterprise systems interoperability. In: BDVA. IEEE (2017)
15. de Oliveira, E.C., de Oliveira, L.C., Cardoso, A., Mattioli, L., Junior, E.A.L.: Metamodel of information visualization based on treemap. Univ. Access Inf. Soc. **16**(4), 903–912 (2017)
16. (OMG), O.M.G.: Model driven architecture guide rev. 2.0 (2014). https://www.omg.org/cgi-bin/doc?ormsc/14-06-01
17. (OMG), O.M.G.: MOF 2.0 query/view/transformation specification (2016). https://www.omg.org/spec/QVT/1.3/PDF
18. Peña, L.E.V., Mazahua, L.R., Hernández, G.A., Zepahua, B.A.O., Camarena, S.G.P., Cano, I.M.: Big data visualization: review of techniques and datasets. In: International Conference on Software Process Improvement, pp. 1–9. IEEE (2017)
19. Shi-Nash, A., Hardoon, D.R.: Data analytics and predictive analytics in the era of big data. In: Internet of Things and Data Analytics Handbook, pp. 329–345 (2017)
20. Vartak, M., Huang, S., Siddiqui, T., Madden, S., Parameswaran, A.: Towards visualization recommendation systems. ACM SIGMOD Record **45**(4), 34–39 (2017)
21. Vartak, M., Rahman, S., Madden, S., Parameswaran, A., Polyzotis, N.: SEEDB: efficient data-driven visualization recommendations to support visual analytics. Proc. VLDB Endowment **8**(13), 2182–2193 (2015)

Don't Tune Twice: Reusing Tuning Setups for SQL-on-Hadoop Queries

Edson Ramiro Lucas Filho[1]([⊠]), Eduardo Cunha de Almeida[1],
and Stefanie Scherzinger[2]

[1] Universidade Federal do Paraná, Curitiba, Brazil
{erlfilho,eduardo}@inf.ufpr.br
[2] OTH, Regensburg, Brazil
stefanie.scherzinger@oth-regensburg.de

Abstract. SQL-on-Hadoop processing engines have become state-of-the-art in data lake analysis. However, the skills required to tune such systems are rare. This has inspired automated tuning advisors which profile the query workload and produce tuning setups for the low-level MapReduce jobs. Yet with highly dynamic query workloads, repeated re-tuning costs time and money in IaaS environments. In this paper, we focus on reducing the costs for up-front tuning. At the heart of our approach is the observation that a SQL query is compiled into a query plan of MapReduce jobs. While the plans differ from query to query, single jobs tend to be similar between queries. We introduce the notion of the *code signature* of a MapReduce job and, based on this, our concept of job similarity. We show that we can effectively *recycle* tuning setups from similar MapReduce jobs already profiled. In doing so, we can leverage any third-party tuning adviser for MapReduce engines. We are able to show that by recycling tuning setups, we can reduce the time spent on profiling by 50% in the TPC-H benchmark.

1 Introduction

More than a decade after the publication of the MapReduce paper [7], we observe a clear preference among Hadoop or Spark users for higher-level languages [11] (e.g., Hive [21] and SparkSQL [2]). Typically, writing queries for SQL-on-Hadoop systems is more productive than custom-coding MapReduce jobs for MapReduce frameworks: SQL-on-Hadoop systems compile declarative queries into a query plan of MapReduce jobs. Naturally, this greatly improves the productivity of data scientists. Yet compiling queries to query plans, and then allocating their jobs onto nodes in a cluster is only half the battle: The underlying MapReduce framework needs to be tuned for performance.

The expertise required for allocating the right mix of physical resources (main memory, disk space, bandwidth, etc.) to jobs, and for twiddling with the right tuning knobs is rare. This was already the case roughly 10 years ago, when the first automatic tuning advisers for MapReduce frameworks were proposed, e.g. [8]. Ever since, SQL-on-Hadoop engines and MapReduce frameworks have

© Springer Nature Switzerland AG 2019
A. H. F. Laender et al. (Eds.): ER 2019, LNCS 11788, pp. 93–107, 2019.
https://doi.org/10.1007/978-3-030-33223-5_9

94   E. R. L. Filho et al.

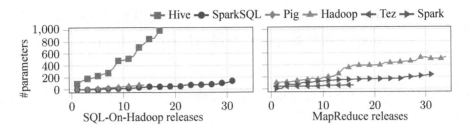

Fig. 1. Number of tuning parameters growing over time [10]. (The releases are: Hadoop from 0.23.11 to 2.8.0, Spark from 0.5.0 to 2.2.0, Tez from 0.5.0 to 0.8.5, Hive from 0.3.0 to 2.3.0, Pig from 0.1.0 to 0.16.0, and SparkSQL from 1.1.0 to 2.2.0.)

grown in complexity, manifesting in the number of tuning parameters. As Fig. 1 shows, Hive [21] currently has about a thousand tuning parameters. Manual tuning is quite out of the question.

Tuning advisers for MapReduce frameworks rely on profiling of the query workload [1,8,12]. Naturally, profiling imposes an overhead. For instance, the Starfish tuning adviser causes an overhead of up to 50% [12]. When the query workload is highly dynamic, re-tuning becomes a cost factor in pay-as-you-go IaaS environments.

In this paper, we model the static information of Hive to match jobs with similar resource consumption patterns and reuse the same tuning setup to reduce their total cost of tuning. Our model relies on two observations regarding the query plans compiled from SQL queries: (a) The jobs within a query plan execute different query operators, and often have different resource requirements. (b) Since the jobs are generated automatically, MapReduce jobs tend to be similar *across* query plans.

Let us consider a specific example regarding observation (a). Figure 2 shows the resource consumption of TPC-H query 5. The Hive engine (version 0.6.0) compiles this query into a sequence of seven MapReduce jobs. For each job, we track main memory and CPU consumption, as well as the amount of data in physical reads and writes.

Let us now consider observation (b). We regard two MapReduce jobs in two query plans as similar from the perspective of tuning, if they have the same *code signature*. Intuitively, the code signature of a MapReduce job captures the SQL operators implemented by this job, as well as the expected size of the input. This information is available through the Hive query compiler. Our hypothesis (which we can confirm in our experiments) is that jobs that share the same code signature benefit from the same tuning setups. We therefore *reuse* tuning setups for similar jobs to reduce profiling time.

Let us illustrate this point. Compiling the TPC-H queries in Hive-0.6 yields 123 MapReduce jobs. For 75% of these jobs, there is at least one other job with the same code signature. Only a quarter of all jobs has a unique code signature.

In fact, once we have profiled enough jobs, we may even be able to assign tuning setups for ad-hoc queries. These are queries that we have not encountered (or

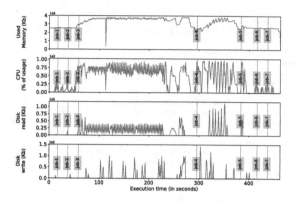

Fig. 2. CPU, memory, disk write and disk read consumption for TPC-H query 5 across the 7 MapReduce jobs. (We executed the experiments on a cluster of 3 nodes (Intel(R) Core(TM) i3-3240 CPU @ 3.40 GHz, 4 GB of RAM and 1 TB of disk space each). Details are provided in Sect. 4.)

profiled) yet. In fact, ad-hoc queries are prevalent in many query workloads [23], yet tuning advisers for MapReduce frameworks rely on profiling the workload up front. Thus, our approach can be used in environments where, traditionally, tuning advisers fail.

In Sect. 2, we review the state-of-the-art on SQL-on-Hadoop engines, as well as MapReduce frameworks and their tuning advisers. In Sect. 3, we motivate and define the notion of the code signature of a MapReduce job, and introduce the code signature cache. We conduct our experiments using the TPC-H queries in Sect. 4. In Sect. 5, we discuss related work in the context of our approach. We conclude with Sect. 6.

2 State-of-the-Art

We briefly sketch the control flow of compiling queries in SQL-on-Hadoop engines. We then describe how automatic tuning advisers for MapReduce frameworks proceed.

2.1 SQL-on-Hadoop Engines

The generic workflow within a SQL-on-Hadoop engine starts when a SQL query is submitted to the *Driver*. This component manages session handlers and tracks statistics. The *Compiler* then translates the query into a logical query plan. The *Optimizer* rewrites the logical plan in order to find a good execution plan in terms of execution costs. For instance, joins sharing the same join predicate may be merged, or data partitions irrelevant to query evaluation may be disregarded. The *Executor* then receives the DAG of MapReduce jobs. It queues the jobs in the MapReduce framework for processing. The MapReduce jobs are nodes in a directed acyclic graph (DAG). The directed edges denote dependencies between jobs.

```
insert overwrite table q5_local_supplier_volume
select n_name, sum(l_extendedprice * (1 − l_discount)) as revenue
from customer c join
    ( select n_name, l_extendedprice, l_discount, s_nationkey, o_custkey
      from orders o join
        ( select n_name, l_extendedprice, l_discount, l_orderkey, s_nationkey
          from lineitem l join
            ( select n_name, s_suppkey, s_nationkey from supplier s join
                ( select n_name, n_nationkey from nation n join region r
                  on n.n_regionkey = r.r_regionkey and r.r_name = 'ASIA'
                ) n1 on s.s_nationkey = n1.n_nationkey
            ) s1 on l.l_suppkey = s1.s_suppkey
        ) l1 on l1.l_orderkey = o.o_orderkey
        and o.o_orderdate >= '1994−01−01' and o.o_orderdate < '1995−01−01'
    ) o1 on c.c_nationkey = o1.s_nationkey and c.c_custkey = o1.o_custkey
group by n_name order by revenue desc;
```

(b) Query plan.

(a) TPC-H query 5.

Fig. 3. Query and query plan of TPC-H query 5, as compiled by Hive 0.6.0.

Example 1. Figure 3b shows the final query plan produced by Hive v0.6.0 for TPC-H query 5 (presented in Fig. 3a). Each job is responsible for executing one or more SQL operators in the query, like sort and aggregation.   □

The DAG declares a partial order, which the *Execution Engine* considers when deploying the jobs. However, the MapReduce framework needs to be configured for performance: A *tuning setup* is registered with the MapReduce framework before the jobs can be executed. Today's SQL-on-Hadoop engines assign a single tuning setup to all jobs of a query. However, technically, the underlying MapReduce framework allows each job to run with its own tuning setup.

Tuning advisers for MapReduce frameworks, on the other hand, have not been designed to tune a DAG of jobs, such as a query plan compiled from SQL queries. Rather, they produce one tuning setup per MapReduce job, as discussed next.

2.2   Tuning Advisers for MapReduce Frameworks

In general, there are different strategies for obtaining a profile of the resource requirements of a MapReduce job. For instance, tuning advisers consider MapReduce JobCounters [15,16], real-time statistics [22], job execution time [3] or phases execution time [4], instrumentation of the JVM [12,17], or perform log analysis [19,20].

Inevitably, profiling adds an overhead to the execution time of a MapReduce job. For instance, Starfish [12] instruments the JVM. When Starfish monitors all of the JVM tasks, the authors report a profiling overhead of 50%. To speed up tuning, Starfish can be configured to profile only a sample of the JVM tasks. For instance, when profiling only 20% of the JVM tasks, the profiling overhead drops to 10%. However, not sampling but profiling all tasks will lead to more effective tuning setups.

Reusing job profiles is a way to reduce the cost of tuning. The authors of PStorM [9] propose a form of sampling to reduce the tuning overhead. They

Table 1. Tuning advisers for MapReduce frameworks in comparison: Reported speedup, supported Hadoop version, and the heuristics used to determine tuning setups.

Tuning System	Speed up	Hadoop Version	Heuristics
MR-COF [17]	up to 41%	0.20.2	Genetic Algorithm
Gunther [16]	up to 33%	0.20.3	Genetic Algorithm
Starfish [12]	up to 46%	0.20.2	Random Recursive Search
MRTuner [19]	1x	1.0.3 and 1.1.1	PTC-Search
Panacea [18]	1.6x up to 2.9x	-	Exhaustive Search
RFHOC [4]	2.11x-7.4x	1.0.4	Genetic Algorithm
GeneExpression [14]	46%-71%	1.2.1	Particle Swarm Optimization
MROnline [15]	30%	2.1.0	Hill Climbing
MEST [3]	-	2.6.0	Genetic Algorithm
JellyFish [22]	up to 74%	YARN	Hill Climbing

sample only a single map and reduce task. This produces a *tiny-profile*, which they match against a history of profiles. After PStorM finds a match to its tiny-profile, it feeds the Tuning Adviser (e.g., Starfish) with the match in order to generate a tuning setup.

Internally, tuning advisers maintain a representation of the tuning parameters and their domains, as well as a cost model to predict the execution time of a given job. They also apply heuristics. It is beyond the scope of this paper to do a more thorough survey, especially as we employ tuning advisers as black box systems. However, in order to give an idea of both the complexity of the problem, as well as the plethora of solutions proposed, we list prominent tuning advisers in Table 1. The reported speedups range from 24% up to 7.4x, depending on the workload. Note the richness of heuristics applied in the various tools.

3 The Code Signature Cache

At the heart of our approach is a data structure called the *code signature cache*. It assigns tuning setups to MapReduce jobs. The tuning setups are produced by a third-party tuning adviser. We use the *code signature* of a MapReduce job as lookup key in the code signature cache. We introduce the notion of a code signature shortly. We then discuss how the code signature cache manages tuning setups.

3.1 Code Signatures

The SQL-on-Hadoop engine Hive compiles SQL queries to query plans. During query compilation, the resulting MapReduce jobs are annotated with several descriptive properties. The Hive Java API makes these annotations accessible: Each job is annotated with a list of the physical query operators that are implemented by this job. For each operator, a *cardinality* is given. For instance, a job may execute two *Filter*-operations (i.e. selection in relational algebra), as well as one aggregation. Each job is further annotated with the estimated size of its input.

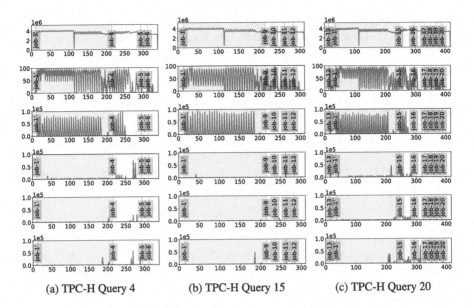

(a) TPC-H Query 4　　　　(b) TPC-H Query 15　　　　(c) TPC-H Query 20

Fig. 4. Execution of selected TPC-H queries. The jobs labeled 1' share the same code signature and apparently have similar resource profiles. This suggests that they would benefit from the same tuning setup.

Example 2. TCP-H query 1 is compiled by Hive into two jobs. The first job is annotated with the operators Filter, Select, and GroupBy. Each operator has cardinality 2. The job is further annotated with the operators TableScan, ReduceSink, and FileSink, each with a cardinality of 1. In the setup of our experiments (see Sect. 4) the estimated input size is stated as 7.24 GB.　□

Our assumption is that these declarative annotations are related to the resource profile of these jobs. Further, we hypothesize that jobs with the same annotations may be executed with the same tuning setups, even though they differ in their Java code. In our experiments, we are able to confirm this. For now, we argue on an intuitive level.

Example 3. Let us consider Fig. 4, where we have run selected TPC-H queries with a default tuning setup. For each query, we execute the MapReduce jobs according to the query plan. Evidently, the queries have different query plans, and therefore a different number of jobs. However, visual inspection suggests that certain jobs have similar resource profiles. Thus, we have highlighted these jobs with a shaded background. Incidentally, these jobs also share the same code signature. In Fig. 4, we have labeled jobs with a unique code signature with a unique job identifier (e.g., jobs 2, 3, and 4), and we have labeled the jobs with the same code signature as job 1'.

Thus, this suggests that tuning setups may be shared between jobs with the same code signature: Once one instance of job 1' has been profiled, we reuse its

tuning setup for the other jobs with the same signature. Thus, we simply skip profiling these jobs. □

In fact, similarity of resource consumption between common MapReduce jobs (e.g., sort, grep, WordCount) has already been identified [13]. However, we believe to be the first wort to model Hive jobs specifically to identify this similarity. The main difference of our model is that it calculates the code-signature of a given job at compiling time, instead of running or sampling it.

Since the MapReduce jobs are compiled from queries, the query plans of syntactically different queries nevertheless often contain jobs with the same query annotations. Formally, we capture these annotations by the *code signature* of a job, as defined next.

3.2 Definitions

We now embark on the formal definitions. Let us define a *query plan* as a directed acyclic graph $G = (V, E)$, where the set of vertices V represents the MapReduce jobs, and the set of edges E denotes the precedence between two jobs. More precisely, a vertex (job) $j \in V$ is a tuple of the form $v = (O_j, T_j, C_j)$ in which O_j is the set of physical *query operators* it executes (the set of physical query operators is fixed, $O_j = \{o_1, \ldots, o_n\}$. For instance, Hive version 0.6.0 knows 16 different physical operators), T_j is the set of *associated input tables*, and C_j is the set of *configurations* used to allocate resources. Each directed edge $e \in E$ is an ordered pair of vertices defined as $e = (i, j)$ and connects the jobs i to j, when the execution of i directly precedes j.

The query compiler assigns the implemented physical query operators, as well as their cardinalities, to each node in the query plan. We thus consider the annotation function $ops : V \times O \rightarrow \mathbb{N}_0^+$, where

$$ops(j, o) = \begin{cases} n \text{ job } j \text{ implements operator } o \text{ exactly } n \text{ times} \\ 0 \text{ otherwise.} \end{cases}$$

We also consider the annotation function $ord : V \rightarrow \mathbb{N}_0^+$, which returns the order of magnitude of the expected input data for the given MapReduce job.

We are now in the position to define the code signature of a MapReduce job.

Definition 1. The *code signature* of a MapReduce job j in V is a $(|O| + 1)$-tuple,

$$codesignature(j) = \langle ord(j), o_1 : c_1, \ldots, o_i : c_i, \ldots, o_n : c_n \rangle$$

where $c_i = ops(j, o_i)$, the cardinality of this operator. □

In the following example, we omit operators from the code signature with a cardinality of zero, for the sake of brevity.

Example 4. We continue with TPC-H query 1. The code signature of the first job is

$\langle 9, Tablescan : 1, Filter : 2, Select : 2, Groupby : 2, Reducesink : 1, Filesink : 1 \rangle$

The order of magnitude of the input size is 9. □

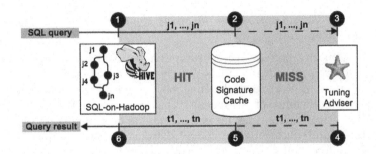

Fig. 5. Lookups in the code signature cache. For a cache miss, a third-party tuning adviser is run to produce a tuning setup.

3.3 Cache Hits and Misses

Figure 5 visualizes the code signature cache. Initially, the cache is empty. A SQL query is compiled by Hive into the query plan (Step 1). For each of the jobs $j_1, \ldots, j_n$ in this query plan, we look up the tuning setup in the code signature cache (Step 2). For each cache miss, we employ the Starfish tuning adviser for profiling the job and generating a tuning setup (Step 3). The tuning setups, denoted $t_1, \ldots, t_n$, are stored in the code signature cache, with the code signatures of the jobs as lookup keys (Step 4). As the cache becomes populated, we observe more cache hits (Steps 5 and 6). In the best case, we have cache hits for all jobs in the query plan. Then we can simply reuse the tuning setups of similar jobs, and need not turn to Starfish for profiling at all.

4   Experiments

We have implemented the code signature cache in Java, and integrated it with Apache Hive. We leverage tuning setups generated by the Starfish tuning adviser [12]. Unless explicitly stated otherwise, we run Starfish with sampling turned off (i.e., a sampling rate of 100%), to obtain high-quality tuning profiles. Using Starfish 0.3.0[1], we are tied to Hadoop 0.20.2 and Hive 0.6.0. We point out that the code signature cache is a generic data structure and not restricted to any particular version of Hive or Hadoop.

We evaluate the TPC-H queries provided for Hive[2]. The data has been generated with a scale factor of 10. This amounts to 10.46 GB of data when stored on disk.

Our experiments were executed in a cluster with three physical machines. We isolate the master node on one machine, so that it does not influence with the profiling of jobs.

In particular, each machine has a Intel(R) Core(TM) i3-3240 CPU @ 3.40 GHz, 4 GB of RAM, 1 TB of disk. We used the *collectl* tool[3] tool to measure CPU, memory, network, and disk consumption. The reported execution times

---

[1] The Starfish binary is available at https://www.cs.duke.edu/starfish/release.html.

[2] See https://issues.apache.org/jira/browse/HIVE-600 for the verbatim SQL queries.

[3] http://collectl.sourceforge.net.

are averaged over 10 runs. All our profiling runs are configured with the out-of-the-box tuning setup that we refer to as "Hadoop Standard". We first consider the reuse of tuning setups at the level of single MapReduce jobs, and later at the level of SQL queries.

4.1   Recycling Tuning Setups at the Job Level

We first study the distribution of code signatures in the query plans of TPC-H queries. We then confirm that the code signature is indeed a viable basis for recycling tuning setups among jobs.

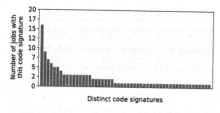

(a) MapReduce jobs compiled from TPC-H queries: Counting jobs that share the same code signature.

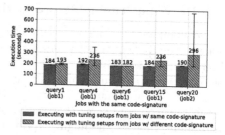

(b) Jobs with the same code signature tend to benefit from the same tuning setups. This effect cannot be repeated for jobs with different code signatures.

Fig. 6. Recycling tuning setups among jobs with the same code signature.

Repeating Code Signatures. We have compiled the TPC-H queries into query plans. Figure 6a shows the number of jobs with the same code signature. There is one code signature that is actually shared by 16 jobs. In fact, this job occurs in over 70% of all TPC-H queries. Moreover, for 75% of all MapReduce jobs, there is at least one other job with the same code signature. Only a quarter of all jobs has a unique code signature. Thus, there is a considerable share of recurring code signatures.

Justifying the Recycling of Tuning Setups. We experimentally examine our hypothesis, stating that we may recycle tuning setups for jobs with the same code signature in Fig. 6b. We choose 5 representative MapReduce jobs that all share the same code signature. When compiled into query plans, we obtain 20 MapReduce jobs. For each job j of those five jobs, we define two groups of jobs:

1. The five jobs that share the same code signature. For these jobs, we obtain the 5 tuning setups from Starfish.
2. The remaining jobs within the same query plan. These have different code signatures. Again, we obtain the tuning setups from Starfish.

We then execute job 1 of query 1 with all the tuning setups from groups (1) and (2), shown in the first and second bar respectively. We repeat this procedure

for the other jobs listed. In general, the jobs executing with the tuning setups of group (1) show better performance than with the tuning setups of group (2). The reported execution times are averaged over 10 runs. The error bars mark the minimum and maximum execution times. There is noticeably less variance in the execution times of group (1).

Overall, we see that for jobs with the same code signature, we may use the tuning setups interchangeably. When jobs have different code signatures, this is not necessarily the case. We have conducted this experiment for all recurring code signatures, and we have made the same observations in the other cases as well. For the sake of conciseness, we show only the case portrayed in Fig. 6b.

4.2   Recycling Tuning Setups at the Query Level

We now employ the code signature cache for profiling the TPC-H queries. We first profile all 22 queries in the order specified by the benchmark and discuss the benefits of applying the code signature cache. We then contrast this with the total time spent on profiling if Starfish only samples the JVM tasks. We also consider different execution orders in profiling the TPC-H queries with the code signature cache, and show that the query order does not have as much impact on profiling time as one might expect. Finally, we compare the execution time of non-uniform tuning when we have the code signature cache available during profiling and when we profile all jobs with Starfish.

Profiling the TPC-H Queries in Order. We profile the 22 TPC-H queries in the order of the TPC-H benchmark specification. Figure 7a shows the profiling time per query. In total, over ten thousand seconds are spent on profiling.

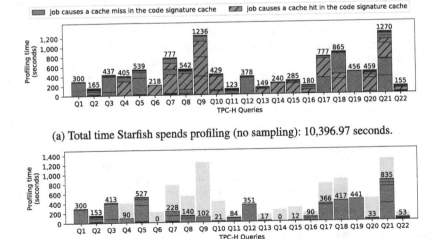

(a) Total time Starfish spends profiling (no sampling): 10,396.97 seconds.

(b) Reduced profiling time leveraging the code signature cache. Total time spent profiling: 4,679.66 seconds.

Fig. 7. The code signature cache reduces the profiling time by over 50% for TPC-H.

Even though the runs in Fig. 7a do not make use the code signature cache, for the purpose of illustration, we visually distinguish two groups of jobs:

1. Jobs which cause a cache miss in the code signature cache,
2. and jobs which cause a cache hit in the code signature cache.

We can observe that for the first TPC-H query, all jobs would cause a cache miss. Yet already for the second and third queries, we'd have cache hits, even though the savings are minor. With the code signature cache becoming more populated, we get more cache hits, and in some cases, some substantial savings in the profiling time. For instance, for queries Q6 and Q14, we can recycle all tuning setups from the cache. Thus, they require no profiling at all.

Let us now turn to the quantitative assessment. In Fig. 7b, we use the code signature cache. Thus, we employ Starfish only for the jobs from group (1), and recycle the tuning setups for the jobs from group (2). The shaded grey area indicates the height of the original bars from Fig. 7a, for easier comparison.

Using the code signature cache reduces the total time spent on profiling from over ten to below five thousand seconds. Overall, we can cut down the time spent profiling by more than 50%.

Recycling vs. Starfish Sampling. Starfish has its own strategy for reducing the profiling time, by sampling only a share of the JVM tasks. We compare this strategy with our approach of using Starfish (without sampling) in combination with the code signature cache. In Fig. 8a, we compare the total accumulated time spent on profiling for different modes of operation. The topmost line denotes profiling with Starfish, where sampling is turned off. This summarizes the experiment of Fig. 7a.

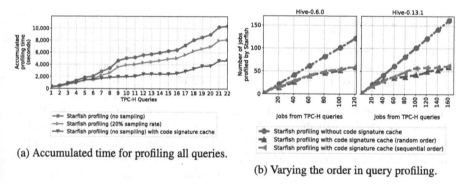

(a) Accumulated time for profiling all queries.

(b) Varying the order in query profiling.

Fig. 8. Accumulated time for profiling.

When we run Starfish with a sampling rate of 20% (nevertheless executing all tasks of the query), the total time spent on profiling is effectively reduced. However, sampling increases the error rate in the resulting tuning profiles [12].

In the given chart, the profiling time is lowest for the combination of Starfish and recycling from the code signature cache. Thus, we can profile in half of the time, without having to make the sacrifices due to sampling.

Varying the Query Order. The recycling rate of tuning setups in the code signature cache, as reported in Fig. 7b, is influenced by the order in which the TPC-H queries are profiled.

In Fig. 8b, we vary the order of queries. Moreover, we contrast the MapReduce jobs produced by two different versions of Hive. On the horizontal axis, the charts show the total number of MapReduce jobs compiled from the TPC-H queries by the Hive query compiler. On the vertical axis, we denote the number of jobs which had to be profiled by Starfish.

The tuning adviser Starfish, when used stand-alone, profiles all jobs. We further compare Starfish in combination with the code signature cache. Regardless whether the queries are encountered in order of their specification or in a randomly generated order, for this query workload, we can recycle tuning setups from the cache for about half of the jobs.

Thus, while the query compilers of Hive 0.6.0 and 0.13.1 produce a different number of jobs, the benefits of recycling is independently of the submission order.

Comparing Execution Times. Finally, we execute the TPC-H queries with non-uniform tuning. In one scenario, the tuning setups for all jobs have been generated by Starfish. In a second scenario, we have recycled tuning setups from the code signature cache.

In total, this yields a speedup (or rather, slowdown) of 0.93 for the TPC-H queries. Thus, thanks to the code signature cache, we only spend about half the profiling time, with a tolerable impact on query execution times.

This is a good result, considering that Starfish with sampling turned on imposes a higher error rate (e.g., an error rate of 15% when sampling merely 10% of the JVM tasks [12]).

4.3   Discussion

In summary, we can experimentally support our hypothesis that jobs with the same code signatures benefit from the same tuning setups. Therefore, we may recycle tuning setups. By reducing the number of jobs to be profiled, we can effectively cut down on the time required for physical-level performance tuning.

Even when Starfish profiles only a sample of 20% of the tasks in the JVM, it does not reach this speedup (while the quality of tuning setups produced by Starfish degrades). Thus, coupling a third-party tuning advisor with the code signature cache is a winning strategy for reducing profiling time.

For some queries, we were even able to directly assign tuning setups to MapReduce jobs, requiring no profiling at all. This is promising for processing ad-hoc queries, which normally do not benefit from up-front tuning. In our experiments with the TPC-H queries, we were able to cut down profiling time by half. Moreover, the mechanism is quite robust when the order of TPC-H queries varies.

5 Related Work

Performance tuning for database management systems is an evergreen in database research, and a profitable consultancy business in industry. As stated by Bonnet and Shasha [5]: "An under-appreciated tuning principle asserts start-up costs are high; running costs are low."

There are several projects aiming at reducing the profiling time in physical-level tuning. In Sect. 2, we have already described how Starfish [12] samples the JVM tasks executing MapReduce jobs. This reduces the profiling time, but at the cost of tuning effectiveness.

The PStorM [9] system is closest to our work. As in our approach, PStorM leverages Starfish as a third-party tuning adviser. Also similar to our idea of caching tuning setups, similar jobs are mapped to existing tuning setups in a profile store.

However, our notion of job similarity based on code signatures is much simpler, since we rely on the declarative annotations that the Hive query compiler adds to MapReduce jobs. In contrast, PStorM considers code similarity metrics, and compares control flow graphs (CFG) as well as feature vectors. PStorM avoids computing a code signature (e.g., by hashing the source code or byte code), because of the risk of mismatching source code with similar behaviour, but different code primitives (e.g., for-loop vs. while-loop).

In particular, PStorM analyzes the byte code for static features and samples map tasks for dynamic features to probe the profile store for matching profiles. Thus, the matching accuracy depends on the size of the sample and the maintenance of the features, which also incur an execution overhead. After all, creating, maintaining and testing feature vectors is time consuming.

Our code signature cache is less complex, yet nevertheless highly effective: The lookup key is based on declarative query operators. Thus, we operate on a higher level of abstraction, instead of on the underlying code primitives.

Another related system is Kambatla [13], that monitors the execution of a given job using a pre-defined number of intervals. It computes the average consumption for each resource within each interval and matches it with similar profiles. MrEtalon [6] is another related system that profiles a given job on a sample of the data set. MrEtalon builds a similarity matrix to this profile and compares it to the pre-established similarity matrices, that will generate the recommended tuning setup. All in all, the drawback of these systems is that they increase the time spent on the tuning activity due to the effort to sample the number of MapReduce tasks or the data set to match similar jobs.

6 Conclusion

Automated tuning of SQL-on-Hadoop engines and MapReduce frameworks is a highly topical research area. Tuning adviser tools profile MapReduce jobs to produce suitable tuning setups. Naturally, profiling introduces an overhead. In pay-as-you-go environments, profiling can drive up the operational costs considerably. Therefore, ways for reducing the time spent on tuning are of great interest to the research community and practitioners alike.

Existing tuning advisers cut down the profiling time by sampling, either monitoring only a share of the JVM tasks (as done by Starfish), by monitoring only a specific sample of MapReduce jobs (as done by PStorM), or running the jobs with a sample of its data set. Thus, they trade time for the effectiveness of the resulting tuning setup.

In this paper, we reduce the profiling time by skipping profiling altogether for MapReduce jobs where we can recycle the tuning setups from similar jobs. To this end, we rely on our model of the code signature as a means for identifying similar jobs, and to populate the code signature cache.

Our approach is appealingly simple, yet effective, and lets us cut back on profiling by nearly 50% in case of the TPC-H queries, without major sacrifices to the quality of tuning setups. Provided that we have successfully profiled enough similar queries (or rather, their MapReduce jobs), we may even supply ad-hoc queries with tuning setups, skipping up-front profiling altogether.

As future work, we plan to refine the code signature cache by integrating the selectivity of query operators into the code signature. Moreover, we hope to be able to use the code signature cache for application-level tuning as well: By caching power hints for MapReduce jobs, we might be able to automatically suggest performance hints for similar jobs. This could be a great relief to the data analyst who has no prior background in database administration.

Acknowledgments. We thank Herodotos Herodotou for all the support with Starfish. This study was financed in part by the Coordenação de Aperfeiçoamento de Pessoal de Nível Superior - Brasil (CAPES) - Finance Code 001.

References

1. Aken, D.V., Pavlo, A., Gordon, G.J.: Automatic database management system tuning through large-scale machine learning. In: SIGMOD (2017)
2. Armbrust, M., et al.: Spark SQL: relational data processing in spark. In: SIGMOD (2015)
3. Bei, Z., Yu, Z., Liu, Q., Xu, C., Feng, S., Song, S.: MEST: a model-driven efficient searching approach for mapreduce self-tuning. IEEE Access **5**, 3580–3593 (2017)
4. Bei, Z., et al.: RFHOC: a random-forest approach to auto-tuning hadoop's configuration. IEEE Trans. Parallel Distrib. Syst. **27**(5), 1470–1483 (2016)
5. Bonnet, P., Shasha, D.E.: Application-level tuning. In: Liu, L., Özsu, M.T. (eds.) Encyclopedia of Database Systems. Springer, Boston (2009). https://doi.org/10.1007/978-0-387-39940-9
6. Cai, L., Qi, Y., Li, J.: A recommendation-based parameter tuning approach for hadoop. In: International Symposium on Cloud and Service Computing, SC2 2017 (2018)
7. Dean, J., Ghemawat, S.: MapReduce: simplified data processing on large clusters. In: OSDI (2004)
8. Duan, S., Thummala, V., Babu, S.: Tuning database configuration parameters with iTuned. ReCALL **2**(1), 1246–1257 (2009)
9. Ead, M.: PStorM: profile storage and matching for feedback-based tuning of mapreduce jobs. In: EDBT (2014)
10. Filho, E.R.L., de Melo, R.S., de Almeida, E.C.: A non-uniform tuning method for SQL-on-hadoop systems. In: AMW (2019)

11. Floratou, A., Minhas, U.F., Özcan, F.: SQL-on-hadoop: full circle back to shared-nothing database architectures. PVLDB **7**, 1295–1306 (2014)
12. Herodotou, H., et al.: Starfish: a self-tuning system for big data analytics. In: CIDR (2011)
13. Kambatla, K., Pathak, A., Pucha, H.: Towards optimizing hadoop provisioning in the cloud. Design (2009)
14. Khan, M., Huang, Z., Li, M., Taylor, G.A., Khan, M.: Optimizing hadoop parameter settings with gene expression programming guided PSO. Concurrency Comput. Pract. Expereience **29**, e3786 (2017)
15. Li, M., et al.: MRONLINE: mapreduce online performance tuning. In: HPDC (2014)
16. Liao, G., Datta, K., Willke, T.L.: Gunther: search-based auto-tuning of MapReduce. In: Wolf, F., Mohr, B., an Mey, D. (eds.) Euro-Par 2013. LNCS, vol. 8097, pp. 406–419. Springer, Heidelberg (2013). https://doi.org/10.1007/978-3-642-40047-6_42
17. Liu, C., Zeng, D., Yao, H., Hu, C., Yan, X., Fan, Y.: MR-COF: a genetic mapreduce configuration optimization framework. In: Wang, G., Zomaya, A., Perez, G.M., Li, K. (eds.) ICA3PP 2015. LNCS, vol. 9531, pp. 344–357. Springer, Cham (2015). https://doi.org/10.1007/978-3-319-27140-8_24
18. Liu, J., Ravi, N., Chakradhar, S., Kandemir, M.: Panacea: towards holistic optimization of mapreduce applications. In: CHO (2012)
19. Shi, J., Zou, J., Lu, J., Cao, Z., Li, S., Wang, C.: MRTuner: A toolkit to enable holistic optimization for mapreduce jobs. PVLDB **7**, 1319–1330 (2014)
20. The Apache Software Fundation: Rumen: a tool to extract job characterization data form job tracker logs (2013). https://hadoop.apache.org/docs/r1.2.1/rumen.html
21. Thusoo, A., et al.: Hive - a petabyte scale data warehouse using hadoop. In: ICDE (2010)
22. Ding, X., Liu, Y., Qian, D., et al.: JellyFish: online performance tuning with adaptive configuration and elastic container in hadoop YARN. In: ICPADS (2016)
23. Chen, Y., Alspaugh, S., Katz, R.: Interactive query processing in big data systems: a cross industry study of mapreduce workloads. Technical report 12, University of California, Berkeley, August 2012

A Graph Model for Taxi Ride Sharing Supported by Graph Databases

Dietrich Steinmetz[1], Felix Merz[1], Hui Ma[2], and Sven Hartmann[1(✉)]

[1] Clausthal University of Technology, Clausthal-Zellerfeld, Germany
{dietrich.steinmetz,felix.merz,sven.hartmann}@tu-clausthal.de
[2] Victoria University of Wellington, Wellington, New Zealand
hui.ma@ecs.vuw.ac.nz

Abstract. The emergence of more complex, data-intensive applications motivates a high demand of effective data modeling for graph databases to support efficient query answering. In this paper, we develop an intuitive graph data model for dynamic taxi ride sharing. We argue that our proposed data model meets the data needs imposed by three fundamental tasks associated with taxi ride sharing. An experiment consisting of a taxi ride sharing simulation with real-world data demonstrates the effectiveness of our modelling approach.

Keywords: Graph database · Data modelling · Ride sharing

1 Introduction

With the increasing number of complex, data-intensive problems emerged, not only are data sets getting bigger, but also data is getting more and more connected. For example, cyber-traffic analysis is a domain where the size and interconnectivity of data is massively increasing due to the still rising usage of the Internet [6]. A typical example of such complex, data-intensive problems is the Dynamic Taxi Ridesharing Problem (DTRP) [8]. This problem aims to find taxi routes and allocate passengers to taxis with the objectives of maximizing the number of serviced passengers and minimizing the operating cost and passenger inconvenience [1]. Due to the current rise of companies like Uber and Lyft and the possible utilization in autonomous driving it is quite popular. The DTRP is NP-hard [20], so solving it is computationally challenging. This problem also attracts attention because historic taxi trip records, e.g., from New York City (NYC) are openly available, which can be used to generate problem instances for experiments. Besides NYC [8,16,19] data from other cities like Shanghai and Beijing are frequently used for research [4,5,24].

To efficiently answer queries against large interconnected datasets, data should be organized carefully so that it does not become a bottleneck for applications. In particular, we need not only effectively store data but also consider the relationships among data and how this affects the performance of queries.

© Springer Nature Switzerland AG 2019
A. H. F. Laender et al. (Eds.): ER 2019, LNCS 11788, pp. 108–116, 2019.
https://doi.org/10.1007/978-3-030-33223-5_10

While relational databases are still the most common database technology for data-intensive storage and retrieval applications, they are not very efficient for queries of interconnected data due to the expensive joins [10]. To efficiently answer structural queries for complex, data-intensive problems, graph databases are a better choice since they provide native support not only for data but also for relationships between data [18,23]. Graph databases consist of nodes and relationships where nodes represent objects and relationships represent relations between objects [17, Sect. 1]. With them the retrieval of related objects or entire paths is often surprisingly efficient. This makes graph databases attractive for the DTRP where a lot of path calculations are needed to compute solutions.

For interconnected data there are many ways to store them in a graph database. To make best use of the capabilities of graph databases, data should be organized in a way that important queries can be performed efficiently. However, since the appearance of graph databases in the 1980s there has been far less research on conceptual modeling for them than for the relational databases [2]. The intuitive way of data modeling is to identify relevant concepts in the application domain and to abstract them as nodes and relationships [17, Sect. 3]. The following objectives will be achieved:

- To provide proper support of the fundamental tasks (e.g., finding taxi routes, allocating travelers to taxis) of the DTRP by a graph database. Based on the requirements we propose an intuitive model for the graph database.
- To evaluate our modeling approach we conduct a theoretical analysis of the data needs of the DTRP that are met by our proposed graph model as well as an experiment that explores the travel request satisfaction rate for different numbers of taxis. For that we model real-world datasets of the DTRP according to our proposed approach and store them in a graph database. For our prototype implementation, we use Neo4j to store and retrieve the data of the DTRP since it is currently the most popular graph database system [18,21], and road network data can be easily imported from Open Street Map (OSM) [22].

Organization. This paper is organized as follows. In Sect. 2 we briefly discuss related work and outline the DTRP and its subproblems (allocating travelers to taxis, sequencing the taxi schedule) to understand the requirements. In Sect. 3 we propose an intuitive graph model for the DTRP. In Sect. 4 we report on the experiment that we have conducted. In Sect. 5 we give conclusions and an outlook on future work.

2   Background

2.1   Data Modeling for Graph Databases

A graph model is a data model for graph databases and refers here to the labeled property graph model presented in [17, Sect. 3]. Data modeling for graph

databases has not been researched as thoroughly as for relational databases. Primarily an intuitive modeling approach is chosen, because the data often already exists in a graph-like structure in cases where a graph database is used. Neo4j lists multiple examples in their GraphGists list [12]. Some more sophisticated examples for the most common use cases of Neo4j are given at [11]. Intuitive graph modeling is also used in the literature in areas like cyber-traffic analysis [6], healthcare [14] and biology [3,7].

2.2 Traveler-Taxi Allocation and Taxi Schedule Sequencing

Our work is motivated by the DTRP, cf. [8,9,20]. In this problem, a set of taxis is running in a road network to serve customers, that is, to pick them up from their location and to drop them off at another location. Customers can share a taxi to save costs. Taxis have a limited seat capacity. To a certain extend taxis can make detours but taxi drivers need to account for the interests of other passengers. The objective of the DTRP is to achieve a high travel request satisfaction rate while minimizing the total travel distance (or cost) of taxis. The DTRP is an online problem since travel requests are coming on the fly and taxis need to be scheduled in real-time. The information on travel requests is unknown until the request is received.

NP-hard problems like the DTRP are particularly challenging, since problems in this class are suspected to have no polynomial-time algorithms. Therefore, heuristics are widely used to ensure scalability. The DTRP is a scheduling problem where taxis are resources and travel requests are tasks. Scheduling problems are very popular in many application domains, and often tackled by decomposing them into an allocation problem and a sequencing problem [15, Chap. 1].

Therefore, the DTRP is often treated as a composition of two subproblems: the traveler-taxi allocation problem and the taxi schedule sequencing problem. When a travel request is received, the goal is to allocate it to a taxi that is close enough to pick up the traveler while satisfying the constraints of the request as well as the constraints due to the seat capacity of the taxi and the requirements of other travelers who are already on board of the taxi. Once a taxi has a new request allocated to it, the schedule of this taxi has to be reorganized to account for the potential detour and waiting time. Traveler-taxi allocation and taxi schedule sequencing are not independent subproblems, since finding the best candidate taxi for a request depends on how that request affects the taxi route.

2.3 Requirements for Our Graph Model

To solve the DTRP efficiently, we aim to design a graph model for it. A review of the state-of-the-art literature on the DTRP resulted in the following set of important tasks that should be supported by our graph model, cf. [8,9,20]:

Task 1 *Retrieve the minimum travel time between the pickup and dropoff location for a specified travel request.*

Task 2 *Retrieve suitable taxis that can reach the pickup location of a request in a specified timeframe.*

Task 3 *Retrieve the remaining capacity and the remaining slack time at a specified point in the taxi schedule.*

These tasks are fundamental for the traveler-taxi allocation and the taxi schedule sequencing. The minimum travel time of a request is the basis of calculation of the maximum detour time for this request. Moreover, based on the time of a request, the minimum travel time and the maximum detour time it is possible to compute the latest arrival time of a request. This is crucial in order to decide for a candidate taxi whether it can arrive in time at the pickup location of a travel request. Finding suitable taxis for a request is the central aim for the traveler-taxi allocation. The maximum slack time of involved trips and the remaining capacity of a taxi are used when checking if a request can be inserted into a taxi schedule. Among the candidate taxis the best one will be selected, i.e., the one that causes the least increase of the overall travel distance or cost.

3   An Intuitive Graph Model for the DTRP

Based on the requirements discussed above we will now design a graph model for the DTRP that can meet the data needs of the three important tasks.

For the DTRP the following real-world entities are relevant: travel requests, taxis and a road network. We regard a *road network* as a directed graph $G = (V, E)$ where V is a set of road points and E a set of road segments. The road points are used to model intersections, terminal nodes and other points of interest, in particular potential pickup and dropoff locations of passengers. The road segments are used to model roads or part of roads. In our graph model, road points $v \in V$ are represented by nodes with label *RoadPoint*. For each road point we store the properties latitude and longitude. Road segments $e \in E$ are represented by relationships with type ROAD_SEGMENT between road points. For each road segment we store the property travel time.

Travel requests $r \in R$ are represented as nodes with label *TravelRequest*. Requests come from potential passengers with a desired pickup and dropoff location. For each request we store the properties datetime, passenger count and maximum slack time. Furthermore, each request is linked to two road points through two relationships with types IS_PICKED_UP_ AT and IS_DROPPED_OFF_AT for the pickup and dropoff location, respectively.

Taxis $h \in T$ are represented by nodes with the label *TaxiShift*. We regard a taxi as a shift of a taxi driver.[1] For each taxi we store the properties passenger capacity, shift start and shift end. We model the schedule of a taxi h as a set S_h of taxi states. Taxi states $\sigma_h \in S_h$ are represented by nodes with label *TaxiState*. Each taxi state is linked to a road point through a relationship with type IS_LOCATED_AT. The next taxi state $next_{S_h}(\sigma_h) \in S_h$ and the previous taxi state $prev_{S_h}(\sigma_h) \in S_h$ are linked through relationships with type IS_BEFORE.

---

[1] For simplicity, we assume in this work that each taxi has just one taxi shift.

Furthermore, there are relationships with type IS-SCHEDULED-BY between a taxi shift h and each of its taxi states $\sigma_h \in S_h$.

We regard a taxi state σ_h as a stay of taxi h at the road point v_{σ_h}. For each taxi state we store the properties number of passengers n_{σ_h}, period start t_{s,σ_h} and period end t_{e,σ_h}. They need to satisfy the constraint that the period end of a taxi state differs from the period start of the next taxi state by the travel time between their respective road points. Furthermore, for every taxi state we store a property s_{σ_h} whether a pickup or dropoff is happening. A *taxi stop* is a taxi state with a pickup or dropoff of some passenger. This causes a certain delay of γ called the change time.[2] Taxi stops have higher priority than other taxi states since they have to be passed while other taxi states connecting the stops can be replaced by different routes. To optionally skip the states there is an additional relationship with type IS-BEFORE-STOP at each stop connecting it to the next stop $next_{s,S_h}(\sigma_h)$ and previous stop $prev_{s,S_h}(\sigma_h)$ if existent.

Trips are represented by nodes with label *Trip*. For each trip we store the property remaining slack time. Once a request is accepted, it results in a trip of the traveler. Each trip is linked to a request through a relationship with type IS-INITIALIZED-BY. We regard the trip schedule as a subset of the schedule of its assigned taxi. Hence, there are relationships with type IS-SCHEDULED-BY between a trip and each taxi state that it shares with its assigned taxi.

After the definition of the nodes and relationships we can now assemble them in our intuitive graph model for the DTRP shown in Fig. 1.[3]

Proposition 1. *Using our intuitive graph model in Fig. 1, it is possible to meet all data needs of Tasks 1, 2 and 3*

Sketch of Proof. We will demonstrate that based on our intuitive graph model it is possible to solve the three important tasks.

For Task 1 we want to retrieve minimum travel time between the pickup and dropoff location of a request. To compute the minimum travel time between two road points $v_1, v_2 \in V$ we find the path P with the lowest total travel time $\omega(P)$ in the road network. We refer to this path P as the shortest path[4] $p(v_1, v_2)$. It can be computed using a shortest path algorithm like Dijkstra's or the A^*-heuristic.

For Task 2 we want to retrieve suitable taxis that are close to the pickup location of a request. We can use Dijkstra's algorithm with a maximum path weight to find the schedule states close to the pickup location of the request.

For Task 3 we want to retrieve the remaining capacity and the remaining slack time of a taxi in a given taxi state. The remaining seat capacity for a taxi

---

[2] This change time is not considered in some publications on the DTRP even though it has severe implications on ride sharing efficiency, since picking up passengers causes a schedule delay even if the pickup location is on the taxi route.

[3] For a better overview, we show the graph model with its nodes and relationships, but do not visualize the properties stored for nodes and relationships.

[4] In the literature this term is often used based on travel distance. Road segments, however, can have different travel speeds which leads to the invalidity of the triangle inequality on the road network. The path with the lowest total travel distance between two locations might not necessarily be the shortest path between them.

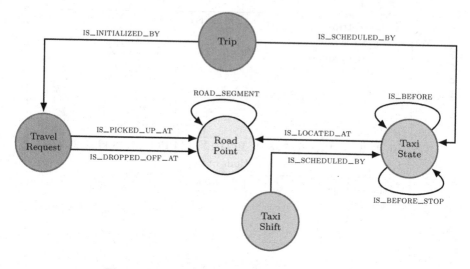

Fig. 1. Our intuitive graph model for the DTRP.

state can be computed from the total capacity (stored as a property of the taxi node) and the current passenger number (stored as an aggregated property of the taxi state node). The remaining slack time can be computed by inspecting the current taxi state and all future taxi stops, and finding the minimal value of the remaining slack times of the trips connected to them (stored as an aggregated property of the trip node).

4   Experimental Evaluation

To evaluate our modeling approach we have implemented our proposed graph model using Neo4j. In addition, we adapted the taxi ride sharing algorithms from [8,9,20] and implemented them as a plugin for Neo4j. Our experiment was based on real-world data of NYC utilizing OSM data and historic taxi trip data from NYC [13]. The imported road network consisted of 605,828 road points and 694,102 road segments, increasing to 927,621 road points and 1,931,503 road segments after data preprocessing, which included data cleaning and integration.

For our experiment we used data for the week from January 4 to 10, 2016 involving 319,081 travel requests after preprocessing 328,643 taxi trips. After the experiment the results were verified against our proposed graph model and the time and seat capacity constraints, to check for the correctness of the implemented algorithms.

Figure 2 shows the satisfaction rate of travel requests given by the number of trips that are shared or completed without sharing and the travel requests that are rejected on January 4, 2016 for 250, 500 and 1000 taxis. We observe that significantly less travel requests can be handled when using 250 taxis compared to 500 taxis, while 1000 taxis yield no significant improvement compared to 500 taxis.

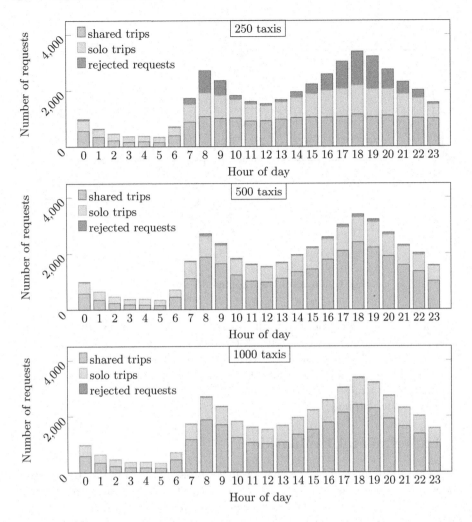

Fig. 2. Plots of the cumulative number of shared trips, solo trips and rejected requests for January 4, 2016 with 250, 500 and 1000 taxis, respectively.

5   Conclusion and Future Work

In this paper, we have proposed a labeled graph property model for the DTRP. Based on a review of state-of-the-art solutions for the DTRP we identified fundamental tasks for solving the problem and developed an intuitive graph model for the DTRP. We then verified that our proposed graph model has the capability to satisfy the requirements imposed by the fundamental tasks. In addition, we provided a prototype impelmentation of our graph data model and the respective taxi ride sharing algorithms, which we then utilised for a taxi ride sharing simulation with real-world data.

For the future, we plan to conduct further experiments to explore the performance and scalability of our approach. Moreover, we will investigate possible design alternatives for our intuitive graph model in order to further improve the support provided by the graph database backend for dynamic taxi ride sharing.

References

1. Agatz, N., Erera, A., Savelsbergh, M., Wang, X.: Optimization for dynamic ridesharing: a review. Eur. J. Oper. Res. **223**, 295–303 (2012)
2. Angles, R., Gutierrez, C.: Survey of graph database models. ACM Comp. Surv. **40**, 1 (2008)
3. Graves, M., Bergeman, E.R., Lawrence, C.B.: Graph database systems. IEEE Eng. Med. Biol. Mag. **14**, 737–745 (1995)
4. Hou, Y., et al.: Towards efficient vacant taxis cruising guidance. In: IEEE GLOBE-COM, pp. 54–59 (2013)
5. Huang, Y., Bastani, F., Jin, R., Wang, X.S.: Large scale real-time ridesharing with service guarantee on road networks. PVLDB **7**(14), 2017–2028 (2014)
6. Joslyn, C., Choudhury, S., Haglin, D., Howe, B., Nickless, B., Olsen, B.: Massive scale cyber traffic analysis: a driver for graph database research. In: International Workshop Graph Data Management Experiences and Systems, p. 3. ACM (2013)
7. Lysenko, A., Roznovăţ, I.A., Saqi, M., Mazein, A., Rawlings, C.J., Auffray, C.: Representing and querying disease networks using graph databases. BioData Min. **9**(1), 23 (2016)
8. Ma, S., Zheng, Y., Wolfson, O.: T-share: a large-scale dynamic taxi ridesharing service. In: IEEE ICDE, pp. 410–421 (2013)
9. Ma, S., Zheng, Y., Wolfson, O., et al.: Real-time city-scale taxi ridesharing. TKDE **27**, 1782–1795 (2015)
10. Mishra, P., Eich, M.H.: Join processing in relational databases. ACM Comp. Surv. **24**, 63–113 (1992)
11. Neo4j: Graph database use cases. https://neo4j.com/use-cases/
12. Neo4j: Neo4j GraphGists. https://neo4j.com/graphgists/
13. NYC Taxi & limousine commission: trip record data. http://www.nyc.gov/html/tlc/html/about/triprecorddata.shtml
14. Park, Y., Shankar, M., Park, B.H., Ghosh, J.: Graph databases for large-scale healthcare systems. In: IEEE ICDE Workshops, pp. 12–19 (2014)
15. Pinedo, M.L.: Scheduling: Theory, Algorithms, and Systems. Springer, Heidelberg (2016)
16. Qian, X., Zhang, W., Ukkusuri, S.V., Yang, C.: Optimal assignment and incentive design in the taxi group ride problem. Trans. Res. B: Meth. **103**, 208–226 (2017)
17. Robinson, I., Webber, J., Eifrem, E.: Graph Databases. O'Reilly, Sebastopol (2013)
18. Sahu, S., Mhedhbi, A., Salihoglu, S., Lin, J., Özsu, M.T.: The ubiquity of large graphs and surprising challenges of graph processing. PVLDB **11**, 420–431 (2017)
19. Santi, P., Resta, G., Szell, M., Sobolevsky, S., Strogatz, S.H., Ratti, C.: Quantifying the benefits of vehicle pooling with shareability networks. Proc. Nat. Acad. Sci. **111**, 13290–13294 (2014)
20. Santos, D.O., Xavier, E.C.: Dynamic taxi and ridesharing: A framework and heuristics for the optimization problem. In: IJCAI, vol. 13, pp. 2885–2891 (2013)
21. solidIT: DB-engines ranking - popularity ranking of graph DBMS. https://db-engines.com/en/ranking/graph+dbms

22. Steinmetz, D., Dyballa, D., Ma, H., Hartmann, S.: Using a conceptual model to transform road networks from OpenStreetMap to a graph database. In: Trujillo, J.C., et al. (eds.) ER 2018. LNCS, vol. 11157, pp. 301–315. Springer, Cham (2018). https://doi.org/10.1007/978-3-030-00847-5_22

23. Vicknair, C., Macias, M., Zhao, Z., Nan, X., Chen, Y., Wilkins, D.: A comparison of a graph database and a relational database: a data provenance perspective. In: ACM Southeast Conference, p. 42 (2010)

24. Yuan, N.J., Zheng, Y., Zhang, L., Xie, X.: T-Finder: a recommender system for finding passengers and vacant taxis. IEEE TKDE **25**, 2390–2403 (2013)

Process Modeling and Analysis

Comprehensive Process Drift Detection
with Visual Analytics

Anton Yeshchenko[1]([✉]) [ID], Claudio Di Ciccio[1] [ID], Jan Mendling[1] [ID],
and Artem Polyvyanyy[2] [ID]

[1] Vienna University of Economics and Business, Vienna, Austria
{anton.yeshchenko,claudio.di.ciccio,jan.mendling}@wu.ac.at
[2] The University of Melbourne, Parkville, VIC 3010, Australia
artem.polyvyanyy@unimelb.edu.au

Abstract. Recent research has introduced ideas from concept drift into
process mining to enable the analysis of changes in business processes
over time. This stream of research, however, has not yet addressed the
challenges of drift categorization, drilling-down, and quantification. In
this paper, we propose a novel technique for managing process drifts,
called Visual Drift Detection (VDD), which fulfills these requirements.
The technique starts by clustering declarative process constraints discovered from recorded logs of executed business processes based on their
similarity and then applies change point detection on the identified clusters to detect drifts. VDD complements these features with detailed visualizations and explanations of drifts. Our evaluation, both on synthetic
and real-world logs, demonstrates all the aforementioned capabilities of
the technique.

Keywords: Process mining · Process drifts · Declarative process
models

1 Introduction

The availability of data has extended conceptual modeling as a research field of
manually created models with automatic techniques for generating models from
data. Process mining is one of these recent extensions that is concerned with
providing transparency of how the businesses operate based on real-world event
data. Process discovery algorithms have proven to be highly effective in generating process models from data of stable behavior [1]. However, many processes are
not stable but are subject to various forms of change over time. In data mining,
such change over time is called a *drift*. A drift is a concept that process mining
has addressed only to a limited extent so far.

Recent works have focused on integrating ideas from research on concept
drift from data mining into process mining [7,12,18,22,26]. The arguably most
advanced technique is proposed in [14], where Maaradji et al. present a framework for detecting process drifts based on tracking behavioral relations over time

A. H. F. Laender et al. (Eds.): ER 2019, LNCS 11788, pp. 119–135, 2019.
https://doi.org/10.1007/978-3-030-33223-5_11

using statistical tests. A strength of this approach is its statistical soundness and ability to identify a rich set of drifts, which makes it a suitable tool for verifying if an intervention at a known point in time has resulted in an assumed change of behavior. However, in practice, the existence of different types of drifts in a business process is not known beforehand, and the analysts are interested in distinguishing what has and what has not changed over time. This need calls for a more fine-granular analysis.

In this paper, we present a novel technique for process drift detection, called Visual Drift Detection (VDD), which addresses the identified research gap. More specifically, our technique facilitates the *visual interpretation* [25] of process drifts founded in the formal rigor of temporal logic of DECLARE constraints [2,10] and time series analysis [6]. Key strengths of our technique are clustering, i.e., grouping, of declarative behavioral constraints that exhibit similar trends of changes over time and automatic detection of changes, i.e., drift points. These features allow us to detect and explain drifts that would otherwise sneak undetected by other techniques. The paper presents an evaluation that demostrates these capabilities.

The remainder of the paper is structured as follows. Section 2 illustrates the problem of process drift detection and formulates five requirements for its analysis. Then, Sect. 3 states the preliminaries. Section 4 presents our drift detection technique, while Sect. 5 evaluates the technique using synthetic and real-world benchmark data. Finally, Sect. 6 summarizes the results and concludes with an outlook on future research.

2   Process Drift Analysis

This section discusses and motivates the problem of process drift analysis (Sect. 2.1), and specifies requirements for its solution (Sect. 2.2).

2.1   Motivating Example

Various logs of real-world business process executions have been recently made available for research. As an example, consider the log of the Italian process for handling the collection of road ticket fines [16]. This process starts with a ticket being issued. In the best case, which covers a third of all the cases, the fine is directly paid. In roughly half of the other cases, a fine notification is sent to the accused driver. Some of these drivers appeal, while some ignore the notice, such that a considerable share of cases sees a penalty being added. Partially, these are further appealed, paid or eventually sent for credit collection. The authority is now interested in this question: Has the process of handling road ticket fines, specifically for the accused drivers, changed over time, and which parts of the process now work differently than in the past?

The described problem is typical for many domains. The objective is to explain the change of the system's behavior in a dynamically changing nonstationary environment based on some *hidden context* [11]. In this setting, a

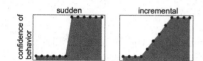

Fig. 1. Different types of drifts, cf. Fig. 2 in [11]; note that an outlier is not a drift.

concept drift is a change of the conditional distribution of the output given a specific input. Research in data mining and machine learning distinguishes techniques for uncovering drifts in an *online* or *offline* manner [23], with applications in prediction and fraud detection.

In process mining, *process drift* is a notion for analyzing changes of business processes over time. Classical process mining techniques have implicitly assumed that logs are not sensitive to time in terms of systematic change [1]. Sampling-based techniques explicitly build on this assumption for generating a process model with a subset of the event log data [5]. A significant challenge for adopting concept drift for process mining is to represent behavior in a time-dependent way. The approach reported in [14] uses causal dependencies and tracks them over time windows. The specific challenge is to not only spot a drift but also to classify it. Figure 1 shows established drift classes from data mining. Next, we use the example of the road ticket fines process to illustrate the potential causes of drifts.

A *sudden drift* is typically caused by an intervention. A new law could eliminate the right of an accused driver to lodge a second appeal. As a result, we would not see second appeal events in our log in the future. An *incremental drift* might result from a stepwise introduction of self-service terminals for paying fines at toll stations. A *gradual drift* may yield from a new policy to show less indulgence with drivers who marginally violated speeding rules. Finally, a *reoccurring drift* might result from specific measures taken in the holiday season from June to August, like flagging down drivers directly on the highway to have them pay right on the spot. Existing process mining techniques support these types of drifts partially.

The following are four cases from the Italian road ticket fines log[1]:

1. 10 Jan. 2011: ⟨Lodging ticket, Appeal, Appeal, Payment, Close ticket⟩
2. 15 Jan. 2011: ⟨Lodging ticket, Appeal, Appeal, No payment, Close ticket⟩
3. 04 Feb. 2011: ⟨Lodging ticket, Appeal, Payment, Close ticket⟩
4. 06 Feb. 2011: ⟨Lodging ticket, Appeal, No payment, Close ticket⟩

We observe a sudden drift here due to the introduction of a new law. After 4 Feb. 2011, it is not possible to lodge a second appeal. Therefore, in formal terms, from case 3 onwards, the behavioral rule that multiple appeals occur before the ticket closes abruptly decreases in confidence. In DECLARE, we denote this rule as ALTERNATERESPONSE(Appeal, Close ticket).

---

[1] https://doi.org/10.1007/s00607-015-0441-1.

2.2 Requirements

Based on the analysis of process change scenarios from the literature, like the road ticket fines discussed previously, we identified five requirements for process drift analysis:

R1. Identify drifts: The points at which a business process undergoes drifts should be identified based on precise criteria;

R2. Categorize drifts: Process drifts should be according to their types;

R3. Drill down and roll up analysis: Process drifts should be characterized at different levels of granularity, e.g., drifts that concern the entire process or only its parts;

R4. Quantitative analysis: Process drifts should be associated with a degree of change, a measure that quantifies to which extent the drift entails a change in the process;

R5. Qualitative analysis: Process drifts should convey changes in a business process to process analysts effectively.

Table 1 provides an overview of the state-of-the-art methods to process drift analysis with the reference to the requirements. Note that collectively these methods implement all the requirements, whereas each individual methods addresses only a subset thereof.

Table 1. Process drift detection in process mining.

Approach	R1	R2	R3	R4	R5
ProDrift [14,18]	+	+/-	-	-	-
TPCDD [26]	+	-	-	-	-
Process trees [17]	+	-	-	-	+
Performance spectra [7]	-	-	+	-	+
Comparative Trc. Clustering [12]	-	-	-	+	+
Graph metrics on Proc.Graphs [22]	+	-	-	+	+
VDD approach (this paper)	**+**	**+**	**+**	**+**	**+**

Approaches like ProDrift [14] and Graph Metrics on Process Graphs [22] put an emphasis on requirement R1. The evaluation of ProDrift in [14] shows that two types of drifts are found with high accuracy (sudden and gradual drifts), hence partly addressing requirement R2; note that the authors report high sensitivity of the technique to the choice of the method parameters. The approach relies on the automated detection of changes in business process executions, which are analyzed based on causal dependency relations studied in process mining [24]. The Tsinghua Process Concept Drift Detection approach (TPCDD) [26] uses two kinds of behavioral relationships (direct succession and weak order). The approach computes those relations on every trace, so as to later identify the change points through their merge and clustering. The sole type of drift that TPCDD detects is the sudden drift.

The other approaches emphasize requirement R5. The approach based on Process Trees [17] uses ProDrift for drift detection, and aims at explaining how sudden drifts influence behavior of the process. To this end, process trees for pre-driftand post-drift sections of the log are built and used to explain the change.

The Performance Spectra approach [7] focuses on drifts that show seasonality. The technique filters the control-flow and visualizes identified flow patterns. It is evaluated against a real-world log, in which recorded business processes show year-to-year seasonality. A strength of the Comparative Trace Clustering approach [12] is its ability to include non-control-flow characteristics in the analysis. Based on these characteristics, it partitions and clusters the log. The differences between the clusters, then, indicate the quantitative change in the business processes, refer to requirement R4. The Graph Metrics on Process Graphs approach [22] discovers a first model, called a reference, using the Heuristic Miner on a section of the log [1]. Then, it discovers models for other sections of the log and uses graph metrics to compare them with the reference model. The technique interprets significant differences in the metrics as drifts. The reference model and detection windows get updated, once a drift is detected.

This discussion, summarized in Table 1, witnesses that none of the state-of-the-art methods addresses all the five requirements. Thus, the work at hand, to address the gap.

3   Preliminaries

In this section, formal preliminaries of the approach are given. Section 3.1 discusses DECLARE specification as the main body of process mining research we build upon. Section 3.2 describes clustering and change point detection methods, which are the main instruments of our approach.

An event log L (*log* for short) is a collection of recorded traces that correspond to process executions. In this paper, we abstract the set of activities of a process as a finite non-empty alphabet $\Sigma = \{a, b, c, \ldots\}$, and we define a trace as a finite sequence of activities $a_i \in \sigma, 1 \leq i \leq n$. Case 1 of the road ticket process from Sect. 2.1 is an example of a trace. Cases 1–4 are an example of an event log. In the following examples, we shall also resort on the string-representation of traces (i.e., $\sigma = a_1 a_2 \cdots a_n$) defined over Σ. Event log L is a multiset of traces, as the same trace can be repeated multiple times in the same log: denoting the multiplicity $m \geq 0$ as an exponent of the trace, we have that $L = \{\sigma_1^{m_1}, \sigma_2^{m_2}, \ldots, \sigma_N^{m_N}\}$ (if $m_i = 0$ for some $1 \leq i \leq N$ we shall simply omit σ_i). The size of the log is defined as $|L| = \sum_{i=1}^{N} m_i$, i.e., the sum of its traces' multiplicities. For example, the size of the Italian help desk log is 150370. A sub-log $L' \subseteq L$ of L is a log $L' = \{\sigma_1^{m_1'}, \sigma_2^{m_2'}, \ldots, \sigma_N^{m_N'}\}$ such that $m_i' \leq m_i$ for all $1 \leq i \leq N$. A log consisting of cases 1–3 from the example log L in Sect. 2.1 is a sub-log of L.

3.1   DECLARE Modeling and Mining

A declarative process specification represents the behavior of a process by means of *constraints*, i.e., temporal rules that specify the conditions under which activities may, must, or cannot be executed. In this paper we focus on DECLARE, one of the most well-established declarative process modeling languages to date [2].

Table 2. Example DECLARE constraints.

Constraint	Explanation	Examples			
ATMOSTONE(a)	If a occurs, then it occurs at most once	✓bcc	✓bcac	✗bcaac	✗bcacaa
RESPONSE(a, b)	If a occurs, then b occurs eventually after a	✓baabc	✓bcc	✗caac	✗bacc
ALTERNATERESPONSE(a, b)	If a occurs, then b occurs eventually afterwards, and no other a recurs in between	✓cacb	✓abcacb	✗caacb	✗bacacb
CHAINRESPONSE(a, b)	If a occurs, then b occurs immediately afterwards	✓cabb	✓abcab	✗cacb	✗bca
PRECEDENCE(a, b)	If b occurs, then a must have occurred before	✓cacbb	✓acc	✗ccbb	✗bacc
ALTERNATEPRECEDENCE(a, b)	If b occurs, then a must have occurred before and no other b recurs in between	✓cacba	✓abcaacb	✗cacbba	✗abbabcb
CHAINPRECEDENCE(a, b)	If b occurs, then a occurs immediately beforehand	✓abca	✓abaabc	✗bca	✗baacb
NOTSUCCESSION(a, b)	a occurs if and only if b does not occur afterwards	✓bbcaa	✓cbbca	✗aacbb	✗abb

DECLARE provides a standard library of templates (*repertoire* [9,20]), i.e., constraints parametrized over activities. Examples of DECLARE constraints are RESPONSE(a, b) and CHAINPRECEDENCE(b, c). The former constraint applies the RESPONSE template on tasks a and b, and states that if a occurs then b must occur later on within the same trace. In this case, a is named *activation*, because it is mentioned in the "if" clause, thus triggering the constraint, whereas b is named *target*, as it is in the consequent clause [9]. CHAINPRECEDENCE(b, c) asserts that if c (the activation) occurs, then b (the target) must have occurred immediately before. Given an alphabet of activities Σ, we denote the number of all possible constraints that derive from the application of DECLARE templates to all activities in Σ as $\#_{cns} \subseteq O(\Sigma^2)$ [9]. For the Italian road ticket fine log, $\#_{cns} = 1584$. Table 2 shows some of the templates of the DECLARE repertoire, together with the examples of traces that satisfy (✓) or violate (✗) them.

Declarative process mining tools can measure to what degree constraints hold true in a given event log [15]. To that end, diverse measures have been introduced. Among them, we consider here *support* and *confidence* [10]. Their values range from 0 to 1. In [10], the support of a constraint is measured as the ratio of times that the event is triggered and satisfied over the number of activations. Let us consider the following example event log: $L = \{\sigma_1^4, \sigma_2^1, \sigma_3^2\}$, having $\sigma_1 = $ baabc, $\sigma_2 = $ bcc, and $\sigma_3 = $ bcba. The size of the log is $4+1+2 = 7$. The activations of RESPONSE(a, b) that satisfy the constraint amount to 8 because two a's occur in σ_1 that are eventually followed by an occurrence of b, and σ_1 has multiplicity 4 in the event log. The total amount of the constraint's activations in L is 10 (see the violating occurrence of a in σ_3). The support thus is 0.8. By the same line of reasoning, the support of CHAINPRECEDENCE(b, c) is $\frac{7}{8} = 0.875$ (notice that in σ_2 only one of the two occurrences of c satisfies the constraint). To

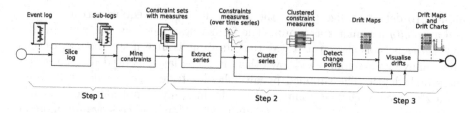

Fig. 2. The VDD approach.

take into account the frequency with which constraints are triggered, confidence scales support by the ratio of traces in which the activation occurs at least once. Therefore, the confidence of RESPONSE(a, b) is $0.8 \times \frac{6}{7} \approx 0.69$ because a does not occur in σ_2. As b occurs in all traces, the confidence of CHAINPRECEDENCE(b, c) is 0.875.

3.2 Clustering and Change Point Detection Algorithms

In this paper, we focus on the analysis of time-series data. A *time series* is a sequence of ordered data points $\langle t_1, t_2, \cdots, t_d \rangle = T \in \mathbb{R}^d$ consisting of $d \in \mathbb{N}^+$ real values. Figure 3(f) illustrates an example of time series. A *multivariate time series* is a set of $n \in \mathbb{N}^+$ time series $D = \{T_1, T_2, \ldots, T_n\}$. We assume a multivariate time series to be piece-wise stationary except for its *change points*. In our approach, we take advantage of the following techniques.

Time series clustering is an unsupervised data mining technique for organizing data points into groups based on their similarity [4]. The objective is to maximize data similarity within clusters and minimize it across clusters. More specifically, the *time-series clustering* is the process of partitioning D into non-overlapping clusters of multivariate time series, $C = \{C_1, C_2, \ldots, C_m\} \subseteq 2^D$, with $C_i \subseteq D$ and $1 \leq m \leq n$, for each i such that $1 \leq i \leq m$, such that homogeneous time series are grouped together based on a *similarity measure*. A *similarity measure* $\text{sim}(T, T')$ represents the distance between two time series T and T' as a non-negative number. Time-series clustering is often used as a subroutine of other more complex algorithms and is employed as a standard tool in data science for anomaly detection, character recognition, pattern discovery, visualization of time series [4].

Change point detection is a technique to detect the points in which multivariate time series exhibit changes in their values [6]. Let D^j denote all elements of D at position j, i.e., $D^j = \{T_1^j, T_2^j, \ldots, T_n^j\}$, where T^j is a j-th element of time series T. The objective of change point detection algorithms is to find $k \in \mathbb{N}^+$ changes in D, where k is previously unknown. Every element D^j for $0 < j \leqslant k$ is a point at which the values of the time series undergo significant changes. In Fig. 3(f), e.g., each vertical black dashed line is one of the $k = 9$ change

points. To detect change points, the search algorithms require a *cost function* and a *penalty* parameter as inputs. The former describes how homogeneous the time series is. It is chosen in a way that its value is high if the time series contains many change points and low otherwise. The latter is needed to constrain the search depth. The supplied penalty should strike a good balance between finding too many change points and not finding any significant ones. Change point detection is a technique commonly used in signal processing and, more in general, for the analysis of dynamic systems that are subject to changes [6].

4   Technique

In this section, we introduce the VDD approach. First, we derive a multivariate time series from an event log, where each time series represents how the confidence values of some DECLARE constraint evolve over time. We prefer confidence over support to prevent that sporadically occurring activities bias our detection algorithms. Then, we cluster sub-sets of time series to group together the constraints that expose a similar trend in their confidence value. Next, using change point detection techniques, we identify the process drifts, i.e., the points in which significant changes in the confidence of behavioral rules occur. Finally, we assess and explain behavioral changes through visual diagrams and numerical reports on drift metrics. Figure 2 illustrates the multi-step VVD approach.

Step 1: Mining DECLARE Windows. In this step, we split the log into sub-logs. From each sub-log, we mine the set of DECLARE constraints and compute their confidence.

Step 2: Slicing the DECLARE Constraints Space into Time and Behavior Sub-spaces. This step begins with the extraction of multi-variate time series that represent the trends of the constraints' confidence. Thereupon, we cluster those time series to find groups of constraints that exhibit similar confidence trends (henceforth, *behavior clusters*). The step ends by returning the detected change points both in the entire multi-variate time series and in each cluster, so as to find overall and behavior-specific drifts, respectively.

Step 3: Explaining Drifts. In the last step, we plot Drift Maps and Drift Charts to visually identify and characterize the detected drift. In the following, we detail those steps.

4.1   Mining DECLARE Windows

The first step takes as input a log L, and two additional parameters (win_{size} and win_{step}). It returns a multivariate time series D based on the confidence of mined DECLARE constraints.

First, we sort the traces in the event log L by the timestamp of their respective first events. Thereupon, we extract a sub-log from L as a window of size $\text{win}_{\text{size}} \in \mathbb{N}^+$, with $1 \leqslant \text{win}_{\text{size}} \leqslant |L|$. We subsequently shift the sub-log window by a given step ($\text{win}_{\text{step}} \in \mathbb{N}^+$, with $1 \leqslant \text{win}_{\text{step}} \leqslant \text{win}_{\text{size}}$). Notice that we have sliding

windows if $\text{win}_{\text{step}} < \text{win}_{\text{size}}$ and tumbling windows if $\text{win}_{\text{step}} = \text{win}_{\text{size}}$. Thus, the number of produced sub-logs is equal to: $\#_{\text{win}} = \left\lfloor \frac{|L| - \text{win}_{\text{size}} - \text{win}_{\text{step}}}{\text{win}_{\text{step}}} \right\rfloor$. Having win_{size} set to 5000 and win_{step} set to 2500, $\#_{\text{win}}$ amounts to 57 on the Italian road fine ticket log.

For every sub-log $L_j \subseteq L$ thus formed $(1 \leqslant j \leqslant \#_{\text{win}})$, we check all possible DECLARE constraints that stem from the activities alphabet of the log, amounting to $\#_{\text{cns}}$ (see Sect. 3.1). For each constraint $i \in 1..\#_{\text{cns}}$, we compute its confidence over the sub-log L_j, namely $\text{Conf}_{i,j} \in [0,1]$. This generates a time series $T_i = (\text{Conf}_{i,1}, \ldots, \text{Conf}_{i,\#_{\text{win}}}) \in [0,1]^{\#_{\text{win}}}$ for every constraint i. In other words, every time series T_i describes the confidence of all the DECLARE constraints discovered in the i-th window of the event log. The multivariate time series $D = \{T_1, T_2, \ldots, T_{\#_{\text{cns}}}\}$ encompasses the full spectrum of all constraints. Next, we detail the steps of slicing the DECLARE constraints and explaining the drifts.

4.2 Slicing the DECLARE Constraints Space into Time and Behavior Sub-spaces

The second step processes the previously generated multivariate time series D to derive (i) a set C of clusters exhibiting similar confidence trends, and (ii) a set of $k \in \mathbb{N}^+$ change points representing the process drifts.

Change Point Detection. To detect change points, we use the *Pruned Exact Linear Time (PELT)* algorithm [13]. This algorithm performs an exact search, but requires the input dataset to be of limited size. Our setup is appropriate as by design the length of the multivariate time-series is limited by the choice of parameters win_{size} and win_{step}. Also, this algorithm is suitable for cases in which the number of change points is unknown a priori [6, p. 24], as in our case. We use the *Kernel cost function*, detailed in [6], which is optimal for our technique, and adopt the procedures described in [13] to identify the optimal *penalty* value.

Clustering Time Series of DECLARE Constraints. By applying a change point detection algorithm on the entire multivariate time-series, we are able to pinpoint the window (i.e., the sub-log) where overall behavior changes occur. However, the level of granularity may be inappropriate as we could not single out the phenomena that are local to certain behavioral rules. That would interfere with the accuracy of results. Therefore, we use time-series clustering techniques [4] to group together similarly changing pockets of behavior of the process. One time series describes how one constraint changes its confidence over time. By clustering, we find all the time series that share similar trends of values, hence, we find all similarly changing constraints. We use *hierarchical clustering*, as it is reportedly one of the most suitable algorithms when the number of clusters is unknown [4]. As a result, we obtain a partition of the multivariate time series of DECLARE constraint confidence values into behavior clusters.

4.3 Explaining Drifts

After clustering the behavior of the log and finding the change points, we expand the classification of the types of drifts found in the literature by being able to identify, pinpoint, and categorize the drifts within behavior clusters. We also allow for an assessment of how erratic the clusters are by means of the novel measure described next.

Finding Erratic Behavior Clusters. The behavioral changes in one cluster can be visually depicted by a plot like that in Fig. 3(f). Thus, in order to find and pinpoint the most interesting (erratic) behavior clusters, we define a measure inspired by the idea of finding the length of a poly-line in a plot. The rationale is, straight lines denote a regular trend and have the shortest length, whilst more irregular, wavy curves evidence more behavior changes and their length is higher. We are, therefore, mostly interested in longer lines.

We compute our measure as follows. We calculate for all constraints i such that $1 \le i \le \#_{\mathrm{cns}}$ the Euclidean distance $\delta : [0,1] \times [0,1] \to \mathbb{R}_+$ between consecutive values in the time series $T_i = (T_{i,1}, \ldots, T_{i,\mathrm{win}_{\mathrm{size}}})$, i.e., $\delta(T_{i,j}, T_{i,j+1})$ for every j s.t. $1 \le j \le \mathrm{win}_{\mathrm{size}}$. For every time series T_i, we thus derive the overall measure $\Delta(T_i) = \sum_{j=1}^{\mathrm{win}_{\mathrm{size}}-1} \delta(T_{i,j}, T_{i,j+1})$. Thereupon, to measure how erratic a behavior cluster is, we devise the following measure:

$$\mathrm{Ertc}(C) = \sum_{j=1}^{|C|} \sqrt{1 + (\Delta(T_i) \times \#_{\mathrm{win}})^2} \qquad (1)$$

The most erratic behavior cluster has the highest Ertc value.

Visual Drift Classification. We enable the visual identification of the patterns illustrated in Fig. 1 with a graphical representation that we name Drift Maps: they depict clusters and their constraints' confidence measure evolution along the time series, together with the drift points. We allow the user to inspect every single cluster and its drifts in dedicated diagrams that we name Drift Charts.

Drift Maps, such as those illustrated in Figs. 3(a) or 4(b), plot all drifts data on a two-dimensional plane. The visual representation we adopt is inspired by [25]. The x-axis is the time axis, while every constraint corresponds to a point along the y-axis. We add vertical lines to mark the identified change points, i.e., drift points, and horizontal lines to demark clusters. Constraints are sorted by the similarity of the confidence trends. The values of the time series are represented through the plasma color-blind friendly color map [25], from blue (low peak) to yellow (high peak).

To analyze the time-dependent trend of specific clusters, we build Drift Charts, such as those depicted in Figs. 3(f) or 4(c). They have time on the x-axis and average confidence of the constraints in a cluster on the y-axis. We add vertical lines as in Drift Maps.

Drift Maps permit the users to have a global picture of the clusters and of the process drifts. Drift Charts allow for a visual categorization of the drifts according to the classification introduced in [11] (Fig. 1). The following section demonstrates applications of this visual-aided approach on synthetic and real-world logs.

5 Evaluation

This section presents our evaluation setup, its results on detecting and explaining drifts, and a discussion of the results.

5.1 Evaluation Setup

We evaluate our approach both on synthetic and real-world event logs.[2, 3, 4] We also compare the obtained results with the state-of-the-art methods. Table 3 summarizes the event logs used in the evaluation and indicates related work which used these logs. To discover DECLARE

Table 3. Event logs used in the evaluation.

Origin	Event log	Related work
Synthetic	ConditionalMove	ProDrift 2.0 [18]
Synthetic	ConditionalRemoval	ProDrift 2.0 [18]
Synthetic	ConditionalToSequence	ProDrift 2.0 [18]
Synthetic	Loop	ProDrift 2.0 [18]
Real-world	Italian help desk[1]	Process Trees [17]
Real-world	BPI2011[3]	ProDrift 2.0 [18]

constraints, we used MINERful[5] because of its high performance [10]. We opted for the *ruptures* python library[6] for change point identification. We used the *scipy* library[7] for the clustering of time-series, including the hierarchical clustering. By experimenting with the clustering algorithm, we tuned the parameters to attain the best outcome, such as the weighted method for linking clusters (distance between clusters defined as the average between individual points), and the correlation metric (to find individual distances between two time-series). To enhance Drift Map visualizations, we sort the time-series of each cluster with the mean squared error distance metric. We implemented our approach in Python 3. Its source code is publicly available.[8]

---

[2] https://doi.org/10.4121/uuid:0c60edf1-6f83-4e75-9367-4c63b3e9d5bb.

[3] https://doi.org/10.4121/uuid:a7ce5c55-03a7-4583-b855-98b86e1a2b07.

[4] https://doi.org/10.4121/uuid:d9769f3d-0ab0-4fb8-803b-0d1120ffcf54 (preprocessed as in [18]).

[5] https://github.com/cdc08x/MINERful.

[6] https://github.com/deepcharles/ruptures.

[7] https://docs.scipy.org/doc/scipy/reference/generated/scipy.cluster.hierarchy.linkage.html.

[8] https://github.com/yesanton/Process-Drift-Visualization-With-Declare.

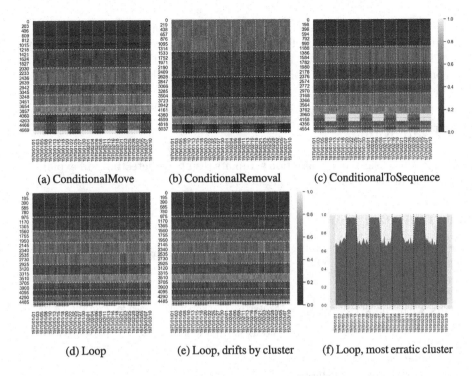

(a) ConditionalMove (b) ConditionalRemoval (c) ConditionalToSequence

(d) Loop (e) Loop, drifts by cluster (f) Loop, most erratic cluster

Fig. 3. Evaluation results on synthetic logs.

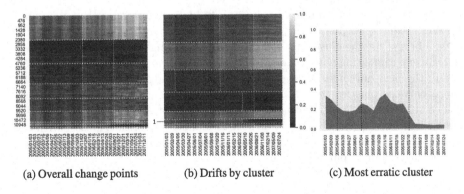

(a) Overall change points (b) Drifts by cluster (c) Most erratic cluster

Fig. 4. BPIC2011 hospital log VDD visualizations.

5.2 Detecting Drifts

To demonstrate the accuracy with which our technique detects drifts, we first test it on synthetic data in which drifts were manually inserted, to show that we detect drifts at the points in which they occur. Thereafter, we compare our results with the state-of-the-art algorithm ProDrift [18] on real-world event logs.

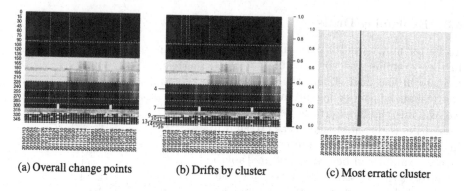

(a) Overall change points   (b) Drifts by cluster   (c) Most erratic cluster

Fig. 5. Italian help desk log VDD visualizations.

Synthetic Data. Ostovar et al. [18] published a set of synthetic logs that they altered to artificially include drifting behavior: ConditionalMove, Conditional-Removal, ConditionalToSequence, and Loop.[9] Figure 3 illustrates the results of the application of the VDD technique on these logs. By measuring *precision* as the fraction of correctly identified drifts over all the ones retrieved by VDD and *recall* as the fraction of correctly identified drifts over the actual ones, we computed the F-score (harmonic mean of precision and recall) of our results for each log. Using the default settings and no constraint set clustering, we achieve the F-score of 1.0 for logs ConditionalMove, ConditionalRemoval, Conditional-ToSequence, and 0.89 for the Loop log. When applying the cluster-based change detection for the Loop log, we achieve the F-score of 1.0. The Drift Map for the *Loop* log is depicted in Fig. 3(e). In contrast to [18] we can see which behavior in which cluster contributes to the drift. The Drift Chart in Fig. 3(f) illustrates the trend of confidence for the most erratic cluster for the *Loop* log.

Real-World Data. Figure 4(a) illustrates the Drift Map constructed for the BPIC2011 event log.[3] As in [18], two drifts are detected towards the second half of the time span of the log. However, in addition, our technique identifies drifting behavior at a finer-granular level. Figure 4(b) shows the drifts pertaining to clusters of constraints. The trend of the confidence measure for the most erratic cluster is depicted in Fig. 4(c).

Our technique correctly detects drifts in the Italian help desk log, by identifying the same two drifts that were found by ProDrift [17], approximately in the first half and towards the end of the time span. As illustrated by the VDD visualization in Fig. 5(a), in addition we detected another sudden change in the first quarter. Following on that, we analyzed the within-cluster changes (Fig. 5(b)) and noticed that the most erratic cluster contains an outlier, as is shown by the spike in Fig. 5(c).

---

[9] http://apromore.org/platform/tools.

5.3 Explaining Drifts

To better understand a particular drift, we further examine the constraints that participate in the drift. Using the example of the Italian help desk log presented above, we examine the most erratic behavior clusters' drifts (calculated using Eq. (1)), shown in Table 4. In Fig. 6, we present the most erratic examples of behavior, and in Table 5 we present the constrains that describe that specific behavior after applying the constraint minimization algorithm.

Table 4. Italian help desk log erratic clusters.

Drift number	Ertc measure
without drift	89
9	780.041
11	328.881
14	293.887
10	292.712
13	289.103
7	232.401
4	196.012
15	171.012
16	166.111

Figure 6(a) shows an erratic behavior, which visually corresponds to the *reoccurring concept* classification from Fig. 1. Examining the constraints that constitute this behavior, the analyst could conclude that in the dates of the peak in Fig. 6(a) the activity Create SW anomaly always had Take in charge ticket executed immediately beforehand, and otherwise in the other parts of the plot. Also, she could conclude that before Create SW anomaly the Assign seriousness activity was executed, and no other Create SW anomaly occurred in between.

Table 5. Italian ticket log constraints; including min, max, and mean confidence.

Cluster	Constraint	Activity 1	Activity 2	Min	Max	Mean
9	CHAINPRECEDENCE	Take in charge ticket	Create SW anomaly	0.0	100	42.8
	ALTERNATEPRECEDENCE	Assign seriousness	Create SW anomaly	0.0	100	49.0
11	CHAINPRECEDENCE	Take in charge ticket	Schedule intervention	0.0	100	9.9
	ALTERNATEPRECEDENCE	Assign seriousness	Schedule intervention	0.0	100	9.9
4	CHAINRESPONSE	Take in charge ticket	Wait	9.4	69.6	23.2
	NOTSUCCESSION	Resolve ticket	Wait	10	77.2	26
	NOTSUCCESSION	Wait	Assign seriousness	10	78	26.6
	NOTSUCCESSION	Wait	Take in charge ticket	9.8	73.3	22.1
	ALTERNATERESPONSE	Assign seriousness	Wait	9	72.3	23.8
	ALTERNATERESPONSE	Wait	Closed	8.3	61.4	22.5
	ALTERNATERESPONSE	Wait	Resolve ticket	8.3	61.4	22.8
	ATMOSTONE	Wait		9.8	68.6	25.1

Figure 6(b) has four spikes, where Schedule intervention activities occurred. Immediately before Schedule intervention, Take in charge ticket occurred. Also, Assign seriousness occurred had to occur before Schedule intervention recurred. We notice, however, that this cluster shows *outlier* behavior, due to its rare changes.

Finally, Fig. 6(c) depicts a *gradual* drift until June 2012, and the *incremental* drift afterward. We notice that all constraints in the cluster have Wait either as an activation (e.g., with ALTERNATERESPONSE(Wait, closed)) or as a target (e.g., with CHAINRESPONSE(Take in charge ticket, Wait)).

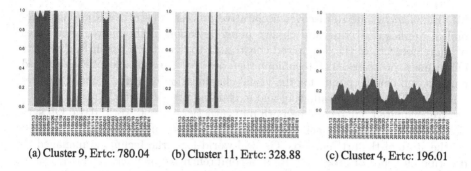

(a) Cluster 9, Ertc: 780.04   (b) Cluster 11, Ertc: 328.88   (c) Cluster 4, Ertc: 196.01

Fig. 6. Italian help desk log detailed clusters.

5.4   Discussion

Our method addresses all the five requirements for process drift detection presented in Sect. 2.2 as follows:

R1 We evaluated our method with the synthetic logs showing its ability to identify drifts precisely;

R2 We developed a visualization approach based on Drift Maps and Drift Charts for classification of process drifts and have shown its effectiveness for real-world logs. Our enhanced approach based on change point detection has yielded effective to automatically discover the exact points at which *sudden* and *reoccurring concept* drifts occur. The indicative approximation of long-running progress of *incremental* and *gradual* drifts was also found. *Outliers* were detected via time series clustering;

R3 Using clustering, Drift Maps, and Drift Charts, the method enables the drilling down into (rolling up out) sections with a specific behavior (general vs. cluster-specific groups of constraints);

R4 We introduced, and incorporated into our technique, a drift measure called Ertc that quantifies the extent of the drift change;

R5 To further qualitatively analyze the detected drifts, VDD shows how the process specification looks before and after the drift (as a list of DECLARE constraints, refer to Table 5).

We found that the size of the window does not introduce significant difference in results for the automatic evaluation of the VDD, so we recommend using the number of windows that will guide the visual search best, that is around 60 windows should be produced for one graph. That means the recommended parameters are: $win_{step} = \frac{|L|}{60+1}$ and $win_{size} = 2 \cdot win_{step}$ for smooth visual representation.

6   Conclusions

In this paper, we presented a visual technique for detecting and analyzing process drifts in logs of executed business processes. First, the technique uses the

MINERful technique to discover declarative process constraints from logs. Second, it applies clustering and change point detection methods over time series of characteristics of the discovered constraints to detect process drifts (in parts of) business processes. The technique then devises visualizations of the detected clusters and change points for the visual classification of drifts. Finally, we presented a technique for evaluating and explaining process drifts.

We evaluated our technique both on synthetic and real-world data. On synthetic logs, the technique achieved an average F-score of 0.96 and outperformed all the state-of-the-art methods. On real-world logs, the technique managed to describe all types of process drifts in a comprehensive manner. Also, the evaluation reported that our technique can identify outliers of process behavior.

Limitations of the work at hand naturally give rise to future research. First, one can study the problem of automatic classification of process drifts; we plan to use shapelets [3] to solve this problem. Second, one can study how the use of other declarative process constraints, e.g., the 4 C spectrum [21] or branched DECLARE [8], impacts the effectiveness of the technique. Third, an empirical evaluation with the potential users of the technique can provide further insights for improving the usability of the approach. Finally, we argue that, based on the identified past process drifts, and using time-series prediction algorithms, one can predict future drifts to prepare for forecasted changes [19].

Acknowledgements. This work is partially funded by the EU H2020 program under MSCA-RISE agreement 645751 (RISE_BPM). Artem Polyvyanyy was partly supported by the Australian Research Council Discovery Project DP180102839.

References

1. van der Aalst, W.M.P.: Process Mining - Data Science in Action. Springer, Heidelberg (2016). https://doi.org/10.1007/978-3-662-49851-4
2. van der Aalst, W.M.P., Pesic, M., Schonenberg, H.: Declarative workflows: balancing between flexibility and support. CS - R&D **23**(2), 99–113 (2009)
3. Abanda, A., Mori, U., Lozano, J.A.: A review on distance based time series classification. DMKD **33**(2), 378–412 (2019)
4. Aghabozorgi, S., Seyed Shirkhorshidi, A., Ying Wah, T.: Time-series clustering - a decade review. IS **53**(C), 16–38 (2015)
5. Bauer, M., Senderovich, A., Gal, A., Grunske, L., Weidlich, M.: How much event data is enough? A statistical framework for process discovery. In: CAISE, pp. 239–256 (2018)
6. Truonga, C., Oudre, L., Vayatis, N.: Selective review of offline change point detection methods (2019). arxiv:1801.00718
7. Denisov, V., Belkina, E., Fahland, D.: BPIC 2018: Mining Concept Drift in Performance Spectra of Processes (2018)
8. Di Ciccio, C., Maggi, F.M., Mendling, J.: Efficient discovery of target-branched declare constraints. Inf. Syst. **56**, 258–283 (2016)
9. Di Ciccio, C., Maggi, F.M., Montali, M., Mendling, J.: Resolving inconsistencies and redundancies in declarative process models. IS **64**, 425–446 (2017)
10. Di Ciccio, C., Mecella, M.: On the discovery of declarative control flows for artful processes. ACM TMIS **5**(4), 24:1–24:37 (2015)

11. Gama, J., Zliobaite, I., Bifet, A., Pechenizkiy, M., Bouchachia, A.: A survey on concept drift adaptation. ACM Comput. Surv. **46**(4), 44:1–44:37 (2014)
12. Hompes, B., Buijs, J.C.A.M., van der Aalst, W.M.P., Dixit, P., Buurman, H.: Detecting change in processes using comparative trace clustering. SIMPDA **2015**, 95–108 (2015)
13. Killick, R., Fearnhead, P., Eckley, I.A.: Optimal detection of changepoints with a linear computational cost. J. Am. Stat. Assoc. **107**(500), 1590–1598 (2012)
14. Maaradji, A., Dumas, M., La Rosa, M., Ostovar, A.: Detecting sudden and gradual drifts in business processes from execution traces. IEEE TKDE **29**(10), 2140–2154 (2017)
15. Maggi, F.M., Mooij, A.J., van der Aalst, W.M.P.: User-guided discovery of declarative process models. In: CIDM, pp. 192–199. IEEE (2011)
16. Mannhardt, F., de Leoni, M., Reijers, H.A., van der Aalst, W.M.P.: Balanced multi-perspective checking of process conformance. Computing **98**(4), 407–437 (2016)
17. Ostovar, A., Leemans, S.J., La Rosa, M.: Robust drift characterization from event streams of business processes (2018). https://eprints.qut.edu.au/121158/
18. Ostovar, A., Maaradji, A., La Rosa, M., ter Hofstede, A.H.M., van Dongen, B.F.: Detecting drift from event streams of unpredictable business processes. In: ER, pp. 330–346 (2016)
19. Poll, R., Polyvyanyy, A., Rosemann, M., Röglinger, M., Rupprecht, L.: Process forecasting: towards proactive business process management. In: Weske, M., Montali, M., Weber, I., vom Brocke, J. (eds.) BPM 2018. LNCS, vol. 11080, pp. 496–512. Springer, Cham (2018). https://doi.org/10.1007/978-3-319-98648-7_29
20. Polyvyanyy, A., Armas-Cervantes, A., Dumas, M., García-Bañuelos, L.: On the expressive power of behavioral profiles. Formal Asp. Comput. **28**(4), 597–613 (2016)
21. Polyvyanyy, A., Weidlich, M., Conforti, R., La Rosa, M., ter Hofstede, A.H.M.: The 4C spectrum of fundamental behavioral relations for concurrent systems. In: Ciardo, G., Kindler, E. (eds.) PETRI NETS 2014. LNCS, vol. 8489, pp. 210–232. Springer, Cham (2014). https://doi.org/10.1007/978-3-319-07734-5_12
22. Seeliger, A., Nolle, T., Mühlhäuser, M.: Detecting concept drift in processes using graph metrics on process graphs. In: S-BPM, p. 6 (2017)
23. Tsymbal, A.: The problem of concept drift: definitions and related work. Comput. Sci. Depart. Trinity College Dublin **106**(2), 58 (2004)
24. van der Aalst, W., Weijters, T., Maruster, L.: Workflow mining: discovering process models from event logs. TKDE **16**(9), 1128–1142 (2004)
25. Ware, C.: Information visualization: perception for design. Elsevier, Amsterdam (2012)
26. Zheng, C., Wen, L., Wang, J.: Detecting process concept drifts from event logs. In: OTM CoopIS, pp. 524–542 (2017)

A Probabilistic Approach to Event-Case Correlation for Process Mining

Dina Bayomie[1]([envelope]) [iD], Claudio Di Ciccio[1] [iD], Marcello La Rosa[2] [iD],
and Jan Mendling[1] [iD]

[1] Vienna University of Economics and Business, Vienna, Austria
{dina.sayed.bayomie.sobh,claudio.di.ciccio,jan.mendling}@wu.ac.at
[2] University of Melbourne, Melbourne, Australia
marcello.larosa@unimelb.edu.au

Abstract. Process mining aims to understand the actual behavior and performance of business processes from event logs recorded by IT systems. A key requirement is that every event in the log must be associated with a unique case identifier (e.g., the order ID in an order-to-cash process). In reality, however, this case ID may not always be present, especially when logs are acquired from different systems or when such systems have not been explicitly designed to offer process-tracking capabilities. Existing techniques for correlating events have worked with assumptions to make the problem tractable: some assume the generative processes to be acyclic while others require heuristic information or user input. In this paper, we lift these assumptions by presenting a novel technique called *EC-SA* based on probabilistic optimization. Given as input a sequence of timestamped events (the log without case IDs) and a process model describing the underlying business process, our approach returns an event log in which every event is mapped to a case identifier. The approach minimises the misalignment between the generated log and the input process model, and the variance between activity durations across cases. The experiments conducted on a variety of real-life datasets show the advantages of our approach over the state of the art.

Keywords: Event correlation · Simulated annealing · Process mining

1 Introduction

Recent years have seen a drastically increasing availability of process execution data from various data sources [16]. Process mining offers different analysis techniques that can help to extract business insights from these data, known as event logs. To this end, each event in an log must have at least three attributes [17]: *(i)* the *event class* referring to a specific activity in the process (e.g., "Order checked" or "Claim assessed"), *(ii)* the *end timestamp* capturing the completion time for that activity, and *(iii)* the *case identifier* (e.g., the order number in an order-to-cash process, or the claim ID in a claims handling process). Data lake

© Springer Nature Switzerland AG 2019
A. H. F. Laender et al. (Eds.): ER 2019, LNCS 11788, pp. 136–152, 2019.
https://doi.org/10.1007/978-3-030-33223-5_12

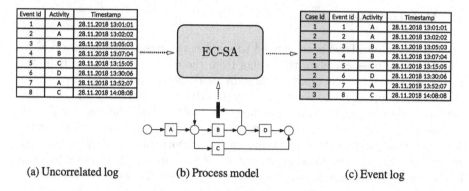

(a) Uncorrelated log   (b) Process model   (c) Event log

Fig. 1. Overview of the EC-SA approach.

infrastructures, though, often put more emphasis on storing and synchronising data than on structuring them in a way that process mining can be readily applied [6,11].

Prior research has described the problem of missing case identifiers as a correlation problem, because the connections between different events has to be reestablished based on heuristics, domain knowledge or payload data. In essence, the correlation problem is concerned with identifying which events belong together to the same case when a unique case identifier is missing. Existing correlation techniques face the challenge of operating in a large search space. For this reason, previous proposals have introduced assumptions to make the problem tractable. Some techniques assume the generative processes to be acyclic [9,14] while others require heuristic information about the execution behavior of activities in addition to the process model [7]. Beyond that, performance has been an issue.

In this paper, we address the correlation problem as a multi-level optimization problem. We propose a novel technique called *EC-SA* (Events Correlation by Simulated Annealing), which is based on simulated annealing. As illustrated in Fig. 1, the technique takes as input a set of uncorrelated events and a (normative or descriptive) process model that captures knowledge of the underlying business process, and produces an event log as output. The technique revolves around two nested objectives. First, it seeks to minimize the misalignment between the generated log and an input process model; second, it seeks to minimize the activity execution time variance across cases. This latter objective builds on the assumption that same activities tend to have similar duration across cases.

The remainder of this paper is organized as follows. Section 2 discusses the related work. Section 3 presents the different phases of our novel EC-SA event correlation technique. Section 4 then discusses the experimental evaluation on real-life logs before Sect. 5 concludes the paper.

2 Related Work

Several techniques have been defined to address the event correlation problem. The following ones correlate the events from the control flow perspective. The greedy approach in [9] estimates a Markov model for an uncorrelated event log. It does not support cyclic behavior. It is sensitive to concurrency and the number of overlapping cases at a given point in time. In [18], the authors provide an approach that uses sequence partition to search the solution space for the minimal set of patterns that can represent the uncorrelated event log. The approach does not support cyclic. As an output, it produces the behavioral patterns of the log. The Correlation Miner (CMiner) approach [14] works in two phases. The first phase is discovering an acyclic process model from the uncorrelated log using linear programming. In the second phase, the discovered model is used to correlate the events by solving quadratic programming constraints. It does not support cyclic models. The performance of the approach is highly sensitive to the amount of uncorrelated events mainly because of the quadratic-constraints based phase. The Deducing Case Ids (DCI) approach in [7] searches the solution space for the possible correlation between the events, and prunes the search space based on the given input in terms of the process model and heuristic data on activity execution behavior. DCI supports the cyclic processes. It is sensitive to the quality of the input data and not computationally efficient.

Our approach has common factors with CMiner and DCI. The three techniques consider the activity duration to find a solution, and they use the control flow to identify the correlation between the events.

Two techniques tackle the correlation problem by considering the data perspective have been devised to date. In [13] the authors address the correlation problem in the web service environment. Their semi-automated approach correlates events of the service logs as process views based on a correlation condition using the event data from different data layers. In [15], the authors address the problem of having the event data stored in databases. They mine the association and correlation rules over the different attributes in the database. Then, they measure the support of these rules over the data and use the most supported rules for correlating the events. They use the MapReduce technique to improve the performance of applying the correlation constraints.

In summary, these recent techniques make assumptions about process behavior, available information and size of search space. Our *EC-SA* technique lifts those assumptions.

3 Event Correlation Technique

We treat the problem of automatically correlating events as a multi-level optimization problem. Specifically, our technique, EC-SA, is based on population-based simulated annealing [2]. The technique revolves around two nested objectives: *(i)* minimizing the misalignment between the generated event log and the input process model, and *(ii)* minimizing the activity execution time variance

across cases. In order to describe our technique precisely, we first introduce a number of preliminary concepts.

3.1 Preliminaries

We introduce the basic notions of event, uncorrelated event log, case and projection of a case over an event attribute. Thereupon, we present the definitions of event log and trace.

An *event* e is an atomic unit of execution. Events bear *attributes*. In particular, we assume the following attributes to be mandatory: activity name Act (string) and timestamp Ts (date-time). The value of attribute X on event e shall be denoted as $e.X$, e.g., $e.$Ts refers to the timestamp of e. We assume a total order $\preccurlyeq$ to be defined over the universe of events. Therefore, we assign to every event a unique integer index (or *event id* for short), induced by $\preccurlyeq$ on the events. We shall denote the index i of an event e as a subscript, e_i. We assume the assignment of Ts to be coherent with $\preccurlyeq$, i.e., if $e \preccurlyeq e'$ then $e.$Ts $\leqslant e'.$Ts. In Fig. 1(a), e.g., event e_3 is such that $e_3.$Act $=$ B and $e_3.$Ts $=$ 28.11.2018 13:05:03.

An *uncorrelated event log* (or *uncorrelated log* for short) UL is a finite set of events with total order $\preccurlyeq$. Figure 1(a) depicts an uncorrelated event log UL.

A *case* $\sigma = \langle e_{\sigma_1}, \ldots, e_{\sigma_n} \rangle$ is a finite sequence of length n of events e_{σ_i} with $1 \leqslant i \leqslant n$ induced by $\preccurlyeq$, i.e., such that $e_{\sigma_i} \preccurlyeq e_{\sigma_k}$ for every $i \leqslant k \leqslant n$. We assume every case to be assigned a unique case identifier (case id for short), namely an integer in a convex subset. The value of attribute X over case σ shall be denoted as $\sigma.X$. In Fig. 1(c), $\sigma_2 = \langle e_2, e_4, e_6 \rangle$. We write $L(e) = \sigma$ to indicate that the case of event e in log L is σ. In the example of Fig. 1(c), $L(e_2) = L(e_4) = L(e_6) = \sigma_2$.

An *event log* $L = \{\sigma_1, \ldots, \sigma_n\}$ is a finite non-empty set of non-overlapping cases, i.e., if $e \in \sigma_i$, then $e \notin \sigma_j$ for all $i, j \in [1 \ldots n]$, $i \neq j$. We denote its cardinality as $|L| = N$ with $N \geqslant 1$. Figure 1(c) shows an event log consisting of cases σ_1, σ_2, and σ_3. Notice that the union of all events of every case of a log L, together with the total order defined on them, is an uncorrelated log. For the sake of conciseness, we denote this totally ordered events set as $UL(L)$. A *trace* t is a projection of a case σ over the activity names: $t = \text{Act}(\sigma)$. In Fig. 1(c), $\text{Act}(\sigma_2) = \langle \text{A}, \text{B}, \text{D} \rangle$.

3.2 The Problem

Given an uncorrelated log UL as input (like the one in Fig. 1(a)), the output of EC-SA is an event log L that partitions UL into a set of cases, i.e., such that for every event $e \in UL$ there exists one and only one case $\sigma \in L$ s.t. $e \in \sigma$. Figure 1(c) shows such a log. To derive L from UL, EC-SA considers as an additional input a process model (e.g., the Workflow net depicted in Fig. 1(b)), which drives the mapping of events to cases. We assume the process model to have exactly one start activity (initially, only one activity is enabled) and to expose terminating conditions (at some stage of the run, no activity is enabled any longer).

3.3   Multi-level Optimization

The event correlation problem can be solved by optimization metaheuristic techniques. EC-SA uses a multi-level simulated annealing as optimization technique. *Simulated Annealing* (SA) is a metaheuristic that searches for the nearest approximate global solution in the search space of the optimization problem, by simulating the cooling process of metals through the annealing process. Using SA to solve the event correlation problem helps in finding a global optimal correlated log in reasonable time.

SA explores the search space through the following steps. It starts by creating the initial *population*, as we are using the population-based SA [2]. A population (pop) is a non-empty set of individuals ($|\text{pop}| \geqslant 1$). The population is formed by generating random *individuals*. Then SA initializes the current step $S_{\text{curr}} = 1$ and the current temperature with an initial temperature, $\tau_{\text{curr}} = \tau_{\text{init}}$. The annealing process begins with the generation of a neighbor solution x' for the current individual x. Next, SA computes the *energy cost function* between x and x', namely $\delta f_c(x, x')$. Both $\delta f_c(x, x')$ and τ_{curr} are used as input to compute the *acceptance probability* of the new neighbor solution, which we denote as $\text{prob}(x')$. $\text{prob}(x')$ determines if the new neighbor, x', can be used as the next individual. Notice that $\text{prob}(x')$ may select x' even though it performs worse than x in order to increase the chances to skip the local optimum and let the algorithm further explore the search space. At each iteration, SA compares the global optimal solution x_G at step $S_{\text{curr}} - 1$, i.e., the best solution over the iterations $[0, S_{\text{curr}}[$, with the local optimal solution x_L in pop at S_{curr} based on $\delta f_c(x_G, x_G)$. Thus, SA can return the best solution over all the iterations. Finally, SA uses a cooling schedule that defines the rate at which the temperature (τ_{curr}) cools down, and increments S_{curr} by 1. SA repeats the annealing and cooling process till S_{curr} reaches the maximum number of iterations (S_{max}).

SA has a set of parameters that influence the annealing process: *(i)* the initial temperature (τ_{init}), *(ii)* the maximum number of steps (S_{max}), and *(iii)* the population size ($|\text{pop}|$). In addition to these parameters, SA requires the following main functions to be defined: *(i)* the creation of a new neighbor (x'), *(ii)* the energy cost function ($\delta f_c(x, x')$), *(iii)* the acceptance probability ($\text{prob}(x')$), and *(iv)* the cooling schedule. We implement those functions to resolve the event correlation problem. In the rest of this section, we discuss the SA steps using the defined functions.

The cooling schedule simulates the cooling-down technique of the annealing process by controlling the computation of the current temperature τ_{curr}. We use the logarithmic function schedule, as follows: $\tau_{\text{curr}} = \frac{\tau_{\text{init}}}{\ln(1 + S_{\text{curr}})}$.

Figure 2 shows the steps of EC-SA. Aside of the aforementioned SA-specific parameters, it requires as input *(i)* an uncorrelated event log (e.g., the one depicted in Fig. 1(a)) and *(ii)* a process model (e.g., the one of Fig. 1(b)). The approach generates a (correlated) event log as its output (depicted, e.g., in Fig. 1(c)). We discuss the steps in details through the following subsections.

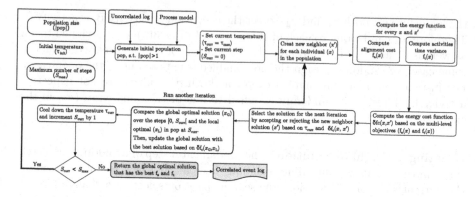

Fig. 2. The EC-SA technique

Creating the Initial Population. As shown in Fig. 2, the first step is the generation of the initial population, pop, of size $|pop| \geq 1$. An individual represents a possible event log, such as the one depicted in Fig. 3(a). We use a dedicated data structure for such individuals that we name log array.

A *log array LA* is an associative array mapping every event to a case. The size of the log array is $|LA| = |UL|$. We write $LA(e) = \sigma$ to indicate that event e is mapped to case σ by log array LA. In Figs. 3(a) and 4, the log array elements are labeled with the corresponding event (e.g., B_4 is event e_4, where $e_4.Act = B$). The content of each cell is the assigned case id (e.g., B_4 is assigned with case id 2, i.e., $LA(e_4) = \sigma_2$). LA is created by replaying the uncorrelated events on the process model. The replaying step is repeated based on the population size. In our example, we assume $|pop| = 1$ for readability purposes.

To generate the log array, we replay all events on the process model. Every run from the initial activity to the termination conditions will correspond to a case. We name the cases corresponding to non-terminated runs as *open cases*. We figure three scenarios when replaying an event e over the input process model:

1. e corresponds to the execution of the start activity of the process model (we name it *start event*); then, a new run starts and a new case is open, accordingly;
2. e corresponds to the execution of an enabled (non-starting) activity on one (or more) runs (*enabled event*); then, e is assigned to the case of the run that enables its activity, or, if more runs enable it, it is assigned randomly to one of those.
3. e does not correspond to any enabled activity (*non-enabled event*); then, e is assigned randomly to one of the open cases, although its activity was not enabled. This way, we guarantee to correlate all the events even when the log has deviated from the model.

The replaying of the uncorrelated events in Fig. 1(a) on the process model in Fig. 1(b) generates the LA_1 individual in Fig. 3(a). In the example, upon e_1 we generate σ_1, and upon e_2, σ_2 starts. Afterwards, there are two open cases within

the log before e_3: both σ_1 and σ_2 expect the execution of activity B or activity C. Therefore, e_3 can belong to each of those cases. In Fig. 3(a), e_3 is assigned to σ_2, as well as e_4 and e_5. To guarantee the assignment of all uncorrelated events to some case, we randomly assign the non-enabled events to one of the open cases. For instance, e_6 is a non-enabled event, as both σ_1 and σ_2 are not expecting activity D. Thus, e_6 is randomly assigned to one of the open cases (σ_2, in the example).

Creating a Neighbor Solution. The fundamental step of exploring the search space in the simulated annealing technique is creating a new neighbor based on the current solution. We explore the search space by selecting a changing point in the current individual (x) and replay the events on the model from that point on in order to find a different solution (x'). The selection of the changing point is based on the current step (S_{curr}) to determine from which part of the LA the change may occur. For instance, when $S_{curr} = 1$ the changing point is randomly selected from the beginning of the log, i.e., the first few events. Instead, when $S_{curr} = S_{max} - 1$ the changing point is randomly selected from the end of the log, i.e., the last few events. The continuous increment of S_{curr} leads to reducing the number of events to be replayed at each iteration; this is in line with the cooling down mechanism of the simulated annealing approach.

Energy Cost Function. The *energy function* is a fundamental part of simulated annealing. As shown in Fig. 2, this function is divided into two components to support a bilevel objective and solve the correlation problem. The first-level objective ($f_a(x)$) aims at minimizing the misalignment between the output log and the given process model. The second-level objective ($f_t(x)$) aims at minimizing the activity execution time variance within the log.

To measure the model-log misalignment we use the well-established *alignment cost* function proposed in [1]. Figure 3 shows an example of the alignment computation. The first step is to extract the cases from the log array as shown in Fig. 3(b). Then, we project the traces from the cases as shown in Fig. 3(c). For each trace within the log, we compute the raw alignment cost ($\delta_A(t_i)$) of the trace w.r.t. the process model. For example, Fig. 3(d) shows that the model cannot execute activity D in t_2, so it is considered as a move in the log. On the other hand, activity C in t_1 is considered as a move in the model as it does not occur in the trace although the model would require it. The third trace has no deviations. The raw cost of the log is the summation of the traces' alignment cost. For instance, the raw cost of the log array in Fig. 3(a) is $f_a(LA_1) = \delta_A(t_1) + \delta_A(t_1) + \delta_A(t_3) = 1 + 1 + 0 = 2$.

The second objective of EC-SA is to minimize the activity execution time variance. We assume that the same activities tend to have similar execution duration across cases. We thus calculate the time variance using the Mean Square Error (MSE) as in Eq. (2). MSE measures the deviation between the expected activities durations and the correlated events durations. Given an activity a, we compute the average of the activity durations as the expected value $Time_{avg}(a)$.

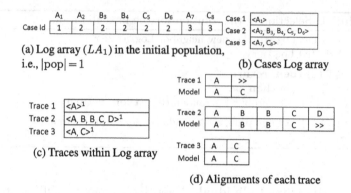

(a) Log array (LA_1) in the initial population,
i.e., $|pop| = 1$

(b) Cases Log array

(c) Traces within Log array

(d) Alignments of each trace

Fig. 3. Alignment computation of LA_1

Given a case $\sigma = \langle e_{\sigma_1}, \ldots, e_{\sigma_n} \rangle$, we compute the Elapsed Time (ET), i.e., the event duration, of an event $e_{\sigma_i} \in \sigma$ (with $1 \leqslant i \leqslant n$) as follows:

$$\mathrm{ET}(\sigma, e_{\sigma_i}) = \begin{cases} e_{\sigma_i}.\mathrm{Ts} - e_{\sigma_{i-1}}.\mathrm{Ts} & \text{if } 1 < i \leqslant n \\ 0 & \text{otherwise} \end{cases} \tag{1}$$

Recalling that with $LA(e)$ we indicate the case to which e is assigned by log array LA, the (time-)MSE is computed as follows.

$$\mathrm{MSE}(LA) = \frac{1}{|LA|} \sum_{i=0}^{|LA|} (\mathrm{Time}_{\mathrm{avg}}(e_i.\mathrm{Act}) - \mathrm{ET}(LA(e_i), e_i))^2 \tag{2}$$

The MSE is used as the second-level objective function, f_t. For example, the average execution times (in minutes) of each activity in the log array of Fig. 3(a) are $\mathrm{Time}_{\mathrm{avg}}(\mathsf{B}) = 2.52$, $\mathrm{Time}_{\mathrm{avg}}(\mathsf{C}) = 12.02$, and $\mathrm{Time}_{\mathrm{avg}}(\mathsf{D}) = 15.02$. Considering the expected time values for each of the events, we have that $f_t(LA_1) = \mathrm{MSE}(LA_1) = 4.1\,\mathrm{min}$.

Based on the energy function, i.e., on objective functions f_a (alignment cost) and f_t (time-MSE), the *energy cost function*, $\delta f_c(x, x')$, is computed as follows.

$$\delta f_c(x, x') = \begin{cases} f_a(x') - f_a(x) & \text{if } f_a(x') > f_a(x) \\ f_t(x') - f_t(x) & \text{otherwise.} \end{cases} \tag{3}$$

$$\mathrm{prob}(x') = \exp^{\frac{-\delta f_c(x,x')}{\tau_{\mathrm{curr}}}} \tag{4}$$

The acceptance probability, $\mathrm{prob}(x')$, is computed using $\delta f_c(x, x')$ and the current temperature (τ_{curr}) as shown in Eq. (4). EC-SA compares the value of $\mathrm{prob}(x')$ with a random value in the interval $[0, 1]$ to accept (if higher) or reject (if lower) the new neighbor. In this way, we simulate the annealing process, enforced by the fact that the decrease of the τ_{curr} temperature also diminishes the randomness of the choice. Furthermore, notice that the memory-less stochastic perturbation makes it possible to skip the local optimal.

Algorithm 1. Selection of the solution for the next iteration

---

input : Current LogArray x; new neighbor LogArray x'
output: Selected LogArray

1 **if** $f_a(x') \leqslant f_a(x)$ **then return** x' ;
2 **else if** $f_a(x') = f_a(x)$ **then**
3 $\quad\lfloor$ **if** $f_t(x') \leqslant f_t(x)$ *or* $\text{prob}(x') \geqslant \text{random}(0,1)$ **then return** x' ;
4 **else if** $f_a(x') > f_a(x)$ *and* $\text{prob}(x') \geqslant \text{random}(0,1)$ **then return** x' ;
5 **return** x

Selection of the Next Individual. Algorithm 1 shows the full selection procedure of the individual for the next iteration. Its decision between x and x' is based on the objective functions, f_a (first-level) and f_t (second-level), and $\text{prob}(x')$ (perturbation). If the new neighbor (x') has a lower alignment cost, then it is selected. If the new neighbor (x') and current individual (x) have the same alignment cost, then we check the activity time variance. We alter the final decision with a random selection weighed by $\text{prob}(x')$ which, in turn, is calculated on the basis of the current temperature, τ_{curr}, and $\delta f_c(x, x')$. As Eq. (3) shows, also $\delta f_c(x, x')$ considers $f_t(x)$ and $f_t(x')$ in this case. On the contrary, if the new neighbor has a higher alignment cost than the current individual, we calculate $\delta f_c(x, x')$ based on $f_a(x)$ and $f_a(x')$. The acceptance probability, again, may alter the decision. This process is repeated for each individual within the population.

Running Example. Figure 4 shows the intermediate results within the EC-SA iterations. We assume that $S_{\max} = 4$ and $\tau_{\text{init}} = 100$. Figure 4(a) shows the new individual created from the initial individual $x = LA_1$. Since $f_a(x) = f_a(x')$ and $f_t(x) < f_t(x')$, then $\delta f_c(x, x')$ is computed considering f_t. $\delta f_c(x, x')$ is equal to 0.4. Thus, $\text{prob}(x')$ is calculated on the basis of $\tau_{\text{curr}} = 100$ and $\delta f_c(x, x')$. Upon the comparison of $\text{prob}(x')$ against a random value in $[0, 1]$, we assume that x' is selected and replaces x in the population. Figure 4(b) shows the second iteration, where $f_a(x') = 0 \leqslant f_a(x) = 2$. Therefore, x' is directly selected without computing the acceptance probability as it performs better than the current individual (x). Figure 4(c) shows the last iteration. The new neighbor achieves a higher $f_a(x') = 1$ than the current individual $(f_a(x) = 0)$. Thus, $\delta f_c(x, x')$is computed on the basis of f_a. Based on $\text{prob}(x')$ at $\tau_{\text{curr}} = 91$ and a selection against the random value, we assume that x' is rejected and x is kept in the population.

Finally, EC-SA returns the solution that has the best f_a and f_t over all the iterations, i.e., the global optimal solution x_G till $S_{\max}$, as shown in Fig. 1(c). Following the EC-SA steps in Fig. 2, the algorithm proceeds until $S_{\text{curr}} = S_{\max}$. The replaying of the events from different changing points in the log over the iterations grows the search space to explore. Accepting a worse solution than

(a) Iteration 1 ($S_{curr} = 1$, $\tau_{curr} = 100$, prob$(x') = 0.99$)

Case Id	A_1	A_2	B_3	B_4	C_5	D_6	A_7	C_8	
	1	2	2	2	2	2	3	3	$f_a(x) = 2$, $f_t(x) = 4.1$
	1	2	1	1	1	1	3	3	$f_a(x') = 2$, $f_t(x') = 4.5$

(b) Iteration 2 ($S_{curr} = 2$, $\tau_{curr} = 144.9$, prob(x') is irrelevant)

Case Id	A_1	A_2	B_3	B_4	C_5	D_6	A_7	C_8	
	1	2	1	1	1	1	3	3	$f_a(x) = 2$, $f_t(x) = 4.5$
	1	2	1	2	1	2	3	3	$f_a(x') = 0$, $f_t(x') = 2.4$

(c) Iteration 3 ($S_{curr} = 3$, $\tau_{curr} = 91$, prob$(x') = 0.98$)

Case Id	A_1	A_2	B_3	B_4	C_5	D_6	A_7	C_8	
	1	2	1	2	1	2	3	3	$f_a(x) = 0$, $f_t(x) = 2.4$
	1	2	1	1	1	2	3	3	$f_a(x') = 1$, $f_t(x') = 4.5$

Fig. 4. EC-SA iterations, with $S_{max} = 3$ and $\tau_{init} = 100$

the current solution in some iterations helps to skip the optimal local solution and reach the optimal global solution.

4 Evaluation

We implemented EC-SA in a freely available prototype tool.[1] Using this tool we conducted two experiments to evaluate the accuracy and time performance of our approach, and compared the results with the state-of-the-art approach DCI [7].

4.1 Design

Given an event log with correlated events (the "original log"), we removed the case identifiers and created an uncorrelated set of events. Using the latter log as input, we conducted two experiments (see Fig. 5). First, we measured the accuracy of the log generated by our approach against the original log, by taking as input process knowledge the set of distinct traces extracted from the original log itself. The purpose of this first experiment was to measure the loss of accuracy in the log produced by EC-SA, when using as input the equivalent of a perfectly fitting and precise process model (as represented by the set of traces of the original log). In the second experiment, instead of the distinct traces of the original log, we used as process knowledge the process model mined from the original log using two state-of-the-art automated discovery methods: Split Miner [4] and Inductive Miner [10]. These two methods strike different tradeoffs in terms of fitness, which captures the degree to which the discovered process model is able to recognize the traces in the event log, and precision, which captures the extent to which the behavior allowed by the process model is observed in the event log. The purpose of this second experiment was to measure how well our approach is able to correlate events, in spite of an input model that is not perfectly fitting

---

[1] Available at https://github.com/DinaBayomie/EC-SA/releases/tag/v1.0.

nor precise. This second scenario is closer to reality, where a process model may be available within the organisation, though this model is not a faithful representation of the behavior captured by the set of uncorrelated events we want to correlate. Finally, we compared the results of the second experiment with the DCI approach as a baseline.

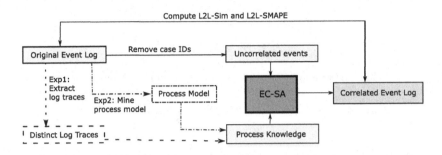

Fig. 5. Evaluation steps

Table 1. Example illustrating L2L$_{\text{sim}}$ computation steps

(a) L_1 traces	(b) L_2 traces	(c) Iteration 1		
$t_{1,1} = \text{Act}(\sigma_{1,1}) = \langle A,B,C \rangle$	$t_{2,1} = \text{Act}(\sigma_{2,1}) = \langle A,B,B,D \rangle$	$\Delta^{\text{ins}}_{\text{del}}(t_{1,3}, t_{2,2}) = 0$	$\Delta^{\text{ins}}_{\text{del}}(t_{1,3}, t_{2,3}) = 0$	$\Delta^{\text{ins}}_{\text{del}}(t_{1,1}, t_{2,3}) = 1$
$t_{1,2} = \text{Act}(\sigma_{1,2}) = \langle A,B,D \rangle$	$t_{2,2} = \text{Act}(\sigma_{2,2}) = \langle A,C \rangle$	$\Delta^{\text{ins}}_{\text{del}}(t_{1,2}, t_{2,1}) = 1$	$\Delta^{\text{ins}}_{\text{del}}(t_{1,1}, t_{2,2}) = 1$	$\Delta^{\text{ins}}_{\text{del}}(t_{1,2}, t_{2,2}) = 3$
$t_{1,3} = \text{Act}(\sigma_{1,3}) = \langle A,C \rangle$	$t_{2,3} = \text{Act}(\sigma_{2,3}) = \langle A,C \rangle$	$\Delta^{\text{ins}}_{\text{del}}(t_{1,2}, t_{2,3}) = 3$	$\Delta^{\text{ins}}_{\text{del}}(t_{1,1}, t_{2,1}) = 3$	$\Delta^{\text{ins}}_{\text{del}}(t_{1,3}, t_{2,1}) = 4$

To measure the accuracy of the event log generated by EC-SA w.r.t. the original log, we used two measures: L2L$_{\text{sim}}$ and L2L$_{\text{SMAPE}}$. L2L$_{\text{sim}}$ is a log-to-log similarity measure, defined as the average string-edit distance between each trace of the generated log and its closest trace in the original log, weighted by the relative frequency of each trace in the two logs (cf. Definition 1). In essence, this measure is the transposition of the alignment-based fitness measure between a model and a log [1] to the case of two logs. L2L$_{\text{SMAPE}}$ is the symmetric mean absolute error of the events elapsed time between the two logs (cf. Definition 2). We used this measure to assess the time deviation between the events in the generated log and those in the original log. Finally, we measured the time taken by our approach and by DCI to complete the correlation task, using a timeout of 24 h.

Definition 1 (L2L$_{\text{sim}}$). *Let $\Delta^{\text{ins}}_{\text{del}}$ be the string-edit distance allowing only for insertions and deletions [12]. Let L_1 and L_2 be two event logs of same cardinality N, $L_1 = \{\sigma_{1,1}, \sigma_{1,2}, \ldots, \sigma_{1,N}\}$ and $L_2 = \{\sigma_{2,1}, \sigma_{2,2}, \ldots, \sigma_{2,N}\}$. We define the pair of trace-closest cases of L_1 and L_2, $(\sigma_{1,\star}, \sigma_{2,\star})$, as follows:*

$$(\sigma_{1,\star}, \sigma_{2,\star}) = \underset{\substack{\sigma_{1,i} \in L_1 \\ \sigma_{2,j} \in L_2}}{\arg\min} \left\{ \Delta^{\text{ins}}_{\text{del}}(\text{Act}(\sigma_{1,i}), \text{Act}(\sigma_{2,j})) \right\} \text{ with } 1 \leqslant i, j \leqslant N \quad (5)$$

The log-to-log similarity distance L2L$_{sim}$ *is thus inductively defined as follows:*

$$N \times \text{L2L}_{sim}(L_1, L_2) = \begin{cases} \Delta_{del}^{ins}(\text{Act}(\sigma_{1,1}), \text{Act}(\sigma_{2,1})) & \textit{if } |L_1| = |L_2| = 1 \\ \text{L2L}_{sim}(L_1 \setminus \{\sigma_{1,\star}\}, L_2 \setminus \{\sigma_{2,\star}\}) & \textit{otherwise} \end{cases}$$

(6)

Operationally, L2L$_{sim}$ is computed as follows: we first sort L_1 and L_2 by their trace-closest pairs of cases, then we sum up the respective Δ_{del}^{ins} distances till saturation, and finally we derive L2L$_{sim}$ by averaging the sum over the number of cases in the logs. Table 1 shows two example logs, L_1 in Table 1(a) and L_2 in Table 1(b), and the computation of L2L$_{sim}(L_1, L_2)$. We compute Δ_{del}^{ins} for each pair of traces, and sort them as in Table 1(c). For instance, $\Delta_{del}^{ins}(t_{1,3}, t_{2,2})$ is 0 as there is no deviation between the two traces. By selecting this pair, $\Delta_{del}^{ins}(t_{1,3}, \sigma_{2,\star}))$ and $\Delta_{del}^{ins}(t_{1,\star}, \sigma_{2,2})$ are removed (the marked cells in Table 1(c)). Thus, L2L$_{sim}(L_1, L_2) = \frac{2}{3} \approx 0.67$.

Definition 2 (L2L$_{SMAPE}$). L2L$_{SMAPE}$ *is the Symmetric Mean Absolute Error of the events Elapsed Time (ET) between two event logs,* L_1 *and* L_2, *such that their events are equivalent, i.e.,* $UL(L_1) = UL(L_2)$. *Let* $ET(L(e), e)$ *be the Elapsed Time of event* e *in log* L *as per Eq. (1). We define* L2L$_{SMAPE}$ *as follows:*

$$\text{L2L}_{SMAPE}(L_1, L_2) = \frac{1}{\sum_{i=0}^{|L_1|} |\sigma_i|} \times \sum_{e \in UL(L_1)} \frac{|\text{ET}(L_1(e), e) - \text{ET}(L_2(e), e)|}{|\text{ET}(L_1(e), e)| + |\text{ET}(L_2(e), e)|}$$

(7)

In the following, we will use the original log as L_1 and the generated log as L_2.

4.2 Datasets

We used a dataset of model-log pairs from a recent benchmark of automated discovery methods [3]. This collection contains twelve public real-life event logs extracted from the 4TU Centre for Research Data.[2] These logs record executions of business processes from a variety of domains, such as healthcare, finance, government and IT service management. They are the *BPI Challenge* (BPIC) logs from 2012 to 2017, the *Road Traffic Fines Management Process* (RTFMP) log, and the *SEPSIS Cases* log.[3]

Table 2 reports the logs characteristics. These logs are widely heterogeneous ranging from simple to very complex, with a log size ranging from 681 traces (for the BPIC152f log) to 150,370 traces (for the RTFMP log). A similar variety can be observed in the percentage of distinct traces, ranging from 0.2% to 80.6% of

---

[2] https://data.4tu.nl/repository/collection:event_logs_real.
[3] Seven of these logs, namely the BPIC14 log, the five BPIC15 logs and the BPIC17 log, were filtered in [3] using the technique in [8] to remove infrequent behavior. We kept this filtering to be able to use the models associated with these logs in the benchmark dataset.

Table 2. Descriptive statistics of public logs

Evt. log	Traces		Events		Tr. length		
	Total	Dst. %	Total	Dst. %	m.	avg	M.
BPIC12	13087	33.4	262200	36	3	20	175
BPIC13$_{cp}$	1487	12.3	6660	7	1	4	35
BPIC13$_{inc}$	7554	20.0	65533	13	1	9	123
BPIC14$_f$	41353	36.1	369485	9	3	9	167
BPIC15$_{1f}$	902	32.7	21656	70	5	24	50
BPIC15$_{2f}$	681	61.7	24678	82	4	36	63
BPIC15$_{3f}$	1369	60.3	43786	62	4	32	54
BPIC15$_{4f}$	860	52.4	29403	65	5	34	54
BPIC15$_{5f}$	975	45.7	30030	74	4	31	61
BPIC17$_f$	21861	40.1	714198	41	11	33	113
RTFMP	150370	0.2	561470	11	2	4	20
SEPSIS	1050	80.6	15214	16	3	14	185

Table 3. Results of Exp. 1

Evt. log	L2L$_{sim}$	L2L$_{SMAPE}$
BPIC12	0.87	0.13
BPIC13$_{cp}$	0.85	0.20
BPIC13$_{inc}$	0.91	0.21
BPIC14$_f$	0.86	0.28
BPIC15$_{f1}$	0.89	0.22
BPIC15$_{f2}$	0.82	0.09
BPIC15$_{f3}$	0.91	0.02
BPIC15$_{f4}$	0.83	0.21
BPIC15$_{f5}$	0.94	0.02
BPIC17	0.96	0.31
RTFMP	0.96	0.32
SEPSIS	0.91	0.11

the total number of traces, and the number of event classes (i.e., the activities executed within the process), ranging from 7 to 82. Finally, the length of a trace also varies from very short, with traces containing only one event, to very long, with traces containing 185 events.

For each log, we used the process model obtained by Split Miner (SM) and Inductive Miner (IM), both with noise filtering enabled and default parameters, as per the benchmark in [3]. These two methods strike different tradeoffs between fitness and precision: IM tends to create models with higher fitness but low precision; SM tends to create smaller models with an overall higher F-Score (the harmonic mean of fitness and precision), though with lower fitness. This led to a total of 24 log-model pairs for our evaluation.

4.3   Results

Tables 3 and 4 show the results of the two experiments, respectively. From Exp. 1 we can see that using a perfectly accurate input (the distinct traces of the original log), the average loss of accuracy is only 10% (average L2L$_{sim}$ = 0.901, min = 0.82, max = 0.96). This is consistent with the events elapsed time, which is relatively low across all twelve logs (average L2L$_{SMAPE}$ = 17.6%, mix = 2%, max = 28%). Overall, these results indicate the robustness of the specific optimization technique chosen (multi-level simulated annealing), which proves to be appropriate for the problem at hand. These results were achieved by setting the initial temperature to 1,000 and the maximum number of steps to 100.

As expected, when comparing the results of the two experiments (cf. Tables 3 and 4), the logs generated in Exp. 1 using as input the distinct log traces of the original log have higher L2L$_{sim}$ and lower L2L$_{SMAPE}$ values than the logs generated in Exp. 2 using a process model as input. However, the loss in L2L$_{sim}$ between the two experiments is only 4.42% on average, barring a modest increase in L2L$_{SMAPE}$ (16.67% on average). These differences are attributable to the fact that the models used as input are not perfectly accurate. Specifically, fitness

Table 4. Results of Exp. 2 with Split Miner (SM) and Inductive Miner (IM)

Source log	SM-mined model		SM-based output log		IM-mined model		IM-based output log	
	Fitness	Precision	L2L$_{sim}$	L2L$_{SMAPE}$	Fitness	Precision	L2L$_{sim}$	L2L$_{SMAPE}$
BPIC12	0.97	0.72	0.83	0.44	0.98	0.50	0.82	0.42
BPIC13cp	0.90	0.93	0.78	0.41	0.82	1.00	0.78	0.40
BPIC13inc	0.98	0.92	0.92	0.61	0.92	0.54	0.89	0.57
BPIC14f	0.77	0.84	0.77	0.40	0.89	0.64	0.77	0.42
BPIC15f1	0.90	0.88	0.81	0.30	0.97	0.57	0.79	0.35
BPIC15f2	0.77	0.90	0.77	0.12	0.93	0.56	0.74	0.21
BPIC15f3	0.94	0.78	0.85	0.18	0.95	0.55	0.82	0.15
BPIC15f4	0.73	0.91	0.77	0.33	0.96	0.58	0.74	0.30
BPIC15f5	0.79	0.94	0.90	0.14	0.94	0.18	0.60	0.32
BPIC17	0.96	0.81	0.94	0.45	0.98	0.70	0.92	0.47
RTFMP	1.00	0.97	0.96	0.47	0.99	0.70	0.93	0.52
SEPSIS	0.76	0.77	0.89	0.27	0.99	0.45	0.72	0.40

and precision affect the L2L$_{sim}$ measure negatively. Given that in general the precision of IM is much lower than that of SM, while its fitness is slightly higher, we obtain better results both in terms of L2L$_{sim}$ and L2L$_{SMAPE}$ when using as input the models discovered by SM. For example, the precision of the SM model for BPIC15f5 is 0.94 as opposed to 0.18 in the case of IM, while the two fitness measures are much closer to each other (0.79 for SM, 0.94 for IM). A very low precision as in the case of IM for this log, provides a large number of possibilities to replay the process and thus to correlate events in ways that are different than those in the original log. In the specific case of the BPIC15f5 log, this leads to a difference of 30% in L2L$_{sim}$ between SM and IM.

Leaving aside the specific differences between SM and IM, the average L2L$_{sim}$ across all 24 model-log pairs is still relatively high (0.82), which means that in most cases we can correlate events correctly. The average L2L$_{SMAPE}$ is also relatively low (0.36), meaning that the event times in the generated log deviate by 36% on average from those of the original log. In other words, we correctly assign events to their specific cases on 64% of the cases on average.

Table 5 compares the results of the second experiment with DCI using the models generated by SM. This table also reports the time performance of the two approaches. Looking at the accuracy, we can see that EC-SA outperforms DCI in all except three logs where L2L$_{sim}$ is higher for DCI, and one log where L2L$_{SMAPE}$ is lower for DCI. In those logs where EC-SA outperforms DCI, the differences in L2L$_{sim}$ range from small to substantial increases. For example, in the case of the BPIC15f5 log, our approach's L2L$_{sim}$ is 22% higher than that of DCI. In this case, the discovered model has a fitness of 0.79. As DCI strictly depends on the process model behavior, it cannot assign the deviating events to any case, thus around 22% of the events will not be correlated and thus excluded from the generated log. EC-SA handles this problem by randomly assigning these events to one of the open cases, i.e. cases started before the event occurrence.

On the contrary, when the model has very high fitness, DCI is able to correlate all the events to their possible cases because it builds a complete representation of the solution space, which will thus include the optimal solution. On the other hand, EC-SA's degree of randomness may lead to escaping the global optimum if the number of steps set is not sufficiently high, for the model-log at hand. As a result, DCI can have a slightly higher $L2L_{sim}$ than EC-SA, as in the case of BPIC12 where the discovered model has fitness of 0.97, and DCI's $L2L_{sim}$ is 6% higher than that of EC-SA. In reality, though, we cannot assume the input model to be highly fitting. Rather, we expect this model not to be very accurate both in terms of fitness and precision, given that it would be a model created manually by process analysts through interviews and workshops (so it may be biased towards the perspective of particular process participants), and may in addition be out-of-date.

Table 5. Results of Exp. 2 with EC-SA and DCI (using the SM-mined model)

	EC-SA output (SM)			DCI output (SM)		
Source log	$L2L_{sim}$	$L2L_{SMAPE}$	Exec. [h]	$L2L_{sim}$	$L2L_{SMAPE}$	Exec. [h]
BPIC12	0.83	**0.44**	5	**0.89**	0.47	18.5
BPIC13cp	0.78	0.41	1.1	**0.81**	**0.30**	5
BPIC13inc	**0.92**	**0.61**	2.2	0.77	0.50	19
BPIC14f	**0.77**	**0.40**	2.7			>24
BPIC15f1	**0.81**	**0.30**	5.2	**0.81**	0.43	21.9
BPIC15f2	**0.77**	**0.12**	4	0.71	0.54	22.3
BPIC15f3	0.85	0.18	6	**0.89**	0.20	23.7
BPIC15f4	**0.77**	**0.33**	6	0.71	0.53	22.7
BPIC15f5	**0.90**	**0.14**	5	0.74	0.50	23.5
BPIC17	**0.94**	**0.45**	8			>24
RTFMP	**0.96**	**0.47**	7			>24
SEPSIS	**0.89**	**0.27**	1.6	0.84	0.25	17

Looking at the time performance, we can observe that DCI suffers from significant performance issues as it takes close to 20 h for the majority of logs, timing out at 24 h for three logs. Specifically, DCI takes 4× the average execution time of EC-SA. In effect, DCI requires as input extra information such as minimum, average and maximum execution time for each activity. For our evaluation, we calculated this heuristic data based on the three quartiles of the activities execution time in the original log. The quality of the DCI output is affected by the quality of its inputs. The heuristic data affects the $L2L_{SMAPE}$ and $L2L_{sim}$ because it is used to prune the various correlation possibilities assessed by the approach.

5   Conclusion

We presented a novel approach called EC-SA to address the problem of correlating events that belong to the same case. Our approach uses multi-level objective

simulated annealing for mapping each event to a case. For optimization, we use trace alignment cost and activity execution time variance. Our evaluation in terms of log-to-log similarity, symmetric mean absolute error of event elapsed times and overall time performance on a range of real-life model-log pairs shows that our approach outperforms the state of the art. A possible avenue for future work is to include the payload of uncorrelated events to improve correlation accuracy, e.g. data inputs/outputs of process activities. Another avenue for future work is to explore different forms of process knowledge as input to EC-SA, e.g., declarative rules [5].

Acknowledgements. This research is partly funded by the Australian Research Council (DP180102839) and by the EU H2020 programme under agreement 645751 (RISE_BPM).

References

1. Adriansyah, A., van Dongen, B., van der Aalst, W.: Conformance checking using cost-based fitness analysis. In: Proceedings of EDOC. IEEE (2011)
2. Askarzadeh, A., dos Santos Coelho, L., Klein, C., Mariani, V.C.: A population-based simulated annealing algorithm for global optimization. In: Proceedings of SMC. IEEE (2016)
3. Augusto, A., et al.: Automated discovery of process models from event logs: review and benchmark. IEEE TKDE **31**(4), 686–705 (2019)
4. Augusto, A., Conforti, R., Dumas, M., La Rosa, M., Polyvyanyy, A.: Split miner: automated discovery of accurate and simple business process models from event logs. Knowl. Inf. Syst. **59**(2), 251–284 (2019). https://doi.org/10.1007/s10115-018-1214-x
5. Baier, T., Di Ciccio, C., Mendling, J., Weske, M.: Matching events and activities by integrating behavioral aspects and label analysis. SoSyM **17**(2), 573–598 (2018)
6. Bala, S., Mendling, J., Schimak, M., Queteschiner, P.: Case and activity identification for mining process models from middleware. In: Buchmann, R.A., Karagiannis, D., Kirikova, M. (eds.) PoEM 2018. LNBIP, vol. 335, pp. 86–102. Springer, Cham (2018). https://doi.org/10.1007/978-3-030-02302-7_6
7. Bayomie, D., Awad, A., Ezat, E.: Correlating unlabeled events from cyclic business processes execution. In: Nurcan, S., Soffer, P., Bajec, M., Eder, J. (eds.) CAiSE 2016. LNCS, vol. 9694, pp. 274–289. Springer, Cham (2016). https://doi.org/10.1007/978-3-319-39696-5_17
8. Conforti, R., La Rosa, M., ter Hofstede, A.: Filtering out infrequent behavior from business process event logs. IEEE TKDE **29**(2), 300–314 (2017)
9. Ferreira, D.R., Gillblad, D.: Discovering process models from unlabelled event logs. In: Dayal, U., Eder, J., Koehler, J., Reijers, H.A. (eds.) BPM 2009. LNCS, vol. 5701, pp. 143–158. Springer, Heidelberg (2009). https://doi.org/10.1007/978-3-642-03848-8_11
10. Leemans, S.J.J., Fahland, D., van der Aalst, W.M.P.: Discovering block-structured process models from event logs containing infrequent behaviour. In: Lohmann, N., Song, M., Wohed, P. (eds.) BPM 2013. LNBIP, vol. 171, pp. 66–78. Springer, Cham (2014). https://doi.org/10.1007/978-3-319-06257-0_6

11. Meroni, G., Di Ciccio, C., Mendling, J.: An artifact-driven approach to monitor business processes through real-world objects. In: Maximilien, M., Vallecillo, A., Wang, J., Oriol, M. (eds.) ICSOC 2017. LNCS, vol. 10601, pp. 297–313. Springer, Cham (2017). https://doi.org/10.1007/978-3-319-69035-3_21

12. Navarro, G.: A guided tour to approximate string matching. ACM Comput. Surv. **33**(1), 31–88 (2001)

13. Nezhad, H., Saint-Paul, R., Casati, F., Benatallah, B.: Event correlation for process discovery from web service interaction logs. VLDB J. **20**(3), 417–444 (2011)

14. Pourmirza, S., Dijkman, R., Grefen, P.: Correlation miner: mining business process models and event correlations without case identifiers. IJCIS **26**(02), 1742002 (2017)

15. Reguieg, H., Toumani, F., Motahari-Nezhad, H.R., Benatallah, B.: Using Mapreduce to scale events correlation discovery for business processes mining. In: Barros, A., Gal, A., Kindler, E. (eds.) BPM 2012. LNCS, vol. 7481, pp. 279–284. Springer, Heidelberg (2012). https://doi.org/10.1007/978-3-642-32885-5_22

16. Soffer, P., Hinze, A., Koschmider, A., Ziekow, H., et al.: From event streams to process models and back: challenges and opportunities. Inf. Syst. **81**, 181–200 (2019)

17. van der Aalst, W.: Process Mining - Data Science in Action, 2nd edn. Springer, Heidelberg (2016). https://doi.org/10.1007/978-3-662-49851-4

18. Walicki, M., Ferreira, D.: Sequence partitioning for process mining with unlabeled event logs. DKE **70**(10), 821–841 (2011)

DCR-KiPN a Hybrid Modeling Approach for Knowledge-Intensive Processes

Flávia Santoro[1][✉], Tijs Slaats[2], Thomas T. Hildebrandt[2], and Fernanda Baiao[3]

[1] University of the State of Rio de Janeiro, Rio de Janeiro, Brazil
flavia@ime.uerj.br
[2] University of Copenhagen, Copenhagen, Denmark
{slaats,hilde}@di.ku.dk
[3] Pontifical Catholic University of Rio de Janeiro, Rio de Janeiro, Brazil
fbaiao@inf.puc-rio.br

Abstract. Hybrid modeling approaches have been proposed to represent processes that have both strictly regulated parts and loosely regulated parts. Such process is so-called Knowledge-intensive Process (KiP), which is a sequence of activities based on intense knowledge use and acquisition. Due to these very particular characteristics, the first author previously proposed the Knowledge-intensive Process Ontology (KiPO) and its subjacent notation (KiPN). However, KiPN still fails to represent the declarative perspective of a KiP. Therefore, in this paper, we propose to improve KiPN by integrating it with the declarative process modeling language DCR Graphs. DCR-KiPN is a hybrid process modeling notation that combines a declarative process model language (activities and business rules) with the main aspects of a KiP, such as cognitive elements (decision rationale towards goals, beliefs, desires and intentions), interactions and knowledge-exchange among its participants.

Keywords: Knowledge-intensive Process · Hybrid process notation

1 Introduction

Process models are typically represented using visual notations founded on well-established metamodels that define constructs of the language and structural rules among them. Notations comprise a set of graphical diagrams and symbols constrained by those rules. Such symbols and rules should ideally be enough for expressing important aspects of the business processes, both completely and correctly. Popular visual notations for modeling business processes include the industry standard Business Process Modeling Notation (BPMN), which focuses on the representation of (imperative) structured control-flow oriented processes.

When it comes to flexible processes (whose control flow is not rigid), other modeling approaches, such as declarative (constraint-based) notations, focus on what "can" be done rather than on what "should" be done. Declare [11] and

© Springer Nature Switzerland AG 2019
A. H. F. Laender et al. (Eds.): ER 2019, LNCS 11788, pp. 153–161, 2019.
https://doi.org/10.1007/978-3-030-33223-5_13

DCR Graphs [5] are examples of declarative modeling languages that support a higher degree of flexibility in business process modeling. However, many processes in real life are neither totally unstructured nor ad-doc; thus, hybrid modeling approaches [2,10,13] have been proposed to address such processes. Many examples of such scenarios are classified as a Knowledge-intensive Process (KiP).

A KiP is a sequence of activities based on intense knowledge use and acquisition. It is dynamic, lack a predefined control-flow, and is highly dependent on the experience and knowledge of stakeholders [1]. Due to these very particular characteristics, Franca et al. [12] proposed an ontology for the definition of KiP, the Knowledge-intensive Process Ontology (KiPO). Based on this metamodel, Netto et al. [9] developed the Knowledge-intensive Process Notation (KiPN). The original metamodel was extended to incorporate constructs related to declarative constraints [6], but the notation was not properly updated.

We investigate how to represent the integration of the main components of KiPO using a declarative paradigm in KiPN. This is the classic problem of how to define a hybrid modeling approach that combines flexibility with constraints in a process model, but more than this, including many other elements that cannot be represented in one single diagram. From the other side, DCR Graphs is a declarative approach for flexible business process modeling in which both the constrains as well as the run time state can be visualized and also it allows an effective process execution [5]. So, we argue that bringing together DCR Graphs and KiPN addresses the problem of hybrid modeling in the context of KiP.

The goal of this paper is to discuss the conceptual modeling of KiP and present DCR-KiPN which is a hybrid process modeling notation that combines a declarative process model language (activities and business rules) with the main aspects of a KiP (decision rationale towards goals, beliefs, desires and intentions, interactions and knowledge-exchange). Our main contribution is advancing the potential understanding of KiPs by providing the foundations for a rich conceptual modeling approach.

2 Preliminaries

2.1 Running Example

We use a knowledge-intensive process example from the literature to illustrate the problem and the proposal, as well as to serve as a preliminary evaluation. Vaculin et al. [14] described the "Solution Builder" (SB) application that supports supply chain teams "to simplify, streamline, and standardize idea to market deployment of cross-brand solutions". The process behind this application is related to the complex development of a new solution involving team members working collaboratively to understand the structure, requirements, and constraints of the solution. The outcome - a Prescribed Action Course (PCA) - consists of parameterized actions to enable the solution. To create a PCA, many parameters and issues need to be considered and, depending on the nature of the solution, different sets of decisions need to be made. The basic process (Question-Answer - QA) is to respond to questions formulated by the SB, previously mod-

eled as individual elements of knowledge. Usually, answering a question requires research, and moreover, an answer can be reworked, postponed or committed.

This is a typical KiP scenario that presents the challenges of modeling not only the tasks to be done (answer questions) but also the decisions (which could be based on rules). Since the decisions are dependent on the participant expertise, each instance might take different paths. For example, one expert could opt to delay an answer in order to start a research about the topic, and this could add a non-expected delay to that process instance. In order to have a complete understanding of the process, it is also necessary to represent the interactions among the participants, the cognitive aspects and alternatives they consider.

2.2   Modeling Knowledge-Intensive Processes

KIPs encompass various interconnected knowledge-intensive decision making tasks conducted by human workers [1]. Some examples of KiPs are customer support, design of new products/services, and IT governance [7]. An important aspect of a KiP is the large number of exceptions that can occur in different instances. Franca et al. [12] proposed the KiPO, a metamodel to define KiP concepts formalized in an ontology well-founded in UFO [4]. KiPO [12] contemplates the various perspectives of a KiP, especially related to cognitive aspects, business rules, decision making and collaboration. Moreover, Netto et al. [9] presented its subjacent notation (KiPN) which stands for the graphical representation of the KiPO elements. KiPN is a visual syntax (graphic vocabulary and grammar rules) that comprises a set of 6 interrelated diagrams, which in turn are composed by symbols that altogether represent the main perspectives of a KiP.

KiP Diagram is the main diagram, which aims to provide an overview of the process by showing its activities and goal. Unlike a BPMN representation, there is no predefined order of execution for the activities. Business Rules Diagram documents the constraints that, in normal circumstances, should be considered in a decision-making task. The purpose of this diagram is to visualize the business rules considered in each alternative. Socialization Diagram represents aspects of collaboration and knowledge exchange among agents. Decision Map describes the decision-making dynamics, allowing the visualization of the rationale that leads to a decision. Agent Matrix maps the skills and experience of the agents. Intention Panel depicts the intrinsic characteristics of agents which might influence the main activities and goals of the process, such as, desires that motivate agents to act, beliefs and feelings when participating in a socialization or decision.

KiPO was recently extended by Lyrio [6] who introduced the concepts of Linear-time Temporal Logic (LTL) Declare templates. Moreover, the characteristic of unpredictability in KiP can lead to the violation of constraints. These violations should be represented, so that they could be managed. Levels of enforcement assign a minimum degree of compliance to be respected by process agents. The enforcement level (EL) of a business rule is defined at design time (Conceived EL) but violations are only identified at runtime (Perceived EL). Up to now, KiPN did not provide elements to model such concepts.

2.3 Modeling Declarative Processes with DCR Graphs

The theory of Dynamic Condition Response (DCR) Graphs [5] was developed independently from the notation Declare, sharing inspiration from LTL and the early work on declarative constraint patterns used for formal verification [8]. DCR Graphs offer several advantages: (1) provides a clear notation of state of the process as it is executed, (2) uses only a handful of basic relations (constraints and effects), (3) provides strong formal expressiveness results [3].

Figure 1 shows an example of a DCR Graph for the QA process. The boxes in the diagram represent the (completion of) activities of the process, the bottom part contains the name of the activity, the top bar may contain a number of executing roles. DCR Graphs support 5 basic relations between activities: condition, response, milestone, exclusion and inclusion. The *condition relation*, indicated in orange with a bullet at the target, represents that the activities Rework answer and Commit Answer cannot execute before the activity Answer question has been done. Condition relations may also have an associated *delay* depicted by a number next to the arrow, in the example, Commit Answer can only happen at least 3 days after the last execution of Answer question, i.e. leaving time to do more research and possibly decide to rework the answer.

The *response relation*, indicated in blue with a bullet at the source, indicates that the execution of activity Answer question requires the activity Commit Answer to happen at some later time. Responses are not immediate and should not be confused with the notion of flow: we may wait with committing the answer, and execute any other enabled activity in the meantime. The *exclusion relation*, indicated in red and with a % sign at the target, represents that when the activity at the source is executed, the activity at the target is excluded from the process. In the example, this means that when Answer question is executed, Postpone answer is excluded, and when Commit Answer is executed, Do research, Rework answer and Answer question are excluded. Dually, the *inclusion relation*, indicated in green and with a + sign at the target, indicates that the activity at the target is included when the activity at the source is executed. So, after deciding to rework the answer, the postpone activity is included again.

Boxes also carry a marking consisting of three parts indicating a state of each activity. The first part is if an activity has been executed (and how long ago) - indicated with a green check mark. The second part is if the activity is a pending response, required to happen in the future (and possibly a deadline for when) - marked with a blue exclamation mark. The third part is if it is currently included in the process - indicated by marking excluded (not included) with a dashed border.

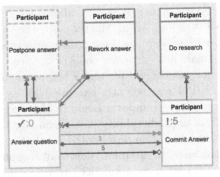

Fig. 1. Marking of timed DCR Graph after the execution of Answer question. (Color figure online)

3   DCR-KiPN

DCR-KiPN is a hybrid notation to represent the dynamic aspect of KiP. DCR graphs provide the representation of flexible execution of tasks in a dynamic way, in which we add violations and their respective enforcement levels. KiPN brings the diverse perspectives of KiP, then, composing the hybrid model.

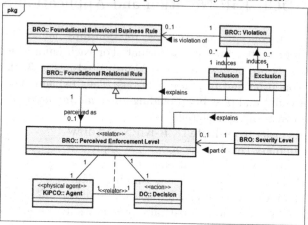

The perception of a business rule by an Agent occurs during the analysis of the alternatives in the decision-making process [6], i.e., the Agent perceives the business rule through the consent of its compliance level. The Perceived EL of a rule in a decision-making represents the consensus among all the agents who participated in the action. The individual perceptions of the agents are represented by the Feelings or Beliefs that influence the decision. The event that might cause the rule violation is unpredictable and, therefore, cannot be described in a process model. This does not however exempt it from being represented to provide a better understanding of what happened in a specific instance. The violation of a business rule occurs when, during the execution of a process instance, it is no longer possible for the rule to be satisfied. E.g. a rule given by a condition relation is violated if the activity at the target of the relation is executed before the activity at the source. While violation of condition relations can be immediately detected, it is not possible to determine that a response relation is violated in finite time. A violation of a response relation with a time deadline can, however, be detected.

Fig. 2. Extended metamodel

DCR graph allows events to run multiple times. The conflict relation is generalized to two relations of dynamic exclusion and inclusion of events. This ensures that the dynamic characteristic of a KiP will be explicit in the model because events can be re-executed and skipped, as well as constraints can be re-defined for specific cases. The most important is the representation of such possibilities. In this sense, the proposed incorporation of DCR Graphs as the main KiPN diagram presents two requirements: 1. Extension of the KiPO to incorporate the inclusion and exclusion relations and the concepts of Enforcement Levels for conditions and responses; and, 2. Extension of DCR Graphs notation to represent EL on conditions and responses. We modified KiPO by adding the Classes Include and Exclude as the concepts formally defined in [5]. As we will see in the next section, sometimes, the Classes Include and Exclude, when dynamically

instantiated in a running case of a process by adding or excluding events, shows a Decision made by the Agent, which implies in a Perceived EL. Thus, making inclusions and exclusions explicit provides an enhanced understanding of the decision made and its consequences. Figure 2 depicts KiPO extension.

4   DCR-KiP Notation and Application Scenario

The EL concepts and the new relationships defined in the metamodel should be represented in a visual format. For each enforcement level adopted in the ontology, we propose an icon, as presented in Fig. 3, that is added to modifiers on condition and response relations. They explain the enforcement level of the constraint and possibly providing an *escalation activity* to be carried out in case the constraint is violated.

In order to evaluate DCR-KiPN and draw preliminary conclusions about how representative the extended notation is, we have modeled the KiP scenario of our running example and we discuss its advantages and limitations. Figure 4 shows a partial representation of this scenario, showing the representation of posting and answering questions.

EL	Description	Symbol DCR-KiPN
Strict	If the rule is violated, a penalty is applied	⊘ (red)
Deferred	It is strict but its fulfillment may be delayed	⊘ (purple)
Pre-authorized	Exceptions are allowed only if pre-approved	⊘ (gray)
Post-justified	Exceptions are allowed if justified after the event	⊘ (brown)
Override	A comment should be provided if the rule violation occurs	⊘ (yellow)
Guideline	Just a suggestion	⊘ (green)

Fig. 3. Representation of EL

After a question is posted, it should be answered within the deadline of 14 days. However, two of the possible violations are allowed in the model: either the answer can be postponed before the deadline passes (but still the answer is required eventually) or the deadline can be violated and subsequently justified.

The behaviour of this example can in fact be encoded as the plain timed DCR graph in Fig. 5. While the latter can be executed directly by the current DCR tools (e.g. https://dcrgraphs.net), the former is likely easier to understand by an end-user.

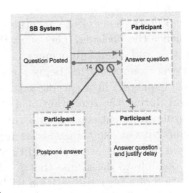

Fig. 4. Example DCR graph with violations and enforcement levels

4.1   Discussion

This proposal aims at using all the representativeness that KiPN offers to model a KiP allied to the possibility of representing the dynamics of a running process embedded in a process model, i.e., choosing the next activity to be performed even if the agent has to "break a business rule", which is in fact the reality of such type of processes. This hybrid language integrates the declarative paradigm with all the other elements and diagrams that compose the KiPN. Consequently, in our running example, it would be possible to model the beliefs, desires and

intentions associated to the respondent (the innovation agent) as shown in Fig. 6, the Intention Panel of KiPN.

The process of answering a question involves decisions that leads the respondent, for example, to rework on his/her initial solution for the problem. In this case, he/she will do some research as many times as he/she finds necessary to provide ground for his/her activity. The Decision Map Diagram supports the representation of his/her rationale, as in Fig. 7. The decision on how to answer a question is an important element of this KiP. Thus, when we look at the diagrams of Figs. 4 and 5, we can see the paths chosen to execute a task related to the

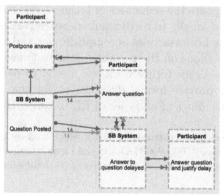

Fig. 5. Encoding of violations and EL

business rules, and the impact on the process, but the diagrams in Figs. 6 and 7 enhance our understanding of the domain by making explicit the knowledge involved and the cognitive rationale of the participants.

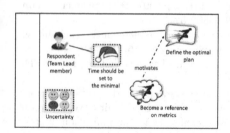

Fig. 6. Intention panel for QA process

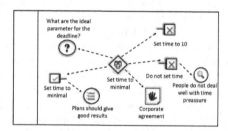

Fig. 7. Decision map for QA process

Furthermore, the Business Rules diagram of KiPN may be replaced by the extended DCR Graphs. The integration in terms of metamodel opens opportunities to explore the different views in many scenarios.

5 Conclusion

The paper motivates and outlines the integration of KiPN, which is a rich notation for KiP, and the declarative modeling language of timed DCR Graphs. The aim was to fill a gap of a proper way to capture the essence of the fulfillment and violation of business rules in a KiP, which stands for its real dynamics, but still allowing the integrated representation of the diverse concepts that supports

KiP understanding. Our main contribution is on adding to the body of knowledge of the conceptual modeling of knowledge-intensive processes to formally capture the semantics of business rule enforcement and violation. We contribute specifically to its dynamic perspective and to the visualization of the impacts of the business rules accomplishment and violation by the agents while they make decisions on the possible paths to follow.

As for future work, we intend to perform case studies in real scenarios and to provide formal descriptions for the solution proposed, in particular formal encodings of all types of EL to timed DCR graphs.

Acknowledgments. Work supported by the Innovation Fund Denmark project *Eco-Know* (7050-00034A) and the Danish Council for Independent Research project *Hybrid Business Process Management Technologies* (DFF-6111-00337).

References

1. Ciccio, C.D., Marrella, A., Russo, A.: Knowledge-intensive processes: characteristics, requirements and analysis of contemporary approaches. J. Data Semant. 4(1), 29–57 (2015)
2. Debois, S., Hildebrandt, T., Marquard, M., Slaats, T.: Hybrid process technologies in the financial sector: the case of BRFkredit. In: vom Brocke, J., Mendling, J. (eds.) Business Process Management Cases. MP, pp. 397–412. Springer, Cham (2018). https://doi.org/10.1007/978-3-319-58307-5_21
3. Debois, S., Hildebrandt, T.T., Slaats, T.: Replication, refinement & reachability: complexity in dynamic condition-response graphs. Acta Inf. 55(6), 489–520 (2018)
4. Guizzardi, G.: Ontological foundations for structural conceptual models. Ph.D. thesis, University of Twente, October 2005
5. Hildebrandt, T.T., Mukkamala, R.R.: Declarative event-based workflow as distributed dynamic condition response graphs. In: Proceedings Third Workshop on Programming Language Approaches to Concurrency and communication-cEntric Software, PLACES, pp. 59–73 (2010)
6. Lyrio, R.: DecKiPO: Extending the semantic expressivity of the business rules representation in knowledge-intensive processes scenarios. Master's thesis, UNIRIO, (in Portuguese) (2018)
7. Marjanovic, O., Freeze, R.D.: Knowledge intensive business processes: theoretical foundations and research challenges. In: 44th Hawaii International International Conference on Systems Science, HICSS-44 2011, pp. 1–10 (2011)
8. Dwyer, M.B., Avrunin, G.S., Corbett, J.C.: Property specification patterns for finite-state verification. In: 2nd Workshop on Formal Methods in Software Practice, March 1998
9. Netto, J.M., Barboza, T., Baião, F.A., Santoro, F.M.: KiPN a visual notation for knowledge-intensive processes. Int. J. Bus. Process Integr. Manage. (IJBPIM) 9(3), 197–219 (2019). X(Y4), 000–000
10. Parody, L., López, M.T.G., Gasca, R.M.: Hybrid business process modeling for the optimization of outcome data. Inf. Softw. Technol. 70, 140–154 (2016)
11. Pesic, M., van der Aalst, W.M.P.: A declarative approach for flexible business processes management. In: Business Process Management Workshops, BPM, pp. 169–180 (2006)

12. dos Santos França, J.B., Netto, J.M., do E Santo Carvalho, J., Santoro, F.M., Baião, F.A., Pimentel, M.G.: KIPO the knowledge-intensive process ontology. Softw. Syst. Model. **14**(3), 1127–1157 (2015)
13. Slaats, T., Schunselaar, D.M.M., Maggi, F.M., Reijers, H.A.: The semantics of hybrid process models. In: On the Move to Meaningful Internet Systems: OTM, pp. 531–551 (2016)
14. Vaculín, R., Hull, R., Heath, T., Cochran, C., Nigam, A., Sukaviriya, P.: Declarative business artifact centric modeling of decision and knowledge intensive business processes. In: Proceedings of the 15th IEEE International Enterprise Distributed Object Computing Conference, EDOC 2011, Helsinki, Finland, 29 August–2 September 2011, pp. 151–160 (2011)

Exploring the Modeling of Declarative Processes Using a Hybrid Approach

Amine Abbad Andaloussi[1]([✉]), Jon Buch-Lorentsen[1], Hugo A. López[2,5],
Tijs Slaats[3], and Barbara Weber[1,4]

[1] Software and Process Engineering, Technical University of Denmark,
2800 Kongens Lyngby, Denmark
amab@dtu.dk
[2] Department of Computer Science, IT University of Copenhagen,
Copenhagen, Denmark
[3] Department of Computer Science, University of Copenhagen,
Copenhagen, Denmark
[4] Institute of Computer Science, University of St. Gallen,
St. Gallen, Switzerland
[5] DCR Solutions A/S, Copenhagen, Denmark

Abstract. Process modeling aims at providing an external representation of a business process in the shape of a process model. The complexity of the modeling language, the usability of the modeling tool, and the expertise of the modeler are among the key factors defining the difficulty of a modeling task. Following a qualitative analysis approach, this work explores a hybrid modeling technique enhanced with a tool (i.e., the Highlighter) to guide the transition from informal text-based process descriptions to formal declarative process models. The exploratory results suggest that this technique provides cognitive support to modelers and hint towards an enhanced quality of process models in terms of alignment, traceability of process requirements and availability of documentation. The outcome of this work shows a clear opportunity for future work and provides a framework for further empirical studies.

1 Introduction

A process model is a visual/graphical representation of the different components of a business process, as well as their interrelations. The full understanding of a process tends to be a joint construction between different process design artifacts (process artifacts for short), including the business process model. In this paper, we examine an approach used to relate textual process artifacts and business process models during the Process of Process Modeling (PPM for short). This

Work supported by the Innovation Fund Denmark project *EcoKnow* (7050-00034A), the Danish Council for Independent Research project *Hybrid Business Process Management Technologies* (DFF-6111-00337), and the European Union's Horizon 2020 research and innovation programme under the Marie Sklodowska-Curie grant agreement BehAPI No. 778233.

A. H. F. Laender et al. (Eds.): ER 2019, LNCS 11788, pp. 162–170, 2019.
https://doi.org/10.1007/978-3-030-33223-5_14

process is regarded as a "design activity" where a modeler develops an internal representation of the business process and externalizes it through one or many process artifacts [3]. Throughout this process, three levels of cognitive load are induced. *(1)* Intrinsic load is associated with the complexity of the material being processed, while *(2)* extraneous load is rising from the unnecessary representational complexity of the task. *(3)* Germane load, in turn, is associated with the effort invested in building an appropriate scheme to organize new information efficiently [5]. During a modeling session, intrinsic load emerges from the complexity of inferring a mental model from a set of process specifications. Extraneous load raises from the formulation of the textual process description and the complexity of the modeling tool. While intrinsic load is inherent to the task and thus unavoidable, efforts can be made to reduce the extraneous load by improving the quality of the tool-support and enhancing the PPM experience.

When considering the declarative modeling paradigm, the requirement for lowering extraneous load in favor of extra intrinsic processing becomes more stringent. This is due to the understandability of declarative languages, which is shown to be controversial especially for novice end-users [8]. A hybrid modeling approach can, in turn, be used to facilitate the modeling of declarative business processes and provide additional channels to support the PPM through a set of interrelated process artifacts. In this vein, the Highlighter [11] was introduced.

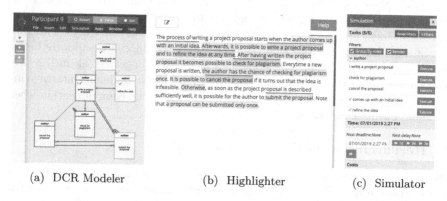

(a) DCR Modeler   (b) Highlighter   (c) Simulator

Fig. 1. A hybrid process artifact combining the Modeler, the Highlighter and the simulation tools. Available online as part of the DCR platform at https://dcrgraphs.net/

The Highlighter (cf. Fig. 1b) is integrated with the default Dynamic Condition Response (DCR [10]) graphical modeling tool (shortly, the Modeler, cf. Fig. 1a) and a guided simulation (cf. Fig. 1c). The tool displays a process model and an annotatable textual description side-by-side allowing to map the specifications in the textual process description with the corresponding model elements (i.e., activities, roles and relations). During a typical modeling session, end-users can design process models by highlighting activities, roles and relations in the

process description, then intertwine with the Modeler and the guided simulation to reconcile and validate the process model. Following a qualitative research approach, this work aims at exploring the understandability of such a hybrid process artifact. The remainder of this paper is organized as follows. Section 2 provides an overview of the existing hybrid process artifacts. Section 3 explains the research method. Section 4 reports the obtained findings. Section 5 provides a discussion, while Sect. 6 wraps up the key findings and presents future work.

2   Background and Related Work

Hybrid process representations are introduced in the literature in two contexts: *(a)* to designate hybrid languages (e.g., [14]) or *(b)* to describe hybrid process artifacts. While hybrid languages combine existing languages to enable a concise and precise representation of business processes, hybrid process artifacts combine two or more process artifacts overlapping in the description of some aspects of the business process [1]. The emergence of hybrid process artifacts is driven by three main motivations: *(1)* supporting the understandability of process models (cf., [1,2]), *(2)* enhancing the maintainability of process models (cf., [16]), and *(3)* improving the modeling of business processes.

Similar to this work, Dengler and Denny, in [7], propose a hybrid process artifact that combines process models and textual descriptions, embedded in a wiki-based platform. The proposed representation aims at improving the PPM experience by enabling different stakeholders to extract process knowledge and to express business processes using both formal and informal constructs. The findings of a qualitative analysis show that the proposed approach supports better knowledge elicitation. With the same idea in mind, Pinggera et al. in [12] propose the Literate Process Modeling (LiProMo) approach aiming at interweaving annotations and graphical process models to enhance the communication when modeling business processes.

3   Research Method

This section introduces the research questions, presents the subjects who took part in this study, describes the material and the procedure followed to run the study and explains the approach used to analyze the collected data.

Research Questions: The Highlighter aims at enhancing the PPM experience by providing a tool-support allowing to facilitate the transition from a textual process description to a graphical process model. In order to investigate this support, it is necessary to understand the way the Highlighter is used in practice. To this end, the first research question is formulated as follows: **RQ1: How do users engage with a modeling task using the Process Highlighter?**

By enhancing the PPM experience, the Highlighter is expected to positively affect the perceived quality of the produced models. To explore this angle, the second research question is formulated as follows: **RQ2: In what aspects can the Highlighter help to improve the quality of process models?**

Participants. The participants who took part in this study included novice subjects from industrial and education environments. In the former, 7 employees from the Syddjurs municipality in Denmark, and from the latter, 10 students from the Technical University of Denmark (DTU).

Material. The material used to conduct this study originates from a process introduced by Reichert and Weber in [13, p. 349]. This process describes the writing of a project proposal. The material was presented in Danish at Syddjurs municipality and in English at DTU. A copy of the material is available online at http://andaloussi.org/papers/ER2019/material.pdf.

Procedure. The study was conducted in both Syddjurs municipality and DTU. Participants were introduced to the modeling notation and the use of the Highlighter in both locations. Then, participants were given a familiarization task on PPM using the tool and the notation. Next, the participants were given the description of the *project proposal* process and were asked to use the Highlighter to derive the corresponding process model.

We collected participant's insights about their experience with the tool from retrospective think-aloud sessions.

Analysis Approach. In order to address our research questions, two different analyses have been performed. At the first stage, we have extracted the interactions of the users with the DCR modeling platform. This data were filtered to keep only the interactions associated with adding activities, roles and relations. Next, these interactions were split between those using the Highlighter, and those using the Modeler. During the analysis, the interactions were aggregated over all the modeling sessions and projected according to their time-occurrence into a rhythm eye chart [9]. An example of such a visualization is shown in Fig. 2. The ring structure represents a time-line, the different percentages refer to the progress in relative time. Events (i.e., interactions) are projected as thin lines onto the ring and events of similar type (e.g., interaction with the Highlighter) are depicted with the same color. Besides the user interactions, the collected verbal data were transcribed and analyzed following a qualitative coding approach based on concepts from grounded theory [6].

4   Findings

This section reports the findings. Section 4.1 scrutinizes the way users engage with a modeling task using the Highlighter. Section 4.2 explores whether the proposed hybrid modeling approach can improve the quality of process models.

4.1 How Do Users Engage with a Modeling Task Using the Process Highlighter? (RQ1)

The users' interactions collected throughout the modeling sessions provide deepened insights into the way end-users engaged with the Highlighter. As shown in Fig. 2, most of the interactions with the Highlighter occurred during the first quarter of the modeling session, which in turn, suggests that most end-users initiated the modeling using the Highlighter and then progressively moved to the Modeler. To further substantiate this modeling pattern, the users' interactions were scrutinized to identify the common interactions within each of the process artifacts. As shown in Fig. 3a, a larger portion of activities were appended to the model using the Highlighter. Similarly, Fig. 3b shows that most roles were added using the Highlighter. Unlike activities and roles, Fig. 3c shows that relations were mostly added using the Modeler, which in turn suggests that the Highlighter was not extensively used to add relations. These users' interactions come in line with the subjective insights provided by the participants during the think-aloud. Indeed, most participants affirmed using the Highlighter to identify activities and roles from the process description and resort to the Modeler to add relations. These insights raise the following questions: *(1) Why is the Highlighter perceived more efficient to identify and add activities and roles? (2) What makes the use of the Modeler tool more attractive for adding relations to the model?*

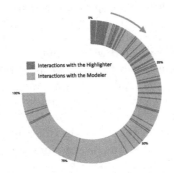

Fig. 2. The interactions associated with the Highlighter and the Modeler tool.

To answer both questions, we turn to the qualitative coding of the verbal data. In respect to *(1)*, the participants mentioned that the tool provides a kickstart to process modeling and helps in developing an overview of the business process (e.g., *"Definitely, I think it is way easier to use the Highlighter to create the activities and it gives a better overview"*). Moreover, some participants have associated the use of the Highlighter with its ability to provide structure and to decompose the complexity of the process description (e.g., *"it is* [referring to the Highlighter] *a nice way to structure the text"*). Other participants mentioned that the Highlighter can help to memorize the process specifications and to draw attention to specific fragments of the process description (e.g., *"It was faster that*

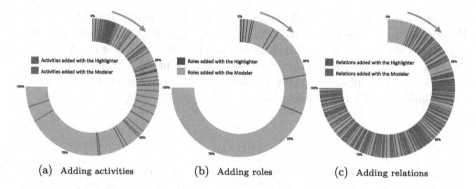

(a) Adding activities (b) Adding roles (c) Adding relations

Fig. 3. Interactions associated with adding activities, roles and relations.

was the main focus. at least I feel that [it] *helps speed things up. I did not really notice that text was highlighted because I already knew what I had highlighted myself, so I mainly focused on the relations that could be between them"*).

In respect to *(2)*, while the identification of activities and roles was straightforward for most participants, many of them faced difficulty when trying to add relations in the Highlighter. Some participants justified their abstention with the argument that the Modeler tool provides a two-dimensional visualization allowing to perceive the interplay between the different activities (e.g., *"It just seemed easier once the visual aspect of the activities were done, then you could just connect them directly"*). In addition, some participants struggled to locate the exact textual fragment referring explicitly to a specific constraint in the process description. This struggle might be due to the phrasing of the process description (e.g., *"For the relations, I'm not sure it's the problem of the Highlighter or on the formulation of the text"*). Unlike activities and roles which are often explicit in the process description, relations may not be always explicit in the text.

4.2 In What Aspects Can the Highlighter Help to Improve the Quality of Process Models? (RQ2)

From the think-aloud, it has emerged that the mapping between the process model and the process description supports better traceability of the process specification (e.g., *"Using the Highlighter makes sense in the sense that it adds traceability ... it helped me map the relations to the requirements"*) and enables a wider coverage of the requirements in the process description (e.g., *"It would be useful after and it is also useful during because I can see whether I already covered some piece of text"*). In addition, the participants' quotes indicate that the Highlighter was used to check the alignment between the process description and the process model (e.g., *"It* [referring to the Highlighter] *becomes indispensable as a method to verify whether the process fits with what has been described"*[1]).

---

[1] Quote translated from Danish.

Last but not least, some participants emphasized the importance of using the Highlighter as a mans to document their process models (e.g., *"I think it is very useful as a documentation tool and documentation can also be very useful during the process"*). Indeed, the explicit links between the process model and the textual process description can serve for documenting the semantics of the model and enabling modelers to justify their modeling choices [12].

5   Discussion

The findings of this exploratory study provide several indications about the perceived benefits of the Highlighter. Both the subjective insights obtained from the participants and the user interactions extracted from the modeling platform show that the Highlighter was perceived more efficient to identify and append activities and roles to the model. These insights fall in line with the conclusions drawn from cognitive psychology. Indeed the use of the Highlighter to mark-up specific fragments of the process description (e.g., activities, roles) can be associated with a well-known phenomenon referred in cognitive psychology as the *isolation effect* [15]. This effect is shown to increase the reader attention on specific parts of the text and help memorizing them [4,15]. This, in turn, can potentially explain the participants' insights related to the increased memory and attention when using the Highlighter and to some extent support the other insights about the ability of the Highlighter to provide overview and structure as well as to reduce the complexity of the process description (cf. Sect. 4.1). In addition to that, the quotes of several participants indicate that the Highlighter can support increased traceability, enhanced coverage and better alignment between the process model and the corresponding process description. However, when it gets to identify relations in the model, the Highlighter was challenging. As mentioned in Sect. 4.1, This challenge is associated with the difficulty in identifying the right text reflecting a certain constraint in the process model, which can be due to the phrasing of the process description.

All these insights provide indications about the extraneous load arising from using the tool. Indeed, the cognitive support provided by the Highlighter can reduce the complexity of the modeling task and contribute to an enhanced PPM experience. However, the implicitness of some constraints in the process description can add an extra layer of complexity when trying to map them to DCR relations, which in turn can induce a higher extraneous load. Hence, the use of the Highlighter can be presumably more effective with process descriptions comprising explicit constraints.

Finally, it has to be noted that the outcome of this exploratory work can be subject to limitations mainly with regards to the number of participants who participated in the study. Therefore, it is hard to generalize the reported findings and draw strong conclusions about the use of hybrid process artifacts in general and the Highlighter in particular. Nevertheless, the outcome of this work provides interesting insights emerging from the users' experience and sheds light on the direction of subsequent empirical investigations.

6   Conclusion and Future Work

This work summarizes the findings of an exploratory study investigating the modeling of DCR graphs with the support of the Highlighter. The results suggest that the use of the Highlighter is associated with increased support in PPM and hints toward an enhanced quality of process models. The outcome of this study provides strong indications for the direction of future work. Based on the conclusions drawn from cognitive psychology, we hypothesize that *(a)* the Highlighter reduces the cognitive load induced during a modeling task. Moreover, following the insights about the explicit mapping between the process specifications and the corresponding model elements we hypothesize that *(b)* the Highlighter improves model comprehension and clarifies the semantics of the model. Concerning the quality of process models, we hypothesize that *(c)* the Highlighter provides better alignment between the process description and the process model and enables covering the majority of the requirements mentioned in the text.

These hypotheses define our direction for future work. Following a quantitative analysis approach, we are planning a series of experiments to test and validate each of these hypotheses in controlled experimental settings. Moreover, it would be worth to investigate in the up-coming studies the support offered by the Highlighter when integrated with other process modeling languages from both the declarative and the imperative paradigms. The findings will serve as a basis to validate the usability of the Highlighter and will help to improve the design of similar hybrid process artifacts.

References

1. Abbad Andaloussi, A., Burattin, A., Slaats, T., Petersen, A.C.M., Hildebrandt, T.T., Weber, B.: Exploring the understandability of a hybrid process design artifact based on DCR graphs. In: Reinhartz-Berger, I., Zdravkovic, J., Gulden, J., Schmidt, R. (eds.) BPMDS/EMMSAD -2019. LNBIP, vol. 352, pp. 69–84. Springer, Cham (2019). https://doi.org/10.1007/978-3-030-20618-5_5
2. Abbad Andaloussi, A., Slaats, T., Burattin, A., Hildebrandt, T.T., Weber, B.: Evaluating the understandability of hybrid process model representations using eye tracking: first insights. In: Daniel, F., Sheng, Q.Z., Motahari, H. (eds.) BPM 2018. LNBIP, vol. 342, pp. 475–481. Springer, Cham (2019). https://doi.org/10.1007/978-3-030-11641-5_37
3. Burattin, A., et al.: Who Is behind the model? Classifying modelers based on pragmatic model features. In: Weske, M., Montali, M., Weber, I., vom Brocke, J. (eds.) BPM 2018. LNCS, vol. 11080, pp. 322–338. Springer, Cham (2018). https://doi.org/10.1007/978-3-319-98648-7_19
4. Cashen, V.M., Leicht, K.L.: Role of the isolation effect in a formal educational setting. J. Educ. Psychol. 61(6p1), 484 (1970)
5. Chen, F., et al.: Robust Multimodal Cognitive Load Measurement, pp. 13–32. Springer, Cham (2016). https://doi.org/10.1007/978-3-319-31700-7
6. Corbin, J., Strauss, A.: Basics of Qualitative Research: Techniques and Procedures for Developing Grounded Theory. SAGE Publications, Thousand Oaks (2014)

7. Dengler, F., Vrandečić, D.: Wiki-based maturing of process descriptions. In: Rinderle-Ma, S., Toumani, F., Wolf, K. (eds.) BPM 2011. LNCS, vol. 6896, pp. 313–328. Springer, Heidelberg (2011). https://doi.org/10.1007/978-3-642-23059-2_24

8. Fahland, D., et al.: Declarative versus imperative process modeling languages: the issue of understandability. In: Halpin, T., et al. (eds.) BPMDS/EMMSAD -2009. LNBIP, vol. 29, pp. 353–366. Springer, Heidelberg (2009). https://doi.org/10.1007/978-3-642-01862-6_29

9. Gulden, J.: Visually comparing process dynamics with rhythm-eye views. In: Dumas, M., Fantinato, M. (eds.) BPM 2016. LNBIP, vol. 281, pp. 474–485. Springer, Cham (2017). https://doi.org/10.1007/978-3-319-58457-7_35

10. Hildebrandt, T.T., Mukkamala, R.R.: Declarative event-based workflow as distributed dynamic condition response graphs. EPTCS **69**, 59–73 (2011)

11. López, H.A., Debois, S., Hildebrandt, T.T., Marquard, M.: The process highlighter: from texts to declarative processes and back. In: BPM (Dissertation/Demos/Industry), volume 2196 of CEUR, pp. 66–70. CEUR-WS.org (2018)

12. Pinggera, J., Porcham, T., Zugal, S., Weber, B.: LiProMo-Literate process modeling. In CAiSE Forum, volume 855 of CEUR, pp. 163–170. CEUR-WS.org (2012)

13. Reichert, M., Weber, B.: Enabling Flexibility in Process-Aware Information Systems. Springer, Heidelberg (2012). https://doi.org/10.1007/978-3-642-30409-5

14. Slaats, T., Schunselaar, D.M.M., Maggi, F.M., Reijers, H.A.: The semantics of hybrid process models. In: Debruyne, C., et al. (eds.) OTM 2016. LNCS, vol. 10033, pp. 531–551. Springer, Cham (2016). https://doi.org/10.1007/978-3-319-48472-3_32

15. von Restorff, H.: Über die wirkung von bereichsbildungen im spurenfeld. Psychologische Forschung **18**, 299–342 (1933)

16. Zugal, S., Pinggera, J., Weber, B.: The impact of testcases on the maintainability of declarative process models. In: Halpin, T., et al. (eds.) BPMDS/EMMSAD -2011. LNBIP, vol. 81, pp. 163–177. Springer, Heidelberg (2011). https://doi.org/10.1007/978-3-642-21759-3_12

Query Approaches

Negation in Relational Keyword Search

Qiao Gao$^{(\boxtimes)}$, Mong Li Lee, and Tok Wang Ling

National University of Singapore, Singapore, Singapore
{gaoqiao,leeml,lingtw}@comp.nus.edu.sg

Abstract. Keyword search in relational databases frees users from writing complicated SQL queries. However, negation is still not allowed in keyword queries, limiting its expressiveness. This work addresses the problem of supporting negation in keyword queries. Our solution considers the keyword matches and the scope of negation. This enables us to correctly translate the negation using either NOT or NOT EXISTS SQL operator, and allows us to determine the user's search intention. We also support multiple negation and nested negation in keyword queries, further increasing the expressive ability.

1 Introduction

Keyword search over relational databases has become a popular search paradigm, relieving non-expert database users of the need to write complex error-prone SQL queries. Existing relational keyword search has focused on improving the efficiency of the query processing [2,4,6], ranking the query results [8,10,12] or extending the expressive power of the keyword query, e.g., allowing metadata [13], aggregate functions [15] or temporal predicates [5] in keyword queries.

A keyword query typically has some search target and search conditions. For example, in the query {Department Employee Skill Java} that finds departments which have employees with the skill Java, the keyword "Department" indicates the search target, while the keywords "Employee Skill Java" indicate the search condition. However, there is no support for negation in search conditions, e.g., find departments which have some employee who does *not* have the skill Java.

A naive approach to support negation in relational keyword search is to allow the reserved word NOT in keyword queries, and translate it into the NOT operator in the corresponding SQL queries. This approach will retrieve correct results when the negation is applied to search conditions involving single valued attributes. However, incorrect results may be retrieved when multivalued attributes are involved in the search conditions. Figure 1 shows an company database with relations Employee, Department and Project. Relation EmployeeSkill captures the multivalued attribute Skill of employees, while relation WorkFor captures the projects that employees work for. Suppose we issue a keyword query {Department Employee NOT Skill Java} to find departments which have some employee who does not have the skill Java. The naive approach would translate this query to the following SQL statement and retrieve departments $D01$ and $D02$.

© Springer Nature Switzerland AG 2019
A. H. F. Laender et al. (Eds.): ER 2019, LNCS 11788, pp. 173–188, 2019.
https://doi.org/10.1007/978-3-030-33223-5_15

SELECT D.* FROM Department D, Employee E, EmployeeSkill ES
WHERE D.Did = E.Did AND E.Eid = ES.Eid AND **NOT** ES.Skill contains 'Java';

Employee

Eid	Name	Salary	Address	Did	JoinDate
E01	Smith	3.5k	Brown Street	D01	2010
E02	Green	4.2k	Queen Street	D01	2009
E03	Brown	5.5k	Smith Street	D02	2006

Project

Pid	Name	Budget
P01	Safety for Java	40k
P02	RDB	50k
P03	AI	60k

WorkFor

Eid	Pid
E01	P01
E02	P02
E02	P03
E03	P02
E03	P03

EmployeeSkill

Eid	Skill
E01	Java
E02	C++
E03	Java
E03	PhP

Department

Did	Name	Address
D01	Computing	Brown Street
D02	Marketing	Queen Street

Fig. 1. Example company relational database.

We observe that the answer $D02$ is not correct because its only employee Brown ($E03$) has two skills Java and PhP. This is because Skill is a multivalued attribute, and the NOT operator in SQL cannot handle negation over multiple tuples. The correct SQL statement requires us to use NOT EXISTS to ensure that none of the skills of an employee is Java:

SELECT D.* FROM Department D, Employee E
WHERE D.Did = E.Did AND **NOT EXISTS** (SELECT * FROM EmployeeSkill ES
WHERE E.Eid = ES.Eid AND ES.Skill contains 'Java');

Translating keyword queries involving negation over multivalued attributes using NOT EXISTS guarantees that the negation in the search condition is applied to multiple tuples. This requires us to understand *matches* of the keywords in a query. If the keyword matches some tuple value that belongs to a single-valued attribute, then the negation is applied to a single tuple, and a NOT operator suffices. Otherwise, if the keyword matches some tuple value that belongs to a multivalued attribute, then the negation has to be applied to a set of tuples, and a NOT EXISTS operator is needed.

Supporting negation in keyword queries also requires us to consider the *scope* of negation to identify the search intention. Consider two queries which have the same set of keywords, but the position of NOT differs: {Department NOT Employee Project AI} and {Department Employee NOT Project AI}. The first query aims to find departments which do not have any employee who participates in some AI project because the scope of negation is "Employee Project AI". This query will return no results. In contrast, the second query finds departments which have some employee who does not participate in any AI project since the scope of negation is "Project AI". This query would return department $D01$ that has employee $E01$ who does not participate in any AI project.

In this work, we propose a solution to support negation in keyword queries. We consider two important aspects: (a) the matches of keywords, and (b) the scope of negation. The former enables the correct SQL translation using either

NOT or NOT EXISTS depending on whether the negation is applied to search conditions involving single tuple or multiple tuples. The latter allows us to identify the user's search intention. Our solution also supports multiple negation and nested negation. We evaluate the effectiveness of our approach to increase the expressiveness of keyword queries and retrieve correct results.

2   Preliminaries

A keyword query involving negation is a sequence of keywords $\{k_1 \ k_2...k_n\}$ where k_i may be a *data-content* keyword, a *metadata* keyword or the reserved word *NOT*. A data-content keyword matches tuple values, and there may be several such matches, e.g., *Java* may match a project name or an employee skill. This ambiguity leads to different query interpretations. A metadata keyword matches either a relation name or an attribute name, and provides the context of a data-content keyword, e.g., *Skill* matches the attribute name in relation EmployeeSkill and having this keyword before *Java* indicates that the user is interested in employees with the Skill *Java* rather than projects related to Java. The reserved word NOT indicates negation. For a query to be meaningful, we impose the constraint that if a keyword k_i is the NOT reserved word, then k_{i+1} is either a data-content or a metadata keyword, $1 < i < n$. Further, we also allow the use of brackets in the query to define the scope of the negation.

We adopt the semantic approach in [13] to process keyword queries. This approach uses an Object-Relationship-Mixed (ORM) schema graph to capture the Object-Relationship-Attribute (ORA) semantics in a relational database which will enable us to distinguish single-valued attributes, multivalued attributes and object/relationship types in database when we analyze the matches of query keywords. Query patterns are constructed based on the ORM schema graph to depict different query interpretations. Each query pattern is subsequently used to generate a SQL statement.

2.1   ORM Schema Graph

An ORM schema graph $G = (V, E)$ captures the object types, relationship types and attributes in a relational database. Each node $u \in V$ is an object/relationship/mixed node comprising of an object/relationship/mixed relation and its component relations. An object (or relationship) relation captures the single-valued attributes of an object type (or a relationship type). Multivalued attributes are captured in component relations. A mixed relation contains information of both an object type and its many-to-one relationship types. Two nodes u and v are connected by an undirected edge $(u, v) \in E$ if there exists a foreign key-key constraint from the relations in u to those in v.

Figure 2 shows the ORM schema graph for the database in Fig. 1. Note that an ORM node may contain multiple relations, e.g., node Employee contains object relation *Employee* and component relation *EmployeeSkill*.

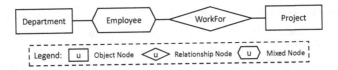

Fig. 2. ORM schema graph of Fig. 1.

2.2   Query Patterns

Based on the ORM schema graph, a set of query patterns can be generated to capture the different interpretations of the query keywords. Details of pattern generation process are in [13]. We illustrate the key ideas with an example.

Consider the query {Department Employee Java}. The keyword *Department* matches the relation name Department, while the keyword *Employee* matches the relation name Employee. These relations are mapped to the nodes Department and Employee in the ORM schema graph in Fig. 2. Based on Fig. 1, we have two matches for the keyword *Java*, namely, the value of attribute Skill in the component relation EmployeeSkill, and the value of attribute Name in the object relation Project. Figure 3 shows the query patterns generated to capture these matches. Query pattern P_a depicts the interpretation to find departments which have employees with the skill Java, while P_b depicts the interpretation to find departments which have employees participating in some project Java.

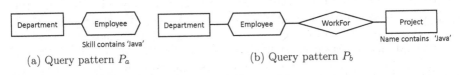

(a) Query pattern P_a (b) Query pattern P_b

Fig. 3. Two query patterns generated for query {Department Employee Java}.

2.3   SQL Generation

Each query pattern is used to generate an SQL statement [13]. The *target nodes* are first identified as they indicate the query search target. These are usually the nodes matched by the first few metadata keywords in the query. The SELECT clause has all or specific attributes from the relations corresponding to the target nodes. The FROM clause contains the relations of all the nodes in the query pattern. The WHERE clause contains the join conditions for the relations in FROM clause and also the attribute value conditions in the query pattern.

Consider the query pattern P_a in Fig. 3(a). The node Department is the target node as it is matched by the first metadata keyword in the query. The SQL statement generated for P_a is as follows:

```
SELECT D.* FROM Department D, Employee E, EmployeeSkill ES
WHERE D.Did =E.Did AND E.Eid = ES.Eid AND ES.Skill contains 'Java';
```

Note that all the attributes in the relation *Department* are added to the SELECT clause. The component relation *EmployeeSkill* is included in the FROM clause, since there is an condition over its attribute Skill.

3   Proposed Solution

Given a keyword query Q that contains negation, we first derive a query Q' that contains only data-content and metadata keywords in Q, and generate a set of query patterns from Q'. Then we annotate each query pattern P with NOT or NOT EXISTS operator by analyzing if the negation should be applied to attributes or objects/relationships. Finally, we generate SQL statements from the annotated query patterns. We describe the details of the last two steps.

3.1   Annotating Query Patterns

To simplify discussion, we first assume that query Q has only one NOT reserved word. Suppose k_1 and k_2 are keywords before and after NOT in Q respectively. We analyze the matches of these keywords to determine if the negation is over an attribute or some object/relationship. Let P be a query pattern generated from Q by omitting the NOT.

Case 1. k_1 and k_2 match the same node n in P. In this case, the NOT in Q indicates a negation over some attribute of the object/relationship that corresponds to the node n.

Case 2: k_1 and k_2 match different nodes in P. In this case, the NOT in Q indicates a negation over some object/relationship.

3.1.1 Negation over Attributes

Here, we distinguish whether the negation is applicable to a single-valued or multivalued attribute. If k_2 matches the value or name of a single-valued attribute A, then the negation is applied to only one tuple, and we annotate the node n in P with a NOT operator, i.e., *NOT A contains 'value'*. Otherwise, if k_2 matches the value or name of a multivalued attribute A, then the negation needs to be applied to multiple tuples, and we annotate n with a NOT EXISTS operator, i.e., *NOT EXISTS A contains 'value'*.

Example 1 (Negation over single-valued attribute). Consider the query

$$Q_1 = \{\text{Department Employee NOT Name Smith}\}$$

We first generate a query pattern P_1 from {Department Employee Name Smith} (see Fig. 4(a)). Then we examine the keywords before and after the NOT in Q_1. The keyword *Employee* matches the object node Employee in P_1, while *Name* matches the single-valued attribute name Name of the same object node Employee. Hence, the negation is over a single tuple and we annotate P_1 with a NOT operator before the condition *Name contains 'Smith'* (see Fig. 4(b)).   □

(a) Query pattern P_1 (b) Annotated query pattern for Q_1

Fig. 4. Example query pattern annotated with NOT operator.

Example 2 (Negation over multivalued attribute). Suppose we have the query:

$$Q_2 = \{\text{Department Employee NOT Skill Java}\}.$$

We generate a query pattern P_2 from {Department Employee Skill Java} (see Fig. 5(a)). The keyword *Skill* after the NOT in Q_2 matches the multivalued attribute name Skill of Employee, indicating that the negation is applicable to multiple tuples. As such, we annotate P_2 with a NOT EXISTS operator before the condition *Skill contains 'Java'* as shown in Fig. 5(b). □

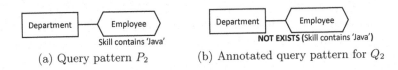

(a) Query pattern P_2 (b) Annotated query pattern for Q_2

Fig. 5. Example query pattern annotated with NOT EXISTS operator.

Note that a keyword query can have negation over more than one attributes in an object/relationship. In this situation, users should use brackets to specify which attribute(s) the negation is applicable to.

Example 3 (Negation involving more than one attributes). Consider the following queries which have brackets over different attributes:

$$Q_3 = \{\text{Department Employee NOT (Name Smith Skill Java)}\}$$
$$Q_4 = \{\text{Department Employee NOT (Name Smith) Skill Java}\}$$

Figure 6(a) shows the query pattern generated from {Department Employee Name Smith Skill Java}. The node Employee has two search conditions on its attributes *Name* and *Skill*. The brackets in Q_3 indicate that the negation should be applied to both attributes, while those in Q_4 imply that the negation is applicable only to *Name*. Figure 6(b) shows the annotated query pattern for Q_3 with a NOT EXISTS operator over attributes *Name* and *Skill* in the node Employee since *Skill* is a multivalued attribute. In contrast, the annotated query pattern for Q_4 has a NOT operator over the single-valued attribute *Name*. □

3.1.2 Negation over Object/Relationship

Let n be the object/relationship node in P that corresponds to the relation R matched by k_2. In this case, the NOT in Q indicates a negation over multiple tuples of R, and we annotate the node n with a NOT EXISTS operator.

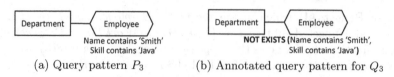

(a) Query pattern P_3 (b) Annotated query pattern for Q_3

Fig. 6. Example query pattern with NOT EXISTS operator over multiple attributes.

Example 4 (Negation over object). Consider the following query:

$$Q_5 = \{\text{Department NOT Employee Name Smith}\}.$$

Figure 7(a) shows a query pattern P_5 generated from {Department Employee Name Smith}. P_5 is the same as P_1 in Fig. 4(a) because Q_5 and Q_1 in Example 1 have the same set of metadata and data-content keywords. The difference is the keywords before and after the NOT. Here, the keyword *Department* matches the node Department in P_5, while the keyword *Employee* matches another node Employee. There is a one-to-many relationship between nodes Department and Employee, implying that each tuple in the relation *Department* can be associated with multiple tuples in the relation *Employee* via the key-foreign key reference. Hence, we annotate P_5 with a NOT EXISTS operator over the Employee node to indicate that the negation is applied to multiple tuples (see Fig. 7(b)).   □

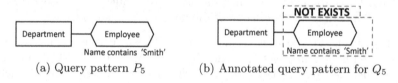

(a) Query pattern P_5 (b) Annotated query pattern for Q_5

Fig. 7. Annotating an object node in a query pattern with NOT EXISTS operator.

When the negation is over some object/relationship, the scope of the negation may include other objects/relationships depending on the position of the NOT. Users can use brackets to specify the scope of the negation. By default, we use all the keywords after NOT to find the scope of the negation.

Example 5 (Scope of negation). Consider the following queries which have the same set of keywords, but the position of NOT differs:

$$Q_6 = \{\text{Department NOT Employee Project AI}\}$$
$$Q_7 = \{\text{Department Employee NOT Project AI}\}$$

Query pattern P_6 in Fig. 8(a) is generated from {Department Employee Project AI}. The search intention of Q_6 is to find departments that do not have employees working for project AI. The set of keywords that comes after NOT in Q_6 is $W =$

{Employee, Project, AI} which match the nodes *Employee* and *Project* in P_6. The minimal connected subtree $T = \{Employee - WorkFor - Project\}$ in P_6 that contains these nodes gives the scope of the negation. Figure 8(b) shows the annotated query pattern where NOT EXISTS is applied to T.

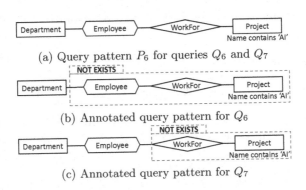

(a) Query pattern P_6 for queries Q_6 and Q_7

(b) Annotated query pattern for Q_6

(c) Annotated query pattern for Q_7

Fig. 8. Example to illustrate the scope of negation.

On the other hand, the search intention of Q_7 is to find departments which have some employee that does not work for project AI. The set of keywords that comes after NOT in the query is $\mathcal{W}' = \{$Project, AI$\}$ which match the same node *Project* in P_6. Figure 8(c) shows the annotated query pattern where NOT EXISTS is applied to the minimal connected subtree $T' = \{WorkFor - Project\}$, indicating that the scope of the negation in Q_7 is T'. □

Note that the node *Workfor* is included in T', since it is an intermediate node between node *Employee* (matched by the keyword before NOT) and node *Project* (matched by the keyword after NOT) in the query pattern. Including the intermediate node *WorkFor* in T' ensures that departments which have employees that do not work for any project are also retrieved. This is because such departments also satisfy the search intention – an employee who does not work for any project certainly does not work for project AI. If we do not include the node *WorkFor* in T', then we can only retrieve departments which have some employee working for some project not named AI. This search intention can be expressed by the query {Department Employee WorkFor NOT Project AI} where the keyword *WorkFor* is specified explicitly before NOT to indicate that it is outside the scope of the negation and the employee must work for some project.

Algorithm 1 gives the details to find the scope of negation when an object/relationship is involved. The input is a query Q, a query pattern P and the position of NOT in Q. The output is an annotated query pattern depicting the minimal connected subtree where NOT EXISTS should be applied to. We first find a minimal connected subtree T that is matched by the set of keywords following the NOT reserved word (Lines 1–6). Then we expand T to include adjacent nodes that are not matched by any keywords in Q (Lines 7–13).

Algorithm 1. Scope of negation when an object/relationship involved

---

Input: query $Q = \{k_1...k_n\}$, query pattern P, position i of NOT in Q
Output: annotated query pattern P'

1 **if** k_i *is followed by a bracket* **then**
2 $\quad$|$\quad$ Add all the keywords in the bracket into a set W;
3 **else**
4 $\quad$|$\quad$ Add all the keywords after k_i in to a set W;
5 Let $V = \{v_1 \; v_2...v_m\}$ be the set of nodes in P matched by keywords in W;
6 $T = findMinimalSubtree(V, P)$;$\qquad$ // Find minmal connected subtree T
7 Add all the nodes adjacent to T in P to a queue $Queue$;
8 **while** $Queue$ *is not empty* **do**$\qquad$ // Expand the minimal subtree T
9 $\quad$|$\quad$ $u = Queue.poll()$;
10 $\quad$|$\quad$ **if** u *is not matched by any keywords in Q* **then**
11 $\quad$|$\quad$|$\quad$ $T = T \cup \{u\}$;
12 $\quad$|$\quad$|$\quad$ **foreach** *node $u' \notin T$ and adjacent to u in P* **do**
13 $\quad$|$\quad$|$\quad$|$\quad$ $Queue.add(u)$;
14 $P' = annotateNotExists(T, P)$;$\qquad$ // Annotate NOT EXISTS over T
15 **return** P';

3.1.3 Handling Multiple Negation in a Query

We have analyzed whether the negation is over attributes (Case 1) or over object/relationship (Case 2). These two types of negation can be handled independently, even if they occur at the same time in a query. For example, in the query {Department NOT Employee NOT Name Smith}, the first negation is applied to the object *Employee* while the second negation is applied to the attribute *Name*. We handle each negation independently as described in Examples 1 and 4. Figure 9 shows the final annotated query pattern which is essentially obtained by merging the annotations in Fig. 4(b) and Fig. 7(b).

Fig. 9. Annotated query pattern for {Department NOT Employee NOT Name Smith}.

A keyword query with multiple negation involving attributes only can also be handled independently. Note that if we have multiple negation involving the same multivalued attribute, e.g., {Project Employee NOT Skill Java NOT Skill C++}, we can use the OR operator in SQL to reduce the number of multiple NOT EXISTS operators as shown in Fig. 10.

On the other hand, when a keyword query has multiple negation over objects/relationships only, each negation has its own scope and may involve different nodes in the query pattern, leading to different search intentions. Again, we

Fig. 10. Annotated query pattern with multiple negation over the same multivalued attribute for query {Project Employee NOT Skill Java NOT Skill C++}.

use brackets to define the scope of each negation. For each negation in keyword query, we use Algorithm 1 to identify its scope and generate an annotated query pattern. These annotated query patterns are then merged to one final annotated query pattern. Note that the merging is carried out differently depending on whether the negation is nested or independent in the keyword query.

Example 6 (Nested negation over objects). Suppose we want to find departments which do not have employees named Smith and these employees also do not participate in project AI. We can issue the following query with nested negation:

$$Q_8 = \{\text{Department NOT (Employee Smith NOT (Project AI))}\}$$

For each negation, we call Algorithm 1 to identify its scope and generate an annotated query pattern. These annotated query patterns are merged to a final annotated query pattern with nested NOT EXISTS operators (see Fig. 11).   □

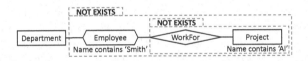

Fig. 11. Final annotated query pattern with nested negation for query Q_8.

Example 7 (Independent negation over objects). Consider a query with two negation, one over the object Employee and another over the object Project:

$$Q_9 = \{\text{Department NOT (Employee Smith) NOT (Project AI)}\}$$

The search intention is to find departments which do not have employees named Smith and these departments also do not have any employees participating in project AI. Here, we generate one subquery for each negation as follows:

$$S_1 = \{\text{Department NOT Employee Smith}\}$$
$$S_2 = \{\text{Department NOT Project AI}\}$$

For each subquery, we call Algorithm 1 to identify the scope of the negation and generate the corresponding annotated query pattern (see Fig. 12(a) and Fig. 12(b)). These annotated query patterns are combined by merging the *Department* node which is outside the scope of both negation. Figure 12(c) shows the final annotated query pattern obtained.   □

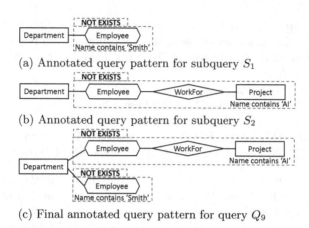

(a) Annotated query pattern for subquery S_1

(b) Annotated query pattern for subquery S_2

(c) Final annotated query pattern for query Q_9

Fig. 12. Annotated query pattern with independent negation over objects.

3.2   Generating SQL Statements

We generate an SQL statement for each annotated query pattern P. We first ignore the NOT annotations in the query pattern and use the method in [13] to generate the main SQL query (recall Sect. 2.3). Then for each NOT operator in P, we add a NOT operator in front of the corresponding attribute value condition in the SQL statement.

For each NOT EXISTS operator in P, starting from the outermost NOT EXISTS, we add a NOT EXISTS operator together with a subquery to the WHERE clause of the main SQL query. We identify the relations in the nodes under the scope of this NOT EXISTS operator, and move these relations from the FROM clause of the main SQL query to the FROM clause of the subquery. The joins and select conditions involving these relations are also moved from the WHERE clause of main SQL query to that of the subquery. If this NOT EXISTS operator has other nested NOT EXISTS operators in the annotated query pattern, we generate a second-level subquery in the first-level subquery and move the relations in a similar way.

Example 8 Recall query $Q_1 = \{$Department Employee NOT Name Smith$\}$. Its annotated query pattern in Fig. 4(b) has one NOT operator. We first obtain the main SQL query and then add a NOT operator before $E.Name$ as follows:

SELECT D.* FROM Department D, Employee E
WHERE D.Did = E.Did AND **NOT** E.Name contains 'Smith';   □

Example 9 Recall query $Q_8 = \{$Department NOT (Employee Smith NOT (Project AI))$\}$. Its final annotated query pattern in Fig. 11 has two NOT EXISTS operators. We first obtain the main SQL query:

SELECT D.* FROM Department D, Employee E, WorkFor WF, Project P
WHERE E.Did = D.Did AND E.Name contains 'Smith' AND WF.Eid = E.Eid
        AND WF.Pid = P.Pid AND P.Name contains 'AI';   Then we process the

NOT EXISTS operators in the query pattern and add subqueries. Note that relations in node Employee are in the first level subquery and relations in nodes WorkFor and Project are in the second level subquery. The final SQL statement generated is as follows:

```
SELECT D.* FROM Department D
WHERE NOT EXISTS (SELECT * FROM Employee E
    WHERE E.Did = D.Did AND E.Name contains 'Smith'
    AND NOT EXISTS (SELECT * FROM WorkFor WF, Project P
        WHERE WF.Eid = E.Eid AND WF.Pid = P.Pid AND P.Name contains 'AI'));
```

The generated SQL statement can be executed in any relational DBMS to retrieve query results. Some DBMS such as Oracle has optimized the NOT EXISTS operator as anti-join operator based on negation as failure theory [3]. For example, for the select statement in the second NOT EXISTS operator in the above SQL query, if an answer satisfying this select statement is found, the second NOT EXISTS operator will fail and the rest of the answers will not be tested.

4   Evaluation

We evaluate the expressive ability of our proposed approach to supporting negation in keyword queries. For comparison, we implement a baseline by extending the work in [13] to allow for the NOT reserved word in a keyword query, and translating the negation into the NOT operator in the SQL statement. We use two datasets in our evaluation: the TPC-H database[1] (TPCH) and the ACM Digital Library publication[2] (ACMDL). Table 1 gives the schemas.

Table 1. Database schemas.

TPCH	ACMDL
Part (partkey, name, type, size, retailprice)	Paper (paperid, title, keywords, date, procid)
Supplier (suppkey, name, nationkey, acctbal)	Proceeding (procid, acronym, title, date,
PartSupp (partkey, suppkey, availqty, supplycost)	country, publisherid)
Lineitem (partkey, suppkey, orderkey, quantity)	Publisher (publisherid, code, name, country)
Order (orderkey, custkey, status, totalamount)	Author (authorid, name)
Customer (custkey, name, nationkey, mktsegment)	Author_aff_history (authorid, affiliation)
Nation (nationkey, name, regionkey)	Editor (editorid, name)
Region (regionkey, name)	Write (authorid, paperid)
	Edit (editorid, procid)

Table 2 shows the keyword queries we design for the TPCH database and the user search intention. Queries T_1 and T_2 involve negation over single-valued

---

[1] http://www.tpc.org/tpch/.
[2] http://dl.acm.org/.

Table 2. Keyword queries over the TPCH database.

	Keyword query	Search intention	Baseline	Ours
T_1	customer order NOT totalamount >300,000	Find customers who have orders with total price not larger than 300,000	✓	✓
T_2	customer part type steel NOT name brown	Find customers who bought steel that is not named brown	✓	✓
T_3	part name rose NOT supplier region Africa	Find parts named rose and not from a supplier in Africa	✗	✓
T_4	customer NOT order	Find customers who do not have any orders	✗	✓
T_5	customer part steel NOT (part copper) NOT (part tin)	Find customers who bought steel and not copper or tin	✗	✓
T_6	customer NOT (part copper NOT (supplier S1))	Find customers who did not buy copper that is not supplied by S1	✗	✓

attribute totalamount and name respectively. Both the baseline and our approach correctly generate SQL statements with NOT operator over these attributes.

Queries T_3 and T_4 involve negation over object/relationship supplier and order respectively. The baseline approach translates the negation into NOT SQL operators over the attributes in supplier (for T_3) and order (for T_4), which leads to incorrect results. In contrast, our solution first identifies the scope of the NOT reserved word and uses the NOT EXISTS operator in the generated SQL queries to retrieve correct results. Query T_5 has two independent negation over the object part, while T_6 has nested negation. Only our proposed solution is able to handle such queries and retrieve correct results.

Table 3 shows the queries we design for ACMDL database. Query A_1 involves negation over a single-valued attribute, and both the baseline and our solution can generate the correct SQL statement. Query A_2 has a negation over the multivalued attribute affiliation. Only our proposed solution can retrieve the correct results since we use the NOT EXISTS operator to check all the affiliations for each author in the proceeding SIGMOD. This guarantees that all the 3918 authors retrieved do not have any affiliation matching "NUS". In contrast, the baseline uses the NOT operator and retrieve 29 additional incorrect authors.

For query A_3, our solution can identify that the scope of the negation is the object paper and generates an SQL query that uses the NOT EXISTS operator to retrieve the correct results (470 distinct authors). However, the baseline retrieves 14 additional incorrect results, since it can only guarantee that each author in the results has at least one paper that is not related to database.

Queries A_5 and A_6 have multiple negation. Our solution retrieves correct results for both queries, while the baseline cannot handle negation over multivalued attributes and object/relationship. Further, the baseline could not generate

the correct query pattern and identify the scope of the NOT reserved words for queries with nested negation.

In summary, our proposed solution improves the expressive ability of keyword queries by allowing for negation over attributes, object/relationship, as well as multiple negation including nested negation.

Table 3. Keyword queries over the ACMDL database.

	Keyword query	Search intention	Baseline	Ours
A_1	proceeding name publisher NOT name Springer	Find the name of proceeding whose publish is not Springer	✓	✓
A_2	author NOT affiliation NUS paper proceeding SIGMOD	Find authors not with affiliation from NUS and published paper in SIGMOD	×	✓
A_3	author affiliation Harvard NOT paper database	Find the authors with affiliation Harvard and have not written paper related to database	×	✓
A_4	author affiliation Berkeley NOT edit proceeding	Find the authors from Berkeley and not edit any proceedings	×	✓
A_5	paper NOT title database NOT (author affiliation NUS) proceeding VLDB	Find the papers neither with title database nor with authors from NUS, and published in VLDB	×	✓
A_6	paper SIGMOD NOT (author NOT (affiliation Stanford))	Find the papers from SIGMOD and none of their authors not from Stanford	×	✓

5   Related Work

Early works in relational keyword query support keywords that match tuple values [1,2,6]. [11] increases the expressiveness of keyword query with aggregates and GroupBy functions for users to retrieve statistical information. [7] extends keyword queries with temporal predicates and time periods for users to specify conditions over the time dimension of the database. All these works do not distinguish the Object-Relationship-Attribute (ORA) semantics in the database, which may lead to missing, incomplete, meaningless, duplicated and incorrect results [14].

A semantic approach is proposed in [13] which utilizes an Object-Relationship-Mixed (ORM) data graph to capture ORA semantics, and extends keyword queries with metadata keywords to reduce the inherent ambiguity of keyword queries. [15] shows the importance of ORA semantics for the correct

evaluation of keyword queries with aggregates and GroupBy. [5] provides support for temporal predicates in keyword queries, and uses ORA semantics to capture the multiple interpretations of temporal conditions.

To the best of our knowledge, none of the existing keyword search approaches over relational database support negation in keyword queries. The work in [9] provides support for NOT semantics in keyword queries over XML. However, the evaluation is based on the hierarchical structure of XML trees and is not applicable to the general graph model of relational data. Further, [9] does not differentiate the object, relationship and attribute semantics in the XML documents. Our proposed solution extends the semantic approach in [13] as it is able to address the problem of incomplete and incorrect results, etc., by capturing the ORA semantics in relational database.

6   Conclusion

Existing keyword search over relational databases do not allow users to specify negation in search conditions, which limits the expressiveness of the keyword query. Processing keyword queries with negation is complex and we cannot simply translate the negation in a keyword query to the corresponding SQL NOT operator as this may lead to incorrect query results. In this work, we have extended keyword queries to include the NOT reserved word so that negation over search conditions can be expressed. Our solution analyzes the scope of each NOT reserved word, and determines whether it should be translated to the SQL NOT or NOT EXISTS operator to ensure that correct results are retrieved. We also support multiple negation and nested negation in keyword queries. Evaluation on two datasets shows the effectiveness of our solution to identify user's search intention and retrieve correct results.

References

1. Agrawal, S., Chaudhuri, S., Das, G.: DBXplorer: a system for keyword-based search over relational databases. In: IEEE ICDE (2002)
2. Bhalotia, G., Hulgeri, A., Nakhe, C., Chakrabarti, S., Sudarshan, S.: Keyword searching and browsing in databases using BANKS. In: IEEE ICDE (2002)
3. Clark, K.L.: Negation as failure. In: Gallaire, H., Minker, J. (eds.) Logic and Data Bases. Springer, Boston (1978). https://doi.org/10.1007/978-1-4684-3384-5_11
4. Ding, B., Yu, J.X., Wang, S., Qin, L., Zhang, X., Lin, X.: Finding top-k min-cost connected trees in databases. In: IEEE ICDE (2007)
5. Gao, Q., Lee, M.L., Ling, T.W., Dobbie, G., Zeng, Z.: Analyzing temporal keyword queries for interactive search over temporal databases. In: Hartmann, S., Ma, H., Hameurlain, A., Pernul, G., Wagner, R.R. (eds.) DEXA 2018. LNCS, vol. 11029, pp. 355–371. Springer, Cham (2018). https://doi.org/10.1007/978-3-319-98809-2_22
6. Hristidis, V., Papakonstantinou, Y.: Discover: keyword search in relational databases. In: VLDB (2002)

7. Jia, X., Hsu, W., Lee, M.L.: Target-oriented keyword search over temporal databases. In: Hartmann, S., Ma, H. (eds.) DEXA 2016. LNCS, vol. 9827, pp. 3–19. Springer, Cham (2016). https://doi.org/10.1007/978-3-319-44403-1_1

8. Kargar, M., An, A., Cercone, N., Godfrey, P., Szlichta, J., Yu, X.: Meaningful keyword search in relational databases with large and complex schema. In: IEEE ICDE (2015)

9. Lin, R.-R., Chang, Y.-H., Chao, K.-M.: Identifying relevant matches with NOT semantics over XML documents. In: Yu, J.X., Kim, M.H., Unland, R. (eds.) DAS-FAA 2011. LNCS, vol. 6587, pp. 466–480. Springer, Heidelberg (2011). https://doi.org/10.1007/978-3-642-20149-3_34

10. Luo, Y., Lin, X., Wang, W., Zhou, X.: SPARK: top-k keyword query in relational databases. In: ACM SIGMOD (2007)

11. Tata, S., Lohman, G.M.: SQAK: doing more with keywords. In: ACM SIGMOD (2008)

12. Yu, X., Shi, H.: CI-Rank: ranking keyword search results based on collective importance. In: IEEE ICDE (2012)

13. Zeng, Z., Bao, Z., Le, T.N., Lee, M.L., Ling, T.W.: ExpressQ: identifying keyword context and search target in relational keyword queries. In: ACM CIKM (2014)

14. Zeng, Z., Bao, Z., Lee, M.L., Ling, T.W.: A semantic approach to keyword search over relational databases. In: Ng, W., Storey, V.C., Trujillo, J.C. (eds.) ER 2013. LNCS, vol. 8217, pp. 241–254. Springer, Heidelberg (2013). https://doi.org/10.1007/978-3-642-41924-9_21

15. Zeng, Z., Lee, M.L., Ling, T.W.: Answering keyword queries involving aggregates and group by on relational databases. In: EDBT (2016)

Answering GPSJ Queries in a Polystore: A Dataspace-Based Approach

Hamdi Ben Hamadou[1] , Enrico Gallinucci[2] , and Matteo Golfarelli[2]([envelope])

[1] Institut de Recherche en Informatique de Toulouse, Toulouse, France
hamdi.ben-hamadou@irit.fr
[2] University of Bologna, Cesena, Italy
{enrico.gallinucci,matteo.golfarelli}@unibo.it

Abstract. The discipline of data science is steering analysts away from traditional data warehousing and towards a more flexible and lightweight approach to data analysis. The idea is to perform OLAP analyses in a *pay-as-you-go* manner across heterogeneous schemas and data models, where the integration is progressively carried out by the user as the available data is explored. In this paper, we propose an approach to support data analysis within a polystore supporting relational, document and column data models by automatically handling both data model and schema heterogeneity through a dataspace layer on top of the underlying databases. The expressiveness we enable corresponds to GPSJ queries, which are the most common class of queries in OLAP applications. We rely on Nested Relational Algebra to define a cross-database execution plan. The plan is composed of several local plans, to be executed on the distinct databases, and a global plan, which combines and possibly aggregates inter-database data. The system has been prototyped on Apache Spark.

Keywords: Polystore · NoSQL · Dataspace · GPSJ · Schemaless · OLAP

1 Introduction

With the rise of Big Data, NoSQL systems have effectively provided different ways to address the scalability issues of relational database management systems (RDBMSs) and the variety aspect of Big Data. As companies move towards *polyglot persistence* [20] (i.e., employing several DBMSs to exploit the best features of each) to optimize the operational workload, new challenges arise from an analytical perspective, because the analyst needs a transparent way to access these fragmented and differently-shaped data. At the same time, the discipline of data science is steering analysts away from traditional data warehousing and towards a more flexible and lightweight data analysis approach. The idea is to relax the rigidity of traditional integration approaches to perform OLAP (OnLine Analytical Processing) analyses in a *pay-as-you-go* manner [14], where the integration is

© Springer Nature Switzerland AG 2019
A. H. F. Laender et al. (Eds.): ER 2019, LNCS 11788, pp. 189–203, 2019.
https://doi.org/10.1007/978-3-030-33223-5_16

progressively carried out by the user as the available data is explored. This calls for new approaches to enable effective analyses on a polyglot system without performing a complex integration phase.

The main challenges to address in this context are related to the heterogeneity of the data in terms of data model and schema. *Data model heterogeneity* is intrinsic in a polyglot database; it requires to distribute the computation of a query across the different databases (which adopt different query languages) and to possibly rely on a middleware to combine and further elaborate the results. *Schema heterogeneity* is a common type of heterogeneity in most NoSQL systems as they abandon the traditional *schema-first, data-later* approach of RDBMS (which requires all record in a table to comply with a predefined schema) in favour of a *soft-schema* approach, in which each record embeds its own schema definition. For instance, two records in the same collection may contain different attributes or the same attributes following different naming conventions. Schema heterogeneity is mainly due to schema evolution and to the acquisition of data from sources adopting different schema representations for the same entities.

State-of-the-art proposals for polyglot systems mainly include *multistores* (which provide a unique query language to separately query different DBMSs) and *polystores* (which additionally enable cross-DBMS query processing) [23]. Current solutions mostly focus on addressing data model heterogeneity and on optimising the query processing, but they do not consider schema heterogeneity. This prevents analysts from taking full advantage of the data, as several instances may be missed by queries that do not take schema variations into consideration. In this paper we propose an approach to support data analysis within a polystore by handling both data model and schema heterogeneity through a dataspace layer on top of the underlying databases. A dataspace is a lightweight integration approach providing basic query expressive power on a variety of data sources, bypassing the complexity of traditional integration approaches and possibly returning best-effort or approximate answers [7]. Consistently with the pay-as-you-go philosophy, the dataspace is first built by applying simple matching rules and is progressively enriched by the users as they discover new relationships among data structures through exploratory queries.

The query expressiveness we enable corresponds to GPSJ queries (i.e., generalized projection, selection and join [12]), i.e., the most common class of queries in OLAP applications. State-of-the-art works typically delegate to the user the formulation of adequate queries with the risk of getting inconsistent answers to the envisioned questions. In contrast, GPSJs enforce a query semantics to prevent the user from getting misleading results leading to ambiguous or potentially incorrect interpretation in the analytical context. The possibility to extend the approach to a broader class of queries is considered as future work. For a given GPSJ, our approach defines a cross-database execution plan in Nested Relational Algebra (NRA) [24], which is compatible with the expressiveness of document stores' query language [3] and SQL (as it is a superset of relational algebra), with the latter being used by both RDBMSs and column-based systems. The cross-database execution plan is composed of several local plans, to be executed

on the distinct underlying databases, and a global plan, which combines and possibly aggregates inter-database data. The resolution of schema heterogeneity is handled in the local plans, where the knowledge of the dataspace is exploited to properly query all schema variations of the involved data. This activity is supported by previous research efforts on enabling schema-independent querying on heterogeneous schemas [1,2,9,10], which focus only on single collections of records in a particular data model. A prototypical implementation of the approach has been carried out on Apache Spark [26].

The paper outline is as follows. After discussing related work in Sect. 2, in Sect. 3 we formalize the dataspace and the query expressiveness. Then we present the formulation of the execution plan in Sect. 4. Finally, in Sect. 5 we briefly discuss the prototypical implementation and we draw the conclusions.

2   Related Literature

The importance of transparently querying multistore systems has been highlighted by contexts such as federated databases [21] and, more recently, soft-schema support in NoSQL systems [5]. Here we classify state-of-the-art work by focusing on the considered levels of data model and schema heterogeneity.

Data Model Transformation. Generally, these works store document data model into a relational one [6,22]. They offer relational views built on top of the new relational data model to assist the user while formulating queries. This strategy implies that several data model transformation should be performed. Hence, this process requires additional resources, such as an external relational database [15]. Users of these systems have to learn new schemas every time new data are inserted (or updated) in the collection, because it is necessary to re-generate the relational views.

Multistore and Polystores. Most of the approaches provide integrated access to a number of heterogeneous database systems [8,16] through one [16] or more query language [8] using a middle-ware layer. However, they still require the user to either define the global schema or to specify a particular data source to use, e.g., BigDAWG [8] requires user to use the adequate querying language for each data model. Furthermore, they consider neither schema mapping during the query rewriting steps, nor schema heterogeneity.

Multimodel Systems. These systems offer a single platform to store and query data in different data models (e.g., OrientDB, http://orientdb.com/orientdb/). Multimodel systems excel in term of data governance, management, and access. However, they are limited to a pre-defined set of data models and extending support to new data models is challenging.

Schema-Independent Querying. In document-based stores *structural heterogeneity* points to the existence of several paths to access the same attribute. A transparent querying mechanisms to overcome this heterogeneity is introduced in [2]. A recent research work [9] resolves the problem of having semantically equivalent

attributes but with a *different naming convention*, as highlighted in [25], using a set of schema mappings. Most of these approaches consider the heterogeneity problem inside one collection at a time for a particular data model only. Moreover, the same information could be represented using *different data types*, and transcoding functions are required to resolve this heterogeneity [11].

Schema Inference. A second line of work focuses on the representation of the different schemas within the same collection of documents. In [25] the authors recommend summarizing all document schemas under a skeleton to discover the existence of fields or sub-schemas inside the collection. In [13] the authors suggest extracting collection structures to help developers in the process of designing their applications. The limitation with such a logical view is that it requires a manual process in order to build the desired queries by including the desired attributes and all their possible navigational paths.

All mentioned works handle either data model or schema heterogeneity. To the best of our knowledge, this is the first work to handle both of them.

3   Dataspace and Query Modeling

In this work we consider a polystore comprising databases in three data models: relational, document-based and column-based[1]. Our running example is a variation of Unibench [18], i.e., a benchmark multimodel dataset based on an e-commerce application. The conceptual schema is shown in Fig. 1. With respect to Unibench we exclude the graph and key-value databases and we extend the benchmark by injecting some heterogeneity into the schemas. We remark that schema heterogeneity is possible only in the document-based and column-based data models. In particular, we cover the following kinds of schema heterogeneity.

- Missing attributes: attributes that exist in some records and not in others (e.g., the gender and birthday of the Client are not always specified).
- Different data types: attributes with varying data types (e.g., the id in Client is a number, but the personId in Order is stored as string).
- Semantic equivalence: attributes with varying naming conventions (e.g., order-Line.cost and orderLine.price in Order are alternative attributes representing the same information).

In the polystore, the data is split among a set of databases DB. We exploit the concept of dataspace to provide a global representation of the available attributes in the different databases and to hide the underlying schema heterogeneity. In particular, the dataspace plays the role of the abstraction level enabling the user to formulate queries. As data model heterogeneity entails terminology heterogeneity, Table 1 explains the terminology used in the remainder of the paper to generally refer to schema elements (e.g., tables, columns), independently of their declination in the different data models. The basic information we consider is the *attribute*, which we define as follows.

---

[1] We remark that column-based NoSQL systems (e.g., BigTable [4]) are different from column-oriented DBMS (e.g., Vertica).

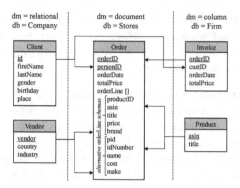

Fig. 1. Running example of a multi-store e-commerce application, based on Unibench [18]; orderLine is an array in the Order collection whose objects come in two schema variations (i.e., attributes from orderLine.productID to orderLine.brand are alternative to those from orderLine.pid to orderLine.make).

Table 1. The adopted terminology VS the terminology used in different data models.

Relational	Column-based	Document-based	Reference term
Table	Column-family	Collection	Collection
Tuple	Object	Document	Record
Attribute	Column	Attribute	Attribute
Attribute name	Column name	Path	Name

Definition 1 (Attribute). *Given a polystore DB, we define an attribute as* $a = (dm, db, col, name)$, *where* $dm = $ [relational|column|document] *is the data model,* $db \in DB$ *is the database name, col is the collection name in db, name is the name of the attribute in the collection col.*

We refer to A^* as the set of all attributes within all databases in the polystore DB; given an attribute a, we use $db(a)$, $col(a)$, $name(a)$ and $array(a)$ to respectively refer to its database db, its collection col, its name $name$ and (possibly) the $array$ attribute in which it is contained. In fact, attributes in document-based stores can appear in a *nested* form. In such cases, the name of the attribute corresponds to a path in dot notation that contains the ordered list of $array$ attributes and ends with the attribute itself; accessing a simple attribute requires to *unnest* all the arrays in which it is contained.

Example 1. With respect to Fig. 1, consider the following reference attributes:

- a_1 : (relational, Company, Client, id)
- a_2 : (relational, Company, Client, firstName)
- a_3 : (relational, Company, Client, lastName)
- a_4 : (document, Stores, Order, personID)
- a_5 : (document, Stores, Order, orderLine)
- a_6 : (document, Stores, Order, orderLine.productID)

- a_7 : (document, Stores, Order, orderLine.pid)
- a_8 : (document, Stores, Order, orderLine.price)
- a_9 : (document, Stores, Order, orderLine.cost)
- a_{10} : (document, Stores, Order, orderLine.brand)
- a_{11} : (document, Stores, Order, orderLine.make)

It is $db(a_4)$ = Stores and $col(a_4)$ = Order; also, $array(a_6) = array(a_7) = array(a_8) = array(a_9) = a_5$; attributes a_6, a_8 and a_{10} belong to the first schema variation of orderLine, while attributes a_7, a_9 and a_{11} belong to the second schema variation of orderLine.

In a polystore, attributes do not provide a global representation that hides the inherent schema heterogeneity as several syntactically different attributes may represent the same type of information. Relationships between attributes can be either manually inserted or automatically discovered. The automatic retrieval of such relationships is out of scope in this paper. Nonetheless, the literature on this topic is abundant; we refer the reader to a survey on common techniques for schema matching [17] and to an existing work for automatic discovery of primary-foreign key relationships [19]. Whether they are obtained either automatically or manually, which is likely when an incremental approach is adopted, relationships can be formalized as follows:

Definition 2 (Mapping). *A mapping is a relationship between two attributes* a' *and* a''. *We define a mapping as* $m = (a', a'', \phi, \varphi, \psi)$, *where* $a', a'' \in A^*$, $\phi = [sameAs|fk]$ *is the type of the mapping, and* φ *is a transcoding function to express* a' *values in* a'' *format (if necessary; otherwise,* $\varphi = I()$ *where* $I()$ *is the identity function). Finally,* ψ *is the semantics describing the meaning of the relationship (limitedly to* fk *mappings).*

The mapping type sameAs resolves semantic equivalence by indicating that there is an exact match between a' and a'', i.e., both attributes represent the same information for a given entity; a sameAs mapping can exist only if, for any given record, a' and a'' never coexist. Conversely, fk indicates that the values in a' correspond to the values in a'' (i.e., a relationship that, in RDBMSs, is modeled as a' being a *foreign key* to a''). Consequently, a'' must be a key; for the sake of simplicity, all keys are not composite. Mappings are assumed to be consistent; for example if $\exists\ m' = (a', a'', fk, \varphi, \psi)$, then $\nexists\ m'' = (a', a'', sameAs, \varphi')$.

The sameAs mappings are used to capture schema heterogeneity within a collection (thus, $db(a') = db(a'')$ and $col(a') = col(a'')$) whereas fk mappings are used to establish join relationships between collections (thus, $col(a') \neq col(a'')$). The semantics is necessary when the same attribute is referenced by several fk mappings to disambiguate the relationships. Note that while fk mappings are oriented, sameAs mappings are not oriented in principle, but they become oriented in practice when we consider the function φ that transcodes from a' to a'' and not viceversa.

Example 2. Consider the following mappings between the attributes defined in Example 1: $m_1 = (a_4, a_1, fk, toInt(), \text{“client order”})$, $m_2 = (a_6, a_7, sameAs, I())$, $m_3 = (a_8, a_9, sameAs, I())$, $m_4 = (a_{10}, a_{11}, sameAs, I())$.

The presence of several attributes that semantically represent the same concept can be hidden by an abstract representation called *feature*, which is based on the sameAs mappings.

Definition 3 (Feature). *A feature is a representation of a set of attributes in the polystore that semantically model the same concept. We define a feature as $f = (name, a, M)$, where a is the representative attribute of the feature, name is the name of the feature (possibly different from $name(a)$), and M is a set of* sameAs *mappings, in the form $(a', a,$ sameAs$, \varphi)$, linking all the feature's attributes to the representative attribute a. $M = \varnothing$ when a concept is modeled by a single attribute.*

The name of each feature is derived from the names of the represented attributes. However, it is up to the end user to specify a different name.

Example 3. Given the mappings in Example 2 we obtain the following features:

- $f_1 = ($id, $a_1,\ \varnothing)$
- $f_2 = ($firstName, $a_2,\ \varnothing)$
- $f_3 = ($lastName, $a_3,\ \varnothing)$
- $f_4 = ($personId, $a_4,\ \varnothing)$

- $f_5 = ($orderLine, $a_5,\ \varnothing)$
- $f_6 = ($orderLine.productID, $a_6,\ \{m_2\})$
- $f_7 = ($orderLine.price, $a_8,\ \{m_3\})$
- $f_8 = ($orderLine.brand, $a_{10},\ \{m_4\})$

We refer to $attr(f)$ as the set of attributes represented by f (i.e., the representative attribute plus those derived from the mappings). An attribute is always represented by one and only one feature; thus, for any two features f' and f'', it is $attr(f') \cap attr(f'') = \varnothing$. We refer to the feature of an attribute a as $feat(a)$ and to the name of a feature as $name(f)$.

Ultimately, we simply define the dataspace as follows.

Definition 4 (Dataspace). *A dataspace $\mathcal{D}$ is a set of features.*

We remark that, since features represent only attributes, there is no notion of collection in the dataspace (i.e., at the feature level). This is a substantial difference with a traditional integration approach, which would have required to define global collections and to model them (and their respective attributes) consistently with the modelings used in the different databases. Instead, features simply highlight the semantically distinct concepts that are available in the dataspace. In the next Section we explain the query mechanism based on the dataspace of features.

The query expressiveness that we consider covers a wide class of queries by composing three basic SQL operators: selection, join and generalized projection. The combination of these three operators determines GPSJ (Generalized Projection / Selection / Join) queries that were first studied in [12]. We provide the following definition of a query, which is based on the features of the dataspace.

Definition 5 (Query). *Given a dataspace $\mathcal{D}$, we define a query as $q = (q_\pi, q_\gamma, q_\sigma)$, where: $q_\pi \subseteq \mathcal{D}$ specifies the features to be projected; q_γ specifies optional aggregations as a set of couples (f, op), where $f \in \mathcal{D}$ and op is an aggregation function; q_σ is an optional set of selection predicates in the form of triplets (f, ω, v), where $f \in \mathcal{D}$, $\omega \in \{=; >; <; \neq; \geq; \leq\}$ and v is a value.*

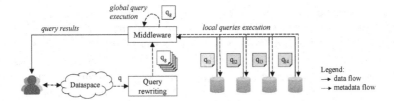

Fig. 2. Query execution process: the query q (formulated on the dataspace) is translated into a set of local queries ($q_{l1} \ldots q_{l4}$) to be executed in separate databases, and a global query (q_g) that operates in the middleware on the results of the local queries.

GPSJ queries are the most common class of queries in OLAP applications. Attributes in q_γ are measures of the event that is the target of the OLAP analysis. The single events are measured at the finest level of granularity, possibly filtered by conditions expressed on q_σ and then grouped at the coarser granularity defined by q_π. It is not mandatory that all the three operators are present, thus simple selection queries and join queries are also covered. We refer to $feat(q)$ as the set of features involved in q; also, we will use $attr(q)$ as short for $attr(feat(q))$.

Example 4. Let us suppose that we want to measure the average price orderLine.price of the products orderLine.productID of brand orderLine.brand "ABC" by a client called "John Smith" from the dataspace $\mathcal{D}$. Therefore the group-by set is $q_\pi = \{f_6\}$; the aggregation set is $q_\gamma = \{(f_7, \mathsf{avg})\}$ and the set of selection predicates is $q_\sigma = \{(f_2, =, "John"), (f_3, =, "Smith"), (f_8, =, "ABC")\}$.

4   Execution Plan Formulation

The execution of the query requires the definition of an execution plan that potentially includes different databases. We model the execution plan in NRA, as it is compatible with SQL and document stores' query languages [3]. Given a query execution plan, we distinguish between the single *local plans* (i.e., the parts that can be executed directly on a single database) and the *global plan* (i.e., the part to be executed in the middleware to join the data coming from different databases). While the local plans directly access the collections of the polystore, the global plan accesses the intermediary results of the local plans (i.e., *views* on the single databases). An intuition of the process is given in Fig. 2. We remark that schema variability is managed by the local plans.

4.1   Determining the Query Graph

The information necessary to build the query plan can be modeled by means of a supporting structure we call *datagraph*. Indeed, a query involves a set of features which, in turn, represent several attributes in the dataspace. The datagraph is used to find the connections between these attributes and to obtain the execution plan for a given query.

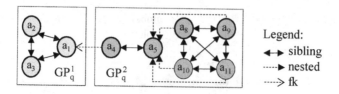

Fig. 3. Query graph of the query in Example 4, with the query graph partitions GP_q^1 and GP_q^2 highlighted; bold circles correspond to representative attributes of a feature.

Definition 6 (Datagraph). *The datagraph G is a graph $G = (A^*, E)$ where A^* is the set of all the attributes of all databases (representing the vertexes of the graph) and E is the set of edges connecting the attributes.*

An edge $e \in E$ between two attributes a' and a'' indicates the existence of a relationship, which is described by its type, i.e., $type(e)$; its value is one of the following three:

- sibling: represented as $a' \leftrightarrow a''$, it indicates that a' and a'' are in the same collection and at the same nesting level;
- nested: represented as $a' \xrightarrow{n} a''$, it indicates that a' is nested inside a'';
- fk: represented as $a' \xrightarrow{fk} a''$, it indicates that the values of a'' are referred to the values of a'.

Edges of type sibling and nested are automatically derived from the schema, while those of type fk can be either derived from the original schemas or defined by the user through mappings. Noticeably, nested edges can only come from databases whose data model supports nested attributes (i.e., document- and column-based). Figure 3 shows a portion of the datagraph representing the attributes from Example 1. The existence of a directed path from a' to a'', represented as $a' \Rightarrow a''$, implies the existence of a *-to-one* (i.e., either *one-to-one* or *many-to-one*) relationship from a' to a'' through a chain of join and unnesting operations. For instance, it is $a_9 \Rightarrow a_2$, while $a_1 \not\Rightarrow a_4$.

Definition 7 (Query graph). *Given a datagraph G and a query q, we define the query graph $G_q = (A' \subseteq A^*, E' \subseteq E)$ as the minimally connected subgraph of G such that i) $A' \supseteq attr(q)$, and ii) there exists $A'' \subseteq A'$ s.t. $A'' \neq \varnothing, A'' \supseteq q_\gamma, \forall (a \in A'', a' \in A'),$ it is $a \Rightarrow a'$.*

Condition (i) ensures that all attributes belonging to the features involved in the query are included in A'. Condition (ii) entails the *answerability* of query q on D with the GPSJ semantics, that is, there exist one or more attributes representing the events at the finest level of granularity (i.e., a *-to-one* relationship exists with all the others attributes in q). More than one query graphs could exist for a given query as more than one *-to-one* paths could exist each associated to a different semantics (e.g., a sale could be associated to both the *date of sale* and *date of shipping*). In this case the user is asked to identify the adequate query graph to execute.

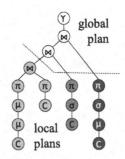

Fig. 4. Sample execution plan for a generic GPSJ; different shades of grey represent different databases.

Algorithm 1. Definition of the NRA execution plan for a query q.

Input $q = (q_\pi, q_\gamma, q_\sigma)$: a query; $G_q = (A', E')$ the query graph for q.
Output P: the NRA plan of q.
1: $P \leftarrow \varnothing$
2: $LP \leftarrow \varnothing$ ▷ Empty array of local plans
3: $GP_q \leftarrow partitionQueryGraph(G_q)$
4: **for all** $GP_q^i \in GP_q$ **do**   ▷ One local plan is created for every partition of G_q
5:     $CP \leftarrow \varnothing$ ▷ Empty array of collection plans
6:     $C \leftarrow identifyAccessedCollections(GP_q^i)$
7:     **for all** $col \in C$ **do**   ▷ One collection plans is created for every partition of GP_q^i
8:         $CP_{col} \leftarrow defineCollectionPlan(col, GP_q^i)$
9:     $LP_i \leftarrow defineLocalJoins(CP, GP_q^i)$
10: $P \leftarrow defineGlobalPlan(LP, G_q)$
11: **return** P

4.2 Defining the Nested Relational Algebra Execution Plan

The full structure of a GPSJ query is shown in Fig. 4 and, as discussed in Sect. 3, is composed of an aggregation[2], over a set of joins, over a set of filtering operators. The process to translate a query graph G_q into an NRA execution plan is described by Algorithm 1 and requires to: (1) partition G_q in several subgraphs, each corresponding to a local plan (line 1); (2) define each local plan (lines 4–9); (3) collate the local plans into the global one (line 3).

Query Graph Partitioning. Intuitively, a local plan includes all and only the operators that apply to the same database. More formally, this corresponds to partitioning G_q based on the edges of type fk in E' (denoted as E'_{glo}) such that $a' \xrightarrow{\text{fk}} a''$ and $db(a') \neq db(a'')$ (see Fig. 3). Let us define GP_q as the set of partitions, where $|GP_q| = |E'_{\text{glo}}| + 1$. Noticeably, if two edges in E'_{glo} refer to the same database db, it will determine two local plans. For instance, with reference to the running example, this happens if both Client and Vendor tables are accessed on the relational database through the Stores collection in the document database.

---

[2] We define the aggregation with the operator γ declared as $_X\gamma_Y$, where X is the group-by set (i.e., a set of features) and Y is the set of aggregations (where each aggregation is composed of a feature and an aggregation function).

Local Plan Definition. At this point, for each query graph partition GP_q^i, we define the corresponding local plan by applying in sequence the following steps.

1. *Identify accessed collection* Similarly to the query graph partitioning step, the collections to be accessed are identified by partitioning G_q^i based on the edges of type fk. It is possible that the same collection needs to be accessed twice (e.g., given a collection of cities, both the birth city and the residence of customers are requested by the query); this happens when G_q^i includes two fk edges between the same collections and with different semantics.
2. *Define collection plan* For each collection *col* we define a plan by applying in sequence the following steps.
   (a) *Collection accesses* A collection access C(*col*) is added to the local plan to denote the collection to be accessed.
   (b) *Unnest operators* Given a feature $f \in feat(q)$, it may happen that some of the $attr(f)$ belong to a nested structure. To retrieve them it is mandatory to flatten the structure by recursively unnesting the arrays. More formally, if $\exists\ a \in attr(f) \mid array(a) \neq \varnothing$, the unnest operator μ on $array(a)$ is necessary. For instance, given $a''' \in attr(f)$ in the collection *col*, if $array(a''') = a''$, $array(a'') = a'$ and $array(a') = \varnothing$, then C(*col*) in the local plan becomes $\mu_{a''}(\mu_{a'}(\mathsf{C}(col)))$. Notice that, due to schema heterogeneity, several arrays may need to be unnested, thus the unnesting rule is applied to each $a \in attr(f)$.
   (c) *Selection operators* for each feature $f \in feat(q_\sigma)$, a selection operator σ_p must be added to the local plan, where $p = (f, \omega, v)$ is the selection predicate on f. Clearly, p must be actually formulated on $attr(f)$; however, if $|attr(f)| > 1$ due to schema heterogeneity, the same predicate must be applied to several attributes. The predicate must be true for any of the schema variations of f. Each record fits a specific schema variation including only one of the attributes in $attr(f)$, thus p is defined as a disjunction of conditions on $attr(f)$: $p = (\bigvee_{\forall a_i \in attr(f)} \varphi_{a_i}(name(a_i)), \omega, v)$, where φ is the function transcoding a_i into the representative attribute of f. For the sake of optimization, a single selection operation is generated for predicates that must be applied to the same collection, e.g., given $p_1 = \{f', \omega_1, v_1\}$ and $p_2 = \{f'', \omega_2, v_2\}$, if $col(attr(f')) = col(attr(f''))$ then the applied selection operator is $\sigma_{p_1 \wedge p_2}$.
   (d) *Projection operators* The role of projection operator is threefold: (1) it keeps only the features required by the following join and aggregation operators; (2) it solves the semantic equivalence by combining all the attributes in $attr(f)$ and renaming them in $name(f)$; (3) it solves data format heterogeneity by applying φ to transcode values from the original format to the one of the representative attribute. Consider $F_\pi = \{feat(q_\pi) \cup feat(q_\gamma) \cup F_{\bowtie}\}$ the set of features to be projected, where $F_{\bowtie}$ is the set of features whose attributes are involved in fk edges in G_q. Also, consider $F_\pi^{col} = \{f \in F_\pi \mid attr(f) \in col\}$. $|F_\pi^{col}|$ projections are added to the previously defined access plan for *col*. The projection for $f \in F_\pi^{col}$ is defined as $\left(\bigvee_{\forall a_i \in attr(f)} \varphi_{a_i}(name(a_i))\right) / name(f)$. The role

of $\bigvee$ is to select the only non-null value among $attr(f)$; it is expressed with the CASE statement in SQL, or with the $ifNull operator in the MongoDB query language. Finally, "/" represents the renaming of the result with the feature's name.

3. *Define local joins* For each edge $a' \xrightarrow{fk} a''$ in a query graph partition G_q^i, a join operator $\bowtie_{name(feat(a'))=name(feat(a''))}$ is added to join the different collection plans. Please note that for the sake of simplicity we did not consider projections aimed at removing features that are necessary only for joins.

Global Plan Definition. Similarly to the addition of local joins, a join operator $\bowtie_{name(feat(a'))=name(feat(a''))}$ is added for each edge $a' \xrightarrow{fk} a''$ between two query graph partitions to join the different local plans. We remark that the optimization of join ordering is out of the scope of this paper. Ultimately, the aggregation operator $_{q_\pi}\gamma_{q_\gamma}$ after the last join operator, where q_π is the group-by set of the query and q_γ is the set of aggregations functions applied on the features. We remind the reader that the final aggregation or projection is optional.

Example 5. The execution plan of the query in Example 4 is shown in Fig. 4. Noticeably, the aggregation and global join operators directly reference the resolved feature names.

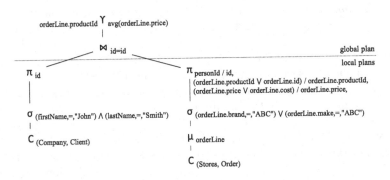

Fig. 5. Execution plan of the query in Example 4.

5   Discussion and Conclusions

Data science and BI 2.0 expect more flexible and lightweight approaches to data analysis. Our proposal extends previous polystore solutions by handling schema heterogeneity and ensuring consistent answer for GPSJ queries, i.e., a wide class of queries that is the most common in OLAP.

Although the main contribution of this paper is the introduction of the formal framework, we carried out a preliminary experimentation through a prototype to verify the correctness and effectiveness of our findings. With reference to Fig. 2 we adopted Spark SQL as the middleware, MySQL, MongoDB and Cassandra as relational, document-based and column-based DBMSs, respectively. The polystore we implemented is based on Unibench and has been extended with schema heterogeneity. All the classes of heterogeneity discussed in the paper have been injected and two different schemata for the Order collection are present. Maximal schema cardinality is 142k records for the Order and Invoice collections. We also defined the minimal set of features to answer a workload of 4 queries. In particular, query in Example 4 (whose plan is reported in Fig. 5) retrieves 23% of the orders, and allows to transparently access the related order lines that are evenly distributed on different schemata of the document DB. Overall query execution requires 6.9 s: 0.2 s are necessary to create the plans, 1.2 s to run in parallel the local plans, 2.7 s to generate Spark dataframes and 2.8 s to run the global one. Other queries perform at comparable times and all results correctly correspond to those of a manual execution.

Future extensions will cover different aspects. First, we plan to cover horizontal partitioning of the data, that is, the same collection can span on several collections on potentially different DBs. This introduces a new level of heterogeneity, as features may represent attributes that do not belong to the same collection. We will also extend our approach (1) to support additional data models (e.g., key-value and graph), and (2) to enable a broader set of queries than GPSJs (e.g., [1]). In terms of effectiveness, we will consider the introduction of KPIs to provide further insights to the user with respect to the underlying heterogeneity of the data (e.g., [10]). Finally, we intend to run larger experimentation over real datasets to better study the efficiency and boundaries of our approach.

References

1. Ben Hamadou, H., et al.: Schema-independent querying for heterogeneous collections in NoSQL document stores. Inf. Syst. (2019, in press). https://doi.org/10.1016/j.is.2019.04.005
2. Ben Hamadou, H., Ghozzi, F., Péninou, A., Teste, O.: Towards schema-independent querying on document data stores. In: 20th International Workshop on Design, Optimization, Languages and Analytical Processing of Big Data Co-Located with EDBT/ICDT. CEUR-WS.org (2018)
3. Botoeva, E., Calvanese, D., Cogrel, B., Xiao, G.: Expressivity and complexity of MongoDB queries. In: 21st International Conference on Database Theory, pp. 9:1–9:23. Schloss Dagstuhl - Leibniz-Zentrum fuer Informatik (2018). https://doi.org/10.4230/LIPIcs.ICDT.2018.9
4. Chang, F., et al.: Bigtable: a distributed storage system for structured data. ACM Trans. Comput. Syst. 26(2), 4:1–4:26 (2008)
5. Corbellini, A., Mateos, C., Zunino, A., Godoy, D., Schiaffino, S.N.: Persisting big-data: the NoSQL landscape. Inf. Syst. 63, 1–23 (2017)

6. DiScala, M., Abadi, D.J.: Automatic generation of normalized relational schemas from nested key-value data. In: 2016 ACM SIGMOD International Conference on Management of Data, pp. 295–310. ACM (2016). https://doi.org/10.1145/2882903. 2882924

7. Franklin, M.J., Halevy, A.Y., Maier, D.: From databases to dataspaces: a new abstraction for information management. SIGMOD Rec. **34**(4), 27–33 (2005)

8. Gadepally, V., et al.: The BigDAWG polystore system and architecture. In: 2016 IEEE High Performance Extreme Computing Conference, pp. 1–6. IEEE (2016)

9. Gallinucci, E., Golfarelli, M., Rizzi, S.: Variety-aware OLAP of document-oriented databases. In: 20th International Workshop on Design, Optimization, Languages and Analytical Processing of Big Data Co-Located with EDBT/ICDT. CEUR-WS.org (2018)

10. Gallinucci, E., Golfarelli, M., Rizzi, S.: Approximate OLAP of document-oriented databases: a variety-aware approach. Inf. Syst. (2019, in press). https://doi.org/10.1016/j.is.2019.02.004

11. Golfarelli, M., et al.: OLAP query reformulation in peer-to-peer data warehousing. Inf. Syst. **37**(5), 393–411 (2012). https://doi.org/10.1016/j.is.2011.06.003

12. Gupta, A., Harinarayan, V., Quass, D.: Aggregate-query processing in data warehousing environments. In: 21th International Conference on Very Large Data Bases, pp. 358–369. Morgan Kaufmann (1995)

13. Herrero, V., Abelló, A., Romero, O.: NOSQL design for analytical workloads: variability matters. In: 35th International Conference on Conceptual Modeling, pp. 50–64 (2016). https://doi.org/10.1007/978-3-319-46397-1_4

14. Jeffery, S.R., Franklin, M.J., Halevy, A.Y.: Pay-as-you-go user feedback for dataspace systems. In: 2008 ACM SIGMOD International Conference on Management of Data, pp. 847–860. ACM (2008). https://doi.org/10.1145/1376616.1376701

15. LeFevre, J., et al.: MISO: souping up big data query processing with a multistore system. In: 2014 ACM SIGMOD International Conference on Management of Data, pp. 1591–1602. ACM (2014). https://doi.org/10.1145/2588555.2588568

16. Ong, K.W., Papakonstantinou, Y., Vernoux, R.: The SQL++ semi-structured data model and query language: a capabilities survey of SQL-on-Hadoop, NoSQL and NewSQL databases. CoRR abs/1405.3631 (2014)

17. Rahm, E., Bernstein, P.A.: A survey of approaches to automatic schema matching. VLDB J. **10**(4), 334–350 (2001). https://doi.org/10.1007/s007780100057

18. Rolls, D., Joslin, C., Scholz, S.: Unibench: a tool for automated and collaborative benchmarking. In: 18th IEEE International Conference on Program Comprehension, pp. 50–51. IEEE Computer Society (2010). https://doi.org/10.1109/ICPC.2010.36

19. Rostin, A., et al.: A machine learning approach to foreign key discovery. In: 12th International Workshop on the Web and Databases (2009)

20. Sadalage, P.J., Fowler, M.: NoSQL Distilled: A Brief Guide to the Emerging World of Polyglot Persistence. Pearson Education, London (2013)

21. Sheth, A.P.: Federated database systems for managing distributed, heterogeneous, and autonomous databases. In: 17th International Conference on Very Large Data Bases, p. 489. Morgan Kaufmann (1991)

22. Tahara, D., Diamond, T., Abadi, D.J.: Sinew: a SQL system for multi-structured data. In: 2014 ACM SIGMOD International Conference on Management of Data, pp. 815–826. ACM (2014). https://doi.org/10.1145/2588555.2612183

23. Tan, R., et al.: Enabling query processing across heterogeneous data models: a survey. In: 2017 IEEE International Conference on Big Data, pp. 3211–3220. IEEE Computer Society (2017). https://doi.org/10.1109/BigData.2017.8258302

24. Thomas, S.J., Fischer, P.C.: Nested relational structures. Adv. Comput. Res. **3**, 269–307 (1986)
25. Wang, L., et al.: Schema management for document stores. PVLDB **8**(9), 922–933 (2015). https://doi.org/10.14778/2777598.2777601
26. Zaharia, M., et al.: Apache Spark: a unified engine for big data processing. Commun. ACM **59**(11), 56–65 (2016). https://doi.org/10.1145/2934664

Ontology-Schema Based Query by Example

Lucas Peres, Ticiana L. Coelho da Silva[✉], Jose Macedo[✉],
and David Araujo[✉]

Insight Data Science Lab, Fortaleza, CE, Brazil
{lucasperes,ticianalc,jose.macedo,david}@insightlab.ufc.br

Abstract. The Web has evolved from a network of linked documents to one where both documents and data are linked, resulting in what is commonly known as the Web of Linked Data, that includes a large variety of data usually published in RDF from multiple domains. Intuitive ways of accessing RDF data become increasingly important since the standard approach would be to run SPARQL queries. However, this can be extremely difficult for non-experts users. In this paper, we address the problem of question answering over RDF. Given a natural language question or a keyword search string, our goal is to translate it into a formal query as SPARQL that captures the information needed. We propose Von-QBE which is a schema-based approach to query over RDF data without any previous knowledge about the ontology entities and schema. This is different from the-state-of-art since the approaches are instance-based. However, it can be unfeasible using such approaches in big data scenarios where the ontology base is huge and demands a large amount of computational resource to keep the knowledge base in memory. Moreover, most of these solutions need the knowledge base triplified, which can be a hard task for legacy bases. Von-QBE results are promising for the two real benchmarks evaluated, considering that only the ontology schema is used to generate SPARQL queries.

1 Introduction

The Web has evolved from a network of linked documents to one where both documents and data are linked, resulting in what is commonly known as the Web of Linked Data, that includes a large variety of data usually published in RDF from multiple domains. Intuitive ways of accessing RDF data become increasingly important since the standard approach would be to run structured queries in triple-pattern-based languages like SPARQL [12]. This can be extremely difficult for non-experts users.

Consider the example question, such as "Find the title of action movies produced in Eastern Asia and the name of their company". A possible SPARQL formulation, assuming a user familiar with the schema of the underlying knowledge base, could consist of the following:

© Springer Nature Switzerland AG 2019
A. H. F. Laender et al. (Eds.): ER 2019, LNCS 11788, pp. 204–212, 2019.
https://doi.org/10.1007/978-3-030-33223-5_17

```
SELECT DISTINCT ?x ?title ?company_name WHERE {
?x a mo:Movie; mo:title ?title;
 mo:isProducedBy ?y; mo:belongsToGenre [ a mo:Brute_Action ] .
?y :companyName ?company_name .
?y :hasCompanyLocation [ a mo:Eastern_Asia ] . }
```

This complex query, which involves multiple joins, is difficult for the user to come up with specific relations, classes and entities. This would require familiarity with the knowledge base, which in general, no user should be expected to have. In this paper, we address the problem of question answering over RDF. Given a natural language question Q_N and an underlying ontology O, our goal is to translate Q_N into a formal query Q_S as SPARQL that captures the information need to be expressed by Q_N. We focus on queries that emphasize classes and relations between them. We do not consider aggregation, disjunctive and negation queries.

A considerable number of question answering approaches for RDF data has been proposed, to name a few [1,8,9,11,13] and [12]. They address the same problem of this paper. However, they present several limitations: [1,9,13] and [11] are instance-based approaches, which can be unfeasible in big data scenarios where the ontology base is huge and demands a large amount of computational resource to keep the knowledge base in memory. Moreover, most of those solutions need the knowledge base triplified, which can be a hard task for legacy bases. [12] requires a pre-processing phase to constructed a phase-concept dictionary as part of the knowledge base, and [8] is based on SPARQL templates. In this paper, we propose Von-QBE (stands for Virtual Ontology Query By Example) that overcome such limitations. Von-QBE derives from the term virtual ontology, since it is not instance-based and it can use an ontology virtualized by other tools like Ontop [3] instead of RDF stores.

Von-QBE is a schema-based approach to query over RDF data without any previous knowledge about the ontology entities and schema. Von-QBE lets the user queries using natural language questions or by using a keyword search and translates the query into SPARQL. Furthermore, Von-QBE assists the user to construct his/her query search interactively. The remainder of the paper is structured as follows: Sect. 2 introduces our proposal Von-QBE. Section 3 presents the experimental evaluation, and finally Sect. 4 draws the final conclusions.

2   Von-QBE Framework

In this section, we introduce our proposal. Given a natural language question Q_N (or a keyword search string) and an ontology base O, Von-QBE translates Q_N into a SPARQL query Q_S that can capture the same information expressed by Q_N. Beyond that, Von-QBE also helps the user to construct its keyword search interactively. For the sake of brevity, from now on we will use Q_N in place of the natural language question, and the keyword search string since each word in the natural language question is tackled as a keyword.

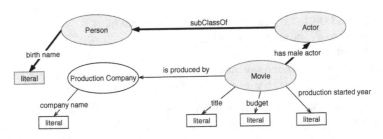

Fig. 1. Part of IMDB ontology schema with the highlighted fragment for the search: *movies and their actors birth name*

Suppose the ontology schema in Fig. 1[1] represented as an RDF graph based on [4], where the classes are graph nodes and the properties, edges. Imagine a user that starts Q_N with the keyword *movie*. Von-QBE suggests improving Q_N using concepts from the ontology schema and whenever Q_N represents what the user is searching for, the user can submit Q_N to Von-QBE. Then, Von-QBE transforms Q_N into a SPARQL query Q_S and returns the answers.

Von-QBE comprises three main components: (1) *Fragment Extractor* responsible to, from Q_N, identify the ontology subset involved in the query. Throughout this paper, we call such subset as *fragment*; (2) *Fragment Expansor* which expands the fragment with classes and properties, i.e. ontology concepts. Based on this expansion, *Fragment Expansor* suggests new ontology concepts to the user expands Q_N; and finally, (3) *Query Builder* which transforms the fragment into a SPARQL query Q_S. In what follows, we describe in details each Von-QBE component.

Fragment Extraction. As we mentioned before a *fragment* from the underlying RDF graph corresponds to the classes and properties of the ontology schema involved on Q_N. The *Fragment Extraction* is made up by two main components: (1) *Keyword Matcher* that identifies the ontology concepts mentioned on Q_N, and (2) *Fragment Constructor* that discovers how these concepts are related on the ontology schema. Consider the ontology schema presented in Fig. 1 and Q_N as "Give the movie actors". The *Keyword Matcher* would identify the classes *Movie* and *Actor* that yield the highest similarity value with the terms of Q_N. From these classes, the *Fragment Constructor* would extract the fragment *Movie has male actor Actor*, once the class *Movie* directly achieves *Actor* in the RDF graph.

Now consider Q_N as "Find the birth name of actors from movies". The *Keyword Matcher* would identify the classes *Actor* and *Movie*, and the property *birth name*. However, *birth name* is not a property of *Actor* neither a property of *Movie* in the RDF graph. So *Fragment Constructor* identifies the class *Person* and the property *subClassOf* to relate *birth name* with *Actor*. Finally, the fragment is built by means of the relation *has male actor* that relates *Movie* and *Actor*, the relation *subClassOf* that relates *Actor* and *Person*, and the relation

---

[1] https://sites.google.com/site/ontopiswc13/home/imdb-mo.

birth name which is a property of *Person*. The generated fragment is highlighted in Fig. 1.

Algorithm 1 performs the *Keyword Matcher*. First of all, we prefer to use Jaro-Winkler [10] as the similarity measure since it is widely used. Algorithm 1 receives as input a list of *words* from Q_N, the ontology schema (*RDFSchema*) and a similarity threshold ρ. It outputs the ontology concepts (classes and/or properties) that match with *words*. For each word (line 3) in Q_N, *testWord* appends such word with the previous words (*composedConcept*) in Q_N such that they together are similar to a concept in *RDFSchema* (Line 4). So, Line 5 checks if there is any concept on *RDFSchema* such that the similarity between *testWord* is greater than a threshold ρ. If so, the algorithm updates *composedConcept* (Line 6) in order to keep in such variable a sequence of words in Q_N that matches an ontology concept according to ρ. If the similarity is not greater than ρ, the algorithm adds into *elements* list the highest similar ontology concept with *composedConcept* (Lines 8 and 9), and updates the *composedConcept* variable to the current analyzed word. The intuition behind is from that word the algorithm might start a new sequence of words that match with any ontology concepts. Algorithm 1 needs to check if there is any ontology concept that is similar to the last value assigned to *composedConcept* at Line 13. If so, such concept is added into the *elements* list (Lines 14 and 15). Line 17 returns the output of the algorithm.

The output of Algorithm 1 is given as input *Fragment Constructor* module, which builds the fragment that relates the ontology concepts involved in Q_N according to the RDF Schema (also given as input). First, it computes the closure

---

Algorithm 1. Algorithm Keyword Matcher

Data: *words, RDFSchema, ρ*
Result: elements //ontology elements
1 elements := {}; n :=(words.length-1); composedConcept := "" ;
2 **for** $i := 0$ *to* n-1 **do**
3   word = words[i] ;
4   testWord = composedConcept + word ;
5   **if** *similarConcept(testWord, RDFSchema) $> \rho$* **then**
6 | composedConcept = testWord ;
7   **else**
8 | concept := RDFSchema.getMostSimilarConcept(composedConcept);
9 | elements.add(concept) ;
10 | composedConcept = word ;
11   **end**
12 **end**
13 **if** *similarConcept(composedConcept, RDFSchema) $> \rho$* **then**
14   concept := RDFSchema.getMostSimilarConcept(composedConcept) ;
15   elements.add(concept) ;
16 **end**
17 **return** *elements*

---

graph [5] which is a subgraph constructed by using the shortest paths (obtained by running Dijkstra algorithm) among all the pair of ontology concepts returned by Algorithm 1. This graph might have cycles which are often found on RDF ontologies. Imagine two properties that are one inverse of another, like *has male actor* that connects *Movie* to *Actor* and *is male actor in*, connecting *Actor* to *Movie*. To remove these cycles, the module applies Prim's algorithm [6] to find the Minimum Spanning Tree(MST). Prim outputs a fragment smaller or equal than the closure graph. This means that such a fragment contains only the minimal number of paths to connect all the ontology concepts outputted by Algorithm 1. Of course, the closure graph might have multiple MSTs. However, Prim only takes one of them.

After the computation of the fragment, Von-QBE starts two other components: (1) *Fragment Expansor* which expands the fragment with ontology classes and properties. Based on this expansion, *Fragment Expansor* suggests new ontology concepts to the user expands Q_N; (2) *Query Builder* which transforms the fragment into a SPARQL query Q_S.

Fragment Expansor. Von-QBE suggests the user expands Q_N using the ontology classes and properties that are directly connected to the fragment. The *Fragment Expansor* expands the fragment with all edges (of course, the ones that are not already in the fragment) that come in (or out) from the fragment nodes. Remember that our ontology is represented as an RDF graph, and the fragment nodes are ontology classes. Let Q_N be "Find the movies and their actors" and the underlying ontology is the RDFSchema represented in Fig. 1. The fragment nodes derived from Q_N are *Movie* and *Actor*. From the node *Movie*, *Fragment Expansor* can find the following properties: *title, budget, production started year, is produced by* and *has male actor*. However, the *has male actor* is already in the fragment. So, only the other properties should be presented as a suggestion to the user expands Q_N. The node *Actor* contains a particular case. Consider the property *has male actor* is already in the fragment. In this case, *Fragment Expansor* can only suggest *subClassOf*. However, when a class is a subclass of another, it must inherit the properties from the parent class. So, instead of suggesting *subClassOf*, *Fragment Expansor* suggests to the user *birth name*.

Query Builder works as follows: each edge in the fragment (output of *Fragment Constructor* module or expanded with the suggestions outputted by *Fragment Expansor* module and accepted by the user) is added as a clause (or triple pattern), and the source and the target nodes are named as variables. Since the ontology schema might have properties that present multiple domains and ranges, *Query Builder* also adds a clause to inform the instance type (class) of each variable. All the clauses (or triple patterns) are given as input to Apache Jena library[2] which generates Q_S according to the SPARQL syntax. Let Q_N be: "Find the birth name of actors from movies" and the fragment with the following relations: *Movie has male actor Actor, Actor subClassOf Person* and *Person birth name*. The second edge relates to the property *subClassOf*. Whenever *Query*

---

[2] http://jena.apache.org.

Builder finds an edge with *subClassOf*, it replaces such edge by other new edges that have the parent class as a source. So considering the *RDF Schema* represented in Fig. 1, *Query Builder* generates the following edges: *E1: Movie has male actor Actor* and *E2: Actor birth name*.

The edge *E1* is a relation connecting two classes. Since this is the first edge to be processed, we have two new variables (one for *Movie* and one for *Actor*). *Query Builder* also adds three clauses: a definition for the *Movie* variable, a definition for the *Actor* variable and the connection of both variables using the property *has male actor*. So, the edge *E1* corresponds to the three following triple patterns: *TP1: ?Movie a imdb:Movie*, *TP2: ?Actor a imdb:Actor* and *TP3: ?Movie imdb:has_ male_ actor ?Actor*. The edge *E2* is a property that points to a literal value (also called attribute or, in RDF, *DataTypeProperty*). This kind of edge needs to use also two variables, but only the first one is a class instance, the other variable is a literal value (strings, numbers, dates, among others). Since the *Actor* variable is already defined, *Query Builder* only needs to add one more triple pattern: *TP4: ?Actor imdb:birth_ name ?Actor_ birth_ name*. Once all the triple patterns are generated from the fragment edges, Apache Jena generates the SPARQL query Q_S as follows:

```
SELECT ?Movie ?Actor ?Actor_birth_name WHERE{
?Movie a imdb:Movie .
?Actor a imdb:Actor .
?Movie imdb:has_male_actor ?Actor .
?Actor imdb:birth_name ?Actor_birth_name .}
```

3 Experiments

In this section, we provide the details about the experimentation performed with Von-QBE. No experiments were made to compare Von-QBE to other solutions previously mentioned since these works use the ontology data instances to improve their performance, which would not be a fair comparison. From the authors' knowledge, OptiqueVQS [7] and Von-QBE are the only solution schema-based, but OptiqueVQS does not accept natural language or keyword search then we can not compare with OptiqueVQS as well. Instead, we experimented Von-QBE with two real benchmarks. For each benchmark, we evaluate each question is evaluated according to well-established metrics, i.e., *recall* and *precision*.

3.1 Datasets

Our experiments are based on two collections of questions: IMDB Movie Ontology[3] virtualized[4] using Ontop [3] with questions formulated in SPARQL query[4]. IMDB provides data about actors, movies, directors, and production company.

---

[3] https://sites.google.com/site/ontopiswc13/home/imdb-mo.
[4] https://raw.githubusercontent.com/wiki/ontop/ontop/attachments/Example_
MovieOntology/movieontology.q.

Another collection of questions are the QALD[5] task for question answering over linked data. It comprises two sets of questions over DBpedia [2], annotated with SPARQL queries and answers. We used QALDs 5, 6, 7 and 9 training questions which are provided with a SPARQL benchmark. For both benchmarks, the questions out-of-scope for Von-QBE were not considered, like ASK type questions, aggregation, and counting. Moreover, the ones that no entities are available (empty results).

After removing these questions, our test set consists of 12 QALD-(5, 6, 7, 9) training questions and 29 Ontop questions out of 37. The number of evaluated questions in QALD-(5, 6, 7, 9) reduces by much, because these questions comprise information about instances, like people names, country names, aggregations, sorting, while Von-QBE works with conceptual questions, using classes and properties names only.

3.2 Evaluation Results

Table 1 lists the results of each experiment using IMDB and QALD datasets. To both benchmarks, we set 0,9 as the similarity threshold (ρ) in the *Keyword Matcher* algorithm. IMDB contains some questions with low results for precision, like the keyword search question 24: "title movies company name production company located East Asia", for example, demands the movie title and company names located in East Asia. Von-QBE generates a SPARQL query that projects all properties and entities used in the triple-patterns on the SELECT clause, then the movies and companies URIs, titles, and names are returned. However, there exist movies with the same title but different IDs, so Von-QBE retrieves more answers than the benchmark. This decreases precision.

Table 1. Experiment results for IMDB and QALD-(5, 6, 7, 9) datasets.

Dataset	Questions	Select-project questions	Answerable questions	Recall (R)	Precision(P)
IMDB	37	37	29	0.96	0.69
QALD-5	286	269	1	0.2	$1 \times 10e - 4$
QALD-6	335	308	5	0.55	0.001
QALD-7	215	193	2	0.39	$3 \times 10e - 5$
QALD-9	408	371	4	0.66	0.013
Weighted mean				0.53	0.0047

Another drawback is for questions that use entities to filter the results, like question 271 from QALD-9: "Which awards did Douglas Hofstadter win?". The SPARQL gold standard retrieves only the awards from *Douglas Hofstader* while the SPARQL generated from Von-QBE retrieves all the awards. This happens because VON-QBE is schema-based only, and *Douglas Hofstader* is an entity,

---

[5] http://qald.aksw.org.

not a concept. This has a major impact in the QALD results, since only a really small portion of the questions, Von-QBE can retrieve any result. Analyzing only the queries with answers, we still get some acceptable recall results using only the schema. We plan to enhance VON-QBE by using, for instance, Named Entity Recognition tools to detect for each entity described in the query (like *Douglas Hofstader*) its corresponding class. The evaluation data can be found at[6] and a demonstration of Von-QBE can be found at[7].

4   Conclusion and Future Work

In this paper, we propose Von-QBE to address the problem of translating a natural language question or a keyword search over RDF data into SPARQL query. From the authors' knowledge, Von-QBE is the first work to address such a problem using only the ontology schema. We believe our results are promising for the two real benchmarks evaluated, considering that only the ontology schema was used to generate SPARQL queries. As future work, we aim at using natural language processing tools to detect entities described in the query and find its corresponding concept over the ontology schema. Moreover, we aim at expanding Von-QBE to process different types of queries, like aggregation.

Acknowledgments. This work has been supported by FUNCAP SPU 8789771/2017 research project.

References

1. Arnaout, H., Elbassuoni, S.: Effective searching of RDF knowledge graphs. J. Web Semant. **48**, 66–84 (2018)
2. Auer, S., Bizer, C., Kobilarov, G., Lehmann, J., Cyganiak, R., Ives, Z.: DBpedia: a nucleus for a web of open data. In: Aberer, K., et al. (eds.) ASWC/ISWC -2007. LNCS, vol. 4825, pp. 722–735. Springer, Heidelberg (2007). https://doi.org/10.1007/978-3-540-76298-0_52
3. Calvanese, D., et al.: Ontop: answering SPARQL queries over relational databases. Semant. Web **8**(3), 471–487 (2017)
4. World Wide Web Consortium, et al.: RDF 1.1 concepts and abstract syntax
5. Kompella, V.P., Pasquale, J.C., Polyzos, G.C.: Multicast routing for multimedia communication. IEEE/ACM Trans. Netw. (TON) **1**(3), 286–292 (1993)
6. Prim, R.C.: Shortest connection networks and some generalizations. Bell Labs Tech. J. **36**(6), 1389–1401 (1957)
7. Soylu, A., Kharlamov, E., Zheleznyakov, D., Jimenez-Ruiz, E., Giese, M., Horrocks, I.: OptiqueVQS: ontology-based visual querying. In: VOILA@ ISWC, p. 91 (2015)
8. Unger, C., Bühmann, L., Lehmann, J., Ngonga Ngomo, A.-C., Gerber, D., Cimiano, P.: Template-based question answering over RDF data. In: Proceedings of the 21st International Conference on World Wide Web (2012), pp. 639–648. ACM (2012)

---

[6] https://github.com/InsightLab/linked-graphast/tree/evaluation.
[7] https://github.com/InsightLab/von-qbe.

9. Usbeck, R., Ngomo, A.-C.N., Bühmann, L., Unger, C.: HAWK – hybrid question answering using linked data. In: Gandon, F., Sabou, M., Sack, H., d'Amato, C., Cudré-Mauroux, P., Zimmermann, A. (eds.) ESWC 2015. LNCS, vol. 9088, pp. 353–368. Springer, Cham (2015). https://doi.org/10.1007/978-3-319-18818-8_22

10. Winkler, W.E.: The state of record linkage and current research problems. Statistical Research Division, US Census Bureau, Citeseer (1999)

11. Xu, K., Zhang, S., Feng, Y., Zhao, D.: Answering natural language questions via phrasal semantic parsing. In: Zong, C., Nie, J.Y., Zhao, D., Feng, Y. (eds.) Natural Language Processing and Chinese Computing. CCIS, vol. 496, pp. 333–344. Springer, Heidelberg (2014). https://doi.org/10.1007/978-3-662-45924-9_30

12. Yahya, M., Berberich, K., Elbassuoni, S., Ramanath, M., Tresp, V., Weikum, G.: Natural language questions for the web of data. In: Proceedings of the 2012 Joint Conference on EMNLP and CoNLL, pp. 379–390. Association for Computational Linguistics (2012)

13. Yih, S.W.-T., Chang, M.-W., He, X., Gao, J.: Semantic parsing via staged query graph generation: question answering with knowledge base

Query Rewriting for Continuously Evolving NoSQL Databases

Mark Lukas Möller[1]([✉]), Meike Klettke[1], Andrea Hillenbrand[2], and Uta Störl[2]

[1] University of Rostock, Rostock, Germany
{mark.moeller2,meike.klettke}@uni-rostock.de
[2] University of Applied Sciences Darmstadt, Darmstadt, Germany
{andrea.hillenbrand,uta.stoerl}@h-da.de

Abstract. In agile software development settings, applications are typically backed by schema-flexible NoSQL databases. New application code frequently implies data model changes to the effect of multiple schema versions within the NoSQL database. Here, a query rewriting approach can handle the issue of how to access legacy data, otherwise datasets in previous schema versions would seem to disappear for the application. Our NoSQL query rewriting approach for multi-versioned databases takes evolution operations into account, their reverse operations as well as the heterogeneity of data. For that purpose we specify four NoSQL heterogeneity classes from relational up to completely unstructured NoSQL records. Furthermore, we propose a NoSQL query rewriting algorithm that generates subqueries compatible to all existing structural versions.

Keywords: Multi-versioned NoSQL databases · NoSQL query rewriting · NoSQL Schema Evolution · NoSQL data heterogeneity classes

1 Introduction

All successful software products permanently underlie changes. This includes frequent schema evolutions of data structures which in turn implies the necessity to eventually adapt legacy data to such data model changes. Schemaless NoSQL databases that do not prescribe structural and semantic constraints allow applications to store different structural versions in the same database. If applications are evolved, then the issue of multi-versioned databases has to be addressed. *NoSQL query rewriting (QR)* allows the application to access data entities in different structural versions. Our approach for QR distributes such queries onto the pertained different structural versions as shown in Fig. 1.

Query rewriting can be applied in two directions. *Forward Query Rewriting* assumes a legacy application and handles queries in case that the legacy application is not aware of an already evolved database schema. *Backward Query Rewriting* assumes an evolved application and fetches entities according to legacy

A. H. F. Laender et al. (Eds.): ER 2019, LNCS 11788, pp. 213–221, 2019.
https://doi.org/10.1007/978-3-030-33223-5_18

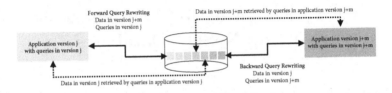

Fig. 1. Forward and Backward Query Rewriting for versioned databases

schema versions. For implementing lazy data migration, a backward QR approach has to be applied, which turns out to be the common use-case.

We first define the *semantics* of evolution operations, introduce an *evolution history graph* which contains information on schema versions and evolution operations, and then develop a QR algorithm for multi-versioned NoSQL databases.

2   Foundations

In this section we summarize the formal foundations for the QR algorithm while particularly focusing on the NoSQL characteristics.

NoSQL Heterogeneity Classes. NoSQL databases can store heterogeneous datasets within the same collection. Heterogeneity has to be considered in all algorithms that process NoSQL data. We have to take into account structural heterogeneity, varying cardinalities, and the existence of so-called dangling tuples. Therefore, we are introducing four *heterogeneity classes* (HC).

HC1 contains datasets in different structural versions, yet all datasets in the same version have exactly the same structure. Further, we can assume 1:1 cardinalities and no dangling tuples between two entity types.

HC2 extends HC1 by adding 1:n cardinalities. Dangling tuples can occur and have to be considered during data migration.

HC3 extends HC2 to arbitrary cardinalities (1:1, 1:n, n:1, n:m).

HC4 represents databases that can have different structures within the same version. Here, optional properties can occur. NoSQL databases allow this heterogeneity even if an explicit schema, e.g., a JSON schema, is present.

Formal Semantics. NoSQL data with an equal or similar set of properties is called a *kind*. A kind named A is defined by a *schema* S_A and a *set of entities* E_A, i.e., $\mathcal{K}_A = (S_A, E_A)$. The schema S_A consists of a set of property names $S_A = \{A_1, \ldots, A_n\}$. The set of entities over S_A is defined as $E_A := \{e_1, \ldots, e_m\}$ where m is the number of entities. Each entity in E_A consists of up to n attributes called a_{i_j}, so $e_i = \{a_{i_j} \mid i \in \{1, \ldots, m\}, j \in \{1, \ldots n\}\}$. Here, i represents the index for the i-th entity of E_A and j is the j-th attribute of the entity.

Each attribute a_{i_j} consists of an attribute name and an attribute value, i.e., $a_{i_j} = (A_{i_j} : v_{i_j}) \in S_{A_i} \times \mathcal{D}(A_i)$ whereby $S_{A_i} \subseteq S_A$ and $\mathcal{D}(A_i) \subseteq \mathcal{D}(A)$.

Thus, $S_{A_i} \times \mathcal{D}(A_i)$ represents the property domain. The property value v_{i_j} is either a null value, a boolean, a string, a number, an array, or it can contain nested properties, as is typical in NoSQL applications. If v_{i_j} contains the nested property w, the value of w is accessible by the *path expression* $v_{i_j}.w$. In case of nested properties, all paths are assumed to be available in the schema as well.

Example 1. Let us consider a database of a research institute for storing sensor data with three different kinds: projects, metadata, and the sensor values for each test run. The kind *projects* is defined as $\mathcal{K}_{\text{projects}} = \{S_{\text{projects}}, E_{\text{projects}}\}$. The according schema is $S_{\text{projects}} = \{$ "p_id", "station_name", "funder", "budget" $\}$. A set of possible entities could read as follows:

```
E_projects = {{("p_id": 1), ("station_name": "Baltic Sea"), ("funder": "DFG"), ("budget": "5
↪    Mil")}, {("p_id": 2), ("station_name": "Baltic Sea")}}
```

Lastly, we introduce $X?$ as a notation to mark X as an optional property. Analogously, the set operator $\overset{?}{\in}$ exists. The notation $X \overset{?}{\in} S_A$ predicates that X is part of the schema, yet not all entities necessarily have a property X.

Evolution Operations. The semantics of an evolution operation has to consider the HC. As an example, we discuss the `rename` operation for HC4 (see Fig. 2). In version v_A, both optional property names X and Z are considered to be part of the schema $S_{A_{[v_A]}}$. Here, $[v_A]$ represents the version number. On the *schema level*, it is required to distinguish the cases resulting from whether X and Z is present or not for each entity. For example, if both the new and old property names are present, the current value is kept. The properties $A_2, \ldots, A_n$ represent the other properties of the kind which do not affect the operation. After the operation, the now non-optional property Z is part of the schema while X is not part of the schema anymore. Here, $[v_A + 1]$ states that the version number is incremented. The given four cases describe the migration of all entities in E_A.

The evolution operations are defined accordingly across all HCs. For example, in HC1, only the first case has to be considered. In [5], we specified the complete definitions for the operations `add`, `delete`, `rename`, and the even more complex multi-type operations `move` and `copy` with a more detailed explanation.

3   Rewriting NoSQL Data

Based on the above definitions, we can now develop an algorithm for NoSQL query rewriting regarding all heterogeneity classes.

Evolution History Graph. For query rewriting it is necessary to store information about the *history* of schema versions and the *evolution operations* which transform each schema version into its successor schema version. The information is stored in a graph-based model, $G = (H, OP)$. The history H contains the

HC4: RENAME IGNORE A.X TO Z

$$global\ precond : \{X \overset{?}{\in} S_A, Z \overset{?}{\notin} S_A\}$$

$$S_A(X?, Z?, A_3, \ldots, A_n)_{[v_A]} \to S_A(Z, A_3, \ldots, A_n)_{[v_A+1]}$$

$\forall e_i \in E_{A[v_A]} :$

$case: X \in e_{i[v_A]} \wedge Z \notin e_{i[v_A]}$
$\begin{cases} case\ precond : \{X \in e_{i[v_A]} \wedge Z \notin e_{i[v_A]}\} \\ e_i((X{:}x), a_{i_3}, \ldots, a_{i_n})_{[v_A]} \to e_i((Z{:}x), a_{i_3}, \ldots, a_{i_n})_{[v_A+1]} \\ case\ postcond : \{X \notin e_{i[v_A+1]} \wedge Z \in e_{i[v_A+1]}\} \end{cases}$

$case: X \in e_{i[v_A]} \wedge Z \in e_{i[v_A]}$
$\begin{cases} case\ precond : \{X \in e_{i[v_A]} \wedge Z \in e_{i[v_A]}\} \\ e_i((X{:}x), (Z{:}z), a_{i_3}, \ldots, a_{i_n})_{[v_A]} \to e_i((Z{:}x), a_{i_3}, \ldots, a_{i_n})_{[v_A+1]} \\ case\ postcond : \{X \notin e_{i[v_A+1]} \wedge Z \in e_{i[v_A+1]}\} \end{cases}$

$case: X \notin e_{i[v_A]} \wedge Z \in e_{i[v_A]}$
$\begin{cases} case\ precond : \{X \notin e_{i[v_A]} \wedge Z \in e_{i[v_A]}\} \\ e_i((Z{:}z), a_{i_3}, \ldots, a_{i_n})_{[v_A]} \to e_i((Z{:}z), a_{i_3}, \ldots, a_{i_n})_{[v_A+1]} \\ case\ postcond : \{X \notin e_{i[v_A+1]} \wedge Z \in e_{i[v_A+1]}\} \end{cases}$

$case: X \notin e_{i[v_A]} \wedge Z \notin e_{i[v_A]}$
$\begin{cases} case\ precond : \{X \notin e_{i[v_A]} \wedge Z \notin e_{i[v_A]}\} \\ e_i(a_{i_3}, \ldots, a_{i_n})_{[v_A]} \to e_i((Z{:}\bot), a_{i_3}, \ldots, a_{i_n})_{[v_A+1]} \\ case\ postcond : \{X \notin e_{i[v_A+1]} \wedge Z \in e_{i[v_A+1]}\} \end{cases}$

$$global\ postcond : \{X \notin S_{A[v_A+1]}, Z \in S_{A[v_A+1]}\}$$

Fig. 2. Semantics of the `rename` operation in HC4 with **ignore** strategy

schema versions of each kind from the oldest available to the most recent version. The history of a kind $\mathcal{K}$ is denoted as $H_{\mathcal{K}}$, so $H = \{H_{\mathcal{K}_1}, \ldots, H_{\mathcal{K}_n}\}$. For each version, a tuple with the version number and the superset of the property names of the schema in this version is stored. It is denoted as $H_{\mathcal{K}} = \{(v, \{props\})\}$.

The set of evolution operations OP is defined as a set of tuples (s, t, v_s, v_t, op) for storing evolution information. Each tuple contains the name of the *source* and the *target kind* (s and t), the *current version of the source*, the *new version of the target kind* (v_s and v_t), and the *parameterized evolution operation*. Executing an evolution operation results in a new tuple in OP. For single-type operations, a tuple is added to the corresponding history H, while for multi-type one tuple is added to each of the histories of the source and of the target kind.

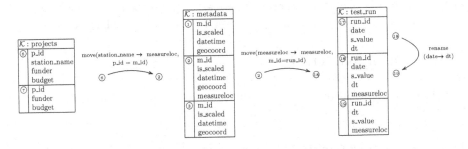

Fig. 3. Evolution history graph for rewriting queries

As an example, we use a part of an evolution history graph with three kinds $\mathcal{K}_{\text{projects}}$, $\mathcal{K}_{\text{metadata}}$, and $\mathcal{K}_{\text{test\_run}}$. These are available in different versions due to past schema evolution operations. This graph is visualized in Fig. 3. Circled numbers represent the respective schema versions, each associated with a group of properties in that schema version. Evolution operations are visualized as arrows, labeled with parameterizations of exemplary evolution operations.

The graph is explained using $\mathcal{K}_{\text{test\_run}}$. Initially, the schema of this kind consists of the properties "run_id", "date", "s_value", and "dt", and there are no entities in older versions than 17 (*oldest materialized version*). Two move and one rename operation are executed, which generate the following result set:

```
H_test_run = {(17, {run_id, date, s_value, dt}), (18, {run_id, date, s_value, dt,
↪   measureloc}), (19, {run_id, s_value, dt, measureloc})},
OP = {(projects, metadata, 6, 2, move(projects.station_name → metadata.measureloc, p_id =
↪   m_id)), (metadata, test_run, 2, 18, move(metadata.measureloc → test_run.measureloc,
↪   m_id = run_id)), (test_run, test_run, 18, 19, rename(test_run.date → test_run.dt))}
```

Analogously, H_{project} and H_{metadata} are created. The property names in the history sets are the superset of all property names of the entities of a kind in a particular version.

The Query Rewriting Algorithm. The task of the QR routine is to transparently look up entities and their property values as if they were eagerly migrated. The QR algorithm is provided in Algorithm 1.

For each version in $H_\mathcal{K}$ of a queried kind $\mathcal{K}$, the operation is looked up in OP that led to this particular version. Then, the query is rewritten based on rules given in Sect. 2 and in [5]. If one of the multi-entity operations is applied, affected kinds that are not part of the original query need to be joined. If the joined kind is affected by an evolution operation that has not been migrated until now, a rewriting cascade is triggered. This process is continued recursively based on the resulting rewritten queries.

The QR process is demonstrated by querying $\mathcal{K}_{\text{test\_run}}$ in the latest version 19. For illustration, we use SQL as the query language. Without additional knowledge of the data, we have to assume HC4. As an example, all entities are selected, expressed by **SELECT * FROM test_run**. Data in the latest version is queried directly. Only the star-operator is expanded to the list of properties. We assume the presence of a system-handled property called _v for each entity, denoted as a circled number in Fig. 3. Figure 4 contains the whole query for all versions of $\mathcal{K}_{\text{test\_run}}$. The query for the latest version is given in line 1.

For each older schema version of a queried kind, operations are looked up, which lead to the least recently inspected, that is, to the chronologically newest version. In Fig. 3, operations are depicted as inbound edges. On the formal level, the information can be found by inspecting the tuples in OP. The generated query of the last iteration is rewritten. Eventually, other kinds have to be rewritten recursively if they were part of a multi-entity operation. In the running example, the query for $\mathcal{K}_{\text{test\_run}}$ in version 18 is generated next. Since data is

Algorithm 1. QR Algorithm

procedure SELECT QUERY REWRITE
input:
    $G = (\text{H}, \text{OP})$
    $Q \leftarrow Query\ against\ kind\ \mathcal{K}$
5: **init:**
    $Q_{all} \leftarrow Q$ ▷ Collects Queries for all versions, global
    $Q_{ver} \leftarrow Q$ ▷ Query to modify per iteration
 main:
    for each version $v' < v$ of $\mathcal{K}$ **do**
10:       $Q_{ver} \leftarrow rewrite(\mathcal{K}, Q_{ver}, v')$
    return Q_{all}
  rewrite(*Kind* $\mathcal{K}$, *Query* Q, *Version* v):
    $s \leftarrow lookup\ schema\ of\ \mathcal{K}\ in\ \text{H}\ in\ version\ v$
    $op \leftarrow lookup\ edge\ in\ OP\ which\ led\ \mathcal{K}\ to\ previously\ inspected\ version$
15:    **if** op *was single-type operation* **then**
        $Q' \leftarrow Apply\ rules\ on\ Q\ proposed\ in\ [5]$
        $Augment\ version\ information\ in\ where\ clause:\ \mathcal{K}.\_v = v$
        $Q_{all} \leftarrow Q_{all} \cup Q'$ ▷ $\cup$ = UNION operation
        return Q'
20:    **else**
        $\mathcal{K}_{src} \leftarrow source\ kind\ of\ multi\text{-}entity\ operation\ op$
        $Join\ Kind\ \mathcal{K}_{src}\ with\ Kinds\ in\ Q\ (condition\ in\ op)$
        $Q' \leftarrow Apply\ rules\ proposed\ in\ [5]$ ▷ Rewrites latest version of $\mathcal{K}_{src}$
        $Augment\ version\ information\ in\ where\ clause:\ \mathcal{K}.\_v = v$
25:       $Q_{all} \leftarrow Q_{all} \cup Q'$
        if $\mathcal{K}_{src}$ *was lazily evolved* **then**
            for each version $v'_{\mathcal{K}_{src}} < v_{\mathcal{K}_{src}}$ of $\mathcal{K}_{src}$ **do**
                $Q' = rewrite(\mathcal{K}_{src}, Q', v'_{\mathcal{K}_{src}})$ ▷ Recursive rewrite
        return Q'

present in HC4, four subqueries are generated from the query of the previous iteration and can be found in lines 2–9 of Fig. 4.

This query is recursively modified in the following iteration. The next QR step is the move operation that migrates $\mathcal{K}_{test\_run}$ from version 17 to 18 and takes $\mathcal{K}_{metadata}$ into account. Here, the **move ignore** approach is applied, which joins only the first match and is abbreviated by JOIN FIRST MATCH ONLY as introduced in [5]. The four subqueries given in lines 10–21 in Fig. 4 are generated.

In contrast to the single-type operation, the QR of the multi-type operation must not be interrupted. The moved property "measureloc" is affected by another evolution operation and entails a *QR cascade*. Recursively, the versions and applied operations on $\mathcal{K}_{metadata}$ are checked if they influence the query. This is the case, because a **move** operation on $\mathcal{K}_{project}$ affects "measureloc". The fully rewritten query for $\mathcal{K}_{test\_run}$ in version 17, the lines 22–41 of Fig. 4, have to be part of the query as well. Recursively, it is checked whether there is an operation on $\mathcal{K}_{projects}$ that influences properties in the query. In the example, the QR process terminates because there are no pending operations left.

Yet, the QR algorithm is able to rewrite read-only queries with arbitrary projection and selection attributes. Aggregations can be handled in two steps. First, the affected kinds from all schema versions are read, and second the aggregation operation is executed. Write operations can be executed, too. In that case, all affected entities are migrated to their latest version first.

```
 1  SELECT run_id, dt, s_value, measureloc FROM test_run WHERE _v=19
 2  UNION SELECT run_id, date AS dt, s_value,measureloc
 3  FROM test_run WHERE _v=18 AND EXISTS(date) AND NOT EXISTS(dt)
 4  UNION SELECT run_id, date AS dt, s_value, measureloc
 5  FROM test_run WHERE _v=18 AND EXISTS(date) AND EXISTS(dt)
 6  UNION SELECT run_id, dt, s_value, measureloc
 7  FROM test_run WHERE _v=18 AND NOT EXISTS(date) AND EXISTS(dt)
 8  UNION SELECT run_id, NULL AS dt, s_value, measureloc
 9  FROM test_run WHERE _v=18 AND NOT EXISTS(date) AND NOT EXISTS(dt)
10  UNION SELECT run_id, date AS dt, s_value, measureloc
11  FROM test_run JOIN FIRST MATCH ONLY metadata ON m_id = run_id
12  WHERE test_run._v=17 AND metadata._v = 3 AND EXISTS(date) AND NOT EXISTS(dt)
13  UNION SELECT run_id, date AS dt, s_value, measureloc
14  FROM test_run JOIN FIRST MATCH ONLY metadata ON m_id = run_id
15  WHERE test_run._v=17 AND metadata._v = 3 AND EXISTS(date) AND EXISTS(dt)
16  UNION SELECT run_id, dt, s_value, measureloc
17  FROM test_run JOIN FIRST MATCH ONLY metadata ON m_id = run_id
18  WHERE test_run._v=17 AND metadata._v = 3 AND NOT EXISTS(date) AND EXISTS(dt)
19  UNION SELECT run_id, NULL AS dt, s_value, measureloc
20  FROM test_run JOIN FIRST MATCH ONLY metadata ON m_id = run_id
21  WHERE test_run._v=17 AND metadata._v = 3 AND NOT EXISTS(date) AND NOT EXISTS(dt)
22  UNION SELECT run_id, date AS dt, s_value, station_name AS measureloc
23  FROM test_run JOIN FIRST MATCH ONLY metadata ON m_id = run_id
24      JOIN FIRST MATCH ONLY projects ON p_id = m_id
25  WHERE test_run._v=17 AND metadata._v = 2 AND projects.p_id = 6
26      AND EXISTS(date) AND NOT EXISTS(dt)
27  UNION SELECT run_id, date AS dt, s_value, station_name as measureloc
28  FROM test_run JOIN FIRST MATCH ONLY metadata ON m_id = run_id
29      JOIN FIRST MATCH ONLY projects ON p_id = m_id
30  WHERE test_run._v=17 AND metadata._v = 2 AND projects.p_id = 6
31      AND EXISTS(date) AND EXISTS(dt)
32  UNION SELECT run_id, dt, s_value, station_name as measureloc
33  FROM test_run JOIN FIRST MATCH ONLY metadata ON m_id = run_id
34      JOIN FIRST MATCH ONLY projects ON p_id = m_id
35  WHERE test_run._v=17 AND metadata._v = 2 AND projects.p_id = 6
36      AND NOT EXISTS(date) AND EXISTS(dt)
37  UNION SELECT run_id, NULL AS dt, s_value, station_name AS measureloc
38  FROM test_run JOIN FIRST MATCH ONLY metadata ON m_id = run_id
39      JOIN FIRST MATCH ONLY projects ON p_id = m_id
40  WHERE test_run._v=17 AND metadata._v = 2 AND projects.p_id = 6
41      AND NOT EXISTS(date) AND NOT EXISTS(dt);
```

Fig. 4. Result of the query rewriting algorithm for HC4

4 Related Work

The main focus of this paper lies on combining the notions of heterogeneity of datasets and evolution in NoSQL databases for query rewriting. For this task, we have regarded the following related work.

Schema evolution with complex schema modification operations (SMOs), automated data migration operations, and automated rewriting of queries for relational databases, has been studied by Moon et. al. in the PRISM project [4]. In [2], a language is defined for bidirectional schema evolution and forward and backward delta code generation in relational databases.

There are several tools for NoSQL databases schema evolution. Most of them implement an eager migration, for instance, *Mongeez*, *Flyway*, and *Liquibase*. The foundation of lazy NoSQL data migration has been proposed in [7]. A similar approach is introduced in [6], where the performance of lazy migration in NoSQL data stores has been studied in particular. In [3] first ideas for hybrid approaches

and an estimation of their complexity are given. The foundations on QR in our tool *Darwin* have been developed in [8]. Here, operations are translated into DEDs and in that context, forward and backward mappings are defined. For HC1 and HC2, prototypical implementations have been made in this work. Another QR approach *EasyQ* [1] uses a dictionary with paths to properties with the same information but different names for expanding queries.

To the best of our knowledge, the combination of input data in different HCs, versioning, and multi-type evolutions has not been studied before.

5 Summary and Future Work

In *lazy data migration*, datasets are only updated on demand. Consequently, NoSQL databases contain datasets in different schema versions. For querying these versioned NoSQL data, we developed QR techniques so that queries against the latest version of the schema are rewritten against previous schema versions.

We have shown that *query rewriting* in HC4 has to consider all structural variants of the entire dataset. Without any additional knowledge about the NoSQL database, we can merely assume HC4. In case that the datasets are in another HC, query rewriting turns out much simpler. Consequently, information about the HC can significantly improve the performance of the rewriting process. In NoSQL databases with a rigid *schema management*, we can even guarantee that datasets are in NoSQL HC1.

The overall aim of the *Darwin* project is the development of a *migration adviser* in order to support users to choose the optimal migration strategy in a certain scenario. The HC of the NoSQL data influences this choice. In case of HC1, a lazy migration can be recommended. For datasets in HC4, eager data migration is more advantageous than lazy or hybrid approaches.

The tool *Darwin* [9] currently covers query rewriting for HC1 and HC2. In the next step, we will extend *Darwin* to rewrite queries for datasets in all HCs.

Acknowledgements. The article is published in the scope of the project *"NoSQL Schema Evolution und Big Data Migration at Scale"* which is funded by the *Deutsche Forschungsgemeinschaft (DFG)* under the number 385808805. A special thanks goes to Stefanie Scherzinger, Dennis Marten, Tanja Auge, and Hannes Grunert for their support, comments on this work, and several discussions.

References

1. Hamadou, H.B., Ghozzi, F., Péninou, A., et al.: Towards schema-independent querying on document data stores. In: Proceedings of EDBT/ICDT (2018)
2. Herrmann, K., Voigt, H., Rausch, J., et al.: Living in parallel realities: co-existing schema versions with a bidirectional database evolution language. In: Proceedings of SIGMOD 2017 (2017)
3. Klettke, M., Störl, U., Shenavai, M., et al.: NoSQL schema evolution and big data migration at scale. In: Proceedings of SCDM@Big Data 2016 (2016)

4. Moon, H.J., Curino, C.A., Zaniolo, C.: Scalable architecture and query optimization for transaction-time DBs with evolving schemas. In: Proceedings of SIGMOD 2010 (2010)

5. Möller, M.L., Klettke, M., Störl, U.: Formal semantics of NoSQL evolution operations under different heterogeneity levels. Technical report, Rostock University (2018)

6. Saur, K., Dumitras, T., Hicks, M.W.: Evolving NoSQL databases without downtime. In: Proceedings of ICSME 2016 (2016)

7. Scherzinger, S., Klettke, M., Störl, U.: Managing schema evolution in NoSQL data stores. In: Proceedings of DBPL@VLDB (2013)

8. Stenzel, J.: Query rewriting in NoSQL-Datenbanksystemen. Master's thesis, University of Applied Sciences Darmstadt (2017)

9. Störl, U., et al.: Curating variational data in application development. In: Proceedings of ICDE 2018 (2018)

Big Data Technology II

Relaxed Functional Dependency Discovery in Heterogeneous Data Lakes

Rihan Hai[1(✉)], Christoph Quix[2,3], and Dan Wang[1]

[1] RWTH Aachen University, Aachen, Germany
{hai,wang}@dbis.rwth-aachen.de
[2] Hochschule Niederrhein, University of Applied Sciences, Krefeld, Germany
christoph.quix@hs-niederrhein.de
[3] Fraunhofer Institute for Applied Information Technology FIT,
Sankt Augustin, Germany

Abstract. Functional dependencies are important for the definition of constraints and relationships that have to be satisfied by every database instance. Relaxed functional dependencies (RFDs) can be used for data exploration and profiling in datasets with lower data quality. In this work, we present an approach for RFD discovery in heterogeneous data lakes. More specifically, the goal of this work is to find RFDs from structured, semi-structured, and graph data. Our solution brings novelty to this problem in the following aspects: (1) We introduce a generic metamodel to the problem of RFD discovery, which allows us to define and detect RFDs for data stored in heterogeneous sources in an integrated manner. (2) We apply clustering techniques during RFD discovery for partitioning and pruning. (3) We performed an intensive evaluation with nine datasets, which shows that our approach is effective for discovering meaningful RFDs, reducing redundancy, and detecting inconsistent data.

1 Introduction

Data lakes (DLs) have been proposed to tackle the problem of data access by providing a comprehensive repository, in which the raw data from heterogeneous sources is ingested in its original format [5]. Although DLs have been generally considered as a promising solution, they face the challenges that the ingested raw data often lack sufficient metadata or have inadequate data quality.

Functional dependencies (FDs) specify that attributes functionally depend on some other attributes, e.g., in Fig. 1b, the working years of employees determine their levels: $Years \rightarrow Level$. In contrast to such an *exact* FD, we might also be interested in discovering *relaxed* functional dependencies (RFDs). RFDs are relaxed in the sense that they do not apply to all tuples of a relation, or that *similar* attribute values are also considered to be equal [2]. In Fig. 1b we can have a RFD: $Years \rightarrow Salary$, if we consider 24.8 and 24.9 to be similar. RFDs are especially useful in cases where the source data have lower quality with inconsistencies and incorrect values. By using RFDs, we can detect additional relationships among data items for data exploration or profiling; on the other

© Springer Nature Switzerland AG 2019
A. H. F. Laender et al. (Eds.): ER 2019, LNCS 11788, pp. 225–239, 2019.
https://doi.org/10.1007/978-3-030-33223-5_19

```
{"Genre":
  {
   "name":"Symbolism",
   "Painter": [{
    "name":"Gustav Klimt",
    "Painting": [{
     "title":"The Lady in Gold",
     "History": [
      {
       "year":    ,
       "museum":"Belvedere",
       "city":"Vienna"},
      {
       "year":    ,
       "museum":"Neue Galerie",
       "city":"New York"} ]
     }] }]
  } }
```

(a) JSON document: Art genre

	EID	Years	Level	Salary(k€)
t_1	1011	2	1	24.8
t_2	1008	2	1	24.9
t_3	846	5	2	45
t_4	845	5	2	45
t_5	107	10	3	60
t_6	23	11	3	60

(b) Relational table: *Employee*

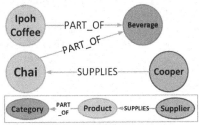

(c) Graph: Supply chain

Fig. 1. Running example: heterogeneous data in a data lake

hand, we can identify the data objects that violate the detected constraints, which can be useful for data cleaning.

Problem Definition. We tackle the problem of discovering RFDs in DLs with structured data (relations), semi-structured data (JSON) and graphs. Figure 1 shows our running example with JSON, relational, and graph data. JSON is a popular data model for semi-structured data, but it has not yet been investigated for RFD discovery. Discovery of FDs or RFDs in graphs often focuses on linked data in RDF (Resource Description Framework) [18], but not for labeled property graphs of Neo4j, which we address in our work.

Related Works. Most existing solutions for FD discovery [12] focus on handling only one type of data, e.g., relational [9,16], XML [4,17], or graphs [18]. In this work we propose an approach based on a generic metadata model, which handles heterogeneous data in a unified manner and thus avoids the need for specific algorithmic solutions for each data type. It also leads to a clearer RFD definition, which simplifies the understanding over different data structures.

A number of RFD definitions and discovery solutions have been proposed [2]; they can be classified into three categories. To tolerate inconsistent data, the first type of RFDs [9] require that "almost" all tuples satisfy the dependency; usually an error threshold ε indicates the degree to which the dependency is allowed to be violated. The second category of RFDs [1] relax on how the attribute values are compared. Instead of grouping identical values, they group similar attribute values by using similarity functions (e.g., *Years → Salary* in our example). The third category of RFDs [4] are the hybrids of the previous two types. A recent approach [11] discovers RFDs based on sampling and a novel search space traver-

sal strategy, which is efficient, yet the possibilities of supporting heterogeneous data and applying clustering techniques are not considered as in this work.

Our Solution. We propose a clustering-based RFD discovery method for heterogeneous data such that we can find the "hidden" relationships among attributes in various datasets. To support inconsistent or incomplete data, our approach tolerates a certain degree of tuple violation. Our main contributions are: (1) We propose a generic metamodel and RFD definition, which facilitates an integrated method to perform RFD discovery over heterogeneous data. (2) We provide clustering-based algorithms to discover RFDs. (3) We propose a pruning procedure based on agglomerative clustering, which can effectively reduce the search space and thereby improve the performance. (4) We show experimentally that our approach produces more meaningful RFDs with less redundancy, and the discovered RFDs can be effectively used for error detection.

The remainder of the paper is organized as follows: first we introduce preliminary concepts in Sect. 2; we explain our proposed generic metadata model and definition of RFD in Sect. 3; then we discuss the overall approach in Sect. 4; we evaluate our solutions in Sect. 5, before we conclude the paper in Sect. 6.

2   Preliminaries

We define FDs and relevant concepts as in [9,12]. Given a relational schema R and its instance r, for a tuple $t_i \in r$ and a set of attributes $X \subseteq R$, $t_i[X]$ denotes the projection of t_i on X. For a set of attributes $X \subseteq R$ and an attribute $A \in R$, the FD $X \rightarrow A$ *holds* iff for all pairs of tuples $t_i, t_j \in r$, if $t_i[X] = t_j[X]$, then $t_i[A] = t_j[A]$. We refer to X as the left-hand side (LHS) and A as the right-hand side (RHS).

A FD $X \rightarrow A$ is *minimal* if by removing any attribute from X, the FD is no longer satisfied. A FD $X \rightarrow A$ is *non-trivial* if $A \notin X$. Given two attributes $A, B \in R$, if we have $X \rightarrow A$ and $X \rightarrow B$, then $X \rightarrow AB$. Thus, it is sufficient to detect dependencies with singleton RHS. Like most existing works, our approach generates *minimal, non-trivial* RFDs with *singleton* RHS.

Partition. Given a set of attributes X, we group tuples with identical values projected on X, and obtain *equivalent classes*. In Fig. 1b, $\{t_1, t_2\}$ is an equivalence class regarding $Years$. By grouping all tuples in r into equivalent classes, we obtain a *partition* π_X of r regarding X. The number of equivalent classes $|\pi_X|$ is its *rank*. In Fig. 1b, $\pi_{Years} = \{\{t_1, t_2\}, \{t_3, t_4\}, \{t_5\}, \{t_6\}\}$, $\pi_{Level} = \{\{t_1, t_2\}, \{t_3, t_4\}, \{t_5, t_6\}\}$, and $|\pi_{Years}| = 4$, $|\pi_{Level}| = 3$. If we already have the partitions of π_X and π_Y, we can obtain a new partition of the attribute set $X \cup Y$ by computing the *product* of π_X and π_Y, i.e., $\pi_{X \cup Y} = \pi_X \cdot \pi_Y$ (Lemma 3.6, [9]). For instance, $\pi_{\{Years, Level\}} = \pi_{Years} \cdot \pi_{Level} = \{\{t_1, t_2\}, \{t_3, t_4\}, \{t_5\}, \{t_6\}\}$. If a set of attributes X has no two identical tuple values, we call X a *superkey*. If none of the strict subsets of X is a superkey, X is a *key*, e.g., EID in Fig. 1b. By removing equivalent classes whose sizes are one, we obtain *stripped partitions*, denoted as $\hat{\pi}$. For example, $\hat{\pi}_{Years} = \{\{t_1, t_2\}, \{t_3, t_4\}\}$. $||\hat{\pi}_X||$ is the sum of the sizes of equivalent classes in $\hat{\pi}$, e.g., $||\hat{\pi}_{Years}|| = 4$.

FD Inference. Given $\widehat{\pi_X}$, the error measure $e(X) = (||\widehat{\pi_X}|| - |\widehat{\pi_X}|)/|r|$, indicates the minimum fraction of tuples to be removed from r such that X becomes a superkey. A FD $X \to A$ holds iff $e(X) = e(X \cup A)$ (Lemma 3.5, [9]). For example, $e(Years) = e(\{Years, Level\}) = \frac{4-2}{6}$, thus we have the FD: $Years \to Level$. Given a set of FDs (denoted as Σ) over schema S, a *cover* of Σ (denoted as σ) is a set of FDs satisfying: (1) $\sigma \subseteq \Sigma$; (2) any FD in Σ is either also in σ, or can be implied by σ, denoted as $\sigma \models \Sigma$.

3   Metadata Model and RFD Definition

In order to discover the RFDs for heterogeneous data sources, a primary step is to have a proper representation of the schemas. FD or RFD discovery usually works on relational structures. The tree-structured data models such as JSON, could be represented in a universal relation that contains all attributes of the JSON document with normalized atomic values. However, such a normalization causes failures to detect dependencies including array-based elements, and massively increases the number of tuples, which puts a huge burden on performance [17]. Therefore, our approach for RFD discovery preserves the hierarchical relationships among schema elements by applying a generic metadata model, which can also represent the schema of relational tables and Neo4j graphs.

Our metadata model is inspired by our previous model *GeRoMe* [10], but the present model is much simpler as we focus on RFD discovery. The model is similar to extended entity-relationship models with explicit types for attributes which might also be complex types to represent nested objects.

Definition 1. *A generic schema S is a tuple $\langle T, C, P, A \rangle$ with*

- *T is a set of atomic types, e.g., $\{number, string, boolean, \ldots\}$;*
- *C is a set of complex types $\{c_1, \ldots, c_n\}$ where each c_i has a set of properties $prop(c_i) \subseteq P$ and super types $super(c_i) \subseteq C$;*
- *P is a set of properties $\{p_1, \ldots, p_m\}$ where each p_i has a type, i.e., $type(p_i) \in C \cup T$, and each p_i might be unique $(unique(p_i) \in \{true, false\})$ or multi-valued $(multi(p_i) \in \{true, false\})$;*
- *A is a set of binary association types $\{a_1, \ldots, a_k\}$ where each a_i has a set of properties $prop(a_i) \subseteq P$, a source and a target type $(source(a_i) \in C$ and $target(a_i) \in C)$.*

A dataset as an instance of a schema is logically represented by a set of tuples of different arities. For example, if the schema has a complex type c with n properties, then an instance of c is a tuple with $n + 1$ attributes: $c(id, v_1, \ldots, v_n)$ where id is a unique object identifier and each v_i represents a property value. Instances of an association type a_i with m properties are represented as tuples $a_i(id, o_1, o_2, v_1, \ldots, v_m)$ with id being a unique identifier for this association, o_1/o_2 being the identifier of the source/target object and each v_i is a property value. Note that tuples of complex or association types might have nested structures as the properties might have complex types and/or be multi-valued.

Definition 2. *A generic functional dependency (gFD) for a generic schema* $S = \langle T, C, P, A \rangle$ *is an expression of the form:* $[X_0]X_1, \ldots, X_n \to Y_1, \ldots, Y_m$

- X_0 *is an absolute path expression starting with a complex or association type* $t \in C \cup A$, *defining the* context *of the gFD, resulting in a set of objects O;*
- $X_1, \ldots, X_n, Y_1, \ldots, Y_m$ *are relative path expressions that are evaluated relative to the results of* X_0 *and select for each* $o \in O$ *a single value, i.e., generating a virtual relation R with tuples of the form* $r(o, x_1, \ldots, x_n, y_1, \ldots, y_m)$;
- *a path expression has the form* $s_0.s_1 \ldots .s_k$, *where* $s_0 \in C \cup A$ *is the initial step for an absolute path expression to select the starting type, and* $s_1, \ldots, s_k$ *are steps in absolute or relative path expressions that refer either to properties or association types to navigate in the schema;*
- *the semantics is as for plain FDs:* $\forall t_i, t_j \in R : t_i[X] = t_j[X] \Rightarrow t_i[Y] = t_j[Y]$.

In the following, we briefly explain how different types of data sources are virtually mapped to this generic representation of schemas and FDs.

Representation of JSON. The types of objects in JSON are represented by complex types in our model, as they might have properties and associations. JSON arrays are represented as multi-valued properties.

Example 1. *In Fig. 1a,* Genre *is a complex type with two properties:* name *with an atomic type and* Painter *with a complex type. Some properties (e.g.,* Painting) *are multi-valued. This gFD states that each painting is owned by one museum in the corresponding year:* [Genre.Painter.Painting]title, History.year → History.museum

Representation of Neo4j Graphs. A Neo4j graph separates data into nodes and relationships. A node has a collection of properties in key-value pairs and a set of labels that specify the node type. A relationship is a directed edge connecting two entity nodes. In our metadata model, nodes and their properties are represented as complex types. A node may have multiple labels indicating its domain roles, which we specify as *super types*. We represent a relationship as *association*, whose *source* and *target* identify the corresponding in- and outgoing complex types. A relationship in Neo4j usually also has a set of *properties* that can be attached to the association in our model.

Example 2. *In Fig. 1c, the nodes* Chai *and* Ipoh Coffee *both have the label* Product, *which is a complex type, as well as* Category *and* Supplier. *The relationships* PART_OF *and* SUPPLIES *are association types. In addition to Fig. 1c,* Product *has the properties* productName, unitInStock *and* unitPrice, *while* Supplier *has* ID *and* name, *which all have atomic types. The association* SUPPLIES *has a property* purchasePrice. *The gFD below defines that for each supplied product, the purchase price depends on the supplier ID and the product name:* [Supplier.SUPPLIES]source.ID, target.productName → purchasePrice.

Subsequently, gFDs that relate properties from several complex or association types are referred to as **inter-FDs**, in contrast to **intra-FDs** defined within the scope of one type. Usual FDs in relational schemas are intra-FDs.

Based on our metadata model, we now define RFDs.

Definition 3. *Given a schema* $S = \langle T, C, P, A \rangle$ *and its instance* r, *a RFD* f *is in the form:* $[X_0]X_1, \ldots, X_n \xrightarrow[c_X, c_Y]{\varepsilon} Y_1, \ldots, Y_m$

- *the basic structure of the RFD is as for gFDs defined in Definition 2;*
- ε *is the error threshold that indicates the minimal percentage of objects to be removed from* O *(the result of* X_0*) such that the RFD becomes valid, i.e.,* $\Psi(f) = min\{|O_1| \ |O_1 \subseteq O \text{ and } f \text{ holds for } O \backslash O_1\}/|O| \le \varepsilon$ *[9];*
- c_X *and* c_Y *are values that indicate the clustering over the values of the LHS and RHS of* f*; values within the same cluster are considered to be equal.*

Example 3. *The following examples define RFDs given the relation in Fig. 1b: (a)* $[Employee]Level \xrightarrow[1.0, 1.0]{0.2} Years$ *(b)* $[Employee]Salary \xrightarrow[0.998, 1.0]{0} Level$ *The first example states that the dependency holds if we remove no more than 20% tuples (e.g.,* t_5 *or* t_6*) from the relation; the second example requires all the tuples to satisfy the dependency.*

The values c_X, c_Y are indicators for the clustering applied to the instance values. A higher value indicates that elements are well matched to their own cluster, while lower values indicate that more dissimilar elements are grouped in one cluster. In Sect. 4, we will use the silhouette coefficient (SC) [14] as indicator, which has not been applied in existing RFD discovery approaches. In Example 3b, the salary values 24.8 and 24.9 are grouped in the same cluster, and with a SC of 0.998 we can say *Salary* is "well-clustered".

4 Our Approach

4.1 Approach Overview

Algorithm 1 describes our approach with a dataset D and error threshold ε as input. We first extract the schema of D and represent it in our generic meta-model. The dataset is transformed into a decomposed form, which basically corresponds to the first normal form of the logical instance representation discussed in Sect. 3 (all properties are transformed to atomic values). The original hierarchical structures and relationships are maintained as the schema information (see Sect. 4.2). We refer to the resulting tables as *property tables*, and they are preprocessed in two steps. First, we filter long textual attributes which lead to less interesting RFDs without semantic significance (long texts are often unique). The second step is to group the same values of an attribute using hash partition.

We prune and remove certain attributes, if they are found to be *equivalent* by our feature-based agglomerative clustering (see Sect. 4.3). Then, we discover

---

Algorithm 1. RFD Discovery

Input: Relational/JSON/graph dataset D, threshold ε; **Output:** Set of RFDs

1   $R \leftarrow ExtractSchema(D)$; $D' \leftarrow 1NF\_Decomposition(D, R)$; $\Sigma \leftarrow \emptyset$; $P_r \leftarrow \emptyset$

2   **foreach** *property table* $d \in D'$ **do**

3      $P_0 \leftarrow HashPartition(FilterLongTextualAttrs(d))$; $P \leftarrow \emptyset$ // Preproc.

4      $C \leftarrow FeatureAgglomeration(P_0)$ // Prune equivalent attributes

5   **foreach** *attribute* $c \in C$ **do**

6          $(P_c, s_c) \leftarrow ClusterPartition(P_0, c)$ // Obtain equivalent classes

7   Add P_c to P, add s_c to Φ // Φ: silhouette coefficient

8      $\Sigma \leftarrow \Sigma \cup IntraRFDDiscovery(P, R, \varepsilon, \Phi)$; $P_r \leftarrow P_r \cup P$

9   $\Sigma' \leftarrow InterRFDDiscovery(P_r, R, \varepsilon, \Phi, \Sigma)$

10 **return** $\Sigma \cup \Sigma'$

---

the intra-RFDs by *X-means* clustering (Sect. 4.4). For JSON or graphs, a RFD may also exist among properties of different complex types or association types. Therefore, we also try to discover whether there exist inter-RFDs (Sect. 4.5). The union of intra-RFDs and inter-RFDs is returned as the final result.

4.2 Schema Inference and Dataset Decomposition

A relational dataset can be directly processed for RFD discovery; a JSON or graph dataset needs some preprocessing to generate tables with atomic values only. Our DL system [5,8] loads a JSON document and extracts its schema using Apache Spark[1]. Based on the extracted schema, we decompose the JSON documents into a set of *property tables*. We perform decomposition as follows: **(1)** For each complex type, we create a property table for it with an identifier ID and each property as a column. **(2)** If a complex type c_2 is a property of another complex type c_1, we create a column *parent identifier (PID)* with the identifier of c_1 in the table of c_2. **(3)** If there is an association type (e.g., a relationship in Neo4j graph), we create a new association property table with columns storing its properties, e.g., identifiers of source and target objects. **(4)** If a *Property* is multi-valued, we generate a value table.

Example 4. *Table 1 shows the decomposed property tables, one for each complex type. Except the root node* Genre, *each property table has a column PID. Note that we use **path-based** table names, thus we can uniquely find an attribute in a property table. Graphs of Neo4j are processed similarly, but we retrieve the schema using the APOC library[2]. In addition to the steps above, we create path tables for inter-RFD discovery. In the evaluation, we limit the length of paths to 3, as longer paths often do not lead to meaningful results. Table 2 shows three examples of property tables: the left one for the complex type* Supplier, *the middle one for the association type* SUPPLIES, *and the last one which is a path table including IDs of all nodes and relationships on the path.*

---

[1] https://spark.apache.org/.

[2] https://neo4j-contrib.github.io/neo4j-apoc-procedures/.

Table 1. Decomposed result of Fig. 1a.

Genre		Genre.Painter			Genre.Painter.Painting			Genre.Painter.Painting.History				
ID	name	ID	PID	name	ID	PID	title	ID	PID	year	museum	city
1	Symbolism	11	1	Gustav Klimt	101	11	The Lady in Gold	1001	101	1941	Belvedere	Vienna
								1002	101	2006	Neue Galerie	New York

Table 2. Partial decomposed result of Fig. 1c.

Supplier		Supplier-SUPPLIES-Product				Supplier-SUPPLIES-Product-PART_OF-Category				
ID	name	ID	SrcID	TgtID	purchasePrice	node1_ID	rel1_ID	node2_ID	rel2_ID	node3_ID
12	Cooper	101	12	35	35	12	101	35	102	18

4.3 Pruning Rules

Given a dataset whose number of attributes is m, and number of tuples is $|r|$, the lattice-based FD discovery has the complexity $\mathcal{O}(|r|^2 \left(\frac{m}{2}\right)^2 2^m)$ [12]. Thus, pruning candidate FDs has been intensively conducted in existing works for efficiency. Existing pruning rules [9] mainly check whether an attribute is a key, or whether a candidate FD can be inferred from existing dependencies. Besides implementing the existing pruning rules [9,12,17], we have designed the following pruning procedure based on agglomerative clustering.

Equivalent Attributes. We call two attributes A and B *equivalent* if two RFDs $A \to B$ and $B \to A$ both hold [16]. We can replace A with B in the LHS or RHS of a dependency. In this way, we have less RFDs; yet, it preserves the same information, which leads to a smaller cover of the final RFD set.

Pruning Based on Agglomerative Clustering. To detect equivalent attributes, we use agglomerative (hierarchical) clustering; for generality, we calculate the distances using Ward's method [15] as criterion. The first step is feature selection. Recall in Sect. 2 we introduced that a FD can be inferred from the calculation of $e(X)$, which depends on the values of the stripped partition rank $|\widehat{\pi_X}|$ and its sum $||\widehat{\pi_X}||$. Thus, we calculate the values of $|\widehat{\pi}_A|$ and $||\widehat{\pi}_A||$ for each attribute to form the feature matrix for agglomerative clustering. Given two attributes A and B, their squared Euclidean distance is $d_{AB} = \sqrt{(|\widehat{\pi}_A| - |\widehat{\pi}_B|)^2 + (||\widehat{\pi}_A|| - ||\widehat{\pi}_B||)^2}$. During the hierarchical clustering process, the values of distance among current clusters are monotonic. Thus, we can determine the optimal number of clusters by detecting the change point[3] in the distance slope, and use it as the termination condition. Note that [16] also discovers equivalent attributes, yet it examines strict value equality. In this work we detect equivalence by applying agglomerative clustering, which provides the relaxation. Finally, we set attributes in each cluster as equivalent attributes for pruning.

---

[3] Library used in implementation: https://github.com/deepcharles/ruptures.

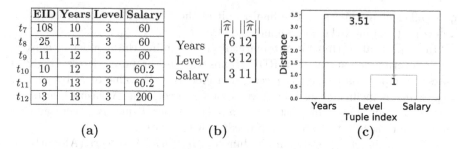

Fig. 2. (a) Added tuples; (b) Feature matrix; (c) Clustering result

Example 5. *Figure 2a shows a few additional tuples which we added to Fig. 1b. Since* EID *is a key and already pruned, we calculate the feature matrix for the remaining attributes (cf. Fig. 2b), e.g., by comparing similar values of* Salary *we obtain stripped partition* $\widehat{\pi}_{Salary} = \{\{t_1, t_2\}, \{t_3, t_4\}, \{t_5, t_6, t_7, t_8, t_9, t_{10}, t_{11}\}\}$ *(t_{12} is stripped out as its equivalent class size is one). Thus, in the third row of the matrix in Fig. 2b we insert* $|\widehat{\pi}_{Salary}| = 3$, $||\widehat{\pi}_{Salary}|| = 11$. *Figure 2c shows the hierarchical clustering result using the matrix, and the red line indicates that the clustering terminates with two clusters when it reaches the change point. Since* Level *and* Salary *are in the same cluster, we have them as equivalent attributes. We can prune* Salary *and only examine RFD candidates including* Level.

4.4 Clustering-Based RFD Discovery

To provide the relaxation in attribute value comparison, for partition we use clustering instead of exact value matching.

Our partition method *ClusterPartition* is invoked from the main algorithm with the previous partition P_0 and the current attribute c as input, and produces the new clustering-based partition P_c. The second output s_c is the silhouette coefficient (SC) for c, which constitutes c_X and c_Y in Definition 3.

Our approach automatically determines the optimal number of clusters by applying the clustering method *X-means* [13], which conducts an initial clustering, then repeatedly performs local *K-means* to split each cluster, and selects the most promising subset of clusters using Bayesian Information Criterion.

The upper bound u for the number of clusters is the rank of the initial partition P_0, the lower bound l is 2. To make *X-means* more efficient for a potentially large number of clusters, we do a preprocessing to narrow down the potential values for the number of clusters. The preprocessing uses a binary search strategy to refine the upper and lower bounds. In each step, a *K-means* clustering is performed with $K = \frac{u+l}{2}$ and the search continues in that part with better SCs. From the intensive experiments over real world datasets, we found that the clustering results become less meaningful with SC below 0.8; thus, we will ignore clusterings with a SC less than 0.8. If the initial rank of P_0 is low (e.g., less than 50), then the preprocessing step is skipped as *X-means* is already

quite efficient in this case. The final result of the *ClusterPartition* procedure is a new partition and the corresponding SC.

In [18], an algorithm for automatically determining the number of clusters for discovering dependencies in RDF graphs was also proposed. However, [18] is based on gap statistics and *K-means*, and increases the value of K by one per step, which is inefficient for a large value of K. In contrast, *X-means* selects the most promising subset of clusters for refinement per *K-means* sweep, and we apply binary search to fasten the procedure with a large K.

After obtaining the partition, the function *IntraRFDDiscovery* (Algorithm 1, line 8) computes the stripped partition and infers the RFD using the error measure in Definition 3. We also generate the RFD candidates based on the attribute lattice similar to TANE [9].

4.5   Inter-RFD Discovery

For JSON documents, a RFD may exist among attributes of different types. Thus, we also need to examine such *inter-RFDs*, whose LHS/RHS are attribute sets from different tables after decomposition. The key challenge in inter-RFD discovery is how to efficiently "group" property tables to avoid an exhaustive search. More specially, regarding partition and RFD inference, discovering inter-RFD is similar to intra-RFD which we have introduced. However, for inter-RFD we need to combine the attributes from a set of property tables, which implies much more RFD candidates than the intra-RFD discovery for a single property table. We mainly developed the following rules extended from [17] to make the inter-RFD discovery more efficient:

(1) If a property table T_2 is generated from a multi-valued property, we group it with its parent table T_1, e.g., *(History, Painting)* in Fig. 1a.

(2) If a RFD created from rule (1) is valid for tuples with the same parents (PIDs), but does not hold in all the tuples, we add the next ancestor table farthest from the root. We repeat this step until we find a valid inter-RFD or we reach the root table. For instance, if the RFD candidates generated from *(History, Painting)* do not hold, we examine *(History, Painting, Painter)*.

(3) We group the parent table with its child tables, or two sibling tables if they have similar number of records. The purpose of this rule is to group property tables with similar number of records ($|r|$ for computing $e(X)$), otherwise there will be a number of null values, and it rarely leads to valid RFDs.

Note that for (1) and (2), [17] has proposed algorithms to compute inter-RFDs from invalid intra-RFDs, which hold for the instance values of each individual complex type, but might not for the whole JSON document or graph. For instance, in the *History* table in the right of Table 1, the intra-RFD: *year* → *museum* holds only for the same painting (e.g., *PID* as 101). It is very likely that there exist other painting records with year 2006 but in other museums, i.e., *year* → *museum* is not valid. However, within the grouping *(History, Painting)*

Table 3. Relational datasets

Name	Rows#	Attr#
Adult	32561	15
Bio	184292	9
Wiki Image	777676	12

Table 4. JSON datasets

Name	Records#	Objects#	Attr#	**L**
TVshows	20	18	47	5
Restaurant	25357	4	13	3
Profile	1561	3	15	2

Table 5. Graph datasets

Name	Nodes#	Rel#	NodeTypes#	NodeProp#	RelTypes#	RelProp#
Movie	171	250	2	5	4	1
Northwind	1035	3139	5	51	4	5
WorldCup	83382	156673	13	30	16	0

Table 6. Number of FDs/RFDs: baseline and our approach ($\varepsilon = 0$)

Name	Adult	Bio	Wiki image	TVshows	Restaurant	Profile	Movie	Northwind	WorldCup
Baseline	78	30	66	603	44	75	27	1749	826
Our approach	46	10	66	259	44	40	27	2105	715

if we add the attribute *title* in LHS, we might find a valid inter-RFD, e.g., $[Genre.Painter.Painting]title, History.year \rightarrow History.museum$.

After obtaining the attributes in the same group, the search space construction, pruning and RFD discovery are similar with intra-RFDs. In particular, for Neo4j property graphs, the inter-RFD discovery procedure is similar but among node/relationship/path tables from the shortest paths to the longest paths.

5 Evaluation

We have evaluated our approach over nine datasets to compare with a baseline approach (Sect. 5.1), and demonstrate that our approach discovers more meaningful dependencies with less redundancy. In Sect. 5.2, we show that our approach is fault-tolerant, and can be used to detect inconsistent data.

Experimental Setting. We have conducted the experiments in a server running Ubuntu 14.04 LTS, with two Intel Xeon X5647@2.93 GHz CPUs (8 logical cores per CPU) and 16G RAM. The tested relational, JSON, and graph datasets are stored in MySQL 5.5.62, MongoDB 3.4.16, and Neo4j 3.4.5, respectively. The decomposed tables are stored in MySQL and the discovered RFDs are stored in MongoDB. We have implemented the decomposition in Java and the other algorithms in Python 3.5, which are embedded in our DL system *Constance* [5].

Tested Datasets[4]. Table 3 shows the name, number of rows and attributes of the relational datasets: *Adult, Bio* and *Wiki Image*. Table 4 provides the number of JSON records, number of objects/attributes and nesting levels (L) in JSON schema for three JSON datasets. Table 5 reports the number of entity nodes and relationships in the data, the number of nodes types and relationship types, and their corresponding properties in the metadata of graph datasets.

5.1   Baseline Comparison of Discovered Dependencies

The main goal of our clustering-based method and pruning procedure in Sect. 4 is to discover meaningful RFDs and reduce redundancy. Thus, we first report the results of discovered RFDs from all the datasets. For comparison, we have implemented a baseline algorithm using the TANE approach [9]. Since TANE only supports relational data, in the baseline we also apply our rules for inter-FD discovery from JSON/graph datasets. Thus, the comparison mainly reflects the effect of relaxation brought by *ClusterPartition* procedure and pruning using agglomerative clustering.

Reduce Redundancy. By allowing a ratio ε of violating tuples, it usually leads to a larger number of RFDs than the exact FDs. To reduce this effect such that we can observe the impact of our pruning method, we set error threshold ε as 0 in this test (Table 6). We can observe that in most datasets, our approach has a smaller or equal number of discovered dependencies, because with the agglomerative clustering we detect equivalent attributes and prune the dependencies accordingly. Thus, our results have less redundancy and imply all the FDs generated by the baseline.

Discover more Meaningful Dependencies. Now we assign ε with typical error threshold values: 0.01, 0.05, and 0.1. Figure 3 depicts the impact of ε on the number of discovered RFDs. For JSON/graph datasets, the upper hatched parts indicate the number of inter-RFDs. For instance, for *TVshows* with $\varepsilon = 0.01$, there are 75 intra-RFDs and 246 RFDs in total (171 inter-RFDs). Combining Fig. 3 and Table 6, we observe that in most datasets there are more RFDs when $\varepsilon > 0$ than $\varepsilon = 0$; these dependencies do not exist in the FD results of the baseline approach. For instance, for *TVshows* with ε as 0.1 we obtain the RFD: $[root.embedded.episodes]name \rightarrow airtime$. It indicates that the episode name (not a key attribute) can functionally determine the episode airtime. Such meaningful dependencies can be found by our RFD discovery approach but not by the baseline approach. Moreover, with a larger value of ε, we often find more RFDs, e.g., the results of datasets *Adult, TVshows* and *Restaurant* in Fig. 3.

Moreover, in some cases we found that the discovered RFDs are "more compact" than FDs, i.e., with less attributes in LHS. For example, in the *Northwind* dataset, there exists a FD f_1 generated by the baseline: $Customer.postalCode, Order.shipRegion \rightarrow Order.shipCountry$. In our approach we produce the RFD f_2: $Customer.postalCode \rightarrow Order.shipCountry$

---

[4] Links: http://dbis.rwth-aachen.de/cms/staff/hai/RFDDiscovery/datasets.

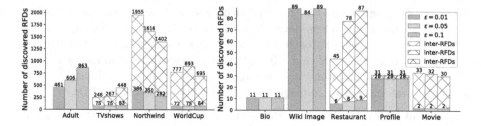

Fig. 3. Number of discovered RFDs in nine datasets with different ε

with ε as 0.05. By clustering similar values instead of exact value matching, and allowing a degree of tuple violation, we find RFDs like f_2. In addition, more RFDs will be pruned as we keep only minimal RFDs. Thus, in Fig. 3 we observe that with a higher value of ε, the number of discovered RFDs decreases in datasets *Northwind* and *Movie*.

5.2 Noise Tolerance and Error Detection

Besides finding interesting RFDs to enrich metadata in data lakes, another goal in this work is to apply our approach over dirty data, then use the discovered RFDs for error detection. We designed the below experiments to examine whether our discovered RFDs meet such a requirement.

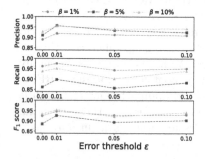

Fig. 4. Fault tolerance results

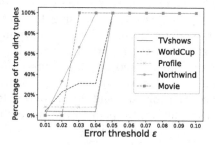

Fig. 5. Error detection results

Noise Tolerance. In line with RFD-based data quality works [3], we obtain *dirty data* by adding Gaussian noise (*mean* = 0.0, standard deviation β = [1%, 5%, 10%]) to the values of 10% of the existing numerical attribute tuples in every dataset. If a RFD discovered from the dirty data can also be found from the clean data, we consider it as the *true positive*. We divide the amount of true positives by the total numbers of RFDs discovered in the dirty data, and obtain

precision; for *recall* we divide the number of true positives by the total number of RFDs in the original clean data. Figure 4 shows the precision/recall/F_1 score results (y-axis) of our approach with error thresholds (x-axis) of the dataset *TVshows*.[5] We can observe that with different values of noises and error thresholds, our approach maintains a satisfying accuracy ($F_1 > 0.85$). Thus, even for a dataset with inaccuracy, our approach can effectively discover RFDs.

Error Detection. In this experiment for each dataset, we insert additional dirty tuples whose values are inconsistent with the original data. Then we use the discovered RFDs to find violating tuples, and examine whether they are the inserted dirty tuples. Figure 5 shows the results of 5 datasets with the percentage of dirty tuples as 5%. The x-axis shows the value of ε used to generate the RFDs, and the y-axis is the percentage of detected true dirty tuples by using these RFDs. In all datasets, we can observe that the percentage of detected error data has a significant increase when ε is getting close to the actual error data rate, although with different varying trends. This indicates that the choice of error threshold value plays a crucial role in finding all inconsistent data. For practical use when the error rate is unknown in a newly imported dataset, we recommend to run our approach with increasing values of error threshold, until the detected error data becomes stable.

6 Conclusion

We have addressed the problem of RFD discovery for heterogeneous data lakes. Our clustering-based approach groups similar attribute values. With our generic metadata model, we provide a unified definition for RFDs, thereby enabling integrated methods for processing different types of data, e.g., relational, JSON, and graph data. We have designed a pruning procedure using agglomerative clustering, which can effectively prune RFD candidates. We have shown experimentally with nine datasets that our approach can find semantically interesting RFDs, which are less redundant compared to the classical approach. Our approach is also fault tolerant, and the discovered RFDs can be used for detecting dirty data. In the future, we plan to use the obtained RFDs for other tasks in data lakes such as schema mapping [6,7].

Acknowledgements. The authors would like to thank the German Research Foundation DFG for the kind support within the Cluster of Excellence "Internet of Production" (Project ID: EXC 2023/390621612).

References

1. Bassée, R., Wijsen, J.: Neighborhood dependencies for prediction. In: Cheung, D., Williams, G.J., Li, Q. (eds.) PAKDD 2001. LNCS (LNAI), vol. 2035, pp. 562–567. Springer, Heidelberg (2001). https://doi.org/10.1007/3-540-45357-1_59

---

[5] Full results: http://dbis.rwth-aachen.de/cms/staff/hai/RFDDiscovery/res.

2. Caruccio, L., Deufemia, V., Polese, G.: Relaxed functional dependencies - a survey of approaches. IEEE Trans. Knowl. Data Eng. **28**(1), 147–165 (2016)
3. Cong, G., Fan, W., Geerts, F., Jia, X., Ma, S.: Improving data quality: consistency and accuracy. In: Proceedings of the VLDB, pp. 315–326 (2007)
4. Fassetti, F., Fazzinga, B.: Approximate functional dependencies for XML data. In: Proceedings of the ADBIS (2007)
5. Hai, R., Geisler, S., Quix, C.: Constance: an intelligent data lake system. In: Proceedings of the SIGMOD, pp. 2097–2100. ACM (2016)
6. Hai, R., Quix, C.: Rewriting of plain SO tgds into nested tgds. Proc. VLDB Endow. **12**(11), 1526–1538 (2019)
7. Hai, R., Quix, C., Kensche, D.: Nested schema mappings for integrating JSON. In: Trujillo, J.C., et al. (eds.) ER 2018. LNCS, vol. 11157, pp. 397–405. Springer, Cham (2018). https://doi.org/10.1007/978-3-030-00847-5_28
8. Hai, R., Quix, C., Zhou, C.: Query rewriting for heterogeneous data lakes. In: Benczúr, A., Thalheim, B., Horváth, T. (eds.) ADBIS 2018. LNCS, vol. 11019, pp. 35–49. Springer, Cham (2018). https://doi.org/10.1007/978-3-319-98398-1_3
9. Huhtala, Y., et al.: TANE: an efficient algorithm for discovering functional and approximate dependencies. Comput. J. **42**(2), 100–111 (1999)
10. Kensche, D., Quix, C., Li, X., Li, Y., Jarke, M.: Generic schema mappings for composition and query answering. Data Knowl. Eng. **68**(7), 599–621 (2009)
11. Kruse, S., Naumann, F.: Efficient discovery of approximate dependencies. Proc. VLDB Endow. **11**(7), 759–772 (2018)
12. Liu, J., Li, J., Liu, C., Chen, Y.: Discover dependencies from data - a review. IEEE Trans. Knowl. Data Eng. **24**(2), 251–264 (2012)
13. Pelleg, D., Moore, A.W., et al.: X-means: extending k-means with efficient estimation of the number of clusters. In: Proceedings of the ICML, pp. 727–734 (2000)
14. Rousseeuw, P.J.: Silhouettes: a graphical aid to the interpretation and validation of cluster analysis. J. Comput. Appl. Math. **20**, 53–65 (1987)
15. Ward Jr., J.H.: Hierarchical grouping to optimize an objective function. J. Am. Stat. Assoc. **58**(301), 236–244 (1963)
16. Yao, H., Hamilton, H.J., Butz, C.J.: FD_Mine: discovering functional dependencies in a database using equivalences. In: Proceedings of the ICDM, pp. 729–732 (2002)
17. Yu, C., Jagadish, H.V.: XML schema refinement through redundancy detection and normalization. VLDB J. **17**(2), 203–223 (2008)
18. Yu, Y., Heflin, J.: Extending functional dependency to detect abnormal data in RDF graphs. In: Aroyo, L., et al. (eds.) ISWC 2011. LNCS, vol. 7031, pp. 794–809. Springer, Heidelberg (2011). https://doi.org/10.1007/978-3-642-25073-6_50

An Ontological Perspective for Database Tuning Heuristics

Ana Carolina Almeida[1]([⊠]), Maria Luiza M. Campos[2],
Fernanda Baião[3], Sergio Lifschitz[3], Rafael P. de Oliveira[3],
and Daniel Schwabe[3]

[1] State University of Rio de Janeiro (UERJ), Rio de Janeiro, RJ, Brazil
ana.almeida@ime.uerj.br
[2] Federal University of Rio de Janeiro (UFRJ), Rio de Janeiro, RJ, Brazil
mluiza@ppgi.ufrj.br
[3] Pontifical Catholic University of Rio de Janeiro (PUC-Rio),
Rio de Janeiro, RJ, Brazil
fbaiao@puc-rio.br,
{sergio,rpoliveira,dschwabe}@inf.puc-rio.br

Abstract. Database tuning is a complex task, involving technology-specific concepts. Although they seem to share a common meaning, there are very specific implementations across different DBMSs vendors and particular releases. Database tuning also involves parameters that are often adjusted empirically based on rules of thumb. Moreover, the intricate relationships among these parameters often pose a contradictory impact on the overall performance improvement goal. Nevertheless, the literature – and practice – on this topic defines a set of heuristics followed by DBAs, which are implemented by the available tuning tools in different ways for specific DBMSs. In this paper, we argue that a semantic support for the implementation of tuning heuristics is crucial for providing DBAs with a higher-level conceptualization, unburdening them from worrying about internal implementations of data access structures in distinct platforms. Our proposal encompasses a set of formally-defined rules based on an ontology, enabling DBAs to define new configuration parameters and to assess the application of tuning heuristics at a conceptual level. We illustrate this proposal with two use case scenarios that show the advantages of this semantic support for the definition and execution of sophisticated DB tuning heuristics, involving hypothetical indexes and what-if situations for relational databases.

Keywords: Database tuning · Ontology · SWRL · Heuristics

1 Introduction

Computational systems are increasingly ubiquitous, producing and consuming large amounts of data. As a consequence, these systems pose a demand for higher performance, especially for lower response time and increased throughput, pushing Database Management Systems (DBMSs) to higher levels of functionalities and control. Database (DB) tuning strategies address this need by supporting the configuration of the physical design of the DB towards improving performance. DB tuning involves

© Springer Nature Switzerland AG 2019
A. H. F. Laender et al. (Eds.): ER 2019, LNCS 11788, pp. 240–254, 2019.
https://doi.org/10.1007/978-3-030-33223-5_20

decisions upon the creation and maintenance of indexes, materialized views, data replication, partitioning, query rewriting, among others. These strategies constitute heuristics for improving the performance of the applications that access this DB [1]. As any other heuristics, DB tuning heuristics may be implemented and automated to assist their users (in this case, the Database Administrator, or DBA) in achieving a goal (i.e., improving performance), and obtaining successful results in most cases [1]. The tools that implement DB tuning heuristics can be semi-automatic (when the DBA makes the final decision on tuning the DB based on the suggestions of the heuristics) or completely automatic (in the case of a self-tuning tool, which implements the decision directly, without the intervention of the DBA).

However, DB tuning heuristics are typically empirically defined, and most lack a precise definition. For example, when the DBA decides on performing a tuning action (*e.g.*, rewriting a query) to improve the database performance, s/he is following reasoning that is present in her/his mind, based on concepts, principles, and previous experiences that only s/he is aware of. This scenario worsens in the presence of self-tuning tools when the DBA is unaware of the rationale followed by the tool since only the final physical design of the tuning process is available. The DBA cannot assess the tuning actions or even backtrack an individual step taken by the tool. For example, the DBA can conclude that a particular index created by the self-tuning tool might degrade the performance of insertion operations in the DB and then may want to undo a tuning action executed by the heuristic. However, the heuristic might have considered that, even while degrading insert operations, the index was still beneficial to the database workload as a whole (the set of all queries and data manipulation commands), as a result of a decision rationale unknown to the DBA. In this case, the rationale and the concepts analyzed by the tool are embedded in its source code, thus making it difficult or even impossible for the DBA to scrutinize.

Also, semi-automatic or self-tuning tools are tailored to suggesting specific actions for particular DBMSs, which makes heuristics experiments difficult in scenarios including several DBMSs and their extension to different structures and parameters. This difficulty does not only occur because the user must understand the source code of the tool, but also because each DBMS employs distinct concepts and terminology for its physical data structures and parameters, as well as for its implementation and syntax.

In this paper, we propose an approach to minimize these problems by explicitly representing the elements and actions involved in the database tuning heuristics using ontologies, as they represent an adequate means to support an accurate semantic record of the heuristics formulation and behavior. The DBA can analyze the tuning heuristics in more detail, as well as compare the different alternatives that each possible heuristic proposes. Also, the DBA can perform (semi-) automatic experiments by combining distinct heuristics. Finally, the use of ontologies also increases the heuristics understanding of the DBA, since they are described using higher-level concepts.

Thus, we present an ontological perspective for DB tuning heuristics. Our approach is developed on top of an ontology-driven conceptual framework[1], which includes an ontology of DB tuning heuristics and an ontology of DB tuning structural concepts.

---

[1] https://github.com/BioBD/outer_tuning, last accessed 2019/04/07.

These ontologies may be extended straightforwardly at the conceptual level to include new concepts and heuristics, without requiring the understanding of the implementation code. The advantage of our approach is that it provides a transparent methodology for tuning databases using multiple heuristics defined through rules based on semantic reasoning. One may create new heuristics by reasoning over the ontologies. We discuss some results of the application of our framework to two real-world case studies.

The remainder of this paper is organized as follows. In Sect. 2 we discuss state of the art in this area; in Sect. 3 we provide an overview of our conceptual framework, and we detail the ontology responsible for defining and executing the heuristics; Sect. 4, we showcase an outline of a demonstration of our framework, using our heuristic ontology. Section 5 concludes this research work.

2   State-of-the-Art

To set the context for discussing the specific contributions of this work, it is important to present different types of initiatives that consider ways of capturing and representing concepts involved in the tuning process, as well as those which offer any tuning support based on the represented concepts for DB or DB Tuning heuristics. As the proposition of specific DB tuning heuristics is not the focus of our proposal, we refrain from citing here such related literature.

The first group of works contemplates those related to conceptual models associated with the DB domain. The Common Warehouse Metamodel (CWM) specification, proposed by the Object Management Group (OMG) as a metadata interchange standard [2] comprises, among others, a package to describe relational data resources, which includes elements associated to indexes, primary keys, and foreign keys. Also supporting interoperability, Aguiar, and colleagues [3] proposed RDBS-O, a well-founded reference ontology covering high-level DB structure concepts. Both initiatives serve as a starting point for more comprehensive efforts covering other aspects of DB physical design, optimization and tuning. Aligned with our work, Ouared and colleagues adopt an approach that proposes a meta-advisor repository for DB physical design [4]. They describe a metamodel with elements dedicated to express optimization algorithms (heuristics), their characteristics and a cost model.

The second group of initiatives addresses tools [5–10] and approaches [11–13], which help the DBA to improve the performance of DBMSs. Considering the use of previously represented knowledge, the research work of Bellatreche and colleagues [14, 15] tracks the relationship between the requirements of the application and the suggestion of physical structures for optimization of the DB in a data warehouse environment. It uses an ontology to formalize domain concepts from data sources and SWRL rules [16] to relate them to the application requirements. Although the strategy supports indexes suggestions, there is no further explanation for them or the proposal of grounded alternatives. Recently, Zhang and colleagues presented the OtterTune tool, which leverages data collected from previous tuning efforts to train machine learning models, and recommends new configurations that are as good as or better than ones generated by existing tools or a human expert [17]. Among the helpful suggestions, they highlight the selection of the best access structures and configuration parameters

for the DBMS. Zhang and colleagues proposed the CDBTune, an end-to-end automatic DBMS configuration tuning system that recommends superior knob settings in cloud environments, using deep reinforcement learning (RL). Through the reward-feedback mechanism in RL instead of traditional regression, they expect to accelerate the convergence speed of their model and improve efficiency of online tuning [18]. Zheng and colleagues presented a neural network-based algorithm for performance self-tuning [19] based on the workload and identify key system performance parameters, suggesting values to tune the DBMS. The reasoning of the algorithms proposed by these works is hidden in the source code or in the constructed model, making it difficult for the DBA to understand it and make adjustments to extend, add or combine heuristics. The decisions are not explained or justified to the DBA. In certain systems, such as Oracle DBMS, there are specific tools for suggesting tuning actions, also making the rationale of their choices available [20, 21]. Nevertheless, they still fail to capture the actual DBA decision process, with justifications for chosen and refused suggested tuning alternatives. Although there are a variety of tools and strategies to support the DBA in the DB tuning task, most works fail to make reasoning and decisions explicit.

Moreover, existing DB tuning tools and approaches suggest actions but do not provide a higher level mechanism for the DBA to verify the effectiveness of their actions and to tailor the rationale to his/her background knowledge. If the DBA disagrees with something suggested by the tool or approach, it may not be feasible for the DBA to include or change any reasoning proposed by the tool. That way, only an experienced DBA would be able to select the best tool to assist him/her according to the established scenario. Besides, the tools and approaches that involve more than one technique or structure do not have enough flexibility to consider additional methods.

3   The Outer-Tuning Conceptual Framework

We have developed Outer-Tuning, an ontology-driven framework for DB Tuning. Outer-Tuning works both in automatic (self-tuning) and in semi-automatic (human intervention) modes, and it may be extended to address new data structures and heuristics because all changes are expressed in the conceptual level using a declarative language.

Outer-Tuning allows the user to enable/disable a set of inference rules (SWRL rules [16]) established by heuristics. This functionality is crucial for the DBA, as s/he can choose, through the interface, which heuristics should be used to tune the DB. The use of a declarative language to define heuristics allows the DBA to focus on "what" the heuristic should do, instead of "how" it should work.

3.1   Outer-Tuning Overview

Figure 1 Illustrates the architecture and execution of the Outer-Tuning framework, using the activity diagram (UML alternative to the BPMN Business Process diagram)[2].

---

[2] https://sparxsystems.com/enterprise_architect_user_guide/14.0/guidebooks/tools_ba_uml_activity_diagram.html, last accessed 2019/04/07.

Outer-Tuning monitors the DB [Step 1] in a non-intrusive and continuous way and captures the workload submitted to the DB. Then, queries are parsed to identify query components and data structures, whose corresponding concepts in the ontology are needed by the tuning heuristics to estimate their processing cost (preconditions) [Step 2]. The rules engine instantiates the concepts [Step 3] and applies the tuning heuristics specified in the ontology rules, thus inferring tuning actions [Step 4] to improve the performance of the queries in the workload.

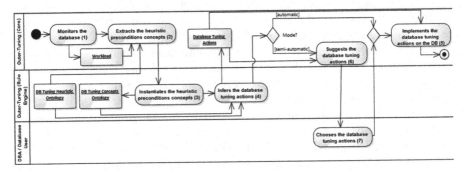

Fig. 1. Outer-tuning execution process

When the framework is set to automatic mode [Step 5], all suggested tuning actions (e.g., creation of indexes and materialized views) are applied to the DB; in semi-automatic mode, the suggested tuning actions are presented to the user [Step 6], who may customize [Step 7] which tuning actions will actually be applied to the DB [Step 5].

3.2   Conceptual Models

The structural conceptual model of the Outer-Tuning framework comprises two independent and complementary (sub)ontologies[3]: the DB tuning concepts ontology (namespace: *tuning*) and the DB tuning heuristic ontology (namespace: *heuristic*). The DB tuning heuristic ontology, which is the focus of the present work, makes references to the concepts described in the DB tuning concepts ontology.

The ontologies are capable of answering the following competency questions: (i) which are the DB concepts involved in the DB tuning process? (ii) what is necessary for each heuristic to know about the DB and to make its decisions? (iii) which are the possible actions that can be performed by a heuristic?

In this paper, we focus on the DB tuning heuristic ontology, which addresses questions (ii) and (iii), and relies on the Unified Foundational Ontology (UFO) [22, 23] as its semantic foundation. Using UFO allows removing the ambiguity of the concepts used in the task of running DB tuning heuristics. This article explains the process of development and use of the ontology.

---

[3] https://www.ime.uerj.br/ontuning/, last accessed 2019/04/07.

The heuristic ontology was designed to support the specification of DB tuning heuristics as rules and the dynamic execution of heuristics during DB tuning, as explained in the following Subsections.

Heuristic Specification

The DBA (which is the role played by a *Person* while tuning a DB) chooses and specifies the heuristics (Fig. 2) that should be considered for DB tuning. Throughout the tuning task, the DBA assumes more specific roles with distinct goals. For example, when defining (and configuring) a heuristic the *heuristic:DBA* plays the role of a *heuristic:specifier*. When configuring a heuristic, a *heuristic:HeuristicSpecification* relationship arises. The *heuristic:Heuristic* exists independently of other concepts.

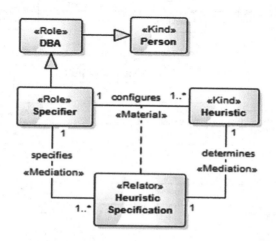

Fig. 2. Fragment of the heuristic ontology – heuristic specification

A *heuristic:Heuristic* takes data structures of the DB schema (defined in DB tuning concepts ontology) and cost estimates of DB operations into account to infer those actions that we should execute for performance improvement. Thus, each precondition of a *heuristic:Heuristic* references existing database concepts (*heuristic:DBConcept*) (Fig. 3). The *heuristic:PreconditionConcept* is derived from the relationship between *heuristic:Heuristic* and *heuristic:Database Concept*. A *heuristic:DBConcept* specializes into *heuristic:TuningAssist* or *heuristic:DBObject*. The *heuristic:TuningAssist* is a database concept required by a heuristic to perform its suggested actions (for example, a heuristic that suggests indexes needs to execute the "create index" DDL statement. So, this heuristic requires the "create index" statement as a precondition). A *heuristic: DBObject* refers to the database concept analyzed by the heuristic to make decisions (for example, the same heuristic suggesting an index may need to examine the *tuning: Where* clause of an SQL statement. So, the *tuning:Where* clause concept is a precondition of this heuristic).

Each *heuristic:DBConcept* defined in the DB tuning concepts ontology needs to be instantiated (Fig. 4) by a *heuristic:Source* (either a *heuristic:Function* or a *heuristic: Rule*). A *heuristic:Function* is a *heuristic:ConceptInstanceFunction* when it instantiates a

heuristic:DBConcept (that is, when it creates a new individual in the DB tuning concepts ontology). For example, a *heuristic:ConceptInstanceFunction* captures the database workload and instantiates a *heuristic:DMLcommand* concept with the specific query command captured. Analogously, a *heuristic:Rule* is a *heuristic:ConceptInstanceRule* when it instantiates a *heuristic:DBConcept*.

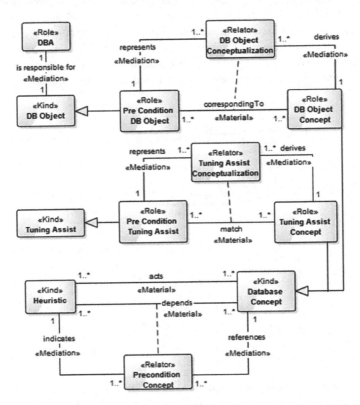

Fig. 3. A fragment of the heuristic ontology – heuristic preconditions definition

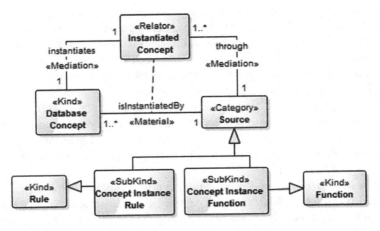

Fig. 4. Fragment of the heuristic ontology – heuristic concepts instantiation definition

Functions differ from rules since a *heuristic:Function* can interact with the DBMS, whereas a *heuristic:Rule* cannot. This is important since some *heuristic:DBConcepts* require accessing the database content to be instantiated, such as DML (Data Manipulation Language) commands. For example, the *tuning:DMLcommand* concept, defined in the domain ontology, requires a function that connects to the DBMS to retrieve the *tuning:DMLcommand* from the workload submitted by the user.

A *heuristic:Function* or method (Fig. 5) is a collection of statements embedded in the database that operate together in a group. It defines input and output parameters. In theory, all these parameters are optional. In our approach, the output parameter (instantiated concept or tuning action) is mandatory. For example, a *heuristic:Function* that retrieves a *tuning:DMLcommand* from the DBMS does not need any input parameters, while a *heuristic:Function* that returns information from an execution plan requires the execution plan as its input parameter. The *heuristic:Parameter* is a concept in the ontology, and its properties indicate if it plays the role of an input or of an output parameter to a *heuristic:Function*. Our approach preferably instantiates concepts through rules rather than functions, so as to make any reasoning explicit. Functions are used in specific situations to instantiate concepts that cannot be derived by rules.

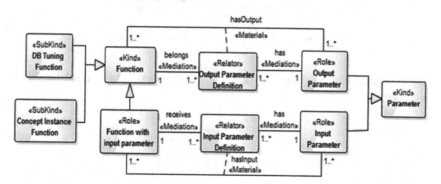

Fig. 5. Fragment of the heuristic ontology – functions definition

A *heuristic:Rule* (Fig. 6) is composed by a *heuristic: condition-action* pair, meaning that when the condition is satisfied, an action is performed. They provide the DBA with the rationale for heuristics application, by keeping track of the way concepts are instantiated when each tuning alternative is evaluated.

A *heuristic:RuleEngine* represents a system that applies inference mechanisms based on given rules, which in our case define DB tuning heuristics. The rule engine component implements the code that selects and executes the heuristics (described in the ontology) to suggest tuning actions (e.g., query rewriting) and the creation of access structures (e.g., materialized views). The instance of *tuning:DMLcommand* comprises the where clauses according to the SQL specification.

To perform the DB tuning task, *heuristic:Heuristic* defines *heuristic:Rules* that must be evaluated by the inference engine. Unlike the *heuristic:ConceptInstanceRule*, this kind of rule (*heuristic:HeuristicDefinitionRule*) corresponds to the definition of the heuristic's actions about the DB behavior. For example, a heuristic of indexes can

simulate indexes, called hypothetical, to know if the optimizer would use it or not. A *tuning:HypotheticalIndex* could exist in the DB (not physically) to improve certain *tuning:DMLcommand* performance.

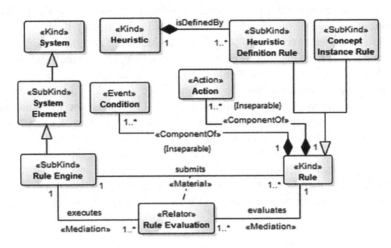

Fig. 6. Fragment of the heuristic ontology – rules definition

The heuristic may only suggests a hypothetical index, as illustrated by the following rule:

```
SingleStatement (?stat) ^ Where (?where) ^ hasClause (?stat, ?where)
^ Predicate (?pred)
^ componentOf (?pred, ?where) ^ SimpleExpression (?pred) ^ Refer-
encedColumn (?refCol)
^ componentOf (?refCol, ?pred) ^ hasName (?refCol, ?nameCol)
^ swrlx:makeOWLThing(?hypInd, ?refCol) ^ swrlb:stringConcat (?name-
Hyp, "hi_", ?nameCol)
-> HypotheticalIndex (?hypInd) ^ hasName (?hypInd, ?nameHyp) ^
originates (?stat, ?hypInd)
^ acts_on (?hypInd, ?refCol) ^ IndexedColumn (?refCol)
```

This rule analyzes the *tuning:SingleStatement* and suggests the indexes according to the columns referenced in the *tuning:Where* clause. Given a *tuning:SingleStatement*, if it has a *tuning:Where* clause predicate that is a simple expression, the rule engine should get the referenced column and its name. As a consequence (the rule action), the machine creates a new individual of type *tuning:HypotheticalIndex* with its relationships with the *tuning:SingleStatement* that caused it (Originates) and the *tuning:Column* being indexed (Acts On). The *tuning:IndexedColumn* is the same as the *tuning: ReferencedColumn*. Additional rules defined in the ontology[4] were not mentioned here, since we described only the ones relevant to the example in the article.

---

[4] http://www.inf.puc-rio.br/~postgresql/conteudo/projeto4/download/OntologiaTuning.owl,   last accessed 2019/04/07.

All the concepts referring to data structured of the DB schema are defined in the DB tuning concepts ontology, to reflect the structures considered by common DB Tuning heuristics [7, 24, 25], and includes *tuning:DMcommand, tuning:DDLcommand, tuning:Clause, tuning:AccessStructure, tuning:Index, tuning:RealIndex, tuning:HypotheticalIndex, tuning:Table, tuning:Column*. If a new DB tuning heuristic needs to refer to a new concept not previously defined, it just needs to extend the DB tuning concepts ontology, defining the semantics of this new concept according to the existing ones.

Execution of Heuristics

The subsequent moment in the DB tuning task is the heuristic execution. The *heuristic:HeuristicExecution* needs the *heuristic:HeuristicDefinition* described in the heuristic ontology since it is responsible for suggesting or applying tuning techniques based on the workload analysis. The user starting the execution process does not have to be an expert, since the heuristics have been specified by an expert (DBA). When a person starts a heuristic execution, s/he chooses which heuristic s/he wants to execute first, assuming the *heuristic:Executor* Role and performing the *heuristic:HeuristicSelection*.

At runtime, the preconditions concepts, defined previously, must be instantiated (*heuristic:InstantiatedConcepts*) and retrieved by a software agent. The software agent is defined since an automated self-tuning strategy (without human DBA intervention) may be used. Then, the *heuristic:Agent* manages the *heuristic:HeuristicExecution*, using *heuristic:InstantiatedConcepts*. During the *heuristic:HeuristicExecution*, each *heuristic:Rule* is checked and evaluated by the rule engine (*heuristic:RuleEvaluation*).

Rule consequents represent suggested Actions, which can be either a *heuristic:TuningAction* or a *heuristic:RuleAction*. When there is a *heuristic:RuleAction*, it becomes a *heuristic:VariablesControl* (*Relator*) managed by the *heuristic:RuleEngine*. We consider *heuristic:VariablesControl* as new instances/individuals of objects or properties in the domain ontology according to the conditions established by the heuristic. For example, a heuristic can add a bonus property to hypothetical indexes each time they are mentioned in an execution plan. This action (adding bonus) cannot be considered a tuning action because it is just a simulation. Therefore, we modeled it as a *heuristic:RuleAction*, as a logical consequence of *heuristic:VariablesControl* (bonus).

A *heuristic:TuningAction* is an action to improve the DB performance, such as the creation of an access structure. To illustrate it, the heuristic may decide to transform the hypothetical index into a real index when it achieves a considerable bonus. Every *heuristic:TuningAction* requires an interaction with the DB, that is achieved via a *heuristic:Function* to perform this interaction, represented as a *heuristic:DBTuningFunction*.

Moreover, every Tuning Action may have an optional Justification, so roles were created (*heuristic:Justifier* and *heuristic:TuningActionJustifier*) to contemplate it. The justification indicates an explanation for the fact that the DBA accepted or not an action.

The DB tuning task can be semi-automatic or fully automatic. To address this, we introduce the concept of *heuristic:Implementer* that aggregates properties from *heuristic:DBA* and *heuristic:Agent*. When the *DBA* implements the action (*DBA Implementer*), it means that it is semi-automatic, i.e., the DBA needs to intervene and

indicate whether or not to accept a suggested action. The DBA will need to analyze all the suggested action. When the agent implements the action (*heuristic:AgentImplementer*), it means that it is fully automatic, i.e. without any human intervention, and the *heuristic:Agent* performs all of the suggested actions.

Whenever the heuristic ontology is instantiated it means that a given heuristic is being performed using concept instances defined in DB tuning concepts ontology according to the workload submitted to the DB.

4   Case Studies

We ran two scenarios in our Outer-tuning framework, using our ontologies. The first scenario applied tuning heuristics that suggest (hypothetical and physical) index structures, and shows the importance of visualizing all the alternatives considered by the tuning heuristics, instead of only the implemented actions. The second scenario illustrates the need of extending the ontologies used by the framework, adding tuning heuristics that suggest materialized views. Ontology extension points are described in [26].

Scenario 1. The DB has a table (EMPLOYEE) with four columns (Identifier, Name, Gender and Salary). Figure 7 shows the query presented in the DB workload that was analyzed by the tuning heuristics defined in the heuristic ontology.

```
SELECT * FROM EMPLOYEE
WHERE salary in (1000, 1500, 2000, 2500, 3000, 3500, 4000, 4500, 5000)
AND  gender = "M"' ;
```

Fig. 7. Query presented in the analyzed workload

The DBA selects two different heuristics (HEIC-A and HEIC-B) to run individually on the same workload and DB. The two heuristics eventually recommended the creation of different indexes in the DB.

At first, the DBA executes the framework using only the rules of the HEIC-A heuristic about hypothetical indexes. Analyzing the DB, the optimizer generates the query execution plan that chooses to use two hypothetical indexes (over the salary column and gender column) created by the HEIC-A heuristic. Later, on the same initial state of the DB (i.e., with no tuning actions performed by HEIC-A), the DBA executes the framework using only the rules of the HEIC-B heuristic. The optimizer generates the query execution plan that does not use any index and, rather, suggests a full table scan operation. From these outcomes, the DBA may be in doubt about which recommendation to follow, either creating the physical index or not. The DBA, then, checks the rule conditions that generated the candidate indexes and identifies that both heuristics consider the columns referenced in the WHERE clause. As the conditions of the rule are the same, the DBA cannot understand why the heuristics generated different recommendations. S/he verifies information about the candidate index suggested by each heuristic. By analyzing the ontology instances created during the execution of

Scenario 1, the DBA concludes that HEIC-B heuristic does not consider bitmap indexes, while HEIC-A does (Table 1). The following SQWRL query [27] recovers all hypothetical indexes suggested per heuristic:

```
Heuristic(?h) ^ DatabaseConcept(?dc) ^ acts (?h, ?dc) ^
TuningAssist(?tunAss)
^ match(?tuna, ?dc) ^ CreateHypothetical(?tunAss) ^
HypotheticalIndex(?hypInd)
^ creates(?tunAss, ?hypInd) ^ hasType(?hypInd, ?indType)
-> sqwrl:select(?h, ?indType)
```

The regular B+tree indexes created by HEIC-B leads to a higher execution cost to the query, justifying the fact that the optimizer does not consider them. The DBA may also assess the decision rationale followed by our proposal (i.e., all alternative considerations, even for those that are not considered for suggesting tuning actions).

Table 1. Hypothetical Indexes considered by heuristics HEIC-A and HEIC-B

Heuristic	Index		
	Name	Creation cost	Type
HEIC-A	HI_GENDER	0.5625	Bitmap
HEIC-A	HI_SALARY	4	Bitmap
HEIC-B	HI_GENDER	13	B+tree
HEIC-B	HI_SALARY	17	B+tree

Scenario 2. Scenario 2 used the TPC-H benchmark for the workload. This benchmark has analytical queries (OLAP), an opportunity for the evaluation of heuristics that consider materialized views (MVs). We considered two types of MVs during the analysis of the results: the beneficial and the malefic. A MV is considered *beneficial* when rewritten queries that use the MV increases the performance of the workload, and *malefic* when their use decreases the performance of the workload. This occurs when the MV size is greater than the number of pages read in the original query.

We ran two additional heuristics [28] in our Framework, which have inferred materialized views for the workload. HMV1 pointed out three beneficial materialized views to the workload (Q01, Q05, Q09) and two malefic (Q04, Q12). HMV2 showed four beneficial materialized views (Q01, Q05, Q06, Q09) and five malefic (Q03, Q04, Q07, Q12, Q14). Both heuristics brought a positive gain equivalent to the workload (12.4% and 12.2%). But the framework showed that HMV1 estimated lower costs than HMV2 for the creation and storage of MVs. While HMV1 proposed the creation of 5 MVs, HMV2 proposed 9. This demonstrates the way the framework shows that the same heuristic can bring benefits or losses depending on the workload received.

Regardless of the result presented by both tuning heuristics, this scenario shows that the framework is able to work simultaneously with more than one heuristic, compare the solutions presented and the inclusion of new heuristics. With the use of our framework, the DBA has sufficient information to assess which heuristics are interesting for his/her workload, in a conceptual level. An experienced DBA may even

extend the heuristics behavior based on his/her experience. For example, composing HMV1 and HMV2 would suggest the beneficial MVs both have inferred and avoid the malefic MVs (Q7, Q3, Q14) suggested by HMV2.

In conclusion, the scenarios show that the Framework is able to: (i) Display all alternatives evaluated, regardless of the decision that the heuristic took. In addition to the alternatives, the DBA may also submit SQWRL queries to view the instances of the ontology that represent all the behavior of the heuristics; (ii) infer useful DB tuning actions. The case studies have demonstrated useful actions to improve database performance; (iii) compare tuning heuristics described with the ontology. The case studies show that the comparison of heuristics is possible through the interpretation of ontology instances, and (iv) support the DBA in the DB tuning task with relevant information which s/he can match the heuristics to the workload or insert new heuristics in the tuning ontology.

5   Conclusion and Future Works

We presented an ontological perspective for DB tuning heuristics execution. Existing proposals hinder both the extension to new heuristics and the transparency of the reasoning used for decision-making. We described a conceptual model (heuristic ontology) to address these points. The extension to new heuristics is facilitated because the user only needs to instantiate the heuristic ontology defining new rules. Although not all database tuning strategies are covered by our ontology, the DB tuning concepts ontology (not detailed in this present paper) can be easily extended (without changing the framework) to include concepts and properties for memory tuning (e.g.: shared_buffers, checkpoint_segments), query tuning (e.g.: rewriting) and transactions tuning (e.g.: locks, isolation levels). The transparency of the reasoning is obtained by defining the rationale described in rules. As the rules are defined in terms of familiar concepts, it becomes easier for the DBA to understand the heuristics proposed behavior. We argue that representing database tuning activities with more formalism through our ontologies allows a more precise discussion and study of the issues behind database tuning—for example, the different ways of working with tuning heuristics (add new structures to existing heuristics, work with different heuristics that suggest the same type of structure)—that are not possible if the concepts involved were not explained through a high-level model.

Future work will address new DB tuning heuristics and how we can compose or combine them, identifying conflicts of the rules (semi) automatically and solving them. Besides, we can create a repository for DB tuning decisions rationale.

References

1. Shasha, D., Bonnet, P.: Database Tuning: Principles, Experiments, and Troubleshooting Techniques. Morgan Kaufmann Publishers, San Francisco (2003)
2. OMG (Object Management Group): Common Warehouse Metamodel (CWM) Specification. Version 1.1, vol. 1, No. formal/03-03-02 (2003)

3. Aguiar, C.Z., Falbo, R.D., Souza, V.E.: Ontological representation of relational databases. In: ONTOBRAS (2018)
4. Ouared, A., Ouhammou, Y., Roukh, A.: A meta-advisor repository for database physical design. In: Bellatreche, L., Pastor, Ó., Almendros Jiménez, J., Aït-Ameur, Y. (eds.) MEDI 2016. LNCS, vol. 9893, pp. 72–87. Springer, Cham (2016). https://doi.org/10.1007/978-3-319-45547-1_6
5. Ding, Z., Wei, Z., Chen, H.: A software cybernetics approach to self-tuning performance of on-line transaction processing systems. J. Syst. Softw. **124**, 247–259 (2017)
6. Noon, N.N., Getta, J.R.: Automated performance tuning of data management systems with materializations and indices. J. Comput. Commun. **4**, 46–52 (2016)
7. Morelli, E., Almeida, A., Lifschitz, S., Monteiro, J.M., Machado, J.: Autonomous re-indexing. In: Proceedings of the ACM Symposium on Applied Computing (SAC), pp. 893–897 (2012)
8. Bruno, N., Chaudhuri, S., König, A.C., Narasayya, V., Ramamurthy, R., Syamala, M.: AutoAdmin project at Microsoft research: lessons learned. Bull. IEEE Comput. Soc. Tech. Comm. Data Eng. **34**(4), 12–19 (2011)
9. Rangaswamy, S., Shobha, G.: Online indexing for databases using query workloads. Int. J. Comput. Sci. Commun. **2**(2), 427–433 (2011)
10. Goasdoué, F., Karanasos, K., Leblay, J., Manolescu, I.: View selection in semantic web databases. Proc. VLDB Endow. **5**(2), 97–108 (2012)
11. Basu, D., et al.: Regularized cost-model oblivious database tuning with reinforcement learning. In: Hameurlain, A., Küng, J., Wagner, R., Chen, Q. (eds.) Transactions on Large-Scale Data- and Knowledge-Centered Systems XXVIII. LNCS, vol. 9940, pp. 96–132. Springer, Heidelberg (2016). https://doi.org/10.1007/978-3-662-53455-7_5
12. Bellatreche, L., Schneider, M., Lorinquer, H., Mohania, M.: Bringing together partitioning, materialized views and indexes to optimize performance of relational data warehouses. In: Kambayashi, Y., Mohania, M., Wöß, W. (eds.) DaWaK 2004. LNCS, vol. 3181, pp. 15–25. Springer, Heidelberg (2004). https://doi.org/10.1007/978-3-540-30076-2_2
13. Bouchakri, R., Bellatreche, L.: On simplifying integrated physical database design. In: Eder, J., Bielikova, M., Tjoa, A.M. (eds.) ADBIS 2011. LNCS, vol. 6909, pp. 333–346. Springer, Heidelberg (2011). https://doi.org/10.1007/978-3-642-23737-9_24
14. Bellatreche, L., Khouri, S., Boukhari, I., Bouchakri, R.: Using ontologies and requirements for constructing and optimizing data warehouses. In: Proceedings of International Convention MIPRO, pp. 1568–1573 (2012)
15. Khouri, S., Bellatreche, L., Boukhari, I., Bouarar, S.: More investment in conceptual designers: think about it! In: Proceedings of the IEEE International Conference on Computational Science and Engineering, pp. 88–93 (2012)
16. Horrocks, I., Patel-Schneider, P.F., Boley, H., Tabet, S., Grosof, B., Dean, M.: SWRL: a semantic web rule language combining OWL and RuleML. National Research Council of Canada, Network Inference, and Stanford University (2004)
17. Zhang, B., et al.: A demonstration of the ottertune automatic database management system tuning service. Proc. VLDB Endow. **11**(12), 1910–1913 (2018)
18. Zhang, J., et al.: An end-to-end automatic cloud database tuning system using deep reinforcement learning. In: Proceedings of the 2019 International Conference on Management of Data, pp. 415–432. ACM (2019)
19. Zheng, C., Ding, Z., Hu, J.: Self-tuning performance of database systems with neural network. In: Huang, D.-S., Bevilacqua, V., Premaratne, P. (eds.) ICIC 2014. LNCS, vol. 8588, pp. 1–12. Springer, Cham (2014). https://doi.org/10.1007/978-3-319-09333-8_1
20. Dias, K., Ramacher, M., Shaft, U., Venkataramani, V., Wood, G.: Automatic performance diagnosis and tuning in oracle. In: Proceedings of CIDR Conference, pp. 84–94 (2005)

21. Alhadi, N., Ahmad, K.: Query tuning in oracle database. J. Comput. Sci. **8**(11), 1889–1896 (2012)
22. Guizzardi, G.: Ontological foundations for structural conceptual models. Thesis presented in the University of Twente (2005). http://doc.utwente.nl/50826
23. Guizzardi, G., Wagner, G., de Almeida Falbo, R., Guizzardi, R.S.S., Almeida, J.P.A.: Towards ontological foundations for the conceptual modeling of events. In: Ng, W., Storey, V.C., Trujillo, J.C. (eds.) ER 2013. LNCS, vol. 8217, pp. 327–341. Springer, Heidelberg (2013). https://doi.org/10.1007/978-3-642-41924-9_27
24. Lohman, G., Valentin, G., Zilio, D., Zuliani, M., Skelley, A.: DB2 advisor: an optimizer smart enough to recommend its own indexes. In: Proceedings of the IEEE International Conference on Data Engineering (ICDE), pp. 101–110 (2000)
25. Bruno, N.: Automated Physical Database Design and Tuning. CRC Press, Boca Raton (2011)
26. Oliveira, R.P., Baião, F., Almeida, A.C., Schwabe, D., Lifschitz, S.: Outer-tuning: an integration of rules, ontology and RDBMS. In: Proceedings of the Brazilian Symposium on Information Systems (SBSI), Aracaju, Sergipe, Brazil (2019)
27. O'Connor, M.J., Das, A.K.: SQWRL: a query language for OWL. In: Proceedings of the 5th International Workshop on OWL: Experiences and Directions, OWLED (2009)
28. Oliveira, R.P.: Ontology-based database tuning: the case of materialized views. Master thesis presented at PUC-Rio, Rio de Janeiro, Brazil (2015)

SkipSJoin: A New Physical Design for Distributed Big Data Warehouses in Hadoop

Yassine Ramdane[1]([⊠]), Nadia Kabachi[2]([⊠]), Omar Boussaid[1]([⊠]),
and Fadila Bentayeb[1]([⊠])

[1] University of Lyon, Lyon 2, ERIC EA 3083,
5, avenue Pierre Mendes, 69676 Bron Cedex, France
{Yassine.Ramdane,Omar.Boussaid,Fadila.Bentayeb}@univ-lyon2.fr
[2] University of Lyon, University Claude Bernard Lyon 1, ERIC EA 3083,
43, boulevard du 11 novembre 1918, 69100 Villeurbanne, France
Nadia.Kabachi@univ-lyon1.fr

Abstract. Hadoop uses horizontal partitioning to improve the performance of a big data warehouse. A major challenge when horizontally partitioning the tables of a big data warehouse is to reduce network traffic for a given workload. A common technique to avoid this issue, when performing a join operation, is to co-partition the tables of the data warehouse on their join key. However, in the existing partitioning schemes, executing a star join operation in Hadoop still needs many MapReduce cycles. In this paper, we combine a data-driven and a workload-driven model to create a new scheme for distributed big data warehouses over Hadoop, called "SkipSJoin". Our approach allows performing the star join operation in only one Spark stage, and allows skipping the loading of some unnecessary HDFS blocks. Our experiments show that our proposal outperforms some approaches in terms of query execution time.

Keywords: Load balancing · Bucket · Sort-merge-bucket join

1 Introduction

Partitioning and Load Balancing (PLB) of the data is an optimization technique which is used to organize tables in Hadoop. It has been used to skip unnecessary data load, for load balancing [11], and to guide the physical design of a DW [3]. In the literature, many works have tackled the problem of the PLB of data with MapReduce. We can distinguish two types of techniques, static and dynamic. In static techniques, the system distributes the database before proceeding with the processing. This technique is based on either a data-driven [6,7] or a workload-driven model [10,11]. In dynamic techniques, the system performs the PLB algorithm at the moment of query processing [5,8]. Hadoop uses different techniques for the PLB of data to enhance queries performances. However,

A. H. F. Laender et al. (Eds.): ER 2019, LNCS 11788, pp. 255–263, 2019.
https://doi.org/10.1007/978-3-030-33223-5_21

the random distribution of Hadoop blocks may slow down the query processing, especially with the OLAP query when joining several tables.

An OLAP query is composed of several operations, such as filtering, star joins, and grouping. The join operation is the most expensive one, and often involves a high communication cost. To minimize the MapReduce cycles and network communication when performing a star join operation, some solutions have been proposed [5,8]. However, to the best of our knowledge, there is no previous proposal that can perform the star join in only one Spark stage.

In this paper, we propose a new physical design for distributed BDW over a cluster of homogeneous nodes, called "SkipSJoin", based on a model that is both data driven and workload-driven, using a static technique for the PLB of the data like [6]. We take into account: the size of the DW, the distribution of the foreign and the primary keys of the fact and dimension tables, the query workload used, and the characteristics of the cluster. Our strategy allows performing the filtering, projection, and star join operations of an OLAP query locally and in a single Spark stage. Moreover, with SkipSJoin, we can avoid reading some data blocks that are not relevant to an OLAP query, based on a given workload. However, instead of using a sophisticated technique such as the max skipping algorithm [11], our heuristic is simple, and based on two main measures, as we will explain in Sect. 3.3. We have evaluated our approach on the TPC-DS benchmark using Hadoop cluster, a Spark engine, and Hive system.

The rest of this paper is structured as follows. Section 2 summarizes related work on horizontal partitioning techniques and different join algorithms with MapReduce. Section 3 presents SkipSJoin's architecture and provides further details. We present our experiments in Sect. 4 and we conclude in Sect. 5.

2   Related Work

Horizontal Partitioning (HP) in databases has been widely studied [1,3,4,11]. The HP technique is used in BlinkDB [3] to guide the physical design of the database and to improve OLAP query runtime. Sun et al. [11] proposed a fine-grained tuple-level partitioning that can achieve the maximal level of skipping of HDFS blocks. Moreover, HP is used to optimize join operation in distributed system. We can notice that almost all of the existing join algorithms in the literature rely on dynamic techniques of PLB of the data, e.g. repartition and broadcast join [4] and multi-way join [1]. Few are based on static techniques, such as HadoopDB [2] and trojan join [6]. This kind of algorithm requires prior knowledge of table schema and join conditions. The dynamic algorithm of Afrati et al. [1] may perform well for star join operation by minimizing the amount of replication of tuples, however it may involve considerable communication cost during tuples transfer. Also, the fully replicating tables used in the broadcast join algorithm [4], can perform star join operation in map side with minimal Spark stages if the dimension tables used in the query are small enough to fit into memory. Purdilă et al. [8] propose a dynamic algorithm that can execute the star join operation in two MapReduce cycles and [5] propose two efficient algorithms

to minimize network communication cost. However these methods still require a shuffle phase. On the other hand, the static technique used in Hadoop++ [6] is not suitable for the star join operation, as it can co-partition two tables. Moreover, HadoopDB [2] attempts to integrate MapReduce and parallel DBMS. Some improvements have been made on both scalability and efficiency. However, the results are still not satisfactory in the star join operation.

3 Proposal Approach

In the first part of our approach, we build horizontal fragments (buckets) of the fact and dimension tables of the DW, using our hash-partitioning method (see Sect. 3.2). Then, we distribute these buckets evenly over the cluster's nodes, in which we can execute the star join of an OLAP query locally and in only one Spark stage. The second part allows skipping the scanning of some unnecessary data blocks, by hash-partitioning some DW tables with frequent attributes of the filters. That is, we extend the first part using a stable workload, i.e. the set of columns used in Where clauses and Group by remains fairly stable over time but the filters may change (the validity of this assumption has been empirically observed in a variety of real-world production workloads [3]). Our approach is composed of 6 steps: (1) Selecting the near-best number of buckets; (2) Adding a new partition key to the fact table; (3) Creating the new dimensions that contain the same bucketed key as the fact table; (4) Retrieving the most frequent attributes from the queries' filters; (5) Partitioning and bucketing the tables of the DW; and finally (6) Balancing the buckets over the cluster's nodes. Before giving the details of our approach, we formulate our problem in the next section.

3.1 Formalization

Suppose, we have a star schema DW $E = \{F, D1, ..., Dk\}$, such that F is the fact table and Dd, $d \in 1...k$, are the dimension tables. We denote by FK the set of all foreign keys of F and by PK the set of primary keys of Dd. We denote by Q the set of distinct queries used, such that $Q = \{q_1, ... q_m\}$, and by φ the set of the use frequencies of the queries q_j, $j \in 1...m$, such that $\varphi = \{f_1, ..., f_m\}$. We define the workload W the set of all queries Q, used by its corresponding use frequencies φ, in a period of time t, such that $|W| = \sum_{j=1}^{m} f_j$. We denote by $R = \{R0 ..., Rk\}$ the set of all frequent attributes used in the queries' filters of the workload W, such that $R0$ is the most frequent attribute selected to hash-partition the fact table F, and Rd, $d \in 1...k$, is the most frequent attribute selected to hash-partition the dimension Dd. We denote by $Bkey$ the partition key used to bucket F and all Dd in $\#B$ buckets, here $\#B$ is the near-best number of the buckets that should be created. We denote by $BF = \{BF_0, ..., BF_{\#B-1}\}$ the set of buckets created by bucketing F with $Bkey$ into $\#B$ buckets, and by $BDd = \{BDd_0, ..., BDd_{\#B-1}\}$, the set of buckets of each dimension Dd, $d \in 1...k$. We denote by $BSF = \{\|BF_0\|, ..., \|BF_{\#B-1}\|\}$ and $BSDd = \{\|BDd_0\|, ..., \|BDd_{\#B-1}\|\}$, $d \in 1...k$, the sets of the buckets'

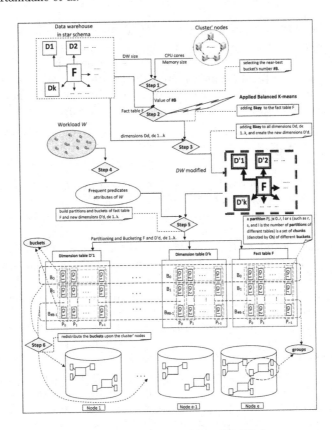

Fig. 1. The steps of building SkpiSJoin

sizes of F and dimensions Dd respectively. We denote by a *group* the set of the buckets that have the same value of $Bkey$: it is composed of one bucket of F and one bucket of each Dd. We denote by $N=\{n_1, \dots, n_e\}$ the set of all homogeneous nodes of the cluster. The first aim is to choose $Bkey$ and $\#B$ for building the buckets of BF and all BDd, $d \in 1 \dots k$, in such a way as to keep them roughly balanced in size, and how to distribute them over N in order to perform the star join, locally and in only one Spark stage. The second objective is to construct R to skip loading some unnecessary HDFS blocks of some DW tables. Figure 1 summarizes the steps of our strategy. In the following, we detail our solution.

3.2 Selecting $\#B$ and $Bkey$

In this section, we explain briefly the steps 1, 2, and 3 of Fig. 1. In step 1, we determine $\#B$; In step 2, we show how to add the $Bkey$ column to fact table F, and how to fill this key; In step 3, we show how to add $Bkey$ to all dimensions.

Selecting $\#B$. We should select $\#B$ from the range $[\#B_{min}, ..., \#B_{max}]$. To determine $\#B_{min}$ and $\#B_{max}$, we follow these rules:

- **Rule 1.** We should use almost all idle CPU cores of the nodes. So, $\#B_{min}$ should be equal to $\#c$, the total number of CPU cores assigned to all Spark executors. Our aim is to assign at least one RDD partition to each CPU core.
- **Rule 2.** Selecting a large number of $\#B$ ($\#B \gg \#c$) can disrupt the distributed system as a result of increasing the I/O operations, and this can incur significant overhead for processing the RDD partition. Hence, and since our processing is in-memory, using Spark, we determine $\#B_{max}$ as follows:

$$\#B_{max} \leq \lfloor \#B_{min} \times max(V_E/V_M, 1) \rfloor \; and \; \#B_{max} \leq |T| \qquad (1)$$

where V_E is the size of E, V_M is the sum of all memory sizes of the data nodes, and T is the smallest dimension in E. The first part of Eq. (1) means that if the memory size is large, we can process a large RDD partition. However, if the memory size is small, then $\#B_{max}$ increases and processing a small RDD partition become preferable. The second part, i.e., $\#B_{max} \leq |T|$, means that, we must not get an empty bucket for all BF and BDd.

- **Rule 3.** To find quickly the near-best value of $\#B$, we execute the queries with $\#B = \#c$, and each time we increment $\#B$, i.e. $\#B = \#B + \#c$, until $\#B = \#B_{max}$ or until the execution time of the queries rises.

Adding $Bkey$ **Column to the Fact Table.** To create a *group* of the buckets, we can add a new key $Bkey$ of integer type to all the tables of the DW E and co-partition the tables of E by this added join key. However, the way to fill the $Bkey$ column remains a challenging task. If the distribution of the values of $Bkey$ is skew, we obtain unbalanced bucket sizes in BSF and all $BSDd, d \in 1 ... k$. In this case, our application seems un-parallelizable. To cure this issue, we should study how to calculate the values of the $Bkey$ column. Moreover, since the sizes of the dimensions are small compared to the fact table, we can focus on only minimizing the standard deviation of BSF and not $BSDd, d \in 1 ... k$, by bucketing F with a simple range partitioning method. However, there is an essential factor that can affect the size of the newly constructed dimensions (denoted $D'd$): the similarity of the tuples in each bucket of BF. This can increase the number of tuples in each bucket of $BD'd, d \in 1 ... k$, as we will show in the following. To overcome this problem we propose the following method.

(1) From the fact table F, we create the matrix MB, such that:

$$MB = \begin{pmatrix} V_{FD11} & V_{FD21} & \cdots & V_{FDk1} \\ \cdots & \cdots & & \cdots \\ & & V_{FDdj} & \\ \cdots & \cdots & & \cdots \\ V_{FD1n} & V_{FD2n} & \cdots & V_{FDkn} \end{pmatrix}$$

where V_{FDdj} is the value of the foreign key fk_d comming from Dd in line j of the fact table F, and $n = |F|$.

(2) After building MB, we clustered it in $\#B$ clusters. Thus, we obtain the values of $Bkey$ column. Our clustering method should trade off between the number of tuples in each bucket against the similarity of the tuples in each bucket. So, we finish by using the balanced K-means algorithm [9]. The first reason to choose this kind of algorithm is to minimize the standard deviation of BSF and the second one is to minimize the size of the newly built dimensions $D'd$ (see why and how to build $D'd$ in next subsection). The output of the algorithm is $(n \bmod \#B)$ clusters of size $\lceil n/\#B \rceil$ and $\#B\text{-}(n \bmod \#B)$ clusters of size $\lfloor n/\#B \rfloor$.

(3) Finally, we affect the cluster values obtained to the $Bkey$ column.

Adding $Bkey$ Column to the Dimension Tables. After adding $Bkey$ to F, and in order to construct a *group*, we must also add $Bkey$ to all the Dd, $d \in 1 \dots k$, and obtaining new dimensions $D'd$. To do this, first, we create an intermediate table IDd corresponding to the dimension Dd. The IDd table is composed of two columns, fk_d and $Bkey$, such that: (1) fk_d is the foreign key of dimension Dd in fact table F and (2) $Bkey$ is the partition key added in F. Initially, we have $|IDd| = |F|$, so, before joining IDd with Dd to obtain $D'd$, we delete all duplicate tuples in IDd. By creating $D'd$ we can build $BD'd$ and $BSD'd$.

3.3   Selecting the Frequent Attributes

In this section (step 4 in Fig. 1), we show how to select the most frequent attributes used in the queries' filters, namely the set R. To construct R, but without using a sophisticated clustering method like the max skipping algorithm [11], we finish by using a simple decision strategy which is based on two essential rules. Note that step 4 is independent of the previous ones.

- **Rule 1.** We consider that a distribution $Dist$ has a heavy data skew if the value of the skewness, denoted by Sk, is more than 2.0 (we choose this value following some recommendations of [12]). There are numerous methods to calculate Sk of a given set. In our case, we use the following formula:

$$Sk = \frac{n}{(n-1)(n-2)} \sum \left(\frac{x_i - \mu}{\sigma} \right)^3$$

where n is the cardinality of $Dist$, x_i is the ith element of $Dist$, σ is the standard deviation of $Dist$, and μ is the average value of $Dist$.

- **Rule 2.** Since our processing is in-memory, using the Spark engine, we assume that an attribute A of a table T has a high density D if $\#B_{min} \le 1/D(A) \le \#B_{max}$, where $D(A) = \frac{1}{number\ of\ distinct\ values\ of\ A\ in\ T}$, $\#B_{min}$, and the $\#B_{max}$ are selected as we have explained in the rules of Sect. 3.2. Our reason for choosing this formula is to decrease the size of the meta-data table persisting in memory by the Name-node when hash-partitioning T by A.

To create R: (1) We retrieve from the queries' filters all the attributes of integer type and we keep only the frequent ones. In our case, we assume that an attribute

is frequent if its rate of occurrence in the workload W is greater than or equal to a threshold Th, which is determined by the administrator of the system; (2) we keep only the most frequent attribute, for each table of the DW E that has a high density D and the lower value of the skewness Sk; Finally (3) we create the set R_i, $i \in 0..k$. For more details, see our previous work in [10].

3.4 Building the Partitions and the Buckets

After adding $Bkey$ to F, building the new dimensions $D'd$, and creating the set R, we can construct BF and $BD'd$, $d \in 1 \ldots k$. Thus, for each table T of E, we hash-partition T by the corresponding attribute $a \in Ri$, $i \in 0 \ldots k$ if one exists, then we bucket T by the $Bkey$ column into $\#B$ buckets. See step 5 of Fig. 1.

3.5 Placement of the Buckets

In this section, see step 6 of Fig. 1, we redistribute the *groups* created evenly over the cluster nodes, using the round robin technique. Formally, we can denote by $group_i = BF_i \uplus_{d=1}^{k} BD'd_i$, $i \in 0 \ldots \#B - 1$. Thus, we start to place the $group_0$ in node 1, $group_1$ in node 2, ..., and the $group_{p-1}$ in the node e, such $e = p \; modulo \; \#B$ and $p <= \#B$. We restarted the operation with same way, we put $group_p$ in node 1, $group_{p+1}$ in node 2, ..., until the last $group_{\#B-1}$.

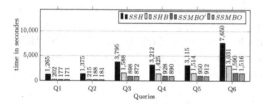

Fig. 2. Runtime of the queries with DW **Fig. 3.** Workload runtime

4 Experiments and Results

To evaluate our approach, we carried out some experiments with a BDW, denoted by DW. We used a cluster of 15 slave data nodes and one master node characterized by CPU Pentium I7 with 8 cores, 16 GB of memory and 2 TB of hard drive. For the workload W, we selected 20 queries from among the 99 queries of the benchmark with use frequencies φ. We divided our experiments into two parts: In the first part, we evaluate our approach without using W. The aim of this is to show how to perform the star join operation in a single Spark stage whatever the used OLAP query. We have selected 6 queries from the TPC-DS benchmark with different levels of complexity. We have compared our approach with different baseline approaches. The approach notations are: SSH

is the default Partitioning and Distributing (P & D) schema of Hadoop/Spark, using Shuffle Hash (SH) join; SHB is the default P & D schema of Hadoop/Spark, using Hash Broadcast (HB) Join; SSMBO is our P & D schema (without based on queries workload), using the balanced K-means and SMB join; and SSMBO' which is similar to SSMBO but instead using the balanced K-means algorithm, we just create roughly equal buckets' size of the fact table, using range-partitioning method. By using the rules of Sect. 3.2, we obtain $\#B = 630$. In the second part, we included our hash-partitioning technique based on the W. So, in *SkipSJoin* we use our bucketing technique as in the *SSMBO* approach and our skipping method as in given in detail in Sect. 3.3. Figure 2 shows, for the different approaches, the execution time of the 6 selected queries. In Fig. 3, we compare the runtimes of W in the approaches SHB, SSMBO, and SkipSJoin.

As shown in Fig. 2, the query execution time with SSMBO approach is up 2 times better over SHB approach. We can see that the worst results were obtained with SSH approach. This is due to the high rate of data shuffling. In $Q1$ and $Q2$, since we only involved two small dimensions, the broadcasting of the RDD partitions become fast and we can see that the execution times of these queries in the SHB approach are roughly the same as with our approaches SSMBO', and SSMBO. However in Q3, Q4, Q5, and Q6, the performance of SHB suffers. The reason is that in the SHB approach when the table is large, the system cannot broadcast it, and must combine with HB join and SH join to perform these queries. We noticed that the runtime of the queries with SSMBO is much better than the SSMBO' approach, and this demonstrates the efficiency of our balanced K-means algorithm. Obviously, the random clustering applied in SSMBO' can increase the size of some new dimensions and degrade the system performances. Moreover, we can see from Fig. 3 that SkipSJoin is much better than SSMBO. The reason is that since we hash-partition some tables by the most frequent attributes used in the filters of W, we can omit loading some chunks into memory.

5   Conclusion and Future Research

In this paper, we have presented a new strategy for partitioning and distributing a big data warehouse over Hadoop cluster. SkipSJoin allows performing the star join operation of an OLAP query locally, in only one Spark stage, without a shuffle phase. Moreover, by taking into consideration the given workload, SkipSJoin can skip loading unnecessary data blocks. We have seen that although we have roughly balanced the split inputs, we get unbalanced intermediate results due to the selectivity of some of the filters. In the future, we aim to add to our hybrid approach SkipSJoin a Multi-Agent-System to balance smartly the reducer loads (i.e. optimize grouping and aggregation operations).

References

1. Afrati, F.N., Ullman, J.D.: Optimizing multiway joins in a map-reduce environment. IEEE Trans. Knowl. Data Eng. **23**(9), 1282–1298 (2011)
2. Abouzeid, A., Bajda-Pawlikowski, K., Abadi, D., Silberschatz, A., Rasin, A.: HadoopDB: an architectural hybrid of MapReduce and DBMS technologies for analytical workloads. Proc. VLDB Endow. **2**(1), 922–933 (2009)
3. Agarwal, S., Mozafari, B., Panda, A., Milner, H., Madden, S., Stoica, I.: BlinkDB: queries with bounded errors and bounded response times on very large data. In: Proceedings of the 8th ACM European Conference on Computer Systems, pp. 29–42 (2013)
4. Blanas, S., Patel, J.M., Ercegovac, V., Rao, J., Shekita, E.J., Tian, Y.: A comparison of join algorithms for log processing in mapreduce. In: Proceedings of the 2010 ACM SIGMOD International Conference on Management of Data, pp. 975–986. ACM (2010)
5. Brito, J.J., Mosqueiro, T., Ciferri, R.R., Ciferri, C.D.: Faster cloud Star Joins with reduced disk spill and network comm. Proc. Comput. Sci. **80**, 74–85 (2016)
6. Dittrich, J., Quiané-Ruiz, J.A., Jindal, A., Kargin, Y., Setty, V., Schad, J.: Hadoop++: making a yellow elephant run like a cheetah (without it even noticing). Proc. VLDB Endow. **3**(1–2), 515–529 (2010)
7. Eltabakh, M.Y., Tian, Y., Özcan, F., Gemulla, R., Krettek, A., McPherson, J.: CoHadoop: flexible data placement and its exploitation in Hadoop. Proc. VLDB Endo. **4**(9), 575–585 (2011)
8. Purdilă, V., Pentiuc, Ş.G.: Single-scan: a fast star join query processing algorithm. Softw.: Pract. Exp. **46**(3), 319–339 (2016)
9. Malinen, M.I., Fränti, P.: Balanced K-means for clustering. In: Fränti, P., Brown, G., Loog, M., Escolano, F., Pelillo, M. (eds.) S+SSPR 2014. LNCS, vol. 8621, pp. 32–41. Springer, Heidelberg (2014). https://doi.org/10.1007/978-3-662-44415-3_4
10. Ramdane, Y., Boussaid, O., Kabachi, N., Bentayeb, F.: Partitioning and bucketing techniques to speed up query processing in Spark-SQL. In: IEEE 24th International Conference on Parallel and Distributed Systems (ICPADS), pp. 142–151 (2018)
11. Sun, L., Franklin, M.J., Krishnan, S., Xin, R.S.: Fine-grained partitioning for aggressive data skipping. In: Proceedings of the ACM SIGMOD International Conference on Management of Data, pp. 1115–1126 (2014)
12. Field, A.: Discovering Statistics using IBM SPSS Statistics. Sage, Thousand Oaks (2013)

Learning k-Occurrence Regular Expressions from Positive and Negative Samples

Yeting Li[1,2], Xiaoying Mou[1,2], and Haiming Chen[1(✉)]

[1] State Key Laboratory of Computer Science, Institute of Software,
Chinese Academy of Sciences, Beijing 100190, China
{liyt,mouxy,chm}@ios.ac.cn
[2] University of Chinese Academy of Sciences, Beijing, China

Abstract. Deterministic regular expressions (DREs) are a core part of XML schema languages such as DTD/XSD and are used in different kinds of applications. Presently the most powerful model to learn DREs is k-occurrence regular expressions (k-OREs for short). However, there has been no algorithms can learn k-OREs from positive and negative samples. In this paper, we propose an efficient and effective algorithm to learn k-OREs from positive and negative samples. Our algorithm proceeds as follows: (1) learning deterministic k-OA from positive and negative samples based on genetic algorithm; (2) converting the k-OA into optimum deterministic k-OREs.

Keywords: XML schema · Deterministic regular expressions · Language learning · Positive and negative samples

1 Introduction

Regular expressions (REs) are a fundamental concept in computer science and widely used in various applications, e.g., programming languages, database and semantic data modeling. Since they play an important role in data processing and matching, REs have always been a popular research topic. Different applications may require REs with various extensions or restrictions, among them are deterministic regular expressions (DREs) [5], which are a core part of XML schema languages such as DTD and XSD, and are used in different kinds of applications, e.g., the SPARQL query language for RDF [18], efficiently evaluating regular path queries [12], AXML [1]. Roughly speaking, a DRE must satisfy that when matching a word from left to right against an expression, a symbol can be matched to only one position in the expression without looking ahead. For instance, given a DRE $E_1 = (a|b)a$, if we input an a, it can efficiently match the first a in E_1 without looking ahead. But for a nondeterministic expression

Work supported by the National Natural Science Foundation of China under Grant Nos. 61872339 and 61472405.

$E_2 = (a|b^?)a$, if we input a symbol a, we cannot decide which position (the first or the second a) in E_2 to match without lookahead. One immediate benefit of using DREs is efficient parsing. Indeed it gives a natural manner to define determinism in REs. As a result, DREs perform better on several decision problems than general ones, for example, language inclusion is tractable for DREs but is PSPACE-complete for general ones [19,20]. It is known that DREs are strictly less expressive than REs [6] and thus not every RE can be defined by a DRE.

Learning DREs is an important research topic, which means, briefly speaking, given samples S, to learn a DRE r satisfying $S \subseteq L(r)$ or returns *null* if no such DRE exists. This problem becomes particularly important for XML schema extraction, since Li et al. [16] showed that XML documents with corresponding DTD/XSD definitions on the Web only account for 30.2%, with the proportion of 24.5% for valid ones. Therefore, it is essential to devise algorithms to learn a suitable schema for XML documents, and previous researches have shown that the fundamental task in schema learning is inferring DREs from given samples (i.e., learning DREs) (e.g., [2,3,8,17]).

Compared with the study of learning REs (or more generally, learning regular languages), which has a relatively long history, the study of learning DREs is relatively new and has been quite insufficient. Presently, most researches can only deal with *single occurrence regular expressions* (i.e., expressions in which each symbol occurs at most once), e.g., [2,3,7,8,14,15,17,22], which is quite restrictive. On the other hand, a more powerful model for learning DREs is the so called k-*occurrence regular expressions* (k-OREs) [2]. It has been observed that in practice, it suffices to learn DREs in which each alphabet symbol occurs at most k times, for some small k. Indeed, according to a study in which the authors gathered large-scale real-world XML data containing $124,326$ DREs extracted from DTDs and $134,816$ DREs from XSDs, the result reveals that DREs in practical schemas satisfy that every alphabet symbol occurs only a small number of times: 99.9% percent of DREs in DTDs and 100% percent of DREs in XSDs satisfy $k \leq 7$ [13]. And single occurrence regular expressions are just a special case of k-OREs, i.e., $k=1$. However, currently there are only few researches on k-OREs, e.g., Bex et al. [2] propose an algorithm to learn k-OREs, and Li et al. [16] provide a learning algorithm for k-OREs with interleaving which is not for DREs. Both of their methods only support learning from positive samples. This shows the needs to further study algorithms for k-OREs. Furthermore, all of the above existing researches learn DREs from positive samples only. However, in the computational learning theory initiated by [9], a seminal result shows that the class of all REs cannot be learned from positive data only. Using the same technique from [9], Bex et al. [2] prove that even the class of DREs cannot be learnable from positive data. Thus it is impossible for an algorithm to infer the full class of DREs from positive data only.

Our Contributions: All existing algorithms for learning DREs consider only positive samples. To the best of our knowledge, our work is the first to address learning DREs from both positive and negative samples. We propose an efficient

and effective algorithm to learn k-OREs from positive and negative samples, which is based on a genetic algorithm.

2   Preliminaries

For the rest of this paper, Σ denotes a finite set of alphabet symbols. The empty word is denoted by ε. The set of all words over Σ is denoted by Σ^*. A standard regular expression over Σ is defined as: $\emptyset$, ε or $a \in \Sigma$ is a regular expression, the union $E_1|E_2$, the concatenation $E_1 \cdot E_2$ or the Kleene star E_1^* is a regular expression for regular expressions E_1, E_2. We also use shorthand operators $E^? = \varepsilon|E$ and $E^+ = E \cdot E^*$. The size of an expression E, denoted by $|E|$, is the number of symbols and operators occurring in E.

For a regular expression E, a marked form of E, denoted by $\overline{E}$, is obtained by marking symbols in E with subscripts, such that each marked symbol occurs only once in $\overline{E}$. For example, given an expression $E = a(a|b)(ab)^*$, one of its marked form is $\overline{E} = a_1(a_2|b_1)(a_3b_2)^*$. The same notation will also be used for dropping of subscripts from the marked symbols: $\overline{\overline{E}} = E$. We extend this notation for words and sets of symbols in the obvious way. The definition of determinism is based on the marked expressions, as follows.

Definition 1 [6]. *A regular expression E is deterministic if and only if for all words $uxv, uyw \in L(\overline{E})$ if $x \neq y$ then $\overline{x} \neq \overline{y}$, where $x, y \in \overline{\Sigma}$ and $u, v, w \in \overline{\Sigma}^*$.*

Definition 2 [2]. *A regular expression E is k-occurrence (called k-ORE), if every alphabet symbol occurs at most k times in E.*

A k-occurrence automaton (called k-OA) is a specific kind of finite state automata defined in the following. Note that states are labeled with symbols but no edges are labeled.

Definition 3 [2]. *A k-OA is a node-labeled graph $G = (V, R, lab)$ where:*

- *V is a finite set of nodes (also called states) with a distinguished source src and sink snk.*
- *R is the edge relation such that src has only outgoing edges; snk has only incoming edges; every $v \in V \setminus \{src, snk\}$ is reachable by a path from src to snk.*
- *lab is the labeling function with $V \setminus \{src, snk\} \to \Sigma$.*
- *there are at most k states with the same symbol in Σ.*

A word $a_1 \cdots a_n$ is accepted by G if there exists a path $src\ v_1 \cdots v_n\ snk$ in G such that $a_i = lab(v_i)$ for $1 \leqslant i \leqslant n$. We denote the set of all words accepted by G as $L(G)$. We use $out_\sigma(v)$ to denote $\{v_1|(v, v_1) \in R$ and $\sigma = lab(v_1)\}$, i.e., the set of states of all direct successors of a state v in G.

Definition 4. *A k-OA is deterministic, if for any $v \in V$ and $\sigma \in \Sigma$, $out_\sigma(v)$ contains at most one state.*

3 The Learning Algorithm

Our algorithm aims to obtain a deterministic k-ORE with some fixed k, which should accept all positive samples S_+ and reject all negative samples S_-. This is mainly achieved by using a genetic algorithm. We show the major technical details of our algorithm in this section. The main algorithm is presented in Sect. 3.1. Generating a deterministic k-OA from samples is introduced in Sect. 3.2. Converting the k-OA into a deterministic k-ORE is given in Sect. 3.3.

3.1 The Main Algorithm

The pseudocode of our learning algorithm is presented in Algorithm 1. We will make many attempts with k varies. The k value can range from 1 to the maximal number of occurrences of alphabet symbols in S_+ and S_-, denoted as k_{max}. Notably, on the basis of practical experience, k_{max} is usually less than 8, since 99.9% of practical DREs satisfy that each symbol occurs at most 7 times [13].

Algorithm 1. $learner_-^+$

Input: positive sample S_+, negative sample S_-

Output: an expression r in k-ORE

1 initialize candidate set $C \leftarrow \emptyset$
2 **for** $k = 1$ *to* k_{max} **do**
3   **for** $n = 1$ *to* N **do**
4        $\mathcal{A} \leftarrow iKOA_-^+ (S_+, S_-, k)$
5        $r \leftarrow iKORE_-^+ (\mathcal{A})$
6   **if** $r \neq \varepsilon$ **then** add r to C;
7 **return** $r \leftarrow bestRE(C, S_+, S_-)$

The function bestRE is used to select the final optimum result with a k value, which ensures to avoid overgeneralization and to be as precise and concise as possible. We introduce two measures for this selection: (a) *A language size measure* [3] and (b) *One part of the minimum description length (MDL)* [21]. Language size measures the precision, which is the language size of an expression r, called $|L(r)|$. Since in general $L(r)$ is infinite and cannot be measured, we only consider the words with length up to $L_{max} = 2m + 1$, where m is the length of r excluding regular expression operators, ε, and $\emptyset$. The function is defined as: $L(r)^{\leqslant L_{max}} = \sum_{l=1}^{L_{max}} |L^l(r)|$, where $|L^l(r)|$ is the number of subset words of $L(r)$ that have length l. The part of *MDL* measures the concision, which is the *length of an expression* r in bits, that is $Len(r) = |r| * \lceil \log_2(|\Sigma| + |\mathcal{M}|) \rceil$, where $|\Sigma|$ is the size of the alphabet and $\mathcal{M}$ is the set of $\{|, \cdot, ?, *, +, (,)\}$. Intuitively, the less the indicator values, the better the RE. Finally, we prioritize *language size* over *expression length*. Since the genetic algorithm may also converge to a local maximum, we also run the algorithms N times to increase the probability of avoiding a local maximum value. In the experiments we set N to 10.

3.2 Generating Deterministic k-OAs from Samples

For a given $k \in [1, k_{max}]$, a deterministic k-OA can be learned from samples based on a genetic algorithm. We show the learning process in Algorithm 2.

Algorithm 2. $i\text{KOA}_-^+$

Input: positive sample S_+, negative sample S_-, a k value
Output: a deterministic k-OA $\mathcal{A}$

1 $P \leftarrow \text{init}(k), C \leftarrow \emptyset$
2 **for** $generation = 1$ to g_{max} **do**
3 $\quad$ $W \leftarrow \text{decode}(P)$
4 $\quad$ $parents \leftarrow \text{select}(P, \text{calcFitness}(W, S_+, S_-))$
5 $\quad$ $P \leftarrow \text{crossover}(parents)$
6 $\quad$ $P \leftarrow \text{mutate}(P)$
7 $\quad$ $\mathcal{A} \leftarrow \text{bestFA}(\text{decode}(P), S_+, S_-)$
8 $\quad$ $\mathcal{A} \leftarrow \text{DISAMBIGUATE}(\mathcal{A}, S_+, S_-)$
9 $\quad$ add $\text{SIMPLIFY}(\mathcal{A}, S_+, S_-)$ to C
10 **return** $\mathcal{A} \leftarrow \text{bestFA}(C, S_+, S_-)$

The Genetic Algorithm. Here, we consider the learning problem as finding an optimum solution in the deterministic k-OREs for some fixed k.

Initialization. We first initialize a population whose size is the number of possible solutions. Each individual in the population is initialized to a k-OA with $k * |\Sigma| + 2$ states and random edge relations. For simplifying the operations on k-OAs, we code each individual into a chain of binary DNA. Take 2-OA as an example to explain the *coding* process, shown in Fig. 1. Actually a k-OA graph of an individual is coded into a chain of string of 0s and 1s, and the length of the string is $(k * |\Sigma| + 1)^2$. Inversely, the process of changing a chain of string into a k-OA graph is called *decoding*.

Selection. In each generation of the population, we select excellent individuals to breed new generations. We measure individuals by a fitness function used for finding preferential solutions. In our algorithm, the function will choose individuals which are good at describing the class of languages of samples.

Crossover and Mutation. They are two ways to generate a second generation of one population based on those selected individuals by the above step. For crossover, we decide a pair of parents from the selected ones for breeding. Mutation can be easily completed by choosing and exchanging one position of one individual. Examples are shown in Fig. 2. As shown in Algorithm 2, the genetic algorithm is the basis of our algorithm. The variable P means a population. We set the size of P as 500, then initialize P by randomly generating 500 individuals (i.e., k-OAs). The function decode can code k-OAs with chains of binary DNA. The population need to evolve $g_{max} = 300$ generations to get a rational solution. The implementations of functions decode, select, crossover and mutate can be referred to the above explanations. The crossover probability is assigned as 0.8 and the mutation rate is 0.003 by experience. To be mentioned, calcFitness will measure individuals by a fitness function, and the fitness value $f(\mathcal{A})$ for an automaton $\mathcal{A}$ is usually defined as follows. $f(\mathcal{A}) = \frac{|T_P| + |T_N| - |F_P| - |F_N|}{|S_+| + |S_-|}$, where $T_P = \{w \in S_+ \mid w \in L(\mathcal{A})\}$, $T_N = \{w \in S_- \mid w \notin L(\mathcal{A})\}$,

---

Algorithm 3. DISAMBIGUATE

Input: positive sample S_+, negative sample S_-, a k-OA $\mathcal{A}$
Output: a deterministic k-OA $\mathcal{A}$

1 initialize queue Q to the initial states of $\mathcal{A}$
2 initialize set of marked states $B \leftarrow \emptyset$
3 **while** Q *is non-empty* **do**
4      $s \leftarrow \text{first}(Q)$
5   **while** some $\sigma \in \Sigma$ has $|\text{out}_\sigma(s)| > 1$ **do**
6          $C \leftarrow \emptyset$
7   **for** t *in* $\text{out}_\sigma(s)$ **do**
8              $\mathcal{A}' \leftarrow \mathcal{A}$
9   **for all** t' *in* $\text{out}_\sigma(s) \setminus \{t\}$ **do**
10   delete edge(s, t') from $\mathcal{A}'$
11   add $\mathcal{A}'$ to C
12          $\mathcal{A} \leftarrow \text{bestFA}(C, S_+, S_-)$
13   add s to marked states B and pop s from Q
14   enqueue all states in $\text{out}(s) \setminus B$ to Q
15 **return** $\mathcal{A}$

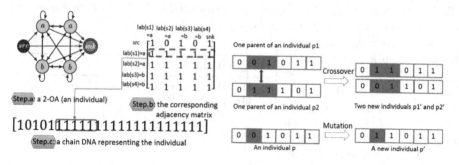

Fig. 1. The process of encoding an individual

Fig. 2. Examples for crossover and mutation operations

$F_P = \{w \in S_- \mid w \in L(\mathcal{A})\}$, $F_N = \{w \in S_+ \mid w \notin L(\mathcal{A})\}$, $|S_+|, |S_-|$ are the size of positive and negative samples, respectively. To be mentioned, the computations of $|T_P|, |T_N|, |F_P|$ and $|F_N|$ involve the process of checking whether a word can be accepted by an automaton. Here, we use the efficient algorithm in [11]. The $f(\mathcal{A})$ can guarantee selected individuals to accept positive samples and reject negative samples as many as possible. For an automaton $\mathcal{A}$, if the value of $f(\mathcal{A})$ is larger, then $\mathcal{A}$ has more possible to be chosen. The function bestFA has the same operations as select, and the only difference between them is that select returns a pair of *parents* from selected individuals based on the fitness function, however, bestFA only returns the best automaton $\mathcal{A}$ (with the largest fitness value is 1, i.e., satisfying $S_+ \subseteq L(\mathcal{A})$ and $S_- \cap L(\mathcal{A}) = \emptyset$).

DISAMBIGUATE can convert a k-OA into a deterministic k-OA. For each state s and symbol $\sigma \in \Sigma$ such that $|out_\sigma(s)| > 1$, we delete edges to keep $|out_\sigma(s)| = 1$, which is guided by the function bestFA. SIMPLIFY is designed to delete useless edges and states according to samples.

3.3   Converting Deterministic k-OAs into k-OREs

The process of converting an automaton into an expression has many results in previous research. We complete Algorithm 4 based on related results.

$Soa2Sore(\mathcal{A})$ implements the conversion of a *single-occurrence* automaton (i.e., 1-OA) into a regular expression. However the *single-occurrence* automaton restricts each symbol to occur at most once. Referring to the notion of marked expressions, we can mark the symbols occurring more than once in the label of states of a k-OA. That is, for every symbol $a \in \Sigma$ and all states $lab(s_i) = a(1 < i \leqslant n)$, we get a marked k-OA such that $lab(s_1) = a_1, \cdots, lab(s_n) = a_n$. Clearly, a marked k-OA is a *single-occurrence* automaton. We can convert the automaton into a single-occurrence regular expression r, then we drop the subscripts for all symbols in r and get a new expression in k-OREs. These series of processes cannot guarantee the resulting k-ORE be deterministic. Hence, we refer to the efficient determinism checking algorithm introduced in [10], and then ensure to obtain a deterministic k-ORE from a deterministic k-OA.

Our learning algorithm calls iKORE$_-^+$ with $k \in [1, k_{max}]$. In these attempts, iKORE$_-^+$ must return at least one deterministic regular expressions since when $k = 1$ the expression converted from a 1-OA will always be deterministic. Therefore, $learner_-^+$ ensures to learn a deterministic expression.

Algorithm 4. iKORE$_-^+$

Input: a deterministic k-OA $\mathcal{A}$
Output: a DRE r in k-ORE or ε

1   $r \leftarrow Soa2Sore(mark(\mathcal{A}))$ [8]
2   **if** r *is not deterministic* **then**
3     $\lfloor \; r \leftarrow \varepsilon$

4   **return** r

---

4   Conclusion

In this paper, we developed an algorithm to learn deterministic k-OREs from positive and negative samples. We first constructed deterministic k-OAs based on a genetic algorithm, to accept positive samples and reject negative ones. Then we converted the k-OAs into deterministic k-OREs.

Although studies show that in practice it suffices to learn DREs from k-OREs, however, for a fixed k value, k-OREs is a subclass of DREs. Therefore it is of both theoretical and practical interests to further investigate new models that can infer the full class of DREs. Further, in fact we also get a version of our algorithm in which the expressions are not restricted to DREs. Then we can compare our algorithm with others like [4], and use our algorithm to applications that require REs rather than DREs. We leave these for future work.

References

1. Abiteboul, S., Milo, T., Benjelloun, O.: Regular rewriting of active XML and unambiguity. In: Proceedings of the 24th SIGMOD, pp. 295–303 (2005)
2. Bex, G.J., Gelade, W., Neven, F., Vansummeren, S.: Learning deterministic regular expressions for the inference of schemas from XML data. TWEB **4**(4), 14:1–14:32 (2010)
3. Bex, G.J., Neven, F., Schwentick, T., Vansummeren, S.: Inference of concise regular expressions and DTDs. ACM Trans. Database Syst. **35**(2), 11:1–11:47 (2010)
4. Bonifati, A., Ciucanu, R., Lemay, A.: Learning path queries on graph databases. In: Proceedings of the 18th EDBT, pp. 109–120 (2015)
5. Brüggemann-Klein, A.: Unambiguity of extended regular expressions in SGML document grammars. In: Lengauer, T. (ed.) ESA 1993. LNCS, vol. 726, pp. 73–84. Springer, Heidelberg (1993). https://doi.org/10.1007/3-540-57273-2_45
6. Brüggemann-Klein, A., Wood, D.: One-unambiguous regular languages. Inf. Comput. **140**(2), 229–253 (1998)
7. Ciucanu, R., Staworko, S.: Learning schemas for unordered XML. In: Proceedings of the 14th DBPL, pp. 31–40 (2013)
8. Freydenberger, D.D., Kötzing, T.: Fast learning of restricted regular expressions and DTDs. Theory Comput. Syst. **57**(4), 1114–1158 (2015)
9. Gold, E.M.: Language identification in the limit. Inf. Control **10**(5), 447–474 (1967)
10. Groz, B., Maneth, S.: Efficient testing and matching of deterministic regular expressions. J. Comput. Syst. Sci. **89**, 372–399 (2017)
11. Hopcroft, J.E., Ullman, J.D.: Introduction To Automata Theory, Languages, and Computation. Addison-Wesley, Boston (2001)
12. Huang, X., Bao, Z., Davidson, S.B., Milo, T., Yuan, X.: Answering regular path queries on workflow provenance. In: Proceedings of the 31st ICDE, pp. 375–386 (2015)
13. Li, Y., Chu, X., Mou, X., Dong, C., Chen, H.: Practical study of deterministic regular expressions from large-scale XML and schema data. In: Proceedings of the 22nd IDEAS, pp. 45–53 (2018)
14. Li, Y., Dong, C., Chu, X., Chen, H.: Learning DMEs from positive and negative examples. In: Li, G., Yang, J., Gama, J., Natwichai, J., Tong, Y. (eds.) DASFAA 2019. LNCS, vol. 11448, pp. 434–438. Springer, Cham (2019). https://doi.org/10.1007/978-3-030-18590-9_61
15. Li, Y., Mou, X., Chen, H.: Learning concise relax NG schemas supporting interleaving from XML documents. In: Gan, G., Li, B., Li, X., Wang, S. (eds.) ADMA 2018. LNCS (LNAI), vol. 11323, pp. 303–317. Springer, Cham (2018). https://doi.org/10.1007/978-3-030-05090-0_26
16. Li, Y., Zhang, X., Cao, J., Chen, H., Gao, C.: Learning k-occurrence regular expressions with interleaving. In: Li, G., Yang, J., Gama, J., Natwichai, J., Tong, Y. (eds.) DASFAA 2019. LNCS, vol. 11447, pp. 70–85. Springer, Cham (2019). https://doi.org/10.1007/978-3-030-18579-4_5
17. Li, Y., Zhang, X., Xu, H., Mou, X., Chen, H.: Learning restricted regular expressions with interleaving from XML data. In: Trujillo, J.C., et al. (eds.) ER 2018. LNCS, vol. 11157, pp. 586–593. Springer, Cham (2018). https://doi.org/10.1007/978-3-030-00847-5_43
18. Losemann, K., Martens, W.: The complexity of regular expressions and property paths in SPARQL. ACM Trans. Database Syst. **38**(4), 24:1–24:39 (2013)

19. Losemann, K., Martens, W., Niewerth, M.: Closure properties and descriptional complexity of deterministic regular expressions. Theor. Comput. Sci. **627**, 54–70 (2016)
20. Martens, W., Neven, F., Schwentick, T.: Complexity of decision problems for XML schemas and chain regular expressions. SIAM J. Comput. **39**(4), 1486–1530 (2009)
21. Quinlan, J.R., Rivest, R.L.: Inferring decision trees using the minimum description length principle. Inf. Comput. **80**(3), 227–248 (1989)
22. Zhang, X., Li, Y., Cui, F., Dong, C., Chen, H.: Inference of a concise regular expression considering interleaving from XML documents. In: Phung, D., Tseng, V.S., Webb, G.I., Ho, B., Ganji, M., Rashidi, L. (eds.) PAKDD 2018. LNCS (LNAI), vol. 10938, pp. 389–401. Springer, Cham (2018). https://doi.org/10.1007/978-3-319-93037-4_31

Domain Specific Models I

What Rocks Are Made of: Towards an Ontological Pattern for Material Constitution in the Geological Domain

Luan Fonseca Garcia(✉)📍, Joel Luis Carbonera📍,
Fabricio Henrique Rodrigues, Cauã Roca Antunes📍, and Mara Abel📍

Informatics Institute - Federal University of Rio Grande do Sul (UFRGS),
Porto Alegre, RS, Brazil
{luan.garcia,joel.carbonera,fabricio.rodrigues,
caua.antunes,marabel}@inf.ufrgs.br
http://www.inf.ufrgs.br/bdi

Abstract. We propose an ontological pattern for dealing with the material constitution relation in Geology domain. This is important because geologists are often interested only in properties that are dependent to the matter (the rock, the minerals) or to the object (a geological unit, a grain). The scale of analysis is very important in Geology and may range from millimeters to kilometers. Differentiating the matter from the object that it constitutes allows one to represent properties from different scales separately. We first provide a short review of the state of the art for the constitution relation and how our vision fits within the existing theories.

Keywords: Ontological pattern · Ontological design pattern · Material constitution · Constitution · Ontology · Geology · Geological domain

1 Introduction

In the Geology domain, in general, geologists have to deal with entities of very different ontological natures and orders of magnitude (or scales), ranging from millimeters to kilometers - e.g., from grains to geological unities. Beyond that, when describing the very same entity under different scales, the geologist focus on very distinct properties. For example, an amount of rock is regarded as a homogeneous mass in macroscopic scale, but reveals a granular, discrete nature when analyzed in microscopic scales[1]. Additionally, it is common to consider that certain geological entities are constituted by certain amounts of rocks. By

---

[1] We use 'macroscopic' here to refer to a scale where entities are large enough to be visible by the naked eye. Conversely, 'microscopic' refers to anything smaller than what can be seen by the naked eye.

© Springer Nature Switzerland AG 2019
A. H. F. Laender et al. (Eds.): ER 2019, LNCS 11788, pp. 275–286, 2019.
https://doi.org/10.1007/978-3-030-33223-5_23

considering this conceptualization, geologists are able to differentiate the properties of the geological objects and the properties of the materials that constitute them. Moreover, the distinctions between the properties of the object and of its material is somewhat related to those between the properties found at different scales of analysis. Bearing this in mind, having a clear understanding of the nature of the material constitution in this context would provide significant help for supporting analysis of the subjects of the domain.

Unfortunately, the notion of constitution is still heavily overloaded and conceptually unclear in computer science, despite the wide number of efforts in the Philosophy literature to properly characterize it ontologically, as discussed in Sect. 2. Today, there is no computational model for Geology that explicitly deals with the notion of constitution and its role in defining the domain concepts in accordance with the conceptualization that is shared among geologists. In this context, building systems that can represent geological data with the suitable semantics becomes a challenge.

In this paper, we discuss the ontological nature of material constitution within Geology and propose an ontological pattern that explicitly captures the semantics underlying this notion and that can be used for supporting the suitable computational manipulation of geological data. In order to achieve that, we establish three main requirements that our model should meet:

1. Integrate different scales of analysis in the same model;
2. Support the distinction between geological entities and the matter that constitute them;
3. Clarify how some entities present different properties at different scales.

The remaining of the paper is organized as follows: Sect. 2 brings a brief review of possible views on constitution in the realm of Philosophy and explicits the notion we adopt in this work; in Sect. 1 we better describe the geological concepts involved on our efforts and develop our model proposal; Sect. 4 presents related work and discusses our finds; finally, our final remarks are presented in Sect. 5.

2   Material Constitution

In [5], constitution is defined as the relation between something and what it is made of. In this sense, we can define material constitution as the relation between some material entity and the physical matter that it is made of. Although this definition looks simple, there is much of a debate about the material constitution relation.

Consider the example of the statue and the clay extracted from [14]. A sculptor buys a lump of clay on Monday and names it 'Lump'. On Tuesday, he sculpts the clay into the form of a statue of the biblical king David and names it 'David'. It is possible to see that Lump differs from David. Lump existed on Monday, David didn't. Lump could survive being squashed, while David couldn't. They also differ in their kinds, since Lump is primarily a lump of clay, while David is primarily a statue. Following this, the following argument is possible:

1. David did not exist on Monday (and it exists on Tuesday).
2. Lump did exist on Monday (and continue to exists on Tuesday).
3. If 1 and 2 are true, then David is not identical do Lump.
4. We conclude then that David is not identical to Lump.

The problem is that this implies that spatially coincident objects exist, which seems absurd at a first glance. This paradox can be broadly analyzed in five perspectives [14]:

1. Accepting that Lump and David are different entities and have different properties (The Constitution View).
2. Denying that 1 is true because David already existed on Monday or that it never existed (The Eliminativist View).
3. Considering 2 false by either denying the existence of Lump (Eliminativist) or denying that Lump could survive the shape transformation (The Dominant Kinds View).
4. Denying 3 by rejecting the standard formulation of Leibniz's Law (The Relative Identity Theory).
5. Insisting that the underlying issues are in some sense verbal and there is no matter of fact about which premise is false (The Deflationist View).

In this paper, we assume the first philosophical view, so-called The Constitution View, because it is the only one that allows us to reflect a common view among geologists, where they often differentiate properties from the matter (rock) from properties of the object constituted by it (a geological unit constituted by that rock, for instance).

According to [2], The Constitution View is a metaphysical view of concrete entities in the natural world that accepts the possibility of existing two different material objects at the same place at the same time. In other words, this is the view that accepts that some object is different from the matter that constitutes it, that they are spatially coincident and that a relation of material constitution holds between them. This philosophical standpoint brings to light properties that are essential for one entity while are only contingent to another entity. For instance, being shaped like a man is a essential property for David, the statue, while it is only contingent for the lump of clay that constitutes it. Suppose that the statue is melted until it has not a man-shape. The David statue would cease to exist, while the lump of clay would remain the same.

It is important to note that even within the Constitution View there are distinct approaches. [5] separates three different approaches according to the relationship between constitution and composition, where composition is the relation holding between something and its parts. All these three views of constitution assume that the entities involved in the relation of constitution are three-dimensional. It also implies that constitution is relative to a specific instant of time - what constitutes something may change over time.

The first approach considers that objects are constituted by their parts, so constitution is identified as composition (i.e. a parthood relation). This is the view of [6, 7, 9–11]. The second one admits that constitution and composition

are distinct relations, but defines constitution in terms of parthood. Usually, in this view, the constituent and constituted entity share all the same parts, but the constituted is more loosely tied to these parts regarding its identity [13,16]. The third one, which is the approach that we follow in this work, says that constitution is not composition and if x constitutes y, then x is not a part of y. This approach is defended by [1,2] and will be detailed in the following.

According to Baker, the fundamental idea of constitution is that when something of one primary kind is in certain circumstances, something of another primary kind (a new thing, with new causal powers) comes to exist. Baker says that everything is of a single primary kind. She says that an object's primary kind answers the question: What is x most fundamentally? In this sense, the primary kind of the Lump would be being a lump of clay, and when it is sculpted in a certain way there are certain circumstances that brings to existence a new thing - David -, with new causal powers and different primary kind (being a statue).

Baker defines 6 conditions for an entity to constitute another at a certain time:

1. The constituent and the constituted entity are from distinct primary kinds.
2. The constituent and the constituted are co-localized in space and nothing can be constituted by two things of the same primary kind at the same time.
3. There must exist a set of favorable circumstances which the constituent must meet in order for the constitution relation to exist.
4. Whenever the constituent meets the favorable circumstances, the constitution relation must exist.
5. There must exist a possible situation where the constituent is not constituting anything of the same primary kind as the constituted entity, that is, whenever it is not in favorable circumstances.
6. Constitution only holds between things of the same basic kind of stuff (material things to material things, immaterial to immaterial, etc.).

Furthermore, Baker concludes that the constitution relation is asymmetric, irreflexive and contingent. For instance, there could be an aggregate of grains of quartz and feldspar that didn't meet favorable circumstances because they are far away from each other and thus do not constitute a sandstone rock.

In the following section, we present definitions for the entities from our domain, discuss which constitution relations hold between them and propose an ontological pattern for representing them.

3   Ontological Pattern for Geological Knowledge Representation

Geologists are acquainted with a variety of different types of entities that they have to deal with to make sense of the geological scenario that is presented to them in order to carry out their reasonings and make their inferences. Among

these entities, some are already evident in macroscopic scales of analysis, while others only become discernible in microscopic scale.

In the group of macroscopic entities we can highlight the concepts of rock and lithological unit. A lithological unit is a body of rock that is sufficiently distinctive and continuous for being mapped, and thus is an object with three-dimensional spatial expression and discernible features [15]. Therefore, we may inspect the position, size, shape and boundaries of a lithologic unit. Amounts of rock, on the other hand, are usually regarded as homogeneous portions of matter which constitute lithological units and other macroscopic geological entities. Accordingly, a rock presents properties which are roughly uniform across all its extension, such as porosity and density.

We shall focus here on a subtype of rock, known as Sedimentary Rock, a rock that is formed by the accumulation of sediments (usually grains). Sediments are particles of rock originated from rocks that previously existed and suffered processes of weathering and erosion. The study of sedimentary rocks is important because most of petroleum reservoirs in the world occur in this kind of rocks. Thus, the properties of sedimentary rocks are interesting for geologists for understanding the lithological units in order to predict the behavior of oil and gas inside the reservoir, as well as for allowing extrapolation of such properties to other geological entities constituted by the same type of rock. The properties of the lithological unit, although influenced by the properties of the rock, are not directly derived from them.

In the microscopic scale, we have entities such as grain and mineral. In our context, grains are small particles made of a single type of mineral. They present types of properties similar to those found in lithologic units (position, size, shape), though in a different scale. These properties are of interest for geologists since they help to explain how different grains would interact. A mineral is a solid chemical compound with a crystalline structure. Moreover, analogously to the case of rock, the mineral that constitutes a grain also present homogeneous properties, such as chemical composition, melting point, and behavior under pressure. Such properties help the geologist to explain certain behaviors of the grain or other larger objects with such mineral in its composition.

The connection between the entities of different scales, however, is usually imprecise. It is generally agreed that sedimentary rocks are "made of" grains, and properties such as grain size distribution are attributed to the rock. However, these properties contradict the homogeneous nature of rocks. This suggests the existence of an intermediate entity which collects the microscopic grains, allowing the analysis of their properties as a group, but without the homogeneity that characterizes the rock. We will refer to such an entity as a collection of grains (i.e. the simple mereological sum of mineral grains which, when arranged in a proper way, give rise to some amount of sedimentary rock). Similarly to how a lithological unit have properties which cannot be directly derived from the rock that constitutes it, rock properties do not rise directly from the properties of the collection of grains. Instead, those properties emerge, in a certain sense, from the way the collection of grains is arranged. That is, the exact same collection

of grains if differently arranged – e.g. due to diverse pressure conditions – would yield a rock with different material properties - e.g. higher pressure would result in 'less permeability'.

The analysis of these concepts from the geological domain (i.e. Lithologic Unit, Sedimentary Rock, Collection of Grains, Grain, Mineral) provides some evidence that we are dealing with three fundamental kinds of entities that are defined in [8], as Objects, Amounts of Matter and Arbitrary Collections. An object is an entity with spatial extension in three dimensions and a unifying relation that holds between all its parts. A car, a brick and a loaf of bread are examples of objects. Examples from geological domain include lithologic units and grains. Amounts of matter are entities which are mereologically invariant - that is, their identity is tied to that of their parts - but have no unifying relation among their parts. Examples of these entities include steel, mud, bread, and air, as well as rock and mineral. Finally, arbitrary collections are groupings of objects, do not have a unifying relation, and are mereologically invariant to a certain extent, in the sense that the identity of a collection is tied to that of its members, which may, however, change some of their parts without changing their identities. A fleet of cars, a pile of bricks and a collection of grains are examples of Arbitrary Collection.

By distinguishing these three main kinds of entities, our ontological pattern elucidates which properties belong to each type of entity. For example, spatial properties such as position, size and shape always come from objects. Thus, a geologist may refer the boundaries of a lithologic unity, but not of a sedimentary rock, or to the shape of a grain, but not of some mineral amount. Similarly, material's properties[2], like permeability, density and melting point, are always properties of amounts of matter. For example, a sedimentary rock has a certain porosity which cannot be verified in the underlying collection of grains without considering its arrangement, in the same way as a mineral presents a certain melting point that is not simply a function of its underlying collection of molecules, but results from the particular way in which they are bonded together. In these cases, we have properties of the "upper level" entity which do not arise directly from the properties of the underlying entity. These new properties suggest that there may be some constitution relations playing a part here. More specifically, there seems to be constitution relations between:

A Sedimentary rock and lithological unity.
B Collection of grains and sedimentary rock.
C Mineral and grain.
D Collection of molecules and mineral.

In order to verify whether or not it is really the case, we can check them against Baker's six conditions (enumerated in Sect. 2). constitution relations supporting the existence of such new properties.

---

[2] Here understood as a local physical property of a system that does not depend on the system size or the amount of material in the system.

Considering what we discussed so far, some of Baker's conditions are promptly fulfilled by all cases. First of all, it is clear that we are dealing with entities of distinct primary kinds in each of the considered relations, what fulfills condition (1). It is also clear that, in each of the cases, the related entities are spatially coincident. Additionally, Amounts of Matter (such as rocks and minerals) have their identities determined by that of their parts, we have that if two instances of amounts of matter spatially coincide, they would share all the same parts, and then they would actually be the same entity. A similar case can be made for Arbitrary Collections (such as collections of molecules and grains). Thus, it would not be possible to have two spatially coincident amounts of matter (or arbitrary collections) giving rise to the same constituted entity, which fulfills condition (2). Moreover, the relations involve just material entities, which arguably corresponds to a single basic type of stuff, fulfilling condition (6). The remaining conditions must be verified for each case.

According the condition (3), the constituent entity must be in some favorable circumstance that makes it give rise to the constituted entity. Additionally, by condition (4) whenever something of the type of the constituent is in such favorable circumstance, it must give rise to the corresponding constituted entity. Finally, by condition (5), there must be some possible situation in which a potential constituent do not gives rise to the corresponding constituted entity.

Lithological unit is defined as a body of rock that is sufficiently distinctive. Thus, in case (A), a sedimentary rock gives rise to a lithological unity whenever it is in some condition that results in the referred 'sufficient distinctiveness', which is provided by some material discontinuity between the rock amount and its surrounds - for example, being delimited by a geological fault or being surrounded by rocks of different types. By the definition of lithological unity, the rock that constitutes it is always in such condition, what fulfills condition (3). Likewise, whenever an amount of rock is in such circumstances, it becomes sufficiently distinctive and then gives rise to some lithological entity, what fulfills the condition (4). Finally, whatever sufficiently large rock amount we take into account contains smaller, inner amounts of rock of the same type. For such inner amounts there is no material discontinuity that can make it distinguishable from the larger rock amount. Thus, in these cases, the inner amounts cannot be said to give rise to any lithological unit, and that provides a possible case to fulfill condition (5).

In case (B), for a collection of grains to give rise to a rock, they must present some high degree of consolidation (i.e. they must be tied strongly enough together). Such degree of consolidation is the favorable circumstance required by condition (3). Additionally, it is this degree of consolidation that gives rise to the properties that rocks exhibit (e.g. it fixes the grains in the specific structure that results in the porosity characteristic of the rock). Therefore, whenever a collection of grains reaches such adequate degree of consolidation, an amount of rock comes into existence - what meets condition (4). Finally, right after the sediment deposition (i.e. when the grains are deposited at some surface) and before lithification (i.e. the process that consolidates the sediment into rock), we

already have the collection of grains gathered together at the same place, but we do not yet have a rock - which fulfills condition (5).

Case (C) is analogous to case (A). Being a small particle of a single type of mineral, a grain is a small individuated portion of mineral. Thus, a grain arises from an amount of mineral when such amount presents a material discontinuity in relation to its surroundings (e.g. as a result of a crack in a larger amount of mineral, so that the two amounts are no longer tied together by the chemical bonds characteristic of the mineral type). This material discontinuity is the favorable circumstance required by condition (3). Conversely, whenever a sufficiently small amount of mineral is surrounded by a material discontinuity, it becomes a small individuated portion of mineral and, thus, a grain - what meets condition (4). Again, analogously to case (A), every sufficiently large mineral amount contains some inner non-individuate amount of the same mineral that, lacking the required material discontinuity to its surroundings, does not give rise to a grain - as required by condition (5).

Finally, case (D) is analogous to case (B). Since a mineral is a solid chemical compound with a crystalline structure, the arrangement of the molecules of such chemical compound into the referred crystalline structure is precisely the favorable circumstance that makes a mineral rise from a collection of molecules, as required by condition (3). Moreover, whenever a collection of molecules of a particular type is arranged into the crystalline molecular structure that characterizes a mineral, there exist a mineral amount corresponding to such arrangement, so that case (D) also meets condition (4). Finally, since a given collection of molecules may be arranged in diverse structures (which would give rise to minerals of different types), or not arranged at all (e.g. the mereological sum of separate artificially created molecules), case (D) also meets condition (5).

Distinctly from the entirely new properties in cases (A), (B), (C) and (D) - which do not derive from the underlying constituent entities -, no new property arises when grouping objects in a collection. The properties of a collection are simply statistical data over the objects they collect, being directly derived from the properties of those objects. In our example, the mode, the average and distribution of the size of the grains are properties of the collection which are directly derived from the size of each grain. Thus, there is a clear distinction among the relation that holds between the collection and the objects it groups and the relations of constitution holding between objects and amounts of matter or between amounts of matter and collections. Additionally, if the relation between the collection and each object were a constitution relation, it would contradict our definition of constitution both by having more than one constituent for a single constituted entity and by having a constituent entity that do not spatially coincides with the constituted entity. Therefore, we identify the relation of a collection and each of its objects as one of membership, a specific type of parthood.

Given the definition of the concepts of the domain, their classification into three upper-level types, and the identification of the constitution relations among such concepts, we come up with the full model presented in Fig. 1. It meets the

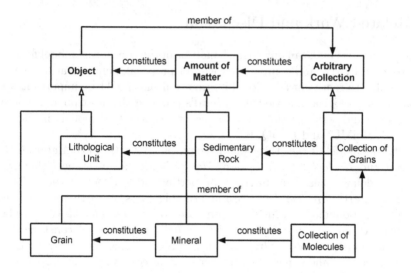

Fig. 1. Ontological pattern for material constitution in the geology domain.

three requirements defined in introduction: (1) it integrates different scales of analysis in the same model (e.g. dealing with molecules, grains and lithological units), (2) it supports the distinction between geological entities and the matter that constitutes them (i.e. lithological units being constituted by sedimentary rock and grains being constituted by mineral amounts), and (3) clarify how some entities present different properties in different scales (i.e. by acknowledging the existence of collections of objects as constituents of amounts of matter, we establish a link between discrete particles that we observe in smaller scales, e.g. grains or molecules, with the homogeneous amounts of matter we observe in larger scales, e.g. rocks or minerals).

In addition to using this pattern as a model for generically modeling the geological domain, it may be used as a pattern for specific scenarios (for example, substituting/specializing Sedimentary Rock, Grain, Mineral and so on with the specific types of rock, grain and mineral with which one is working).

Finally, our model reveals an interesting pattern. For the cases we considered, Objects are constituted by Amounts of Matter, which are in turn constituted by Arbitrary Collections. Thus, it seems to be the case the constitution relations delimit "constitution levels", with each entity being constituted by something in the level directly below, that is, constitution relations may not "skip" levels. Furthermore, there may exist several successive chains of constitution relations, that seems to agree with different scales of observation (e.g. each grain in a collection is constituted by a portion of mineral, which is in turn constituted by a collection of molecules). We observe this occurrence of this pattern in this specific domain, but it may serve as insight for pursuing similar patterns in other domains or as a possible general rule.

4   Related Work and Discussion

In this section, we make an ontological analysis of the conceptual model for Geology proposed by [12] and compare it with our proposal, demonstrating how our model is able to represent additional information that might be important when dealing with geological knowledge. Richard's is one of the most popular conceptual models and serve as the basis for notorious standard models in Geology such as GeoSciML[3] and RESQML[4].

Richard's model defines three main geological concepts: *EarthMaterial*, *GeologicUnit* and *GeologicStructure*. *EarthMaterials* are the substances that make up Earth, defined based on intrinsic properties independent of their disposition within Earth. *GeologicUnits* are identifiable parts of Earth with definable and locatable boundaries, which are 'composed of' *EarthMaterial*. We note here that what Richard calls 'composition' is actually a relation of constitution as defined previously. *GeologicStructures* are configurations of matter in Earth, defined based on inhomogeneities, patterns or discontinuities in a rock mass. They are dependent entities whose existence relies on an underlying *GeologicUnit* or *EarthMaterial*.

As the author notes, an *EarthMaterial* not associated with any *GeologicUnit* or *GeologicStructure* "would have to be homogeneous, isotropic and lack any sort of internal discontinuities" [12]. In this sense, *EarthMaterial* matches our notion of Amount of Matter. However, the author also defines *CompoundMaterial* as an *EarthMaterial* that has parts which are, in turn, "composed of" other *EarthMaterials*. He names these parts *EMConstituents*, and claims that they have types such as "clast" and "crystal" and roles that specify how the constituent relates to the *CompoundMaterial* as a whole, such as "phenocryst". Two main aspects of this definition come to our attention. First, if the *CompoundMaterial* has parts with different types and roles regarding the whole, then it is not homogeneous, even when not associated to any *GeologicUnit* or *GeologicStructure*. Secondly, the *EMConstituent* types and roles resemble more closely our notion of Objects than that of Amounts of Matter, since clasts, crystals and phenocrysts are not necessarily homogeneous and have non-essential parts which may change without altering their identities. This contradiction between an "homogeneous" whole and its inhomogeneous parts highlights an attempt at representing entities of different constitution levels (i.e., the *CompoundMaterial* and the *EMConstituents*) without actually individuating such levels.

Another issue with Richard's model is related to the properties of *EarthMaterials*. It is not always clear when a property such as *GeologicAge* or *Genesis* refers to the *EarthMaterial* itself, to the particles that make it up or to the object it 'composes' - *EMConstituents*, for example, have neither of these properties, however it is clear that the age of formation and history of a clast are usually different from the same properties of the *EarthMaterial* that 'composes' it. A similar problem is faced by the property *ChemichalDescription*, which,

---

[3] http://www.geosciml.org/.

[4] https://www.energistics.org/resqml-current-standards/.

for *CompoundMaterials*, actually derives from the properties of its constituents, although this is not described by the model. Finally, it is also not clear which *PhysicalProperties* are actually from the *EarthMaterial* and which belong to the *GeologicalUnit*, neither how the ones from GeologicalUnit are derived from the properties of its *EarthMaterial*, if they are derived at all. The same is true for Color, which is a property from both concepts, even though the color of the *GeologicalUnit* is certainly related to the Color of the *EarthMaterial*.

As we have discussed in the previous section, our ontological framework allows us to model both the homogeneous rock and the underlying inhomogeneous collection of grains without falling in contradiction by expliciting the change in scale between two constitution levels. Thus, we may describe a rock with its uniform properties and the collection of grains and their varied attributes, recognizing both as different entities (i.e., the rock is not the collection of grains and vice versa) and stressing the relation between them.

Additionally, our framework guides the attribution of properties to entities according to their ontological nature, preventing confusion regarding to what entity a particular property must belong. For example, the *ChemicalDescription* which is assigned to a Rock is actually a property of the underlying collection of grains, which, on its turn, is a statistical description of the chemical compositions of the minerals which constitute the grains in the collection.

5   Conclusion

We have presented an ontological pattern for geological knowledge representation. Our pattern discerns three main kinds of geological entities, Objects, Amounts of Matter and Arbitrary Collections. We have identified that, in the Geology domain, constitution relations always occur either between Amounts of Matter and Objects (rock/lithological unit and mineral/grain) or between Arbitrary Collections and Amounts of Matter (collection of grains/rock and collection of molecules/mineral).

The pattern allows the integration between distinct scales of analysis which are common to the domain and the distinction between geological entities and the matter that constitute them, helping to clarify how some entities present different properties in different scales. The pattern also guides the assignment of properties to entities according to their nature as Objects, Amounts of Matter or Arbitrary Collections, helping to prevent mismatching of properties, i.e., entities with properties that actually belong to a different constitution level.

We restricted our study of the use of the material constitution relation to the geological domain. In Geology, most of the time geologists are interested in natural kinds. Natural kinds reflect the structure of the natural world, instead of intentions and actions of human beings [3]. As a future work we would like to investigate the possibility to generalize the proposed pattern to other domains, but this will require a careful examination of the constitution relation that occurs in the artifacts domain, as discussed in [4].

Our work relies on the view where the matter and the object constituted by it are distinct entities. This view is specially useful in the geological domain

because it reflects the shared view of geologists where they differentiate the rock from the objects that are constituted by it and identify properties that are exclusive for each one of them. As a future work, we intend to extend this ontological pattern for other domains, however, it might not be true that every domain would benefit modeling separated the object from the matter that constitutes it.

Acknowledgments. We would like to thanks the Informatics Institute from the Federal University of Rio Grande do Sul (UFRGS), the Brazilian National Research Council (CNPq) and the Coordination for the Improvement of Higher Education Personnel (CAPES) for supporting our research.

References

1. Baker, L.R.: Persons and Bodies: A Constitution View. Cambridge University Press, Cambridge (2000)
2. Baker, L.R.: The Metaphysics of Everyday Life. Cambridge University Press, Cambridge (2007)
3. Bird, A., Tobin, E.: Natural kinds. In: Zalta, E.N. (ed.) The Stanford Encyclopedia of Philosophy. Metaphysics Research Lab, Stanford University, spring 2018 edn. (2018)
4. Borgo, S., Vieu, L.: Artefacts in formal ontology. In: Philosophy of Technology and Engineering Sciences, pp. 273–307. Elsevier (2009)
5. Evnine, S.J.: Constitution and composition: three approaches to their relation. ProtoSociology **27**, 212–235 (2011)
6. Fine, K.: Things and their parts. Midwest Stud. Philos. **23**(1), 61–74 (1999)
7. Fine, K., et al.: Acts, events and things. In: Sixth International Wittgenstein Symposium, Kirchberg-Wechsel (Austria), pp. 97–105 (1982)
8. Gangemi, A., Guarino, N., Masolo, C., Oltramari, A., Schneider, L.: Sweetening ontologies with DOLCE. In: Gómez-Pérez, A., Benjamins, V.R. (eds.) EKAW 2002. LNCS (LNAI), vol. 2473, pp. 166–181. Springer, Heidelberg (2002). https://doi.org/10.1007/3-540-45810-7_18. http://dl.acm.org/citation.cfm?id=645362.650863
9. Johnston, M.: Constitution and identity. In: The Oxford Handbook of Contemporary Philosophy (2005)
10. Johnston, M.: Hylomorphism. J. Philos. **103**(12), 652–698 (2006)
11. Koslicki, K.: The Structure of Objects. Oxford University Press on Demand, Oxford (2008)
12. Richard, S.M.: Geoscience concept models. Spec. Pap.-Geol. Soc. Am. **397**, 81 (2006)
13. Thomson, J.J.: The statue and the clay. Noûs **32**(2), 149–173 (1998)
14. Wasserman, R.: Material constitution. In: Zalta, E.N. (ed.) The Stanford Encyclopedia of Philosophy. Metaphysics Research Lab, Stanford University, fall 2017 edn. (2017)
15. Werlang, R., Abel, M., Perrin, M., Carbonera, J.L., Fiorini, S.R.: Ontological foundations for petroleum application modeling. In: 18th International Conference on Petroleum Data, Integration and Data Management (2014)
16. Zimmerman, D.: Theories of masses and problems of constitution. Philos. Rev. **104**(1), 53–110 (1995)

Role-Based Clustering for Collaborative Recommendations in Crowdsourcing System

Qiao Liao[1,3], Xiangmin Zhou[2], Daling Wang[1(✉)], Shi Feng[1], and Yifei Zhang[1]

[1] School of Computer Science and Engineering,
Northeastern University, Shenyang, China
liaoqiaogtl@outlook.com, {wangdaling,fengshi,zhangyifei}@cse.neu.edu.cn
[2] School of Science, RMIT University, Melbourne, Australia
xiangmin.zhou@rmit.edu.au
[3] Tianjin Artificial Intelligence Innovation Center, Tianjin, China

Abstract. Crowdsourcing as a distributed problem-solving and business production model has attracted much attention in recent years. In crowdsourcing systems, task recommendation can help workers to select suitable tasks on crowdsourcing platforms as well as help requesters to receive good outputs. However, as one of the most successful recommendation approaches, current clustering-based models in crowdsourcing are challenged by multi-preference and cold-start problems. This paper proposes a role-based clustering model, which transforms a large-sparse worker-task rating matrix into a set of role-based clusters that are small, independent and rating intensive worker-task rating matrices, leading to better quality and performance in task recommendation. Specifically, we first cluster a worker-task rating matrix into a set of clusters in terms of the role identification and distribution operations. The clusters are further extended to include all their external worker (task) roles. Then, the task recommendation results with respect to a worker are generated by operating over the clusters involving the worker's activities, which captures the worker's preferences in multiple areas. Moreover, the model discovers the structure information from the clustering results and crowdsourcing datasets, by which tasks can be recommended to new workers interactively without their interest profiles. We evaluated our method over the benchmark dataset from NAACL 2010 workshop. The results show the high superiority of our proposed recommendation method over crowdsourcing platforms.

Keywords: Role-based clustering · Task recommendation · Cold-start · Multi-preference · Crowdsourcing system

1 Introduction

Crowdsourcing as a distributed problem-solving and business production model has attracted much attention in recent years [14,15]. Popular crowdsourcing system examples include Amazon Mechanical Turk (or MTurk) and Crowd Flower

© Springer Nature Switzerland AG 2019
A. H. F. Laender et al. (Eds.): ER 2019, LNCS 11788, pp. 287–301, 2019.
https://doi.org/10.1007/978-3-030-33223-5_24

etc. There is however a challenge in crowdsourcing system that a worker has to select a task from more than thousands of tasks. In September 2017, the number of available Human Intelligence Tasks (HITs) for qualified workers on MTurk was about 259000 in average per day[1]. Obviously, it is impossible for workers to select their most suitable tasks by browsing the extremely long task list. Fortunately, task recommendation helps workers to select tasks from an automatically generated short list and helps requesters to receive good outputs [18].

We study the problem of collaborative recommendation in crowdsourcing system. Given a worker and a set of tasks, we aim to identify a list of tasks that best meets the preferences of this worker. In the field of crowdsourcing, two challenges need to be addressed. First, a worker in crowdsourcing may be interested in one or more fields of crowdsourcing. For example, one may be interested in both "mathematics" and "music". If the recommendation is limited to a single field, quite a lot opportunities for task recommendation will be excluded. Second, the workers to be recommended must include the workers who have no history behaviors on crowdsourcing at all. Ignoring these workers will be a serious barrier of improving the quality of crowdsourcing systems.

Many approaches have been developed for task recommendation. A well-known method is the collaborative filtering (CF) that uses the pure rating data to estimate or learn a model to make recommendation [4,13]. Typical example of the CF approaches for crowdsourcing is Probability Matrix Factorization (PMF) [9]. PMF may generate recommendation from a large worker-task rating matrix derived from the crowdsourcing datasets [18]. However, the scalability of CF approaches is limited as the approach has to generate recommendation by using the entire worker-task rating matrix. For solving the scalability issue, the clustering-based model was adopted as one of the most successful approaches in recommender systems and has been applied in various cases [3,8]. Task recommendation aims at recommending the proper tasks to workers so that the workers are interested in the tasks. Normally, a clustering-based model first groups a worker-task rating matrix into a set of clusters and then apply PMF to the clusters for recommendation. However, as the common CF-based recommendation, current clustering-based models are facing two challenges: multi-preference and cold-start problems.

- Multi-preference problem: According to the cluster-based method, a worker must be located in a single cluster and receives the task recommendation from the cluster, while the worker might do the tasks of other clusters and a task might be done by the workers of other clusters as well, excluding quite a lot opportunities for task recommendation [3,5,12].
- Cold-start problem: As the recommendation above is limited to the workers located in a cluster, it is hardly to recommend to new users who are not located in any clusters at all. Though existing works addressed the cold-start problem by taking into account the user profiles or by providing the most popular tasks of the whole system to new users, the former is hardly available

---

[1] https://worker.mturk.com/.

in the most crowdsourcing practice, while the latter is limited by low success rates of the recommendation [16–18].

In this paper, we consider a worker (task) as roles, and propose a role-based clustering approach that allows a worker (task) to play roles in multiple clusters. A worker (task) may be replaced by multiple worker (task) roles if the worker (task) plays roles in more than one cluster, resulting in a set of extended clusters. Applying CF to the extended clusters enables the recommendations to a single worker from more than one cluster, regaining the missing opportunities to the worker in recommendation. Additionally, in contrast with the current methods for cold-start recommendation [16–18], the role-based clustering recommendation may improve the success rate of cold-start recommendation dramatically by providing workers with the structure information about the crowdsourcing. Our contributions in this work are summarized as follows.

1. We propose a role-based clustering approach that transforms a large-sparse worker-task rating matrix into a set of small, independent and rating intensive ones. Operating over the small, independent and rating intensive matrices enables fast system response, while the effect of unrelated ratings is reduced.
2. We propose to generate recommendation for a worker from all the clusters where the worker plays role in, leading to better opportunities in task recommendation. As such, the multi-preferences of workers can be well exploited.
3. We propose to publish structure information and allow workers to request recommendation from the areas of their interests, leading to high success rate in the task recommendation to new workers.
4. We conduct extensive experiments on the benchmark dataset from NAACL 2010 workshop. The results show that our method is feasible and superior for recommendation in crowdsourcing systems.

The structure of the rest of the paper is as follows. Section 2 surveys the related work. Section 3 describes the framework of our recommendation solution for crowdsourcing system. Section 4 presents our proposed role-based clustering for task recommendation, followed by the experimental evaluation in Sect. 5. Finally, we conclude the whole paper in Sect. 6.

2 Related Work

We review existing literature on collaborative recommendation approaches in crowdsourcing system, particularly the approaches about the multi-preference and cold-start problems.

Collaborative filtering (CF) approaches rely on the worker behaviors in recommendation. A typical CF-based approach for crowdsourcing is Probability Matrix Factorization (PMF) [5], which generates recommendation from a large worker-task rating matrix derived from the crowdsourcing datasets successfully [17]. However, this approach incurs the scalability issue as its recommendation is generated based on the entire worker-task rating matrix. The problem may

be solved by clustering-based model [7,10,11] that first preprocesses the worker-task rating matrix into a set of small clusters and then conducts collaborative filtering over these clusters. Usually, the clusters are interrelated rather than independent of each other, reflecting the fact that workers may have multiple preferences and thus worked in multiple clusters. Currently popular clustering-based approach only generates recommendation to a worker based on the tasks of the cluster where the worker is located, excluding quite some opportunities in recommendation [3]. Moreover, this approach ignores the multi-preferences of workers, leading to the contradiction that a worker with interests in multiple areas can get task recommendation from a single area only.

Cold-start problem has been studied in traditional recommender systems [19,20]. The cold-start problem in crowdsourcing platform is common when the recommendations are generated for new workers. Under this situation, there is no any rating between the new workers and the tasks of the crowdsourcing platform. Yuen et al. [18] applied the PMF approach in crowdsourcing system to solve the cold-start problem. This approach analyzes the relationships between users and inter-dependencies among products to identify new worker-task associations [18]. However, the success rate of such a recommendation may be still challenged due to lacking of penalization in the recommendation, thus no worker personal preference is considered at all. Li et al. [6] solved the cold-start problem by using the degree of social influence to recommend tasks to the new workers. The condition of this recommendation is that the new worker has friends who did the tasks ever. However, the conditions it requires are hard to be satisfied in many crowdsourcing systems.

We propose a clustering-based model that allows each worker (task) to play roles in multiple clusters of their interests and generates recommendation to this worker from all his related clusters. Our method relies on the worker behaviors, e.g., submitting or completing tasks in crowdsourcing, and does not require the creation of explicit profiles. It provides a new solution to cold-start problem in terms of structure information that is recovered via matrix reconstruction.

3   Framework of Our Solution

This section describes the framework of our proposed role-based clustering for task recommendation. Let $[R]_{M \times N}$ be a worker-task rating matrix with M workers and N tasks, and each $R_{ij} \in R$ be the behavior value of worker W_i to task T_j, which includes 1, 2, 3, 4, 5, and null according to the extent of W_i favoring T_j [17]. The framework of our approach is shown in Fig. 1.

In Fig. 1, the left part is a role-based clustering mechanism that transforms a worker-task rating matrix R into a set of small and rating intensive clusters, each cluster is a small worker-task rating matrix that consists of a set of workers, a set of tasks and the ratings between them. The transformation from the original R to a set of small worker-task rating matrices $(R_1, R_2, \ldots, R_n)$ does not change the semantics of the original R. The semantics of a worker-task rating matrix in this paper refers to all the workers, tasks and the ratings

between them. The clusters are rating intensive because the principle "high coherent and low coupling" was applied to the clustering. Each R_i is potentially a professional working group (PWG). According to task description, all PWGs, namely $PMG_1, PMG_2, ..., PMG_n$ as in Fig. 1 form the structure information of $R_1, R_2, ..., R_n$, respectively. The significant change from R_i (i = 1, 2, ..., n) to PMG_i (i = 1, 2, ..., n) is the labeling and specification, including the name and a short description of the R_i. Thus, a PMG_i refers to a named and specified R_i. Yet, the structure information to be used in the recommendation is only about the name and specification, without necessarily looking into the content of the R_i, and normally published in the outsourcing platform.

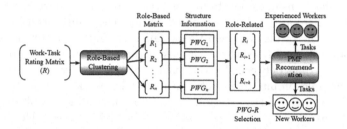

Fig. 1. Framework of role-based clustering for task recommendations

The recommendation is performed using Probability Matrix Factorization (PMF). The PMF as shown in the right part of Fig. 1 is the recommendation mechanism that takes R_i as input and provides recommendation to workers as output. However, the way used to generate recommendation to experienced workers is different from that to new workers. The tasks recommended to an experienced worker may come from one or more clusters where the worker has played roles. The tasks recommended to a new worker may come from one or more clusters selected by him in terms of structure information.

4   Role-Based Clustering for Task Recommendation

This section discusses the details on our role-based clustering for collaborative recommendations in crowdsourcing system, including the role-based clustering and the collaborative filtering-based task recommendation.

4.1   Role-Based Clustering

Many clustering methods are available for item summarization [3,21]. We propose role-based clustering to allow users to play two roles. We create the worker-task rating matrix first. The content of the rating matrix can be derived from the working records of a crowdsourcing system. The ratings between workers and tasks are captured as in [17]. If a worker's work is accepted by requester,

the rating value is set as 5. If it is rejected by requester, the rating value is set as 4. If a worker completes a task and submits the work done, the rating value is set as 3. If a worker browses the detailed information of a task, the rating value is set as 1. If a worker does not browse the detailed information of a task, set the rating value as 0. The result matrix is depicted in Fig. 2(a), where the rows $W_{01}, W_{02}, ..., W_{12}$ are workers; the columns $T_{01}, T_{02}, ..., T_{09}$ are tasks. The rating between a worker and a task is one of the values in 1, 2, 3, 4, 5, null.

Taking the worker-task rating matrix as input, the process of role-based clustering consists of two steps. First, it transforms the worker-task rating matrix into a set of interrelated clusters, as shown by the transformation from Fig. 2(a) to (b). Secondly, it transforms the interrelated clusters into a set of independent clusters, as the transformation from Fig. 2(b) to (c). The interrelated clusters, shown in Fig. 2(b), are worker/task-based because each cluster consists of workers, tasks and the ratings between them. The independent clusters as shown in Fig. 2(c), are role-based because each cluster consists of the worker-roles, task-roles and the ratings between them. Considering multi-preference, a worker may play multiple roles in multiple clusters if the worker worked on the tasks of the multiple clusters. Similarly, a task may play multiple roles in multiple clusters if the task was conducted by the workers of multiple clusters. The role-based clustering makes a worker (task) be replaced by multiple roles whenever necessary. The worker (task)-ID is therefore replaced by the IDs of multiple roles. For example, the worker-ID W_{02} in Fig. 2(b) is replaced by the worker-role-ID W_{02} and W_{021} in Fig. 2(c); the task-ID T_{09} in Fig. 2(b) is replaced by task-role-ID T_{09} and T_{091} in Fig. 2(c). Arranging all the roles into the clusters where they played in, we transform the Fig. 2(b) into (c).

The matrix reconstruction as a term in this paper refers to a process to reorganize a task-worker rating matrix into a set of smaller and relatively rating intensive matrices preserving the meaning of original matrix. The matrix reconstruction can be performed by exchanging the positions of the rows in the matrix, as well as that of the columns. The exchanging does not change the meaning of the matrix according to elementary number theory, while the distributions of workers, tasks and ratings of the matrix will be changed. The matrix reconstruction for clustering aims at driving the distribution into clusters. There are two criteria for the driving: (1) a worker must be moved into a cluster if the tasks completed by the worker are mostly located in the cluster; (2) a task must be moved into a cluster if the workers doing the task are mostly located in the cluster. As a result, a large sparse worker-task rating matrix is transformed into a set of small and rating intensive worker-task rating matrices, shown as the conversions from Fig. 2(a) to (b).

The clusters are *"high coherent and low coupling"*. The interconnections between workers and tasks of the same cluster are high while those of different clusters are minimized. The interconnection between workers and tasks may be identified by the ratings between them. There is interconnection between two workers working on the same tasks. Likewise, there is interconnection between two tasks conducted by the same worker. Moreover, the interconnection between

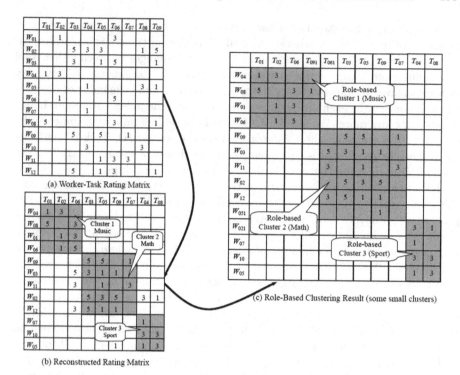

Fig. 2. Process of role-based clustering

any items (workers or tasks) is transitive. The matrix reconstruction is a process to rearrange the positions of rows and columns, resulting in a set of clusters of *"high coherent and low coupling"*, see also Fig. 2(b).

Considering the information behind clusters, the workers and tasks of each cluster constitute a professional working group, see also that of labeled by 'Math', 'Music' and 'Sport' in Fig. 2. All the groups and the relationships between them further form the organizational structure of a crowdsourcing platform. A cluster is considered as a professional working group because the criteria about the clustering is based on the behaviors of the workers rather than the similarity between the tasks. To reuse the concepts and organizational structure mined from the original rating matrix, we use the term structure information to describe all the professional groups and the relationship between them. The structure information is not only useful for task providers to add new tasks into the system in a structured way, but also useful for new workers to understand the organizational structure of the crowdsourcing. With the structure information, new workers have an opportunity to request the mechanism of the platform to generate recommendation from the professional groups of their preference.

In addition to the structure information, we must take into account the performance of matrix reconstruction as well. Considering the transformation process from Fig. 2(a) to (b), there could be a lot of exchanges between either rows or columns. For a large worker-task rating matrix, the exchanges could be very time expensive. To improve the performance, one may build the index of the rows and columns, so the exchange is only performed over the index until no exchange is necessary any more. We use a list of records instead of matrix to improve the exchange performance, where a record consists of worker-ID, Task-ID and rating value. The record list is equivalent to the worker-task rating matrix because both of them describe the same entities and their relationships.

For the clustering via matrix reconstruction, we extract the first cluster from the whole matrix, then extract the second one from the rest of the data. The process is recursively conducted until the size of the remained data is equivalent to the prior estimated size of a reasonable cluster. Thus, the original large sparse matrix is converted into a number of interrelated clusters. These clusters are not independent of each other, as some workers of one cluster may also work on the tasks of other clusters, and some tasks of one cluster may be conducted by the workers contained in other clusters. The interconnection can be simply identified by the ratings located outside of the clusters as shown in Fig. 2(b). To remove the interconnection between clusters, the matrix reconstruction must be performed by role-based restructuring. To do this, we first identify all internal and external roles of the clusters, and then move the external roles together with the corresponding ratings into the clusters in which they played. Here, a role of a cluster refers to a worker who did one or more tasks of the cluster, or a task completed by one or more workers of the cluster. In terms of role-based clustering, all the clusters become role-based ones and the interrelationship between them are disappeared from structure point of view. Algorithm 1 presents the process of the role-based clustering.

All the roles are originated from workers and tasks. A worker of a cluster will become an internal role of the cluster with the same ID. For example, the worker $W_1, W_2, ..., W_{12}$ and the task $T_1, T_2, ..., T_9$ are internal roles of the clusters containing them as shown in Fig. 2(c). While W_{021} and W_{051} are external worker-roles derived from worker W_{02} and W_{05}, T_{061} and T_{091} are external task roles derived from task T_{06} and T_{09}. When we move all the external roles into existing clusters, all external ratings will be moved as well. As a result, each role belongs to one and only one cluster and all the external ratings are cleaned. All the clusters are independent of each other as in Fig. 2(c). In addition, the external role IDs must be rooted by the IDs of original workers or tasks so that all the clusters containing a worker may be identified easily. This helps to generate recommendations from all the clusters for a worker with multi-preferences.

Algorithm 1: Role-Based Clustering

Input: Initial Matrix A, cluster number k
Output: Cluster [] (i=1, 2, ..., k)
/*Part1: Clustering via Matrix Reconstruction*/
  1) **For** i=1 to k
  2)   {(A, Cluster [i])=Cluster Initiation (A, i) //**Model 11**
  3)   **Repeat**
  4) C=Cluster [i]
  5)   (A, Cluster [i])=Cluster Reduction(Cluster Expansion(A, C)) //**Model 12-13**
  6)   **Until** C= Cluster [i]
  7) }
/*Part2: Clustering via Role Identification and Distribution*/
  1) For i=1 to k
  2)   {(A, Cluster [i])=Role Distribution (Role Identification (A, Cluster [i])) //**Model 21-22**
  3) }

4.2 Applying CF to the Role-Based Clusters

In this section, we discuss how to generate recommendation via CF approach. Given a cluster C_k, we do probabilistic matrix factorization (PMF) [9] as follow. Suppose there are M tasks, N workers, and a set of integer rating values from 1 to 5 and null in the cluster C_k. Let R_{ij} represent the rating of worker W_i for task T_j, $W \in R^{D \times N}$ and $T \in R^{D \times M}$ be latent worker and task feature matrices, with column vectors W_i and T_j representing worker-specific and task-specific latent feature vectors respectively. Since model performance is measured by computing the root mean squared error (RMSE) on the test set, we first adopt a probabilistic linear model with Gaussian observation noise. The conditional distribution over the observed ratings is defined as below:

$$p(R|W,T,\sigma^2) = \prod_{i=1}^{M} \prod_{j=1}^{N} [N(R_{ij}|W_i^Y T_j, \sigma^2)]^{I_{ij}} \tag{1}$$

where $N(x|\mu, \sigma^2)$ is the probability density function of the Gaussian distribution with mean μ and variance σ^2, and I_{ij} is the indicator function that equals to 1 if worker w_i rated task t_j and 0 otherwise. We also place zero-mean spherical Gaussian priors [7,10] on worker and task feature vectors.

$$p(W|\sigma_W^2) = \prod_{i=1}^{M} N(W_i|0, \sigma_W^2 I), p(T|\sigma_T^2) = \prod_{j=1}^{N} N(T_j|0, \sigma_T^2 I) \tag{2}$$

The log of the posterior distribution over the worker and task features is given as below:

$$\ln p(W,T|R,\sigma^2,\sigma_T^2,\sigma_W^2) = -\frac{1}{2\sigma^2} \sum_{i=1}^{M} \sum_{j=1}^{N} I_{ij}(R_{ij} - W_i^Y T_j)^2$$
$$-\frac{1}{2\sigma_W^2} \sum_{i=1}^{M} W_i^Y W_i - \frac{1}{2\sigma_T^2} \sum_{i=1}^{N} T_j^Y T_j$$
$$-\frac{1}{2}((\sum_{i=1}^{M} \sum_{j=1}^{N} I_{ij}) \ln \sigma^2 + ND \ln \sigma_W^2 + MD \ln \sigma_T^2) + C \tag{3}$$

where C is a constant that does not depend on the parameters. Maximizing the log-posterior over task and worker features with fixed hyper-parameters (i.e. the observation noise variance and prior variances) is equivalent to minimizing the sum-of-squared-errors objective function with quadratic regularization terms:

$$E = -\frac{1}{2}\sum_{i=1}^{M}\sum_{j=1}^{N}I_{ij}(R_{ij}-W_i^YT_j)^2 + \frac{\lambda_W}{2}\sum_{i=1}^{M}\|W_i\|_{Fro}^2 + \frac{\lambda_T}{2}\sum_{j=1}^{N}\|T_j\|_{Fro}^2 \quad (4)$$

where $\lambda_W = \sigma^2/\sigma_W^2, \lambda_T = \sigma^2/\sigma_T^2$, and $\|\ \|_{Fro}^2$ is the Frobenius norm. A local minimum of the objective function given by Eq. 4 can be found by performing gradient descent in W and T. This model can be viewed as a probabilistic extension of the SVD model, since the objective given by Eq. 4 is simplified as the SVD objective in the limit of prior variances going to infinity if all ratings have been observed. In this work, instead of using a simple linear-Gaussian model, which can make predictions outside of the range of valid rating values, the dot product between the worker-specific and task-specific feature vectors is passed through the logistic function $g(x) = 1/(1 + exp(-x))$, which bounds the range of predictions:

$$p(R|W,T,\sigma^2) = \sum_{i=1}^{M}\sum_{j=1}^{N}[N(R_{ij}|g(W_i^YT_j),\sigma^2)]^{I_{ij}} \quad (5)$$

We let null into 0 and map the ratings 1, 2, ..., 5 to the interval $[0, 1]$ using the function $t(x) = (x - 1)/(5 - 1)$, so the range of valid rating values matches the range of predictions our model makes. Minimizing the objective function given above using steepest descent takes linear time cost to the number of observations.

4.3 Recommendation Construction and Delivery

In this part, we describe how to generate recommendations to both experienced workers and new workers. The role-based clustering model provides additional opportunities in recommendation. Given an experienced worker of crowdsourcing, multiple recommendations may be generated by applying CF to the role-based clusters containing this worker. The percentage number of the tasks recommended to the worker may be provided according to the percentage of the roles played by him.

We adopt two alternative solutions, recommendation from multiple clusters and recommendation from worker selected clusters, for generating recommendations to new workers.

1. **Recommendation from multiple clusters.** A worker may get multiple popular tasks from multiple clusters. As each cluster is corresponding to a professional working group (PWG), likely corresponding to a field of interest, it is more likely to meet a new worker's preference by allocating tasks from multiple clusters while not from the most popular tasks of the global worker-task rating matrix, as proved by in Sect. 5.5.

2. **Recommendation from worker selected clusters.** To solve the cold-start problem, we publish the structure information in the crowdsourcing platform in advance so that all the new workers have a chance to select the *PWG*s of their interests and request the system for task recommendation from the groups selected. Although cold-start problem is really'cold', we find a chance in crowdsourcing to make the problem'warmer' with structure information. As a result, the quality of the recommendation to new workers may be improved significantly.

In fact, the matrix reconstruction on the worker-task rating matrix is a kind of machine learning, which recovers the knowledge, a global picture about the crowdsourcing, resulting in a basis for online active learning [2, 22] for worker preference. In practice, most new workers in the crowdsourcing are eager to see the global picture in advance instead of receiving a recommendation blindly.

5 Experimental Evaluation

5.1 Experiment Setup

We conduct the experiments on the benchmark dataset collected by the NAACL 2010 workshop on crowdsourcing, which has been publically available [16–18]. The data was collected within a month from multiple requesters, including the data for a diverse variety of tasks on MTurk. The numbers of the workers, tasks and ratings are 1654, 10357 and 27971 respectively.

5.2 Evaluation Methodology

We evaluate our model, namely the role-based clustering for collaborative recommendations in crowdsourcing system in terms of effectiveness. First of all, we evaluate the effect of the role-based clustering and, then, the effect of the role-based recommendation. Moreover, we compare the effect of our model with that of a few other existing competitors. Finally, we evaluate the effect of our recommendation for cold start workers. The models for the comparison are as follows.

1. **PMF-based** model exploits low-rank approximations to model the total user-item rating matrix for further predictions [16].
2. **K-means** model uses k-means clustering to cluster users and, uses the PMF-based model, to generate recommendation [3].
3. **Hierarchical** model uses hierarchical clustering to cluster users and, uses the PMF-based model, to generate recommendation [3].
4. **Role-based** as proposed by us uses the role-based clustering method to cluster the worker-task-rating matrix and uses the PMF-based model to generate recommendation.

To conduct task recommendation for each experienced worker, we applied PMF [1,9] to all the clusters in which the worker played roles. The recommendation quality is evaluated based on four metrics: root mean square error (RMSE), mean squared error (MSE), mean absolute error (MAE), and mean percentage error (MPE), which are calculated by: $RMSE = \sqrt{(\sum_{w,t} \widehat{R}_{w,t} - R_{w,t})/N}$, $MSE = (\sum_{w,t}(\widehat{R}_{w,t} - R_{w,t})^2)/N$, $MAE = (\sum_{w,t} |\widehat{R}_{w,t} - R_{w,t}|)/N$, $MPE = \frac{100\%}{N} \sum_{w,t} \frac{\widehat{R}_{w,t} - R_{w,t}}{R_{w,t}}$ respectively. Here, $R_{w,t}$ is the worker-task rating value of test set, $\widehat{R}_{w,t}$, the predicting value of worker-task rating, and N the total number of (worker, task, rating) triplets.

The recommendation quality for cold start workers is evaluated based on Success Rate, namely the ratio of the new workers completing a recommended task to all the new workers receiving recommendations. The success rate can be calculated by $SR = NWD/NWR$, where, NWD is the number of the new workers who have done a recommended task successfully, NWR the number of new workers who got recommendations, and SR a short for Success Rate.

5.3   Experimental Results

Effect of Role-Based Clustering. We test the effect of role-based clustering to the rating density of the worker-task rating matrix. We generate 10 clusters using our role-based clustering over the worker-task rating matrix derived from MTurk dataset, and calculate the density of each cluster and that of the original whole matrix. The comparison results are reported in Table 1. Here the number of workers (tasks) refers to the number of the roles that the workers (tasks) play in one or more clusters and the density is the ratio between the number of ratings and the size of the matrix. Clearly, comparing with the original rating matrix, the clusters achieve 4–37 times higher density, which saves 90% of memory cost and is suitable for efficient task recommendation.

Table 1. Result of role-based clustering

	C_1	C_2	C_3	C_4	C_5	C_6	C_7	C_8	C_9	C_{10}	Original
Workers	136	372	324	51	251	179	283	365	234	162	1654
Tasks	1379	886	773	3027	374	770	896	876	519	867	10357
Ratings	2764	1932	1457	9162	1363	3686	1843	3063	1432	1269	27971
Density	1.47%	0.59%	0.58%	5.93%	1.45%	2.67%	0.73%	0.96%	1.18%	0.90%	0.16%

To further analyze these clusters, we extract the structure information from each of them. The cluster structures are described as Table 2. As we can see, different clusters represent different working areas of crowdsourcing, which is helpful to locate the right tasks for interested workers.

Table 2. Structure information of crowdsourcing

Group	Field	Description
C_1	Definition Compare	Compare the definitions of two dictionaries
C_2	English-Afrikaans	Check English-Afrikaans word translations
C_3	Wikipedia Question	Read a Wikipedia sentence and answer questions
C_4	Spanish Annotation	Annotation of positive and negative opinions (Spanish)
C_5	Sentence Labelling	Label sentences as "Important" or not
C_6	Fact Confirmation	Read a sentence and say whether it expresses a fact
C_7	Clouds Tag Ranking	Rank tag clouds for queries
C_8	Twitter Labelling	Label named entities in Twitter data
C_9	English Writing	English creative writing
C_{10}	Subject Identify	Identify subjects for given verbs in English sentences

Effect of Role-Based Recommendation. We evaluate the effect of role-based model to the recommendation quality by conducting the recommendation over different clusters and the original worker-task matrix. We randomly select 80% of ratings from the dataset as training data, and leave the remaining 20% for recommendation prediction. The comparison results are shown in Table 3. Comparing the pure PMF-based recommendation over the original worker-task rating matrix, those over the role-based clusters achieve higher effectiveness in terms of four metrics, RMSE, MPE, MSE and MAE. The smaller RMSE, MPE, MSE or MAE indicates the better performance.

Table 3. Recommendation performance for different groups

	C_1	C_2	C_3	C_4	C_5	C_6	C_7	C_8	C_9	C_{10}	Original matrix
Ratings	2764	1932	1457	9162	1363	3686	1843	3063	1432	1269	27971
RMSE	0.103	0.142	0.405	0.41	0.395	0.403	0.457	0.629	0.231	0.605	0.424
MSE	0.021	0.023	0.184	0.107	0.156	0.163	0.197	0.395	0.053	0.366	0.18
MAE	0.008	0.014	0.099	0.154	0.126	0.238	0.202	0.266	0.033	0.183	0.162
MPE	0.038	0.016	0.089	0.352	0.287	0.273	0.174	0.423	0.032	0.091	0.394

Effectiveness Comparison. In this test, we evaluate the effectiveness of our role-based model by comparing with existing competitors, PMF-based [16], K-means model [3], and Hierarchical model [3]. As shown in Fig. 3, our role-based model is superior to that of existing competitors in terms of RMSE, MSE and MAE. This is because the role-based model can well handle the multiple-preference problem of workers. Although hierarchical model achieves smaller MPE than our role-based model, it incurs high time cost due to its pair-wise user comparison during clustering process. Thus our role-based model is more practical.

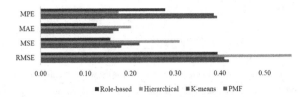

Fig. 3. Performance comparison of different methods

Effect to Cold Start Workers. We test the recommendation quality of our role-based model and that of PMF-based model by conducting recommendation to new workers. We recommend tasks to new workers by providing the most popular tasks of the professional working groups. As shown in the Table 4, the success rate of our role-based model is much higher than that of pure PMF method for cold start recommendation. This has proved that our role-based model can well handle the cold start problem in recommendation.

Table 4. Result of cold start solution

Cluster	C_1	C_2	C_3	C_4	C_5	C_6	C_7	C_8	C_9	C_{10}	Role	PMF
Workers	109	298	259	41	200	143	226	292	187	130	2357	2357
Tasks	1103	709	618	2422	299	616	717	700	415	694	10367	10367
Ratings	1945	1332	1120	6373	932	2556	1287	2094	1101	867	27971	27971
Tasks Rec	3	2	2	8	2	4	2	3	2	2	30	30
Suc Rate	0.325	0.304	0.204	0.206	0.483	0.283	0.246	0.432	0.058	0.302	0.355	0.147

6   Conclusion

In this paper, we proposed a role-based clustering approach for collaborative recommendations in crowdsourcing system. We first transform a large sparse worker-task rating matrix into a set of small, rating intensive and independent rating matrices and structure information. Then, the recommendation is generated by collaborative filtering over these small rating matrices. The test results prove the high effectiveness of our solution.

Acknowledgements. The work was supported by the National Key R&D Program of China under grant 2018YFB1004700, and National Natural Science Foundation of China (61772122, 61872074).

References

1. Dueck, D., Morris, Q.D., Frey, B.J.: Multi-way clustering of microarray data using probabilistic sparse matrix factorization. Bioinformatics **21**(Suppl. 1), i144–i151 (2005)

2. Elahi, M., Ricci, F., Rubens, N.: Active learning in collaborative filtering recommender systems. Comput. Sci. Rev. **20**(C), 29–50 (2016)
3. Gao, M., Cao, F., Huang, J.Z.: A cross cluster-based collaborative filtering method for recommendation. In: ICIA, pp. 447–452 (2013)
4. Jannach, D., Zanker, M., Felfernig, A., Friedrich, G.: Recommender Systems: An Introduction (2010)
5. Klašnja-Milićević, A., Ivanović, M., Nanopoulos, A.: Recommender systems in e-learning environments: a survey of the state-of-the-art and possible extensions. Artif. Intell. Rev. **44**(4), 571–604 (2015)
6. Li, N., Mo, W., Shen, B.: Task recommendation with developer social network in software crowdsourcing. In: ISEC, pp. 9–16 (2017)
7. O'Connor, M.: Clustering items for collaborative filtering. In: ACM SIGIR Workshop on Recommender Systems: Algorithms and Evaluation (1999)
8. Qin, D., Zhou, X., Chen, L., Huang, G., Zhang, Y.: Dynamic connection-based social group recommendation. TKDE 1–14 (2019)
9. Salakhutdinov, R., Mnih, A.: Probabilistic matrix factorization. In: NIPS, pp. 1257–1264 (2007)
10. Sarwar, B.M., Riedl, J., Konstan, J.: Recommender systems for large-scale e-commerce: scalable. In: ICCIT (2002)
11. Ungar, L.H.: Clustering methods for collaborative filtering. In: AAAI Workshop on Recommendation Systems (1998)
12. Xu, B., Bu, J., Chen, C., Cai, D.: An exploration of improving collaborative recommender systems via user-item subgroups. In: WWW, pp. 21–30 (2012)
13. Yue, S., Larson, M., Hanjalic, A.: Collaborative filtering beyond the user-item matrix:a survey of the state of the art and future challenges. ACM Comput. Surv. **47**(1), 1–45 (2014)
14. Yuen, M.C., Chen, L.J., King, I.: A survey of human computation systems. In: CSE, pp. 723–728 (2009)
15. Yuen, M.C., King, I., Leung, K.S.: A survey of crowdsourcing systems. In: PASSAT, pp. 766–773 (2012)
16. Yuen, M.C., King, I., Leung, K.S.: Task recommendation in crowdsourcing systems. In: CrowdKDD, pp. 22–26 (2012)
17. Yuen, M.-C., King, I., Leung, K.-S.: TaskRec: probabilistic matrix factorization in task recommendation in crowdsourcing systems. In: Huang, T., Zeng, Z., Li, C., Leung, C.S. (eds.) ICONIP 2012. LNCS, vol. 7664, pp. 516–525. Springer, Heidelberg (2012). https://doi.org/10.1007/978-3-642-34481-7_63
18. Yuen, M.C., King, I., Leung, K.S.: TaskRec: a task recommendation framework in crowdsourcing systems. Neural Process. Lett. **41**(2), 223–238 (2015)
19. Zhou, X., Chen, L., Zhang, Y., Cao, L., Huang, G., Wang, C.: Online video recommendation in sharing community. In: SIGMOD, pp. 1645–1656 (2015)
20. Zhou, X., et al.: Enhancing online video recommendation using social user interactions. VLDB J. **26**(5), 637–656 (2017)
21. Zhou, X., Zhou, X., Chen, L., Bouguettaya, A.: Efficient subsequence matching over large video databases. VLDB J. **21**(4), 489–508 (2012)
22. Zhu, J., Shen, B., Hu, F.: A learning to rank framework for developer recommendation in software crowdsourcing. In: APSEC, pp. 285–292 (2015)

A Reference Conceptual Model for Virtual Network Function Online Marketplaces

Renata Guizzardi[1(✉)], Anderson Bravalheri[2], Giancarlo Guizzardi[3],
Tiago Prince Sales[4], and Dimitra Simeonidou[2]

[1] Ontology and Conceptual Modeling Research Group (NEMO),
Federal University of Espirito Santo, Vitoria, Brazil
`rguizzardi@inf.ufes.br`
[2] High Performance Networks Group, University of Bristol, Bristol, UK
`{a.bravalheri,Dimitra.Simeonidou}@bristol.ac.uk`
[3] Conceptual and Cognitive Modeling Group,
Free University of Bozen-Bolzano, Bolzano, Italy
`gguizzardi@unibz.it`
[4] DISI, University of Trento, Trento, Italy
`tiago.princesales@unitn.it`

Abstract. Recently, we witnessed a shift in the Networking paradigm, with large part of the network control moving from hardware to software. This move has been accompanied by an increase of interest in declarative software models (conceptual models) for the domain. Moreover, novel architectures allow services to be deployed in multiple domains. These changes call for new business models to allow the commercialization of Virtual Network Functions (VNFs). This paper proposes the creation of an ontology-based reference conceptual model to support VNF Marketplaces, allowing VNF vendors and infrastructure providers to commercialize VNFaaS (VNFs as services). The proposed reference model has been engineered by using foundational ontology techniques (UFO/OntoUML), it has been formally validated by using model simulation techniques, and it has been implemented in OWL.

Keywords: Ontology-based conceptual modeling · Virtual Network Function · Marketplace · UFO-S

1 Introduction

In the past few years, we have been observing a shift in the Networking paradigm, with large part of the network control moving from hardware to software in the context of an increased virtualisation of networks. This move has been accompanied by an increase of interest in declarative software models (conceptual models) for the domain [1]. Additionally, we have witnessed the migration of network services to profit from the growing adoption of distributed cloud computing

© Springer Nature Switzerland AG 2019
A. H. F. Laender et al. (Eds.): ER 2019, LNCS 11788, pp. 302–310, 2019.
https://doi.org/10.1007/978-3-030-33223-5_25

technologies in 5G networks. In this setting, new business models are needed to enable the different market players to profit from these changes. Along with the changes in the business models, comes the need for novel platforms to support the development and commercialization of Virtual Network Functions (VNFs) and Network Services (NSs).

In this paper, we discuss the case of a VNF Marketplace to enable VNF vendors and infrastructure providers to commercialize VNFaaS (VNFs as services). This marketplace is based on the architecture of the 5G Exchange Hub [4], which consists of the interconnection of different testbed islands, allowing the orchestration and deployment of multi-domain NSs. In this marketplace, service developers may create new NSs through the combination of VNFs offered by different vendors and deployed at distinct sites, according to the requirements of the service being developed. In other words, we do not assume that the developer owns a particular infrastructure, but rather allow the services to be run in third-parties infrastructures, which are owned by infrastructure providers.

Our proposed business model requires that prior to the service development per se, a contract is established between the VNF vendor and the infrastructure provider, regulating VNF deployment. For that, the infrastructure provider must acquire a license to deploy, through a service agreement with the VNF vendor. For deploying the VNF, the infrastructure provider charges from the developer a deployment cost, which is defined with basis on how much the infrastructure provider spends with the VNF license, and the infrastructure running and maintenance.

The proposed marketplace is based on a Reference Conceptual Model to support the aforementioned business model, besides allowing NS developers to design and deploy NSs. This particular paper reports on an excerpt of this Conceptual Model, making explicit the involved market players (i.e. VNF vendors, infrastructure providers and NSs developer), and how a service is established between the different parties. In order to do that, we build our work on the basis of a Core Ontology of Services (UFO-S) [8]. UFO-S is a well-founded ontology based on the Unified Foundation Ontology (UFO), and by reusing it, we profit from its already established semantics. Furthermore, as demonstrated in [8], UFO-S is expressive enough to harmonize the different views of service found in the literature of Service Computing, Service Sciences and Enterprise Modeling.

We here claim that an ontology-based Reference Conceptual Model is more suitable than other kinds of conceptual models, such as ER and traditional UML models. Our main justification is that besides making the domain knowledge explicit, an ontology supports reasoning capabilities, i.e. the ability to navigate in the ontology model, finding answers to specific queries. Moreover, if there is a need to interoperate the marketplace with other systems (e.g. commercial portals from specific VNF vendors), ontologies are particularly advisable, especially if based on a foundational ontology, formalizing the real-world semantics behind the domain concepts.

Following the best practices in the area of Ontology-Driven Conceptual modeling [7], our proposed reference model has been engineered by using foundational

ontology techniques (UFO/OntoUML). Moreover, it has been formally validated by using the OntoUML support for model simulation and anti-pattern detection, and it has been implemented in the description logics SHROIQ (OWL). The proposed model is then used to support the development of a proof of concept of the proposed marketplace and allows for a number of reasoning tasks regarding different aspects concerning its business model and its operation.

The remaining of this paper is organized as follows: Sect. 2 presents UFO-S, the core ontology reused in this work; Sect. 3 describes the Marketplace Reference Conceptual Model; Sect. 4 discusses validation and codification of the proposed model, as well as the a proof of concept developed for the Marketplace; Sect. 5 discusses some related works; and finally, Sect. 6 presents our final considerations.

2   The UFO-S Core Ontology of Services

UFO-S [8] is a Core Ontology grounded on UFO [6] and as such, it is meant to capture a structure that is recurrent in several domains [3]. UFO-S accounts for a conceptualization of services independent of a particular application domain and is designed with the main goal of supporting meaning negotiation among different views on services held, for example, in Service Computing, Service Sciences and Enterprise Semantics. In our work, we use only an excerpt of UFO-S, and for the description of its remaining concepts, we refer to [8]. UFO-S is based on the UFO foundational ontology. For reasons of space, we are not able to present the definition of the categories comprehending UFO, and we thus also refer the reader to [6].

In UFO-S, agent is a category that represents the essential properties of any type of agentive object (e.g. person, organization, or software agent). Service provider is the role played by agents when these agents commit themselves to offer a service to a target customer community. As a role mixin, service provider can be instantiated by agents of different kinds, e.g., persons and organizations [6].

Target customer community is a collective representing the group of agents that constitute the community to which the service is being offered. The criteria for defining the target customer community membership are included in the content of the service offering. This may range from offerings with no restrictions to strictly targeted service offerings. The target customers are members of a target customer community and, therefore, have claims for the fulfillment of the service provider's *commitments* when offering a service. The social relator aggregating the aforementioned commitments of the service provider and the corresponding claims by the target customers is named service offering.

After the service is negotiated, a service agreement is established, and the service provider becomes a hired service provider, while the target customer effectively is turned into a service customer. As in a service offering, a service agreement is composed of commitments and claims. However, in contrast to the service offering, a service agreement involves not only commitments from the hired service provider towards the service customer, but may also involve

commitments from the service customer towards the hired service provider (for example, the commitment of providing a monetary compensation in case of service delivery). In any case, a service agreement should conform to the previous service offering, in a sense that the commitments established by the former should be compatible to the ones predefined in the latter.

3   VNF Marketplace Reference Conceptual Model

Figure 1 presents the concepts and relations that allow an `Infrastructure Provider` to deploy and commercialize a `Virtual Network Function (VNF)` developed by a third-party vendor, here named `Virtual Network Function Provider` (VNF Provider). A VNF is the role played by a `Software` when commercialized by a particular vendor (see the offers relation from `Virtual Network Function Offering` to VNF). A VNF instantiates a `VNF Type` (e.g. the Cisco ASA 5500-X Firewall is an instance of the Firewall type).

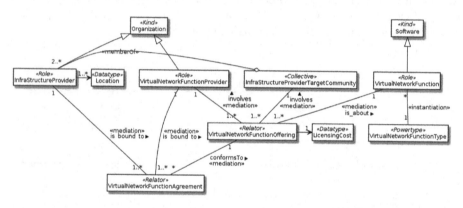

Fig. 1. Concepts involved in the contract between an Infrastructure Provider and a VNF Provider to deploy and commercialize a VNF

Both VNF Provider and Infrastructure Provider are roles played by `Organizations`. The Infrastructure Provider has a `Location` (this information is important to enable the NS Developer to select the best placement for a particular service). The VNF Provider represents the vendors of VNFs, while the Infrastructure Provider is the role responsible for actually deploying the VNFs that compose the NSs in the Marketplace. For that, a service agreement (in the sense of UFO-S) is established between the VNF Provider and the Infrastructure Provider, according to the concepts defined by UFO-S. Thus, first, a VNF Provider provides a service offering (again, in the sense of UFO-S) to a `Target Infrastructure Provider Community`.

The `VNF Offering` offers a particular VNF (e.g. Cisco ASA 5500-X Firewall), having a specific `License Cost`. If an Infrastructure Provider member of

the target community is interested in the offering, a `VNF Agreement` may be established, conforming to such VNF Offering (see the UFO-S *conforms to* relation between the VNF Agreement and VNF Offering). Having established this VNF Agreement, the Infrastructure Provider gains the right to commercialize the deployment of such VNF in the Marketplace.

Figure 2 presents the concepts and relations that allow a service developer to acquire the right to *deploy* a particular VNF as part of a developed service. To enable the `Developer` to use the VNF as part of an NS, the Infrastructure Provider delivers a service to the Developer, following the same service structure as the one described above. The Infrastructure Provider makes a `Virtual Network Function Deployment Offering` to a `Target Developer Community`, having a particular `VNF Deployment cost`. Note that the VNF Deployment Offering requires an existing VNF Agreement (refer to *requires* relation). This avoids that Infrastructure Providers commercialize the deployment of VNFs for which they have not yet acquired a licensing agreement. An interested Developer, member of the target community, may then make a VNF Deployment Agreement (`Virtual Network Function Deployment Agreement`) *conforming to* the VNF Deployment Offering, thus gaining the right to execute that particular VNF in a service developed through the Marketplace.

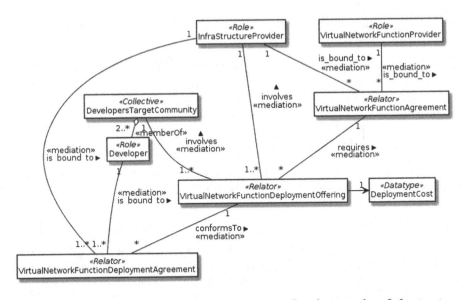

Fig. 2. Concepts involved in the contract between a Developer and an Infrastructure Provider to deploy a VNF as part of a developed service

Please note that the excerpts of our reference conceptual model presented in Figs. 1 and 2 are based on UFO-S. As previously stated, Core Ontologies are general enough to allow the creation of ontologies in more specialized domains. Thus, our reference model applies the UFO-S concepts described in Sect. 2 by

analogy. In other words, for all UFO-S described notions, we created concepts that are specific to the Marketplace domain. For instance, in Fig. 1, the VNF Provider plays the role of UFO-S service provider (provides VNF Offering) and then the role of hired service provider (once a VNF Agreement is established), at the same time that the Infrastructure Provider plays the roles of target customer and service customer. In Fig. 2, the Infrastructure Provider is the one that offers the service (see VNF Deployment Offering), hence playing the role of UFO-S service provider and then the role of hired service provider (once a VNF Deployment Agreement is established). Meanwhile, in the context of this last figure, the Developer plays the role of target customer and service customer. Moreover, our reference model shows two collectives based on UFO-S target customer community (namely, the Infrastructure Provider Target Community and the Developers Target Community), two relators based on UFO-S service offering (i.e. VNF Offering and VNF Deployment Offering), and other two relators based on UFO-S service agreement (i.e. VNF Agreement and VNF Deployment Agreement).

4 Implementation and Validation of the Reference Model

The Marketplace Reference Model proposed in the previous section has been developed according to domain-specific knowledge elicited from (and validated by) experts of the High Performance Networks Group of the University of Bristol. Besides that, the reference model has been implemented in the Description Logics SHROIQ (OWL) and verified using Protégé. Moreover, the derivation rules and integrity constraints complementing the model have been specified using SWRL rules (Horn Logic). Then, the ontology has been populated with instances. This allowed for the verification of *logical consistency* and *satisfiability* of the model.

With this implemented version of the model in Protégé, once the reasoner is turned on, some extra information is inferred about the individuals, based on the implemented SWRL rules. For supporting the Marketplace's functionalities, it is important to know, for instance, what VNF type a particular VNF Deployment Agreement agrees to deploy; and what are the possible Deployment Costs (related to the VNF Deployment Offering) associated to a specific VNF. This information (among other) may not be known by the way the Reference Model's concepts are directly related, thus requiring the creation of SWRL rules that enable such information inference based on the navigation of several concepts and relations.

Besides this formal verification, the model has been *validated* via visual simulation discussed in [7]. This strategy allows for systematically analyzing the mode instances generated by the simulator in contrast with the set of intended instances of the model developers. If the simulator generates unintended instances, it is necessary to constrain the model to avoid them; and, on the other hand, if some intended instances are missing, we need to verify if there are existing constraints that should be relaxed to allow for them. To employ this strategy, we have used the Alloy simulator of the OntoUML model-based

editor [5]. Such simulator takes as input the OntoUML model and a set of OCL restrictions, generating as output the instances of the developed model.

Finally, an important validation is to understand if the model is able to adequately support the class of applications for which it was created, in our case, VNF Marketplaces. Figure 3 shows a screenshot of a proof of concept that we developed for a VNF Marketplace. The prototype was implemented with basis on the proposed reference model, which was taken as an analysis model to help shape the developed interface, functionalities and knowledge base. In this case, the implemented ontology was not used, since, as a design decision, we favored a widely popular architecture for single-page web applications, known as the MERN (MongoDB, Express, React, Node.js) stack. MongoDB is an open-source NoSQL database, which allows us to store data about the marketplace (e.g. available VNFs, NSs, infrastructure providers, etc.). Express and Node.js are being used in the server side of the marketplace, particularly to implement a RESTful API to persist and query application data stored in MongoDB. Lastly, we used React - a well known Javascript library developed by Facebook - to build the graphical user interface of the marketplace.

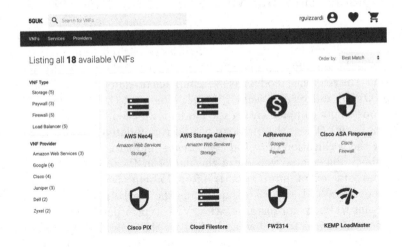

Fig. 3. Screenshot of the proof of concept homepage

5   Related Works

In the past few years, there have been a couple of initiatives proposing VNF Marketplaces in the sense discussed in this article. D'Oro, Palazzo, and Schembra [2] propose a VNF Marketplace to enable customers behaving as third-party sellers with their hardware and software resources providing VNFaaS (Virtual Network Functions as a Service). The paper describes the marketplace's architecture and propose a mathematical model to regulate the network flows. Xilouris et al. [9]

describe the T-Nova approach, which includes a VNF marketplace to enable buying, composing, and deploying "virtual" services on the fly. In that paper, the authors describe some VNFs they have developed and how they may be combined with the assistance of the marketplace. Moreover, they discuss about VNF Lifecycles, Monitoring and Networking.

These works, however, despite discussing architectural and implementation aspects of VNF marketplaces, do not propose an explicit *reference model* for this domain. In fact, despite the recent interest in conceptual models in the area of computer networks (e.g., [1]), to the best of our knowledge, the proposal presented here is the first explicit, reusable, ontology-grounded Reference Conceptual Model for VNF marketplaces. We also highlight that, in both these existing works in the literature, the focus is on *scalability* issues, while our proposed reference model targets the marketplace *business model*. In particular, we do that by demonstrating that Network Services are indeed Services, in the sense of the term employed in Service Science and related areas, i.e., in a sense that takes service to be more than mere *behavior* (service delivery) and function (the expected outcome of service delivery. Instead, this view essentially involves aspects such as *Service Offering* and *Service Agreement*. As such, besides these functional aspects, our model addresses the multiple aspects of contractual relationship management that are needed to make such a marketplace work. This is done here by systematically reusing the central pattern of the UFO-S Core Ontology of Services.

6   Conclusions

This paper presents a Reference Conceptual Model to support the development of a VNF Marketplace to enable VNF vendors, and infrastructure providers to commercialize VNFaaS. The proposed model has been developed using a well-founded approach for modeling, verifying, validating and implementing ontology-driven conceptual models. We believe that this model not only offers a solution to the immediate problem at hand, but it also contributes to demonstrate the practical usefulness of conceptual modeling techniques in the domain of Network Services and Functions.

Our proposed conceptual model mainly focuses on Service Design and Deployment via the appropriate configuration (binding) of VNFs and VNF types. As such, the model ignores the infrastructure providers' deployment capacity. In a future version of this model (and its DL implementation), we should address this aspect, thus improving its reasoning capabilities for supporting network orchestration and management.

Acknowledgments. This work was supported by the EPSRC grant EP/L020009/1: Towards Ultimate Convergence of All Networks (TOUCAN).

References

1. Barcelos, P.P.F., et al.: On the importance of truly ontological distinctions for standardizations: a case study in the domain of telecommunications. Comput. Stan. Interfaces **44**, 28–41 (2016)
2. D'Oro, S., et al.: Orchestrating softwarized networks with a marketplace approach. In: Proceedings of the 14th MobiSPC)/12th FNC/Workshop, Leuven (2017)
3. de Almeida Falbo, R., Barcellos, M.P., Nardi, J.C., Guizzardi, G.: Organizing ontology design patterns as ontology pattern languages. In: Cimiano, P., Corcho, O., Presutti, V., Hollink, L., Rudolph, S. (eds.) ESWC 2013. LNCS, vol. 7882, pp. 61–75. Springer, Heidelberg (2013). https://doi.org/10.1007/978-3-642-38288-8_5
4. Gkounis, D., et al.: Towards sustainable end-to-end multi-domain orchestration of softwarized 5g networks (forthcoming). IEEE Commun. Mag. Spec. Issue Future Internet: Archit. Protoc. (2018)
5. Guerson, J., et al.: OntoUML lightweight editor: a model-based environment to build, evaluate and implement reference ontologies. In: IEEE 19th EDOC Workshops. IEEE (2015)
6. Guizzardi, G.: Ontological foundations for structural conceptual models. CTIT, Centre for Telematics and Information Technology (2005)
7. Guizzardi, G.: Ontological patterns, anti-patterns and pattern languages for next-generation conceptual modeling. In: Yu, E., Dobbie, G., Jarke, M., Purao, S. (eds.) ER 2014. LNCS, vol. 8824, pp. 13–27. Springer, Cham (2014). https://doi.org/10.1007/978-3-319-12206-9_2
8. Nardi, J.C., et al.: A commitment-based reference ontology for services. Inf. Syst. **54**, 263–288 (2015)
9. Xilouris, G., et al.: T-NOVA: a marketplace for virtualized network functions. In: Proceedings of the EuCNC 2014, Bologna (2014)

Intuitive Understanding
of Domain-Specific Modeling Languages:
Proposition and Application
of an Evaluation Technique

Dominik Bork[✉], Christine Schrüffer, and Dimitris Karagiannis

Faculty of Computer Science, University of Vienna,
Waehringer Street 29, 1090 Vienna, Austria
dominik.bork@univie.ac.at

Abstract. For correct utilization of a modeling language and comprehension of a conceptual model, the graphical representation, i.e.,
the notation, is of paramount importance. A graphical notation, especially for domain-specific languages, should be aligned to the knowledge,
beliefs, and expectations of the intended model users. More concretely,
the notation of a modeling language should support computational
offloading for the human user by increasing perceptual processing (i.e.,
seeing) and reducing cognitive processing (i.e., thinking and understanding). Consequently, method engineers should design intuitively understandable notations. However, there is a lack of support in evaluating
the intuitiveness of a notation. This paper proposes an empirical evaluation technique for bridging that research gap. The technique comprises
three independent experiments: term association, notation association,
and case study. Usefulness of the technique is shown by an exemplary
evaluation of a business continuity management modeling language.

Keywords: Conceptual modeling · Domain-specific modeling ·
Modeling language · Notation · Evaluation · Business continuity
management

1 Introduction

Due to their abstracting power, conceptual models are excellent in decreasing
complexity of a system under study, thereby highlighting its relevant aspects for
means of understanding and communication by human beings [21]. In order to
achieve this ambitious goal, the demand for intuitively understandable graphical notations advances, consequently asking to fill a research gap of specialized
design and evaluation techniques [8,9]. This affects both, "standard" modeling
languages (see [4,5,7]) and domain-specific modeling languages (DSMLs).

For efficient model-based communication, the notation plays an important
role [6,21] as it establishes the *"first contact of the users with the modeling language"* [7, p. 123] and a first precondition for its adoption and correct usage [4].

© Springer Nature Switzerland AG 2019
A. H. F. Laender et al. (Eds.): ER 2019, LNCS 11788, pp. 311–319, 2019.
https://doi.org/10.1007/978-3-030-33223-5_26

A notation should thus support the modeler in creating and the user in interpreting a model. An *intuitive* notation should moreover account for *computational offloading*, i.e., shifting some of the *cognitive tasks* to *perceptual tasks* [18] which ultimately leads to an intuitive understanding of a modeling language [17]. Intuitivity refers to *Semantic Transparency* as proposed in [18], i.e., the extent to which the graphical representation encodes the meaning of a modeling language concept. Intuitiveness is also referred to by *readability* - models are represented *"in a natural way and can be easily understood without the need for further explanations"* [2, p. 214], *pragmatic quality* - *"correspondence between the model and the audience's interpretation of the model"* [14, p. 94], or *understandability* - *"the ease with which the concepts and structures in the [..] model can be understood by the users of the model"* [20].

Evaluation of modeling languages is very subjective and difficult [11,16,19]. *"While the finished product (the software system) can be evaluated against the specification, a conceptual model can only be evaluated against people's (tacit) needs, desires and expectations"* [19, p. 245]. The difficulty further increases when focusing on intuitive understanding. We believe intuitive understanding can only be evaluated when the user's knowledge, beliefs, and aptitudes are known - a prerequisite for designing a DSML. Another open issue emerges when combining method chunks in situational method engineering [10] to select one or integrate existing notations. Consequently, our research question was: *"How to efficiently evaluate the intuitiveness of a domain-specific modeling language notation?"*

This paper builds upon the foundations of conceptual modeling and visualization (Sect. 2) and proceeds by proposing a new evaluation technique in Sect. 3. Section 4 then reports on an exemplary application of the technique. Eventually, Sect. 5 provides conclusions and directions for future research.

2 Foundations

Domain-Specific Conceptual Modeling. A conceptual modeling method comprises [12]: A *modeling language*, a *modeling procedure*, and *mechanisms & algorithms*. The modeling language encompasses the language syntax, i.e., the grammar of the language; the language semantics, i.e., the meaning of the language concepts; and the language notation (also referred to as concrete syntax), i.e., the visual representation of the language. Based on the application, general-purpose modeling languages (GPMLs) like BPMN and UML can be differentiated from DSMLs as e.g., realized within the OMiLAB [3,13]. Evaluating the intuitiveness of GPML notations is problematic because of the diverse stakeholders involved and their modeling purposes addressed with such languages. When designing a new DSML, on the other hand, evaluating intuitiveness becomes feasible because the potential users and their purposes of using the DSML are part of the design process [8]. Thus, DSML method engineers should respect domain-specificity not only in the syntax but also in an intuitive notation.

Visual Aspects in Conceptual Modeling. [22] developed a decoding theory considering humans as information processing entities. Information processing

can be divided into: *Perceptual Processing (seeing)* which is fast and automatic, and *Cognitive Processing (understanding)* which is slow and resource-intensive. Diagrams aim for *computational offloading* by replacing some cognitive tasks by perceptual ones. The objective of designing cognitive effective notations thus needs to be to reduce cognitive processing. Similarly, [18, p. 761] states *"Designing cognitively effective visual notations can [..] be seen as a problem of optimizing them for processing by the human mind"*.

In conceptual modeling, an intuitive visual representation is vital for acceptance and adoption of the modeling method [7, p. 123]. *"The extent to which diagrams exploit perceptual processing largely explains differences in their effectiveness"* [18, p. 761] (see also [15,23]). A comprehensive foundation for empirical research on conceptual modeling notations was proposed by Daniel Moody's impactful Physics of Notation [18]. Moody developed nine design principles for designing cognitive effective notations. The motivation for his research was that *"cognitive effectiveness of visual notations is one of the most widely held (and infrequently challenged) assumptions in the IT field. However, cognitive effectiveness is not an intrinsic property of visual representations but something that must be designed into them"* [18, p. 757].

Semantic Transparency. The semantic transparency design principle is defined as *"the extent to which the meaning of a symbol can be inferred from its appearance"* [18, p. 765]. In literature, semantic transparency is often considered synonymous to an intuitive understanding, i.e., novice users having no training on a modeling language are capable of intuitively deriving the meaning of the language elements from looking at their notation [18]. A notation with a high semantic transparency moves cognitive processing toward perceptual processing as users can infer the meaning of a symbol/model from their working and/or long term memory. Consequently, method engineers should design semantically transparent (mnemonic) visual notations.

3 An Evaluation Technique for Notation Intuitiveness

A new evaluation technique assessing the intuitiveness of modeling language notations is proposed in the following. The technique builds upon participatory design [24] while aiming to be efficiently customized and utilized by method engineers. The evaluation technique's core consists of three sequential phases, each of which conducting a specific experiment with participants. The core phases are preceded by an *initiation* and concluded by a *conclusion* phase (see Fig. 1).

Initiation Phase. Participants are briefly introduced to the domain and the building blocks of the modeling method to be evaluated. This primarily concerns the definition of the relevant domain terms and an introduction to the individual model types of the modeling method (if more than one model type is given). This introduction needs to be textually or orally, i.e., without showing any visual aspects like language concepts or sample models. Moreover, useful information for analyzing the results of the experiments like demographics and previous experience in modeling and the domain to be addressed is collected.

Fig. 1. Procedure of the evaluation technique

Phase 1 – Term Association Experiment. Participants are provided terms that refer to names of modeling language concepts. Each participant then individually drafts one or more graphical representations for each term he/she deems most intuitive. For this task, participants are provided blank papers that only list the terms and coloured pencils for the sketches. As a conductor of this experiment, one needs to classify the returned notation drafts into groups of similar graphics with respect to the *most frequent shapes and colors*. Comparing the gained drafts with the current modeling language notation might identify inadequacies and point to potential improvements.

Phase 2 – Notation Association Experiment. Participants are presented notations of the current modeling language. They are then asked to record their up to three intuitive associations that pop out when looking at the notations. It is important to note, that participants are only presented the notation without any hint of e.g., the name or the semantics of this concept. As a conductor of this experiment, one needs to classify all responses to measure the percentage of participants that intuitively associated the correct semantics to a provided notation. If one of the named terms of one participant matches with the true name or semantics of the concept, the notation is classified *identified*. For instance, if one of the named terms for a class 'Recovery activity' of one participant is 'recovery activity' or 'rollback activity', the notation is correctly identified. In the case that one of the named terms nearly fits the semantics, it is categorized as *partially identified*. In the example of a class 'Recovery activity', the terms 'task' or 'recovery measure' nearly fit to the true semantics. If none of the provided terms expresses the semantics, the notation is classified as *not identified*.

Phase 3 – Case Study Experiment. The case study should be as focused and short as necessary to test whether participants are able to intuitively combine the modeling language concepts in order to solve the presented case. It should be textually introduced and participants shall be provided a modeling tool if applicable. As a conductor of this experiment, one needs to classify the provided models according to their semantic and syntactic correctness. Three error categories are distinguished: *application error*, considers a wrong application of a concept or a wrong definition of a concept property; *procedural error*, covers a wrong sequence of concepts and a wrong/missing application of a relation; and *incomplete model*, covers missing concepts or missing properties of a concept.

Concluding Phase. The conductor presents the solution of the case study before the participants are asked to fill out a feedback survey. The survey covers the *Intuitivity of the notations* and optionally also the *Usability of the modeling*

tool (not in scope of this paper). Eventually, participants are asked to provide positive and negative feedback, and improvement suggestions e.g., using post-its.

4   Application of the Evaluation Technique

This section describes an application of the technique to a DSML for business continuity management (BCM) which is under development in the scope of an international research project. BCM is defined as a *"holistic management process that is used to ensure that operations continue and that products and services are delivered at predefined levels"* [1]. It includes the identification of possible risks of regular business processes and of processes which handle the consequences of an occurred risk. The evaluation aimed to assess the intuitiveness of the graphical notation of the first version of the BCM modeling language.

In total, 15 information science Master students participated in the evaluation. Most participants are male (87%), between 25 and 29 years old, and are in the second semester of their Masters. The initiating survey showed, that the participants have solid experience with modeling and meta-modeling, fundamental experience with business process modeling, and no experience in risk management and business continuity management.

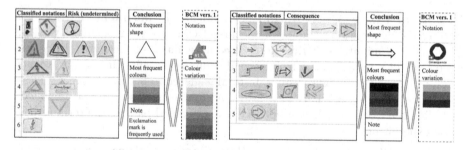

Fig. 2. Term Association experiment results for Risk (undetermined) and Consequence

Results of Phase 1: Term Association Experiment. Participants were provided ten concepts of the BCM modeling language. Within ten minutes, they were asked to draft a notation for each term that they deemed most intuitive. Figure 2 summarizes the classification of the results for the term *Risk (undetermined)* on the left side. The most frequent shape is a triangle and the most frequently used colours are red shades. Furthermore, it can be stated that exclamation marks are frequently used. By comparing these results with the notation realized in version 1 of BCM, it can be concluded that the notation is already intuitive.

Figure 2 (right) summarizes the term association experiment results for the concept *Consequence*. It can be derived, that in most classes an arrow is used whereas the colours vary. By comparing these results it can be concluded, that

shape and colours are different. Therefore, the notation in BCM version 1 is categorized as not intuitive, requiring a major revision for this concept.

Figure 3 classifies excerpts of the results of the term association experiment using a traffic light system. The green light (left circle) indicates that the association is correct, the yellow light (middle circle) that the association is partially correct, and the red light (right circle) that the association is not correct. From the ten concepts tested in total, five associations were correct, four were partially correct, and one was not correct (the concept Consequence).

Element	Term Association	Notation Association	Overall Match
Risk (undetermined)	●○○	●○○	●○○
Risk Trigger	○●○	○○●	○○●
Likelihood	○●○	●○○	●○○
Consequence	○○●	○○●	○○●
Recovery Activity	●○○	○●○	○●○
Other Resource		○○●	○○●
Update Button		○○●	○○●

Fig. 3. Excerpt of term association and notation association experiments results (Color figure online)

Results of Phase 2 – Notation Association Experiment. Participants were given 15 notation samples of the first BCM modeling language version. They had ten minutes to write up to three most intuitive meanings they associate to a given notation. Figure 3 (second column) classifies the gained insights again using the traffic light system. In total, eight concepts were correctly identified, four concepts partially identified, and four concepts were not identified, including the Consequence concept that already failed passing the term association experiment.

Results of Phase 3 – Case Study Experiment. Participants were asked to create five BCM models. For ensuring the test is focusing intuitiveness, a time limit was set. Based on a pre-test with a novice modeler, we decided to give participants 30 minutes to create all five models. The analysis of the models resulted in the following observations: Most errors are *application errors* that are twice as many as *procedural errors* or issues of *incomplete models*. Twenty-two of the thirty-one errors are due to a wrong application of a concept which can be explained by the misunderstood notation of the Risk Trigger or the misunderstood relation between a Risk Trigger and a Risk. Interestingly, while the Consequence notation was not identified in the first two evaluation experiments, it was used correctly in every created model of all participants.

5   Lessons Learned, Implications and Conclusions

The concluding feedback session included a survey and a focus group discussion. Participants proposed to develop new gateways especially for the risk model of

BCM which differ from BPMN gateways. Furthermore, it was mentioned that the allocation of the likelihood was not intuitive. Figure 3 (right column) summarizes an excerpt of the results of the term and notation association experiments. If both experiments categorized a concept in the same colour of the traffic lights, the concept is overall also categorized with this colour. The risk trigger is categorized red since it was not identified ten times in the notation association experiment. The participants applied different colours by drawing the notation of a likelihood, but nevertheless, twelve of fifteen participants correctly identified the likelihood notation. Figure 4 exemplifies how the experiments' led to more intuitive notations.

Fig. 4. Revised notations for four BCM modeling language concepts

By involving the participants in co-creating and evaluating the notation it was possible to improve the first version of the BCM modeling language with respect to its intuitive understanding. A limitation of this research is related to the generalizability of the findings. First, the participants were Master students and not the actual users in the domain. It can be assumed however, that domain experts would produce even better suggestions for improvement. A further limitation targets the limited number of participants (15) and the single application with one modeling language (BCM). However, even under these conditions, the technique proved utility and produced notation improvements.

The technique proposed in this paper targets the empirical evaluation of the intuitiveness of a modeling language notation. Strengths of the technique are its technology-independence and language-customizability enabling efficient adoption. In our future research we plan to apply the technique to further modeling languages and to develop a web-based evaluation environment which enables method engineers to efficiently set-up the experiments for their languages.

Acknowledgment. This research has been partly funded through the Federal Ministry of Education, Science and Research (BMBWF) funded France/Austria Joint Scientific and Technological Cooperation program with the project number FR 01/2019.

References

1. Plain English ISO 22301 2012 Business Continuity Definitions. http://www.praxiom.com/iso-22301-definitions.htm. Accessed 27 July 2019
2. Batini, C., Ceri, S., Navathe, S.B., et al.: Conceptual Database Design: An Entity-Relationship Approach, vol. 116. Benjamin/Cummings, Redwood City (1992)

3. Bork, D., Buchmann, R.A., Karagiannis, D., Lee, M., Miron, E.T.: An open platform for modeling method conceptualization: the OMiLAB digital ecosystem. Commun. Assoc. Inf. Syst. **44**, 673–697 (2019)
4. Bork, D., Karagiannis, D., Pittl, B.: Systematic analysis and evaluation of visual conceptual modeling language notations. In: 2018 12th International Conference on Research Challenges in Information Science (RCIS), pp. 1–11. IEEE (2018)
5. Bork, D., Karagiannis, D., Pittl, B.: A survey of modeling language specification techniques. Inf. Syst. **87**, 101425 (2019)
6. Caire, P., Genon, N., Heymans, P., Moody, D.L.: Visual notation design 2.0: towards user comprehensible requirements engineering notations. In: 21st IEEE International Requirements Engineering Conference (RE), pp. 115–124. IEEE (2013)
7. El Kouhen, A., Gherbi, A., Dumoulin, C., Khendek, F.: On the semantic transparency of visual notations: experiments with UML. In: Fischer, J., Scheidgen, M., Schieferdecker, I., Reed, R. (eds.) SDL 2015. LNCS, vol. 9369, pp. 122–137. Springer, Cham (2015). https://doi.org/10.1007/978-3-319-24912-4_10
8. Frank, U.: Domain-specific modeling languages: requirements analysis and design guidelines. In: Reinhartz-Berger, I., Sturm, A., Clark, T., Cohen, S., Bettin, J. (eds.) Domain Engineering, pp. 133–157. Springer, Heidelberg (2013). https://doi.org/10.1007/978-3-642-36654-3_6
9. Gulden, J., van der Linden, D., Aysolmaz, B.: A research agenda on visualizations in information systems engineering. In: 11th International Conference on Evaluation of Novel Software Approaches to Software Engineering, pp. 234–240 (2016)
10. Henderson-Sellers, B., Ralyté, J.: Situational method engineering: state-of-the-art review. J. Univers. Comput. Sci. **16**, 424–478 (2010)
11. Izquierdo, J.L.C., Cabot, J.: Collaboro: a collaborative (meta) modeling tool. PeerJ Comput. Sci. **2**, e84 (2016)
12. Karagiannis, D., Kühn, H.: Metamodelling platforms. In: Third International Conference on E-Commerce and Web Technologies, EC-Web 2002, p. 182 (2002)
13. Karagiannis, D., Mayr, H.C., Mylopoulos, J. (eds.): Domain-Specific Conceptual Modeling, Concepts, Methods and Tools. Springer, Cham (2016). https://doi.org/10.1007/978-3-319-39417-6
14. Krogstie, J., Sindre, G., Jørgensen, H.: Process models representing knowledge for action: a revised quality framework. Eur. J. Inf. Syst. **15**(1), 91–102 (2006)
15. Larkin, J.H., Simon, H.A.: Why a diagram is (sometimes) worth ten thousand words. Cogn. Sci. **11**(1), 65–100 (1987)
16. Lindland, O.I., Sindre, G., Solvberg, A.: Understanding quality in conceptual modeling. IEEE Softw. **11**(2), 42–49 (1994)
17. Michael, J., Mayr, H.C.: Intuitive understanding of a modeling language. In: Australasian Computer Science Week Multiconference, p. 35. ACM (2017)
18. Moody, D.: The 'physics' of notations: toward a scientific basis for constructing visual notations in software engineering. IEEE Trans. Softw. Eng. **35**(6), 756–779 (2009)
19. Moody, D.L.: Theoretical and practical issues in evaluating the quality of conceptual models: current state and future directions. Data Knowl. Eng. **55**(3), 243–276 (2005)
20. Moody, D.L., Shanks, G.G.: What makes a good data model? Evaluating the quality of entity relationship models. In: Loucopoulos, P. (ed.) ER 1994. LNCS, vol. 881, pp. 94–111. Springer, Heidelberg (1994). https://doi.org/10.1007/3-540-58786-1_75

21. Mylopoulos, J.: Conceptual modelling and Telos. In: Conceptual Modelling, Databases, and CASE: an Integrated View of Information System Development, pp. 49–68. Wiley , New York (1992)
22. Newell, A., Simon, H.A.: Human Problem Solving, vol. 104. Prentice-Hall, Englewood Cliffs (1972)
23. Petre, M.: Why looking isn't always seeing: readership skills and graphical programming. Commun. ACM **38**(6), 33–44 (1995)
24. Recker, J.: Opportunities and constraints: the current struggle with BPMN. Bus. Process. Manag. J. **16**(1), 181–201 (2010)

Domain Specific Models II

A Unifying Model of Legal Smart Contracts

Jan Ladleif[(✉)] and Mathias Weske

Hasso Plattner Institute, University of Potsdam, Potsdam, Germany
{jan.ladleif,mathias.weske}@hpi.de

Abstract. Legal smart contracts have been a subject of research for decades, especially since the fusion of deontic logic with traditional programming poses significant challenges. The issue of how to develop and verify legal smart contracts is growing in importance, not least due to the rapid adoption of blockchain-based smart contracts. In this paper, we want to pave the way towards a model-driven approach at legal smart contract development. To this end, we combine insights from literature in law and legal informatics with capabilities of existing modeling approaches and give a unifying model that encapsulates essential components of legal smart contracts. The unifying model may be used as a reference for language designers aiming at a holistic representation of legal smart contracts in a model-driven architecture. It may further serve as a basis for comparing existing modeling frameworks, which we demonstrate by applying it to a set of eight distinct languages.

Keywords: Smart contracts · Conceptual model · Legal contracts

1 Introduction

The advent of blockchain technology has established smart contracts in the general mainstream. Presented with a global network enabling general-purpose smart contract execution capabilities and an unprecedented capitalization, developers are confronted with entirely new challenges. An often-cited example in this context is the TheDAO bug, in which a programming error was exploited to extract around USD 60 million from a smart contract in 2016 [19]. Thus, the newfound ubiquity of smart contracts calls for a discussion on how the modeling community can use years of experience in model-driven architecture and software design to facilitate a structured development of secure smart contracts, opening the doors for formal verification and dissemination.

This issue becomes even more pronounced when considering the long-term implications of smart contract technology in law and governance. Fusing legal concepts and smart contracts to form legal smart contracts as an enforceable replacement of traditional contract prose and its fulfillment poses a variety of conceptual and technical challenges [5]. One of these is the absence of a widely adopted formal language for designing legal smart contracts that is "simple and

© Springer Nature Switzerland AG 2019
A. H. F. Laender et al. (Eds.): ER 2019, LNCS 11788, pp. 323–337, 2019.
https://doi.org/10.1007/978-3-030-33223-5_27

natural to use, to such an extent that a lawyer could draft contracts using this formalism instead of using traditional legal language" [2].

The issue goes beyond a mere formalization of real-life contract documents, which has been a topic of ongoing research for several decades spawning an impressive amount of approaches [3,17,28]. Instead, a formalization can only be the first step. The core question is how contracts will be drafted in the future, and whether a layer of abstraction can be devised that is suitable for all stakeholders to appreciate—from attorneys through government officials to regular customers.

In this paper, we want to pave the way towards a model-driven design of legal smart contracts by providing a unifying model of their components and respective interplay. The model provides a basis for novel language developments, as well as a baseline for an objective comparison and evaluation of existing approaches. To this end, we give an overview of legal smart contract research and formalizations, based on which we reason about our model. We demonstrate the utility of the unifying model by comparing a set of eight existing language proposals and raise concrete challenges for future research. It is not the goal of this paper to give an exhaustive analysis of all issues regarding smart contracts in practice, e.g., attack vectors or identity management.

The paper is structured as follows: in Sect. 2 we provide background information on the formalization of legal contracts. In Sect. 3, we introduce a number of different modeling languages for contracts. We then present our unifying model of legal smart contracts in Sect. 4, before applying it to the languages discussed before in Sect. 5. We conclude the paper in Sect. 6.

2   Formalizing Legal Contracts

For the remainder of this paper, we will use a stock option contract as an example: An employer might give an employee the opportunity to buy shares in the company at a specific price. The price is only valid until a particular expiration date, though. If the employee does not exercise the option and buy the stock within the receipt of the option and its expiration date, the option expires. In legal terms, this agreement is an example of an American-style call option and one of the most common types of contracts in the financial domain [11].

2.1   Smart Contract Templates

The idea of electronic contracting with smart contracts dates back decades before blockchains or distributed ledgers were devised [17,27]. Smart contracts rely on at least two observations, namely (i) that the validity of real-world contracts can be secured via cryptographic methods and (ii) that they contain operational aspects which can be automated by computers. Based on these observations, Grigg introduced the concept of the *Ricardian contract* in an early electronic payment system [7]. Basically, a Ricardian contract is a text file that is cryptographically signed by a legal issuer and expresses some value to its holders.

The Ricardian contract was further developed to form *Ricardian triples*, which recognize that legal contracts can be roughly divided into three components [2]. They contain clauses describing explicit procedures and actions; the operational parts of the contract automatable via *code*. Some clauses are not immediately automatable, often because they are ambiguous and require interpretation or are intangible in nature, e.g., concepts like rights, obligations and permissions. These constitute the non-operational parts of the contract which are represented as *legal prose*. On top of that, contracts contain *parameters* that are negotiated between all parties, e.g., prices or deadlines.

Figure 1 shows the typical structure of the resulting so-called smart contract template— legal prose and code exist alongside each other and are interlinked. They are both refined by parameters containing concrete agreement details. This concept was picked up by CommonAccord[1], a global initiative towards "codifying and automating legal documents" [9]. It is also used by some blockchain platforms like Corda R3, which allows the deployment of smart contracts that have parametrized legal prose attached to them [10].

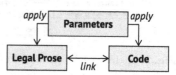

Fig. 1. A smart contract template with the components of the Ricardian triple

Regarding traditional legal prose expressed in natural language as a separate but integral part of the smart contract may be seen as an anachronism, though. In fact, Clack et al. foresee that a common source language may be developed that expresses code and legal prose at the same time [2]. This would require a formal representation of concepts rooted in law, such as creating obligations and liberties or transferring entitlements, all of which must be related to the operational aspects of a contract. For this reason, research has also been focused on formalizing legal prose and relations.

2.2 Formalizing Legal Relations

Legal prose is anchored in deontic logic and contains normative concepts such as permissions, obligations and prohibitions. There are numerous approaches to formalizing subsets of deontic logic capturing institutional and legal domains, such as the seminal institutional grammar (ADICO) of Crawford and Ostrom [3]. More recently, Pace and Schneider developed a language for composing and arguing about deontic notions [25]. However, these approaches do not explicitly model parties and relations between parties, which are integral to contracts.

Thus, several approaches founded in ontology modeling have been proposed. For example, Kabilan and Johannesson contribute a multi-tier ontology framework modeling contract knowledge for the semantic web [15]. Contracts are modeled on three different layers using Unified Modeling Language (UML) class diagrams, from an upper-level view of contract terms down to a template view with limited support for performance and enforcement concepts.

---

[1] http://www.commonaccord.org/, accessed April 10th, 2019.

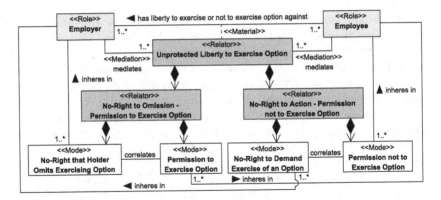

Fig. 2. Reduced UFO-L model of a snapshot legal state in the stock option example contract: after signing, the employee has the unprotected liberty to exercise the option

Griffo et al. present an approach that is more focused on legal relations [6]. They develop an extension to the Unified Foundational Ontology (UFO) called Unified Foundational Ontology for Legal Relations (UFO-L), embracing both standard deontic notions as well as complex legal relators like liberties.

Figure 2 shows an instance of UFO-L representing a simplified view of legal relations between employer and employee in the stock option example. The stock option is modeled as an unprotected liberty of the employee to exercise the option against the employer. In essence, the complex liberty relator is composed of two simple relators, which specify that (i) the employee has the permission to exercise the option, and the employer must not stop them from doing so; and that (ii) the employee has the permission not to exercise the option, and the employer must not demand otherwise. This example shows how simple contracts can already entail complex and non-obvious legal relations.

Additionally, there are open-textured terms in legal prose such as "without delay" that are still difficult to capture precisely [5]. Their actual meaning depends on the jurisdiction the contracts are supposed to comply with, as regional laws and customs might differ. These kinds of modifiers governing the final interpretation of legal relationships are sometimes called meta-rules and need to be considered for fully specified formalizations [16].

3   Contract Modeling Languages

Existing formalizations of contracts are often based in logic. For example, Lee was among the first to use first-order predicate logic to express actions, deadlines, and deontics in his seminal paper on a logic model for e-contracting [17]. The Legalese project[2] is an example for a more recent effort to create a

---

[2] https://legalese.com/, accessed April 10th, 2019.

Domain-Specific Language (DSL) targeting the modal μ-calculus. For an extensive survey of formal languages and models for contracts we refer to Hvitved, who provides a categorization and analysis of several contract languages [12]. Most of these languages use a textual or formulaic concrete syntax for contract specification.

Hazard and Haapio, on the other hand, advocate for a more visual approach to contract modeling, referring to a general trend in law to augment legal prose with figures and clearer structuring [9]. This goes well with the model-driven software development paradigm, in which graphical representations of models are already commonly used on different levels of abstraction to break down complex systems into easily understandable diagrams and shapes. These models have the potential to fully specify legal smart contracts while "not [alienating] the lawyer" [16]. As a consequence, we will limit this section to research that has already been done towards a visual formalization of smart contracts, which largely operates on similar principal components as textual approaches albeit already generalized to a much higher level of abstraction.

Table 1. Selection of modeling approaches in the (smart) contract area

Cat.	Abbr.	Approach	Underlying formalism
(a)	MAV	Mavridou and Laszka (FSolidM) [20]	Finite state machine
	AND	Andrychowicz et al. [1]	Timed automaton
	FLO	Flood and Goodenough [4]	Deterministic finite automaton
(b)	WEB	Weber et al. [29]	BPMN choreography/process
	LOP	López-Pintado et al. (Caterpillar) [18]	BPMN process
	KA1	Kabilan [14]	BPMN collaboration
(c)	KA2	Kabilan and Johannesson [15]	UML class diagram
	REI	Reitwiessner (Babbage) [26]	—

Table 1 shows the approaches to contract modeling we discuss in this paper. They were identified after a review of research literature, development communities and online articles. Our requirements for choosing a language were that it (i) uses a completely or partially graphical notation, and that (ii) the overall approach is applied to legal contract modeling or smart contract modeling, i.e., not necessarily targeting legal applications, in the specific publication. The scope and maturity of the selected approaches varies considerably, from mere concepts up to fully integrated development solutions.

It should be noted that our selection is not meant to be a comprehensive list of all graphical modeling languages for contracts. Especially in the area of blockchain-based smart contracts, many visualization approaches have been explored for various modeling paradigms [13], not all of which are present in our selection. Nevertheless, we believe that we cover a wide range of declarative and imperative approaches with different focuses. We categorize the approaches into three groups: (a) automaton-based, (b) business processes and (c) other

languages. For space reasons, we can not go into detail on each approach, but will summarize their capabilities in Sect. 5.2.

Automaton-Based (a). The first three approaches rely on the observation that contracts have a concept of state, which determines the set of actions that may be performed. An example can be seen in Fig. 3, showing a Finite State Machine (FSM) modeling the stock option example contract using the notation proposed by Mavridou and Laszka [20]. From an initial state ("the agreement has been made"), the employee may fire a transition triggering the exercise of the option if it has not expired yet. Otherwise, only the expire transition may be fired, though it is not specified by whom. The actual smart contract code implementation of the **underlying** function (encapsulating the stock transfer) and the definition of **expiry** need to be available in the context of the model.

All three approaches share some similarities: A contract model has a set of (potentially complex) states, which are connected using edges with temporal and evaluative conditions. The roles within a contract are not represented directly, but through low-level or natural language annotations—or, in case of the timed-automaton approach, through the use of one automaton per role [1]. They especially seem to focus on reachability or complexity analysis of contracts rather than providing a clear and complete visualization for all stakeholders.

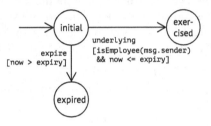

Fig. 3. FSM representing the stock option contract example (syntax from [20])

Business Processes (b). Business Process Model and Notation (BPMN) is an industry-standard modeling framework for business processes, collaborations and choreographies [23]. Conformance, institutional rules and norms as well as inter-organizational communication and agreements are common themes. Thus, the domain lends itself particularly well to smart contracts, which was recognized in a community-wide position paper [21]. Kabilan puts a focus on legal obligations, and extends BPMN elements with a multi-tier contract knowledge ontology (see Sect. 2.2) [14,15]. Weber et al. use BPMN choreography diagrams, laying a bigger focus on inter-organizational communication in the course of business contracts [29]. López-Pintado et al., on the other hand, use BPMN process diagrams with a similar notation [18].

Figure 4 shows an example of a generic BPMN choreography diagram modeling the stock option example. The choice of the employee to exercise the option is modeled by an event-based gateway with a choreography task. The expiration date is included as a timer intermediate catch event. The terms of the actual contract are hidden inside a collapsed sub-choreography named 'underlying'.

Other Languages (c). In their specification of a contract knowledge ontology (see Sect. 2.2), Kabilan and Johannesson also present a method of modeling smart contract templates as UML class diagrams [15]. Legal concepts and activ-

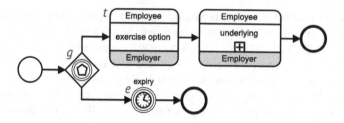

Fig. 4. BPMN choreography diagram representing the stock option contract example

ities (performances) are represented as classes and directly interrelated using associations, giving preconditions and fulfillment triggers.

Finally, Reitwiessner introduces his own notation for modeling smart contracts grounded in blueprints of actual physical machines [26]. Basically, currency flows are represented using pipes triggered by valves and actuators that may "fill up" tanks of currency. By looking at the blueprint of the machine, users are supposed to grasp the flow of currency and the different control flow options more intuitively. As of writing this paper, Babbage is just a proposal and has not spawned any further implementation or research efforts.

4   Unifying Legal Smart Contract Modeling

While the trend of e-contracting is gaining traction, the issue of comprehensively modeling legal smart contracts in a way that is understandable both for humans as well as machines for enforcement and verification remains unsolved [2,9,25]. An initial obstacle is the lack of a common understanding about which contract aspects should be natively reflected in legal smart contract modeling languages. To this end, we develop a unifying model of legal smart contracts that unifies all the essential requirements identified to date. We hope that this model can be used as a reference for evaluating novel language proposals, and give the framework for objective and holistic language comparisons.

4.1   General Reasoning

As a structural basis for our model, we adopt the idea of smart contract templates (see Sect. 2.1) due to its versatility and the fact that various smart contract realizations already use similar structures successfully [10], albeit mostly lacking the legal prose component [30]. We share the view of Clack et al. that there are two sides to a contract: the operational as well as the non-operational side [2].

For both of these sides, we compiled requirements from various sources. These include but are not limited to a discussion on the sequencing and causality of deontic concepts by Pace and Schneider [25]; a proposal on the codification of legal prose in a machine and human-readable way by Hazard and Haapio [9]; as well as an analysis on the legal interpretation and suitability of declarative and imperative contract specifications for blockchains by Governatori et al. [5].

We drew further inspiration from existing modeling approaches (see Sect. 3) and collected a set of unique capabilities such as the strong ties to legal states in two approaches (KA1 [14], KA2 [15]). Lastly, we considered the 16 requirements Hvitved used in his survey of formal languages and models for contracts [12].

For the non-operational aspects, we considered multiple legal ontologies (see Sect. 2.2) [6]. However, they are often limited in that they have no concept of algorithmic execution and the passing of time. Every UFO-L instance, for example, rather represents a snapshot of the legal relations valid at a concrete point in time, without any explicit notion of modeled behavior. Hence, it is not sufficient to provide a singular UFO-L instance for each smart contract to transform it to a legal smart contract. The temporal evolution of legal relations through actions has to be a native component of a formalism [17].

Therefore, we adopt a conceptual approach closely related to the logic model of contracts proposed by Lee [17]. The legal state of the contract is a snapshot of some set of legal relations between a number of entities, which in turn enable some actions. Figure 5 illustrates this understanding of a mutual interplay between actions and legal states using a Petri net modeling the stock option example contract. Places and transitions represent legal states and actions, respectively. Thus, actions may be performed subject to a legal state, transitioning to a new legal state in a well-defined manner.

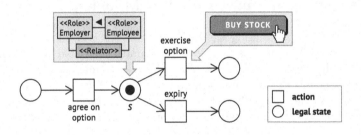

Fig. 5. Interplay of legal states with actions

For example, the place s in the Petri net might represent the legal state of the stock option example pictured in Fig. 2. This enables two actions; (i) the employee may exercise the option if it has not expired yet and (ii) the stock option may automatically expire. Note that we do not distinguish between so-called "happy paths" and reparation/exception paths in our model, as they both rely on the same principles [25].

4.2   Unifying Model of Legal Smart Contracts

Based on the above reasoning, we compiled an overarching unifying model of legal smart contracts as specified in the form of a UML class diagram in Fig. 6. The main artifact is a Smart Contract, which contains sets of Legal States, Actions, Roles, and Data Sources. We also adopt the notion of Meta-Rules as mentioned

by Khalil et al. [16]. A Meta-Rule could be any piece of legislation or regulation which eventually governs the performance of the contract (see Sect. 2.2).

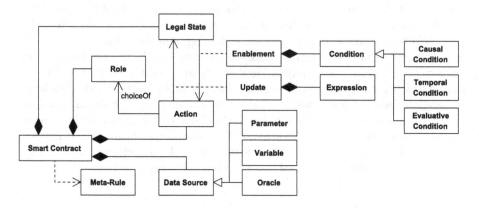

Fig. 6. A unifying model of legal smart contracts

DataSources are specialized into Parameters, Variables and Oracles. Parameters represent parameters negotiated for each contract instance, e.g., the price of stocks in an option. Concrete Parameter instance values may vary in complexity, from simple integer numbers to higher-order functions. Variables are custom runtime state variables similar to parameters, but are not negotiated beforehand and may be set and changed during runtime. An Oracle could be an online service (e.g., providing currency exchange rates), or an event trigger reacting to external events (e.g., a government entity initiating an audit).

Roles specify the number and types of participants in a contract, e.g., the employee and employer similar to their specification in UFO-L (see Sect. 2.2). Roles may refer to humans, but also to organizations or other entities. A Legal State represents a snapshot of the legal relations between the Roles which held at a specific point in time and enable a set of Actions.

Actions in our case refer to any activity that may occur during the execution of a contract. An Action is either performed by one or more Roles, or considered to be autonomous (e.g., the expiration of the stock option). Performing an Action leads to an updated Legal State with the consequences of the Action applied. For example, exercising a stock option (Action) is the choice of the employee (Role) and would lead to a Legal State in which the option may not be exercised again.

Conditions and Expressions refine the interplay between Actions and Legal States. For instance, a stock option might have an expiration date. In this case, allowing the option to expire (an Action without involvement of a Role) would be enabled on the Temporal Condition that the expiration date has been reached. More generally, Temporal Conditions may refer to relative or absolute timers, contingent on a common understanding of time of all participants. Evaluative Conditions may refer to different Data Sources to decide on enablement, e.g., by evaluating the value of Variables using a formal expression. Causal Conditions can

be used to enforce an ordering of Actions, and rely on the history of the legal smart contract. Updates can be refined as well by providing a set of Expressions applied to the resulting Legal State, for example calculating a currency exchange with current data from an Oracle or processing some input given to the Action.

The concrete specification and shape of all classes is deliberately left undefined. We do not aim to impose specific technologies or formalisms on the modeler, but give a predominantly structural view to enable the investigation of different realizations. For example, Legal States could be represented by UFO-L instances, whereas Actions could be defined via BPMN process models. Similarly, there might be formalisms which manage to combine Legal States and Actions into a common language, inching closer to the vision of a single admissible source language by Clack et al. [2]. Additionally, we do not specifically constraint references between classes, e.g., a Legal State will probably reference some or all Roles, while a Condition will need access to Data Sources.

5   Applying the Unifying Model

One goal of our unifying model is to provide a common conceptual understanding of legal smart contracts, so as to mutually compare existing modeling languages. In this section, we want to critically evaluate this goal by applying our unifying model to the languages presented in Sect. 3. It is important to note that the approaches heavily differ in their objectives, markup and degree of formalization. Despite some of them not directly considering legal issues, the evaluation provides valuable insights as to future challenges in legal smart contract modeling.

5.1   Results

Table 2 shows the results of our comparison. All approaches were assessed with regards to our unifying model. A checkmark implies that the approach contains some native modeling element that supports (parts of) the respective aspect. A bracketed checkmark means a partially formal support for the feature through

Table 2. Results of the comparison of the graphical approaches

		roles	data sources			legal states	meta-rules	actions	conditions			expr.	code gen.
			par.	var.	ora.				temp.	eval.	caus.		
automaton-based	MAV	(✓)		(✓)				state transitions	✓	(✓)	✓	(✓)	Solidity
	AND	✓		(✓)				state transitions	✓	(✓)	✓	(✓)	-
	FLO					(✓)	(✓)	state transitions	(✓)		✓		-
business processes	WEB	✓		(✓)	✓			tasks		(✓)	✓	(✓)	Solidity
	LOP	✓		(✓)	✓			tasks		(✓)	✓	(✓)	Solidity
	KA1	✓				✓		tasks	✓		✓		-
other languages	KA2	✓	✓			✓		classes	✓		✓		-
	REI	(✓)						currency flows			✓		-

platform-specific code or natural language annotations. Admittedly, the distinction between native and annotated support involves a degree of estimation.

For example, the FSM approach (MAV [20]) supports the definition of roles through the annotation of platform-specific authentication code (see Fig. 3), whereas BPMN choreography diagrams (WEB [29]) natively model roles through participant bands (see Fig. 4). Note that the assessments made are based on the (claimed) current state of the approach as laid out in the respective publications. Not reflecting a certain part of our unifying model does not mean that the underlying formalism is generally incapable of doing so. For example, BPMN has native support for temporal conditions through timer events, but two approaches (WEB [29], LOP [18]) do not allow their usage for implementation reasons. Further, the degree to which a feature is supported may vary considerably due to the heterogeneity of the approaches, which we attempted to counteract by introducing the two layers of support (native and annotated).

5.2   Discussion

Our results show that support for the conceptual aspects of legal smart contracts is a mixed bag—whereas some enjoy almost universal support, some are largely absent. A good example for the former are actions; they are integral parts of all approaches. Actions are represented through various modeling elements, like transitions/flows, tasks or classes. All languages except one (FLO [4]) provide some support for defining roles. Conditions also enjoy a relatively high level of adoption; especially causal conditions are present in all approaches due to their capability to model orderings of states and actions. Temporal and evaluative conditions are, to some degree, present in around half of the approaches.

On the other hand, some areas seem to be largely missing. Only one language (KA2 [15]) provides support for parameters in the sense of our unifying model, i.e., as characteristic parts of a contract instance that are negotiated between all parties and fixed at contract "signing" or instantiation. Some other approaches emulate this behavior with the specification of variables that are set during runtime using, for example, human tasks with manual inputs (WEB [29]). There appears to be a lack of distinction between parameters and variables despite their conceptual differences. Oracles are only supported by two of the BPMN approaches (WEB [29], LOP [18]) through service and script tasks.

As is apparent from our comparison, evaluative conditions and expressions are only ever present as annotations, i.e., formulas in a possibly platform-specific expression language. These formulas tend to require a solid knowledge of programming concepts such as boolean operators, which can not be expected from non-technical personnel. Languages such as Decision Model and Notation (DMN) decision tables might provide a visual and intuitive alternative for modeling formulas, though complex decisions also require an expression language [24]. Decision tables have been shown to be convertible to smart contract code [8].

Perhaps the most complex parts of contracts are the legal relations they create (see Sect. 2.2). Two approaches model legal relations as a native part of the contract model; either through annotations of ontology-based references to

message flows in BPMN (KA1 [14]), or through fully integrated instances of ontology concepts in a UML class diagram (KA2 [15]). Lastly, one approach (FLO [4]) uses natural language annotations to specify obligations and other deontic notions. In general, though, legal relations are largely absent as explicitly modeled concepts, i.e., dedicated modeling elements or annotations. The same is true for meta-rules, which only one approach (FLO [4]) hints at by referencing concrete New York state laws within natural language annotations.

5.3 Future Challenges

Summarizing the results of the application of the unifying model, we identify six major future challenges in the area of legal smart contract modeling.

Modeling Data Sources. When different parties collaborate on fulfilling a contract, it is of paramount importance that all data used in that process is known and understandable by all participants. There needs to be a common view on the values of data artifacts and, perhaps more importantly, their meaning and semantics. While the structural and semantic modeling of data is a fundamental and well-researched concept in areas such as business choreographies [22], it is mostly missing in contract modeling and the legal smart contract languages we evaluated. Thus, we conclude that (C1) formal definitions of data sources and structures, and (C2) clear distinctions between the different kinds of data sources are essential challenges for future modeling approaches.

Implementing Executable Contracts. While visualization and communication between stakeholders are important goals of model-driven software design, the final intent is to generate a fully executable artifact. Of the evaluated modeling approaches, only three (MAV [20], WEB [29], LOP [18]) explicitly cover this step, providing a generator component for Ethereum smart contracts and discussing the implications of blockchain characteristics such as immutability and transaction cost (see Table 2) [30]. However, the generated smart contracts are limited by constraints of blockchain technology such as the lack of support for native timed triggers in Ethereum. Hence, even though two BPMN-based approaches (WEB [29], LOP [18]) would technically support temporal conditions through timer events, they are omitted due to the aforementioned restrictions.

Thus, more advanced or novel smart contract realizations might be needed. Still, for a legal smart contract modeling language to gain practical importance, it needs to (C3) be founded in clear and complete execution semantics which are (C4) mapped to some actual realization of smart contract technology that enables the enforcement of the contract.

Embedding Legal Relations. To improve support for legal aspects, we assess that (C5) there needs to be a common framework of meta-rules which can be uniquely referenced and (C6) legal states need to be embedded with roles, conditions, expressions and associated with actions directly in the model. Only then can a language be considered a universally acceptable replacement for traditional legal contracts [2]. The embedding of legal states might be accomplished with

(a) native modeling elements or (b) a set of rigorously defined deduction rules founded in a formal framework of legal relations.

The proposal to introduce deduction rules is based on the insight that deontic notions may be deduced from other modeling elements without being explicitly present. Take, for example, the BPMN choreography diagram from Fig. 4 and refer to the legal relations found in the UFO-L instance in Fig. 2. The event-based gateway g models the exclusive choice of the employee to exercise the stock option using task t. The gateway g in conjunction with task t thus implies the no-right to omission relator—the employee has the permission to exercise the option. The second part of the unprotected liberty relator, namely the no-right to action relator, may be deduced from the timer event; i.e., the existence of an alternative path that does not include the exercise of the option. The modes inherent to the employer are technically implied by the closed-world assumption of the modeling paradigm. Other concrete representations of behavioral models and legal relations may exhibit similar mappings.

6   Conclusion

The increasing degree of automation in legal domains calls for a structured and formal modeling approach for legal smart contracts. In this paper, we have developed a unifying model defining the essential components of fully specified legal smart contracts based on literature from law, legal informatics and blockchain research. We also introduced the reader to a set of eight existing modeling languages, and demonstrated how the unifying model can be used as a basis for a holistic comparison of the languages' expressiveness. Our results show that the degree of support for specific legal smart contract concepts varies considerably; ranging from good support for condition modeling to almost non-existing support for legal states, relations or deontic notions. Based on these results, we posed concrete challenges for future endeavors in unambiguously and fully specifying legal smart contracts.

References

1. Andrychowicz, M., Dziembowski, S., Malinowski, D., Mazurek, Ł.: Modeling bitcoin contracts by timed automata. In: Legay, A., Bozga, M. (eds.) FORMATS 2014. LNCS, vol. 8711, pp. 7–22. Springer, Cham (2014). https://doi.org/10.1007/978-3-319-10512-3_2

2. Clack, C.D., Bakshi, V.A., Braine, L.: Smart contract templates: foundations, design landscape and research directions. CoRR **abs/1608.00771** (2016). http://arxiv.org/abs/1608.00771

3. Crawford, S.E.S., Ostrom, E.: A grammar of institutions. Am. Polit. Sci. Rev. **89**(3), 582–600 (1995)

4. Flood, M., Goodenough, O.: Contract as automaton: The computational representation of financial agreements. OFR Working Paper 15–04 (2015). https://doi.org/10.2139/ssrn.2538224

5. Governatori, G., Idelberger, F., Milosevic, Z., Riveret, R., Sartor, G., Xu, X.: On legal contracts, imperative and declarative smart contracts, and blockchain systems. Artif. Intell. Law **26**(4), 377–409 (2018). ISSN 1572-8382, https://doi.org/10.1007/s10506-018-9223-3

6. Griffo, C., Almeida, J.P.A., Guizzardi, G.: Conceptual modeling of legal relations. In: Trujillo, J., et al. (eds.) ER 2018. LNCS, vol. 11157, pp. 169–183. Springer, Cham (2018). https://doi.org/10.1007/978-3-030-00847-5_14

7. Grigg, I.: The Ricardian contract. In: First IEEE International Workshop on Electronic Contracting, pp. 25–31. IEEE (2004)

8. Haarmann, S., Batoulis, K., Nikaj, A., Weske, M.: DMN decision execution on the ethereum blockchain. In: Krogstie, J., Reijers, H.A. (eds.) CAiSE 2018. LNCS, vol. 10816, pp. 327–341. Springer, Cham (2018). https://doi.org/10.1007/978-3-319-91563-0_20

9. Hazard, J., Haapio, H.: Wise contracts: smart contracts that work for people and machines. In: Trends and Communities of Legal Informatics, 20th International Legal Informatics Symposium IRIS 2017, pp. 425–432 (2017)

10. Hearn, M.: Corda: a distributed ledger. Technical White Paper (2016). https://docs.corda.net/_static/corda-technical-whitepaper.pdf

11. Hull, J.: Options, Futures and Other Derivatives. Pearson/Prentice Hall, Upper Saddle River (2009)

12. Hvitved, T.: Contract formalisation and modular implementation of domain-specific languages. Ph.D. thesis, University of Copenhagen (2012)

13. Härer, F., Fill, H.G.: A comparison of approaches for visualizing blockchains and smart contracts. Jusletter IT Weblaw, ISSN 1664-848X, 21 February 2019 (2019). https://doi.org/10.5281/zenodo.2585575

14. Kabilan, V.: Contract workflow model patterns using BPMN. In: 10th International Workshop on Exploring Modeling Methods in Systems Analysis and Design (EMMSAD 2005), CAiSE, vol. 363. CEUR-WS.org (2005)

15. Kabilan, V., Johannesson, P.: Semantic representation of contract knowledge using multi/tier ontology. In: First International Conference on Semantic Web and Databases, pp. 378–397. CEUR-WS.org (2003)

16. Al Khalil, F., Butler, T., O'Brien, L., Ceci, M.: Trust in smart contracts is a process, as well. In: Brenner, M., et al. (eds.) FC 2017. LNCS, vol. 10323, pp. 510–519. Springer, Cham (2017). https://doi.org/10.1007/978-3-319-70278-0_32

17. Lee, R.M.: A logic model for electronic contracting. Decis. Support Syst. **4**(1), 27–44 (1988). ISSN 0167-9236, https://doi.org/10.1016/0167-9236(88)90096-6

18. López-Pintado, O., García-Bañuelos, L., Dumas, M., Weber, I., Ponomarev, A.: Caterpillar: A business process execution engine on the Ethereum blockchain. CoRR **abs/1808.03517** (2018). http://arxiv.org/abs/abs/1808.03517

19. Luu, L., Chu, D.H., Olickel, H., Saxena, P., Hobor, A.: Making smart contracts smarter. In: Proceedings of the 2016 ACM SIGSAC Conference on Computer and Communications Security, pp. 254–269. ACM (2016)

20. Mavridou, A., Laszka, A.: Designing secure Ethereum smart contracts: A finite state machine based approach. CoRR **abs/1711.09327** (2017). http://arxiv.org/abs/abs/1711.09327

21. Mendling, J., Weber, I., Aalst, W.V.D., et al.: Blockchains for business process management - challenges and opportunities. ACM Trans. Manag. Inf. Syst. (TMIS) **9**(1), 4:1–4:16 (2018). ISSN 2158-656X, https://doi.org/10.1145/3183367

22. Meyer, A., et al.: Data perspective in process choreographies: modeling and execution. Technical report BPM-13-29, BPMcenter.org (2013)

23. OMG: Business Process Model and Notation (BPMN), Version 2.0.2, December 2013. http://www.omg.org/spec/BPMN/2.0.2/
24. OMG: Decision Model and Notation (DMN), Version 1.1, December 2016. https://www.omg.org/spec/DMN/1.1/
25. Pace, G.J., Schneider, G.: Challenges in the specification of full contracts. In: Leuschel, M., Wehrheim, H. (eds.) IFM 2009. LNCS, vol. 5423, pp. 292–306. Springer, Heidelberg (2009). https://doi.org/10.1007/978-3-642-00255-7_20
26. Reitwiessner, C.: Babbage – a mechanical smart contract language (2017). https://medium.com/@chriseth/babbage-5c8329ec5a0e
27. Szabo, N.: Formalizing and securing relationships on public networks. First Monday **2**(9) (1997). ISSN 13960466, https://doi.org/10.5210/fm.v2i9.548, https://ojphi.org/ojs/index.php/fm/article/view/548
28. Szabo, N.: A formal language for analyzing contracts (2002). https://nakamotoinstitute.org/contract-language/
29. Weber, I., Xu, X., Riveret, R., Governatori, G., Ponomarev, A., Mendling, J.: Untrusted business process monitoring and execution using blockchain. In: La Rosa, M., Loos, P., Pastor, O. (eds.) BPM 2016. LNCS, vol. 9850, pp. 329–347. Springer, Cham (2016). https://doi.org/10.1007/978-3-319-45348-4_19
30. Wood, G.: Ethereum: a secure decentralised generalised transaction ledger. Technical report EIP-150 (2014)

Formal Specification of Environmental Aspects of a Railway Interlocking System Based on a Conceptual Model

Dalay Israel de Almeida Pereira[1]([envelope]) [ID], Sana Debbech[1] [ID], Matthieu Perin[2] [ID], Philippe Bon[1], and Simon Collart-Dutilleul[1]

[1] Univ. Lille Nord de France, IFSTTAR, COSYS/ESTAS,
59650 Villeneuve d'Ascq, France
{dalay-israel.de-almeida-pereira,sana.debbech,philippe.bon,
simon.collart-dutilleul}@ifsttar.fr
[2] Institut de Recherche Technologique Railenium, 59300 Famars, France
matthieu.perin@railenium.eu

Abstract. Relay-based Railway Interlocking Systems (RIS) are developed with the objective of controlling the movement of trains in a safe manner. However, these systems are generally specified by informal languages whose analyses are made by human inspection, which are error prone. A previous work presented an approach for specifying these systems in a formal language in order to automatically prove safety properties. Nevertheless, despite the impact of the environment over the system operation, the approach allows only the specification of the electrical components behaviour. Hence, the environment must be considered in the system specification in order to guarantee its safety. This paper presents the application of a higher level of modelling abstraction, conceptual modelling, which may provide a conceptual clarification of the RIS environment. This proposed conceptual model allows a semantic analysis of the environmental impact over the system and the description of other safety properties that have not been considered in the formal specification. In this work, an ontology built for the critical systems modelling is used in order to provide a terminological harmonisation between the physical elements of the system and the environment. The conceptual model allows a safety-oriented improvement of the RIS formal specification as well as it provides a common, shared and unambiguous view of both system and environment.

Keywords: Conceptual modelling · Ontology ·
Railway Interlocking Systems · Relay diagrams · UFO · B-method

1 Introduction

Railway Interlocking Systems (RIS) are responsible for controlling trains in a determined track in order to avoid the occurrence of hazards, like collisions.

Supported by the LCHIP (Low Cost High Integrity Platform) project.

© Springer Nature Switzerland AG 2019
A. H. F. Laender et al. (Eds.): ER 2019, LNCS 11788, pp. 338–351, 2019.
https://doi.org/10.1007/978-3-030-33223-5_28

They are considered safety-critical systems, since failures may result in severe consequences like the loss of people lives. A relay-based RIS is the implementation of an interlocking system logic as an electrical circuit whose current flow is controlled by electromechanical components called relays. These systems are generally specified by diagrams representing how the electrical components of the circuit are connected. As a consequence, the safety proof of these systems is a challenging task, since the usual way to verify these models is by manually inspecting and drawing conclusions, which is error prone [10].

In order to automatically verify relay-based RIS, a previous work [2] has presented a methodology for the specification of these systems in a formal language, B-method, whose mathematical background and supporting tools allow the automatic system verification regarding safety properties. In this methodology, one may extract the system behaviour based on the behaviour of its electrical components. Although this methodology provides ways in order to verify the existence of unsafe states during the execution of the system, it fails in disconsider the impact of the environment on the behaviour of these systems. In order to prove the safety of a RIS, the environment must be considered.

The specification of physical electrical components is based on their own meanings and defined behaviours, whereas the environmental specification involves pure knowledge about the field. Furthermore, the impact of the environment over the system is not specified inside relay diagrams. In this work, an example of the conceptual modelling usage is presented in order to conceptualise relations between a RIS and its environment. The use of a conceptual model allows a better understanding of the domain knowledge and provides a shared view with a common vocabulary. Moreover, an improvement of the RIS formal specification may be derived from the captured knowledge. In the literature, conceptual modelling has never been used for assisting the RIS formal specification and creating a direct distinction between the RIS and their environments.

Another benefit of conceptual modelling consists in the use of a top-level ontology in order to provide a conceptualisation in real-world semantics and approximate as well as possible the ideal representation of a domain. In this paper, the conceptual modelling phase is based on the use of the Unified Foundational Ontology (UFO) [9] in order to establish relations between the foundational distinctions of UFO and the system and its environment dependencies. Then, the ontological pattern and the modelling rules proposed by UFO are used for building the ontology.

The next section presents the case study that is used throughout this paper. Then, Sect. 3 discuss about the ontology for modelling critical systems, followed by a presentation of the methodology for the formal specification of RIS. The contribution of this paper, the use of conceptual modelling for the environmental specification in a RIS example, is detailed in Sect. 5 and discussed in Sect. 6. Finally, a conclusion and some previous works are presented.

2   Case Study

Relay-based Railway Interlocking Systems are composed by electrical circuits containing relays, which are electromechanical switching elements comprised by electromagnets (coils) and contacts [15]. When electrified, a relay closes or opens its contacts in a way that it may control the flow of electrical current inside the circuit wires. Before their implementation, these systems are generally modelled by relay diagrams, which are graph-like schemata that present how the electrical components (relays and buttons, for instance) are connected by wires.

In order to exemplify the use of RIS, a simple railway track plan, presented in Fig. 1, depicts two train tracks. This specific track section is used to allow two trains to move in opposite directions without collisions. However, a dangerous situation may be found when a train that arrives at Control Area A must change to the other track because of problems on its own track. The possible collision with a train that comes from Control Area C requires the use of an interlocking system in order to control the movement of these trains. In this industrial example, the diagram presented in Fig. 2 represents a relay-based RIS diagram used by SNCF (the French National Railway Company) in order to control the entrance of trains in Control Area A.

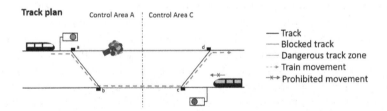

Fig. 1. Track plan from the signalling Control Area A to C

The connection between electrical components are represented by full lines in relay diagrams. These lines are the electrical wires of the circuits. The relation between the relays and their related contacts are represented by vertical semi-doted lines. A relay diagram may contain many different types of electrical components. Some of them are detailed in Table 1.

Relay-based RIS are reactive systems, which means that the electrical activation of a component may trigger the activation of others components. In electrical circuits, a component is activated if it is connected to a positive and a negative sources of energy at the same time. The inputs of this system are usually represented by buttons, levers and independent contacts (whose related relays are not presented). The outputs of these systems are generally understood as the permission or a denial to a train to enter in an specific section of the tracks. Considering the preconditions for each component to be activated and the connections between these components, relay diagrams are graphical representations of the logic behind relay-based RIS behaviour.

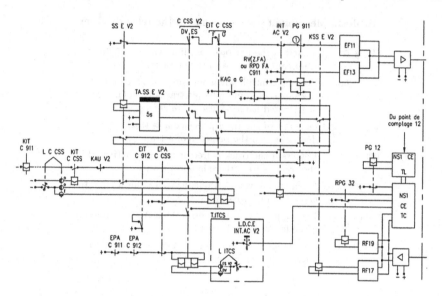

Fig. 2. Part of the relay-based system model of the signalling Control Area A

Table 1. Elements that may be used in a relay-based diagram.

─●─ ─ ─+─●─	Electrical sources of energy poles.
(ES V2 / DV symbol)	Couple button-lever.
(monostable / bistable coil symbols)	Monostable and bistable relays coils, respectively.
5s / 15s (block symbols)	Blocks for relay timed activation and deactivation, respectively.
(normally closed contact / bistable contact symbols)	A normally closed contact related to a monostable relay and a contact related to a bistable relay, respectively.

Due to the critical nature of this example, a thorough RIS safety analysis must be performed in order to avoid hazardous situations. For this purpose, the railway safety community recommends the use of formal specification methodologies [7]. However, although the formal languages mathematical background is capable of proving RIS safety properties, they do not dispose of tools for modelling, organising and harmonising knowledge together with the physical system.

As an example, based on the knowledge about railway systems, the meaning of some components depicted in Fig. 2 are presented in Table 2. However, the system knowledge is related to a high level of expertise of the domain, which may lead to conflicts between the actors. In the formal specification context, there is a lack of a distinction between both system and environmental aspects. This issue complicates the understanding of the formal specification, which may be ambiguous in a collaborative context. Consequently, the need of the knowledge

Table 2. Meaning of some elements of the relay diagram.

KAG a G	Switch in the left position, if activated (TRUE) the train cannot change to the other track
EPA C CSS	Routing control, when activated it allows a train to change its route (change tracks or not), when deactivated it blocks the route change
RPD FA C911	Detector of the train presence in a track, it deactivates in the presence of a train
INT AC V2	Detects if the track is free or not, it is activated if the track is free (there is not a train)
KSS E V2	Permission given by Control Area C for a train to come from Control Area A
EF11	Permission given by Control Area A for a train to come from Control Area C
KIT C 911	Permission for a train in the Control Area A to enter in the dangerous zone

conceptualisation arises in order to clarify and precise the terminology used in the specification.

In fact, we believe in the powerful capacities of the conceptual modelling to provide a shared and non ambiguous view with a common vocabulary. It allows the semantic interpretation of the components of the system, the environment, and relations between them in order to explicitly define a complete taxonomy able to ensure the conceptual clarification of the system and its environment with a high level of abstraction. Based on the definition of the relay diagram elements and the foundational features proposed by UFO, a semantic alignment is performed with the aim to establish an harmonisation between both abstract and concrete domains. In the next section, we briefly present an ontology of dysfunction analysis, which is proposed in a previous work, in order to explain how it is partially reused to satisfy the goal of the present study.

3 An Ontology for the Safe Design of Critical Systems

In order to provide a systematisation of the integration of the dysfunctional analysis into the design process, a domain ontology grounded in the Unified Foundational Ontology (UFO) is proposed in a previous work. It is well-known that the use of foundational ontologies in the development of a domain ontology supports the real-world semantics and improve the clarity, the expressiveness and the truthfulness of a domain conceptualisation. The discussion around the choice of UFO in comparison with other upper ontologies has been made in a previous work [5].

The Dysfunctional Analysis Ontology (DAO) aims to capture the dysfunctional analysis knowledge and it establishes a semantic link between safety constraints to be considered and the Goal-Oriented Requirements Engineering

(GORE) [17]. Furthermore, the related conceptual model improves the conceptual clarification of the safety reasoning and the management of safety decisions in the early stages of the safety critical systems design. Then, it allows an understandable representation of a domain in order to deal with the complexity of the collaborative decision-making.

DAO tackles the semantic heterogeneity issue that may lead to several conflicts between safety analysts and design engineers. The related terminology is based on the extraction of standards definitions such as [4,11,12] since the railway domain is the domain application of DAO. Moreover, the goal-oriented perspective is based on the reuse of a fragment from a reference domain model, the Goal-Oriented Requirements Ontology (GORO), which is grounded in UFO [14]. This improves the completeness, the consistency and the flexibility criterion of DAO. Hence, it supports the communication and the knowledge sharing between both safety and design actors.

In the verification and the validation phases, DAO shows its capabilities to represent several real situations and its taxonomy is relevant for the critical aspect of railway systems. Furthermore, it demonstrates the validity of its reuse for other critical applications such as the development of future autonomous trains [6]. Indeed, DAO considers the socio-technical aspect of railway systems and this is important in the safety improvement. Then, it considers both the safety and the system views in the safety analysis and the system design. This perspective of conceptualisation is relevant for the system specification too, since it support the integration of the environmental properties.

In the present paper, the DAO fragment related to the system and the environment views is reused in order to provide an ontological analysis of the environmental aspect and to capture this knowledge regarding the system specification. This phase seems to be a preliminary activity of the formal specification in order to terminologically systematise the environment notion and its surrounding concepts. One of the issues of formal methods consists in the inability to define the real-world taxonomy with a common vocabulary. In other words, there is a need to clarify the semantics used in the specification based on real-world assumptions and from a high level of abstraction. The present work aims to fill this gap by capitalising and sharing the knowledge in order to satisfy the domain needs. In order to improve the understanding of the DAO scope, Fig. 3 depicts a part of the design pattern of DAO, that is able to address the challenges mentioned above.

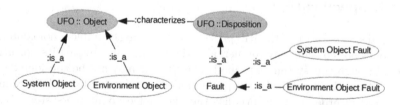

Fig. 3. A part of the DAO design pattern reusable for the relay-based RIS representation

4   A Methodology for the Formal Relay-Based RIS Specification

In order to formally specify the running example, a methodology has been proposed in a previous work [2]. This methodology uses B-method in order to specify the relay diagram logical behaviour based on propositional logic. In the railway domain, B-method is considered one of the strongest approaches for the specification of railway systems [8]. This section presents a methodology for the formal specification of Relay-based RIS using B-method.

The basic building block of a B-method specification is the abstract machine [16]. Inside a machine, the system specification is divided into clauses, like: SETS, VARIABLES, INVARIANT, INITIALISATION and OPERATIONS. Within these clauses, one must specify, respectively, constant information sets, variables, variables properties, the machine initial state (variables initial values), and the operations responsible for changing the machine state. An example of a B-machine is depicted on Fig. 7, explained in detail in Sect. 5.2. Further information about the B-method clauses and notations may be found in [1].

As the RIS state is defined by the state of each electrical component, the running example components must be specified as variables in B-method. Hence, the INVARIANT and INITIALISATION clauses must type each variable and give their initial states, respectively. Some particular types may be defined in the SETS clause, and the initial state of the system is the one represented by the relay diagram itself. Furthermore, inside the INVARIANT clause it is possible to define safety properties that must be met during the system execution. The complete B-specification of the running example is presented in [2], moreover, disconsidering the grey blocks, Fig. 7 also presents this specification.

Considering our running example, in order to avoid possible train collisions, it is possible to specify an invariant in propositional logic. This invariant guarantees that the trains that come from Control Area A and C may never have permission to enter in the dangerous zone at the same time. This property is defined by: "not (PLUS_KIT_C_911 = TRUE & EF11 = TRUE)". The system state transition must be specified by an operation which receives the inputs of the system and changes the values of the variables. This operation calculates the states based on the preconditions for the activation/deactivation of each electrical component.

5   From Conceptual Modelling Towards Environmental RIS Specification

The formal specification of the RIS presented as running example is not complete, since it does not consider environmental variables that may impact its execution. Hence, although this system is formally specified, it may not be considered safe. In this section, the process of conceptual modelling the relay-based RIS example is presented in order to conceptualise the knowledge about the system. Based on this conceptual model, it is possible to structurally capitalise the relation between the system and the environment and formally specify it.

5.1   Conceptual Model of a Relay-Based RIS Case Study

Before modelling the RIS environment, it is necessary to conceptualise the dependence between the electrical components of the system. This dependency reflects how the state of each component may affect the state of other component as a reactive system, i.e., the impact of a component activation/deactivation in the activation/deactivation of other components. This dependency is depicted in the conceptual model presented in Fig. 4.

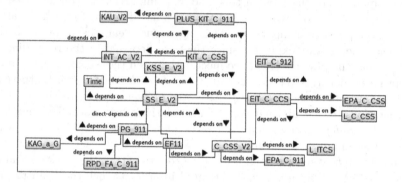

Fig. 4. Conceptual model of the state dependency between the electrical components of the system

However, in real world, some environmental variables may affect the functioning of the system. In this case, the environment is considered as any object/aspect that is external to the system and related to it in some way. In our case study, the environmental objects/aspects related to the execution of the relay-based RIS are: **track**, **train**, **pedal** (which detects the train presence) and **time** (or the variation of time). The conceptualisation of these environmental variables is presented in Fig. 5. In order to improve the readability, concepts and relations are respectively written in bold and italic types.

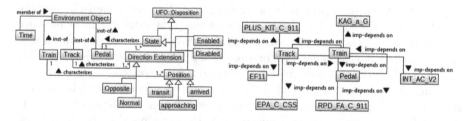

Fig. 5. Conceptual model of the system environment and dependencies between objects

Train, **Track** and **Pedal** may be characterised by their **Dispositions**, which are respectively related to **Position**, **Direction of extension** and **State**. Considering the RIS in Control Area A, a train may be in one of three positions:

"approaching", "in transit" (entering the dangerous zone) or "arrived" (in the dangerous zone). The track between the Control Areas A and C may be extended in two different directions: normal (for the train the comes from Control Area C) or opposite direction (for the train that comes from Control Area A). The Pedal existing in the dangerous zone may be enabled or disabled in order to indicate the presence or absence of a train in this specific location.

Based on the domain knowledge, it is possible to make an explicit representation of the relations between these environmental variables and the electrical components of the RIS. In this case, it is important to consider that the relations associated to environmental variables are different from the relations that connect physical components. The dependence relationship between electrical components are "explicit", since they are depicted in the relay diagram and represent the physical logical connection between these components. In this conceptual model, this relation is called *exp-depends on*. Contrarily, the environmental objects are not explicitly connected or even represented in usual RIS representations, hence, all their dependence relations are modelled as "implicit" and called *imp-depends on*. Figure 5 depicts a part of the complete model which captures these implicit relations.

A condition that must be guaranteed in order to extend the tracks is that the component EPA_C_CSS must be deactivated in order to lock the train routing. The train may not enter in a track if there is the possibility of changing its route during this process. So, the extension of the tracks depends directly of the component EPA_C_CSS state. The extension of the track is also directly related to the permission for the trains to enter in the tracks, so, the state of the track depends on the states of PLUS_KIT_C_911 and EF11.

Regarding the train, its state is directly related to the state of two physical components: KAG_a_G and INT_AC_V2. The former specifies that the switch between tracks is settled to the right position (train not allowed to change tracks) when activated, hence it must be deactivated when the train is "in transit". The latter indicates the occupation of the dangerous zone, hence it must be activated once the train has arrived in this portion of the tracks.

The track and the train are dependent to each other, since a train needs the track to be extended in order to enter in the dangerous zone and the track requires the train to approach in order to extend. Similarly, the train and the pedal are also dependent from each other since the pedal activates in the presence of a train and the train may be considered as "arrived" once the pedal activates. In order to activate the pedal, the component RPD_FA_C_911, which is responsible for the detection of the train presence, must also be activated.

Similarly to what is presented in Fig. 5, the conceptual model fragment related to the instantiation of the physical components is depicted in Fig. 6. After adding the environmental information, the conceptual model of the system is enriched. This step is important to provide a complete and structured view of the system and its environment. Based on the conceptual model representing the relations between the environment and the relay-based RIS, it is possible to improve the formal specification of the system by specifying extra conditions in order to prove the safety of the system.

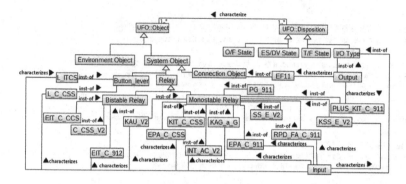

Fig. 6. Conceptual model representing the physical components instantiation

5.2 Formal Specification of Environmental Aspects of the RIS Case Study

Considering the running example B-specification, in order to add more information about the system, it is necessary to redefine the content of each clause. Except for time, which has been already defined as an input of the system in [2], the environmental variables must be defined in the **VARIABLES** clause of the specification, since their states are now considered in the system state. The updated specification is presented in Fig. 7, where all the added information are depicted in blue and inside grey blocks.

Instead of specifying the track as a unique variable, we opted by specifying it in two different variables according to its direction of extension. This may be explained by the fact that the conditions for the extension in each direction are unique and not related to each other. However, the possibility of extension in both directions at the same time may never exist. Hence, this condition must be verified and guaranteed by the invariant "not(track_extension_OD = TRUE & track_extension_ND = TRUE)", considering "track_extension_OD" and "track_extension_ND" the boolean variables related to the opposite and normal direction extensions of the tracks. This invariant may substitute the verification related to the permission to the trains to enter in the dangerous zone, since the extension of the tracks already includes this permission.

The train may be specified by an unique variable train_OD, which may take the values **approaching**, **in_transit** or **arrived**, indicating the position of the train that comes in the opposite direction. These states are specified in the **SETS** clause of the machine. Regarding the pedal, it is specified as a boolean variable, since it may assume only two states: activated (**TRUE**) or deactivated (**FALSE**).

Although the system may give permissions to the train to move, it does not directly controls the train, hence, the train behaviour is independent of the interlocking system. Since the train states are not directly dependent of the system and as an environmental variable, its states may be evolved independently of the RIS and in parallel with it. So, an operation for the state evolution of the train must be created. Furthermore, the operation must consider that in order to

```
MACHINE itcs

SETS O_OU_F = {POS_O, POS_F}; DV_OU_ES = {POS_ES, POS_DV}, TRAIN = {approaching, in_transit, arrived}

VARIABLES KIT_C_CSS, SS_E_V2, TA_SS_E_V2, EIT_C_CSS, C_CSS_V2, PG_911, EF11, PLUS_KIT_C_911
track_extension_OD, track_extension_ND, train_OD, pedal_active

INVARIANT KIT_C_CSS : BOOL & SS_E_V2 : BOOL & TA_SS_E_V2 : BOOL & EIT_C_CSS : O_OU_F & C_CSS_V2 : DV_OU_ES &
PG_911 : BOOL & EF11 : BOOL & PLUS_KIT_C_911 : BOOL & not(track_extension_OD = TRUE & track_extension_ND = TRUE) &
track_extension_OD : BOOL & track_extension_ND : BOOL & train_OD : TRAIN & pedal_active : BOOL

INITIALISATION KIT_C_CSS := FALSE || SS_E_V2 := FALSE || EIT_C_CSS := POS_F || C_CSS_V2 := POS_DV || PG_911 := TRUE ||
TA_SS_E_V2 := FALSE || EF11 := FALSE || PLUS_KIT_C_911 := FALSE ||
track_extension_OD := FALSE || track_extension_ND := FALSE || train_OD := approche || pedal_active := FALSE

OPERATIONS

update_train =
SELECT track_extension_OD = TRUE & train_OD = approaching THEN CHOICE skip OR train_OD := in_transit END
WHEN train_OD = in_transit & pedal_active = TRUE THEN CHOICE skip OR train_OD := arrive END
END;

update_Point_C =
SELECT EF11 = TRUE THEN track_extension_ND :: BOOL
END

update_Point_A(L_C_CSS, INT_AC_V2, EPA_C_CSS, EIT_C_912, KAG_a_G, RPD_FA_C_911, L_ITCS, KAU_V2, KSS_E_V2,
EPA_C_911, TA_SS_E_V2_echue) =
PRE
L_C_CSS : O_OU_F & INT_AC_V2 : BOOL & EPA_C_CSS : BOOL & EIT_C_912 : BOOL & KAG_a_G : BOOL & RPD_FA_C_911 : BOOL &
L_ITCS : DV_OU_ES & KAU_V2 : BOOL & KSS_E_V2 : BOOL & EPA_C_911 : BOOL & TA_SS_E_V2_echue : BOOL
& (train_OD = arrive => INT_AC_V2 = FALSE) & (train_OD = in_transit & pedal_active = TRUE => INT_AC_V2 = TRUE)
& (train_OD = in_transit & RPD_FA_C_911 = FALSE => INT_AC_V2 = TRUE) & (train_OD = in_transit => KAG_a_G = FALSE)
& (train_OD = in_transit & EPA_C_CSS = TRUE => pedal_active = TRUE)
& (KSS_E_V2 = TRUE & TA_SS_E_V2_echue = TRUE & EF11 = FALSE => track_extension_ND = FALSE)

THEN
KIT_C_CSS, PLUS_KIT_C_911, EIT_C_CSS, PG_911, C_CSS_V2, EF11, TA_SS_E_V2, SS_E_V2, track_extension_OD, pedal_active :(
KIT_C_CSS : BOOL & PLUS_KIT_C_911 : BOOL & EIT_C_CSS : O_OU_F & PG_911 : BOOL & C_CSS_V2 : DV_OU_ES & EF11 : BOOL &

SS_E_V2 : BOOL & TA_SS_E_V2 : BOOL & track_extension_OD : BOOL & pedal_active : BOOL &
KIT_C_CSS = bool(SS_E_V2 = TRUE & EIT_C_CSS = POS_O & INT_AC_V2 = TRUE & L_C_CSS = POS_O) &
(...)
TA_SS_E_V2 = bool(SS_E_V2$0 = FALSE & (C_CSS_V2 = POS_ES & EIT_C_CSS = POS_O &
KSS_E_V2 = TRUE) & TA_SS_E_V2_echue = FALSE)
(not(train_OD = approaching & EPA_C_CSS = TRUE) => track_extension_OD = bool(track_extension_OD$0 = TRUE or PLUS_KIT_C_911 = TRUE)) &
(train_OD = approche & EPA_C_CSS = TRUE => track_extension_OD = FALSE) &

pedal_active = bool(pedale_activee$0 = TRUE or (train_OD = transit & RPD_FA_C_911 = FALSE)) )
END
END
```

Fig. 7. Specification improved by environmental aspects (Color figure online)

go from the "approaching" to the "in transit" state, the track must be extended. Following a similar logic, in order to go from the "in transit" to the "arrived" state, the pedal must be activated.

Another variable whose states are not controlled by the RIS at Control Area A is track_extension_ND. Even if Control Area A gives permission to a train to come from Control Area C, it does not extends the track in the normal direction, since this extension is only controlled by the system in Control Area C. So, it is necessary to create an operation for this independent behaviour.

Considering the conceptual model, the operation related to the state evolution of the system itself must be improved. In this case, many preconditions that relate the inputs and the environmental variables may be created. As an example, the component INT_AC_V2 must be always deactivated if the train has arrived, which indicates that this portion of the track is occupied. However, if

the train is still entering in this portion of the track (the train is "in transit" and the pedal is "activated"), INT_AC_V2 is still active, since it is giving permission to the train to enter. Hence, the same occurs if RPD_FA_C_911 is deactivated.

Many other conditions may also be considered. If the train is in transit, the switch between the tracks must continue set to the left position, which means that the component KAG_a_G must be set to FALSE. Furthermore, if the train is "in transit" and EPA_C_CSS is activated, the pedal must also be activated, since the course of the tracks may only be changed if the train has arrived.

Considering that Control Area A cannot control the track extension in the normal direction, a condition must be specified in order to guarantee that the track must not be extended when Control Area A aims to extend it in the opposite direction. This means that, in the moment which the train that comes from Control Area A receives the permission to enter in the dangerous zone, the track must not be extended in the normal way. Hence, if KSS_E_V2 is activated, the time of the block has passed and EF11 is deactivated, the extension in the normal way must be FALSE.

The system in Control Area A is responsible for evolving the state of two environmental variables: the track extension in the opposite way and the pedal activation. The track will be extended in the opposite direction if EPA_C_CSS is deactivated or if the train is already "in transit" or it has been "arrived". Furthermore, if the track is not already extended, the permission for a train to enter in the Control Area A must be given (PLUS_KIT_C_911 activated). Regarding the Pedal, if it is not already activated, it becomes TRUE if the train is "in transit" at the same time that it is detected in the track.

6   Discussion

The specification of the system may be model-checked and simulated by Prob [13] in order to guarantee that the execution of the system may never reach a dangerous state. The model-checking process took 7391 ms, verifying the 85,919 possible transitions between the 62 existing states in a 64 bits Intel(R) Core(TM) i7-7600U 2.80 GHz CPU with 16 Gb RAM and running the Windows 10 operating system in its professional version. The complete simulation of the system execution has shown to be accurate with reality.

The conceptual model related to the environmental aspects of the system allows the reasoning regarding the impact of the environment in the execution of the system. Hence, it is possible to describe many safety conditions that are not explicit in the relay diagram. In this work, the RIS running example presented was improved by adding safety conditions in order to guarantee that, for instance: a train may never enter in the dangerous zone if the course is not locked, the track is never extended in the opposite direction if the switch is set to the right position or that the track is not considered free if the train has arrived.

By adding these safety properties in the system specification, it is possible to improve the safety of the system, since the environmental impact may be verified and analysed. Furthermore, as a result of this work, it is possible to affirm that

the formal specification of a relay-based RIS based on a relay diagram is not enough for guaranteeing safety in some determined conditions. The specification of the knowledge about the system linked to a structured representation of this knowledge is an essential step in order to improve the safety of the railway interlocking system.

7   Conclusion

This paper presents an example of the application of conceptual modelling in order to improve the safety of a railway interlocking system formal specification. The use of a conceptual model allows the reasoning about the impact of environmental variables over the execution of the system. Hence, by using a structured representation of the railway system knowledge, it is possible to derive safety properties in order to improve the safety of the RIS specification.

As a result, the specification of a relay-based RIS that has been presented in a previous work could be improved in order to consider many safety properties that could not be considered before. As a conclusion, it is possible to affirm that the knowledge conceptualisation of the railway domain is essential for the formal specification of relay-based RIS, since relay diagrams do not present all the information about unsafe possible states.

In our near future agenda we aim to perform a dysfunctional analysis of the example presented in this work in order to study the impact of relay failures over the system behaviour by reusing DAO. As a physical component, a relay may fail and break, hence, this behaviour must also be considered in the specification of the system. Furthermore, we aim to automate the formal behavioural specification of relay diagrams based on a graph-like approach (as the one presented in [3]) linked to a complete conceptual model about the known dependence guidelines between the components, environment and inputs of these systems.

Acknowledgements. This work is supported by the LCHIP project and the results presented in this paper are a product of the studies made in this project.

We thank Clearsy LCHIP team for sharing their studies with us, in special, we thank David Deharbe for his availability in explaining their results about the formal specification of relay-based RIS. Besides, we also thank SNCF for providing and allowing us to publish the relay schema in this paper.

References

1. Abrial, J.R.: The B-book: Assigning Programs to Meanings. Cambridge University Press, New York (1996)
2. de Almeida Pereira, D.I., Deharbe, D., Perin, M., Bon, P.: B-specification of relay-based railway interlocking systems based on the propositional logic of the system state evolution. In: Collart-Dutilleul, S., Lecomte, T., Romanovsky, A. (eds.) RSS-Rail 2019. LNCS, vol. 11495, pp. 242–258. Springer, Cham (2019). https://doi.org/10.1007/978-3-030-18744-6_16

3. de Almeida Pereira, D.I., Perin, M., Bon, P., Collart-Dutilleul, S.: A framework for the formal specification of relay-based systems based on a b-method graph specification. Int. J. Comput. Electr. Eng. (IJCEE) **11**(1), 11–19 (2019)
4. CENELEC, NF EN 50129: Applications ferroviaires: Systèmes de signalisation, de télécommunication et de traitement - Systèmes électroniques de écurité pour la signalisation, Mai 2003
5. Debbech, S., Bon, P., Collart-Dutilleul, S.: Towards semantic interpretation of goal-oriented safety decisions based on foundational ontology. J. Comput. (JCP) **14**(4), 257–267 (2019)
6. Debbech, S., Collart-Dutilleul, S., Bon, P.: Cas d'étude de mission ferroviaire télé-opérée. Rapport de recherche, IFSTTAR - Institut Français des Sciences et Technologies des Transports, de l'Aménagement et des Réseaux, November 2018. https://hal.archives-ouvertes.fr/hal-02020997/1
7. Railway applications-communication, signalling and processing systems-software for railway control and protection systems. Std, European Committee for Electrotechnical Standardization (CENELEC), March 2001
8. Fantechi, A., Fokkink, W., Morzenti, A.: B-specification of relay-based railway interlocking systems based on the propositional logic of the system state evolution. In: Formal Methods for Industrial Critical Systems: A Survey of Applications, pp. 61–84 (2013)
9. Guizzardi, G., Wagner, G., Almeida, J.P.A., Guizzardi, R.S.: Towards ontological foundations for conceptual modeling: the unified foundational ontology (UFO) story. Appl. Ontol. **10**(3–4), 259–271 (2015)
10. Haxthausen, A.E., Le Bliguet, M., Kjær, A.A.: Modelling and verification of relay interlocking systems. In: Choppy, C., Sokolsky, O. (eds.) Monterey Workshop 2008. LNCS, vol. 6028, pp. 141–153. Springer, Heidelberg (2010). https://doi.org/10.1007/978-3-642-12566-9_8
11. IEEE, 1012: IEEE Standard for System, Software, and Hardware Verification and Validation (2016)
12. IEEE, 610.12: IEEE Standard Glossary of Software Engineering Terminology (1990)
13. Leuschel, M., Butler, M.: ProB: a model checker for B. In: Araki, K., Gnesi, S., Mandrioli, D. (eds.) FME 2003. LNCS, vol. 2805, pp. 855–874. Springer, Heidelberg (2003). https://doi.org/10.1007/978-3-540-45236-2_46
14. Negri, P.P., Souza, V.E.S., de Castro Leal, A.L., de Almeida Falbo, R., Guizzardi, G.: Towards an ontology of goal-oriented requirements. In: CIbSE, pp. 469–482 (2017)
15. Rétiveau, R.: La signalisation ferroviaire. Presse de l'école nationale des Ponts et Chaussées (1987)
16. Schneider, S.: The B-method: An Introduction. Palgrave, Basingstoke (2001)
17. Van Lamsweerde, A.: Goal-oriented requirements engineering: a guided tour. In: Proceedings of 5th IEEE International Symposium on Requirements Engineering (RE 2001), pp. 249–262. IEEE (2001)

From a Conceptual Model
to a Knowledge Graph for Genomic
Datasets

Anna Bernasconi[✉], Arif Canakoglu, and Stefano Ceri

Dipartimento di Elettronica, Informazione e Bioingegneria,
Politecnico di Milano, Milan, Italy
{anna.bernasconi,arif.canakoglu,stefano.ceri}@polimi.it

Abstract. Data access at genomic repositories is problematic, as data
is described by heterogeneous and hardly comparable metadata. We previously introduced a unified conceptual schema, collected metadata in a
single repository and provided classical search methods upon them. We
here propose a new paradigm to support semantic search of integrated
genomic metadata, based on the Genomic Knowledge Graph, a semantic graph of genomic terms and concepts, which combines the original
information provided by each source with curated terminological content
from specialized ontologies.

Commercial knowledge-assisted search is designed for transparently
supporting keyword-based search without explaining inferences; in biology, inference understanding is instead critical. For this reason, we propose a graph-based visual search for data exploration; some expert users
can navigate the semantic graph along the conceptual schema, enriched
with simple forms of homonyms and term hierarchies, thus understanding the semantic reasoning behind query results.

Keywords: Knowledge graph · Semantic search · Conceptual model ·
Data integration · Genomics · Next Generation Sequencing · Open data

1 Introduction

Next-Generation Sequencing (NGS) technologies and data processing pipelines
are supplying high-quality sequencing data at unprecedented pace [16]. Many
international consortia provide open access to an increasing number of valuable
datasets [6,8,14]. Use of integrated data produced at the various sources is fueling modern biological and clinical research. While the provided sequencing data
is generally of high quality, their metadata are not properly standardized and
normalized, some of them have missing values, and they are organized differently, with no interoperability support across data sources. To alleviate these
problems, we developed the Genomic Conceptual Model (GCM, [1]), covering 8
entities and 37 attributes which describe the most important and complex data
sources, including The Cancer Genome Atlas and Genomic Data Commons [6],

ⓒ Springer Nature Switzerland AG 2019
A. H. F. Laender et al. (Eds.): ER 2019, LNCS 11788, pp. 352–360, 2019.
https://doi.org/10.1007/978-3-030-33223-5_29

the Encyclopedia of DNA Elements [14], Roadmap Epigenomics [8], and others. We currently import 40 million metadata key-value pairs from 8 sources, which describe about 240k genomic items.

In our ongoing effort to provide the genomics community with useful concepts and tools, our next challenge is to make metadata semantically searchable and explorable. Along with GCM, we implemented a multi-ontology semantic knowledge base of genomic terms and concepts, called Genomic Knowledge Graph (GKG). We selected ten attributes from GCM; their values were semantically enriched by using the respective best ontologies, after a careful domain-specific selection process. For each associated ontological term, we described synonyms and other syntactic or semantic variants. We then provided a hierarchy of hypernyms and hyponyms. The focus of this paper is not on the GKG construction, discussed elsewhere [2], but rather in its use for supporting a domain-specific semantic search.

Semantic search technology, which is fueling the main search engines developed by Google, Microsoft, Facebook and Amazon, is empowered by the use of large knowledge graphs, supporting search at the semantic level. In these systems, when the query string can be reliably associated to a given entity, other similar instances associated with that entity are also retrieved and displayed together with the entity properties. Inspired by the successful exploitation of knowledge graph in search engines, we envisioned a semantic search approach empowered by our Genomic Knowledge Graph. However, our approach to semantic search differs from the paradigm used by the main search engines; our semantic search is focused only on *domain specific* outputs, and takes into account the fact that users must check semantic inferences, as they are typically ill-defined and error-prone due to the use of external ontologies. Since some expert users may be willing to spend additional effort on search, we expose to them the structure of the knowledge graph, by offering *exploration capabilities* for accessing entities, relationships and hierarchies, e.g., by navigating from given experiments to the cell lines or tissues of provenance, to the donors with their demography and phenotypes, and to the extraction process with the used technology and device.

This paper is organized as follows. In Sect. 2, we briefly recall the data preparation pipeline to generate the Conceptual Model (GCM) and Knowledge Graph (GKG). Section 3 shows how advanced users can query the knowledge graph according to significant patterns of interaction; we briefly discuss the Neo4j data format to allow exploration queries on GKG. Sections 4 and 5 present related work and conclusions.

2   Building the Genomic Knowledge Graph

The construction of the Genomic Knowledge Graph is performed at the end of a process of data preparation which downloads, transforms, and cleans metadata from original sources, then integrates them in the GCM, performing normalization and enrichment on a number of selected attributes. Such process uses an ETL procedure, which stores data within relational tables; the enrichment process is assisted by tools that minimize the integration designers' efforts.

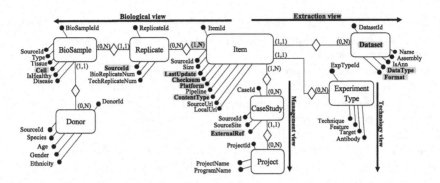

Fig. 1. The genomic conceptual model.

Original Metadata. Metadata are directly downloaded from the original sources and transformed into key-value pairs. In some cases, information is already exposed in this semi-structured format; in other cases, pairs are obtained after flattening hierarchical structures such as JSON or XML.

Genomic Conceptual Model. GCM is an entity-relation schema whose main objective is to recognize a common organization for a limited set of supported by most data sources, although with very different names and formats [1]. In Fig. 1 we show GCM in its current state; additions of new attributes, highlighted with grey background and bold font, are due to the practical experience we gained in the field. The schema is organized as a four-pointed star, centered on the Item entity, which represents an elementary experimental unit: a single file of genomic regions and their attributes. Dimensions (or *views*) respectively describe: (1) the biological phenomena observed in the experiment: the sequenced replicated sample, the biological material and its preparation, its donor; (2) the management aspects of the experiment: the case studies and projects/organizations behind its production; (3) the technological process used for the production of the experimental item; (4) the extraction parameters used for internal selection and organization of items, based on a partitioning strategy acting on different parameter values used in programmatic calls towards the sources.

Ontological Terms. As result of a normalization and enrichment phase, we associate specific values of the GCM with controlled terms. Out of all GCM attributes, we selected ten of them as worthy of enrichment. Then, we selected one or two preferred bio-ontologies for each attribute, and performed an enrichment process. The ontological terms information has been retrieved by using the Ontology Lookup Service [7] "search term" API. We save vocabulary terms with their preferred labels, synonyms (or other semantic variants), iri, descriptions and external references (i.e., identifiers of equivalent terms in alternative ontologies). The details of the annotation process are documented in [2].

Ontological Hierarchy. As a further ontological enrichment, we materialize subsets of the aforementioned ontologies which are relevant to annotate our data

(typically these range up to five hierarchical levels). The terms are linked through relationships which represent subsumption (*IS_A*), thus including hypernyms and hyponyms of the stored terms, and containment (*PART_OF*), thus including their holonyms and meronyms.

3 Exploration of the Genomic Knowledge Graph

The Genomic Knowledge Graph connections can be visually explored by users who understand the entities and relationships of GCM, as well as their linking to the vocabulary, and then to navigate the generalization *IS_A* and the containment *PART_OF* relationships. The user exploration may start from GCM entities or from the vocabulary terms. We next explain 4 typical patterns of exploration: finding items of a given dataset, of a given patient, of a given case study and associated with a given term.

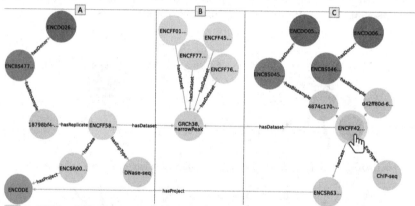

Item <id>: 27927, **item_id:** I294556, **source_id:** ENCFF429VMY, **size:** 5289591 bytes, **last_update_date:** 2017-04-14, **checksum:** a57a4056427e0f1d8324c2e952462a21, **platform:** Illumina Genome Analyzer IIx, **pipeline:** Transcription factor ChIP-seq, **content_type:** peaks and background as input for IDR, **source_url:** https://www.encodeproject.org/files/ENCFF429VMY/@@download/ENCFF429VMY.bed.gz, **local_url:** http://www.gmql.eu/gmql-rest/datasets/public.GRCh38_ENCODE_NARROW_2019_01/ENCFF429VMY/region

Fig. 2. Sequential interaction, from panel (A)—centered on Item ENCFF58—to panel (B)—centered on GRCh38_narrowPeak Dataset—to panel (C)—centered on Item ENCFF42. Note that the items in (A) and (C) share the same Project, ENCODE. (Color figure online)

Finding Other Items from the Same Datasets. A typical three-step exploratory interaction from an Item to a different Item of the same Dataset is shown in Fig. 2. Entity instances are represented as circles which include the value of entity identifiers or some relevant properties; directed edges, carrying the relationship names, connect entity instances. At all times, one of the entity instances is the *navigation handler*, and its attributes can be (on request) extensively represented in a box presented below the diagram. The end of the navigation is shown in Fig. 2(C), where the navigation handler points to entity Item ENCFF42, but the navigation starts from Item ENCFF58 in Fig. 2(A).

We use Fig. 2(A) to illustrate the typical organization of a GCM instance, centred of the Item ENCFF58 (gray color, in the center), connected to the other entities Replicate, BioSample, Donor (colors from pink to dark red, along the biological view), to CaseStudy and Project (yellow colors, along the management view) and to ExperimentType (green color, along the technology view). In Fig. 2(B) we show that the user navigates to the Dataset entity (blue color, along the extraction view), where several other Item instances of the same Dataset are illustrated; then, Fig. 2(C) shows the end of the navigation. Navigation progressively occurs by double-clicking on entity instances, while attributes of a given entity instance (in this case, of Item) are displayed by single-clicking.

Finding All the Datasets of a Given Patient. Another typical search query asks for all data types pertaining to a specific cancer patient; associating the same patient with heterogeneous data types is highly valuable in order to understand the possible research questions that can be asked to the underlying data repository. However, this query must be explored patient by patient, as each patient may be associated to a highly variable number of data types.

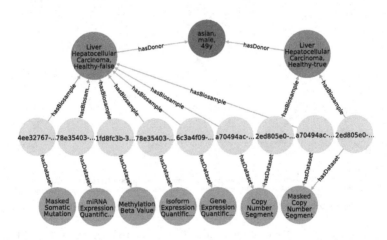

Fig. 3. Exploration starting from a Donor, providing tumoral and normal tissues, which are used to provide Items belonging to different Datasets. Note that here we omit Replicate nodes for space reasons; they have 1:1 correspondence with BioSamples.

As shown in Fig. 3, we represent Donors through their ethnicity, gender, and age (in this specific case through values [asian, male, 49y]). The database stores two biological samples extracted from this patient, who is affected by "Liver Hepatocellular Carcinoma". One sample is tumoral and the other one is healthy (i.e., a control). By further expanding the nodes, the user reaches the Item level, thereby extracting 9 data Items which belong to 7 different Datasets, each showing the type of data described in the region files (e.g., mutations, methylation levels, copy number variations, and RNA or miRNA gene expression).

Exploring the Organization of a Given Case Study. Figure 4 shows another typical exploration. Assume that a user is not aware of what constitutes a case of study in the ENCODE data source and wants to discover it. Thus, she starts with a given CaseStudy entity ENCSR63, shown at the bottom of the figure. This entity represents a set of Items that are gathered together, because they contribute to the same research objective. The interaction first allows to visualize the group of eight Items associated with this case study, belonging to the hg19_narrowPeak and GRCh38_narrowPeak Datasets (respectively having cardinality five and three). Then, the underlying biological views are revealed, by showing that all the Items are associated with chains originating from two distinct Donors.

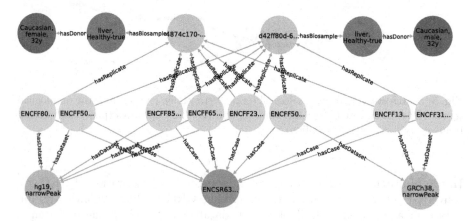

Fig. 4. From bottom to top: a CaseStudy contains multiple Items, which derive from two different Replicates/BioSamples/Donors and are contained in two Datasets based on the reference assembly of the genome.

Ontological Exploration. By starting from terms, the user may see how each term is connected to different entities, thereby typically exploring the hierarchical structure of ontological terms. Figure 5 shows how multiple Items (grey nodes on the right) can be retrieved by using different graph paths starting from the same hierarchical ancestor, ⟨brain⟩. A typical search may start from this entity, which already has a number of connected BioSamples (i.e., samples which have been *annotated* as related to brain concept) and progressively discover all its sub-concepts up to the level where terms annotate other BioSamples. Then, the exploration connects BioSamples to their Replicates and eventually to Items. Note that, in the figure, ⟨brain⟩ directly annotates a BioSample and is an indirect hypernym of ⟨pons⟩ and ⟨globus pallidus⟩, each connected to two BioSamples. Note also that five BioSamples give rise to six Replicates and then to seven Items, and also note that some Items are associated with two Replicates. Once Items are reached, the user may be interested in understanding from which datasets

or experiment types they derive; this is possible by further exploring from the Item nodes, using the first pattern of exploration discussed in this Section.

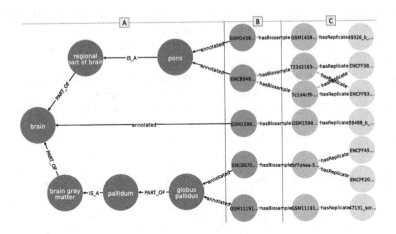

Fig. 5. Search starting from ontological terms. Essentially, (A) contains the ontological terms, (B) contains annotated BioSamples, and (C) the Replicates (pink) and derived Items (grey). (Color figure online)

Implementation Using Neo4j. For supporting the exploration of GKG, we converted the relational database describing GKG content [2] into a graph database; among many available graph databases (e.g., Neptune or Titan[1]), we have chosen Neo4j (https://neo4j.com/), currently the leading open source graph database, used by several companies also in the bioinformatics domain (e.g., EBI, Intermine[2]). We map to Cypher (Neo4j's query language) exploration queries which are progressively built by our query interface.

4   Related Works

Some recent works employ conceptual models' expressive power to explain biological entities and their interactions [11,15], or to characterize the processes and objects during related analysis workflows [13]. The GKG is instead based on a CM [1] that drives the data integration process and exposes the unified view resulting from this effort. A classic work [5] proposed a Genomics Ontology, while a more recent one [4] promotes the use of foundational ontologies to avoid errors while creating and curating genomic domain models for personalized medicine. We instead use ontologies to find a common ground between the descriptions and terminologies used in different sources.

---

[1] https://aws.amazon.com/neptune/, http://titan.thinkaurelius.com/.

[2] https://www.ebi.ac.uk/ols/docs/neo4j-schema,   https://github.com/intermine/neo4j.

Among a number of integrated databases in the bioinformatics domain that employ graph-based paradigms, we cite: BioGraphDB [10], a resource to query, visualize and analyze biological data belonging to several online available sources (focused on genes, proteins, miRNAs, pathways); Bio4j [12], a platform integrating semantically rich biological data (focused on proteins, functional annotations); ncRNA-DB [3], integrating associations among non-coding RNAs and other functional elements.

5   Conclusions

We built an exploration mechanism for supporting semantic queries upon our Genomic Knowledge Graph; we demonstrated the effectiveness of our approach through four examples which are representative of the use of our query interface. Our repository is already storing data coming from eight data sources of genomic data, including datasets relevant for epigenomics, gene expression data, mutation data, deployed in conjunction with an advanced genomic data manager [9], available at http://gmql.eu/gmql-rest/.

Acknowledgement. This research is funded by the ERC Advanced Grant 693174 GeCo (Data-Driven Genomic Computing), 2016-2021.

References

1. Bernasconi, A., Ceri, S., Campi, A., Masseroli, M.: Conceptual modeling for genomics: building an integrated repository of open data. In: Mayr, H.C., Guizzardi, G., Ma, H., Pastor, O. (eds.) ER 2017. LNCS, vol. 10650, pp. 325–339. Springer, Cham (2017). https://doi.org/10.1007/978-3-319-69904-2_26
2. Bernasconi, A., et al.: Ontology-driven metadata enrichment for genomic datasets. In: International Conference on Semantic Web Applications and Tools for Life Sciences, vol. 2275. CEUR-WS (2018)
3. Bonnici, V., et al.: Comprehensive reconstruction and visualization of non-coding regulatory networks in human. Front. Bioeng. Biotechnol. **2**, 69 (2014)
4. Martínez Ferrandis, A.M., Pastor López, O., Guizzardi, G.: Applying the principles of an ontology-based approach to a conceptual schema of human genome. In: Ng, W., Storey, V.C., Trujillo, J.C. (eds.) ER 2013. LNCS, vol. 8217, pp. 471–478. Springer, Heidelberg (2013). https://doi.org/10.1007/978-3-642-41924-9_40
5. Hammer, J., Schneider, M.: The GenAlg project: developing a new integrating data model, language, and tool for managing and querying genomic information. ACM SIGMOD Rec. **33**(2), 45–50 (2004)
6. Jensen, M.A., et al.: The NCI Genomic Data Commons as an engine for precision medicine. Blood **130**(4), 453–459 (2017)
7. Jupp, S., et al.: A new ontology lookup service at EMBL-EBI. In: Malone, J., et al. (eds.) International Conference on Semantic Web Applications and Tools for Life Sciences, vol. 1546, pp. 118–119. CEUR-WS (2015)
8. Kundaje, A., et al.: Integrative analysis of 111 reference human epigenomes. Nature **518**(7539), 317–330 (2015)

9. Masseroli, M., et al.: Processing of big heterogeneous genomic datasets for tertiary analysis of Next Generation Sequencing data. Bioinformatics **35**, 729–736 (2018)

10. Messina, A., et al.: BioGraph: a web application and a graph database for querying and analyzing bioinformatics resources. BMC Syst. Biol. **12**(5), 98 (2018)

11. Palacio, A.L., López, Ó.P., Ródenas, J.C.C.: A method to identify relevant genome data: conceptual modeling for the medicine of precision. In: Trujillo, J., et al. (eds.) ER 2018. LNCS, vol. 11157, pp. 597–609. Springer, Cham (2018). https://doi.org/10.1007/978-3-030-00847-5_44

12. Pareja-Tobes, P., et al.: Bio4j: a high-performance cloud-enabled graph-based data platform. BioRxiv, p. 016758 (2015)

13. Rambold, G., et al.: Meta-omics data and collection objects (MOD-CO): a conceptual schema and data model for processing sample data in meta-omics research. Database **2019**, baz002 (2019). https://doi.org/10.1093/database/baz002

14. Consortium ENCODE. An integrated encyclopedia of DNA elements in the human genome. Nature **489**(7414), 57–74 (2012)

15. Reyes Román, J.F., Pastor, Ó., Casamayor, J.C., Valverde, F.: Applying conceptual modeling to better understand the human genome. In: Comyn-Wattiau, I., Tanaka, K., Song, I.-Y., Yamamoto, S., Saeki, M. (eds.) ER 2016. LNCS, vol. 9974, pp. 404–412. Springer, Cham (2016). https://doi.org/10.1007/978-3-319-46397-1_31

16. Stephens, Z.D., et al.: Big data: astronomical or genomical? PLoS Biol. **13**(7), e1002195 (2015)

Decision Making

Decision-Making in Knowledge-intensive Processes: The Case of Value Ascription and Goal Processing

Pedro H. Piccoli Richetti[1]([⊠]), Fernanda Araujo Baião[2],
and Maria Luiza M. Campos[1]

[1] Graduate Program in Informatics, Federal University of Rio de Janeiro,
Rio de Janeiro, Brazil
pedro.richetti@ufrj.br, mluiza@ppgi.ufrj.br
[2] Pontifical Catholic University of Rio de Janeiro (PUC-Rio),
Rio de Janeiro, Brazil
fbaiao@puc-rio.br

Abstract. Knowledge-intensive Processes (KiPs) are a range of business processes which are rather unpredictable, highly variable, and very dependent on human knowledge and collaboration. Despite the recent efforts to provide comprehensive support for KiP management, there are still few discussions about how human aspects influence process execution. For example, in a disaster management KiP, why someone decides to take action when the action itself may put their own life at stake? This work aims to provide an ontological background for properly understanding human decision-making actions by analyzing cognitive states of agents participating in a KiP. We introduce a novel perspective of decisions seen as value and risk experiences, and a formal characterization of agents' beliefs in a goal processing framework, which paves the way for precisely and systematically explaining decision-making towards process goals. We claim that these value-oriented conceptual models are capable of describing the rationale of decision-making in KiPs in terms of value and risk ascriptions and by a set of belief types that supports goal processing. In a practical example, the proposed conceptual models were applied in the analysis of a real-life KiP instance from the air traffic control domain.

Keywords: Knowledge-intensive Process · Goal Processing · Value Ascription

1 Introduction

Business processes represent core assets of every organization and, as such, need to be managed so as to enable stakeholders to control and guide their evolution. As stated by Dumas et al. [1], the execution of a process leads to several outcomes that should deliver some sort of value to the actors involved in the process. Traditional control-flow oriented – or highly automated – processes typically require less effort to be understood, managed and improved, since each step of these processes can be predefined due to their intrinsic predictability and low variability. However, there exists a range of processes, so called Knowledge-intensive Processes (KiPs), that are rather unpredictable, highly

A. H. F. Laender et al. (Eds.): ER 2019, LNCS 11788, pp. 363–377, 2019.
https://doi.org/10.1007/978-3-030-33223-5_30

variable, and very dependent on human knowledge and collaboration [2]. KiPs are present in several domains, such as in customer support services, air traffic control, design of new products or services, marketing campaigns planning, data quality management, IT governance and strategic planning, disaster management, criminal investigations and healthcare diagnosis [2, 3]. Human agents, and particularly their mental states inhered in them are core elements of KiPs, since they characterize the driving mechanisms for agents to make decisions and take action. Although there exist several works on characterization and management of KiPs [2, 4–7], there are still scarce discussions in the literature on how agents get motivated and decide to act when the process demands ad-hoc decisions, experienced workers and actions to be planned at runtime.

We argue that a precise definition of the cognitive mechanisms that lead agents to participate in a process is of major relevance to explain how agents formulate a proper course of action towards a process goal. Take, as an example, a disaster management process, where the process instance is to save victims from a building on fire. The process involves coordination of many agents, some of them very specialized, to perform activities such as "to isolate the area", "to bring resources to extinguish the fire", "to enter the building and rescue victims", and "to provide medical assistance". Each of these activities are planned and executed specifically for the characteristics of the fire; however, during the execution of some procedures, conditions may change the original course of action (for example, if the building starts to collapse). Consider a firefighter that decides to face the fire and enter the building to search for victims. What motivates the agent to put his/her own life at risk and take this action? What mechanisms make the firefighter decide to act guided by the goal of a process that makes him/her take actions contrary to the natural desire of keeping his/her life safe? In this context, the research question we pursue to answer is: How agents decide to act in order to successfully achieve a goal within a KiP? As we shall claim in this paper, prior to action, agents make decisions among the possible alternatives and then choose the most valuable tasks towards the goals they have previously committed to.

Different notions of value surround business processes contexts. Sales et al. [8] discussed the notions of ethical value, exchange value and use value, being the latter the mostly used in the business literature. Use value is considered a core issue to understand why customers choose a particular product or service and how companies differentiate themselves from their competitors. The notion of use value is relative to one or more experiences (future, current or past) and results from the valuation of such experiences, where a value ascription relationship may take place between an agent and a value object [9]. It is also important to consider the opposite effect of value ascription, that is risk ascription. Risk contemplates future experiences whose chances of happening should be mitigated because their occurrence may imply some kind of loss. Sales et al. [8] proposed that risk shares some similarities with value, such as goal-dependency, context-dependency, uncertainty and impact, thus most of what is applied to the use value notion also can be applied to the risk notion.

A goal can be defined as an anticipatory mental representation of a state of affairs that governs and constrains the behavior of an agent towards its realization [10]. Goals drive human desires and intentions that push agents towards actions, as proposed in the seminal BDI framework [11]. Castelfranchi and Paglieri [10] argued that goals are

central for understanding human cognition, since a goal is a mental representation with a given use, function, role or application. Thus, the value or risk ascribed by agents to a business process activity depends entirely on the goals the agents have represented in their mind and how the experiences provided by that activity contribute to achieving these goals.

Major theories of motivation emphasize that different aspects of beliefs, values and goals compose a motivational state that precedes decision-making and further action [12]. Thus, we claim that a discussion about the role of value and risk within beliefs and goals in KiPs is needed to properly define and understand how agents get motivated and decide to act. In this work, as the main contribution, we propose a well-founded conceptual model to characterize and structure the ontological nature of the relationships between two core concepts: on one side, the mental states of agents participating in a KiP; on the other side, the goals that have to be pursued to lead this processes to a successful state. We argue that this conceptualization should consider value and risk ascriptions within decision-making as crucial concepts to explain why agents take actions in a KiP. To support this proposal, we consider the Goal Processing Theory [10] and the Common Ontology on ValuE and Risk (COVER) [8] in favor of KiP decision-making analysis. The Knowledge-intensive Process Ontology (KiPO) [4] is considered as a reference structural conceptual model for KiPs. All proposed conceptual models are anchored on the Unified Foundational Ontology (UFO) [13] in order to provide a sound basis for the conceptualizations. UFO has been used to evaluate, re-design and give real-world semantics to domain ontologies by making them more truthful to reality and by making their ontological commitments explicit [14]. UFO has also been chosen as a reference top-level ontology because it provides basic concepts regarding objects and events, as well as social and intentional phenomena, which are needed to properly model the discussed domain. Regarding validation, we report on empirical evidences gathered from a practical example, were the proposed conceptual model has been successfully applied in the analysis of a real-life KiP instance from the air traffic control domain.

The remainder of the paper is organized as follows: Sect. 2 presents the background on KiPO, Goal Processing and Value Ascription theories. Section 3 presents the conceptual models we propose to explain how goal processing, value and risk ascription influence decision-making in KiPs. Section 4 presents a case study with a real-life KiP instance from the air traffic control domain applying and illustrating the usefulness of our proposed models, and Sect. 5 concludes the paper.

2   KiPO, Goal Processing and Value Ascription

2.1   The Knowledge-intensive Process Ontology (KiPO)

KiPO is a domain ontology comprising key concepts and relationships that are relevant for understanding, describing and managing a Knowledge-intensive Process [4]. KiPO provides a common, domain-independent understanding of KiPs and, as such, it may be used as a meta-model for structuring KiP concepts. This ontology is anchored on UFO, as each KiPO concept is defined according to UFO constructs, which in turn are

described in terms of its metaproperties (sortality, relational dependence, rigidity, among others). It defines the core concepts of a KiP, such as agents, their goals and mental states, Knowledge-intensive Activities (KiAs) the agents perform and the contextual elements involved in KiAs. KiPO argues that a KiP is driven by agents' intentions towards achieving process goals, and the flow of activities, especially decision-making ones, within a KiP is deeply influenced by intentional moments, such as Beliefs, Desires, Intentions and Perceptions [15].

According to KiPO, an Agent is the one who intentionally commits to make a Decision to solve a Question, being a Decision a special type of KiA. A Question is a Contingency event that triggers a Decision to be made. To perform a Decision, an Agent chooses among several Alternatives, which represent potential Situations that could be achieved (Chosen Alternative) or not (Discarded Alternative). Alternatives satisfies Propositions, which are assessed as Advantages or Disadvantages according to Criteria considered by the Agent during the assessment. An Alternative may also pose some Risks, which are to be avoided. Regarding Decisions, KiPO demands improvements on its Risk definition, since it considers Risk as a Proposition that impacts on Decision Alternatives. More recently, the work of Sales et al. [8] considered Risk as a special case of Value. Also, both Value and Risk concepts can be ascribed to Experiences (Events) so that they can be evaluated by an Agent to the extent which of these Experiences satisfy or hurt some Goal. This approach allows to explain why Agents decide to choose an Alternative in preference of others by the notion of Value Ascription, which considers a sense of valuation of the intended experiences a Decision may imply. KiPO also defines two types of Goals, namely Process Goal and Activity Goal. A Process Goal is the ultimate objective to be pursued when a KiP is performed and it is expected that it should not change during process execution. An Activity Goal is the Goal to be achieved by the execution of an Activity (being a single Activity or a KiA) that an Agent commits to perform as part of the KiP, and it contributes to achieve a Process Goal. KiPO does not elaborate on how Activity Goals are activated, pursued or chosen in scenarios where decisions about the course of action are ad-hoc or the KiP is subject to contingencies which force existing goals to be dropped or new goals to be added.

2.2 Goal Processing

UFO defines a Goal as an internal mental representation of a future expected outcome [13]. As such, its existence depends on an Agent having an Intentional Moment, being a Desire or an Intention towards that Goal. A Desire is one kind of goal bearer, a possible origin of Intentions, and it does not imply on any commitment to action. An Intention refers to a Goal an Agent decides to pursue and it is assumed the Agent is committed to act. An Intention can be characterized as a two-stage structure: an intention "to do", i.e., to perform a given action, and an intention "that", i.e., to realize a Goal [10]. For example, in the scenario of a firefighter whose intention is to rescue a victim under debris of a collapsed building, the intention "that" is to rescue a victim and the intention "to do" is the action of removing the debris over the victim. Goals can be just "means", or instrumental, to higher-level goals. These instrumental goals are intermediate steps to achieve higher-level goals, and they can be added or dropped as

part of the planning for the agents to act. The decisions about which goals should be chosen towards a higher-level goal, e.g. a process goal, is acknowledged as Goal Processing [10]. In this processing, beliefs play a major role, acting as test conditions and filters for goals to reach their final stage, where goals become executive and then instantiate actions. Castelfranchi and Paglieri's [10] theoretical proposal stands in contrast with the dominant view of intentions. It suggests how to reduce the number of motivational primitives in BDI logics from two (desires and intentions) to one (goals), providing, at the same time, some insights on their mutual relationship. They propose a list of different types of goal-supporting beliefs that play different functional roles in goal processing, as described below, with illustrative examples of KiP scenarios:

Motivating Beliefs. Goals are often activated by beliefs on the current state of affairs. This category considers two sub-classes: (a) *Triggering Beliefs*: beliefs that reactively activate goals on the basis of a pre-established connection. For example, as a disaster management coordinator, it is my belief that if a flood started in my city it will activate my goal to provide operational support to a disaster response; (b) *Conditional Beliefs*: beliefs that activate a goal on the basis of the conditional nature of the goal itself. For example, as a loan officer, it is my belief that today is the 10th day of a month that activates my conditional goal to check if borrowers paid their monthly debts. The presence of motivating beliefs enables goals to be activated.

Assessment Beliefs. In order to consider a goal as candidate for being pursued, an agent cannot conclude that such goal is either already realized, self-realizing, or impossible to be achieved. Assessment beliefs are divided in three subclasses: (a) *Self-realization beliefs*: beliefs concerning the fact that a goal will come to be autonomously realized in the world. They may not require actions by the agent, e.g. due to natural processes or other agents that guarantee their achievement. For example, as a forensic investigator, it is my belief that a DNA exam obtained from a crime scene can last up to 14 days, which prevents me pursuing the goal of obtaining the results earlier; (b) *Satisfaction beliefs*: beliefs concerning the fact that a goal is already realized, and that it will remain as such without agents' intervention. For example, as a physician, the belief that my patient has been cured prevents me pursuing the goal to continue treating the patient for the same disease; (c) *Impossibility beliefs*: beliefs concerning the fact that a goal is impossible at a given time, or it will never be possible. For example, as an air traffic controller, it is the belief that two aircrafts can collide if they concurrently land on the same runway that unsupports my goal to direct them to the same runway at the same time. The absence of assessment beliefs enables activated goals to be pursued.

Cost Beliefs. Beliefs concerning the costs or resources that an agent expects to sustain as a consequence of pursuing a certain goal. For example, as an architect, it is my belief about the high price of marble stone that makes me decide to not pursue the goal of making an entire staircase with this material within a housing project.

Incompatibility Beliefs. Beliefs concerning different forms of incompatibility between goals, that can force the agent to choose among them. For example, as a product designer, it is my belief that I cannot apply premium materials in a new product to ensure quality, and at the same time I want to offer a low-cost product, that prevents me pursuing both these goals concurrently.

Preference Beliefs. Beliefs concerning which goals should be given precedence over others in the current context. This category splits in two subclasses: (a) *Value beliefs*: concerning the subjective value of a certain goal, given how this goal will benefit the agent. For example, as a doctor, it is my belief that it is more valuable to treat a bone fracture than to treat skin scrapings of a patient that suffered a motorcycle fall that makes me choose first the goal to treat the bone fracture; (b) *Urgency beliefs*: concerning when a goal will "expire", i.e. it will be no more possible to achieve it. For example, as a firefighter, it is my belief that the fire is about to reach a crowded room that makes me pursue the goal to start fighting the fire first in that room.

Precondition Beliefs. Beliefs concerning the necessary preconditions to successfully execute a chosen goal by executing the appropriate action. They are distinguished by two sub classes: (a) *Incompetence beliefs*: mainly concern both the basic competences, the sufficient skills and abilities needed to reach a goal, given agents' convictions on how to achieve the goal. For example, as a doctor, it is my belief that I cannot start the surgery before an anesthetist applies sedation to the patient; (b) *Lack of conditions beliefs*: concern external conditions, opportunities, and resources. They cover both conditions for the execution of the appropriate actions and conditions for the success of a correctly performed action. For example, as a loan officer, it is my belief that I cannot lend money until the client signs the loan contract. The absence of precondition beliefs enables chosen goals to be executed.

Means-end Beliefs. Beliefs concerning the instrumental relation between a goal and an action or an event which is considered to serve to achieve the former, and, therefore, can be assumed as a means to that end. For example, as a customer service officer, it is my belief that I have to place a call to a client to obtain more details about an issue that makes me place the call to achieve the instrumental goal of obtaining more details, during a customer service process instance. Means-end beliefs enable chosen goals to be executive, i.e. they allow an action to be immediately performed.

Each belief type supports a goal in a specific stage [10] as follows. Goal Activation is the stage where the support of *Motivating Beliefs* makes goals active. In the next stage (Goal Evaluation), goals are evaluated by the presence of *Assessment Beliefs*, which verify if the Active Goal is already satisfied, will be autonomously satisfied, or it is impossible to be achieved. In this phase, the Active Goals need not to be coherent, and are subject to conflicts, thus having to be further chosen or to be renounced. If an Active Goal passes this stage, it is a Pursuable Goal. In the sequence, Goal Deliberation is performed, where Pursuable Goals are tested by *Preference and Cost Beliefs* and, if there are no *Incompatibility Beliefs*, they can become Chosen Goals. At this point, a Chosen Goal becomes an intention of an agent towards a future action. In Goal Checking stage, if Chosen Goals have no more *Precondition Beliefs* constraining the intended action and *Means-end Beliefs* support these goals, the goals become executive and the actions can be immediately instantiated.

Another important aspect in Goal Processing is goal revision: each time the set of beliefs changes, their supported goals should also be revised in order to maintain proper goal support considering the "new believed" reality. For example, if the agent believes a goal is unattainable or it is no longer motivated by its condition or higher-level goals, that goal can be dropped. For instance, a KiP is subject to contingencies, that are

defined as unexpected events that interfere in the process execution. A contingency event may bring about to reality a state of affairs that force a change on the agent's beliefs, thus demanding a goal revision. For example, during a coronary bypass surgery, the blood pressure of the patient suddenly drops. Faced by this situation, the leading surgeon, that has the belief that extreme hypotension is a life-threatening condition, stops planned surgical activities to treat and restore the patient's blood pressure (a newly introduced instrumental goal) to normal levels, so the surgery can continue.

2.3 Value Ascription

Goals give value to actions [16] and value can be ascribed to past, current or envisioned experiences, involving or not a value object as the center of analysis [17]. This postulate about Value Experience is corroborated by the marketing domain where it is stated that "Value resides not in the object of consumption, but in the experience of consumption" [18]. The diagram[1] on Fig. 1 presents an excerpt of COVER ontology [8] depicting the relation of *Value Experiences* and *Goals*.

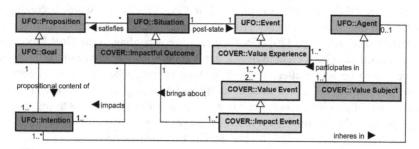

Fig. 1. Relationship between Goals and Value Experiences [8]. (Color figure online)

According to UFO [13], *Events* change reality by changing the state of affairs from one (pre-state) *Situation* to another (post-state) *Situation*. A *Value Experience* aggregates *Value Events*, which can be *Impact Events*, that are a kind of *Value Event* which brings about *Situations* that are *Impactful Outcomes*. Such outcomes may be positive or negative, related to value or risk ascriptions, respectively, and they impact the *Intention* of an *Agent* that is the *Value Subject* participating in the *Value Experience*. Every *Intention* has a *Goal* as propositional content. This brought about *Impactful Outcome* can satisfy a *Goal* to a given degree, which can be determined by the comparison of the

---

[1] From now on, we adopt the following color-coding scheme: events are represented in yellow, objects in pink, qualities and modes in blue, relators in green, situations in orange, propositions in purple and powertypes in white. Italic font style highlights classes' names appearances in the text. For colorful figures, please refer to the online version.

Impactful Outcome and the expected state of affairs to be reached when the *Goal* is achieved. As stated by Azevedo et al. [19], the situations that satisfy a goal are the ones in which value has been produced or their effect is realized.

3   Goal Processing and Value Ascription Roles in KiPs

In this section, we propose a conceptual model to formally define decision-making in KiPs based on Value Ascription and Goal Processing theories. Essentially, a *Decision* is represented as a *Value Experience* which an *Agent* can ascribe value to, referred to the goals supported by the agent's beliefs. Firstly, we provide precise definitions of belief types and goal stages from Goal Processing theory. We anchored these constructs on UFO, so they can also be properly integrated with KiPO and COVER constructs, as these two ontologies are already well-founded on UFO. Figure 2 summarizes the proposed Goal Processing conceptual model that also considers the guidelines for multi-level modeling described in [20].

A *Belief Type* is a specialization of an *UFO::Intrinsic Moment Universal* and categorizes *UFO::Belief*. An instance of a *Belief Type*, like a *Motivating Belief*, is also a specialization of *UFO::Belief*. A *Goal Type* is a specialization of *UFO::Goal Universal* and partitions *UFO::Goal* in one of the four Goal Processing Stages according to Castelfranchi and Paglieri's theory [10]. The partition relation is applied to disjointly categorize a first order type [20] (*Goal Type*), since according to the Goal Processing Theory, a *Goal* must be present in only a single stage at a time. For example, an *Active Goal* ceases to be active after the Goal Evaluation task, when the *Goal* becomes a *Pursuable Goal* and so on. An instance of a *Goal Type*, e.g. an *Active Goal*, is also a specialization of an *UFO::Goal*. Each instance of a *Belief Type* relates to instances of *Goal Type* according to the Goal Processing stages (Fig. 2), e.g., a *Pursuable Goal* is evaluated by *Assessment Beliefs* during the Goal Evaluation task.

Goal-orientation is a characteristic of KiPs. As stated by Di Ciccio et al. [2] for a KiP: "The process evolves through a series of intermediate goals or milestones to be achieved. Process participants continuously assess process progression and then act or plan the actions to be performed, depending on the process status and the available data and knowledge elements". It is also important to consider that goals do not only derive from internal motives, but they may originate from duties, obligations or may also be imported, in forms of requests, orders, norms, and roles [21]. KiPs occur in the context of organizations, which may have their own business rules, norms and roles. As the focus of this work is on existing KiPs rather on design of new ones, it is assumed that KiP goals are already existing. In these scenarios, whenever agents participate in a KiP, it is expected that the agents are aware of the normative structures of the organization they belong to. Thus, some goals of the organization may be imported by the agents that participate in a KiP. This goal adoption can be seen as an agent doing something for others, even though there is no sincere desire towards that goal. Thus, what motivates an agent to act, even when there is no genuine desire to act, can be either a desire to pursue a higher-level goal or a norm/obligation due to a commitment to the organization.

The Self-Determination Theory (SDT) [16] is one of many motivation theories that explains the origins of agents' initiatives to act by specifying different types of motivation [22]. Gagné and Deci [23] affirm that activities that are not interesting (i.e., that are not intrinsically motivating) require extrinsic motivation, such as implicit approval or tangible rewards, which are called external regulations in SDT. According to Eccles and Wigfield [22], a task can be ascribed a positive value by a person because it facilitates important future goals, even if this person is not interested in the task for his/her own sake. For instance, students often take classes they do not particularly enjoy but that they need to take in order to pursue other interests, for example, to please their parents, or to obtain an academic degree.

Once an agent is committed towards a goal, an intentional structure is formed. The intention "to do" may converge into a complex intentional action, performed by subactions. In a KiP, this "to do" structure can be seen as a KiA, which is essentially a complex action (Event) and, as such, may also be composed by other KiAs.

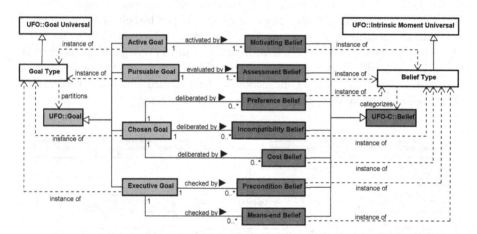

Fig. 2. Goal types and their respective supporting beliefs [10] anchored on UFO.

Decisions in a KiP are considered a special case of KiAs, where agents ponder the possible alternatives and then choose the ones they believe will mostly satisfy a goal. We argue that decisions heavily depend on the value or risk agents ascribe to that decision experience based on the possible outcomes of the decision. The following diagrams (Figs. 3 and 4) present the proposed formalization of the notion of value ascription and decision-making in the context of KiPs. Each introduced new concept is well-founded on an UFO construct. As KiPO and COVER are already anchored on UFO, and due to space limitations, we omit their respective UFO specializations and apply namespaces to refer to reused classes from their founding ontologies. As stated by COVER, *Value* inheres in a *Value Ascription*. It is worth noting that COVER considers that the notion of *Risk* is irreducibly intertwined with the notion of *Value*, that is, *Risk Ascription* is a particular case of *Value Ascription*. In this sense, the *Risk* specialization from *Value* concept aims to emphasize a counter-value position, where

the outcomes of an event may generate a negative impact or a loss for the *Value Subject*, that is the participant of a *Value Experience*. A *KiA*, being an Event, can be a specialization of a *Value Experience*, and a *Decision*, as a specialization of a KiA, inheres the same properties of a *Value Experience*. *Value Ascription* is a relation that also involves a *Value Assessor*, i.e. the one who judges the value of a *Value Ascription*. This ascription is also directly affected by the intrinsic properties of the *Value Objects* that may participate in a *Value Experience*. In a KiP setting, the agents that participate in the process are called *Participants*, and they can be both *Value Assessor Participants*, judging the value of a *KiA* or a *Decision*, or *Value Subject Participants*, participating in a *KiA* or making a *Decision* to solve a *Question* (Fig. 3).

According to KiPO, an *Impact Agent*, which is also a KiP *Participant*, is responsible for executing *KiAs* and for identifying *Questions* that trigger *Decisions*. KiPO defines *Alternatives* as situations that are brought about by making a *Decision*. Some *Alternatives* can be discarded due to lack of supporting beliefs, such as when participants do not believe that they can cause any impact that will contribute to achieve a *Goal* or when these *Alternatives* are to be brought about by a negative *Impact Event* (a *Loss Event*). Conversely, a *Chosen Alternative* is supported by beliefs that it can cause an impact that contributes to achieve a *Goal*. The situation brought about by a *Chosen Alternative* is a pre-state for action, thus, from this point, a *Participant* can manifest an *Intention* to act, with the propositional content of a *Chosen Goal*. If there are no more precondition beliefs preventing the action to be executed, the *Goal* becomes an *Executive Goal* and an *Activity* can be immediately performed (Fig. 4).

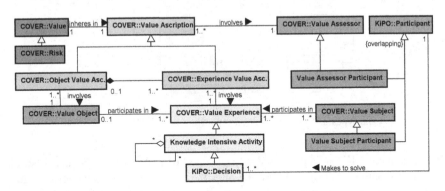

Fig. 3. Value Ascription to Knowledge-intensive Activities and Decisions.

The following scenario presents an example of the presence of value concepts and belief support to process a goal during the execution of a KiP. In a disaster management process, Anne, a firefighter, has to rescue people from a building on fire. It is undoubtedly true that she does not inhere the desire of putting her own life at risk, what would be an inevitable consequence of entering the building. Nevertheless, she adopts the goal of "making people safe" from her role, and as such, she commits herself (that is, she chooses this goal and plans to act) to enter the building. The goal of "entering the building on fire" is an instrumental goal to achieve the higher-level process goal of

"making people safe". This goal adoption may be motivated by an external regulation of not feeling guilty if some victim gets deceased as a consequence of her lack of immediate action and also relates to the use value ascribed to the decision to move and enter the building, needed to help her achieve the process goal. To support this goal, urgency (she believes that the fire will reach the victims very fast) and skill beliefs (she received proper training, and knows she is capable to perform the rescue) are the most important mental moments inhered in her when she chooses the instrumental goal to enter the building.

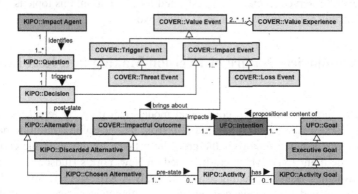

Fig. 4. A Decision in a KiP as a Value Experience.

KiPO defines *Risk* as the propositional content of an *Alternative* that threatens a *Decision*. It does not elaborate on the ontological nature of *Risk* and how it can be of much more interest for KiPs than being constrained to a proposition. As *Risk* can be seen as a special case of *Value* [8], depending on the *Goal* and *Beliefs* inhering in a *Participant*, there can be exclusively a *Risk Ascription* to a *Decision*, instead of a *Value Ascription*. For example, an air traffic control officer has the *Goal* to direct the landing of two aircrafts in the same airport in a very short time window. The demands of two aircrafts landing almost simultaneously is a *Threat Event* (specialization of a *Trigger Event* when it involves *Risk Ascription*) that triggers the *Risk Experience*. It is a *Decision* to be made considering the existing *Alternatives*, and it puts the officer as a *Risk Subject* since it is the *Goal* of air traffic controllers to safely route the aircrafts (the Process Goal). Considering that the occurrence of a *Loss Event* will cause severe consequences, a high *Risk* is ascribed to this *Decision*. For the instrumental *Goal* of orienting two quasi-concurrent landings, the officer must have *Beliefs* supporting this *Goal*. For example, if the *Risk Subject* has an *Incompatibility Belief* that it is unsafe to land two aircrafts in a short time window (a *Discarded Alternative*), the officer decides to authorize one aircraft to land and put the second on hold until it can safely approximate to land.

KiPs are also recognized as collaboration-oriented processes [2], as the participation of multiple agents is expected for the achievement of process goals. In most organizations, strict cooperation is a premise, and incentives, such as material rewards

or social approval, can be offered to foster this behavior, acting as external regulations. By these considerations, it is assumed that KiP participants are committed to cooperate towards the process goals. Beyond the aforementioned case where one agent adopts the organization's goals, there is also a need of a group of agents to form a single whole point of view of beliefs and goals about the process. It is trivial to assume that most of the participants will adhere to a higher-level goal of a KiP due to their commitment to the organization, but for the instrumental goals, it is necessary to establish proper communications among the agents in favor of reaching consensus. Discussions about communications in KiPs have been performed in [24], however, their role in goal processing still deserves a detailed analysis, and for this reason, this topic is left out of the scope of this paper and is planned as future work.

4   The Ontological Nature of Decision-Making in a Real-Life KiP

To exemplify how the proposed conceptual models can properly represent decision-making in KiPs, we inspected a real-life KiP from the air traffic control domain. The specific process instance comprises the procedures taken by the air traffic control and the pilot of the flight 1549, which crash-landed on New York's Hudson River in 2009, with no casualties. This happening was essentially a KiP, since it involved ad-hoc decisions performed by experienced agents, a contingency event and collaboration among all participants. The analysis relies on the inspection of the transcription[2] of the communications among LaGuardia tower, Teterboro tower, New York Terminal Radar Approach Control (TRACON) and the aircraft. Due to space restrictions we focus on specific points of the transcription that contain externalizations of mental states from participating agents or characterizations of decision-making events.

At time 20:27:36 (hh:mm:ss, UTC time), the pilot externalized his Belief that the plane lost thrust in both engines due to a collision with birds: *"...Hit birds, we lost thrust in both engines. We're turning back towards LaGuardia."*. This supporting belief activated an Instrumental Goal to return to LaGuardia airport in order to achieve the higher-level Goal of safely transporting people from a point to another (the Process Goal). At time 20:28:11, the pilot evaluated the Active Goal by the presence of an Impossibility Belief when he stated: *"We're unable (to return to LaGuardia). We may end up in the Hudson."* At that time, he also dropped this first Goal and activated a new unexpected Instrumental Goal: to land on Hudson River.

In 20:29:02-03, the pilot considered an Alternative to try to land at Teterboro airport offered by TRACON. At 20:29:21, TRACON authorized the plane to land at Teterboro. At this point, the pilot had to choose between landing at Teterboro or at the Hudson River. This deliberation was supported by a Value Belief (a subtype of a Preference Belief) that landing at the Hudson River would be less risky (a Risk Ascription) than turning to Teterboro. At 20:29:25 the pilot manifested an unusual

---

[2] The full transcription is available in: https://www.faa.gov/data_research/accident_incident/1549/media/Full%20Transcript%20L116.pdf.

Decision and refused the Alternative to go to Teterboro runway, since he ascribed a higher Risk to this action because it could imply on more severe consequences (a Loss Event), e.g., the plane would crash on ground and in an urban area. In the sequence (20:29:28), the pilot made his last contact: *"We're gonna be in the Hudson."*. This statement represents a Chosen Goal, which turned to be executive since there were no more preconditions prior to the pilot take action and proceed to land on the river.

5 Conclusions

As human agents are a central piece for KiPs execution, shedding light in how agents' mental states drive them to make decisions and perform actions towards goals is of paramount relevance. More specifically, it is interestingly tricky to understand the ontological nature of these cognitive elements and how they relate to the goals adopted from external sources (such as an organization the agent is committed to) in a way that value aggregation is perceived by both parties, in what would be considered contradictory situations at a first sight, such as the outcome of a decision "to land a commercial aircraft on a river" and the goal "to safely transport people".

The main contribution of this work is a conceptual model, in the form of a well-founded ontology, as a novel perspective for precisely explaining how process participants choose goals, make decisions and perform actions based on the notions of goal processing and value ascription. As a practical implication, the model can be of relevance for any organization to help it precisely understand several collaborative and unpredictable critical scenarios. Organizations can benefit of the proposed conceptualization as a reference to analyze their KiPs, now considering that the associated agents perform value ascriptions when making decisions prior to action. Besides, these actions are only formulated after a series of assessments based on agents' beliefs that process instrumental goals needed to achieve business processes successful states.

We are aware that this work did not detail the possible origins of contingency events, which are a main source of questions that trigger decisions. This limits the scope of the present work, by assuming that these events can happen unexpectedly during process execution. The proposed models also do not address neither the social roles of process participants nor the communication perspective within KiPs and goal processing. This perspective is relevant because it is through communication that agents interact with each other, share their beliefs and form a common ground to make collective decisions to achieve process goals. We have focused on agents' internal mental states that make them take individual decisions within the social context of a KiP. This leaves space for further investigations in the future.

We successfully applied the proposed conceptual model to support analysis of a complex and real-life KiP instance, showing the intrinsic and non-intuitive behavior that may emerge from such processes. There is, of course, a need to collect more evidences to demonstrate the descriptive and explanatory power of the proposed model, which will demand a broader empirical evaluation to validate the model under different KiP domains. Domains that are in our agenda to be investigated include: software development and

troubleshooting processes. Future work may also relate value and risk ascription of decisions to process performance outcomes. Since these ascriptions are associated with a goal evaluation function, this should help model process performance of KiPs.

References

1. Dumas, M., La Rosa, M., Mendling, J., Reijers, H.: Fundamentals of Business Process Management. Springer, Heidelberg (2018). https://doi.org/10.1007/978-3-662-56509-4
2. Di Ciccio, C., Marrella, A., Russo, A.: Knowledge-intensive processes: characteristics, requirements and analysis of contemporary approaches. J. Data Semant. **4**, 29–57 (2014)
3. Marjanovic, O., Freeze, R.: Knowledge intensive business processes: theoretical foundations and research challenges. In: 44th International Conference on System Sciences (2011)
4. França, J., Netto, J., Carvalho, J., Santoro, F., Baião, F., Pimentel, M.: KIPO: the knowledge-intensive process ontology. Softw. Syst. Model. **14**(3), 1127–1157 (2014)
5. Işik, Ö., Mertens, W., Van den Bergh, J.: Practices of knowledge intensive process management: quantitative insights. Bus. Process Manag. J. **19**, 515–534 (2013)
6. Vaculin, R., Hull, R., Heath, T., Cochran, C., Nigam, A., Sukaviriya, P.: Declarative business artifact centric modeling of decision and knowledge intensive business processes. In: IEEE 15th International Enterprise Distributed Object Computing Conference (2011)
7. Mundbrod, N., Reichert, M.: Process-aware task management support for knowledge-intensive business processes: findings, challenges, requirements. In: IEEE 18th International Enterprise Distributed Object Computing Conference Workshops and Demos (2014)
8. Sales, T.P., Baião, F., Guizzardi, G., Almeida, J.P.A., Guarino, N., Mylopoulos, J.: The common ontology of value and risk. In: Trujillo, J.C., et al. (eds.) ER 2018. LNCS, vol. 11157, pp. 121–135. Springer, Cham (2018). https://doi.org/10.1007/978-3-030-00847-5_11
9. Guarino, N., Andersson, B., Johannesson, P., Livieri, B.: Towards an ontology of value ascription. In: Formal Ontology in Information Systems, vol. 283, p. 331 (2016)
10. Castelfranchi, C., Paglieri, F.: The role of beliefs in goal dynamics: prolegomena to a constructive theory of intentions. Synthese **155**, 237–263 (2007)
11. Bratman, M.: Intention, Plans, and Practical Reason, vol. 10. Harvard University Press, Cambridge (1987)
12. Wigfield, A., Cambria, J.: Achievement motivation. In: The Corsini Encyclopedia of Psychology, pp. 1–2 (2010)
13. Guizzardi, G.: Ontological Foundations for Structural Conceptual Models. Telematica Instituut/CTIT, Enschede (2005)
14. Guizzardi, G., Wagner, G., Almeida, J., Guizzardi, R.: Towards ontological foundations for conceptual modeling: the unified foundational ontology (UFO) story. Appl. Ontol. **10**, 259–271 (2015)
15. Rao, A.S., Georgeff, M.P.: BDI agents: from theory to practice. In: Proceedings of the First International Conference on Multiagent Systems, vol. 95, pp. 312–319 (1995)
16. Ryan, R., Deci, E.: Intrinsic and extrinsic motivations: classic definitions and new directions. Contemp. Educ. Psychol. **25**, 54–67 (2000)
17. Sales, T., Guarino, N., Guizzardi, G., Mylopoulos, J.: An ontological analysis of value propositions. In: IEEE 21st International Enterprise Distributed Object Computing Conference (EDOC) (2017)
18. Frow, P., Payne, A.: Towards the 'perfect' customer experience. J. Brand Manag. **15**, 89–101 (2007)

19. Azevedo, C., Almeida, J., van Sinderen, M., Quartel, D., Guizzardi, G.: An ontology-based semantics for the motivation extension to archimate. In: IEEE 15th International Enterprise Distributed Object Computing Conference (2011)
20. Carvalho, V., Almeida, J., Fonseca, C., Guizzardi, G.: Multi-level ontology-based conceptual modeling. Data Knowl. Eng. **109**, 3–24 (2017)
21. Castelfranchi, C.: Intentions in the light of goals. Topoi **33**, 103–116 (2014)
22. Eccles, J., Wigfield, A.: Motivational beliefs, values, and goals. Ann. Rev. Psychol. **53**, 109–132 (2002)
23. Gagné, M., Deci, E.: Self-determination theory and work motivation. J. Organ. Behav. **26**, 331–362 (2005)
24. Richetti, P.H.P., de A.R. Gonçalves, J.C., Baião, F.A., Santoro, F.M.: Analysis of knowledge-intensive processes focused on the communication perspective. In: Carmona, J., Engels, G., Kumar, A. (eds.) BPM 2017. LNCS, vol. 10445, pp. 269–285. Springer, Cham (2017). https://doi.org/10.1007/978-3-319-65000-5_16

Conceptualization, Design, and Implementation of EconBPC – A Software Artifact for the Economic Analysis of Business Process Compliance

Stephan Kuehnel[1(✉)], Simon Thanh-Nam Trang[2], and Sebastian Lindner[1]

[1] Martin Luther University Halle-Wittenberg, 06108 Halle (Saale), Germany
{stephan.kuehnel,sebastian.lindner}@wiwi.uni-halle.de
[2] University of Goettingen, 37073 Goettingen, Germany
strang@uni-goettingen.de

Abstract. Business process compliance (BPC) refers to business processes that meet requirements originating from different sources, such as laws, directives, standards, etc. BPC has become a heavy cost driver that requires both technical and economic support. While there are numerous tools for the technical support of compliance with requirements, there is a lack of software artifacts supporting the economic perspective of BPC. Consequently, this paper applies a design science research approach aiming at the conceptualization, design, and implementation of a software artifact for the economic analysis of BPC. In this context, we identify two design requirements on the improvement of decision quality and the reduction of cognitive effort. In addition, we derive five design principles (DP) on the basis of which the software artifact EconBPC is implemented. The five DP are evaluated with regard to comprehensibility, traceability, usefulness, and practicability both as part of an expert survey and in think-aloud sessions.

Keywords: Business process compliance · Economic analysis · Software artifact

1 Introduction

Business process compliance (BPC) refers to business processes that meet requirements originating from various sources, such as laws, directives, etc. [1]. Approaches to BPC verification aim to confirm compliance using formally expressed regulatory requirements by means of process verification tools [2]. Such tools focus on technical methods to support BPC considering a variety of checking scopes like control flows, time, or data [3]. Since BPC has become a heavy cost driver [1], complying with requirements requires both technical and economic support [4]. On the one hand, BPC causes costs

Electronic supplementary material The online version of this chapter (https://doi.org/10.1007/978-3-030-33223-5_31) contains supplementary material, which is available to authorized users.

A. H. F. Laender et al. (Eds.): ER 2019, LNCS 11788, pp. 378–386, 2019.
https://doi.org/10.1007/978-3-030-33223-5_31

for software, hardware, or personnel [5]. On the other hand, BPC prevents violations that could result in negative monetary consequences, e.g., penalties or fines [5]. Both aspects play an important role for the profitability of a company and must remain in an appropriate balance. The investigation of process-based compliance measures (i.e., compliance activities/sequences of business processes) with regard to this balance is a procedure that we call economic analysis of BPC. This analysis includes an economic assessment of process-based compliance measures aimed at identifying inefficiencies and stimulating process enhancements.

The economic analysis of BPC is a complex task for the person in charge of the process (i.e., the process owner), especially if necessary data must be obtained from extensive log files. Studies from the field of decision-making theory suggest the use of software artifacts to support complex tasks and decisions, enabling a reduction of the cognitive effort for the end user [6, 7], e.g., through automation. Although there are design-oriented studies dealing with the economic valuation of business processes (see, e.g., [8–10]), to the best of our knowledge there is a lack of software artifacts dealing with the economic analysis of BPC. Hence, the research question (RQ) of this paper is:

RQ: How to conceptualize and design a software artifact for the economic assessment and analysis of business process compliance?

To answer this question, we apply a design science research (DSR) approach whose details are described in Sect. 2. Section 3 presents design requirements (DR) of a software artifact for the economic analysis of BPC (short: EconBPC) and derives corresponding design principles (DP). Section 4 describes the software architecture and implementation of EconBPC, after which the evaluation results of both think-aloud sessions and an expert survey are discussed in Sect. 5. Section 6 concludes with a summary of contributions and a discussion of limitations.

2   Research Methodology and Preliminary Work

To structure our procedure and ensure scientific rigor when designing EconBPC, we applied a DSR approach inspired by the method described in [11]. It involves five steps: awareness of problem, suggestion, development, evaluation and conclusion. Following Meth et al. [6], our research design includes two design cycles (see Fig. 1).

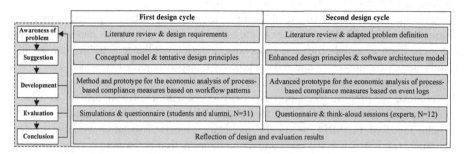

Fig. 1. Design science research approach for EconBPC (according to [6, 11])

A literature review [4] opened the first design cycle, created the awareness that the economic analysis of BPC poses problems and challenges to theory and practice and led to the derivation of the initial DR. The suggestion phase was dedicated to a preliminary conceptualization of EconBPC through a conceptual model [4] and tentative DP. Under consideration of these DP, we developed a method and a first prototype of EconBPC that allows for an economic analysis of compliance utilizing the well-known basic control flow patterns of van der Aalst et al. [12]. The method and the prototype were initially tested with simulated data. As part of a formative evaluation, we interviewed 31 alumni and students at master level in business informatics with a questionnaire on perceived usefulness of EconBPC and asked for expected technical and organizational applicability barriers. The perceived usefulness was asked on a verbal-numeric rating scale with the levels: 1 = "not at all useful", 2 = "hardly useful", 3 = "useful", 4 = "very useful" and 5 = "exceedingly useful". The dataset and further explanations on perceived usefulness can be found in Appendix A. 74% of the respondents rated the approach as exceedingly or very useful, 23% as useful, 3% as hardly useful and 0% as not useful at all. The main expected application barrier was the availability of necessary data and data interfaces in small-sized companies. The evaluation results were used for reflection and prompted us to analyze data availability and data interfaces more closely in the second design cycle.

The second cycle started with an extensive structured literature review of the BPC domain (see [3]). A brief delineation of EconBPC from related work can be found in Appendix B. We examined the search results to determine which data interfaces are used by existing assessment approaches and how they address data availability. As a result, it turned out that log files represent a sound data source [13, 14]. With this in mind, we adapted the conceptualization of EconBPC and implemented an advanced prototype that allows for an economic analysis of BPC utilizing log files. The DR and enhanced DP as well as the advanced prototype and the evaluation results are described in the following sections.

3   Design of the Software Artifact EconBPC

Research has identified the improvement of decision quality and the reduction of cognitive effort as two of the main objectives of human decision makers [6, 7]. We used these findings to derive DR for the tool EconBPC, which is aimed at supporting humans to perform an economic analysis of BPC.

Ensuring BPC requires so-called "compliance activities" that are geared to meeting requirements and added to processes at the initial modeling stage or as part of a process redesign. Even in simple business processes, adding compliance activities can significantly increase complexity and reduce process transparency [2, 15], which makes the economic assessment and analysis of BPC a cognitive challenge for process owners. In this context, we propose to support process owners with a software artifact to reduce their cognitive effort. Therefore, we formulated *DR1* for EconBPC as shown in Fig. 2.

The focus of EconBPC is on the monetary aspects associated with the use of compliance activities. On the one hand, compliance activities serve to prevent costs, as they can prevent compliance violations and resulting monetary consequences. On the

A tool for the economic analysis of business process compliance should...

Design requirement 1		
The artifact is intended to reduce the cognitive effort of process owners in the economic assessment and analysis of business process compliance.	**Design principle 1:** „log file import"	*... provide a log file import interface to enable process (re)constructions, data representations, and economic calculations.*
	Design principle 2: „process modularity"	*... support a modular process interpretation and provide a separate view on compliance acitivites to improve process transparency and enable focused economic analytics.*
	Design principle 3: „monetary input-output ratio"	*... allow the integration of monetary data on input and output factors of process-based compliance measures enabling the calculation of monetary input-output ratios.*
Design requirement 2	**Design principle 4:** „economic assessment and analysis"	*... automatically identify and assess the paths of a process model enabling the calculation of economic indicators for compliance and the analysis of inefficient process paths.*
The artifact is intended to improve the quality of decisions on the use of compliance activities based on economic criteria.	**Design principle 5:** „compliance enhancement support"	*... be capable of both the economic valuation of planned changes to process-based compliance measures and the economic comparison of alternative compliance activities to support economic decisions on compliance enhancements.*

Fig. 2. Design requirements and enhanced design principles of EconBPC

other hand, costs are incurred for their implementation and execution, e.g., for personnel or the acquisition of software and hardware. These costs can significantly affect the economic situation of companies, which is why we suggest to analyze the profitability of compliance activities and to improve the quality of decisions on their use taking into account economic criteria. Consequently, we formulated *DR2* as shown in Fig. 2.

In order to address the DR, we developed a set of five enhanced DP considering the methodological notes of Fu et al. on DP articulation [16]. Figure 2 gives an overview of the DP and their relationships to the respective DR.

The economic analysis of BPC demands the availability of data. As log files represent a sound data source [13, 14] for process (re)constructions, data representations, and economic calculations, we suggest that EconBPC should provide a corresponding import interface. Therefore, *DP1* addresses the import of log files (see Fig. 2).

Complex process models can hamper the distinction between activities serving compliance and activities serving the core business [15]. Consequently, we suggest a modular process interpretation allowing to separate the views on business and compliance activities to improve process transparency and enable focused analytics [15]. Thus, a process can be understood as a composition of components (i.e., activities or sequences) serving different tasks, such as components meeting compliance and components meeting business tasks. The process modularity is addressed by *DP2* (see Fig. 2).

Economic measures, such as the economic efficiency, are generally based on a ratio between the number of resources used (input) and a desired result (output) [17]. Since the economic assessment of BPC requires the calculation of economic ratios, both the input and the output of process-based compliance measures should be recorded in monetary terms [4], as addressed by *DP3* (see Fig. 2). Monetary data of input factors (i.e., costs of compliance activities) should be assigned to the corresponding events of

the log file. Output factors can be expressed in monetary terms as a reduction of the financial risk exposure of BPC (for further details see [5]).

The economic analysis of BPC is based on the assessment of all paths of a process model taking into account compliance costs and path probabilities. Due to space restrictions and since the assessment method is part of previous work [5], we omit further methodical details in this paper. To calculate economic indicators for BPC with little effort and to analyze inefficient paths easily, we suggest that EconBPC should automatically derive and assess all process paths from a log file. Therefore, *DP4* addresses the economic assessment and analysis of BPC considering process paths (see Fig. 2).

If economic inefficiencies are identified, decisions on compliance enhancements must or at least can be made. In order to ensure that planned changes to compliance activities do not lead to a deterioration in profitability, EconBPC should be able to simulate and assess these changes. If alternative compliance activities are available for enhancing BPC, the tool should allow for a selection based on economic criteria. Therefore, *DP5* addresses the compliance enhancement support (see Fig. 2).

4 Implementation of EconBPC

The tool EconBPC was implemented as an R application that builds on the Shiny library [18]. A download link as well as information on installing and using EconBPC can be found at https://bit.ly/2oXZtop. A short screencast of the tool can be downloaded at https://bit.ly/2xwM2wW. Figure 3 illustrates the tool architecture as a component diagram utilizing the Unified Modeling Language (UML).

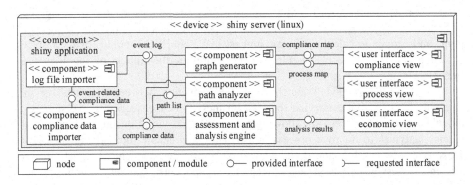

Fig. 3. Architecture of EconBPC illustrated as UML component diagram

We addressed DP1 by developing a *log file importer* for extensible event streams (XES) since XES is a "generally-acknowledged format for the interchange of event log data between tools and application domains" [14]. The *compliance data importer* addresses DP3 since it allows the entering of monetary data of input and output factors of process-based compliance measures required for the determination of monetary input-output ratios. The component *graph generator* enables the visualization of

business processes based on event data. Using the bupaR library [19], a multigraph is created and displayed in the *process view*. By considering compliance data, the graph generator also enables the modular illustration of compliance activities and sequences in the *compliance view*. Thus, the graph generator and the user interfaces address DP2. DP4 and DP5 are jointly addressed by the components *path analyzer, assessment and analysis engine,* and the *economic view*. The path analyzer identifies all paths of a process model from a log file and transfers a path list to the assessment and analysis engine. The engine identifies the compliance events of the paths and assesses them economically, considering monetary compliance data. The results of the path assessment are aggregated for the business process enabling the calculation of economic indicators for BPC. A calculation example can be found in preliminary work [5]. Finally, the assessment and analysis engine transfers the results to the economic view, which displays the outcomes and graphically highlights inefficiencies. If the data of planned changes to process-based compliance measures are imported via the compliance data importer, the engine also enables the economic assessment and analysis of BPC for simulation purposes.

5 Evaluation

The design of EconBPC was evaluated both by an expert survey and think-aloud sessions. Think-aloud sessions are a method for evaluating software designs in which users are asked to complete a series of tasks with the artifact being tested while the users constantly verbalize their thoughts [20]. We oriented towards the so-called "10 ± 2 rule" [21], which states that the problem identification rate of test persons increases only marginally when the sample size exceeds 12. Consequently, we persuaded 12 participants of a regularly occurring compliance expert forum to participate in our evaluation.

The test setup of the think-aloud sessions and a tabular summary of the results can be found in Appendix C. The results can be summarized as follows: The log file import and the compliance data interfaces have been characterized as intuitive to use. The participants commented that the compliance view, which builds on these data, provides a quick overview of the compliance activities. It was particularly emphasized that the automatic path identification and assessment represent a great cognitive relief since the manual evaluation of a large number of instances is practically unfeasible. They also commented that calculation results and identified inefficiencies are clearly presented, which facilitates their use for decision support. Besides these positive aspects, the participants made a total of three significant suggestions for improvement: (1) an option to save modified log files for later analysis or simulation purposes, (2) annotations of compliance activities with cost and reliability data to increase the informative character of the visual representation and (3) a function for importing compliance data along with the log file to simplify data import. To address (1), we added an export interface for log files to the tool. To address (2), we added a function to the graph generator allowing to annotate activities with costs, frequencies and reliabilities. To address (3), we developed an XES extension (see Appendix D) for EconBPC enabling the storage of

compliance data in the log file. The stored values can be used as input data for the economic assessment of BPC.

After the think-aloud sessions, each participant was given a questionnaire containing four questions on each DP about the perceived comprehensibility (C), traceability (T), usefulness (U) and practicability (P). To capture the responses, we used verbal-numeric rating scales with the levels: 1 = "no approval", 2 = "partial approval", 3 = "predominant approval", 4 = "full approval". The questions of the expert survey can be found in Appendix E, the dataset in Appendix F and a complete table of results in Appendix G. The results can be summarized as follows: The respondents agreed fully or predominately with all the statements on C, T, U and P for DP1, DP4 and DP5 in high proportions, i.e., within a range of 83%–100%. The respondents also agreed fully or predominantly in high proportions with the statements on C, T and P for DP2 (83%–92%) and C, T and U for DP3 (92%–100%). However, only 67% fully or predominantly agreed with statement on U for DP2. 25% partially agreed and 8% abstained. Moreover, only 50% agreed completely or predominantly with the statement on P of DP3, whereas 42% agreed partially and 8% did not. As a consequence of the results of U for DP2 and P for DP3, we contacted the respondents again and offered them the opportunity to justify their rating. It turned out that the somewhat lower rating resulted from the improvement potentials identified in the think-aloud sessions. The respondents indicated that the rating of U for DP2 could be increased by improving the informative character of the visual process representation through the proposed annotations. In addition, they argued that the rating of P for DP3 could be increased significantly once the recommended XES extension is realized. Since these improvement suggestions have already been implemented, the criticisms of DP2 and DP3 can already be assumed to be eliminated.

6   Conclusion

This paper is concerned with the conceptualization, design, and implementation of a software artifact for the economic analysis of BPC. In this context, we introduced two DR on the improvement of decision quality and the reduction of cognitive effort. Moreover, we derived five related DP which we evaluated as comprehensible, traceable, useful and practicable. Practitioners and scientists can adapt the DP for developing new tools, e.g., for specific application areas such as data protection, healthcare, or the automotive industry. Thus, the DR and DP contribute to the prescriptive knowledge base of the BPC domain. We implemented the design of EconBPC as a software artifact and evaluated it by 12 test persons in think-aloud sessions. The results showed that the prototype is intuitive to use and that both the automatic path identification and the assessment of process-based compliance measures are perceived as a cognitive relief. In addition, it was found that the clear presentation of inefficiencies and economic results contributes to decision support and can facilitate an improvement in decision quality.

For the theoretical foundation of our DR we used decision-making theory. Choosing a different foundation could result in different DR and related DP. However, decision-making theory is commonly used for design-oriented studies [6, 7]. Since this

paper paid special attention to the design of our software artifact, we followed the recommendations of Fu et al. [16] and focused the evaluation on the DP. Even though the think-aloud sessions provided insights into the cognitive process of tool users, the quantitative evaluation of cognitive effort and decision quality with appropriate metrics is still subject to future research. As with any evaluation, our results depend on our sample, i.e., the choice of other participants, or a different sample size could lead to different results. However, by applying a common evaluation rule and selecting subject-specific experts, we believe to have gained sound insights. Finally, this paper is based on a purely economic view. The simultaneous consideration of other aspects, such as social dimensions, ethics, or sustainability, represents an interesting opportunity for further research.

References

1. Becker, J., Delfmann, P., Dietrich, H.-A., Steinhorst, M., Eggert, M.: Business process compliance checking – applying and evaluating a generic pattern matching approach for conceptual models in the financial sector. Inf. Syst. Front. **18**, 359–405 (2016)
2. Schumm, D., Leymann, F., Ma, Z., Scheibler, T., Strauch, S.: Integrating compliance into business processes: process fragments as reusable compliance controls. In: Proceedings of the Multikonferenz Wirtschaftsinformatik 2010, pp. 2125–2137 (2010)
3. Sackmann, S., Kuehnel, S., Seyffarth, T.: Using business process compliance approaches for compliance management with regard to digitization: evidence from a systematic literature review. In: Weske, M., Montali, M., Weber, I., vom Brocke, J. (eds.) BPM 2018. LNCS, vol. 11080, pp. 409–425. Springer, Cham (2018). https://doi.org/10.1007/978-3-319-98648-7_24
4. Kühnel, S.: Toward a conceptual model for cost-effective business process compliance. In: Proceedings of Informatik 2017, Lecture Notes in Informatics (LNI)), pp. 1631–1639 (2017)
5. Kuehnel, S., Zasada, A.: An approach toward the economic assessment of business process compliance. In: Woo, C., Lu, J., Li, Z., Ling, T.W., Li, G., Lee, M.L. (eds.) ER 2018. LNCS, vol. 11158, pp. 228–238. Springer, Cham (2018). https://doi.org/10.1007/978-3-030-01391-2_28
6. Meth, H., Mueller, B., Maedche, A.: Designing a requirement mining system. JAIS **16**, 799–837 (2015)
7. Wang, B.: Interactive decision aids for consumer decision making in e-commerce. The influence of perceived strategy restrictiveness. MIS Q. **33**, 293 (2009)
8. Magnani, M., Montesi, D.: Computing the Cost of BPMN Diagrams. Technical report UBLCS-07-17. Bologna (2007)
9. Vom Brocke, J., Recker, J., Mendling, J.: Value-oriented process modeling: integrating financial perspectives into business process re-design. BPM J. **16**, 333–356 (2010)
10. Sampathkumaran, P.B., Wirsing, M.: Financial evaluation and optimization of business processes. IJISMD **4**, 91–120 (2013)
11. Vaishnavi, V., Kuechler, W.: Design Science Research Methods and Patterns. Innovating Information and Communication Technology. CRC Press Taylor & Francis, Boca Raton (2015)
12. van der Aalst, W.M.P., ter Hofstede, A.H.M., Kiepuszewski, B., Barros, A.P.: Workflow patterns. Distrib. Parallel Databases **14**, 5–51 (2003)
13. Lu, R., Sadiq, S., Governatori, G.: Measurement of compliance distance in business processes. Inf. Syst. Manag. **25**, 344–355 (2008)

14. Günther, C.W., Verbeek, E.: XES standard definition 2.0. Eindhoven (2014)
15. Betke, H., Kittel, K., Sackmann, S.: Modeling controls for compliance – an analysis of business process modeling languages. In: WAINA 2013. pp. 866–871. IEEE, NJ (2013)
16. Fu, K.K., Yang, M.C., Wood, K.L.: Design principles. Literature review, analysis, and future directions. J. Mech. Des. **138**, 101103 (2016)
17. Kirzner, I.M., Boettke, P.J., Sautet, F.E.: The Economic Point of View. An Essay in the History of Economic Thought. Liberty Fund, Indianapolis (2009)
18. Chang, W., Cheng, J., Allaire, J.J., Xie, Y., McPherson, J.: Shiny: web application framework for R. R package version 1.2.0 (2018). https://CRAN.R-project.org/package= shiny
19. Janssenswillen, G., Depaire, B.: bupaR. business process analysis in R. BPM (2017)
20. Van den Haak, M., de Jong, M., Jan Schellens, P.: Retrospective vs. concurrent think-aloud protocols. Behav. Inf. Technol. **22**, 339–351 (2003)
21. Hwang, W., Salvendy, G.: Number of people required for usability evaluation. Commun. ACM **53**, 130 (2010)

DEMOS: A Participatory Design Approach for Democratic Empowerment of IS Users

Raphaëlle Bour[(⊠)], Chantal Soule-Dupuy,
and Nathalie Vallès-Parlangeau

IRIT, Université Toulouse 1 Capitole, Toulouse, France
{raphaelle.bour, chantal.soule-dupuy,
nathalie.valles-parlangeau}@irit.fr

Abstract. The issue of democracy in society is at the heart of our current concerns. The organizations and their information systems are also concerned by this issue. Democracy in organization requires a debate about norms, values and language encapsulated in the information systems. The participatory design approaches address this issue by proposing a democratic empowerment for users during design phase of projects. To go further, we propose a structured method to integrate democracy into information systems. This method named DEMOS for DEsign Method for democratic information System is described and then illustrated by a real experiment provided by a "lifelong training" service at the University. All aspects of the method are addressed: from elicitation phase to implementation. We particularly focus on techniques and tools used during the design phase.

Keywords: Democracy · Method engineering · Information system design · Requirements engineering · Viewpoint · End-users · Participatory design · Agility · User centered design

1 Introduction

The question of democracy in society is a huge topic. One thing is certain, we can establish a parallelism between democracy in political society and democracy in organizations. The democracy in organizations is built through a participation of co-workers and a "high rate of empowerment" [1]. This process of democratization in organizations requires a particular focus on Information Systems (IS). In fact, an IS is not neutral. In his book Brey speaks about "embedded values" in the IS [2]. Mingers says that IT (Information Technology) systems embed particular values which have a "moral impact" [3]. These embedded values take the form of standards, quantification conventions, indicators. In 2010, Floridi proposed to elicit those embedded values and to take them into account during the IS development [4]. Salles and Colletis describe a "three-level grid" highlighting the link between representations, models and norms [5]. In our view, these observations confirm the need of democracy. On the one hand, those norms and values need to be debated, "deliberated and recognized" [3], in a democratic way. On the other hand, if we agree with Salles to say that « democracy is considered above all else to guarantee access to a plurality of worldviews" [6], a democratic IS has

© Springer Nature Switzerland AG 2019
A. H. F. Laender et al. (Eds.): ER 2019, LNCS 11788, pp. 387–394, 2019.
https://doi.org/10.1007/978-3-030-33223-5_32

to respect viewpoints. For that, the end-users representing different viewpoints have to be considered in the system design. To go further, viewpoints must be implemented in the IS. The IS should not conform only to a dominant viewpoint. In the continuity of Van Den Hoven [7], we propose a "proactive integration" of democracy with a Design Method for demOcratic information System, named DEMOS. Our method proposes to integrate democracy in two ways. Firstly, we propose a democratic design method, which lets users debate about IS values and norms, and to bring out viewpoints. Secondly, we propose a democratic IS, which respects viewpoints identified in the design phase and implements them.

In this article, we first present a state of art divided into two parts. First paragraph is about user involvement in design approaches, second paragraph is about viewpoint concept. Then, we identify specific issues for a democratic IS and present how DEMOS can address them. We illustrate this part with a feedback from a real experiment conducted with the "lifelong training" service at the university.

2   The State of Art

The lack of users input during design has been identified as being a major factor in the failure of IS to be adopted by users [8]. The users' participation is a way to increase functional qualities of the system and to be as close as possible to their needs. It can also be a way of democratic empowerment for users, by a direct participation in decision making [9]. In the IT literature, we find several levels of users' involvement in projects: from considering the users as a "subject of study" in User Centered Design (UCD), to users playing a more collaborative role in co-operative design. With Participatory Design (PD), the user drives the design process himself [10]. With UCD, design team analyses users' interaction, and the direct users' input in design decision making is limited. The software developers still "lead the process", whereas users participate by refining their ideas [11]. The co-operative design seeks to find ways to co-operate with users in the design process [10]. The users interact with a prototype of a system being developed and can provide input in the design process. The user has a consultative role, but it is not sufficient to speak about empowerment. PD is the most involving approach in which participation of people in the co-design [12] of the IS is a "central tenet" [13]. The user is considered as a partner and no more as a subject as in UCD [14]. The aim is to increase system quality, and to empower people by a "higher level of participation in decision making" [15]. As Simonsen says, participation is absolutely necessary. According to him, it is a "basic human right" for users to have the opportunity to influence the design and implementation processes if they are affected by the changes resulting from designing and implementing [16]. Some authors like Sanders defines PD as a "democratic approach" [11]. In fact, PD approaches can provide a democratic empowerment if users participate in "defining project objectives and initial plans" [17]. In this sense, DEMOS can be considered as a PD approach.

In software engineering, viewpoint may have different meanings, as we present in this second paragraph. Today, the importance of involving end-users as stakeholders in the Requirements Engineering (RE) phase is well established [18]. The common point of each participative RE process is that authors make no distinction inside the users

group. They only make a distinction inside the stakeholder's group, like in the IEEE standard where stakeholders are characterized as client, owner, operator, architect, developer and users. Moreover, goal oriented RE is a way to elicit a project motivation, but rarely address norms and values issues with a democratic debate. When authors use the term "viewpoint", they also have different visions. For Kotonya, viewpoints are clients of the system, as in a client-server system [19]. With Sommerville, viewpoints are considered in a multi-perspective way. The aim is to separate stakeholder's concerns. The end-users are again considered as one viewpoint [20]. In the field of computer design, the viewpoints are often attached to different project actors: designers, architects, end-users, etc. For its part, the European Standard CEN recognizes four points of view: functional, informational, resources, organizational. These classifications do not correspond to our problematic, which focuses on the different user's viewpoints only. About user's viewpoint, there are different ways to tackle the problem. In terms of RE, we are talking about user viewpoint modeling [21]. Unfortunately, this form of modeling does not continue beyond the requirements during the design work. The requirements model will not be translated into a conceptual model. With component oriented information systems, viewpoint modeling is managed by base schema and view schema concepts [22]. This form of modeling is primarily a way to architect the system and remains a designer vision. The way to deal with the issue of user views that is closest to ours is handled by Nassar. He proposes an adaptation of the UML diagram with the notion of view extensions [23]. But here again, it is an answer to a technical problem related to access rights, and the solution provided is not at all user-oriented. Then, viewpoint issue is often seen in a technical perspective to separate concerns, or to separate roles, but never as a respect guarantee of democracy.

3   DEMOS: A DEsign Method for demOcratic Information System

DEMOS is presented in the form of a MAP: a "navigational structure" [24] developed by Rolland. It allows presenting the method as a selection of intentions (circles) and appropriate strategies (arrows) to achieve it (Fig. 1).

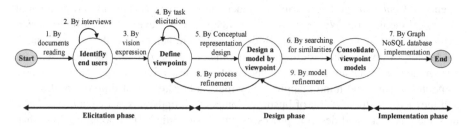

Fig. 1. General view of DEMOS

There are four intentions in the proposed method. Each intention in the MAP is a way to solve an issue that the method addresses:

- *Identify end-users* to **involve end-users in a participatory and democratic process**
- *Define viewpoint* by **allowing a debate to let viewpoints emerge.**
- *Design a model by viewpoint* to **design a democratic IS which considers these viewpoints.**
- *Consolidate viewpoint models* to **provide traceability of viewpoints.**

In the following sections, each strategy is described, with a brief list of means used and expected results. The sections are grouped by intentions, for a better understanding. From January to June 2018, DEMOS has been used for a real project. The project focused on the implementation of an attendance management tool for the Toulouse 1 Capitole university's "lifelong training" service. This experiment was conducted with 8 end-users: 3 teachers, 4 schooling managers and the "lifelong training" service manager. The aim of the project was to develop a prototype to be tested by users. The designed software is currently being implemented. In this paper, third et fourth intention will be illustrated with feedback from this recent experiment.

3.1 First Intention: Identify End-Users

Our first issue is to involve end-users in a participatory and democratic process. For that, the first intention: *Identify end-users*, is the starting point of our participative approach. We developed two strategies to achieve this intention: *by interviews* and *by document reading*. Both strategies are achieved with the client and the main managers concerned by the project. They give information during interviews: motivation of the project, issues to solve and constraints (as brake of users). Business documents complete this information: organigram, specifications. The client must validate the list of end-users obtained. These two strategies have been chosen to be complementary: they give an analysis of prescribed work and real work [25] as said in work ergonomics. Documentation is a representation of the prescribed work and gives a first list of end-users, whereas interviews give information about real work.

3.2 Second Intention: Define Viewpoints

Our second issue is to allow a democratic debate to let viewpoints emerge. The second intention: *Define viewpoints* is crucial. In fact, these viewpoints are the starting point of the rest of the method. We developed two strategies to achieve this intention: *by vision expression* and *by task elicitation*. Both strategies are achieved with end-users and a moderator of the method during the scoping workshop. First, the end-users are encouraged to debate about their visions, and to let viewpoints emerge. Thanks to tools as photolanguage and mind mapping, they make a breakdown of different professions and they express their vision of business domain to propose first viewpoint list. Then, they identify tasks and describe processes with a simplified BPM notation. After that, they consolidate the viewpoint list. During the experiment, two viewpoints were identified: Management viewpoint (with the schooling manager and the lifelong training service managers), and Education viewpoint (with the teachers).

3.3   Third Intention: Design a Model by Viewpoint

Our third issue is to design a democratic IS which takes into account viewpoints. The third intention: *Design a model by viewpoint* corresponds to the design phase starting point. This intention requires a strategy: ***conceptual representation design***. This strategy is achieved during several viewpoint workshop. There are as many workshops as identified viewpoints. The aim is to obtain one conceptual model by viewpoint. During the workshop, each end-user uses his own vocabulary to express concepts he manipulates to achieve his tasks. They do not have to adapt to other norms, values or to use another vocabulary. Because the description of concepts is sometimes confusing for end-users, we proposed several activities to achieve this goal: Photolanguage, brainstorming, markers, etc. The main outputs of these section are simplified class diagrams for each viewpoint. During the ***process refinement*** strategy, work on processes during the viewpoint model designing intention can affect viewpoint identification. For example, end-users can realize at this step that a viewpoint is badly or insufficiently described. In this case, a new definition of the viewpoint is necessary. Figure 2 presents an instantiation of a part of DEMOS meta-model corresponding to the experiment with lifelong training service.

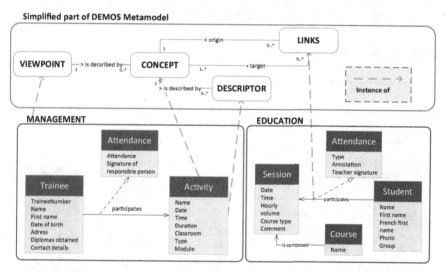

Fig. 2. Instantiation of the strategy ***By conceptual representation design***

We obtained two different conceptual models, and we present here just a little part of them. The vocabulary employed on each model corresponds to the corresponding viewpoint, described with concepts, descriptors and links, using a simplified UML class diagram formalism. Here the structure of the attendance representation is not the same for each viewpoint: the management viewpoint speaks about trainees whereas the education viewpoint is interested in students. Furthermore, while the education

viewpoint is only interested in the class attendance, the management viewpoint needs to attest about attendance for other activities like internships.

3.4 Fourth Intention: Consolidate Viewpoint Models

The fourth intention: *Consolidate viewpoint models*, corresponds to the last step of the design phase. This intention requires a strategy: *searching for similarities*. This strategy is achieved during a sharing workshop where all participants are grouped. This intention is crucial because even if each viewpoint corresponds to a conceptual representation, some elements between these representations are common. Sometimes these elements are identical, sometimes they are named differently but have the same meaning, and sometimes they are simply organized differently. The similarities between models must be identified to share the same IS. For these reasons, after the moderator organizes the models pooling, the end-users can search for similarities. With the *representation refinement* strategy, work on conceptual representation during the viewpoint model consolidation section can affect the previous designed model. In fact, searching for similarities can allow for some new concepts for a viewpoint to emerge. In this case, viewpoint models must be completed.

Figure 3 presents an instantiation of a part of DEMOS metamodel corresponding to the experiment with the lifelong training service.

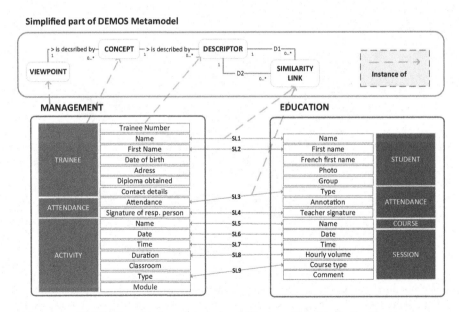

Fig. 3. Instantiation of the strategy *By searching for similarities*

In this illustration, we have selected just a part of the similarity links, corresponding to previous viewpoint models. Here for example, the name of a trainee and the name of a student are similar, so they must be linked. Each similarity link is a way to create a

data repository. It guarantees that even if there is an implementation of several conceptual models, objects are shared through this repository.

The last strategy: **By Graph NoSQL Database implementation** is the purpose of the method because it is an implementation of the viewpoints. To keep viewpoint traceability in the IS, it was necessary to implement a database structure in accordance with viewpoints. Thus, the viewpoints can continue to exist independently during the life of the IS. If a viewpoint evolves, the other viewpoints are not impacted, expected by re-creating similarity links. One efficient solution to implement several linked models is Graph No SQL Database, we have adopted this strategy. In the future, other strategies could be added with other technical solutions.

4 Discussion

We have shown with DEMOS that a structured design method can contribute to integrate democracy in IS, and we have illustrated our proposition with a concrete case. Following the experiment, we have evaluated DEMOS with semi-structured interviews with end-users. After a review of the method and of the results obtained during the experiment, we have conducted an interview with each participant to evaluate the method intentions, the method strategies and the method results. The evaluations revealed that end-users understand intentions of the method. They understand both aspects: a democratic process for a democratic IS which respects their viewpoints. The viewpoint notion that was not obvious to them at first became clearer during the workshops. Moreover, for users, sequencing of steps was coherent according to the intentions. Overall, they were assisted by techniques and tools used during the process, especially by the photolanguage activities. At the end, they are satisfied with the method results, which are consistent with what they have expressed. The final software is under development and was not considered for evaluation.

The issue addressed in this article is democracy in IS. We consider this issue with two different perspectives: how to integrate democracy in IS conception approaches and how to bring democracy into IS. It requires a participative approach involving end-users, respect of viewpoints inside end-users' group, and traceability of these viewpoints. During the experiment, and according to the evaluation, each point has been respected. However, the implementation of viewpoints is guaranteed by the implementation of a database structure. As future work, we want to add other intentions to implement activity model and interface model.

References

1. Jardat, R.: How democratic internal law leads to low cost efficient processes. Soc. Bus. Rev. 3(1), 23–40 (2008)
2. Brey, P.A.E.: Values in technology and disclosive computer ethics. In: Floridi, L. (ed.) The Cambridge Handbook of Information and Computer Ethics, pp. 41–58. Cambridge University Press, Cambridge (2010)
3. Mingers, J., Walsham, G.: Toward ethical information systems: the contribution of discourse ethics. MIS Q. **34**(4), 833–854 (2010)

4. Floridi, L.: The Cambridge Handbook of Information and Computer Ethics. Cambridge University Press, Cambridge (2010)

5. Salles, M., Colletis, G.: How to deal with the conflicting views of the world expressed in regional economic development policies. In: International Conference of Territorial Intelligence, Besançon 2008, Besançon, France, p. 10 (2008)

6. Salles, M.: Decision-Making and the Information System, vol. 3. Wiley, Hoboken (2015)

7. van den Hoven, J.: Moral methodology and information technology. In: Himma, K.E., Tavani, H.T. (eds.) The Handbook of Information and Computer Ethics, pp. 49–67. Wiley, Hoboken (2008)

8. McConnell, S.: Rapid Development: Taming Wild Software Schedules. Microsoft Press, Redmond (2006)

9. Kautz, K.: Investigating the design process: participatory design in agile software development. Inf. Technol. People **24**(3), 217–235 (2011)

10. Andre, K., Christian, N.: Participatory design, user involvement and health IT evaluation. Stud. Health Technol. Inform. **222**, 139–151 (2016)

11. Ferrario, M.A., Simm, W., Newman, P., Forshaw, S., Whittle, J.: Software engineering for 'social good': integrating action research, participatory design, and agile development. In: Companion Proceedings of the 36th International Conference on Software Engineering - ICSE Companion 2014, Hyderabad, India, pp. 520–523 (2014)

12. Sanders, E.B.-N., Stappers, P.J.: Co-creation and the new landscapes of design. CoDesign **4**(1), 5–18 (2008)

13. Kensing, F., Blomberg, J.: Participatory design: issues and concerns. Comput. Support. Coop. Work CSCW **7**(3–4), 167–185 (1998)

14. Dell'Era, C., Landoni, P.: Living lab: a methodology between user-centred design and participatory design: living lab. Creat. Innov. Manag. **23**(2), 137–154 (2014)

15. Kujala, S.: User involvement: a review of the benefits and challenges. Behav. Inf. Technol. **22**(1), 1–16 (2003)

16. Simonsen, J.: Routledge International Handbook of Participatory Design. Routledge, London (2013)

17. Dearden, A., Rizvi, H.: Adapting participatory and agile software methods to participatory rural development. In: Proceedings of the Tenth Anniversary Conference on Participatory Design 2008, Indianapolis, IN, USA, pp. 221–225 (2008)

18. Milne, A., Maiden, N.: Power and politics in requirements engineering: embracing the dark side? Requir. Eng. **17**(2), 83–98 (2012)

19. Kotonya, G., Sommerville, I.: Requirements engineering with viewpoints. Softw. Eng. J. **11**(1), 5 (1996)

20. Sommerville, I., Sawyer, P.: Viewpoints: principles, problems and a practical approach to requirements engineering. Ann. Softw. Eng. **3**, 101–130 (1997)

21. Darke, P., Shanks, G.: User viewpoint modelling: understanding and representing user viewpoints during requirements definition. Inf. Syst. J. **7**(3), 213–219 (1997)

22. Caron, O., Carré, B., Muller, A., Vanwormhoudt, G.: A framework for supporting views in component oriented information systems. In: Konstantas, D., Léonard, M., Pigneur, Y., Patel, S. (eds.) OOIS 2003. LNCS, vol. 2817, pp. 164–178. Springer, Heidelberg (2003). https://doi.org/10.1007/978-3-540-45242-3_16

23. Nassar, M.: VUML: a viewpoint oriented UML extension, pp. 373–376 (2003)

24. Rolland, C., Prakash, N., Benjamen, A.: A multi-model view of process modelling. Requir. Eng. **4**(4), 169–187 (1999)

25. Vilela, R.A.D.G.: et al.: Work ergonomic analysis and change laboratory: similarities and complementarities between interventionist methods (2015, Unpublished)

Complex Systems Modeling

Finding Preferred Objects
with Taxonomies

Paolo Ciaccia[1], Davide Martinenghi[2], and Riccardo Torlone[3]([✉])

[1] Università di Bologna, Bologna, Italy
paolo.ciaccia@unibo.it
[2] Politecnico di Milano, Milan, Italy
davide.martinenghi@polimi.it
[3] Università Roma Tre, Rome, Italy
riccardo.torlone@uniroma3.it

Abstract. Preferences about objects of interest are often expressed at different levels of granularity, not always matching the level of detail of stored data. For instance, we prefer rock to pop music, yet scheduled concerts only cite the name of the performer, with no reference to the musical genre. In this paper we address this common mismatch by leveraging the vast amounts of data organized in taxonomies (such as those found in electronic catalogs and classification systems) for *propagating* preferences from more generic to more specific concepts. This will help users to locate their preferred objects. In spite of its apparent simplicity, this problem requires special care in order to avoid some undesirable effects, e.g., when conflicting preferences at different levels have to be combined (although, generally, we prefer rock to pop music, we would never miss a performance by Madonna). We present a formal model to represent preferences and state the desirable properties of preference propagation, such as the fact that more specific preferences always prevail over more generic ones. We then propose a method for propagating preferences along taxonomies, complying with the stated properties, and show how preferred objects can thereby be efficiently determined.

Keywords: Preferences · Taxonomy · Best results

1 Introduction

The information available in digital form is growing so fast that the search for data of interest (for attending events, buying products, planning a trip, etc.) is becoming increasingly difficult over time. For this reason, there has recently been a huge effort, in both industry and academia, to develop effective methods and tools able to automatically suggest to any individual the items that better match what he/she is looking for [8]. In this framework, the availability of preferences, explicitly expressed by the users or somehow automatically derived from their actions, has been always considered an important ingredient [3,9]. Unfortunately, preferences and data do not always match perfectly, even when they refer to the

© Springer Nature Switzerland AG 2019
A. H. F. Laender et al. (Eds.): ER 2019, LNCS 11788, pp. 397–411, 2019.
https://doi.org/10.1007/978-3-030-33223-5_33

same domain of interest. This is mainly due to the fact that, usually, preferences are expressed in generic terms whereas data is very specific, as shown in the example that follows.

Example 1. We are planning to reserve tickets for a series of concerts for which a general schedule is available, as the one in Fig. 1. We prefer rock to pop concerts, yet we prefer a performance by Madonna to a rock concert. Due to work commitments, we also prefer concerts in August rather than in September. Furthermore, as for the concert venue, during autumn we prefer places indoors to stadiums. And, given two concerts by the same artist, we would prefer to save money (say, if a concert costs $\leq 40\$$, then we prefer it to a concert by the same artist that costs more than 100\$, whereas for intermediate prices other considerations are relevant). For the same reason, we would like to buy tickets only for (a subset of) the "best" available alternatives.

Concerts

Artist	Day	Venue	Price (\$)	
Bruce Springsteen	10/05/2019	Verona Arena	70	t_a
Madonna	24/06/2019	Verona Arena	35	t_b
Madonna	21/07/2019	Blue Note, Milan	120	t_c
Eminem	12/08/2019	Unipol Arena, Bologna	60	t_d
Rihanna	10/10/2019	Blue Note, Milan	50	t_e
Bruce Springsteen	30/10/2019	Stadio Olimpico, Rome	100	t_f

Fig. 1. A set of concerts.

The example highlights that: (i) preferences can be expressed at different levels of detail, even for the same "dimension" of the problem (e.g., seasons vs months for the time dimension), and (ii) in general, preferences do not match the level of detail of data. Moreover, preferences can be conflicting when changing the level of detail (rock is better than pop, yet Madonna, a pop singer, is preferred to rock artists). Finally, additional knowledge is needed to choose the best alternatives using preferences. For instance, we need to know that Unipol Arena is an indoor place, whereas Verona Arena is a Roman amphitheater (thus an outdoor place).

This problem can be tackled by leveraging the great availability of shared and public taxonomies, that is, collection of terms in a domain arranged hierarchically according to an inclusion relationship (e.g., product catalogs, book classifications, biological categorizations, etc.). For instance, the availability of a classification of music artists according to different musical genres would allow us to understand that a preference on rock artists *propagates* to Springsteen.

In this paper we present a principled approach to the problem of finding the best objects stored in a data repository on the basis of a set of preferences that are defined at a level of detail that does not necessarily match that of the data. As

a preliminary step, we adopt a data model for representing taxonomies of values in specific domains (e.g., time or location) and propose a preference model for tuples over attributes defined on a given set of taxonomies. This allows us to formalize preferences between objects at different levels of detail, as those in Example 1. We then identify some general properties of preference propagation in the taxonomies, in particular, the fact that more specific preferences prevail over more generic ones. Thus, in the example above, a Madonna concert takes precedence over a Springsteen concert even if, in general, we prefer rock to pop. We then illustrate an algorithm for propagating preferences along taxonomies, complying with the stated properties. This algorithm takes as input a set of taxonomies and a logic formula describing preferences between tuples over values in the taxonomies and returns another formula describing the preferences that hold on the actual data after propagation. Finally, we present a technique for selecting the best tuples in the data repository according to the propagated preferences. This technique would select tuples t_b and t_d as the best alternatives among the tuples in Fig. 1 given the preferences discussed in Example 1.

The rest of the paper is organized as follows. In Sect. 2 we present a data model for representing tuples of values that belong to the levels of a set of taxonomies whereas, in Sect. 3, we illustrate a preference model over tuples of the data model. In Sect. 4 we investigate the general properties of preference propagation and then propose the algorithm for preference propagation. An algorithm for the selection of the best tuples according to a set of propagated preferences is discussed in Sect. 5. Finally, Sect. 6 briefly concludes. Formal results regarding the correctness and complexity of our approach are omitted in the interest of space.

2   Data Model

In this section we present the essential elements of our data model, which is an adaptation of the model described in [6,7]. For what follows it is useful to remind that a *partial order* $\leq$ on a domain V is a subset of $V \times V$, whose elements are denoted by $v_1 \leq v_2$, that is: reflexive ($v \leq v$ for all $v \in V$), antisymmetric (if $v_1 \leq v_2$ and $v_2 \leq v_1$ then $v_1 = v_2$), and transitive (if $v_1 \leq v_2$ and $v_2 \leq v_3$ then $v_1 \leq v_3$).

Essentially, we consider an extension of the relational model in which each domain can be organized as a *taxonomy*, i.e., a set of values arranged hierarchically. Each taxonomy is organized into a set of *levels* corresponding to different degrees of granularity. For instance, a taxonomy on *time* can be organized in levels such as day, month, season, and year.

Definition 1 (Taxonomy). *A* taxonomy T *is composed of:*

- *a finite set $L = \{l_1, \ldots, l_k\}$ of levels; each level $l \in L$ is associated with a set of values, denoted by $T(l)$;*
- *a partial order $\leq_L$ on L having a bottom element, denoted by $\perp_T$, and a top element, denoted by $\top_T$, such that:*

- $T(\bot_T)$ *contains a set of* ground *values whereas all the other levels contain values that represent sets of ground values;*
- $T(\top_T)$ *contains only a special value* ALL$_T$ *that represents all the ground values;*

- *a family of functions* $\mu_{l_1}^{l_2} : T(l_1) \to T(l_2)$, *called* level mappings, *for each pair of levels* $l_1 \leq_L l_2$ *satisfying the following* consistency conditions:
  - *for each level* l, *the function* μ_l^l *is the identity on the values of* $T(l)$;
  - *for each pair of levels* l_1 *and* l_2 *and for all* l, l' *such that* $l_1 \leq_L l \leq_L l_2$ *and* $l_1 \leq_L l' \leq_L l_2$, *we have:* $\mu_l^{l_2}(\mu_{l_1}^l(v)) = \mu_{l'}^{l_2}(\mu_{l_1}^{l'}(v))$ *for each* $v \in T(l_1)$.

Notice that if $l \leq_L l'$ and $\mu_l^{l'}(v) = v'$, then it is also true that $v \in (\mu_l^{l'})^{-1}(v')$, where $(\mu_l^{l'})^{-1}$ is the *inverse* level mapping from level l' to l.

A partial order $\leq_V$, induced by the level mappings, can also be defined on the values of a taxonomy T.

Definition 2 (Poset on values). *Let T be a taxonomy and v_1 and v_2 be values of levels l_1 and l_2 of T, respectively. We have that $v_1 \leq_V v_2$ if: (i) $l_1 \leq_L l_2$ and (ii) $\mu_{l_1}^{l_2}(v_1) = v_2$.*

Example 2. Portions of the taxonomies relevant to our working example on concerts are shown in Fig. 2. The *time* taxonomy has a bottom level whose (ground) values are all the Days; other relevant levels (considering the preferences in Example 1) are Month and Season, with Day $\leq_L$ Month and Day $\leq_L$ Season. A possible value of the Day level is 23/07/2019, which is mapped by the level mappings to the value 07/2019 of the level Month (i.e., $\mu_{\text{Day}}^{\text{Month}}(23/07/2019) = 07/2019$) and to the value summer of the level Season. Conversely, the inverse level mapping from Month to Day yields for each month all the days in that month (e.g., 23/07/2019 $\in (\mu_{\text{Day}}^{\text{Month}})^{-1}(07/2019)$). As another example, for the *location* of a concert we consider levels Venue, VenueType, and InOut. The values of this taxonomy are organized in the poset shown in Fig. 3, where the level mappings are represented by arrows. For instance, we have Blue Note $\leq_V$ Concert hall $\leq_V$ Indoor and Verona Arena $\leq_V$ Amphitheater $\leq_V$ Outdoor.

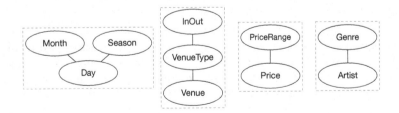

Fig. 2. The taxonomies for our working example

The main construct of the data model is the t-relation, a natural extension of a relational table built over taxonomies.

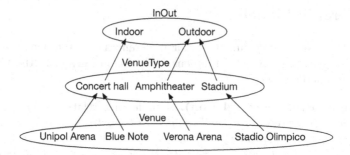

Fig. 3. A taxonomy for concerts' locations

Definition 3 (t-schema, t-tuple, and t-relation). *A* t-schema *(schema over taxonomies) is a set* $S = \{A_1 : l_1, \ldots, A_k : l_k\}$, *where each* A_i *is a distinct attribute name and each* l_i *is a level of some taxonomy* T_i. *A* t-tuple t *over* S *is a function mapping each attribute* A_i *to a value in* $T_i(l_i)$. *A* t-relation r *over* S *is a set of t-tuples over* S.

Given a t-tuple t over a t-schema S and an attribute A_i occurring in S on level l_i, $t[A_i : l_i]$ denotes the value of level l_i associated with t on A_i. In order to simplify the notation, in the rest of the paper we always assume that level names are unique (i.e., the same level name is not used in more than one taxonomy). This makes it possible to understand attribute names, thus also writing $t[l_i]$ in place of $t[A_i : l_i]$.

Example 3. A catalog of concerts in Italy can be represented by the t-schema $S = \{\mathsf{Artist}, \mathsf{Day}, \mathsf{Venue}, \mathsf{Price}\}$. A possible t-relation over S is shown in Fig. 1. Then we have $t_b[\mathsf{Venue}] = \mathtt{Verona\ Arena}$ and $t_e[\mathsf{Artist}] = \mathtt{Rihanna}$.

We conclude with the definitions of the partial order relations for t-schemas and t-tuples.

Definition 4 (Posets on t-schemas and t-tuples). *Let* S_1 *and* S_2 *be two t-schemas. We have that* $S_1 \leq_S S_2$ *if for each* $A_i : l_i \in S_2$ *there is an element* $A_i : l_j \in S_1$ *such that* $l_j \leq_L l_i$. *Let* t_1 *and* t_2 *be t-tuples over* S_1 *and* S_2, *respectively. We have that* $t_1 \leq_t t_2$ *if: (i)* $S_1 \leq_S S_2$, *and (ii) for each* $A_i : l_i \in S_2$ *there is an element* $A_i : l_j \in S_1$ *such that* $t_1[A_i : l_j] \leq_V t_2[A_i : l_i]$.

Notice that, in the above definition, S_2 may have fewer attributes than S_1. However, we can assume without loss of generality that they have the same set of attributes, since we can add to S_2 the missing attributes at the top level.

Example 4. Consider the t-schemas $S = \{\mathsf{Artist}, \mathsf{Day}, \mathsf{Venue}\}$ and $S' = \{\mathsf{Genre}, \mathsf{Season}\}$, and the t-tuples $t = \langle \mathtt{Eddie\ Vedder}, \mathtt{16/04/2019}, \mathtt{Verona\ Arena} \rangle$ and $t' = \langle \mathtt{rock}, \mathtt{spring} \rangle$ over S and S', respectively. Then, $S \leq_S S'$ and $t \leq_t t'$. This is equivalent to considering the t-schema $S'' = \{\mathsf{Genre}, \mathsf{Season}, \top_{location}\}$ in place of S' and the t-tuple $t'' = \langle \mathtt{rock}, \mathtt{spring}, \mathtt{ALL}_{location} \rangle$ in place of t'.

3   Preference Model

In this section, we present our model for preferences on t-relations. We denote as $\mathcal{T} = T_1 \times \ldots \times T_k$ the (multi-dimensional) domain given by the Cartesian product of taxonomies $T_1, \ldots, T_k$.

Definition 5 (Preference relation). *A preference relation over the t-tuples of a domain $\mathcal{T}$ is a preorder $\succeq$ on $\mathcal{T}$, that is, a transitive and reflexive relation. Given a pair of t-tuples t_1 and t_2 in $\mathcal{T}$, if $t_1 \succeq t_2$ then t_1 is (weakly) preferable to t_2. When neither $t_1 \succeq t_2$ nor $t_2 \succeq t_1$ hold, t-tuples t_1 and t_2 are incomparable, denoted $t_1 \sim t_2$. When both $t_1 \succeq t_2$ and $t_2 \succeq t_1$ hold, t-tuples t_1 and t_2 are indifferent, denoted $t_1 \approx t_2$. If $t_1 \succeq t_2$ and $t_2 \not\succeq t_1$ we say that t_1 is strictly preferable to t_2, denoted $t_1 \succ t_2$.*

Notice that $\approx$ is an equivalence relation and $\succ$ is a strict partial order.

Given a set of t-tuples $r \subseteq \mathcal{T}$, the "best" t-tuples in r according to the preference relation $\succeq$ can be selected by means of the *Best* operator β [10]. Although the β operator was originally conceived to deal with strict partial orders, it can also be applied when the preference relation is a preorder, in which case it will return in the result a t-tuple t iff there is no other t-tuple t' that is *strictly* preferable to t:

$$\beta_{\succeq}(r) = \{t \in r \mid \nexists t' \in r, t' \succ t\}$$

Thus, $\beta_{\succeq}(r)$ is not empty for any non-empty instance r, even when preferences define cycles among the t-tuples.

Although the focus of what follows is not on the language used for expressing preferences, it is useful to have one for illustrative purposes. To this end we consider a logic-based language, in which $t_1 \succeq t_2$ iff they satisfy the *preference formula* $F(t_1, t_2)$:

$$t_1 \succeq t_2 \Leftrightarrow F(t_1, t_2)$$

When needed, we denote by $\succeq_F$ the preference relation induced by the formula F, which otherwise will be understood.

As in [3], we only consider *intrinsic preference formulas* (ipf's), i.e., formulas in which only built-in predicates are present (and quantifiers can be omitted as in Datalog). This implies that, in order to evaluate $F(t_1, t_2)$, we only have to look at (the attribute values of) t_1 and t_2. Furthermore, without loss of generality, we assume that F is in Disjunctive Normal Form (DNF) and call each disjunct of F a *preference clause*, i.e.:

$$F(t_1, t_2) = \bigvee_{i=1}^{n} F_i(t_1, t_2).$$

Example 5. The preferences informally stated in Example 1 can be expressed by the DNF formula $F(t_1, t_2) = F_1(t_1, t_2) \lor \ldots \lor F_5(t_1, t_2)$, where the 5 preference clauses are (the **cheap** and **expensive** values of the PriceRange level are the intervals $[0, 40]$ and $(100, +\infty)$, respectively):

$$F_1(t_1, t_2) = (t_1[\mathsf{Genre}] = \mathtt{rock}) \land (t_2[\mathsf{Genre}] = \mathtt{pop})$$
$$F_2(t_1, t_2) = (t_1[\mathsf{Artist}] = \mathtt{Madonna}) \land (t_2[\mathsf{Genre}] = \mathtt{rock})$$
$$F_3(t_1, t_2) = (t_1[\mathsf{Artist}] = t_2[\mathsf{Artist}]) \land$$
$$\qquad\qquad (t_1[\mathsf{PriceRange}] = \mathtt{cheap}) \land (t_2[\mathsf{PriceRange}] = \mathtt{expensive})$$
$$F_4(t_1, t_2) = (t_1[\mathsf{Season}] = \mathtt{autumn}) \land (t_2[\mathsf{Season}] = \mathtt{autumn}) \land$$
$$\qquad\qquad (t_1[\mathsf{InOut}] = \mathtt{indoor}) \land (t_2[\mathsf{VenueType}] = \mathtt{stadium})$$
$$F_5(t_1, t_2) = (t_1[\mathsf{Month}] = \mathtt{august}) \land (t_2[\mathsf{Month}] = \mathtt{september})$$

It might be the case that an ipf leads to a *non-transitive* and/or *non-reflexive* relation $\succeq$.[1] For instance, given the formula:

$$F(t, t') = (t[l] = a \land t'[l] = b) \lor (t[l] = b \land t'[l] = c)$$

and t-tuples $t_1 = (a, \ldots), t_2 = (b, \ldots)$ and $t_3 = (c, \ldots)$, we have $t_1 \succeq t_2$ and $t_2 \succeq t_3$, yet $t_1 \not\succeq t_3$. A simple remedy to this issue is to allow a *transitive (and reflexive) closure* operator, $*$, in the definition of F, i.e.:

$$F(t, t') = [(t[l] = a \land t'[l] = b) \lor (t[l] = b \land t'[l] = c)]^* =$$
$$(t = t') \lor (t[l] = a \land t'[l] = b) \lor (t[l] = b \land t'[l] = c) \lor (t[l] = a \land t'[l] = c)$$

When convenient, we will use the notation $\succeq^*$ to denote the preference relation obtained by transitively closing $\succeq$, and F^* to denote the transitive closure of a formula F. In general, the transitive closure F^* of a formula F with n disjuncts $F_1, \ldots, F_n$ can be computed as:

$$G(t_1, t_2) \leftarrow F_1(t_1, t_2)$$
$$\ldots$$
$$G(t_1, t_2) \leftarrow F_n(t_1, t_2)$$
$$F^*(t_1, t_2) \leftarrow G(t_1, t_2)$$
$$F^*(t_1, t_2) \leftarrow G(t_1, t_3) \land F^*(t_3, t_2).$$

Notice that F^* is finite and is still an ipf [3].

When a (clause of a) formula F compares values of an attribute A at the same level l, it can be used to order t-tuples whose t-schema includes $A : l$. For instance, clause F_1 in Example 5 can be used to order t-tuples whose t-schema includes the Genre level. This is made precise by the following definition.

Definition 6. *A preference formula F applies to a t-schema S if there exist t-tuples t_1, t_2 with t-schema S such that $F(t_1, t_2)$ holds. We denote by $\succeq_S$ the restriction of $\succeq$ to t-schema S, i.e., the subset of $\succeq$ consisting of pairs of t-tuples with t-schema S.*

---

[1] Notice that, although according to Definition 5 $\succeq$ is *not* a preference relation (since it is not a preorder), we still use the same symbol.

When a (clause of a) formula F also compares values of an attribute at *different* levels, we say that F, as well as the corresponding preferences, are *inter-schema*, since the t-tuples ordered by F necessarily have different t-schemas. For instance, in Example 5, clause $F_2(t_1, t_2) = (t_1[\text{Artist}] = \text{Madonna}) \wedge (t_2[\text{Genre}] = \text{Rock})$ is inter-schema. Notice that $\bigcup_i \succeq_{S_i} \subseteq \succeq$, where the inclusion is strict iff inter-schema preferences are present.

4   Propagation of Preferences

In this section we detail how preferences can be *propagated* downward through a set of taxonomies. The scenario we consider assumes that, using some preference language, possibly different from the logic-based one we use in this paper, a binary relation $\succeq$ is defined on the t-tuple domain $\mathcal{T}$. Notice that we *do not* require $\succeq$ to be a preference relation, i.e., transitive and reflexive, since these properties do not need to be enforced at this stage. For instance, the binary relation defined by the preference in Example 5 is neither transitive nor reflexive.

4.1   Propagation Principle and Rules

The $\succeq$ relation completely ignores the structure of the poset on t-tuples $\leq_t$, thus it treats $\mathcal{T}$ as if it were a "flat" domain. This is because $\succeq$ includes all and only those preferences $t_1 \succeq t_2$ such that the attribute values of t_1 and t_2 satisfy the preference formula, yet it does not take into account the taxonomies. The key observation justifying the (downward) propagation of preferences, is that, given a target t-schema S, by exploiting the hierarchical organization of $\mathcal{T}$ it is possible to extend $\succeq_S$, i.e., the relation $\succeq$ restricted to t-schema S, with more preferences that involve t-tuples with t-schemas S_i, with $S \leq_S S_i$.

Therefore, let $\succeq_\downarrow$ denote the binary relation obtained by propagating, in some way to be described, the preferences in $\succeq$. We require that $\succeq_\downarrow \supseteq \succeq$, which implies that all preferences in $\succeq$ are preserved by propagation.

The basic idea underlying propagation could be tentatively captured by the following simple rule:

$$t_1 \succeq_\downarrow t_2 \leftarrow \exists t_1', t_2' ((t_1' \succeq t_2') \wedge (t_1 \leq_t t_1') \wedge (t_2 \leq_t t_2')) \tag{R0}$$

Rule R0 is based on the intuition that, in order to have $t_1 \succeq_\downarrow t_2$, there must exist a preference between t-tuples t_1' and t_2' that generalize t_1 and t_2, respectively: Since the rule also applies when $t_1 = t_1'$ and $t_2 = t_2'$, $\succeq_\downarrow \supseteq \succeq$ always holds. For instance, consider the t-schema in Fig. 1 and the preference clause $F_1(t_1, t_2) = t_1[\text{Genre}] = \text{Rock}) \wedge (t_2[\text{Genre}] = \text{Pop})$. From F_1, using Rule R0 we can propagate the preferences $t_a \succeq_\downarrow t_b$ and $t_a \succeq_\downarrow t_c$, since Bruce Springsteen is a rock artist whereas Madonna is a pop singer.

In spite of its simplicity, Rule R0 can lead to some unwanted effect, as argued by the following example.

Example 6. In our working example, we have a generic preference for rock concerts over pop concerts. With no contradiction with the generic preference, we might have a *more specific* preference stating that a performance by Madonna takes precedence over Springsteen's concerts. In this case, the more specific preference would entail, among others, $t_b \succeq t_a$; yet, rule R0 would keep this preference, but would also propagate the more generic preference on musical genres, thus leading to $t_a \succeq_\downarrow t_b$ and making t_a and t_b become indifferent. However, giving the same importance to both preferences contradicts the intuition, as the more specific preference should take precedence over the more generic one.

Based on the above arguments, we therefore replace Rule R0 with the following one, in which we propagate a preference to t-tuples t_1 and t_2 only if no preference between them is already present in $\succeq$, i.e., t_1 and t_2 are *incomparable*:

$$t_1 \succeq_\downarrow t_2 \leftarrow (t_1 \succeq t_2) \vee [(t_1 \sim t_2) \wedge \exists t'_1, t'_2((t'_1 \succeq t'_2) \wedge (t_1 \leq_t t'_1) \wedge (t_2 \leq_t t'_2))]$$
$$\text{(R1)}$$

It turns out that Rule R1 also suffers from inconsistencies in propagation in more complex cases.

Example 7. Consider clauses F_1 (on musical genres) and $F_2(t_1, t_2) = (t_1[\text{Artist}] = \text{Madonna}) \wedge (t_2[\text{Genre}] = \text{rock})$ from our working example. We have $t_a \sim t_b$, thus using R1 we would propagate both preferences $t_a \succeq_\downarrow t_b$ (thanks to F_1) and $t_b \succeq_\downarrow t_a$ (thanks to F_2), again leading to consider t_a and t_b as indifferent, against intuition.

We can generalize the above observation as follows. Assume $t_1 \sim t_2$ and consider preferences $t'_1 \succeq t'_2$ and $t''_2 \succeq t''_1$, with $t_1 \leq_t t'_1 \leq_t t''_1$ and $t_2 \leq_t t'_2 \leq_t t''_2$. According to Rule R1 both preferences can be propagated, thus leading to $t_1 \succeq_\downarrow t_2$ and $t_2 \succeq_\downarrow t_1$. Even in this case we might argue that only preference $t'_1 \succeq t'_2$ should be propagated, as it is *more specific* than $t''_2 \succeq t''_1$ (since $t'_1 \leq_t t''_1$ and $t'_2 \leq_t t''_2$). We can precisely capture this "specificity" requirement with the following definition.

Definition 7 (More specific preferences). *Given two preferences $t'_1 \succeq t'_2$ and $t''_2 \succeq t''_1$, we say that the first is more specific than the second if both $t'_1 \leq_t t''_1$ and $t'_2 \leq_t t''_2$ hold and $t'_1 \neq t''_1$ or $t'_2 \neq t''_2$.*

Based on the above definition, we can replace Rule R1 with the following one:

$$t_1 \succeq_\downarrow t_2 \leftarrow \exists t'_1, t'_2 ((t'_1 \succeq t'_2) \wedge (t_1 \leq_t t'_1) \wedge (t_2 \leq_t t'_2) \wedge$$
$$\nexists t''_1, t''_2 ((t''_2 \succeq t''_1) \wedge (t''_1 \leq_t t'_1) \wedge (t''_2 \leq_t t'_2) \wedge ((t'_1 \neq t''_1) \vee (t'_2 \neq t''_2))))$$
$$\text{(R2)}$$

where we no longer need to require that $t_1 \sim t_2$, since the case of an existing preference between t_1 and t_2 is captured by the second line of Rule R2.

Example 8. Based on the preferences in Example 5, Rule R2 propagates the following preferences to the t-tuples in Fig. 1, where for each preference we also show the clause exploited for the propagation:

$$F_1 : t_a \succeq_\downarrow t_e, t_f \succeq_\downarrow t_e$$
$$F_2 : t_b \succeq_\downarrow t_a, t_b \succeq_\downarrow t_f, t_c \succeq_\downarrow t_a, t_c \succeq_\downarrow t_f$$
$$F_3 : t_b \succeq_\downarrow t_c$$
$$F_4 : t_e \succeq_\downarrow t_f$$
$$F_5 :$$

Notice that clause F_5 yields no preference, since there is no concert in September.

4.2   Rewriting with Respect to the Target T-Schema

Rule R2 is the basic mechanism used to propagate preferences. However, it does not guarantee that $\succeq_\downarrow$ is a preference relation (i.e., transitivity is not a consequence of R2), even because the very input relation $\succeq$ is not necessarily a preorder. Although one may be tempted to circumvent this problem by adopting an algorithm for non-transitive preferences [2], algorithms of this type can discard a sub-optimal t-tuple t only if the database r contains a t-tuple t' that is *directly* (rather than transitively) better than t. The following example shows the inadequacy of approaches base on non-transitive preferences.

Example 9. Consider the following t-relation r.

Artist	Day	Venue	Price ($)	
Eminem	12/08/2019	Unipol Arena, Bologna	60	t_d
Bruce Springsteen	30/10/2019	Stadio Olimpico, Rome	100	t_f
Chick Corea	25/09/2019	Blue Note, Milan	65	t_g

Since no preference among those in Example 5 applies to the t-schema of r, t-tuples t_d, t_f and t_g are all incomparable. Therefore, Rule R2 can be applied, thus propagating preferences $t_d \succeq_\downarrow t_g$ (through clause F_5) and $t_g \succeq_\downarrow t_f$ (through clause F_4). However, $t_d \not\succeq_\downarrow t_f$, thus $\succeq_\downarrow$ is not transitive.

An algorithm for non-transitive preferences would be able to discover that $\beta_{\succeq_\downarrow}(r) = \{t_d\}$, since there exists a t-tuple in r, namely t_g, that is directly better than t_f. Consider now $r' = \{t_d, t_f\}$. We argue that, even in this case, only t_d should be returned as the best result, since t_g, albeit not in r', is still in the domain of t-tuples. However, no algorithm that just looks at the t-tuples in r' would be able to discard t_f from the result, thus incorrectly returning the set $\{t_d, t_f\}$.

The approach we pursue is based on the idea of *transitively closing the formula F, once this has been rewritten with respect to the target t-schema S by means of level mappings.* The following example illustrates the idea.

Example 10. Consider the same scenario as in Example 9 and the following rewriting, denoted $F'_{S,\downarrow}$, of $F'(t_1, t_2) = F_5(t_1, t_2) \vee F_4(t_1, t_2)$, where F_4 and F_5 are as in Example 5.

$$
\begin{aligned}
F'_{S,\downarrow}(t_1, t_2) = {}& [t_1[\mathsf{Day}] \in (\mu_{\mathsf{Day}}^{\mathsf{Month}})^{-1}(\mathbf{august}) \wedge t_2[\mathsf{Day}] \in (\mu_{\mathsf{Day}}^{\mathsf{Month}})^{-1}(\mathbf{september})] \vee \\
& [t_1[\mathsf{Day}] \in (\mu_{\mathsf{Day}}^{\mathsf{Season}})^{-1}(\mathbf{autumn}) \wedge t_2[\mathsf{Day}] \in (\mu_{\mathsf{Day}}^{\mathsf{Season}})^{-1}(\mathbf{autumn}) \wedge \\
& t_1[\mathsf{Venue}] \in (\mu_{\mathsf{Venue}}^{\mathsf{InOut}})^{-1}(\mathbf{indoor}) \wedge t_2[\mathsf{Venue}] \in (\mu_{\mathsf{Venue}}^{\mathsf{VenueType}})^{-1}(\mathbf{stadium})].
\end{aligned}
$$

in which only values at levels in the t-schema of r are considered. Now, since $(\mu_{\mathsf{Day}}^{\mathsf{Month}})^{-1}(\mathbf{september}) \cap (\mu_{\mathsf{Day}}^{\mathsf{Season}})^{-1}(\mathbf{autumn}) \neq \emptyset$ (i.e., some September days are in autumn), there exists at least one Day value, such as $t_g[\mathsf{Day}] = 25/09/2019$ such that t_d is better than t_g, which in turn is better than t_f. This is sufficient to conclude that $t_d \succeq_\downarrow t_f$.

Then, the transitive and reflexive closure of $F'_{S,\downarrow}(t_1, t_2)$ can be written as:

$$
\begin{aligned}
F'^{*}_{S,\downarrow}(t_1, t_2) = {}& (t_1 = t_2) \vee F'_{S,\downarrow}(t_1, t_2) \vee \\
& [t_1[\mathsf{Day}] \in (\mu_{\mathsf{Day}}^{\mathsf{Month}})^{-1}(\mathbf{august}) \wedge \\
& t_2[\mathsf{Day}] \in (\mu_{\mathsf{Day}}^{\mathsf{Season}})^{-1}(\mathbf{autumn}) \wedge t_2[\mathsf{Venue}] \in (\mu_{\mathsf{Venue}}^{\mathsf{VenueType}})^{-1}(\mathbf{stadium})].
\end{aligned}
$$

Therefore, even if $r' = \{t_d, t_f\}$, we correctly have $\beta_{\succeq_\downarrow^*}(r') = \{t_d\}$.

Besides inverse level mappings, also (direct) level mappings need to be used. This is the case when the preference formula includes *self-join* predicates, in which no values of more generic levels are present (thus inverse level mappings cannot be applied). For instance, if we prefer to pay less, provided the two concerts are of the same musical genre, the corresponding formula will have the following pattern:

$$
F(t_1, t_2) = (t_1[A : l_1] = t_2[A : l_1]) \wedge (t_1[B : l] \leq t_2[B : l]).
$$

Let $S = \{A : l'_1, B : l, \ldots\}$, with $l'_1 \leq_L l_1$. In this case the only possible (and correct) rewriting is:

$$
F_{S,\downarrow}(t_1, t_2) = (\mu_{l'_1}^{l_1}(t_1[A : l'_1]) = \mu_{l'_1}^{l_1}(t_2[A : l'_1])) \wedge (t_1[B : l] \leq t_2[B : l])
$$

Example 11. The preferences described in Example 8 propagate to the t-tuples in Fig. 1 without the need of computing the transitive closure. After computing $F^{*}_{S,\downarrow}$ we also have, among others, the preference $t_d \succeq_\downarrow^* t_f$. Since no t-tuple is preferred to t_b and t_d, we have that $\beta_{\succeq_\downarrow^*}(\mathsf{Concerts}) = \{t_b, t_d\}$.

Algorithm 1 details the steps needed to obtain $F_{S,\downarrow}$ from F. Without loss of generality we assume that all the preference clauses in F refer to attribute levels that are not more specific than the corresponding ones in S, i.e., each preference clause is relevant for obtaining $F_{S,\downarrow}$.

We observe that the rewritten formula $F_{S,\downarrow}$ uses inverse level mappings in order to understand when preferences expressed at different levels can be transitively combined, which is all we need in this paper in order to determine the

---

Algorithm 1. Rewriting of preference formula F with respect to the target t-schema S.

Input: *taxonomies* $T_1, \ldots, T_k$, *target t-schema* $S = \{A_1 : l_1, \ldots, A_k : l_k\}$,
        formula $F = F_1 \vee \ldots \vee F_n$.

Output: $F_{S,\downarrow}$.

  1. **let** $F_{S,\downarrow} := F$

  2. **for each** predicate $t[A_j : l] = c$: // *c is a constant*

  3.   replace $t[A_j : l] = c$ with $t[A_j : l_j] \in (\mu_{l_j}^l)^{-1}(c)$

  4. **for each** predicate $t[A_j : l] \; \theta \; t'[A_j : l]$: // *self-join predicate*, $\theta \in \{=, \neq, <, \leq, >, \geq\}$

  5.   replace $t[A_j : l] \; \theta \; t'[A_j : l]$ with $\mu_{l_j}^l(t[A_j : l_j]) \; \theta \; \mu_{l_j}^l(t'[A_j : l_j])$

  6. **return** $F_{S,\downarrow}$

---

preferred objects in a t-relation. A different issue, which we do not cover in detail in this paper, is to understand the most efficient approach to obtain the transitively closed propagated preference relation. Besides the obvious alternative of materializing inverse level mappings, and then applying the standard transitive closure algorithm, we may also consider, say, to make the transitive closure algorithm aware of level mappings. With respect to the procedure given in (3), the only additional complexity arises for cases like the one illustrated in Example 10. In particular, consider an attribute $A_i : l_i$ in the target t-schema S, and assume that $F_{S,\downarrow}$ contains two predicates P and P' in which the inverse level mappings $(\mu_{l_i}^l)^{-1}(c)$ and $(\mu_{l_i}^{l'})^{-1}(d)$ appear, where c and d are constants, $l_i \leq_L l$, and $l_i \leq_L l'$. In order to transitively combine P and P', as we did in Example 10, it is necessary that the two images of the inverse mappings have a non-empty intersection, i.e., $(\mu_{l_i}^l)^{-1}(c) \cap (\mu_{l_i}^{l'})^{-1}(d) \neq \emptyset$. To this end there are two cases to consider:

$l \leq_L l'$: In this case it is sufficient to check that $\mu_l^{l'}(c) = d$. Similarly, the case $l' \leq_L l$ requires to verify that $\mu_{l'}^l(d) = c$.

$l \not\leq_L l'$ and $l' \not\leq_L l$: When l and l' are incomparable, the way to check that the intersection is not empty depends on how level mappings are implemented. For instance, for **september** and **autumn** the check just requires to compare the definitions of these two concepts, which is an easy task.

5   Computing the Result

In order to compute the best results according to the (transitively closed) rewritten formula $F_{S,\downarrow}^*$ we can use any algorithm developed for returning the best objects in a strict partial order, such as those in [1,10], by suitably adapting it to work with preorders. Algorithm 2 is such an adaptation of the well-known BNL algorithm [1]. Before describing its logic, we need to detail how we can effectively propagate only the most specific preferences.

According to Definition 7, in order to infer that $t_1 \succeq_{\downarrow}^* t_2$ we have to look for t-tuples t_1' and t_2' such that $t_1' \succeq t_2'$, $t_1 \leq_t t_1'$, and $t_2 \leq_t t_2'$. From a practical point of view, since we start with a formula $F_{S,\downarrow}^*$, the materialization of such

t-tuples t_1' and t_2' is not needed at all. Rather, if $F_{S,\downarrow}^*(t_1, t_2)$ holds, we look at the preference clause F_i that evaluates to **true** and, for each involved attribute, we consider the original level it has for both t_1 and t_2 (remind that $F_{S,\downarrow}^*$ has been obtained by applying (inverse) level mappings). If an attribute does not appear in F_i we set its level to the top level of its taxonomy (henceforth simply indicated by $\top$).

Example 12. Consider t-tuples t_a and t_b in Fig. 1 and clause $F_2(t_1, t_2) = (t_1[\mathsf{Artist}] = \mathsf{Madonna}) \wedge (t_2[\mathsf{Genre}] = \mathsf{rock})$. Note that $F_2(t_b, t_a)$ holds and the original levels when evaluating F_2 for t_a are $(\mathsf{Genre}, \top, \top, \top)$, while those for t_b are $(\mathsf{Artist}, \top, \top, \top)$.

Overall, this leads to *a pair of t-schemas*, $\mathsf{spp}(t_1, t_2) = \langle \mathsf{sig}_{1,2}(t_1), \mathsf{sig}_{1,2}(t_2) \rangle$, which we call the *signature of propagated preference*. Notice that $\mathsf{sig}_{1,2}(t_1)$ is the t-schema for t_1 when we test if t_1 is preferred to t_2. Since, in general, this is different from the t-schema for t_1 when we test if t_2 is preferred to t_1, we need to use subscripts, i.e., $\mathsf{sig}_{1,2}$ and $\mathsf{sig}_{2,1}$, respectively, to distinguish the two cases. Now, if also $F_{S,\downarrow}^*(t_2, t_1)$ holds, we compare $\mathsf{spp}(t_1, t_2)$ and $\mathsf{spp}(t_2, t_1) = \langle \mathsf{sig}_{2,1}(t_2), \mathsf{sig}_{2,1}(t_1) \rangle$ and conclude that the first preference is more specific than the second, denoted by $\mathsf{spp}(t_1, t_2) < \mathsf{spp}(t_2, t_1)$ iff $\mathsf{sig}_{1,2}(t_1) \leq_S \mathsf{sig}_{2,1}(t_1)$ and $\mathsf{sig}_{1,2}(t_2) \leq_S \mathsf{sig}_{2,1}(t_2)$, with at least one t-schema being strictly more specific. In Algorithm 2 this "specificity test" is performed by the procedure $\mathrm{MORESPECIFICPREF}(t, t')$, which returns t if the preference $t \succeq_\downarrow^* t'$ is more specific than $t' \succeq_\downarrow^* t$, t' in the opposite case, and **nil** if neither case occurs.

Algorithm 2. Computing the best t-tuples in r according to $F_{S,\downarrow}^*$.

Input: *t-relation r with t-schema $S = \{A_1 : l_1, \ldots, A_k : l_k\}$, formula $F_{S,\downarrow}^*$.*
Output: $\beta_{\succeq_\downarrow^*}$.

1. **let** $Best := \emptyset$
2. **for each** $t \in r$
3.   **let** $Opt := $ **true**
4.   **for each** $t' \in Best$
5.   **cases**
6. $F_{S,\downarrow}^*(t, t') \wedge (F_{S,\downarrow}^*(t', t) \wedge t = \mathrm{MORESPECIFICPREF}(t, t') \vee \neg F_{S,\downarrow}^*(t', t))$:
                              $Best := Best \setminus \{t'\}$
7. $F_{S,\downarrow}^*(t', t) \wedge (F_{S,\downarrow}^*(t, t') \wedge t' = \mathrm{MORESPECIFICPREF}(t, t') \vee \neg F_{S,\downarrow}^*(t, t'))$:
                              let $Opt := $ **false**; **break**
8.   **if** Opt **then** $Best := Best \cup \{t\}$
9. **return** $Best$

Example 13. Assume we are comparing t-tuples t_a and t_b in Fig. 1. Besides the clause F_2 from Example 12, from clause F_1 in Example 5 ($F_1(t_1, t_2) = (t_1[\mathsf{Genre}] = \mathsf{rock}) \wedge (t_2[\mathsf{Genre}] = \mathsf{pop})$) we also derive that $t_a \succeq_\downarrow^* t_b$, whereas $t_b \succeq_\downarrow^* t_a$ follows from clause F_2. For the first preference we have $\mathsf{spp}(t_a, t_b) = \langle (\mathsf{Genre}, \top, \top, \top), (\mathsf{Genre}, \top,$

$\top, \top)\rangle$, whereas for the second we have $\mathsf{spp}(t_b, t_a) = \langle(\mathsf{Artist}, \top, \top, \top), (\mathsf{Genre},$
$\top, \top, \top)\rangle$. Although for t_a the two t-schemas are the same, for t_b Artist is
strictly more specific than Genre, thus $\mathsf{spp}(t_b, t_a) < \mathsf{spp}(t_a, t_b)$ and, consequently,
$t_b = \mathrm{MORESPECIFICPREF}(t_a, t_b)$.

Algorithm 2 keeps the current best t-tuples in the *Best* set. When a new
t-tuple t is read, the *Opt* flag is set to **true** (line 3) and t starts to be compared
with the t-tuples currently in *Best* (line 4). Given $t' \in Best$, when both $F^*_{S,\downarrow}(t, t')$
and $F^*_{S,\downarrow}(t', t)$ hold the MORESPECIFICPREF procedure determines if one of the
two preferences is more specific than the other. If only $t \succeq^*_\downarrow t'$ is propagated
(i.e., $t = \mathrm{MORESPECIFICPREF}(t, t')$) then t' is removed from the result set (line
6), which also happens if only $F^*_{S,\downarrow}(t, t')$ holds. Conversely, when the preference
$t' \succeq^*_\downarrow t$ is more specific (or only $F^*_{S,\downarrow}(t', t)$ holds), then we exit the loop by
setting *Opt* to **false** (line 7). If t exits the loop without having encountered a
strictly better t-tuple t', then t is added to *Best* (line 8). Eventually, we have
$\beta_{\succeq^*_\downarrow}(r) = Best$.

6   Conclusions

In this paper we have studied preference propagation along several taxonomies,
when the levels at which preferences are stated and that of the stored data differ.
The preference model we have proposed is able to deal with conflicting preferences in an effective way, thus propagating only the most specific preferences.

The specificity principle we use in this paper was also considered in [4], albeit
on a different preference model (using strict partial orders rather than preorders)
and a different scenario, in which preferences were to be combined across different
contexts. The problem of dealing with preferences defined on different schemas,
which is the main focus of the present paper, was not addressed at all in [4].

Propagation of preferences in OLAP systems is considered in [5], where an
algebraic language is adopted. Preferences on attributes are of type $\mathsf{POS}(l, v)$,
which means that v is preferred to any other value at the same level l. Propagation occurs along hierarchies of levels, however no issue concerning combination
of conflicting preferences is considered.

Unlike most works studying the problem of managing *qualitative* preference
queries on databases [9], in which the preference relation is a strict partial order
$\succ$, in this paper we have considered "weak" preferences that are modeled as a
preorder $\succeq$. This choice originates from the observation that, while propagating
preferences between different t-schemas, transitivity cannot be guaranteed and a
transitive closure is needed. However, enforcing transitivity might lead to cycles,
which are harmless for preorders but cannot occur in strict partial orders.

Future work includes the study of efficient methods for computing the transitive closure of the preference formula along the lines sketched in Sect. 4, the
development of ad hoc algorithms for determining the best objects, and an experimental evaluation on real-case scenarios.

References

1. Börzsönyi, S., Kossmann, D., Stocker, K.: The skyline operator. In: ICDE, pp. 421–430 (2001)
2. Chan, C.Y., Jagadish, H.V., Tan, K., Tung, A.K.H., Zhang, Z.: Finding k-dominant skylines in high dimensional space. In: SIGMOD, pp. 503–514 (2006)
3. Chomicki, J.: Preference formulas in relational queries. TODS **28**(4), 427–466 (2003)
4. Ciaccia, P., Torlone, R.: Modeling the propagation of user preferences. In: Jeusfeld, M., Delcambre, L., Ling, T.-W. (eds.) ER 2011. LNCS, vol. 6998, pp. 304–317. Springer, Heidelberg (2011). https://doi.org/10.1007/978-3-642-24606-7_23
5. Golfarelli, M., Rizzi, S., Biondi, P.: myOLAP: An approach to express and evaluate OLAP preferences. TKDE **23**(7), 1050–1064 (2011)
6. Martinenghi, D., Torlone, R.: Querying databases with taxonomies. In: Parsons, J., Saeki, M., Shoval, P., Woo, C., Wand, Y. (eds.) ER 2010. LNCS, vol. 6412, pp. 377–390. Springer, Heidelberg (2010). https://doi.org/10.1007/978-3-642-16373-9_27
7. Martinenghi, D., Torlone, R.: Taxonomy-based relaxation of query answering in relational databases. VLDB J. **23**(5), 747–769 (2014)
8. Ricci, F., Rokach, L., Shapira, B.: Introduction to recommender systems handbook. In: Ricci, F., Rokach, L., Shapira, B., Kantor, P.B. (eds.) Recommender Systems Handbook, pp. 1–35. Springer, Boston (2011). https://doi.org/10.1007/978-0-387-85820-3_1
9. Stefanidis, K., Koutrika, G., Pitoura, E.: A survey on representation, composition and application of preferences in database systems. TODS **36**(3), 19:1–19:45 (2011)
10. Torlone, R., Ciaccia, P.: Which are my preferred items? In: RPEC, pp. 217–225 (2002)

Generic Negative Scenarios for the Specification of Collaborative Cyber-Physical Systems

Viktoria Stenkova$^{(\boxtimes)}$ (ID), Jennifer Brings (ID), Marian Daun (ID), and Thorsten Weyer (ID)

paluno – The Ruhr Institute for Software Technology,
University of Duisburg-Essen, Essen, Germany
{viktoria.stenkova,jennifer.brings,marian.daun,
thorsten.weyer}@paluno.uni-due.de

Abstract. Collaborative cyber-physical systems face a plethora of different albeit often similar set-ups they might find themselves in during runtime. While it is necessary to consider each possible configuration to ensure safe operation of a collaborative cyber-physical system, the sheer number of unwanted behaviors makes manual safety assurance tasks daunting. The specification of unwanted behavior in negative scenarios helps identifying and correcting safety-critical design flaws. However, this requires negative scenarios for collaborative cyber-physical systems to be identified and the essential pieces of information therein to be consolidated and reduced to a manageable size. To this end we present a semi-automated approach that (1) generates negative scenarios from main scenarios considering all possible configurations and (2) generates generic negative scenarios using dedicated abstraction mechanisms that provide a condensed view on unwanted behaviors. The application of our approach to a case example from the automotive domain demonstrates its usefulness and appropriateness.

Keywords: Negative scenarios · Message Sequence Charts · Safety analysis · Cyber-physical systems

1 Introduction

Scenarios are commonly used during requirements engineering [1]. In scenario-based requirements engineering, scenarios are used to sketch real world situations the system shall be able to cope with or purposes the system shall fulfill during its operation. Scenarios, however, do not always define the wanted behavior of a system. Scenarios can also be used to document unwanted behavior. These kinds of scenarios are commonly referred to as negative scenarios [2]. Negative scenarios are used to elicit and specify safety requirements [3], as they specify what must not occur. This means that scenarios can also represent behaviors in which the system fails or is misused. The specification of security and safety hazards in negative scenarios allows for improving safety analyses [2] (i.e. by checking whether negative scenarios can occur).

© Springer Nature Switzerland AG 2019
A. H. F. Laender et al. (Eds.): ER 2019, LNCS 11788, pp. 412–419, 2019.
https://doi.org/10.1007/978-3-030-33223-5_34

Scenarios cannot only be used to define the intended user interaction between human users and the system but also to define the intended interaction-based behavior between different systems [4]. This is particularly useful for collaborative CPS as they can form dynamic system groups at runtime [5] to provide more functionality than the individual systems can [6]. The concrete systems collaborating and the number of system instances collaborating in a dynamic system group can vary considerably. This poses challenges for their specification as there is a need to handle an extremely large number of scenarios as system groups with different numbers of individual systems constitute different scenarios [7, 8]. For example, a group of collaborating transport robots jointly working in a smart factory, pose different behavior depending on the number of robots used. If only two robots are responsible for transport tasks, and many transport tasks are assigned to them, the robots pay less attention to their battery status than if the group consisted of ten robots and just as many tasks. This problem is further exacerbated when considering negative scenarios as for each regular i.e., positive main scenario typically more than just one negative scenario needs to be specified, thus, the number of possible negative scenarios can increase rapidly [2, 3].

If negative scenarios are specified for every possible number of systems in the system group that show the same kind of behavior of the system group, the number of scenarios a safety engineer would need to cope with surpasses what can be handled. However, not specifying all scenarios bears the risk of leaving important aspects out during safety analysis.

In this paper, we propose the specification of *generic negative scenarios* to allow for specification of negative scenarios considering all possible numbers of system instances that need to be considered, while at the same time keeping the number of graphical diagrams a safety engineer needs to handle at a reasonable level. Therefore, generic negative scenarios use dedicated abstraction mechanism to reduce complexity. To support safety analysis by structured specification of all relevant negative scenarios collaborative CPS might face during runtime, we propose

(a) an approach for systematic derivation of negative scenarios taking all different configurations of the system group into account and

(b) an approach for generation of generic negative scenarios to specify all relevant negative scenarios for the different configurations in one condensed view.

We use ITU Message Sequence Charts [9] for the specification of main scenarios, negative scenarios and generic negative scenarios, as MSCs or MSC-like languages (e.g., UML sequence diagrams, life sequence charts) are commonly used in the engineering of CPS [3] and have proven useful for comparable tasks [10, 11]. Initial evaluation results from an industrial case example highlight the applicability of the approach and give important insights for enhancing scenario descriptions to account for collaborative CPS.

The paper is structured as follows. Section 2 will briefly introduce the approach for the creation of generic negative scenarios. Section 3 reports findings from our initial evaluation. Section 4 reviews related approaches and Sect. 5 concludes the paper.

2 Generic Negative Scenarios

In this paper, we propose an approach to systematically derive and specify negative scenarios taking the changing morphologies of the system group into account. The approach relies on the structured derivation of negative scenarios and the specification of these derived negative scenarios within one generic negative scenario. The resulting generic negative scenario summarizes a class of similar negative scenarios that differ from each other in the number of instances (as well as in the resulting interactions between system instances due to the number of system instances involved). The approach for generation of generic negative scenarios consists of four steps:

Step 1: Identification of a main scenario and alternative scenarios. Before identifying negative scenarios, a positive main scenario is identified and documented which illustrates a desired behavior of a system group with the smallest possible number of collaborative embedded systems. The main scenario is the standard case in which the system works correctly. Besides the main scenario in many cases alternative scenarios exist, which describe other regular ways of interaction exchange leading to the fulfillment of the same scenario. Therefore, the main scenario is examined for alternative behavior as is commonly done during scenario-based engineering. To avoid confusion, we refer to this kind of alternative scenario as classic alternative scenario in this paper.

Step 2: Identification of alternative configuration scenarios. Beside such classic alternative scenarios, in Step 2 further alternative scenarios are identified that differ in the number of systems involved. These alternative configuration scenarios are created from the main scenario and the classic alternative scenarios by adding further instances representing further systems and the according messages exchanged between the new instance and the already existing instances. We refer to this kind of alternative scenario as alternative configuration scenario in this paper.

Step 3: Identification of negative scenarios. The previously created main scenario and all alternative scenarios (i.e. the classic alternative scenarios and the alternative configuration scenarios) are analyzed for unwanted behavior. This is the case if the system does not achieve its goals or even endangers them, for example, if the behavior of individual system could endanger the system group. In most cases they can be considered light variations from the specified positive scenarios, which result in undesired system states. Consequently, an identified negative scenario for one classic alternative scenario can also be extended to detail this situation considering related alternative configuration scenarios defining the involvement of further system instances. Therefore, for each main and classic alternative scenario, alternative configuration scenarios are created and accordingly negative scenarios depicting the same undesired situation with different numbers of system instances involved can be generated.

Step 4: Generation of generic negative scenarios. To cope with the multitude of negative scenarios, generic negative scenarios are created which abstract from the concrete number of systems in a system group. Individual systems with the same

behavior or tasks are grouped into equivalence classes. Each of these classes requires only one instance in the generic negative scenario model, which enhances readability.

In Fig. 1 the steps for the creation of generic negative scenarios are illustrated. First a main scenario (MS) is created and classic alternative scenarios (CAS 1 – CAS n), are derived for a minimal number of instances. For the main scenario and each of these classic alternative scenarios alternative configuration scenarios with different instance config- urations of the system group (ACS 0.1 – ACS n.1) are created. for the main scenario, all classic alternative scenarios and each alternative configuration scenario negative sce- narios (NS) are specified and the generic negative scenario (GNS) is generated.

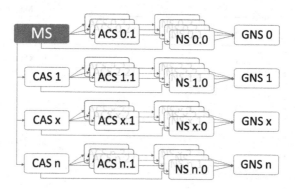

Fig. 1. Generation of generic negative scenarios

3   Application Example

We initially evaluated our approach by applying it to an industrial case example. As application example a cooperative adaptive cruise control system from the automotive industry was used. The specification was provided by our industry partners. Vehicles equipped with cooperative adaptive cruise control systems are enabled to dynamically form platoons during runtime [12]. This allows them to keep a small distance from each other and perform maneuvers together. Platooning offers advantages over single driving such as safety, eco-friendliness, cost savings (time, fuel) as well as advantages for road traffic and the driver himself.

In a platoon two major roles can be distinguished: the lead vehicle and the fol- lowing vehicles. While the lead vehicle initiates maneuvers and is responsible for the organization of the platoon, the following vehicles also exchange information with each other and each follow the preceding vehicle [13]. Therefore, each vehicle senses its environment and exchanges this information with the other vehicles to allow the platoon leader to make decisions taking all available context information into account.

The approach is applied to the platooning case example using the scenario of faulty traffic sign recognition. The recognition of traffic signs depends on many factors, including lighting conditions, weather conditions, obstacles and the condition of the sensors [14]. Therefore, in a platoon, multiple negative scenarios can occur, involving

the erroneous non-recognition of the traffic sign by some vehicles of the platoon and the erroneous detection of different speed limits by different vehicles of the platoon.

Figure 2 shows the resulting generic negative scenario for the detection of faulty traffic signs within a platoon. For a more thorough description of the systematic generation of the generic negative scenario and its comparison to the traditional specification of multiple negative scenarios, please refer to the supplement https://doi.org/10.5281/zenodo.3266992.

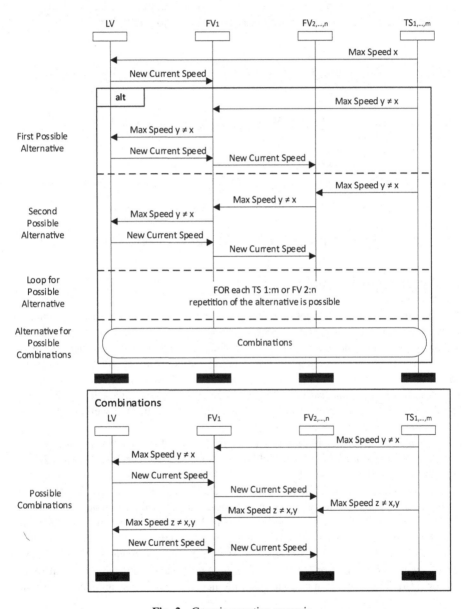

Fig. 2. Generic negative scenario.

The generic negative scenario abstracts from concrete instances but shows instances for different identified instance classes. Instance classes are *lead vehicle (LV)*, *following vehicle 1 (FV$_1$)*, *following vehicle 2-n (FV$_{2,...,n}$)* and *traffic signs (TS $_{1,...,m}$)*. Note that due to their high degree of similarity all following vehicles, but the first following vehicle, are grouped into the class *following vehicle 2-n*.

In the generic negative scenario, the unwanted behavior, which in this case represents the overwriting of the desired speed of the platoon, is caused by the identified generic instances which means that at least one vehicle in position three or higher detects a wrong speed limit and propagates the wrong speed limit to the entire platoon.

The introduction of generic instances representing different classes of instances leads to the need to define several alternatives for the definition of the negative behavior for each possible configuration (e.g., *FV$_3$* or *FV$_4$* fails to detect a traffic sign correctly). Since the alternative inline expression allows only one of the shown behaviors, a loop is used to represent several of the similar alternatives, which depend on the number of instances. The combinations thereof are then specified in a further MSC shown in the lower half of Fig. 2, to express that e.g., *FV$_4$* and *FV$_6$* fail to detect a traffic sign correctly.

Since the explicit specification of all these possibilities leads again to an exhaustive diagrammatic representation, further simplifications are needed. For ITU MSCs the "alt"-operator is defined as exclusive or. We assume that the introduction of a real "or"-operator (i.e. a non-exclusive one) can reduce the complexity of the generic negative scenarios. However, further research is needed to confirm that there are no side effects caused by the introduction of a non-exclusive or operator for MSC.

4 Related Work

There exists a multitude of work in requirements engineering literature dealing with the model-based specification of scenarios and its use during scenario-based requirements engineering approaches (e.g. [1, 2]). Other approaches particularly focus on the specification of negative [15] or misuse [16] scenarios. Recent approaches like [17] propose the formalization of scenarios to foster monitoring negative scenarios at run-time to verify that the negative scenario is not executed in a certain configuration of the collaborative system group. In contrast, generic negative scenarios aim at a proper diagrammatic (i.e. human readable) specification that can then serve for verification purposes.

However, works on scenario-based requirements engineering typically do not take the need for considering multiple closely related scenarios only differing in the number of system instances specified into account. This is the case for approaches on instance level modeling. Instance level modeling can be used, as in Pergl et al. [18], to represent objects in more detail. Instance level modeling does not deal with general classes, but with the objects themselves.

Jahn et al. [19] introduced the language pattern instance specialization which is based on inheritance. It is intended to enable the reuse of properties and facets of an instance by specializing them. Solmi [20] uses language entities for instance modeling. Generic meta levels are used to describe instances. The graphical representation

proposed is similar to mind maps and can, thus, be combined with other languages. Ehrig et al. [21] and Hamsworth et al. [22] propose generating instances to foster testing.

The representation chosen for generic negative scenarios is closely related to the specification of patterns, as no concrete number of instances etc. is given. Hence, pattern matching (e.g., [23]) is to be seen as another related area for this paper.

5 Conclusion

The specification of negative scenarios, which describe safety and security hazards and behavior resulting from these hazards that must not occur during system execution, is an important task. Particularly, negative scenarios are needed to automatically check whether the system correctly mitigates all these hazards. However, in this paper, the case was made that the specification of negative scenarios for collaborative CPS that partake in dynamic system groups at runtime easily becomes challenging due to the many different negative scenarios to be considered. This is caused by the need to consider all possible system group configurations that dynamically form during runtime. Already slight variations in the system group's morphology lead to the need to consider further negative scenarios during safety analysis.

In this paper, we proposed an approach for the specification of generic negative scenarios. Generic negative scenarios contribute to both problematic aspects. First, generic negative scenarios account for the plethora of relevant negative scenarios using only one specification artifact for specifying closely related negative scenarios. Second, by grouping similar behaving system instances in the scenario, the size of the diagrammatic representation can considerably be reduced. Applicability and feasibility have been shown for ITU MSCs for the specification of negative scenarios using an industrial case example from the automotive domain provided by our industrial partners. In this case example, it has shown that the proposed generic negative scenario indeed sufficiently accounts for a variable number of systems and that the use of a single generic negative scenario can considerably reduce complexity and aid in the specification of negative scenarios for collaborative CPS.

Acknowledgements. This research was partly funded by the German Federal Ministry of Education and Research (grant no. 01IS16043V). We like to thank our industrial partners for their support. Namely, we thank Frank Houdek (Daimler AG).

References

1. Weidenhaupt, K., Pohl, K., Jarke, M., Haumer, P.: Scenario usage in system development: a report on current practice. IEEE International Conference Requirements Engineering (1998)
2. Some, S.S.: Use cases based requirements validation with scenarios. In: IEEE International Conference on Requirements Engineering (2005)
3. Sindre, G., Opdahl, A.L.: Eliciting security requirements with misuse cases. Requir. Eng. **10**, 34–44 (2005)

4. Daun, M., Tenbergen, B., Weyer, T.: Requirements Viewpoint. In: Pohl, K., Hönninger, H., Achatz, R., Broy, M. (eds.) Model-Based Engineering of Embedded Systems, The SPES 2020 Methodology, pp. 51–68. Springer, Heidelberg (2012). https://doi.org/10.1007/978-3-642-34614-9_4

5. Broy, M.: Engineering cyber-physical systems: challenges and foundations. In: Aiguier, M., Caseau, Y., Krob, D., Rauzy, A. (eds.) Complex Systems Design & Management, pp. 1–13. Springer, Heidelberg (2013). https://doi.org/10.1007/978-3-642-34404-6_1

6. Yang, W., Xu, C., Pan, M., Ma, X., Lu, J.: Improving verification accuracy of CPS by modeling and calibrating interaction uncertainty. ACM Trans. Internet Technol. **18**, 20 (2018)

7. Gheorghita, S.V., et al.: System-scenario-based design of dynamic embedded systems. ACM Trans. Autom. Electron. Syst. **14**, 3:1–3:45 (2009)

8. Brings, J., et al.: Model-based documentation of dynamicity constraints for collaborative cyber-physical system architectures: findings from an industrial case study. J. Syst. Archit. **97**, 153–167 (2019)

9. International Telecommunication Union: ITU-T Z.120 : Message Sequence Chart (MSC)

10. Daun, M., Brings, J., Krajinski, L., Weyer, T.: On the benefits of using dedicated models in validation processes for behavioral specifications. In: International Conference on Software and System Processes, pp. 44–53 (2019)

11. Daun, M., Weyer, T., Pohl, K.: Improving manual reviews in function-centered engineering of embedded systems using a dedicated review model. Softw. Syst. Model. **18**(6), 3421–3459 (2019)

12. Milanes, V., Shladover, S.E., Spring, J., Nowakowski, C., Kawazoe, H., Nakamura, M.: Cooperative adaptive cruise control in real traffic situations. IEEE Trans. Intell. Transp. Syst. **15**, 296–305 (2014)

13. Ferrara, A.: Scaled experimental study of an automatic collision avoidance system for passenger cars. IFAC Proc. **38**, 301–306 (2005)

14. Ellahyani, A., El Ansari, M., El Jaafari, I.: Traffic sign detection and recognition based on random forests. Appl. Soft Comput. **46**, 805–815 (2016)

15. Uchitel, S., Kramer, J., Magee, J.: Negative scenarios for implied scenario elicitation. **27**, 109–118 (2002)

16. Whittle, J., Wijesekera, D., Hartong, M.: Executable misuse cases for modeling security concerns. In: 30th International Conference on Software Engineering, pp. 121–130 (2008)

17. Greenyer, J., Gritzner, D., König, F., Dahlke, J., Shi, J., Wete, E.: From scenario modeling to scenario programming for reactive systems with dynamic topology. In: 11th Joint Meeting Foundations of Software Engineering, pp. 974–978 (2017)

18. Pergl, R., Sales, T.P., Rybola, Z.: Instance-level modelling and simulation revisited. In: Barjis, J., Gupta, A., Meshkat, A. (eds.) EOMAS 2013. LNBIP, vol. 153, pp. 85–100. Springer, Heidelberg (2013). https://doi.org/10.1007/978-3-642-41638-5_6

19. Jahn, M., Roth, B., Jablonski, S.: Instance specialization-a pattern for multi-level metamodelling. In: MULTI@ MoDELS, pp. 23–32 (2014)

20. Solmi, R.: Instance modeling assisted by an optional meta level. In: International Workshop on Domain-Specific Modeling, pp. 53–57. ACM (2016)

21. Ehrig, K., Küster, J.M., Taentzer, G.: Generating instance models from meta models. Softw. Syst. Model. **8**, 479–500 (2009)

22. Haworth, B., Kirsopp, C., Roper, M., Shepperd, M., Webster, S.: Towards the development of adequacy criteria for object-oriented systems. In: 5th European Conference on Software Testing Analysis and Review. pp. 417–427 (1997)

23. Matsuoka, Y., Aoki, T., Inenaga, S., Bannai, H., Takeda, M.: Generalized pattern matching and periodicity under substring consistent equivalence relations. Theor. Comput. Sci. **656**, 225–233 (2016)

Model Unification

HIKE: A Step Beyond Data Exchange

Sergio Greco[1], Elio Masciari[2,3], Domenico Saccà[1], and Irina Trubitsyna[1(✉)]

[1] DIMES-Università della Calabria, 87036 Rende, CS, Italy
{greco,sacca,trubitsyna}@dimes.unical.it
[2] DIETI-Università degli Studi di Napoli Federico II, 80125 Napoli, NA, Italy
elio.masciari@unina.it
[3] ICAR-CNR, 87036 Rende, CS, Italy

Abstract. The problem of exchanging data, even considering incomplete and heterogeneous data, has been deeply investigated in the last years. The approaches proposed so far are quite rigid as they refer to fixed schema and/or are based on a deductive approach consisting in the use of a fixed set of (mapping) rules. In this paper, we propose HIKE (Highly Intelligent Knowledge Extraction), a framework that addresses this problem. The core of the framework consists of a smart data exchange architecture integrating deductive and inductive techniques to obtain new knowledge. The use of graph-based representation of source and target data, together with the midway relational database and the extraction of new knowledge allow us to manage dynamic databases where also features of data may change over the time. The paper also addresses the problem of computing certain answers in the new setting and reports a precise analysis of its complexity.

1 Introduction

Many proposal have been made for data exchange among heterogeneous sources. However, for the best of our knowledge, no generalization of the consolidated data exchange framework, that supports both the extraction of new knowledge and flexible representation of heterogeneous data has been defined so far. In this paper we present HIKE (Highly Intelligent Knowledge Extraction), an extension of the data exchange framework that addresses the above mentioned issues.

The global scenario is showed in Fig. 1, where (*i*) *Source*, *Target* and *Midway* are three databases, (*ii*) Σ_{SM} and Σ_{MT} are extended TGDs (Tuple Generating Dependencies) mapping data from *Source* to *Midway* and standard TGDs mapping data from *Midway* to *Target*, respectively, (*iii*) Σ_M and Σ_T are extended TGDs defined over the *Midway* database and standard TGDs and EGDs (Equality Generating Dependencies) defined over the *Target* database, respectively.

The idea is that, by allowing an intermediate database and a richer language to derive new information, as well as information obtained by analyzing data, we may define more powerful and flexible tools for data exchange.

To have a flexible and general representation of source and target databases, following the RDF approach, we decided to model them using a graph-based

© Springer Nature Switzerland AG 2019
A. H. F. Laender et al. (Eds.): ER 2019, LNCS 11788, pp. 423–438, 2019.
https://doi.org/10.1007/978-3-030-33223-5_35

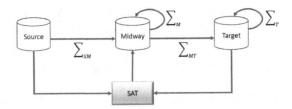

Fig. 1. HIKE architecture

formalism where data are stored into ternary relations. Differently from other formalisms where data are stored into a unique relation [3,17], we consider multiple ternary relations, but analogously to RDF our graph data consist of tuples of the form (i, a, v) with i being a (resource) identifier, a an attribute name and v a value (either a constant or an identifier). The midway database is a relational database containing tuples of any arity that are either imported from the source database using the Σ_{SM} source-midway mapping rules, or are generated by the *Smart Analyzer Tool (SAT)*. Data dependencies denoted by Σ_M are used to generate new information useful to enrich the target database. The target database is graph-based and is built by importing data from the midway database using the mapping rules Σ_{MT}. Finally, as in the standard data exchange scenario, Σ_T consists of a set of TGDs or EGDs.

While we assume that the smart analyzer tool is a black-box aiming to produce new data stored in the midway database (in our prototype it implements several data mining algorithms specific for the domain application), the language used to define Σ_M is a rich logical language that makes use of comparison predicates, *aggregate predicates* and nondeterministic *choice* constructs (well studied in the past by the community of logic databases). This language allows to obtain more realistic information that could be used in a flexible way by both data experts (for analysis purposes) and inexperienced users (for a better navigation through data). We point out that another peculiarity of our framework is that the data exchange takes also advantages of information (under the form of facts) generated by a data analyzer module and stored into the midway database, together with the data extracted from the source database.

For the sake of presentation, in the following we shall denote as *Smart Data Exchange (SDE)* the problem of exchanging data from a source database to a target database using a midway database, which can be also populated by the SAT module.

Example 1. Consider a source and a target databases describing the user's profiles in a social network scenario. These databases contain relations $P_S(\texttt{I, N, V})$ and $P_T(\texttt{I, N, V})$, respectively, with attributes $\texttt{I}$ (profile identifier), $\texttt{N}$ (attribute name) and $\texttt{V}$ (attribute value). The information about profiles' compatibility, extracted from source and target relations (by the SAT module) is stored in the midway database using relation $\texttt{Corr}(\texttt{I}_S, \texttt{I}_T, \texttt{L})$, where the first two attributes contain profile's identifiers taken from tables P_S and P_T, respectively, whereas

L represents the level of compatibility of these profiles. The problem here, is to enrich P_T with some "relevant" attributes from P_S. This scenario can be modelled as follows.

Assume that the source database contains the ternary relation P_S, the target database contains the ternary relation P_T and the midway database contains the relations P_M, P'_M, Tmp and Corr. The mapping from the source to the intermediate databases is defined by the TGD

$$P_S(i,n,v) \rightarrow P_M(i,n,v)$$

saying that all profiles in the source database are imported in the midway database.

To enrich profiles in the midway database we could also use information about compatibilities extracted by the smart analyzer tool. Thus, using full estended TGDs we can define richer profiles as follows:

$$P_M(i_S,n,v) \wedge Corr(i_S,i_T,1) \wedge 1 \geq 0,50 \rightarrow Tmp(i_T,n,v,count(i_S))$$
$$Tmp(i_T,n,v) \wedge w \geq 5 \rightarrow P'_M(i_T,n,v)$$

where the head atom of the first dependency contains the aggregate function count. These extended TGDs say that a target profile with identifier i_T, which is correlated with a ranking of at least 0.5, to at least 5 profiles in the source database having the same attribute n and value v, must be enriched with the feature (i_T,n,v). The mapping from the intermediate to the target database my be expressed using the midway-target TGD

$$P'_M(i,n,v) \rightarrow P_T(i,n,v)$$

□

Once the data of interest have been transferred to the target database they can be checked for consistency and possibly updated using standard TGDs and then analyzed to generate additional data which will be used in possibly next steps.

Contributions and Related Works. Summarizing, in this paper we propose a general framework that supports both analysis and flexible representation of heterogeneous data. The use of graph-based representation of source and target data, together with the extraction of new knowledge made by the SAT tool allow us to manage dynamic databases where also features of data may change over the time. The advantage of using a midway database is that we can use more powerful, logic-based formalisms (using aggregates and nondeterministic functions) to generate new data which are then filtered and imported in the target database. We also study the problem of certain query answering [22] and present a precise complexity analysis of the problem.

The idea to model data analysis during the data mapping is present in Data Posting framework [8] and its simplified version [18]. Differently from HIKE, the

framework proposed in [8,18] does not use graph-based formalisms for source and target data and does not have an intermediate level for data analysis. Moreover, it does not admit the use of existentially quantified variables in the mapping rules and uncertain values in the body of mapping rules can be represented only by means of *non-deterministic* variables, whose values can be selected from specific relations called *domain relations*, possibly restricted by target *count constraints*.

Outline. In the following, we will describe in Sect. 2 the background of our approach. In Sect. 3 we describe our smart data exchange framework. In Sect. 4 we study the complexity of the certain answer problem. In Sect. 5 our strategy for gathering new information from data instances is presented. Finally, in Sect. 6 we will draw our conclusions. For space limitations proofs are omitted.

2   Background

In this section we recall the classical data exchange scenario and an extension of the standard logic query language Datalog with nondeterministic constructs.

2.1   Data Exchange

A schema is a finite collection $R = \{R_1, ..., R_k\}$ of relation symbols. Each relation symbol has an arity, which is a positive integer. A relation symbol of arity n is called n-ary, and has n distinct attributes, which intuitively correspond to column names. An instance I over the schema R is a function that associates to each n-ary relation symbol R_i an n-ary relation $I(R_i)$. With a little abuse of notation we will use R_i to denote both the relation symbol and the relation that interprets it. Given a tuple t occurring in a relation R, we denote by $R(t)$ the association between t and R and call it a fact. An instance can be conveniently represented by its set of facts. $R(\mathbf{v})$, where $\mathbf{v}$ is a vector of variables or constants with the arity of R, is called atom. If R is a schema, then a dependency over R is a sentence in some logical formalism over R.

A *Tuple Generating Dependency (TGD)* is formula of the form: $\forall \mathbf{x}\, \phi(\mathbf{x}) \rightarrow \exists \mathbf{y}\, \psi(\mathbf{x}, \mathbf{y})$, where $\phi(\mathbf{x})$ and $\psi(\mathbf{x}, \mathbf{y})$ are conjunctions of atoms, and $\mathbf{x}, \mathbf{y}$ are lists of variables. *Full TGDs* are TGDs without existentially quantified variables. An *Equality Generating Dependency (EGD)* is a formula of the form: $\forall \mathbf{x}\, \phi(\mathbf{x}) \rightarrow x_1 = x_2$, where $\phi(\mathbf{x})$ is conjunction of atoms, while x_1 and x_2 are variables in $\mathbf{x}$. In our formulae it is common to omit the universal quantifiers, when their presence is clear from the context. The left hand side (w.r.t. the implication symbol) of a data dependency is called *antecedent* or *body*, whereas the right hand side is called *consequent* or *head*.

Let $S = S_1, ..., S_n$ and $T = T_1, ..., T_m$ be two disjoint schemas. We refer to S as the source schema and to the S_i's as the source relation symbols. We refer to T as the target schema and to the T_j's as the target relation symbols. Similarly, instances over S will be called source instances, while instances over T will be called target instances. If I is a source instance and J is a target instance, then

we write $\langle I, J \rangle$ for the instance K over the schema $S \cup T$ such that $K(S_i) = I(S_i)$ and $K(T_j) = J(T_j)$, for $i \leq n$ and $j \leq m$.

The data exchange setting [2,12] is a tuple $(S, T, \Sigma_{st}, \Sigma_t)$, where S is the source relational database schema, T is the target schema, Σ_t are dependencies over the target schema T and Σ_{st} are source-to-target TGDs. The dependencies in Σ_{st} map data from the source to the target schema and are TGDs of the form $\forall \mathbf{x}(\phi_s(\mathbf{x}) \rightarrow \exists \mathbf{y}\, \psi_t(\mathbf{x}, \mathbf{y}))$, where $\phi_s(\mathbf{x})$ and $\psi_t(\mathbf{x}, \mathbf{y})$ are conjunctions of atomic formulas on S and T, respectively. Dependencies in Σ_{st} are also called mapping dependencies. Dependencies in Σ_t specify constraints on the target schema and can be either TGDs or EGDs.

The data exchange problem associated with this setting is the following: given a finite source instance I, find a finite target instance J such that $\langle I, J \rangle$ satisfies Σ_{st} and J satisfies Σ_t. Such a J is called a solution for I.

The computation of an universal solution (the compact representation of all possible solutions) can be done by means of the fixpoint chase algorithm, when it terminates [10]. The execution of the chase involves inserting tuples possibly with null values to satisfy TGDs, and replacing null values with constants or other null values to satisfy EGDs. Specifically, the chase consists of applying a sequence of steps, where each step enforces a dependency that is not satisfied by the current instance. It might well be the case that multiple dependencies can be enforced and, in this case, the chase picks one nondeterministically. Different choices lead to different sequences, some of which might be terminating, while others might not. Unfortunately, checking whether the chase terminates is an undecidable problem [10]. To cope with this issue, several "termination criteria" have been proposed, that is, (decidable) sufficient conditions ensuring chase termination. Some recent works can be found in [7,14,15].

2.2 Datalog Extensions

Queries over relational database can be expressed using Relational Algebra, or alternative equivalent languages such safe Relational Calculus and safe, non-recursive Datalog (with negation). In the following, to state some results, we implicity refer to Relational Algebra (or one of the equivalent formalisms) as query language, even if tables in the target database represent graph-based data (as we will see, they are stored into ternary relations). To make query languages more expressive, several additional feature have been added to these languages including the possibility to manage bags (SQL), aggregates (SQL), recursion (Datalog), existential variables (Datalog$^\pm$) and others. In the following we discuss the extension of Datalog with the nondeterministic choice constructs.

Choice Constructs. The choice constructs [16,20] have been introduced in Datalog to get an increase in expressive power and to obtain simple declarative formulations of classical combinatorial problems, such as those which can be solved by means of greedy algorithms [20].

A *choice atom* is of the form $choice((\mathbf{x}), (\mathbf{y}))$, where $\mathbf{x}$ and $\mathbf{y}$ are lists of variables such that $\mathbf{x} \cap \mathbf{y} = \emptyset$, and can occur in the body of a rule. Its intuitive meaning is to force each initialization of $\mathbf{x}$ to be associated with a unique

initialization of $\mathbf{y}$, thus making the result of executing of a corresponding rule nondeterministic. More formally, a *choice rule* is of the form:

$$A(\mathbf{w}) \leftarrow B(\mathbf{z}), \mathit{choice}((\mathbf{x}), (\mathbf{y}))$$

where $A(\mathbf{w})$ is an atom, $B(\mathbf{z})$ is a conjunction of atoms, $\mathbf{x}, \mathbf{y}, \mathbf{z}$ and $\mathbf{w}$ are lists of variables such that $\mathbf{x}, \mathbf{y}, \mathbf{w} \subseteq \mathbf{z}$. The atom $\mathit{choice}((\mathbf{x}), (\mathbf{y}))$ is used to enforce the *functional dependency* $\mathbf{x} \rightarrow \mathbf{y}$ on the set of atoms derived by means of the rule.

The *choice-least* and *choice-most* constructs [16] specialize the choice construct so as to force greedy selections among alternative choices—these turn out to be particularly useful to express classical greedy algorithms. A *choice-least* (resp. *choice-most*) *atom* is of the form $\mathit{choice\_least}((\mathbf{x}), (c))$ (resp. $\mathit{choice\_most}((\mathbf{x}), (c)))$, where $\mathbf{x}$ is a list of variables and c is a single variable ranging over an ordered domain. A $\mathit{choice\_least}((\mathbf{x}), (c))$ (resp. $\mathit{choice\_most}((\mathbf{x}), (c)))$ atom in a rule indicates that the functional dependency defined by the atom $\mathit{choice}((\mathbf{x}), (c))$ is to be satisfied, and the c value assigned to a certain value of $\mathbf{x}$ has to be the minimum (resp. maximum) one among the candidate values. The body of a rule may contain even more than one choice constructs, but only one choice-least or choice-most atom. For instance, the rule

$$p(x,y,c) \leftarrow q(x,y,c), \mathtt{choice}((x),(y)), \mathtt{choice\_least}((x),(c))$$

imposes the functional dependency $x \rightarrow y,c$ on the possible instances of p. In addition, for each value of x, the minimum among the candidate values of c must be chosen. For instance, assuming that q is defined by the facts $q(a,b,1)$ and $q(a,d,2)$, from the rule above we might derive either $p(a,b,1)$ or $p(a,d,2)$. However, the choice-least atom introduces the additional requirement that the minimum value on the third attribute has to be chosen, so that only $p(a,b,1)$ is derived. The formal semantics is defined by rewriting rules with choice atoms into rules with negated literals and selecting (nondeterministically) one of the stable models of the rewritten program [16,20].

3   Smart Data Exchange

In this section we present the data exchange framework informally discussed in the Introduction. We assume the existence of the following countably infinite sets: *relation names* $\mathcal{R}$, *identifiers* $\mathcal{I}$, *attribute names* $\mathcal{A}$, *constants* $\mathcal{C}$, *nulls* $\mathcal{N}$ and *variables* $\mathcal{V}$. The set of relation symbols (also called predicate symbols) is partitioned into three countable sets denoted by $\mathcal{R}_S$ (source relations), $\mathcal{R}_T$ (target relations) and $\mathcal{R}_M$ (midway relations), whereas $\mathcal{D}_S = \mathcal{I} \cup \mathcal{A} \cup \mathcal{C}$, $\mathcal{D}_T = \mathcal{I} \cup \mathcal{A} \cup \mathcal{C} \cup \mathcal{N}$ and $\mathcal{D}_M = \mathcal{I} \cup \mathcal{A} \cup \mathcal{C}$ denote the domains of relations $\mathcal{R}_S$, $\mathcal{R}_T$ and $\mathcal{R}_M$, respectively. Relations in $\mathcal{R}_S$ and $\mathcal{R}_T$ have arity 3 and take values from $\mathcal{I} \times \mathcal{A} \times \mathcal{I} \cup \mathcal{C}$ and $\mathcal{I} \cup \mathcal{N} \times \mathcal{A} \cup \mathcal{N} \times \mathcal{I} \cup \mathcal{C} \cup \mathcal{N}$ respectively, whereas relations in $\mathcal{R}_M$ may have any arity n and take values from $\mathcal{D}^n_M$. The main difference between the source and the target databases is that the target database may also have nulls (corresponding

to blank nodes in RDF) which are introduced to satisfy constraints. The set of source (resp. target, midway) relations define the source (resp. target, midway) database whose schema is denoted by S (resp. T, M).

The model defined above states that the source and target databases are graph-based databases stored in a relational database (using triples), whereas the midway database is a standard relational database. This choice is due to the fact that we would exchange data among heterogeneous databases and we want model data whose schema may change over the time. The next example shows how relational data are stored into a graph-based database.

Example 2. Consider the below relational database, where attribute dept in relation *employee* is a foreign key for relation *department*, whereas attribute mgr in relation *department* is a foreign key for relation *employee*.

name	dept	sal
john	cs	80
mary	math	90

employee

name	city	mgr
cs	london	john
math	paris	john

department

The database can be represented as a graph-based database as showed below:

id	attr	val
i_1	name	john
i_1	dept	i_3
i_1	sal	80
i_2	name	mary
i_2	dept	i_4
i_2	sal	90

employee

id	attr	val
i_3	name	cs
i_3	city	london
i_3	mgr	i_1
i_4	name	math
i_4	city	paris
i_4	mgr	i_1

department

where each tuple with n values in the original relational database is mapped into n triples sharing the same id. □

In the following, for the sake of simplicity, we often express tuples using facts and assume that $\mathcal{C}$ contains the set of natural numbers.

Extended TGDs. An atom is of the form $p(t_1, ..., t_n)$, where $t_1, ..., t_n$ are terms (standard atom), or of the form $t_1 \theta t_2$, where θ is a comparison predicates and t_1, t_2 are terms (built-in atom). A literal is an atom A (positive literal) or its negation $\neg A$ (negative literal). A conjunction of literals is of the form $B_1 \wedge \cdots \wedge B_n$ where $B_1, ..., B_n$ are literals. A conjunction of literals is said to be *safe* if all variables occurring in built-in atoms and negated literals also appear in positive literals. From now on we assume that whenever we consider conjunctions of literals they are safe.

Definition 1. An extended TGD (ETGD) is a universally quantified implication formula of one of the following forms:

- $\varphi(x) \wedge choice(x') \rightarrow \psi(w)$,
  where $\varphi(x)$ is a safe conjunction of standard and built-in literals, $\psi(w)$ is a conjunction of atoms, $w \subseteq x$ and $choice(x')$, with $x' \subseteq x$, is a possibly empty conjunction of choice-atoms;
- $\varphi(x) \rightarrow q(w_0, c_1\langle w_1 \rangle, ..., c_n\langle w_n \rangle)$ (called aggregate dependency)
  where $\varphi(x)$ is a safe conjunction of standard and built-in literals, $c_1, ..., c_n$ denote aggregate functions (e.g., $min, max, sum, count$), w_0 (called "group-by" variables) and $w_1, ..., w_n$ are lists of variables such that $w_0, ..., w_n \subseteq x$ and $w_0 \cap w_i = \emptyset \ \forall i \in [1, n]$. □

For any set Σ of data dependencies, the *dependency graph* $G_\Sigma = (V, E)$ is built as follows: V consists of the predicate symbols occurring in Σ, whereas there is an edge from p to q if there is a dependency having p in the body and q in the head. Moreover, the edge is labeled with $\neg$ (resp. ag) if p occurs negated (resp. occurs in the head atom which contains aggregate functions). A set of dependency is said to be *stratified* if the depencecy graph does not contain cycles with labeled edges. Observe that since standard dependencies are positive (that is, all body literals are positive), to check stratification it is sufficient to check stratification of ETGDs. From now on we assume that our dependencies are stratified.

The semantics of ETGDs with choice atoms can be defined as in the case of Datalog rules. To this end, in order to eliminate head conjunctions, any ETGDs $r : \varphi(x) \rightarrow p_1(y_1) \wedge \cdots \wedge p_k(y_k)$ having $k > 1$ atoms in the head is rewritten into: (i) k ETGDs $r_i : \varphi(x) \rightarrow p_i(y_i)$ ($i \in [1, k]$), if r does not contain choice atoms, and (ii) $k + 1$ ETGDs $r_0, ..., r_k$ if r contains choice atoms, where $r_0 = \varphi(x) \rightarrow h_r(x)$ and $r_i = h_r(x) \rightarrow p_i(y_i)$ (with $i \in 1, k]$), where h_r is a fresh new predicate. Regarding the semantics of ETGDs with aggregate functions, as the set of ETGDs is stratified, we can partition it into strata so that, if a stratum contains an ETGD with aggregate functions, then it does not contain any other ETGD, and compute one stratum at time following topological order defined over the strata by the dependency graph. The computation of an ETGD with aggregate functions can be carried out in the same way of computing SQL queries with aggregates, as body predicates have been already computed and, therefore, they correspond to database relations in SQL (see also [13]).

Smart Data Exchange. Now we formally define the Smart Data Exchange Framework.

Definition 2. A *Smart Data Exchange (SDE)* is a tuple $(S, M, T, \Sigma_{SM}, \Sigma_{MT}, \Sigma_M, \Sigma_T)$, where:

- S is the source schema containing predicates taken from $\mathcal{R}_S$,
- M is the midway schema containing predicates taken from $\mathcal{R}_M$,
- T is the target schema containing predicates taken from $\mathcal{R}_T$,
- Σ_{SM} is a source-to-midway set of safe ETGDs,
- Σ_M is a midway-to-midway set of safe, stratified ETGDs,

- Σ_{MT} is a midway-to-target set of standard TGDs, and
- Σ_T is a target-to-target set of standard TGDs and standard EGDs.   □

As already pointed out, we assume that the source and target relations are graph-based data and every class of objects is modeled as a named set of triples. RDF graph, microdata and JSON representations are very closed to this description [1]. The midway database is a relational database containing relations of any arity including data in the format of the source and target database.

For any SDE $E = (S, M, T, \Sigma_{SM}, \Sigma_M, \Sigma_{MT}, \Sigma_T)$, we shall use the following notation: $\Sigma_1 = \Sigma_{SM} \cup \Sigma_M$, $\Sigma_2 = \Sigma_{MT} \cup \Sigma_T$, and $\Sigma = \Sigma_1 \cup \Sigma_2$.

Example 3. Consider a graph relation in the source database containing facts of the form $\texttt{graph}(\texttt{id}_1, \texttt{edge}, \texttt{id}_2)$ where $\texttt{id}_1$ and $\texttt{id}_2$ are node identifiers and edge is an attribute value denoting that there is an edge from $\texttt{id}_1$ to $\texttt{id}_2$. The data exchange problem consists in extracting a spanning tree to be stored in the target database. From the source database we can import edges and nodes in the midway database, as defined in the set Σ_{SM} consisting of the below ETGD:

$$\texttt{graph(x, edge, y)} \rightarrow \texttt{edge(x, y)} \land \texttt{node(x)} \land \texttt{node(y)}$$

Assume now that the midway database also contains a fact $\texttt{root}(0)$, for instance generated by the *SAT* module or imported from the source database using another source-to-midway dependency. The next set of ETGDs Σ_M shows how it is possible to generate a spanning tree rooted in the node x denoted by fact $\texttt{root(x)}$.

$$\texttt{root(x)} \rightarrow \texttt{st(nil, x)}$$
$$\texttt{st(z, x)} \land \texttt{edge(x, y)}, \texttt{choice}((y), (x)), \rightarrow \texttt{st(x, y)} \land \texttt{connected(y)}$$
$$\texttt{node(x)} \land \neg\texttt{connected(x)}, \texttt{choice}((), (x)) \rightarrow \texttt{nextRoot(x)}$$

Here the first ETGD is used to start the computation by deriving an edge ending in the root node (the starting node is the dummy node $\texttt{nil}$), whereas the second ETGD, imposing the functional dependency $y \rightarrow x$, guarantees that the set of selected nodes is a spanning tree. The last ETGD in Σ_M gives a node not belonging to the spanning tree if the graph is not connected; this node can be used in the future as a root to compute another spanning tree.

Spanning tree edges and nextRoot facts are then imported in the target database (as triples) using the below set of TGDs Σ_{MT}:

$$\texttt{st(x, y)} \rightarrow \texttt{graph(x, st, y)}$$
$$\texttt{nextRoot(x)} \rightarrow \exists y \; \texttt{graph(nil, root, x)}$$

Information stored in the target database are next analyzed to generate new information which will be stored in the midway database. For instance, from a fact $\texttt{graph(nil, root, x)}$ the SAT module could generate a fact $\texttt{root(x)}$ which, after been stored in the midway database, could generate the computation of another spanning tree rooted in x.   □

Note that the process described in the previous example and showed in Fig. 1 is supervised, that is the activation of the module SAT is performed by the user.

The smart data exchange problem associated with this setting is the following: given a finite source instance I over a schema S and a smart data exchange $E = (S, M, T, \Sigma_{\text{SM}}, \Sigma_{\text{M}}, \Sigma_{\text{MT}}, \Sigma_{\text{T}})$, find finite instances J and K over the schemas M and T, respectively, such that $\langle I, J \rangle$ satisfies Σ_{SM}, J satisfies Σ_{M}, $\langle J, K \rangle$ satisfies Σ_{MT} and K satisfies Σ_{M}. The pair $\langle J, K \rangle$ is called a solution (or model) for $\langle I, E \rangle$, or equivalently for $\langle I, \Sigma \rangle$, where let $\Sigma_1 = \Sigma_{\text{SM}} \cup \Sigma_{\text{M}}$ and $\Sigma_2 = \Sigma_{\text{MT}} \cup \Sigma_{\text{T}}$, $\Sigma = \Sigma_1 \cup \Sigma_2$. The set of solutions for $\langle I, E \rangle$ (or equivalently for $\langle I, \Sigma \rangle$) is denoted by $Sol(I, E)$, (resp. $Sol(I, \Sigma)$). Moreover, J is also called solution (or model) for $\langle I, \Sigma_1 \rangle$ and, in cascade, K is a solution (or model) for $\langle J, \Sigma_2 \rangle$. Thus, the problem of finding solutions can be split into two problems: (i) finding a solutions J for I, and (ii) finding solutions K for J. The set of solutions for $\langle I, \Sigma_1 \rangle$ is denoted by $Sol(I, \Sigma_1)$, whereas the set of solutions for $\langle J, \Sigma_2 \rangle$ is $Sol(J, \Sigma_2)$. Therefore, given a smart data exchange framework, starting from I with dependency Σ_1 we find solutions $J_1, ..., J_m$ and, then starting from every J_i $(1 \leq i \leq m)$ with dependency Σ_2 we find solutions $K_{i_1}, ..., K_{i_n}$. Observe that m is always finite, whereas i_n, in the general case, is not guaranteed to be finite [11].

Certain Answers. Since we have multiple models, the certain answers are those derived from all models.

Definition 3. *Given a query Q, a database I and a smart data exchange $E = (S, M, T, \Sigma_{\text{SM}}, \Sigma_{\text{M}}, \Sigma_{\text{MT}}, \Sigma_{\text{T}})$, the certain answer of Q over $\langle I, E \rangle$ is*

$$Certain(Q, I, E) = \bigcap_{\langle J, K \rangle \in Sol(I, E)} Q(K) \qquad \square$$

Since the certain answer could be equivalently defined as $Certain(Q, I, E) = \bigcap_{J \in Sol(I, \Sigma_1) \wedge K \in Sol(J, \Sigma_2)} Q(K)$, its computation can be optimized by considering the four sets of dependencies separately, that is by first computing solutions J' for $\langle I, \Sigma_{\text{ST}} \rangle$, then solutions J for $\langle J', \Sigma_{\text{M}} \rangle$, next solutions K' for $\langle J, \Sigma_{\text{MT}} \rangle$, and, finally solutions K for $\langle K', \Sigma_{\text{T}} \rangle$. Let us now introduce the concepts of homomorphism and universal model.

A *homomorphism* from a set of atoms A_1 to a set of atoms A_2 is a mapping h from the domain of A_1 (set of terms occurring in A_1) to the domain of A_2 such that: (i) $h(c) = c$, for every $c \in \text{Const}(A_1)$; and (ii) for every atom $R(t_1, \ldots, t_n)$ in A_1, we have that $R(h(t_1), \ldots, h(t_n))$ is in A_2. With a slight abuse of notation, we apply h also to sets of atoms and thus, for a given set of atoms A, we define $h(A) = \{R(h(t_1), \ldots, h(t_n)) \mid R(t_1, \ldots, t_n) \in A\}$.

Definition 4. *A universal model of (I, Σ) is a model $\langle J, K \rangle$ of (I, Σ) such that for every model $\langle J', K' \rangle$ of (I, Σ) there exists a homomorphism from K to K'. The set of all universal solutions of (I, Σ) will be denoted by $USol(I, \Sigma)$.* $\qquad \square$

Proposition 1. *For any positive query Q, database I and SDE $E = (S, M, T, \Sigma_{SM}, \Sigma_M, \Sigma_{MT}, \Sigma_T)$, the certain answer of Q over $\langle I, E \rangle$ is*

$$Certain(Q, I, E) = \bigcap_{J \,\in\, Sol(I, \Sigma_1)} Q(K_J)_{\downarrow}$$

where K_J is any universal solution of $\langle J, \Sigma_2 \rangle$ and $Q(K_J)_{\downarrow}$ is the result of computing naively (i.e. considering nulls as constants) $Q(K_J)$ and deleting tuples with nulls. □

Universal solutions for $\langle J, \Sigma_2 \rangle$ can be easily computed by applying the classical fixpoint algorithm called *Chase* which computes a subset of universal solutions called *canonical* [4,11].

As previously discussed, in several cases we are not interested in all models of $\langle I, \Sigma_1 \rangle$, but only in one selected nondeterministically (e.g. the set of edges of any minimum spanning tree). Thus, we now introduce the definition of *nondeterministic answer*.

Definition 5. *The nondeterministic answer to a query Q over a database instance I and SDE $E = (S, M, T, \Sigma_{SM}, \Sigma_M, \Sigma_{MT}, \Sigma_T)$ is*

$$NonDet(Q, I, E) = \bigcap_{K \,\in\, Sol(J, \Sigma_2)} Q(K)$$

where, J is a model for $\langle I, \Sigma_1 \rangle$ selected nondeterministically. □

Observe that the nondeterministic choice of the model is applied only to dependencies in Σ_1, where users express explicitly that they want select nondeterministically a subset of tuples, whereas for $\langle J, \Sigma_2 \rangle$ we consider all models. Note that, two evaluations of the nondeterministic answers could give different answers (as the choices made could be different) and that the responsibility of computing nondeterministic answers, instead of certain answers, is left to the user. Indeed, in several cases the user is not interested in specific models, but only in one model satisfying some properties (e.g. any spanning tree). Therefore, we introduce the concept of universal nondeterministic model.

Definition 6. *A universal nondeterministic model for $\langle I, \Sigma \rangle$ is any universal model in $USol(D, \Sigma)$ selected nondeterministically.* □

Proposition 2. *For any positive query Q, database I and SDE $E = (S, M, T, \Sigma_{SM}, \Sigma_M, \Sigma_{MT}, \Sigma_T)$, the nondeterministic answer of Q over $\langle I, E \rangle$ is*

$$NonDet(Q, I, E) = Q(K_J)_{\downarrow}$$

where, let J be any model for $\langle I, \Sigma_1 \rangle$ selected nondeterministically, K_J is a universal solution of $\langle J, \Sigma_2 \rangle$ □

4   Complexity Analysis

After having defined certain and nondeterministic answers we now study the complexity of these problems.

First of all observe that computing answers to queries over databases and SDEs is an undecidable problem. This comes out from the fact that the problem of computing certain answers to queries over database with standard TGDs is undecidable. In these cases the problem of deciding whether the chase algorithm terminates (i.e. computes a finite model in finite time) is undecidable. Thus, the problem of checking whether a tuple belongs to the certain answers is undecidable as well.

One way of restoring decidability of certain answering is to isolate a fragment of dependencies for which both the cardinality of $USol(D, E)$ and the cardinality of each element therein is finite. Another approach is identify a fragment of dependencies for which certain answering becomes decidable, regardless of the finiteness of $USol(D, E)$ or the elements therein.

In this paper, we assume that dependencies in Σ_T are *terminating*, that is the chase algorithm is able to compute a (finite) canonical universal solution in finite time. To guarantee finiteness of a universal solution several *termination criteria* have been defined in the literature [7,15]. Therefore, we assume that Σ_T satisfies one of these criteria and we say that Σ_T is terminating. Clearly, if Σ_T is terminating, all solutions for $\langle I, \Sigma \rangle$ are finite. Moreover, we say that a SDE $E = (S, M, T, \Sigma_{SM}, \Sigma_M, \Sigma_{MT}, \Sigma_T)$ is terminating, if Σ_T is terminating.

Theorem 1. *Let* $E = (S, M, T, \Sigma_{SM}, \Sigma_M, \Sigma_{MT}, \Sigma_T)$ *be a terminating SDE, I a database instance and Q a positive query. Then, the problems of computing* $Certain(Q, I, E)$ *and* $NonDet(Q, I, E)$ *are both coNPcomplete.*   □

Theorem 2. *Let* $E = (S, M, T, \Sigma_{SM}, \Sigma_M, \Sigma_{MT}, \Sigma_T)$ *be a terminating SDE without EGDs, I a database instance and Q a positive query. Then, the problem of computing* $Certain(Q, I, E)$ *is in coNP, whereas the problem of computing a nondeterministic answer* $NonDet(Q, I, E)$ *is polynomial time.*   □

Theorem 3. *Let* $E = (S, M, T, \Sigma_{SM}, \Sigma_M, \Sigma_{MT}, \Sigma_T)$ *be a terminating SDE without choice atoms, I a database instance and Q a positive query. Then, the problems of computing* $Certain(Q, I, E)$ *and* $NonDet(Q, I, E)$ *are both polynomial time.*   □

We conclude by showing an interesting subclass of SDEs with choice atoms and EGDs. To this end we need to introduce a refinement of the dependency graph, called propagation graph, to analyze how values are propagated during the evaluation of dependencies.

Propagation Graph. The *Propagation Graph* Γ_Σ of a set of data dependency Σ is a graph (V, E) where V is the set of predicate symbols occurring in Σ, whereas E is built as follows. There is an edge from p to q if either: (*i*) there is

an (E)TGD Σ having q in the head and p in the body, or (ii) there is an EGD having in the body two (not necessarily distinct) atoms $p(\overline{u})$ and $p(\overline{v})$ containing, respectively, the two variables occurring in the head. Moreover, in case (i) the edge is labeled with ch if Σ contains a choice atom, whereas in case (ii) the edge is labelled with eq.

Definition 7. *A SDE $E = (S, M, T, \Sigma_{SM}, \Sigma_M, \Sigma_{MT}, \Sigma_T)$ is said to be* confluent *if the propagation graph of $\Sigma = \Sigma_{SM} \cup \Sigma_M \cup \Sigma_{MT} \cup \Sigma_T$ does not have paths containing both edges labeled with ch and edges labeled with eq.* □

Theorem 4. *Let E be a decidable, confluent SDE, I a database instance and Q a positive query. Then, the problem of computing $NonDet(Q, I, E)$ is polynomial time.* □

5 Smart Analyzer Tool: Building New Data from Data Instances

The analysis of data instances can lead to the discovery of features not modeled in the initial data that could be of potential interest from the user point of view. This information could lead to the introduction of new predicates and, in order to address this problem, we leverage on different data mining techniques [5,9,21], to extract novel knowledge useful for the scenario at hand. A prototype of the SAT module implementing both (supervised) descriptive rule induction techniques [19] and clustering techniques is under development; a preliminary version implementing only specific clustering algorithms is described in [8].

As an example, assume to have a set of social network users exhibiting the following properties: (i) *sex* (either `male` or `female`); (ii) list of *prefered hobbies* (e.g. `sport`, `shopping` or `culture`); (iii) list of *friends*.

These features can be extracted and stored into ground facts using adhoc wrappers and data analyzers that leverages schema information and possibly ontologies associated to data being analyzed. Assuming that the following instances are extracted[1]:

$S(i_1, contains, o_1)$	$S(i_1, contains, o_2)$	$S(i_1, contains, o_3)$
$S(i_1, contains, o_4)$	$S(i_1, contains, o_5)$	$S(i_1, contains, o_6)$
$S(o_1, sex, female)$	$S(o_2, sex, male)$	$T(o_3, sex, male)$
$S(o_4, sex, female)$	$S(o_5, sex, male)$	$T(o_6, sex, male)$
$S(o_1, prefer, shopping)$	$S(o_2, prefer, shopping)$	$S(o_3, prefer, shopping)$
$S(o_4, prefer, sport)$	$S(o_5, prefer, sport)$	$S(o_1, friend, o_2)$
$S(o_1, friend, o_3)$	$S(o_4, friend, o_5)$	$S(o_4, friend, o_6)$

Based on the instances shown above, the SAT module derives, among others, the following pattern:

$$S(Z, contains, X) \land S(Z, contains, Y) \land S(X, friend, Y) \land$$
$$S(X, prefer, P) \rightarrow S(Y, prefer, P)$$

---

[1] Clearly the shown snapshot is very small and it is reported just to give an idea of the type of data, but the technique works for relatively large datasets.

Using this pattern, new facts regarding users' preferences can be inferred. Considering the above facts, the fact S(o6,prefer,sport) is derived.

As a further example, consider the application scenario where users interact with a social network by posing queries, posting comments and uploading (tagged) files. For instance, a user may issue the following query: *Find a restaurant in Milan*. Traditional search engines provide answers on the basis of their default criteria. However, the output could be ineffective as users may not be satisfied by query answers, as these are mainly based on proximity search and some fixed categorizations (e.g. number of stars, price).

To improve this solution, we can perform data pre-processing by clustering user comments stored in our system. As a result, we obtain a set of comment groups from which it is possible to derive new search *dimensions* (to be provided to users) previously hidden in the data. In our example the algorithm could provide the quality of the dishes served in restaurants that meet the conditions of the query (restaurants located in the Milan area) and the new predicate describing this dimension could be *Quality*[2]. As users interact with the system and new enquiries and comments are made, some other additional dimensions and refinements of those previously obtained could arise. For instance, the predicate *Quality* could be further refined by using additional predicates like *fresh-fish* with suitable instance values: bad/good/excellent.

Regarding clustering techniques, it is worth noticing that, (*i*) the above mentioned reasoning is independent from the specific algorithm (we provide several options to take into account the possibly different data features); (*ii*) assignments of clusters to instances are made on a probabilistic basis for soft clustering (e.g. a given instance X belongs to a cluster C with probability $P(X,C)$). For the sake of simplicity, we assign X only to the highest probability cluster C.

Considering Example 1, as a cluster partitioning is produced, we can populate the compatibility table Corr in the midway database, by simply adding instances as follows: if X and Y are assigned to the same cluster C, we add the tuple (X,Y,l) if $l = P(X,C) * P(Y,C)$ is greather than a given threshold (defined by users). The SDE can then refine our pattern search strategy as explained in Sect. 1, i.e. we can search only for patterns that are supported by a minimum number of occurrences.

6   Conclusion and Future Work

In this paper we addressed the problem of enriching the data representation in a Big data environment. We introduced the Smart Data Exchange setting in order to overcome the limitations of the classical data representation approaches. It is a more powerful representation strategy for extracting information from data while integrating them. We analyzed the theoretical complexity of the approach and its applicability in practical scenarios. As a future work, we plan to extend our framework in order to integrate it with further data mining and deep learning

---

[2] We recall that the predicate name can be obtained by using ad-hoc wrappers and domain based ontologies.

algorithms and to enrich data by also extracting information from the web and from social media [6] or health data.

Acknowledgements. Authors have been supported by D-ALL and ProtectID projects, Elio Masciari has been supported by POR FESR Campania project Remiam.

References

1. Angles, R., Gutierrez, C.: An introduction to graph data management. Graph Data Management. DSA, pp. 1–32. Springer, Cham (2018). https://doi.org/10.1007/978-3-319-96193-4_1
2. Arenas, M., Barceló, P., Fagin, R., Libkin, L.: Locally consistent transformations and query answering in data exchange. In: PODS (2004)
3. Arenas, M., Gottlob, G., Pieris, A.: Expressive languages for querying the semantic web. ACM Trans. Database Syst. **43**(3), 13:1–13:45 (2018)
4. Beeri, C., Vardi, M.Y.: A proof procedure for data dependencies. J. ACM **31**(4), 718–741 (1984)
5. Bianchini, D., Antonellis, V.D., Franceschi, N.D., Melchiori, M.: Prefer: a prescription-based food recommender system. Comput. Stand. Interfaces **54**, 64–75 (2017)
6. Brambilla, M., Ceri, S., Valle, E.D., Volonterio, R., Salazar, F.X.A.: Extracting emerging knowledge from social media. In: WWW Conference, pp. 795–804 (2017)
7. Calautti, M., Greco, S., Molinaro, C., Trubitsyna, I.: Exploiting equality generating dependencies in checking chase termination. PVLDB **9**(5), 396–407 (2016)
8. Cassavia, N., Masciari, E., Pulice, C., Saccà, D.: Discovering user behavioral features to enhance information search on big data. TiiS **7**(2), 7:1–7:33 (2017)
9. Castano, S., Ferrara, A., Montanelli, S.: Exploratory analysis of textual data streams. Futur. Gener. Comp. Syst. **68**, 391–406 (2017)
10. Deutsch, A., Nash, A., Remmel, J.B.: The chase revisited. In: Proceedings of PODS Conference, pp. 149–158 (2008)
11. Fagin, R., Kolaitis, P.G., Miller, R.J., Popa, L.: Data exchange: semantics and query answering. Theor. Comput. Sci. **336**(1), 89–124 (2005)
12. Fagin, R., Kolaitis, P.G., Popa, L.: Data exchange: getting to the core. ACM Trans. Database Syst. **30**(1), 174–210 (2005)
13. Greco, S.: Dynamic programming in datalog with aggregates. IEEE Trans. Knowl. Data Eng. **11**(2), 265–283 (1999)
14. Greco, S., Spezzano, F., Trubitsyna, I.: Stratification criteria and rewriting techniques for checking chase termination. PVLDB **4**(11), 1158–1168 (2011)
15. Greco, S., Spezzano, F., Trubitsyna, I.: Checking chase termination: cyclicity analysis and rewriting techniques. IEEE Trans. Knowl. Data Eng. **27**(3), 621–635 (2015)
16. Greco, S., Zaniolo, C.: Greedy algorithms in datalog. TPLP **1**(4), 381–407 (2001)
17. Libkin, L., Reutter, J.L., Soto, A., Vrgoc, D.: Trial: a navigational algebra for RDF triplestores. ACM Trans. Database Syst. **43**(1), 5:1–5:46 (2018)
18. Masciari, E., Saccà, D., Trubitsyna, I.: Simplified data posting in practice. In: Proceedings of 23rd International Database Engineering and Applications Symposium (IDEAS 2019), Athens, Greece (2019, to appear)
19. Novak, P.K., Lavrac, N., Webb, G.I.: Supervised descriptive rule induction. In: Sammut, C., Webb, G.I. (eds.) Encyclopedia of Machine Learning and Data Mining, pp. 1210–1213. Springer, Boston (2017). https://doi.org/10.1007/978-1-4899-7687-1_808

20. Saccà, D., Zaniolo, C.: Stable models and non-determinism in logic programs with negation. In: Proceedings of PODS Conference, pp. 205–217 (1990)
21. Tan, P., Steinbach, M., Karpatne, A., Kumar, V.: Introduction to Data Mining. Addison-Wesley, Boston (2017)
22. ten Cate, B., Fontaine, G., Kolaitis, P.G.: On the data complexity of consistent query answering. In: ICDT Conference, pp. 22–33 (2012)

Unified Management of Multi-model Data
(Vision Paper)

Irena Holubová[1] [iD], Martin Svoboda[1(✉)] [iD], and Jiaheng Lu[2] [iD]

[1] Faculty of Mathematics and Physics, Charles University, Prague, Czech Republic
{holubova,svoboda}@ksi.mff.cuni.cz
[2] University of Helsinki, Helsinki, Finland
jiaheng.lu@helsinki.fi

Abstract. The variety of data is one of the most challenging issues for research and practice in data management. The so-called multi-model data are naturally organized in different and mutually interlinked data formats and logical models, including structured, semi-structured, and unstructured. In this vision paper, we discuss the so far neglected, but for correct and efficient management of multi-model data critical issues and challenges: conceptual modeling of multi-model data, inference of multi-model schemas, unified and conceptual querying, evolution management, and, last but not least, autonomous multi-model data management.

Keywords: Multi-model databases · Conceptual modeling · Schema inference · Query languages · Evolution management · Autonomous systems

1 Introduction and Motivation

In recent years, the Big Data movement has broken down borders of many technologies and approaches that have so far been widely acknowledged as mature and robust. One of the most challenging issues is the *variety* of data. It means that data may be present in multiple types and formats – structured, semi-structured, and unstructured – and independently produced by different sources as well as natively conform to various models, schemas or ontologies.

Although traditional relational databases have been the systems of the first choice for decades, with the arrival of Big Data, their capabilities have become insufficient in many aspects, and so new types of systems, such as NoSQL or NewSQL, have appeared. The variety of *multi-model data* itself brings another dimension of complexity since multiple distinct models must be efficiently supported at a time. Currently, there exist more than 20 representatives of so-called *multi-model databases* [15], involving well-known tools, both traditional relational and novel NoSQL (such as Oracle DB, Cassandra, or MongoDB).

This work was partially supported by the Charles University project PROGRES Q48 and the Academy of Finland project number 310321.

A. H. F. Laender et al. (Eds.): ER 2019, LNCS 11788, pp. 439–447, 2019.
https://doi.org/10.1007/978-3-030-33223-5_36

The main open problems of these systems are: (1) The level of support for multi-model data varies greatly, with different extent of ability to query across different models, index internal structures or optimize query evaluation plans. (2) Since these systems originate mainly in the IT industry, the existing solutions are determined and significantly limited by the specifics of the original underlying single-model systems. (3) For the same reason, there is a lack of necessary formal background, unified approaches, and generally applicable methods allowing to work with multi-model data in full possible extent.

In this vision paper, we discuss these critical open problems and envision the core research areas closely related to the conceptual modeling and data management that need to be appropriately targeted. Namely, we describe, justify, as well as outline possible solutions for the following five key challenges: (1) proposal of a formal background for conceptual modeling of multi-model data and mapping and transformation of such data into individual models, (2) algorithms for inference of multi-model schemas, (3) unified and conceptual querying over multi-model data, (4) correct propagation of changes to data, schemas, and queries induced by the evolution management, and, finally, (5) autonomous multi-model data management in general.

The rest of the paper is structured as follows: In Sect. 2, we provide a brief overview of the existing mainly single-model approaches to data management. In Sect. 3, we discuss the open problems and challenges of multi-model databases, while we conclude in Sect. 4.

2   Related Work

There are basically two existing general approaches to manipulate and query multi-model data: (1) *polyglot persistence*, and (2) *multi-model databases* [17].

The main strategy of the first kind of systems is to leverage different databases to store different models of data and then develop a mediator to integrate them together. While this idea can be traced back to not only federated databases studied during the 1980s, recently, several research prototypes developed on the polyglot persistence paradigm were also introduced. For example, DBMS+ [12] targets at embracing several database platforms with unified declarative processing, while BigDAWG [9] provides an architecture supporting location transparency and a middleware providing a uniform multi-island query interface.

The second kind of systems incorporates only one single database to manage different data models, and provides a fully integrated backend to handle the system demands for performance, scalability, and fault tolerance [18]. The idea of an integrated system can be traced back to the concept of *object-relational databases*, which borrow and adapt the object-oriented programming principles into the world of relational databases.

With the dawn of Big Data, the challenge of handling variety has recently inspired a new generation of dedicated *multi-model databases*, capable of storing and processing structurally different data by supporting several data models

within just a single database. This way of solving the polyglot persistence problem offers advantages in data modeling, allowing to represent data in its most native from. While this approach can be considered as opposite to the *one size does not fit all* argument [26], it can also be understood as a way of re-architecting traditional database models to address new requirements [13]. If nothing else, it was (correctly) assumed that, by 2017, the majority of leading database systems would offer multiple data models within just a single platform.

3   Research Challenges

While the existing multi-model databases pursue the bottom-up design principles, and so essentially represent kind of a trade-off solution, where a core model is more-or-less painfully adapted to additional new models, a top-down approach that would provide a systematically designed and robust conceptual multi-model solution backed by a precise formalism is still missing. In particular, we see the following main issues:

1. *Formal background definition:* There is a need for a complex formal apparatus for multi-model data representation, storing and querying, including proofs of its features and complexity of algorithms.
2. *Data processing unification:* Unified and generally applicable methods and approaches for data processing tasks at the conceptual level (together with necessary mappings and extensions to the logical level) need to be proposed.
3. *Practical impact preservation:* All the proposed languages, methods, and algorithms must still preserve a tight relation to the existing systems so that they can be exploited in real-world scenarios and implementations.

In this section, we discuss in detail five particular key areas we see as the primary research targets for the conceptual modeling and database communities.

3.1   Conceptual Modeling of Multi-model Data

When data across distinct models are to be processed together, their schemas inferred, or query expressions evaluated, kind of a unified data abstraction has to be established first. These models often mutually share a couple of the same principles on the one hand, while can also have certain specifics on the other.

For this purpose, widely used modeling languages ER [6] and UML [22] could be utilized and in a *top-down* way adjusted to the needs of individual logical models. While the former language exists in several notations yet provides more complex constructs better grasping the real-world relationships among entities, the latter one is standardized but, unfortunately, only too data-oriented and concealing important details (e.g., weak entity types). On the contrary, *bottom-up* approaches could find an inspiration in NoSQL AbstractModel [5], a system-independent model for so called *aggregate-oriented* databases.

Regardless of the adopted strategy, the theory of categories [14], associative arrays [11], or description logics [1] could be utilized to internally model the data

in a formal, abstract, and rigorous way. Complex non-relational systems often involve a variety of heterogeneous and interrelated models – models that are, unfortunately, expressed using several modeling languages. Moreover, if there are only a few solutions targeting at conceptual modeling of NoSQL databases in general, modeling of graph databases is even more non-trivial [21].

The key aspect of multi-model data is mutual links between the distinct models. Their semantics and features can differ depending on the types of interlinked models. Also, within the single-model systems, these links can have different representations, involving, e.g., foreign keys in the relational model, pointers in the object model, or embedding and references in document models.

To sum up, the first core issue of multi-model data management is to define and formally describe a way how multi-model data can be modeled and further processed at a conceptual level in a unified means abstracting specific features and technical details of individual models. Next, mapping rules and transformation operations need to be defined so that the proposed conceptual constructs can be mapped to data structures provided by individual logical models, as well as data directly transformed from/to at least the widely used models.

3.2   Inference of Multi-model Schemas

With multi-model data and databases, we may distinguish several levels of schema support ranging from *schema-full* (where a schema description is provided explicitly and its requirements must be satisfied) to *schema-less* (where a schema is neither provided nor required).

In reality, however, even in schema-less databases, there typically exists an implicit schema, i.e., kind of an agreed structure of the data expected by the application. Hence, the idea of schemalessness is often rather characterized as *schema-on-demand*. This observation motivates the necessity of research in the area of multi-model schema inference.

In case of a single-model schema inference, there exists a number of techniques. As a consequence of Gold's theorem [10], e.g., XML schema languages are not identifiable from positive examples only (i.e., sample data). Hence, either an *identifiable* subclass of such a language has to be inferred, or heuristics must be utilized. Naturally, a large set of inference approaches, both heuristic [20] and grammar-inferring [3], can be found for XML data. With the dawn of NoSQL databases, there appeared approaches inferring, e.g., (big) JSON data [2] or general approaches for aggregate-oriented databases [24].

When dealing with multi-model schema inference, we can primarily focus on heuristic approaches. Apart from multi-model extensions of the existing verified single-model approaches, mutual links between records across the models can bring another piece of important information. Inference approaches may thus benefit from information extracted from related data in distinct models.

The second issue of multi-model data management can hence be summarized as the need of a universal multi-model schema-inference method that would provide near real-world schemas and which would be able to infer a correct schema at least for the majority of real-world use cases.

3.3   Multi-model Data Querying

There already exist proposals of proprietary multi-model query languages [16]. For example, AQL provided by ArangoDB enables one to access both graph and document data. However, these languages have numerous limitations, often lack the desired level of documentation and formalism, and not only because of that, it is still an open challenge to develop a full-fledged query language for multi-model data.

In pursuit of such a language, it is only natural to take into account features of the existing languages used both in multi-model as well as single-model databases. Despite they assume different data models and thus have certain specifics, some of their aspects are rather surprisingly shared by more of them. For example, results of SPARQL and Neo4j Cypher query expressions are tables analogous to the relational model, even though these languages are intended for RDF triples and property graphs respectively. Expressions of the majority of languages are often decomposed into clauses, yet their structure and order are fixed in case of SQL, while in Cypher these clauses can almost arbitrarily be chained together. If usage of sub-queries in SQL is straightforward, not all the languages support such a concept. In XQuery for XML data, expressions of all kinds act like functions, and so can be arbitrarily embedded into each other, on the contrary. Even expressions at a higher level of abstraction based on lambda functions are provided in case of XQuery.

It is apparent that in a long-range perspective, it is highly unlikely that such a variety of models and query languages could reasonably be maintained and harnessed. And while the integration at the level of data has already begun as plenty of formerly single-model systems are being enriched with additional data formats, proposal of robust, unified, and even conceptual query languages with appropriate expressive power should obviously be considered as the next step, while other challenges, such as, e.g., multi-model indexing techniques, efficient query evaluation and optimization etc., will in turn follow.

Even though the idea of conceptual querying is not new [4,28], contemporary multi-model databases require a new point of view. Therefore, the third challenging issue is to overcome the outlined obstacles and research on the possibilities of introducing such a unified, well-formalized, and still user-friendly query language for the multi-model environment, so that the data could be processed uniformly from a conceptual perspective concealing representation details of individual logical models and their physical implementations.

3.4   Evolution Management in Multi-model Environment

Efficient management of schema evolution and propagation of changes to relevant parts of a database system, such as data instances, queries, indices, or even storage strategies, is a difficult task in general. In smaller applications, a company can rely on a skilled database administrator, but in most cases, it is still a complicated and error-prone job.

Currently, there exists a number of approaches dealing with single-model systems or systems with closely related models, namely aggregate-oriented NoSQL databases [23,27]. There also exists a nontrivial set of approaches focusing primarily on the evolution management of XML documents, as well as comprehensive analyses of changes of real-world database schemas over time.

In the case of multi-model databases, this task is even more subtle and difficult, not only because we need to distinguish between *intra-model* and *inter-model* changes. In the former case, we can re-use the existing single-model approaches, while in the latter one, however, these cannot be straightforwardly applied. In addition, the challenge of query rewriting [7,19], i.e., propagation of changes to queries, also becomes more complex in case of inter-model changes, which then require changes in data access constructs.

The fourth issue, therefore, is a proposal of a solution dealing with multi-model evolution management covering both intra-model and inter-model changes and ensuring their correct and complete (at least) semi-automatic propagation to all affected parts of the system. This requires a definition of a set of schema modification operations, their precise semantics, as well as the corresponding algorithms for their correct and efficient propagation to not only data instances.

3.5 Autonomous Multi-model Data Management

Autonomous data management provides special features that enable databases to self-tune and self-heal [8,25]. This service relieves database administrators of the remaining operational tasks (that include advanced tuning functions, database security, and troubleshooting), and so they can focus more time on design and development activities instead of administering the database installation and configuration.

Considering the environment of multi-model data, one application can store data in one data model, whereas later the same data can be queried by another application using a different model via *multi-model data views* [14]. Hence, multi-model data transformation can exploit the genuine value of multi-model databases which enable applications requiring different data models to share the same platform. Multi-model databases are supposed to transparently provide different access interfaces (views) of the same data adaptive to each application requirement. Autonomous multi-model databases can recommend suitable data models as such, while at a more advanced level, they can also provide data model virtualization via controlling of physical multi-model data materialization and transformation adaptively.

To conclude, the fifth issue is a proposal of a solution building autonomous multi-model databases to automatically handle the evolution of data models, selecting the best models for physical storage of data, and performing automatic transformations between the involved models. In general, it is the responsibility of databases (not users) to find the best way to organize and store the data in order to fulfill and optimize inter-data model queries and modification requests.

4   Conclusion

As the current trends indicate, multi-model databases represent a dignified and promising successor of the traditional approaches for the newly emerging and challenging use cases. Yet they first need to gain solid foundations and reach the same level of both applied and theoretical maturity in order to become a robust alternative to the relational databases.

We hope to entice the database and conceptual modeling communities to deal with the identified multi-model data management challenges related to the conceptual view of this domain. In particular and as we hope we have shown and argued in this paper, we believe especially the following areas are calling for attention and should be appropriately tackled so that the envisioned functionality of database systems could be pursuit:

- Conceptual modeling of multi-model data enabling their further unified processing, while abstracting specific features of widely used logical models and still preserving the practical usability.
- Universal multi-model schema inference methods that will be able to provide near real-world schemas for at least the majority of real-world use cases and widely used constructs.
- User-friendly, yet well-formalized query language allowing for the unified processing of multi-model data at a conceptual layer concealing details of individual logical models.
- Evolution management covering both intra-model and inter-model schema changes and ensuring their correct and complete propagation to all the affected parts of the multi-model system.
- Autonomous multi-model database management solution allowing to select suitable logical models, handle the evolution of schemas, as well as transformation of both data and query expressions.

References

1. Baader, F., Calvanese, D., McGuinness, D., Patel-Schneider, P., Nardi, D.: The Description Logic Handbook: Theory, Implementation and Applications. Cambridge University Press, Cambridge (2003)
2. Baazizi, M.-A., Colazzo, D., Ghelli, G., Sartiani, C.: Parametric schema inference for massive JSON datasets. VLDB J. **28**, 497–521 (2019)
3. Bex, G.J., Neven, F., Schwentick, T., Vansummeren, S.: Inference of concise regular expressions and DTDs. ACM Trans. Database Syst. **35**(2), 11:1–11:47 (2010)
4. Bloesch, A.C., Halpin, T.A.: ConQuer: a conceptual query language. In: Thalheim, B. (ed.) ER 1996. LNCS, vol. 1157, pp. 121–133. Springer, Heidelberg (1996). https://doi.org/10.1007/BFb0019919
5. Bugiotti, F., Cabibbo, L., Atzeni, P., Torlone, R.: Database design for NoSQL systems. In: Yu, E., Dobbie, G., Jarke, M., Purao, S. (eds.) ER 2014. LNCS, vol. 8824, pp. 223–231. Springer, Cham (2014). https://doi.org/10.1007/978-3-319-12206-9_18

6. Chen, P.: The entity-relationship model - toward a unified view of data. ACM Trans. Database Syst. **1**(1), 9–36 (1976)
7. Curino, C.A., Moon, H.J., Zaniolo, C.: Graceful database schema evolution: the PRISM workbench. Proc. VLDB Endow. **1**(1), 761–772 (2008)
8. Elmagarmid, A.K., Rusinkiewicz, M., Sheth, A., Sheth, A.: Management of Heterogeneous and Autonomous Database Systems. Morgan Kaufmann, Burlington (1999)
9. Elmore, et al.: A demonstration of the BigDAWG polystore system. PVLDB **8**(12), 1908–1911 (2015)
10. Gold, E.M.: Language identification in the limit. Inf. Control **10**(5), 447–474 (1967)
11. Kepner, J., et al.: Associative array model of SQL, NoSQL, and NewSQL databases. In: HPEC 2016, pp. 1–9. IEEE (2016)
12. Lim, H., Han, Y., Babu, S.: How to fit when no one size fits. In: CIDR (2013). www.cidrdb.org
13. Liu, Z.H., Gawlick, D.: Management of flexible schema data in RDBMSs - opportunities and limitations for NoSQL. In: CIDR (2015). www.cidrdb.org
14. Liu, Z.H., Lu, J., Gawlick, D., Helskyaho, H., Pogossiants, G., Wu, Z.: Multi-model database management systems - a look forward. In: Gadepally, V., Mattson, T., Stonebraker, M., Wang, F., Luo, G., Teodoro, G. (eds.) DMAH/Poly -2018. LNCS, vol. 11470, pp. 16–29. Springer, Cham (2019). https://doi.org/10.1007/978-3-030-14177-6_2
15. Lu, J., Holubová, I.: Multi-model data management: what's new and what's next? In: EDBT, pp. 602–605 (2017)
16. Lu, J., Holubová, I.: Multi-model databases: a new journey to handle the variety of data. ACM Comput. Surv. (2019, accepted)
17. Lu, J., Holubová, I., Cautis, B.: Multi-model databases and tightly integrated polystores: current practices, comparisons, and open challenges. In: CIKM, pp. 2301–2302 (2018)
18. Lu, J., Liu, Z.H., Xu, P., Zhang, C.: UDBMS: road to unification for multi-model data management. CoRR, abs/1612.08050:285–294 (2016)
19. Manousis, P., Vassiliadis, P., Papastefanatos, G.: Automating the adaptation of evolving data-intensive ecosystems. In: Ng, W., Storey, V.C., Trujillo, J.C. (eds.) ER 2013. LNCS, vol. 8217, pp. 182–196. Springer, Heidelberg (2013). https://doi.org/10.1007/978-3-642-41924-9_17
20. Mlýnková, I., Nečaský, M.: Heuristic methods for inference of XML schemas: lessons learned and open issues. Informatica, Lith. Acad. Sci. **24**(4), 577–602 (2013)
21. Pokorný, J.: Conceptual and database modelling of graph databases. In: IDEAS 2016, pp. 370–377. ACM, New York (2016)
22. Rumbaugh, J., Jacobson, I., Booch, G.: Unified Modeling Language Reference Manual. Pearson Higher Education, London (2004)
23. Scherzinger, S., Cerqueus, T., de Almeida, E.C.: Controvol: a framework for controlled schema evolution in NoSQL application development. In: ICDE 2015, pp. 1464–1467. IEEE Computer Society (2015)
24. Sevilla Ruiz, D., Morales, S.F., García Molina, J.: Inferring versioned schemas from NoSQL databases and its applications. In: Johannesson, P., Lee, M.L., Liddle, S.W., Opdahl, A.L., López, Ó.P. (eds.) ER 2015. LNCS, vol. 9381, pp. 467–480. Springer, Cham (2015). https://doi.org/10.1007/978-3-319-25264-3_35
25. Sheth, A.P., Larson, J.A.: Federated database systems for managing distributed, heterogeneous, and autonomous databases. ACM Comput. Surv. (CSUR) **22**(3), 183–236 (1990)

26. Stonebraker, M., Cetintemel, U.: "One size fits all": an idea whose time has come and gone. In: ICDE 2005, pp. 2–11. IEEE Computer Society, Washington, DC (2005)
27. Störl, U., Müller, D., Klettke, M., Scherzinger, S.: Enabling efficient agile software development of NoSQL-backed applications. In: BTW 2017, pp. 611–614 (2017)
28. ter Hofstede, A.H., Proper, H.A., Van Der Weide, T.P.: Formal definition of a conceptual language for the description and manipulation of information models. Inf. Syst. 18(7), 489–523 (1993)

Schema Validation and Evolution
for Graph Databases

Angela Bonifati[1]($\boxtimes$)(ID), Peter Furniss[2], Alastair Green[2], Russ Harmer[3](ID),
Eugenia Oshurko[3], and Hannes Voigt[2]

[1] Lyon 1 University & CNRS Liris, Villeurbanne, France
angela.bonifati@univ-lyon1.fr
[2] Neo4j, London, UK
{peter.furniss,alastair.green,hannes.voigt}@neo4j.com
[3] UdL, CNRS, ENS Lyon, UCBL1, Lyon, France
{russell.harmer,ievgeniia.oshurko}@ens-lyon.fr

Abstract. Despite the maturity of commercial graph databases, little consensus has been reached so far on the standardization of data definition languages (DDLs) for property graphs (PG). Discussion on the characteristics of PG schemas is ongoing in many standardization and community groups. Although some basic aspects of a schema are already present in most commercial graph databases, full support is missing allowing to constraint property graphs with more or less flexibility.

In this paper, we show how schema validation can be enforced through homomorphisms between PG schemas and PG instances by leveraging a concise schema DDL inspired by Cypher syntax. We also briefly discuss PG schema evolution that relies on graph rewriting operations allowing to consider both prescriptive and descriptive schemas.

Keywords: Graph databases · Graph schema modelling · Graph schema validation

1 Introduction

Property graph databases are modern data management systems that use graph structures, such as nodes, edges and properties, to encode semantically complex data [3]. Graph database technology has made tremendous progress with many commercial products—such as Neo4j, Oracle PGX, SAP HANA Graph, Redis Graph, Cypher for Apache Spark and TigerGraph—and yet little consensus has been reached so far on the standardization of graph data querying and manipulation or of data definition languages (DDLs).

The aim of ISO SC32/WG3 is to develop a new international standardized query language—called GQL[1]—for property graphs, with support from

---

[1] https://www.gqlstandards.org/.

© Springer Nature Switzerland AG 2019
A. H. F. Laender et al. (Eds.): ER 2019, LNCS 11788, pp. 448–456, 2019.
https://doi.org/10.1007/978-3-030-33223-5_37

the activities of the wider community such as OpenCypher[2] and G-Core [1]. Standardization of graph data querying and manipulation is therefore well under way.

At present, there are only a few examples of property graph systems offering schema and DDL, e.g. Neo4j's Cypher for Apache Spark and TigerGraph. Neo4j 3.5 already provides the means to express certain basic aspects of schemas, e.g. the use of *unique property* and *property existence* constraints enables us to *enforce* nodes (or edges) to have certain properties. However, this does not allow users to express more advanced aspects of schemas such as specifying, for a given node or edge label, the collection of all possible associated properties; or constraining whether or not an edge may exist between nodes with certain labels.

In this paper, we make the following specific contributions: (i) a schema model (and corresponding DDL) specifying labels and (mandatory) properties for nodes and edges with mixed composition and facilitating strict typing of every graph element (Sect. 2); (ii) a mathematical framework for schema validation allowing us to construct both instances and schemas as property graphs and to enforce schema validation through the existence of a homomorphism from instance to schema (Sect. 3); and (iii) graph rewriting rules [5] and their application to propagate changes from schema to instance (or vice versa) while keeping the instance and schema consistent at all times (Sect. 4).

2 PG Schema Language

We introduce in this section an OpenCypher-based[3] schema DDL for Property Graphs (PG). Although informing and feeding the ongoing standardization process, our DLL must not be intended as a standard proposal since its main purpose is to substantiate the algorithmic contributions presented in the paper. The basic components of a schema definition assume a finite set of *labels* $\mathcal{L}$, a set of *property keys* $\mathcal{K}$ and a finite set of data types $\mathcal{T}$.

Property Graph Type. A property graph type is a triple $(\mathcal{BT}, \mathcal{NT}, \mathcal{ET})$ where $\mathcal{BT}$ is a set of element types, $\mathcal{NT}$ is a set of node types and $\mathcal{ET}$ is a set of edge types. A property graph type provides the schema for a PG. Multiple PGs can share a property graph type to the effect that they will have the same schema.

Property Type. A property type is a pair (k, t), where $k \in \mathcal{K}$ is the property key and $t \in \mathcal{T}$ is its data type.

Element Type. An element type $b \in \mathcal{BT}$ is a 4-tuple (l, P, M, E), where $l \in \mathcal{L}$ is a label, P is a set of property types, $M \subseteq P$ is a subset of mandatory property types and $E \subseteq \mathcal{BT}$ is the set of element types that b extends.

Hence, "`Message {content: STRING?, length: INTEGER}`" is a declaration of the element type m = (`Message`, $\{pt_1, pt_2\}$, $\{pt_2\}, \emptyset$), where pt_1 = (`content, STRING`) and p_2 = (`length, INTEGER`); while

---

[2] http://www.opencypher.org/.

[3] https://s3.amazonaws.com/artifacts.opencypher.org/openCypher9.pdf.

"`Post :: Message {language: STRING?}`" declares the element type $p = (\text{Post}, \{pt_3 = (\text{language}, \text{STRING})\}, \emptyset, \{m\})$.

An element type is allowed to extend multiple other element types, but must not extend itself either directly or indirectly. All element types of a property graph type must be disambiguated by their label. Where clear from context, we use the label to denote the corresponding element type.

Exposed (Mandatory) Property Types and Labels. The set of exposed property types of an element type $b = (l, P, M, E)$ is defined as $\text{prop}(b) := P \cup \bigcup_{c \in E} \text{prop}(c)$, i.e. all the property types that b possesses, either directly or through inheritance. Similarly, we define $\text{mand}(b)$ to be the set of exposed mandatory property types of b and $\text{labels}(b)$ to be the set of exposed labels of b. For instance, for element type p from above we have $\text{prop}(p) = \{pt_1, pt_2, pt_3\}$, $\text{mand}(p) = \{pt_2\}$, and $\text{labels}(p) = \{\text{Post}, \text{Message}\}$.

For an element type b to be valid, $\text{prop}(b)$ must not have two or more property types with the same property key, i.e. all properties types of a element type are disambiguated by their property key. Where clear from context, we will use the property key to denote the corresponding property type. For instance, for the element type p above, we have $\text{prop}(p) = \{\text{content}, \text{length}, \text{language}\}$, $\text{mand}(p) = \{\text{length}\}$ and $\text{labels}(p) = \{\text{Post}, \text{Message}\}$. Note that $\text{labels}(b)$ is unambiguous for all element types b of a property graph type.

Node Type. A node type $nt \in \mathcal{ET}$ is a 1-tuple (b), where $b \in \mathcal{BT}$ is an element type. For a node type $nt = (b)$, we define $\text{prop}(nt) = \text{prop}(b)$, $\text{mand}(nt) = \text{mand}(b)$, and $\text{labels}(nt) = \text{labels}(b)$.

Edge Type. An edge type $et \in \mathcal{ET}$ is a triple (s, b, t), where s, b, and t are element types. Exposed (mandatory) property and label sets are defined analogously to node types based on b. Note that s and t need not be node types. This allows a single edge type to be inherited by multiple node types.

Example. The following snippet of the OpenCypher PG schema DDL creates a property graph type that captures an excerpt of the LDBC SNB [8] schema [4].

```
CREATE GRAPH TYPE snb (
// element types
Person {
  firstName : STRING, lastName : STRING
},
Message {
  creationDate : TIMESTAMP, browserUsed : STRING
},
Comment <: Message {},
Post <: Message {
  imageFile : STRING?
},
// node types
(Person), (Post), (Comment),
```

---

[4] The complete PG schema encoding of LDBC SNB is reported in [4].

```
// edge types
(Person)-[KNOWS]->(Person),
(Person)-[LIKES]->(Message),
(Message)-[HAS_CREATOR]->(Person),
(Comment)-[REPLY_OF]->(Message)
)
```

3   Schema Validation

In this section, we provide a mathematical formalization of our schema notion that, in particular, allows us to interpret a DDL specification as a PG. We present the mathematical definitions of schemas and instances as property graphs in Sect. 3.1 and then discuss the application of homomorphisms to the schema validation problem in Sect. 3.2.

3.1   Schemas and Instances as Property Graphs

We fix countable sets $\mathcal{O}$, $\mathcal{K}$ and $\mathcal{V}$ of *objects*, *keys* and *values* respectively. For the purposes of this paper, we assume that $\mathcal{V}$ contains (at least) basic types of integers, booleans, strings and dates.

A *property graph* is defined to be a tuple (N, E, η, P, ν, M) where N and E are disjoint, finite subsets of $\mathcal{O}$ called *nodes* and *edges*; $\eta : E \to N \times N$ is a function assigning a source and target node to each edge; $P \subseteq (N \cup E) \times \mathcal{K}$ is a finite set of *properties*; $\nu \subseteq P \times \mathcal{V}$ is a finite relation, assigning *sets of values* to properties; and $M \subseteq P$ is a set of *mandatory* properties. The requirement that ν be finite means that each node and each edge has finitely many properties, each of which has a finite set of associated values.

A schema $(\mathcal{BT}, \mathcal{NT}, \mathcal{ET})$ specified in our DDL from Sect. 2 can be interpreted as a property graph S in the following way. The nodes N_S are the node types $\mathcal{NT}$ and we have an edge $e \in E_S$ from n_1 to n_2 in E_S if, for some $l_1 \in \texttt{labels}(n_1)$ and $l_2 \in \texttt{labels}(n_2)$, there is an edge type $(n_1, e, n_2) \in \mathcal{ET}$. Note that a node type always gives rise to a single node of S whereas an edge type may give rise to many edges in the schema graph; this is how inheritance in the DDL syntax is 'expanded out' in the schema graph S interpreting the property graph type. Each node and edge has the (mandatory) properties specified by its corresponding node or edge type. As an example, the schema defined in Sect. 2 and interpreted as a property graph is illustrated in Fig. 1.

3.2   Schema Validation via Graph Homomorphisms

Let G and S be property graphs where $N_G \cup E_G$ and $N_S \cup E_S$ are disjoint. A *homomorphism* $h : G \to S$ is a function $h_N : N_G \to N_S$ and a function $h_\mathcal{E} : E_G \to E_S$, mapping nodes and edges of G to nodes and edges of S, such that $\eta_S \circ h_\mathcal{E} = (h_N \times h_N) \circ \eta_G$. We write $h := h_N \cup h_\mathcal{E}$. We further require that (i) if $(x, k) \in P_G$ then $(h(x), k) \in P_S$; (ii) if $((x, k), v) \in \nu_G$ then $((h(x), k), v) \in \nu_S$; and (iii) if $(h(x), k) \in M_S$ then $(x, k) \in M_G$.

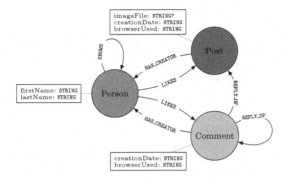

Fig. 1. An extract from the SNB schema

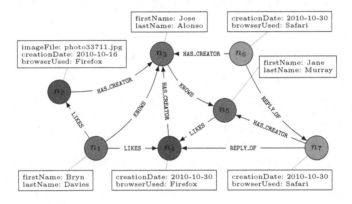

Fig. 2. A valid instance of the SNB schema extract

We can view a homomorphism $h : G \to S$ as a formalization of the notion *schema validation*, i.e. that G respects the 'schema' S: each node/edge x of G is an instance of the schema node/edge $h(x)$; edges in S constrain which edges can exist in G; and properties that are mandatory in the schema S are mandatory (so must occur) in G. In the example instance G of Fig. 2, we have used colours to encode the homomorphism h, i.e. all yellow nodes are Comments, etc. In the DDL of Sect. 2, the fact that all element types are disambiguated by their label would also allow us to determine h provided we include these labels in the instance G.

The ReGraph Library. The Python library ReGraph[5] provides an implementation of the presented system. It enables us to construct property graphs and structure them into hierarchies (DAGs) of graphs via homomorphisms. In this paper we limit our use of the library to the special case of two graphs connected by a single homomorphism, i.e. $h : G \to S$ as this is sufficient to express that G respects the schema S. Our system thus provides an *abstraction barrier* that gives the illusion that the underlying Neo4j graph is, in fact, two separate

---

[5] https://github.com/Kappa-Dev/ReGraph.

graphs—a data graph and a schema—related by a homomorphism that guarantees schema validation. In the next section, we explain briefly how *updates* to either of these graphs are performed in such a way as to maintain the invariant of schema validation.

4   Property Graph Rewriting

In our approach, the data graph *and* its schema are represented as PGs; as such, we can use graph rewriting rules [5] to perform updates of either. Informally, a rewriting rule consists of a *pattern*—of which there can be zero, one or many *instances* in the graph G we wish to modify—together with a collection of modifications to be effected. In the case of PGs, these operations are: addition and deletion of elements; cloning and merging of nodes; and modification of the set of values associated with a property. The rule is applied by selecting an instance in G and performing the associated operations. The effect of a rule application remains localized to the subgraph of G picked out by the choice of instance which, in practice, is very small compared with G itself.

In general, an update invalidates the homomorphism that previously existed and which guaranteed compliance of the data to the schema. In our mathematical formulation, and its associated implementation discussed briefly below, we *automatically* recompute a canonically updated homomorphism that restores compliance [9]. The way in which compliance can be broken—and the process by which we restore it—depends on whether the update was made to the data graph or to the schema.

In the first case, compliance can be broken by the addition of nodes, edges or properties or by the merging of nodes in the data graph. By default, the addition of a new element e is *propagated* to the schema, i.e. we add a new element to the schema to type e in the data graph. We can further specify that e is actually typed by an existing element of the schema; this can be done explicitly by the user or, more commonly, computed automatically through the use of labels. However, in the case of the merge of two nodes, their associated typing nodes in the schema *must* be merged—unless they already had the same type (in which case no change to the schema is necessary).

In the second case, compliance can be broken by the deletion of an element or by the cloning of nodes in the schema. By default, the cloning of a node n is *propagated* to the data graph, i.e. we clone *all* instances of n in the data graph. For some or all instances of n, we may not wish to propagate but rather specify the particular clone of n that should be used to type it, i.e. a *concept refinement*; again, this can be specified directly by the user or computed automatically through the use of labels. However, in the case of the deletion of an element, we *must* delete *all* its instances in the data graph.

An update of the data graph that propagates to the schema can be *blocked* in our implementation. This would be appropriate in situations where the schema is already well-developed and we expect all incoming data to comply, i.e. we consider our schema to be *prescriptive*. However, in an earlier phase of development,

the ability to propagate *automatically* new elements to the schema enables the user to focus simply on gathering their data of interest and allows the schema to adapt appropriately, i.e. the schema is considered to be *descriptive*. As such, our approach—in addition to providing the guarantee that updates never break schema compliance—also provides support for the natural development cycle of an application.

In our implementation, a rewriting rule is translated into a Cypher query that manipulates the underlying Neo4j graph in such a way as to preserve the correspondence with the data and schema graphs. As outlined above, an update of one graph may—but need not necessarily—induce a further update of the other to maintain schema validation. A detailed account will be included in the long version of this paper and can be found in the arXiv preprint [4].

5   Related Work

Schema evolution [17] is a well established topic in data management. A set of principles ruling out schema and instance evolution under schema constraints was discussed in [10]. Various approaches exist to increase usability and efficiency, e.g. schema evolution-aware query languages [18] or providing a general framework to describe database evolution in the context of evolving applications [7]. Meta Model Management 2.0 [2] introduced tools to match, merge and diff given relational schema versions. The resulting mappings couple the evolution of the schema and the data; however, they are complex relationships between heterogeneous schemas, as in data integration and ETL scenarios, i.e. they only deal with schema evolution after the fact. Recently, PRISM [6] and InVerDa [11] have provided advanced database schema evolution tools. PRISM focuses on plain database evolution but allows the answering of queries using former schema versions with respect to the current data. InVerDa provides co-existing schema versions via bidirectional transformations with symmetric relational lenses [12]. However, none of the above approaches goes beyond a prescriptive schema.

SHACL [14] is a language for validating RDF graphs. Shapes are used to validate RDF instances against a set of conditions. SHACL supports RDF term restrictions, cardinality constraints, and predicate constraints. Research on ontologies also considered the problem of update propagation to instances using Description Logic mappings [13]. However, such mappings are quite complex when contrasted with the implicit homomorphisms considered in our work. The distinction between descriptive and prescriptive schemas as carried out in our paper is reminiscent of open and close tuple types as used for instance in JSON [16]. In particular, the schema flexibility pointed out in our work affects not only types but entire portions of the schemas and as such is more general.

Graph rewriting has been used in a variety of areas related to knowledge representation and meta-modelling. For example, triple graph grammars [15,19]—which correspond very closely to our rewriting rules—provide a means to specify bidirectional model transformations and have been used in various applications such as conformance testing and model synchronization.

6   Concluding Remarks

We have presented a schema DDL for PGs following the ASCII-art syntax of Cypher and shown how schema validation and evolution can be simulated via a mathematical framework that enforces and maintains schema validation.

Our next step is to enrich the DDL for the expression of finer constraints and to define a DML for our graph update operations.

Acknowledgements. We would like to thank Petra Selmer (Neo4j) for her careful proof reading and useful feedback. This work was partially funded by a grant from the Fédération Informatique de Lyon.

References

1. Angles, R., et al.: G-CORE: a core for future graph query languages. In: SIGMOD, pp. 1421–1432 (2018)
2. Bernstein, P.A., Melnik, S.: Model management 2.0: manipulating richer mappings. In: SIGMOD, pp. 1–12 (2007)
3. Bonifati, A., Fletcher, G., Voigt, H., Yakovets, N.: Querying Graphs. Synthesis Lectures on Data Management. Morgan & Claypool Publishers, San Rafael (2018)
4. Bonifati, A., et al.: Schema validation and evolution for graph databases. CoRR arXiv:1902.06427 (2019)
5. Corradini, A., Heindel, T., Hermann, F., König, B.: Sesqui-pushout rewriting. In: Corradini, A., Ehrig, H., Montanari, U., Ribeiro, L., Rozenberg, G. (eds.) ICGT 2006. LNCS, vol. 4178, pp. 30–45. Springer, Heidelberg (2006). https://doi.org/10.1007/11841883_4
6. Curino, C., Moon, H.J., Zaniolo, C.: Graceful database schema evolution: the PRISM workbench. PVLDB 1(1), 761–772 (2008)
7. Domínguez, E., Lloret, J., Rubio, A.L., Zapata, M.A.: MeDEA: a database evolution architecture with traceability. DKE 65(3), 419–441 (2008)
8. Erling, O., et al.: The LDBC social network benchmark: interactive workload. In: SIGMOD, pp. 619–630 (2015)
9. Harmer, R., Oshurko, E.: Knowledge representation and update in hierarchies of graphs. In: Guerra, E., Orejas, F. (eds.) ICGT 2019. LNCS, vol. 11629, pp. 141–158. Springer, Cham (2019). https://doi.org/10.1007/978-3-030-23611-3_9
10. Hartung, M., Terwilliger, J.F., Rahm, E.: Recent advances in schema and ontology evolution. In: Schema Matching and Mapping, pp. 149–190 (2011)
11. Herrmann, K., Voigt, H., Pedersen, T.B., Lehner, W.: Multi-schema-version data management: data independence in the twenty-first century. VLDB J. 27(4), 547–571 (2018)
12. Hofmann, M., Pierce, B.C., Wagner, D.: Symmetric lenses. In: POPL (2011)
13. Kharlamov, E., Zheleznyakov, D., Calvanese, D.: Capturing model-based ontology evolution at the instance level: the case of DL-Lite. J. Comput. Syst. Sci. 79(6), 835–872 (2013)
14. Knublauch, H., Kontokostas, D.: Shapes Constraint Language (SHACL). W3C Recommendation 20 July 2017
15. Königs, A., Schürr, A.: Tool integration with triple graph grammars - a survey. Electron. Notes Theoret. Comput. Sci. 148(1), 113–150 (2006)

16. Ong, K.W., Papakonstantinou, Y., Vernoux, R.: The SQL++ semi-structured data model and query language: a capabilities survey of SQL-on-hadoop, NoSQL and NewSQL databases. CoRR arXiv:1405.3631 (2014)
17. Rahm, E., Bernstein, P.A.: An online bibliography on schema evolution. SIGMOD Rec. **35**(4), 30–31 (2006)
18. Roddick, J.F.: SQL/SE - a query language extension for databases supporting schema evolution. SIGMOD Rec. **21**(3), 10–16 (1992)
19. Schürr, A.: Specification of graph translators with triple graph grammars. In: Workshop on Graph-Theoretic Concepts in Computer Science, pp. 151–163 (1994)

Grounding for an Enterprise Computing Nomenclature Ontology

Chris Partridge[1,2]([⊠]) [iD], Andrew Mitchell[1] [iD],
and Sergio de Cesare[2] [iD]

[1] BORO Solutions Ltd., London, UK
{partridgec,mitchella}@borogroup.co.uk
[2] University of Westminster, London, UK
s.decesare@westminster.ac.uk

Abstract. We aim to lay the basis for a unified architecture for enterprise computer nomenclatures by providing the grounding ontology based upon the BORO Foundational Ontology. We start to lower two significant barriers within the computing community to making progress in this area; a lack of a broad appreciation of the nature and practice of nomenclature and a lack of recognition of some specific technical, philosophical issues that nomenclatures raise. We provide an overview of the grounding ontology and how it can be implemented in a system. We focus on the issue that arises when tokens lead to the overlap of the represented domain and its system representation – system-domain-overlap – and how this can be resolved.

Keywords: Enterprise computing nomenclature ontology · Nomenclature · Identifier · Identifier inscription · Identifying space · Foundational Ontology · BORO · System-domain-overlap · Type-token distinction · Type-token-occurrence distinction · Use-mention distinction · Paper tools

1 Introduction

An examination of a legacy enterprise system's data schemas will usually reveal, among other things, that a substantial proportion of the data are identifiers; many of the field/attribute names will have a tell-tale suffix; such as code, short name, and identifier. Typically, the identifier fields in the data schemas, such as 'Alpha Currency Code', mark out a column of identifiers in (what we call) a nomenclature, a formalised system of identifiers. When one starts to examine the ways in which the nomenclatures have been implemented, there seem to be a variety of patterns, driven by a combination of established practices and requirements, with little theoretical foundation.

Given the scale and ubiquity (and, as we shall show below, importance) of these nomenclatures, it is not surprising that there have been attempts to try to organise them across the enterprise (e.g. [1]). However, none of these have yet produced either a general, unified architecture or an ontology for computer nomenclatures. In this paper, we aim to lay the basis for such a unified architecture by providing the grounding for an nomenclature ontology.

© Springer Nature Switzerland AG 2019
A. H. F. Laender et al. (Eds.): ER 2019, LNCS 11788, pp. 457–465, 2019.
https://doi.org/10.1007/978-3-030-33223-5_38

We believe that there have been two significant barriers within the computing community to making progress in this area. Firstly, a lack of a broad appreciation of the nature and practice of nomenclature. In the first part of the paper, we develop this through a brief historical review. Secondly, a lack of recognition of some specific technical, philosophical issues that nomenclatures raise. In the second part of the paper, we outline these issues. Next, we provide an overview of the ontology and how it can be implemented in a system. In the third part, we describe a nomenclature ontology that addresses the issues identified. In the fourth part, we describe a significant issue that arises when implementing the ontology in a system and how to address it.

2 A Brief History of Nomenclatures

In this paper, our focus is on nomenclatures in enterprise computer systems. However, these are the result of a long and broad evolution that started well before computing technology or enterprises emerged. We look at this evolution to provide a better understanding of their general nature and see more clearly where and how concerns have shaped them. Nomenclatures are dependent upon classifications. Initial classifications were developed without the formality and structure of nomenclatures, which emerged when classifications start to scale. The combination of classifications and nomenclatures, particularly in biology, are often called taxonomies – the Linnaean taxonomy being the original example.

There is ample evidence of classification from early history; examples include Ancient Egyptian onomastica (such as the Onomasticon of Amenope), Aristotle's Categories and Theophrastus's Historia Plantarum. In the 15th century, the invention of printing introduced the technology to support larger classification systems. In the 16th and 17th centuries, this led to an increase in works classifying plants and animals. In Species Plantarum (1753), Carl Linnaeus started modern formal binomial nomenclature with two types of names; genus and species – these are early examples of what we call *identifying spaces*. Over time, nomenclature management was formalised. For many scientific nomenclatures, a two-part process evolved; firstly, providing an accessible example of the identified entity – a type specimen – and then secondly publishing its name, publicly providing an example of the name. Both the type specimens and published names were exemplars provided for examination and comparison. This formalisation aimed to make the process more efficient, allowing the nomenclature to scale effectively. This formalisation was part of a broader emergence of bureaucracy, which aims for a rational and efficient way of organising human activities. As Weber [2, Chap. 6] noted, this mechanises the organisation. As well as being subjected to bureaucratisation, nomenclatures played a significant role in enabling it. As they developed more formal processes, enterprises found their efficiency depended heavily upon standardised classifications and their associated standardised nomenclatures; modern examples include ISO 3166 Country Codes and ISO 4217 Currency Codes.

In many ways, computing technology offered an opportunity to create the ultimate bureaucracy – a living embodiment of the 'iron cage' (Weber's characterisation of bureaucracy). It enables far more efficient rational calculation and control than its predecessor, writing technology. Nomenclatures seem a natural fit for computing,

whether storing the codes or handling the rules for managing them. Though there is a recognition that the paper-based rules might need tightening up to take advantage of computing's capabilities – see, for example [3].

3 Nomenclature's Type-Token Architecture

For sound pragmatic reasons nomenclatures are streamlined. For example, within an identifying space, the identifiers typically aim to be unique (no duplicates) and distinct (no object with two identifiers), making algorithmic identification feasible. It is the identifiers that are unique rather than the individual inscriptions. When the algorithmic rules are executed, the process of identifying and reidentifying does not involve the identifier directly. Let's say we are matching an identifier in an article with the nomenclature's list. We match two inscriptions, a portion of text in a copy of the article with an entry in a copy of the list. Clearly, neither inscription is the identifier (if it were, we could simply destroy it and then the identifier would no longer exist). The processes work with the identifiers indirectly through their distinct member inscriptions.

This distinction between the identifier and the inscription is known as the *type-token distinction*. It was introduced by Peirce [4, sec. 4.537]; where (roughly) types are general, and tokens are their concrete instances; typically written (inscriptions) or spoken (utterances). So, for example, in this sentence – Rose is a rose is a rose is a rose – one could say that there are three different word-types ('rose', 'is' and 'a') and ten different word-token inscriptions. (There are also three occurrences of 'rose', but we don't have enough space to discuss this here). From a nomenclature's perspective, identifiers are word-types and identifier inscriptions are word-tokens. The nomenclature rules are typically framed in terms of word-types, though the execution of the rules typically involve word-tokens. However, the design, particularly of computer nomenclatures, does not usually make explicit the type-token distinction.

4 Outlining a Nomenclature Ontology

Here we provide an example of what a general nomenclature ontology would look like. We base this upon the BORO Foundational Ontology [5]. Hopefully, it will inspire alternative nomenclature ontologies based upon different foundations. There is a good argument that a nomenclature ontology should be included within a foundational ontology as it spans multiple (if not most) domains.

One of the critical requirements is to capture the type-token distinction, to clearly identify identifier inscriptions (tokens) and separate them from identifiers (types). This is done by showing that they are different types of objects. There is also a less obvious requirement to characterise what the third type of nomenclature component, identifying spaces, are. Identifier inscriptions (tokens) manually written on paper, carved in stone or metal are visibly concrete, existing in space and time. Identifier inscriptions (tokens) written by the computer into computer storage (whether a magnetic tape or disk or solid-state memory), while not directly visible, are also plainly concrete and spatio-temporal. The identifier inscriptions (tokens) belong to an identifier (type). Under the

BORO extensional view, these types are the set of tokens (all possible tokens in all possible worlds). For example, all GB inscriptions that are ISO Country Code inscriptions make up the type that is the GB ISO Country Code. This extensional view is common, though not universal, in philosophy [6–11]. On this view, identifier inscriptions (tokens) and identifiers (types) are clearly different kinds of thing. Identifiers (types) belong to identifying spaces. For example, the GB ISO Country Code belongs to the ISO 3166-1 alpha-2 codes identifying space. Under the extensional view, these identifying spaces are the set of appropriate identifiers (types).

In this view, the objects in the nomenclature ontology are recursively grounded in a series of levels. As shown in Fig. 1, at ground level, the identifier inscriptions are of spatio-temporal particulars. At the next level, identifiers are grounded in their member inscriptions; then, the identifying spaces are grounded in their member identifiers.

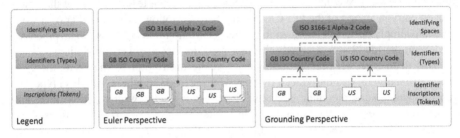

Fig. 1. Grounding levels

The purpose of an identifier is to refer to an object – the identified object. Furthermore, every identifier (type) and all its identifier inscriptions (tokens) refer to the same object. From an engineering perspective, there are two main architectural options for how this reference could work; firstly, that only the identifiers (types) refer directly and the identifier inscriptions (tokens) refer indirectly via their types or secondly, that both identifiers (types) and the identifier inscriptions (tokens) refer directly. The second option has the disadvantage of needing a mechanism to ensure that all the identifier inscriptions (tokens) consistently refer to the same object as their identifier (type) – a typical example of data redundancy.

5   Implementing a Nomenclature Ontology System

When using the BORO methodology (bCLEARer) to mine the ontologies from legacy systems, the relevant data, as well as their data schemas, are extracted and transformed into the ontology. Typically, the legacy systems contain domain nomenclatures, so these are extracted, transformed and stored in the ontology. Our experience is that this raises a theoretical issue with design implications. The underlying issue is that the represented domain and its representation overlap (as shown graphically later in Fig. 3); the actual real identifier inscriptions (parts of the domain, and not some representation of them) are stored and processed in the system. We call this a 'system-

domain-overlap'. The situation repeats in models of the system, where tokens are typically used in naming – a kind of a 'model-domain-overlap' or more generally a 'representation-represented – overlap'.

5.1 Lessons Learnt from Mention and Use

The issues that this kind of overlapping raise have been recognised in philosophy, though mostly in the context of written text (so writing technology). Quine [12, pp. 23–26] describes a *use-mention distinction*. He contrasts two sentences; (1) Boston is populous and (2) 'Boston' is disyllabic. He notes that in the first sentence the name is being used, and in the second sentence it is being mentioned – and suggests we follow the practice of always using quotation to distinguish use and mention, saying it is more convenient but needs "special caution" as a "quotation … designates its object not by describing it in terms of other objects, but by picturing it."

While Quine is surely correct to distinguish between use and mention, his proposal for the use of quotation has been questioned. Tarski [13] and Church [14, Chap. 8] examine the use of quotations in natural language and decide against using them. Davidson [15] also examines this, noting several issues arising from how to interpret the use of a name-token inside the quotation marks. He proposes an alternative 'demonstrative theory' in which quotation marks help to refer to a name-type by pointing to (showing) a token of one. He suggests one reads them as 'the expression a token of which is here' – a 'word-type-reference to word-token-reference to word-token' pattern. The benefit with this approach is that anything that looks like a token is one. There is no need to view some tokens as pictures. A good lesson here is to let tokens be tokens.

Quine's quotation analysis assumes that each inscription of a name can be categorised as a use or a mention – this is necessary if mentions are to be enclosed in quotation marks. Davidson [15] suggests that one could both use and mention at the same time. The lesson here seems to be that one cannot usefully assume that a token in the published nomenclatures is exclusively a use or a mention. So, Quine's quotational approach cannot be applied directly to nomenclatures – they are more about ways of using their identifiers. One final consideration is technology. One can write quotation marks, but there is no easy way of directly pronouncing them. The possibility of quotation marks is created by writing technology; emerging technologies create new opportunities for representation. Both Quine and Davidson's proposals are plainly tied to writing technology. This suggests that there may be opportunities for a new mode of nomenclature representation suitable for computing technology.

5.2 The Current Patterns of Implementation – A Baseline

Current system implementations contain tokens and successfully work with them. Examination of enterprise systems shows two main patterns illustrated in Fig. 2 (Identifiers as Attributes and Identifiers as Objects), neither of which resemble Quine and Davidson's approaches mentioned above. It is not uncommon to find examples of both patterns in a single system. The figure shows the pattern for a single entity type – Countries. In an enterprise system, this pattern is repeated for each entity type –

resulting in a multiplicity of nomenclature infrastructures. Our goal here is to find a way of unifying them.

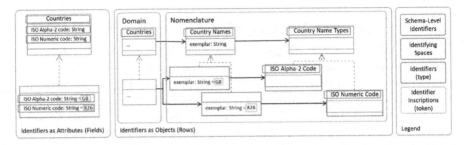

Fig. 2. Patterns of current identifier implementation for an entity

In Fig. 2, the main data-level nomenclature components have been marked out, as far as it is feasible. Hopefully, this makes clear that this classification is implicit, that there is no way to work it out from just the explicit structure. Also, the components are all, in a way, second class citizens [16]; in that, as attributes or objects they do not have access to the same range of resources as classes; for example, they cannot be super- or sub-typed. In the models of the domain, the representations of the three components of the nomenclature are explicitly marked out. They also clearly separate the "pure" domain and the nomenclature. As we use this as a basis for our implemented system, we keep this architecture.

5.3   A Proposed Implementation

Figure 2 makes clear that the system contains 'real' identifier inscriptions (tokens). These play a critical role in the operation of the system as they are exemplars of their types, used to identify and reidentify tokens of the same type. The nomenclature ontology needs to be extended with tokens. Given the earlier analysis, we want to introduce the tokens as just tokens, with no additional commitments to sometimes treating the tokens as pictures of themselves. We also want to avoid committing to a token being either exclusively for use or mention. The simplest design is to add the token as a new kind of representation and connect them to their representation in the model. This is similar in some ways to Davidson's 'word-type-reference to word-token-reference to word-token' pattern (mentioned above), in that the word-type and word-token are referred to and the actual token demonstrated. One outstanding issue is that the non-token picture uses of the inscriptions remain in the representations. The next step is to remove these, leaving the representations as bare nodes.

When humans wish to review the model, it is useful to present the nodes with labels. To achieve this, one needs first to make a clear distinction between what is stored internally and what is viewed (a kind of ANSI-SPARC or model-view architecture). In the view layer, one presents a framed copy of the token (in a similar manner to Quinean quotations) with agreed framing glyphs. The view can recover the names/labels of these nodes algorithmically by navigating from the bare node to their

'real' identifier inscriptions. One can present the name/label using a bare copy of the 'real' identifier inscriptions; we have done this for the schema level representations in our models – nodes such as 'Identifiers' and 'Countries'.

This gives us a system such as that modelled in Fig. 3, which illustrates both ways of presenting the tokens; firstly, reflecting the way they are stored in the ontology data structure with tokens and bare nodes and secondly, as bare nodes that are adorned with an inferred name. In the latter case, this notation needs to be read as shorthand for the fuller first case.

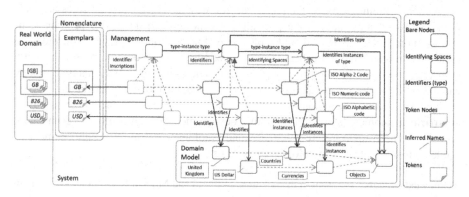

Fig. 3. Proposed implementation structure

In this approach, all the nomenclature management is handled in the same way; there is no schema-data names distinction as in Fig. 2. Moreover, all the representations of nomenclature components are bare nodes and so are first-class citizens; they have access to the same resources as the domain's bare nodes. Tokens are always tokens, as there is no need for framing devices such as quotation marks; hence, there are no pictures of tokens. This resolves the issues identified earlier.

This way of managing tokens has a history. For example, in the semantic network SNePS, [17, 18], inscriptions are a special kind of thick node joined to the rest of the semantic network of thin bare nodes by LEX arcs (see also [19]). Schapiro [18] rightly compares the resulting separation of thick (token) and thin (bare) nodes with Carnap's [20, sec. 14] example of structural definite descriptions. However, the thick inscription nodes are held at arm's length via the LEX arc, without access to the resources of the bare nodes, making them second class citizens [16].

6   Conclusions

We believe that the grounding for an enterprise computing nomenclature ontology, described above, lays the basis for a unified architecture for nomenclatures in computer systems. We provided the grounding in four ways. Initially, we made clearer what a nomenclature is (and so its requirements). Then we looked at the critical technical issues faced when specifying such an ontology. We focused on the distinction between

type (identifiers) and token (inscriptions). Then, we provided an example of a nomenclature ontology based upon the BORO Foundational Ontology that explicitly makes the distinction between inscriptions, identifiers and identifying spaces and specifies their identity criteria. It also clearly distinguishes between the domain and the nomenclature. Finally, we provided an example of an implementation of a nomenclature ontology. We identified the treatment of tokens as a significant issue, illustrating this with the analysis of the proposed use-mention distinction. We related this to system-domain-overlap and showed how this can be accommodated by treating tokens as token.

A theme running through the paper was the way in which nomenclatures are tools both shaped by and shaping the prevailing technology. In the era of printing technology, nomenclatures in lists and tables were 'paper tools' deployed alongside scientific taxonomic and bureaucratic classifications. These tools were subsequently embedded in computer enterprise systems. In this narrative, the nomenclature ontology can be used to design computer tools for a computer-based nomenclature, unconstrained by writing technology. We hope this paper will both encourage a unified approach to nomenclatures though the development of alternative nomenclature ontologies based upon different foundational ontologies and an increasing number of implementations of these ontologies in systems.

Acknowledgements. We want to thank Salvatore Florio and Mesbah Khan for all their help in developing this paper.

References

1. Business Scenario: Identifiers in the Enterprise. The Open Group (2006)
2. Weber, M.: Economy and Society. Bedminister Press, New York (1922)
3. McMurry, J.A., et al.: Identifiers for the 21st century: how to design, provision, and reuse persistent identifiers to maximize utility and impact of life science data. PLoS Biol. **15**, e2001414 (2017)
4. Peirce, C.S.: Collected Papers of Charles Sanders Peirce. Harvard University Press, Cambridge (1932)
5. De Cesare, S., et al.: BORO as a foundation to enterprise ontology. J. Inf. Syst. **30**, 83–112 (2016)
6. Ramsey, F.P.: Foundations of Mathematics and Other Logical Essays. Routledge, Abingdon (1931)
7. Whitehead, A.N., et al.: Principia Mathematica, to *56. Cambridge University Press, Cambridge (1925)
8. Quine, W.V.: Quiddities: An Intermittently Philosophical Dictionary (1987)
9. Haack, S.: Philosophy of Logics. Cambridge University Press, Cambridge (1978)
10. Hugly, P., et al.: Expressions and Tokens. Analysis **41**, 181–187 (1981)
11. Ayer, A.J.: Language, Truth and Logic. Courier Corporation, Mineola (1946)
12. Quine, W.: Mathematical Logic. Harvard University Press, Cambridge (1940)
13. Tarski, A.: The concept of truth in formalized languages. Log. Semant. Metamathematics **2**, 152–278 (1956)

14. Church, A.: Introduction to Mathematical Logic. Princeton University Press, Princeton (1996)
15. Davidson, D.: Quotation. Theory Decis. **11**, 27–40 (1979)
16. Strachey, C.: Fundamental concepts in programming languages. High.-Order Symb. Comput. **13**, 11–49 (2000)
17. Maida, A.S., et al.: Intensional concepts in propositional semantic networks. Cogn. Sci. **6**, 291–330 (1982)
18. Shapiro, S.C., Rapaport, W.J.: SNePS considered as a fully intensional propositional semantic network. In: Cercone, N., McCalla, G. (eds.) The Knowledge Frontier. SYMBOLIC, pp. 262–315. Springer, New York (1987). https://doi.org/10.1007/978-1-4612-4792-0_11
19. Partridge, C.: Business Objects: Re-engineering for Re-use (1996)
20. Carnap, R.: The Logical Structure of the World: Pseudoproblems in Philosophy (1967)

Big Data Technology III

Events as Entities in Ontology-Driven Conceptual Modeling

João Paulo A. Almeida[1(✉)], Ricardo A. Falbo[1], and Giancarlo Guizzardi[1,2]

[1] Ontology and Conceptual Modeling Research Group (NEMO),
Federal University of Espírito Santo (UFES), Vitória, Brazil
jpalmeida@ieee.org, falbo@inf.ufes.br
[2] Conceptual and Cognitive Modeling Research Group (CORE),
Free University of Bozen-Bolzano, Bolzano, Italy
giancarlo.guizzardi@unibz.it

Abstract. The Unified Foundational Ontology (UFO) has been used to provide foundations for the major conceptual modeling constructs. This ontology has led to the OntoUML Ontology-Driven Conceptual Modeling language, a UML class diagram profile reflecting the ontological micro-theories comprising UFO. So far, the focus of OntoUML has been on the representation of structural aspects of a domain (endurant types and their relations), corresponding to a fragment of UFO dubbed UFO-A. This paper extends OntoUML by addressing the representation of event types, reflecting the UFO-B foundational ontology of events. Based on the ontological distinctions and axiomatization provided by UFO-B, we define new OntoUML constructs and guidelines for the conceptual modeling of events and event relations in structural conceptual models.

Keywords: OntoUML · Events · Ontology-driven conceptual modeling

1 Introduction

There has been a growing interest in the use of foundational ontologies to evaluate and (re)design conceptual modeling languages. With such use as a key motivation, a community of researchers has contributed for over a decade now to the development of the Unified Foundational Ontology (UFO), providing theoretical foundations underlying all major conceptual modeling constructs. UFO has been used to systematically design an ontology-driven conceptual modeling (ODCM) language termed OntoUML [10,14], which has been successfully employed in academic, industrial and governmental settings to create conceptual models in a variety of domains [14].

The observation of the application of OntoUML over the years, conducted by several groups in a number of domains, amounted to a fruitful empirical source of knowledge regarding the language and its foundations. In particular, we have observed how modelers would slightly subvert the language's syntax, ultimately creating what we call *"systematic subversions"* [14]. These "subversions" would produce models that were

© Springer Nature Switzerland AG 2019
A. H. F. Laender et al. (Eds.): ER 2019, LNCS 11788, pp. 469–483, 2019.
https://doi.org/10.1007/978-3-030-33223-5_39

grammatically incorrect, but which were needed to express the intended conceptualizations. Moreover, they were "systematic" because they recurred in the works of different authors in similar manners and with the same modeling intent.

One of these "language subversions" concerns the representation of events and their relations [16,21]. Dealing with the representation of events is key to conceptual modeling and knowledge representation, given the importance of events in cognition, language and, in fact, most human endeavours. Despite their importance, the current version of OntoUML does not address event types explicitly, as it focuses on the modeling of structural aspects of the domain in accordance with the fragment of UFO that was first defined (UFO-A, an ontology of endurants).

Recently, there has been a growing interest in the explicit modeling of events in structural conceptual models. This trend can be observed in the so-called *event reification approach* in conceptual modeling [1,2,17] and in *behavioral modeling* in Object-Oriented structural models (class diagrams) [5]. For example, Olivé [17] writes: *"When events are entities, they are modeled in a way similar to ordinary entities: they are instance of event types (a special kind of entity type), they may participate in relationships, they can be specialized or generalized, and so on..."*. Moreover, empirical studies show the benefits of explicitly representing events in structural models. For example, Allen and March [2] show the benefits of explicit event representation in terms of faster learning about the semantics of queries over a conceptual model, and in terms of better supporting casual users in accurately recognizing when these queries are correct. They argue that effective analysis and design require *"a more substantive ontological definition of an event as an entity having both identity and properties."*

Following the same ontology-based language engineering approach that was used to create the original version of OntoUML [10], we employ here a well-founded theory of events (UFO-B) to advance an extension of OntoUML to address events and their relations. We introduce specialized stereotypes to capture event types, their (mereological and historical) relations, as well as their relations to the existing endurant types in OntoUML. Syntactic constraints in the profile guide the creation of sound models capturing event types and adhering to the rules of the underlying foundational ontology.

The remainder of this paper is organized as follows: Sect. 2 presents some background on OntoUML and the UFO-B ontology of events. The notions in UFO-B are used in Sect. 3 to introduce constructs and syntactic constraints for event modeling in OntoUML. In Sect. 4, to demonstrate the expressivity of the profile, we employ it in the representation of a reference ontology of software testing [20]. Section 5 positions our contribution with respect to related work and Sect. 6 presents some conclusions.

2 Background

OntoUML is a language whose meta-model has been designed to comply with the ontological distinctions and axiomatization put forth by UFO [10]. The ontological distinctions present in the ontology are reflected in the modeling primitives of the language via stereotypes, providing thus precise semantics grounded in the underlying ontology. In addition to that, the metamodel of the language is enriched with a number of *semantically motivated syntactic formal constraints* [7] that reflect the axiomatization of the

underlying ontology. This combination of stereotypes and constraints enforces confor-mance, making every valid OntoUML model compliant to UFO.

The original version of OntoUML reflects a particular layer of UFO termed UFO-A, which is the *Ontology of Endurants* in UFO. Endurants are entities that exist in time and can change in a qualitative way while maintaining their identity. They are endowed with both essential and accidental properties and, for this reason, they can instantiate certain types in a *necessary* manner (static classification) while instantiating other types in a *contingent* manner (dynamic classification). Substantials (e.g., Mick Jagger, his car, the moon), relators (e.g., Bill and Ana's marriage, Mary's enrollment in Yale) and qualities (e.g., John's knowledge of Greek, Paul's Fever) are examples of endurants. Roughly speaking, they are the ontological counterparts of Objects, Reified Relationships and Weak Entities in the literature of Conceptual Modeling [9, 10].

Figure 1 exemplifies an OntoUML model. In this model, we have two *kinds* of sub-stantials: `Organization` and `Person`. Kinds are types that classify their entities nec-essarily (in a modal sense) and that provide a uniform principle of identity for their instances. Instances of a kind can (contingently) instantiate different *roles* in differ-ent relational contexts. For example, a person can move in the extension of the role `Employee` by participating in `Employment` *relators*. This distinction between neces-sary and contingent types applies to all endurants and not only to substantials. For example, while an `Employment` is necessarily so, it can contingently be classified as a `TemporaryEmployment` and as a `PermanentEmployment`, i.e., the same instance of `Employment` (e.g., the one connecting John Smith and the UN) can move from the extension of the former to the extension of the latter. Relators (as well as qualities) are existentially dependent entities. In this example, the Employment of John Smith in the UN can only exist if both John Smith and the UN exist. This particular relation of multiple existential dependency is termed in OntoUML *mediation* [10].

Beyond the Ontology of Endurants, UFO also comprises an Ontology of Events (UFO-B). It has been formalized and model checked in [13] and, in [4], systematically mapped to the description logics SHROIQ. It has been extensively tested in practice and employed as a reference model for addressing problems from enterprise architecture [16], software engineering [20], as well as complex media management and event mod-eling in petroleum exploration [13]. UFO-B is composed of five sub-theories: (i) mere-ology – events can form partonomies. In this sub-theory, the relations between events and their parts are characterized by the axioms of the so-called *extensional mereology*; (ii) participation – events are existentially dependent on endurants. The maximal part of an event that is exclusively dependent on a particular endurant is called a *participation*

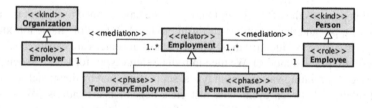

Fig. 1. OntoUML model capturing endurant types

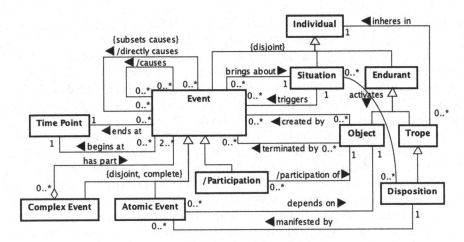

Fig. 2. A summary of UFO-B and its relations

(of that endurant in that event). Events can be partitioned into a set of exhaustive and mutually disjoint participations in this sense. For example, in Brutus' stabbing of Caesar, we have the participations of Brutus, of Caesar, and of the dagger; (iii) temporal relations – events occur in time accumulating temporal parts. Their primary properties are temporal properties. In particular, their *begin* and *end points*. Based on these properties, this theory defines all of the so-called *Allen Relations* [3] between events; (iv) events as manifestation of dispositions – this sub-theory connects endurants and events by characterizing how events are *manifestations* of particular endurants called *dispositions*, which can themselves inhere in other endurants. For example, the passing of an electrical current in a conductor is an event that is a manifestation of a disposition (electrical conductivity) inhering in a conductor. Dispositions are said to be *triggered by* certain *situations*; (v) change – events map the world from situations (that *activate* the dispositions of which they are manifestations) to situations (which are *brought about* the occurrence of that event). If an event E brings about a situation S that activates the dispositions that are manifested as event E', then we say that: S *triggers* E' and that E *causes* E'. Figure 2 summarizes these aspects of UFO-B. For a complete presentation and full formalization of this ontology, one should refer to [4, 13].

3   Extending OntoUML with Event Types

This section presents the extension of OntoUML we have defined to support the modeling of event types and their relations according to UFO-B. First of all, we introduce the stereotype ≪*event*≫ to identify those classes whose instances are events (i.e., to identify the event types in a model). We then introduce stereotypes for UML associations to provide rules for relating various event types, supporting thereby the modeling of mereological relations between events and historical dependence relations. We also introduce stereotypes to model the participation of endurants in events (≪*participation*≫, ≪*creation*≫, ≪*termination*≫), effectively connecting the extension for events we

introduce here with the endurant types that had been defined previously for OntoUML ($\ll$*kind*$\gg$, $\ll$*subkind*$\gg$, $\ll$*phase*$\gg$, $\ll$*role*$\gg$, $\ll$*relator*$\gg$, $\ll$*quality*$\gg$, etc.).

3.1 Introducing Event Types with the $\ll$*event*$\gg$ Stereotype

The stereotype $\ll$*event*$\gg$ identifies those classes whose instances are events (past occurrences). These classes are disjoint from any classes that model endurant types, and whose instances are endurants. As a consequence, no class may be stereotyped with both $\ll$*event*$\gg$ and any of the other stereotypes defined for endurant types in OntoUML. For the same reason, no class may specialize simultaneously a class stereotyped $\ll$*event*$\gg$ and a class stereotyped with any of the other OntoUML stereotypes representing endurant types.

Classes stereotyped $\ll$*event*$\gg$ may be given special attributes to reflect an event's temporal properties in a suitable temporal quality structure. We consider two options here: (i) the use of two attributes, one stereotyped $\ll$*begin*$\gg$ and the other stereotyped $\ll$*end*$\gg$ to identify the boundaries of events; or (ii) the use of a single attribute stereotyped with both stereotypes ($\ll$*begin*$\gg$ and $\ll$*end*$\gg$) in case begin and end coincides systematically for that class. The choice of temporal value space (and thus corresponding datatypes) is application-dependent, and typically reflects a particular model's granularity requirements. In models in which these alternatives can be applied uniformly to all event classes, the temporal attributes can be included in an abstract Event superclass (stereotyped $\ll$*event*$\gg$). (This solution is similar to what is proposed by [6] with a single $\ll$*timestamp*$\gg$ stereotype.)

The use of these temporal attributes forms the basis of the support for the well-known time interval relations proposed by Allen [3]. All these relations can be derived directly from the temporal attributes [13]. Helper OCL operations reflecting each of the temporal relations are defined in the profile (before, meets, overlaps, starts, during, finishes, after, metBy, overlappedBy, startedBy, contains, finishedBy and equals) and thus can be used in constraints involving event classes.

3.2 Relations Between Event Types and Endurant Types

Participation. In order to model the participation of endurants in events, we use the stereotype $\ll$*participation*$\gg$. An association stereotyped $\ll$*participation*$\gg$ always relates a class stereotyped with $\ll$*event*$\gg$ with a class denoting an endurant type. If an endurant and an event are linked through a $\ll$*participation*$\gg$ association, then, either: (i) the event is a manifestation of a disposition of the participating endurant, or (ii) the event is composed of such a manifestation. The lefthand side of Fig. 3 illustrates the use of the stereotypes showing the participation of persons into acts of composition. In this particular model, an act of composition is always dependent on a single person (the composer). Moreover, a person may participate in one or more acts of composition.

Creation and Termination of an Endurant. A special kind of participation is the creation of an endurant. This is identified with the $\ll$*creation*$\gg$ stereotype. If an endurant is related to an event through an association stereotyped $\ll$*creation*$\gg$ then that endurant

Fig. 3. Creation of a Musical Piece in an Act of Composition

is created in that event. In the example shown in Fig. 3, a `Musical Piece` is created in an `Act of Composition` (or in an event that is part of it).

Note that we are concerned here only with the modeling of events as past (as opposed to ongoing) occurrences. Using Lyons' distinction between experiential and historical modes of description ([15] apud [8]), we adopt the historical mode, i.e., we are concerned with "the fixed history of events as *faits accomplis*, as it were the fossil record of once-active processes." [8]. Because of this, instances of classes stereotyped with ≪*event*≫ are classified by those classes necessarily ("rigidly" or "statically"). For the same reason, any features of events are immutable (and should be marked `readOnly`), including the association ends attached to endurants in participation and creation associations (An `Act of Composition` will never have a different `Person` as composer or produce a different `Musical Piece` than it has produced. A `Person`, on the other hand, may participate in new acts of composition in time—but always accumulating past acts of composition if any).

The introduction of (past) events in a model has an important consequence to the interpretation of the endurant types in a model: since events are immutably tied to the endurants on which they specifically depend, and since events accumulate over time, related endurants must also accumulate over time. In other words, by introducing events in the model, our universe of discourse contains not only the entities that exist in a given circumstance but also all entities that have existed in that history of our universe of discourse up to that point (a view aligned with the so-called *Growing Block Universe theory* [19]), shifting from a purely "current semantics" to a "historical semantics".

A modeling consequence of "historical semantics" is that "termination" of an endurant should be considered a change in phase rather than "removal" from the universe of discourse. The termination of an endurant in the profile is represented with the introduction of the ≪*termination*≫ stereotype which relates an event type to a class stereotyped ≪*phase*≫ which is instantiated by the endurant when it takes on a "historical" nature. In such a phase, endurants have immutable properties not unlike past events. Figure 4 shows an example concerning the creation and termination of pieces of legislation by congress. Pieces of legislation may be terminated by means of a `Legislation Repeal`. When terminated, a `Piece of Legislation` instantiates the `Repealed Piece of Legislation` ≪*phase*≫ permanently.

Roles of Participants. The role an endurant instantiates in virtue of having participated in an event of a particular type can be modeled explicitly with the stereotype ≪*historicalRole*≫. Figure 5 revisits the example in Fig. 3 introducing the `Composer` historical role. A historical role is required to be related to an event type through a ≪*participation*≫ association. In this case, the minimum cardinality of the association end attached to the event type must be one, reflecting that, for an endurant to play the role, it mandatorily has participated in an event of that type. In this model, any

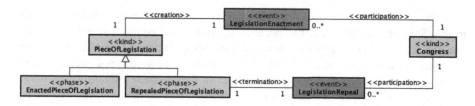

Fig. 4. Creation and Termination of a Piece of Legislation

`Composer` has a participation in at least one `Act of Composition` (which does not apply to `Person` in general as shown in Fig. 3). Further, according to the model, only one `Composer` participates in a certain `Act of Composition`. The pattern of historical role and participation in Fig. 5 makes it explicit that a person is considered a composer in virtue of his/her participation in the act of composition.

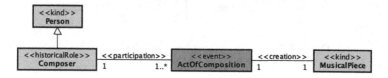

Fig. 5. Participation of a Person into Acts of Composition playing the Composer role

Historical roles can also be used to make explicit the variety of roles that endurants may play in events of a certain type. Figure 6 shows a model in which soccer players participate in soccer matches, along with a possible referee. Participation of referees is optional according to this model to cope with those informal settings when no referee is present. The model makes explicit that a person may participate in a `Soccer Match` in different roles (`Soccer Match Player` or `Referee`). (A constraint enforcing that a person does not participate in both capacities in the same match is usually required.)

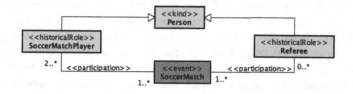

Fig. 6. Participation of Soccer Players and Referees in Soccer Matches

Furthermore, introducing historical roles allows us to distinguish explicitly between role playing in the scope of a (current) relationship and role playing in (past) events. For example, we are able to distinguish the notion of soccer player as a participant

of a Soccer Match, i.e., someone whose dispositions were manifested in a soccer match (Soccer Match Player), and, soccer player as a hired professional, i.e., someone that maintains an employment relationship with a Soccer Club (Hired Soccer Player). As shown in Fig. 7, Hired Soccer Player is stereotyped ≪*role*≫, and is thus associated through a ≪*mediation*≫ to an Employment (≪*relator*≫), while Soccer Match Player is stereotyped ≪*historicalRole*≫ and is thus associated through a ≪*participation*≫ to a Soccer Match (≪*event*≫). If we consider that only "current" employments are represented, when fired by a Soccer Club, a Person no longer instantiates Hired Soccer Player. However, having played in a Soccer Match, a Person will always instantiate Soccer Match Player.

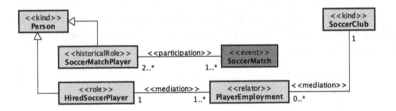

Fig. 7. Roles in virtue of relations versus historical roles

In [12], the authors discuss the duality between relators and events that are their manifestations. For example, a marriage as an event is the manifestation of properties of the marriage as a relator (mutual commitments and claims). As previously discussed, relators (and endurants in general) can change their (contingent) properties while remaining the same; events, in contrast are immutable, i.e., they cannot change in any way while keeping their identity. This aspect of (un)changeability gives us a methodological guideline for chosing to model an event or its endurant counterpart.

3.3   Mereological Relations Between Events

Following Pribbenow [18], we identify different ways in which a whole may be decomposed into parts. Pribbenow discusses that parts may be: (i) "structure dependent", in which case the whole-part relations belong to the definition of the decomposed entity, e.g., the chapters of a book or the functional parts of a machine, (ii) or otherwise "constructed", in which case the whole-part relations are derived or induced using internal features of the parts or external schemes of reference. In the case of "constructed parts", by using internal features, we partition an entity into parts called "portions". For example, we may consider the "portions" of a house according to their colors. In this case, we would identify "red" parts, "brown" parts, "white" parts, etc. By using external schemes, we induce parts called "segments". An example of such external scheme is a spatial frame, so we may decompose a house into its "segment" that lies within 5 m of the road, and the rest of it (the "segment" that lies over 5 m from the road).

We use the classification proposed by Pribbenow to understand the ways in which an event can be decomposed in UFO-B, reflecting ultimately on our modeling recommendations. In the case of structure dependent decompositions (for example, that

between a Soccer Match and a Goal, or between a Soccer Championship and each Soccer Match), no stereotype is used. Differently, for constructed decompositions, we distinguish between participational and temporal decompositions and introduce the ≪*participational*≫ and ≪*temporal*≫ stereotypes for part-whole relations.

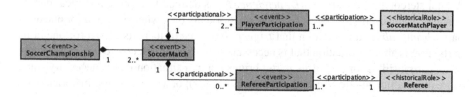

Fig. 8. Structural and participational decompositions involving Soccer Matches

In the case of the decomposition of an event into participations, we have "constructed" "portions", which are projected out of the whole considering their formal relation of dependence on specific endurants. Consider a meeting with multiple participants. The participation of each participant is a "portion" of the meeting in this sense. A portion is maximal with respect to the property under consideration: the portion of the meeting that is John's participation in the meeting covers all events that are part of the meeting and that depend solely from John. It is further disjoint from other portions of the meeting using the same criterion (that must per definition be participations of other participants, and hence disjoint from John's participation.) This kind of event decomposition is marked with the stereotype ≪*participational*≫. The maximum cardinality in the association end attached to the participant is always one, reflecting the rule in UFO-B that participations depend exclusively on a single endurant. Figure 8 shows the combined use of structural and participational decompositions in the soccer example.

In the case of the decomposition of an event into temporal parts, we have "constructed" "segments" using temporal schemes as external reference. For example, the temporal "segments" may be projected out of the whole by reference to a fixed time interval, durations, or temporal relations to other events. Consider segmenting a day-long meeting into two "segments": before and after noon. The meeting's afternoon "segment" is disjoint from the meeting's morning "segment". In addition, similarly to participational portions, temporal segments are maximal with respect to the temporal relations under consideration: in this case, there are no parts of the meeting that are fully contained in the considered time interval that are not part of the segment under consideration. This kind of event decomposition is marked with the stereotype ≪*temporal*≫.

Since events cannot be involved in part-whole relations with endurants (and vice-versa), any class stereotyped with ≪*event*≫ can only participate in part-whole relations with other classes stereotyped ≪*event*≫. Further, temporal relations can be inferred from the part-whole relations between events. More specifically, following UFO-B, the begin point of the whole must precede or coincide with the begin point of the part and the end point of the part must precede or coincide with the end point of the whole. Further, since whole part relations between events follows extensional mereology, the

weak supplementation principle must be enforced. This means that the sum of lower bounds of parts must be equal to or greater than two.

3.4 Historical Dependence Between Events

A final stereotype (≪*historicalDependence*≫) is defined to capture historical dependence between events. An event b depends historically on a whenever: (i) a (or one of its parts) *brings about* the situation that *triggers* b (or one of its parts); (ii) a (or one of its parts) brings about a situation that is necessary—but not sufficient—to *trigger* b (or one of its parts); (iii) a (or one of its parts) brings about a situation that is necessary—and more than sufficient—to *trigger* b (or one of its parts); or, (iv) b depends historically on an event z that depends historically on a.

Condition (i) encompasses direct causation, and, together with (iv), encompass indirect causation, which are grounds for historical dependence. Take, for instance, the relation between penalty kicks and goals. A particular Goal may be historically dependent on a Penalty Kick by being caused by it. Conditions (ii) and (iii) cover the cases of historical dependence in which there is dependence but not causation. Consider, e.g., the relation between penalties and penalty kicks. A penalty is necessary but not sufficient to cause a penalty kick (e.g., because authorization of the referee is required). A model capturing these historical relations between events is shown in Fig. 9. It captures the fact that every penalty kick is historically dependent on a penalty, and that some goals (penalty goals) are historically dependent on a penalty.

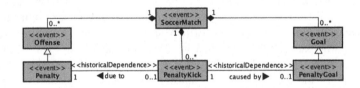

Fig. 9. Historical dependence between events of certain types in a soccer match.

4   Applying the Profile to Model Software Testing Processes

In this section, we revisit the model presented in [20], more specifically the fragment that represents software Testing Processes, the activities that comprise them, artifacts used and produced by those activities, and the people involved. Figures 10 and 11 present this fragment re-engineered using the profile previously discussed.

As Fig. 10 shows, a Testing Processes is structurally decomposed into activities (events) of the following types: Test Case Design, Test Coding, Test Execution, and Test Result Analysis. To uniformly represent the temporal attributes of the events represented in the model, we included an abstract Event superclass that has two attributes, one stereotyped ≪*begin*≫ and the other stereotyped ≪*end*≫, capturing the temporal boundaries of the events (see Sect. 3.1). The historical dependencies shown in Fig. 10 reflect the fact that some activities use artifacts produced

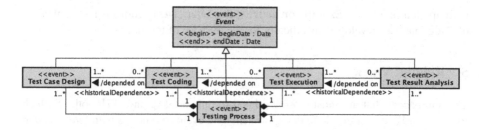

Fig. 10. Software Testing Process Model Revisited – Composition and Dependencies

by others, as shown in Fig. 11. For example, `Test Execution` historically depends on `Test Coding`, since `Test Execution` uses `Test Code` produced in `Test Coding`.

The participations of endurants in the activities that compose the testing process are detailed in Fig. 11. The model makes explicit the historical roles related to the participation of a `Person` (`Test Case Designer`, `Test Coder`, `Test Executor`, `Test Result Analyst`) in each activity of the `Testing Process`. These activities also involve the participation of several types of artifacts (`Document` and `Code`), some of which are created (≪*creation*≫) during the corresponding activity (e.g., `Test Code` was created during `Test Coding`); or simply participated (≪*participation*≫) in the activities (e.g., `Test Code` was used in `Test Execution`). The model omits the historical roles played by those artifacts in the corresponding activities for brevity. An exception is the case of `Tested Code`, which is the historical role of a `Code` when tested in a `Test Execution` activity. This was included to capture the difference between `Tested Code` and `Test Code`. While the former is the historical role played by a `Code` due to its

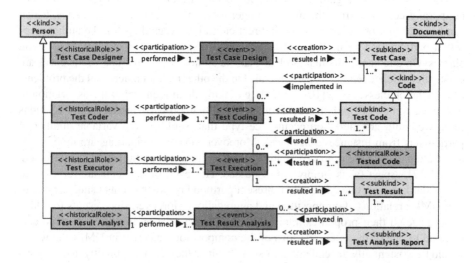

Fig. 11. Software Testing Process Model Revisited – Participations

participation in a Test Execution activity, the latter (Test Code) is a ≪*subkind*≫ of Code that was developed specifically for the purpose of testing.

5 Related Work

The approaches that are most closely related to ours are [5], and [17], both of which focus on UML and, similarly to our approach, treat events as entities with *"identity and properties"* which *"may participate in relationships"* and *"can be specialized"*.

In [5], we have: (a) the representation of part-whole relations between events; (b) the temporal succession of events, also with start and ending events; (c) the modeling of participants of events. Regarding (a), the proposal allows for partonomy structures and define parthood as a subtype of the Allen during relation, a point that is in conformance with UFO-B. The authors, however, are not explicit regarding the semantics of the parthood relations. For example, it is unclear under what conditions two occurrences are the same in their approach and, there seems to be no constraint proscribing the creation of an occurrence A that is composed of one single sub-occurrence B, which is different from A (thus, breaking the so-called *weak supplementation axiom*, a basic axiom in mereology). Since our approach is grounded in UFO-B, it makes clear that our semantics of composition is one of *extensional mereology*. Regarding (b), both approaches can represent Allen relations (although the authors only explicitly consider the case of *before* and *during*). However, we believe the modeling choice adopted here is superior in terms of clarity and flexibility. By marking the begin and end point of events as (immutable) attributes, we can: use different types of datatypes for representing temporal points; easily represent instantaneous events without the need for an extra construct; make explicit that *all* Allen relations are *derived* (and provide OCL derivation rules for all of them). Still regarding (b), our approach differentiates the derived relation of temporal precedence from the much stronger relation of *historical dependence*, which can be used to represent direct and indirect causation. Regarding (c), the authors represent participation by making occurrence types a specialization of UML association classes. On one hand, this makes clear that the author recognizes that occurrences are existentially dependent on its participants. On the other hand, it inherits all the problems of association classes (see [10]), including making them identical to the association to which are connected, and their consequent inability to properly model anadyc relations (e.g., we could not model an occurrence type that would have a variable number of participants from instance to instance). Moreover, since participations are modeled as association ends, there is no systematic connection between participation and parthood.

In [17], aspect (a) is simply not discussed. However, once events are represented as standard classes, one can easily represent parthood between events using, for example, UML's relations of composition and aggregation. Moreover, since events for Olivé et al., have all their properties immutable, the correct relation in this case would correspond to one of the interpretations of the composition construct in UML (the whole would be existentially dependent on its sparts). Since they do not explicitly discuss parthood for events, the authors also do not discuss the semantics on this relation for events. There is, however, an even more problematic issue. For the authors, events are always instantaneous and, hence, even if we can represent mereologically complex events, we

are restrict to events which all parts happen at the exact same instant and, hence, there would be no way to represent events that unfold in time with their parts as well as non-convex events. Regarding (b), the authors represent *effects* of events by invoking operations. This can be seen as a sort of direct causality (which implies temporal precedence of the cause). However, the events that are the effects on an event are not themselves modeled as events in the same sense(!) but as operations of other classes to be invoked. As such they are not subject to all the benefits of explicit event modeling. Additionally, despite implicitly dealing with direct causality and, hence, also implicitly with temporal precedence, the authors do not discuss the modeling of all the remaining Allen relations. Regarding (c), object participation in events is modeled via regular (immutable) associations. Here, once more, there is no connection between participation and parthood and, in particular, also due to the aforementioned limitations, no way to represent mereologically complex participations. Although Olivé et al. [17] briefly considers a semantics for events in which they permanently exist as instances of the model, none of these approaches analyze the (non-trivial) consequences of introducing events in structural models. As discussed in [12], events are locked in the past and, as a consequence, introducing them in structural models changes the semantics of the model to a *historical semantics*, affecting not only them but also the objects to which they are necessarily connected. Here, we make explicit the connection between event participation and (some aspects) of dynamic endurant type instantiation, including phase changes and role playing. However, we make clear the use of events as truthmakers for role playing entails a special semantics of historical role. It is in this latter sense that, for example, in Wikipedia, Paul Newman *"is an actor"* with active years (1953–2008).

6   Final Considerations

This paper makes a contribution to conceptual modeling by proposing a profile for the representation of events in structural conceptual models. This profile was developed to address modeling requirements collected from observing the practice of the OntoUML community while creating ontology-driven conceptual models *(claim to relevance)*. By employing a well-tested language engineering method, this profile was developed to reflect the ontological distinctions and formal semantics put forth by the foundational ontology UFO-B *(claim to ontological adequacy)*. The proposed profile is then employed here to model a fragment of an existing reference model in the area of Software Testing. As this exercise demonstrates, the profile is able to provide specialized semantics to the various relations between events and between events and endurants. The nature of these relations remained implicit in the original model *(claim to applicability)*.

Finally, this work is part of a research program aimed at addressing a fuller evolution of OntoUML [11,14]. As discussed in [14], the development of new ontological foundations for OntoUML and the systematic redesign of its metamodel creates a number of possibilities regarding approaches to mappings from OntoUML to codification languages (e.g., OWL), model verbalization, model simulation, support for patterns and detection of anti-patterns. Revisiting the current modeling support for OntoUML in light of the developments discussed in this paper is part of our current research program.

Acknowledgments. This work has been partially supported by CNPq (407235/2017-5, 312123/2017-5), CAPES (23038.028816/2016-41), FAPES (69382549) and FUB (OCEAN Project).

References

1. Allen, G.N., March, S.T.: The ontological treatment of the 'Event' construct: implications for system analysis and design. In: Proceedings of the 5th Symposium on Research Systems Analysis and Design (2000)
2. Allen, G.N., March, S.T.: The effects of state-based and event-based data representation on user performance in query formulation tasks. MIS Q. **30**, 269–290 (2006)
3. Allen, J.F.: Maintaining knowledge about temporal intervals. Commun. ACM **26**(11), 832–843 (1983)
4. Benevides, A.B., Bourguet, J.R., Guizzardi, G., Peñaloza, R., Almeida, J.P.A.: Representing a reference foundational ontology of events in SROIQ. Appl. Ontol. **14**(3), 293–334 (2019). https://content.iospress.com/articles/applied-ontology/ao190214
5. Bock, C., Odell, J.: Ontological behavior modeling. J. Object Technol. **10**(3), 1–36 (2011)
6. Cabot, J., Olivé, A., Teniente, E.: Representing temporal information in UML. In: Stevens, P., Whittle, J., Booch, G. (eds.) UML 2003. LNCS, vol. 2863, pp. 44–59. Springer, Heidelberg (2003). https://doi.org/10.1007/978-3-540-45221-8_5
7. Carvalho, V.A., Almeida, J.P.A., Guizzardi, G.: Using reference domain ontologies to define the real-world semantics of domain-specific languages. In: Jarke, M., et al. (eds.) CAiSE 2014. LNCS, vol. 8484, pp. 488–502. Springer, Cham (2014). https://doi.org/10.1007/978-3-319-07881-6_33
8. Galton, A.: Processes as continuants (abstract). In: Thirteenth International Symposium on Temporal Representation and Reasoning (TIME 2006), p. 187, June 2006
9. Guarino, N., Guizzardi, G.: "We need to discuss the *relationship*": revisiting relationships as modeling constructs. In: Zdravkovic, J., Kirikova, M., Johannesson, P. (eds.) CAiSE 2015. LNCS, vol. 9097, pp. 279–294. Springer, Cham (2015). https://doi.org/10.1007/978-3-319-19069-3_18
10. Guizzardi, G.: Ontological foundations for structural conceptual models. Ph.D. thesis, CTIT, Centre for Telematics and Information Technology, Enschede (2005)
11. Guizzardi, G., Fonseca, C.M., Benevides, A.B., Almeida, J.P.A., Porello, D., Sales, T.P.: Endurant types in ontology-driven conceptual modeling: towards OntoUML 2.0. In: Trujillo, J., et al. (eds.) ER 2018. LNCS, vol. 11157, pp. 136–150. Springer, Cham (2018). https://doi.org/10.1007/978-3-030-00847-5_12
12. Guizzardi, G., Guarino, N., Almeida, J.P.A.: Ontological considerations about the representation of events and endurants in business models. In: La Rosa, M., Loos, P., Pastor, O. (eds.) BPM 2016. LNCS, vol. 9850, pp. 20–36. Springer, Cham (2016). https://doi.org/10.1007/978-3-319-45348-4_2
13. Guizzardi, G., Wagner, G., Falbo, R.A., Guizzardi, R.S.S., Almeida, J.P.A.: Towards ontological foundations for the conceptual modeling of events. In: Ng, W., Storey, V.C., Trujillo, J.C. (eds.) ER 2013. LNCS, vol. 8217, pp. 327–341. Springer, Heidelberg (2013). https://doi.org/10.1007/978-3-642-41924-9_27
14. Guizzardi, G., et al.: Towards ontological foundations for conceptual modeling: the Unified Foundational Ontology (UFO) story. Appl. Ontol. **10**(3–4), 259–271 (2015)
15. Lyons, J.: Semantics, vol. 2. Cambridge University Press, Cambridge (1977)
16. Nardi, J.C., et al.: A commitment-based reference ontology for services. Inf. Syst. **54**, 263–288 (2015)

17. Olivé, A., Raventós, R.: Modeling events as entities in object-oriented conceptual modeling languages. Data Knowl. Eng. **58**(3), 243–262 (2006)
18. Pribbenow, S.: Parts and wholes and their relations. In: Mental Models in Discourse Processing and Reasoning. Advances in Psychology, vol. 128, pp. 359–382. North-Holland (1999)
19. Sider, T.: Quantifiers and temporal ontology. Mind **115**(457), 75–97 (2006)
20. Souza, E., Falbo, R.A., Vijaykumar, N.: ROoST: reference ontology on software testing. Appl. Ontol. **12**(1), 59–90 (2017)
21. U.S. Department of Defense (DoD): Data Modeling Guide (DMG) for an Enterprise Logical Data Model (ELDM). U.S. Department of Defense (DoD) Report (2011)

Parallel Clique-Like Subgraph Counting and Listing

Yi Yang[1], Da Yan[2], Shuigeng Zhou[1(✉)], and Guimu Guo[2]

[1] Shanghai Key Lab of Intelligent Information Processing,
and School of Computer Science, Fudan University, Shanghai 200433, China
{yyang1,sgzhou}@fudan.edu.cn
[2] Department of Computer Science, The University of Alabama at Birmingham,
Birmingham, USA
{yanda,guimuguo}@uab.edu

Abstract. Cliques and clique-like subgraphs (e.g., quasi-cliques) are important dense structures whose counting or listing are essential in applications like complex network analysis and community detection. These problems are usually solved by divide and conquer, where a task over a big graph can be recursively divided into subtasks over smaller subgraphs whose search spaces are disjoint. This divisible algorithmic paradigm brings enormous potential for parallelism, since different subtasks can run concurrently to drastically reduce the overall running time.

In this paper, we explore this potential by proposing a unified framework for counting and listing clique-like subgraphs. We study how to divide and distribute the counting and listing tasks, and meanwhile, to balance the assigned workloads of each thread dynamically. Four applications are studied under our parallel framework, i.e., triangle counting, clique counting, maximal clique listing and quasi-clique listing. Extensive experiments are conducted which demonstrate that our solution achieves an ideal speedup on various real graph datasets.

Keywords: Dense subgraph mining · Parallel computation · Unified framework

1 Introduction

Dense subgraphs of a network often contain important information about the communities or modules in the network, and as a result, counting and listing dense subgraphs has received a lot of interest from the research community in the last decade [8,9,11,13,22,25]. One example of a dense subgraph is a clique, where every pair of vertices are connected by an edge.

However, these problems have a high computational complexity [17], often NP-hard due to the reduction to the maximum clique problem [18]. Recent studies focus on speeding up the computation by parallel computing [10,12,23, 26]. Since the original problem has an exponential computational complexity,

© Springer Nature Switzerland AG 2019
A. H. F. Laender et al. (Eds.): ER 2019, LNCS 11788, pp. 484–497, 2019.
https://doi.org/10.1007/978-3-030-33223-5_40

after dividing it into multiple subproblems, either the number of subproblems or the time cost of an individual subproblem must be exponential. Accordingly, existing works can be categorized into two aspects.

1. Polynomial Number of Subproblems. This kind of work often uses simple task prepartitioning (e.g., on top of MapReduce [10,23,24] or Pregel-like systems [15,27]). Since the time cost of individual subproblems are exponential, they often suffer from imbalanced workload distribution (e.g., the last-reducer problem) [21] especially on power-law graphs with a heavily skewed degree distribution. However, since the number of subproblems is polynomial, it is not time costly to rearrange the subproblems in order (e.g., vertex ordering schemes are applied [11,25,26]). After rearrangements, the time costly subproblems will be handled in parallel firstly, and the less costly subproblems will be handled in parallel lastly. As a result, the workloads are almost balanced, with the differences between the running time of the last few subproblems.

2. Exponential Number of Subproblems. This kind of work often uses dynamic task partitioning [19] and dynamic load balancing [7,20], or they will suffer from exponential memory consumption storing the fully partitioned subproblems [8]. The dynamics is usually ensured by recursive partitioning, i.e. a subproblem can be further divided into smaller subproblems. Since the number of final subproblems is exponential, the granularity of the partitioning should be carefully chosen (e.g. coarse-grained partitioning leads more load differences and fine-grained partitioning leads more communication cost). The optimal solution usually lays out between extremes, which requires a proper cost model for both communication and computation, and requires an optimization method to find out the optimal solution of the cost model [8].

Contributions. In this paper, we present a unified framework for counting and listing clique-like subgraph in parallel, which takes both of the advantages of the previous two aspects. More specifically, on one hand, we propose a new task partitioning method called *pivot path partitioning*, which gradually partition the original task into a polynomial number of subtasks, then three vertex ordering schemes are compared. On the other hand, the pivot path partitioning method automatically partitions the original task into a proper granularity, without dealing with a cost model and its optimization. More over, the pivot path partitioning method enables general clique counting, which is little explored previously. We focus on the setting of multi-threaded computation within a single machine (i.e., a shared-memory environment). Our contribution can be summarized as follows.

- A unified parallel framework is proposed.
- The pivot path partitioning method is developed.
- First attempt on general clique counting.

2 Preliminaries

This section first defines our graph notations and terminology, and then introduces the clique-like problems that we solve on top of our parallel framework.

2.1 Notations and Terminology

Graphs. Let $G = (V, E)$ be a simple undirected graph with a vertex set V and an edge set E, and let $n = |V|$ and $m = |E|$ be the number of vertices and edges in G, respectively. We use $N(v)$ to denote the set of the neighbors of vertex v, i.e. the set of vertices each of which has an edge connecting to v. We also use $d(v) = |N(v)|$ to denote the degree of vertex v.

Vertex Ordering. We define a total ordering o over the vertices, where $o(v)$ denotes the rank of vertex v, i.e., 1 plus the number of vertices that are before v in the ordering. Obviously, $1 \leq o(v) \leq n$. Given an integer i, we use v_i to denote the vertex with rank i, i.e., $o(v_i) = i$. Given a vertex v, we use $N^-(v) = \{u \mid u \in N(v), o(u) < o(v)\}$ to denote the set of neighbor vertices of v which are ranked before v.

Subgraphs. Given a subset $V' \subseteq V$ of vertices, we define $G(V')$ as the subgraph of G induced by vertex set V', i.e., the edge set of $G(V')$ equals $E' = \{(u, v) \mid u \in V', v \in V', (u, v) \in E\}$. We use $G(v)$ (resp. $G^-(v)$) to denote the subgraph of G induced by vertex set $N(v)$ (resp. $N^-(v)$), i.e., $G(v) = G(N(v))$ (resp. $G^-(v) = G(N^-(v))$).

Cliques. If $G(V')$ is a complete graph where every pair of vertices are connected (i.e. $|E'| = |V'| \cdot (|V'| - 1)/2$), we call $G(V')$ a clique in G, and call $|V'|$ the size of the clique. In particular, if $|V'| = 3$, then we call $G(V')$ a triangle. We use $c(G)$ to denote the size of the largest clique in G.

Maximal Cliques. Let C be a clique in G, and we also abuse the notation C to denote the vertex set of this clique. If there does not exist another clique C' in G, such that $C' \supset C$, then we say that clique C is a maximal clique in G.

Quasi-cliques. Given a density threshold $\gamma \leq 1$ and a subgraph $G(V')$ of G, if for every vertex $v' \in V'$, its degree in the subgraph $G(V')$ satisfies $d(v') \geq \gamma \cdot (|V'| - 1)$, then we say that $G(V')$ is a γ-quasi-clique in G. To ensure the γ-quasi-clique to be a connected graph, we require $\gamma \geq 0.5$.

Intuitively, a quasi-clique relaxes the requirement of a clique where every vertex is connected to every other vertex, into that every vertex is connected to the majority of other vertices in V'. It is a more realistic model for a social community.

k-core. The k-core of a graph G is the maximal subgraph such that every vertex has degree at least k. It can be found by keeping removing vertices that have degree less than k. We call $k(G)$ as the core number of G if k is the largest integer such that the k-core of G is not empty.

2.2 Problem Statement

Without loss of generality, this work studies four specific problems on top of our parallel framework, and we use the graph in Fig. 1 to illustrate the concepts.

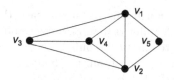

Fig. 1. An example input graph

Triangle Counting. The problem counts the number of triangles in an input graph G. For example, there are 5 triangles $\{v_1, v_2, v_3\}$, $\{v_1, v_2, v_4\}$, $\{v_1, v_2, v_5\}$, $\{v_1, v_3, v_4\}$ and $\{v_2, v_3, v_4\}$ in Fig. 1.

Clique Counting. The problem counts the number of cliques in G with different sizes of $1, 2, 3, \ldots, c(G)$, respectively. In Fig. 1, there are 5 size-1 cliques (i.e., all 5 vertices), 8 size-2 cliques (i.e., all 8 edges), 5 size-3 cliques (i.e., 5 triangles) and 1 size-4 clique (i.e., $\{v_1, v_2, v_3, v_4\}$) in the example graph.

Maximal Clique Listing. The problem lists all the maximal cliques in G. For example, there are 2 maximal cliques $\{v_1, v_2, v_3, v_4\}$ and $\{v_1, v_2, v_5\}$ in Fig. 1.

Quasi-clique Listing. Given a real number $0.5 \leq \gamma \leq 1$ and an integer s, the problem lists all the γ-quasi-cliques in G whose sizes are at least s. For example, there are 3 γ-quasi-cliques $\{v_1, v_2, v_3, v_4\}$, $\{v_1, v_2, v_3, v_5\}$ and $\{v_1, v_2, v_4, v_5\}$ in Fig. 1 with $\gamma = 0.6$ and $s = 4$.

3   The Parallel Framework

Overview. In this section, we introduce our parallel framework generic clique-like subgraph counting and listing, which consists of three phases: tasks partitioning, parallel execution and result aggregation, which are described as follows:

- **Task Partitioning.** The framework first loads an input graph G from a file, and then computes a total ordering of the vertices in G. It then divides the computation workloads into multiple tasks each with a bounded cost, and adds them into a concurrent queue [16] to be fetched and processed concurrently by the computing threads.

  We will discuss the vertex ordering schemes in Sect. 3.1, and introduce our task partitioning method in Sect. 3.2.
- **Parallel Execution.** Multiple threads are executed concurrently in this phase. Threads are numbered with IDs $i = 1, 2, 3, \ldots, t$, where t is the total number of threads. The threads keep fetching tasks from the queue for processing, until the task queue becomes empty.

  We will discuss how to compute the tasks in Sect. 3.3. Once the queue is empty, the idle threads will steal works from the busy threads, so that the workloads are dynamically balanced. The threads will terminate when they all become idle and the task queue is empty.

– **Result Aggregation.** For listing problems, each thread will store the subgraph results in a local buffer of bounded size, and will flush them to disk when the buffer is full, to empty the buffer for keeping more results. After all threads finish running, we can obtain the final results by concatenating the output files of all threads. For counting problems, each thread will maintain its own counter, and their values are summed in the end to get the final count.

3.1 Vertex Ordering Schemes

We assign ranks to vertices using three ordering schemes that are commonly used in existing work [25, 26] as listed below. However, our novelty lies in that we further adjust the resulting ordering by putting a pivot vertex and its neighbors in front of all the other vertices. We will compare all of these ordering schemes in Sect. 4.

– **Scheme 1: Original Ordering.** This ordering scheme simply assigns the rank of the vertices according to the order that they appear in the input file (which is an edge list). Namely, the two end vertices of the first edge in the input file are ranked with 1 and 2, and the two end vertices of the second edge are ranked with 3 and 4 (if they are different from the first two vertices), and so on.
– **Scheme 2: Static Degree Ordering.** This ordering scheme arranges the vertices by descending order of their original degree in the input graph. Namely, the vertex with the highest degree is ranked with 1, and the vertex with the second highest degree is ranked with 2, and so on.
– **Scheme 3: Dynamic Degree Ordering.** This ordering scheme arranges each vertex v according to its degree in the subgraph induced by v plus those vertices ranked before v. Namely, the vertex with the lowest degree in the original graph is ranked with n, and the vertex with the lowest degree in the subgraph induced by the remaining $n - 1$ vertices is ranked with $n - 1$, and the vertex with the lowest degree in the subgraph induced by the remaining $n - 2$ vertices is ranked with $n - 2$, and so on.

Pivot Vertex Reordering. After vertices are ordered as above, we propose to further adjust the order of the vertices by prioritizing a pivot vertex and all of its neighbors to the top. After making this adjustment, a selected pivot vertex v is ranked with 1, and its neighbors are ranked with $2, 3, ..., d(v) + 1$, respectively (in an arbitrary order), and then the remaining vertices are ranked with $d(v) + 2, d(v) + 3, ..., n$ respectively (keeping the same order as in the original ordering scheme). We select the vertex v with the highest degree as the pivot vertex, since v tends to have the heaviest workload and the task partitioning method to be described in Sect. 3.2 will separate it from the rest of the workloads for further divide-and-conquer to distribute the workload among multiple threads.

3.2   Task Partitioning

For simplicity, let $\mathcal{A}(G', S)$ be the task of counting or listing clique subgraphs in G' given that vertices in S are already assumed to be included in a clique subgraph found by the task. Typically, S refers to those vertices already considered.

Let us denote $V_i = \{v_1, v_2, \ldots, v_i\}$. Then, we can divide the "root" task of computing $\mathcal{A}(G, \emptyset)$ into two subtasks as follows:

$$
\begin{aligned}
\mathcal{A}(G, \emptyset) \;=\;& \mathcal{A}(G(V_n), \emptyset) \\
\rightarrow\;& \mathcal{A}(G(V_{n-1}), \emptyset) \;\cup\; \mathcal{A}(G^-(v_n), \{v_n\}).
\end{aligned}
\tag{1}
$$

In other words, we consider two disjoint cases: (1) $\mathcal{A}(G(V_{n-1}), \emptyset)$ finds those clique-like subgraphs that do not contain v_n, where $V_i = \{v_1, v_2, \ldots, v_i\}$, and (2) $\mathcal{A}(G^-(v_n), \{v_n\})$ finds those clique-like subgraphs that contain v_n.

We can similarly divide the first subtask $\mathcal{A}(G(V_{n-1}), \emptyset)$ as follows:

$$
\begin{aligned}
&\mathcal{A}(G(V_{n-1}), \emptyset) \\
&\rightarrow \mathcal{A}(G(V_{n-2}), \emptyset) \;\cup\; \mathcal{A}(G^-(v_{n-1}), \{v_{n-1}\}).
\end{aligned}
\tag{2}
$$

In general, we can keep recursively dividing the first subtask $\mathcal{A}(G(V_{n-i}), \emptyset)$ as:

$$
\begin{aligned}
&\mathcal{A}(G(V_{n-i}), \emptyset) \\
&\rightarrow \mathcal{A}(G(V_{n-i-1}), \emptyset) \;\cup\; \mathcal{A}(G^-(v_{n-i}), \{v_{n-i}\}).
\end{aligned}
\tag{3}
$$

In the end, we will obtain:

$$
\begin{aligned}
&\mathcal{A}(G, \emptyset) \\
&\rightarrow \mathcal{A}(G(V_{d(v_1)+1}), \emptyset) \;\cup\; \bigcup_{i=d(v_1)+2}^{n} \mathcal{A}(G^-(v_i), \{v_i\}).
\end{aligned}
\tag{4}
$$

If v_1 is the pivot vertex with the highest degree, and its $d(v_1)$ neighbors are also ordered right after v_1 as done by our pivot vertex reordering approach, then task $\mathcal{A}(G(V_{d(v_1)+1}), \emptyset)$ in Eq. (4) essentially performs the original listing/counting task on the 1-ego network of v_1. We call this task as the pivot task, and call $\bigcup_{i=d(v_1)+2}^{n} \mathcal{A}(G^-(v_i), \{v_i\})$ the list of minor tasks.

When pivot vertex reordering is used together with our vertex ordering Scheme 3 "dynamic degree ordering", we can show that the size of a minor task is bounded by $k(G)$, the core number of G. This result is formalized by Lemma 1 below.

Lemma 1. *Given a graph $G^-(v_i)$ $(i > d(v_1) + 1)$ of a minor task, the number of vertices in the graph is bounded by $k(G)$.*

Proof. According to our scheme of dynamic pivot vertex reordering, vertex v_n has the lowest degree, followed by v_{n-1}, and so on. Therefore, our recursive division steps are equivalent to iteratively removing a vertex with the lowest degree at a time. This corresponds exactly to the algorithm of k-core decomposition [14], and thus at any step, $d(v_i) \le k(G)$ and thus $G^-(v_i)$ has no more than $k(G)$ vertices.

Table 1. Maximum degree v.s. core number

Dataset	n	m	$d(v_1)$	$k(G)$
Google	875713	4322051	6353	44
Youtube	1134890	2987624	28754	51
Patents	3774768	16518947	793	64
Flixster	2523386	7918801	1474	68
Skitter	1696415	11095298	35455	111
Wiki	2394385	4659565	100032	131

In a real graph, the maximum degree $d(v_1)$ is often much larger than $k(G)$ (which is typically not much larger than 100), and thus most workload is attributed to the pivot task. In other words, the pivot task may need further divide-and-conquer to distribute its workload; while a minor task can directly be processed by a single thread. We show the maximum vertex degree and the core number of the 6 real graphs used in our experiments in Table 1, where we see that $d(v_1) \gg k(G)$.

Even though Lemma 1 may not always hold for the other two vertex ordering schemes, the pivot task is the same and is always the bottleneck of computing workloads, and thus our solution of partitioning the pivot task is still valid. For quasi-cliques, the task partitioning method still works but $G^-(v)$ should be computed using v's two-hop neighborhood (rather than one-hop).

Pivot Task Partitioning. Refer back to Eq. (4) again. For maximal clique/quasi-clique counting/listing, the pivot task $\mathcal{A}(G(V_{d(v_1)+1}), \emptyset)$ is equivalent to $\mathcal{A}(G(V_{d(v_1)+1} - \{v_1\}), \{v_1\})$, i.e., assuming v_1 is in a clique/quasi-clique found and continues to examine the subgraph induced by v_1's neighbors. This is because v_1 is connected to every vertex in $G(V_{d(v_1)+1})$ and thus any clique/quasi-clique in it without v_1 cannot be maximal.

Similarly, for triangle counting, the pivot task $\mathcal{A}(G(V_{d(v_1)+1}), \emptyset)$ can be divided into two cases: (1) count the triangles that contain v_1, which is essentially the number of edges in $G(V_{d(v_1)+1} - \{v_1\})$ (as the two end vertices of an edge also connects to v_1); (2) count the triangles that do not contain v_1, which essentially counts triangles in $G(V_{d(v_1)+1} - \{v_1\})$, another triangle counting task that can be recursively solved. The overall count is just their sum.

To summarize, unlike in Eq. (1) where a task generates two subtasks, a pivot task $\mathcal{A}(G(V_{d(v_1)+1}), \emptyset)$ only generates one subtask computed over the graph $G(V_{d(v_1)+1} - \{v_1\})$.

Since a pivot task can be time-consuming, we can recursively divide the pivot task over $G' = G(V_{d(v_1)+1} - \{v_1\})$ into a new pivot task and a list of minor tasks. Specifically, we can perform dynamic pivot vertex reordering in G'; let v_1' be the new pivot vertex with the maximum degree in G', then we can obtain a level-2 pivot task for v_1' and a list of minor tasks. The pivot task for v_1' can be further partitioned if its graph is still too big.

pivot tasks   minor tasks

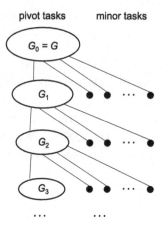

Fig. 2. Task partitioning

In general, for a task with a set S of already-selected vertices, we call $|S| = \ell$ the level of the task. The pivot task at level-ℓ can generate a level-$(\ell + 1)$ pivot task and a list of level-$(\ell+1)$ minor tasks. While a minor task is always processed by a single thread.

Task Representation. After phase 1 "task partitioning" we obtain at most one pivot task at each level, as well as a list of minor tasks. Since there are many minor tasks (e.g., up to n at level-1), it is costly to enqueue them one by one to the task queue, and for computing threads to fetch them one at a time. To reduce this cost, we represent a group of minor tasks at each level by a range; for example, the group of all minor tasks $\bigcup_{i=d(v_1)+2}^{n} \mathcal{A}(G^-(v_i), \{v_i\})$ can be simply denoted by $[d(v_1) + 2, n]$.

Generally, for a minor task at level $\ell = |S|$ over graph G' with n' vertices and v_1' be the pivot vertex, the complete group of tasks at this level can be denoted by range $[d(v_1') + 2, n']$, where we abuse $d(.)$ to measure vertex degree in G'.

While a minor task is usually efficient to compute, a group of them may contain much workload and may need to be distributed to multiple cores for concurrently processing. In this case, we may evenly split the task range into subranges and assign them to different computing threads.

Therefore, in the task queue, it is sufficient to use $\langle \ell, [a, b] \rangle$ to denote a batch of tasks at level-ℓ and with range $[a, b]$, and this is the basic unit to be fetched by computing threads for processing (though the batch can be split to create new batches for fetching when another thread is idle).

Task Initialization. From level 1, we keeps partition the pivot task at each level until when a newly-generated pivot task has an empty graph. Let the last level be ℓ_{max}, then this task initialization approach generates ℓ_{max} group of minor tasks. Figure 2 illustrates this task generation process.

Table 2. Dataset sizes and properties

Dataset	n	m	$d(v_1)$	$k(G)$	$c(G)$
Google	875713	4322051	6353	44	44
Youtube	1134890	2987624	28754	51	17
Patents	3774768	16518947	793	64	11
Flixster	2523386	7918801	1474	68	31
Skitter	1696415	11095298	35455	111	67
Wiki	2394385	4659565	100032	131	26

3.3 Task Computation

As long as the task queue Q is not empty, a computing thread will keep dequeueing a batch of minor tasks $\langle \ell, [a, b] \rangle$ from Q for computation. The thread will compute the tasks within the range $[a, b]$ one by one. Each task is computed by a serial recursive counting/list algorithm, which consumes a stable and small amount of memory as the search space tree is traversed in a depth-first manner.

Subgraph Construction. The pivot tasks' subgraphs $G_1, G_2, ..., G_{\ell_{max}}$ are kept in the memory after task partitioning, so that computing threads can read them whenever needed. The subgraph of a level-ℓ (minor) task can thus be incrementally constructed from $G_{\ell-1}$ for serial processing, rather than constructed from scratch from G. We remark that the former is faster since we only need to examine a smaller graph (and thus less edges/adjacency list items).

4 Performance Evaluation

This section evaluates the performance of the various algorithms on top of parallel framework using large real graph datasets. All the experiments were run on a Linux server with 40 3 GHz CPU cores and 32 GB memory. The programs were written in C++ and compiled with GCC.

For quasi-clique listing, we use parameters $\gamma = 0.8$ and $s = k(G)$ (i.e., G's core number), which essentially finds quasi-cliques from the $\gamma(s - 1)$-core of G. We report computation time in the unit of seconds.

Datasets. We used 6 graph datasets in our experiments as shown in Table 2, which correspond to different types of real-world networks.

Specifically, *Google* [1] is a web graph of Google; *Youtube* [2] is the social network of Youtube users and their connections; *Patents* [3] is the US Patent citation network; *Flixster* [4] is the social network of a movie rating site; *Skitter* [5] is an Internet topology graph; and finally, *Wiki* [6] is a user communication network from Wikipedia.

In Table 2, $d(v_1)$ means the maximum degree, $k(G)$ means the core number, and $c(G)$ means the size of the maximum clique. The datasets are listed in ascending order of their core numbers $k(G)$.

Table 3. The computation cost

Problem	Dataset	Original	Static	Dynamic
Triangle counting	Google	52.86	42.76	**40.03**
	Youtube	64.74	41.07	**38.23**
	Patents	223.32	214.82	**182.26**
	Flixster	181.86	135.34	**119.70**
	Skitter	312.54	210.47	**189.48**
	Wiki	174.88	86.70	**78.90**
Clique counting	Google	66.72	67.84	**63.75**
	Youtube	47.53	47.26	**45.64**
	Patents	190.76	173.27	**155.68**
	Flixster	285.04	238.15	**189.00**
	Skitter	3052.21	2868.00	**2759.43**
	Wiki	2949.47	2823.36	**2179.24**
Maximal clique listing	Google	210.37	**203.82**	211.82
	Youtube	188.20	**185.88**	186.74
	Patents	593.28	**601.10**	606.32
	Flixster	1201.00	1055.19	**905.90**
	Skitter	8287.91	8348.78	**7590.01**
	Wiki	10619.76	10160.41	**7973.61**
Quasi-clique listing	Google	47840.84	**47532.52**	48344.17
	Youtube	**62716.50**	75432.17	65563.62
	Wiki	126553.08	94453.64	**82456.81**

4.1 Experiments on Vertex Ordering Schemes

We first conduct experiments to compare different vertex ordering schemes. For each problem and each dataset, we run a single-threaded program with each of our 3 proposed ordering schemes "original order", "static degree", and "dynamic degree", respectively (c.f. Sect. 3.1). The ordering is adjusted by moving the pivot vertex and its neighbors ahead.

Table 3 reports the computation time of various problems on various datasets using the 3 schemes. We do not report the time of quasi-clique listing on *Patents*, *Flixster* and *Skitter* since they ran over 48 h due to the giant search space [17] and are thus killed.

From Table 3, we can see that the dynamic degree ordering scheme (along with pivot vertex reordering) is a clear and consistent winner, and therefore we adopt this vertex ordering scheme in the following experiments.

Comparison with Existing Work on Clique Counting. The works of [10, 11] proposed an algorithm called FFF_k for counting cliques with small sizes k.

Table 4. Comparison on clique counting

Dataset	FFF_7	Our algorithm	Speedup
Google	**48.62**	70.82	0.69
Youtube	**38.33**	54.10	0.71
Patents	**105.62**	186.21	0.57
Flixster	458.68	**246.38**	1.86
Skitter	5491.22	**2890.53**	2.20
Wiki	4220.07	**2832.20**	1.49

Table 5. Comparison on maximal clique listing

Dataset	Existing approach	Our approach	Speedup
Google	361.07	**244.30**	1.48
Youtube	236.90	**217.01**	1.09
Patents	**769.63**	780.18	0.99
Flixster	1146.16	**972.42**	1.18
Skitter	9571.65	**7693.29**	1.24
Wiki	9676.89	**8017.03**	1.21

The ordering scheme they used is essentially the static degree ordering defined in our Sect. 3.1 (without pivot vertex reordering).

To explore whether pivot vertex reordering reduces the workload, we compare our clique counting algorithm with FFF_k. Since the largest k used in their experiments is $k = 7$, we run our clique counting algorithm with static degree ordering plus pivot vertex reordering as an equivalence to FFF_7. Note that we are counting cliques with very large sizes up to $c(G) = 67$. The results are reported in Table 4, where we can see that our computation time is comparable to FFF_7 when the computation time is short, but much faster when the computation time is long, which justifies the need of pivot vertex reordering.

Comparison with Existing Work on Maximal Clique Listing. The work of [25,26] proposed an algorithm for maximal clique listing. They explored the static and dynamic degree ordering schemes described in our Sect. 3.1. They decompose the task into subtasks $M(G^-(v)) \oplus \{v\}$ for all $v \in V$, and for each subtask, they solve it using pivot vertex reordering. However, pivot vertex reordering is not performed on the root task $M(G)$, and it is interesting to see how this affects the amount of overall workloads.

Table 5 reports the computation time of our algorithm with/without root-task pivot vertex reordering, and we can see that after applying the pivot vertex reordering for the root task, the computation time is consistently improved.

Another problem with [25, 26] is that they do not support recursive partitioning of a pivot task which usually contains a lot of workloads needing parallel computation.

Table 6. Parallel computation on Wiki dataset

Problem	# of threads	1	2	4	8	16	32
Triangle counting	Time	78.89	39.49	21.86	11.09	7.35	5.83
	Speedup	1.00	2.00	3.61	7.12	10.74	13.53
Clique counting	Time	2179.24	1206.20	612.21	323.43	181.88	119.99
	Speedup	1.00	1.81	3.56	6.74	11.98	18.16
Maximal clique	Time	7973.61	4608.41	2311.60	1228.39	657.33	443.84
	Speedup	1.00	1.73	3.45	6.49	12.13	17.96
Quasi-clique	Time	82500.23	45493.54	24127.00	14223.90	8202.75	5139.22
	Speedup	1.00	1.81	3.42	5.80	10.06	16.05

4.2 Experiments on Parallel Computation

We now explore how our parallel framework scales up with the number of threads using various applications and datasets. We run our programs with 1, 2, 4, 8, 16 and 32 threads, respectively, for testing vertical scalability. We report both the computation time and speedup ratio (w.r.t. single-threaded execution). Dynamic degree ordering plus pivot vertex reordering is used for task partitioning in all the following experiments. Due to the space limitation, we only report the results on *Wiki* dataset.

Table 6 shows the computation time and the corresponding speedup ratio w.r.t. single-threaded execution. We can see that the speedup ratio increases near-linearly with the number of threads all the way till 16, but the increment of the speedup trend slows down when we run 32 threads, possibly because the overheads of task generation and fetching stand out compared with the significantly amortized task computation time. The increment of the speedups are similar for clique counting and quasi-clique listing. Overall, our framework demonstrates a near-optimal speedup.

Compared with maximal clique listing where the vertical scalability slows down at 32 threads, triangle counting slows down earlier at 16 threads mainly because the computing workloads of triangle counting is much lower than that of maximal clique listing, and thus the other overheads stand out sooner.

5 Conclusion

In this paper, we proposed a framework of task partitioning and workload balancing for triangle counting, clique counting, maximal clique listing and quasi-clique

listing. For task partitioning, we proposed pivot path partitioning, which recursively explores a node in the search tree which has the most heavily workload. For workload distribution, we dynamically balanced the workload by a work stealing strategy. Our experiments showed that our pivot path partitioning strategy reduced the total amount of work to be computed. We also demonstrated that our parallel executions have a almost ideal speedup ratio for up to 32 threads.

Acknowledgements. Yang and Zhou were supported by National Natural Science Foundation of China (NSFC) under grant No. U1636205, Yan and Guo were partially supported by NSF OAC-1755464 and NSF DGE-1723250.

References

1. https://snap.stanford.edu/data/web-Google.html
2. https://snap.stanford.edu/data/com-Youtube.html
3. https://snap.stanford.edu/data/cit-Patents.html
4. http://konect.uni-koblenz.de/networks/flixster
5. https://snap.stanford.edu/data/as-skitter.html
6. https://snap.stanford.edu/data/wiki-Talk.html
7. Blumofe, R.D., Leiserson, C.E.: Scheduling multithreaded computations by work stealing. J. ACM **46**(5), 720–748 (1999). https://doi.org/10.1145/324133.324234
8. Cheng, J., Zhu, L., Ke, Y., Chu, S.: Fast algorithms for maximal clique enumeration with limited memory. In: The 18th ACM SIGKDD International Conference on Knowledge Discovery and Data Mining, KDD 2012, Beijing, China, 12–16 August 2012, pp. 1240–1248 (2012). https://doi.org/10.1145/2339530.2339724
9. Du, N., Wu, B., Xu, L., Wang, B., Pei, X.: A parallel algorithm for enumerating all maximal cliques in complex network. In: Workshops Proceedings of the 6th IEEE International Conference on Data Mining (ICDM 2006), Hong Kong, China, 18–22 December 2006, pp. 320–324 (2006). https://doi.org/10.1109/ICDMW.2006.17
10. Finocchi, I., Finocchi, M., Fusco, E.G.: Counting small cliques in mapreduce. CoRR abs/1403.0734 (2014). http://arxiv.org/abs/abs/1403.0734
11. Finocchi, I., Finocchi, M., Fusco, E.G.: Clique counting in mapreduce: algorithms and experiments. ACM J. Exp. Algorithmics **20**, 1.7:1–1.7:20 (2015). https://doi.org/10.1145/2794080
12. Khosraviani, A., Sharifi, M.: A distributed algorithm for γ-quasi-clique extractions in massive graphs. In: Pichappan, P., Ahmadi, H., Ariwa, E. (eds.) INCT 2011. CCIS, vol. 241, pp. 422–431. Springer, Heidelberg (2011). https://doi.org/10.1007/978-3-642-27337-7_40
13. Kumpula, J.M., Kivela, M., Kaski, K., Saramaki, J.: Sequential algorithm for fast clique percolation. Phys. Rev. E Stat. Nonlinear Soft Matter Phys. **78**(2), 026109 (2008)
14. Matula, D.W., Beck, L.L.: Smallest-last ordering and clustering and graph coloring algorithms. J. ACM **30**(3), 417–427 (1983). https://doi.org/10.1145/2402.322385
15. McCune, R.R., Weninger, T., Madey, G.: Thinking like a vertex: a survey of vertex-centric frameworks for large-scale distributed graph processing. ACM Comput. Surv. **48**(2), 25:1–25:39 (2015). https://doi.org/10.1145/2818185
16. Michael, M.M., Scott, M.L.: Simple, fast, and practical non-blocking and blocking concurrent queue algorithms. In: Proceedings of the Fifteenth Annual ACM Symposium on Principles of Distributed Computing, Philadelphia, Pennsylvania, USA, 23–26 May 1996, pp. 267–275 (1996). https://doi.org/10.1145/248052.248106

17. Pardalos, P.M., Rebennack, S.: Computational challenges with cliques, quasi-cliques and clique partitions in graphs. In: Festa, P. (ed.) SEA 2010. LNCS, vol. 6049, pp. 13–22. Springer, Heidelberg (2010). https://doi.org/10.1007/978-3-642-13193-6_2

18. Pardalos, P.M., Xue, J.: The maximum clique problem. J. Global Optim. **4**(3), 301–328 (1994)

19. Ribeiro, P.M.P., Silva, F.M.A., Lopes, L.M.B.: Efficient parallel subgraph counting using G-tries. In: Proceedings of the 2010 IEEE International Conference on Cluster Computing, Heraklion, Crete, Greece, 20–24 September 2010, pp. 217–226 (2010). https://doi.org/10.1109/CLUSTER.2010.27

20. Schmidt, M.C., Samatova, N.F., Thomas, K., Park, B.: A scalable, parallel algorithm for maximal clique enumeration. J. Parallel Distrib. Comput. **69**(4), 417–428 (2009). https://doi.org/10.1016/j.jpdc.2009.01.003

21. Svendsen, M., Mukherjee, A.P., Tirthapura, S.: Mining maximal cliques from a large graph using mapreduce: tackling highly uneven subproblem sizes. J. Parallel Distrib. Comput. **79–80**, 104–114 (2015). https://doi.org/10.1016/j.jpdc.2014.08.011

22. Tsourakakis, C.E., Bonchi, F., Gionis, A., Gullo, F., Tsiarli, M.A.: Denser than the densest subgraph: extracting optimal quasi-cliques with quality guarantees. In: The 19th ACM SIGKDD International Conference on Knowledge Discovery and Data Mining, KDD 2013, Chicago, IL, USA, 11–14 August 2013, pp. 104–112 (2013). https://doi.org/10.1145/2487575.2487645

23. Wu, B., Yang, S., Zhao, H., Wang, B.: A distributed algorithm to enumerate all maximal cliques in mapreduce. In: Fourth International Conference on Frontier of Computer Science and Technology, FCST 2009, Shanghai, China, 17–19 December 2009, pp. 45–51 (2009). https://doi.org/10.1109/FCST.2009.30

24. Xiang, J., Guo, C., Aboulnaga, A.: Scalable maximum clique computation using mapreduce. In: 29th IEEE International Conference on Data Engineering, ICDE 2013, Brisbane, Australia, 8–12 April 2013, pp. 74–85 (2013). https://doi.org/10.1109/ICDE.2013.6544815

25. Xu, Y., Cheng, J., Fu, A.W.: Distributed maximal clique computation and management. IEEE Trans. Serv. Comput. **9**(1), 110–122 (2016). https://doi.org/10.1109/TSC.2015.2479225

26. Xu, Y., Cheng, J., Fu, A.W., Bu, Y.: Distributed maximal clique computation. In: 2014 IEEE International Congress on Big Data, Anchorage, AK, USA, 27 June–2 July 2014, pp. 160–167 (2014). https://doi.org/10.1109/BigData.Congress.2014.31

27. Yan, D., Bu, Y., Tian, Y., Deshpande, A.: Big graph analytics platforms. Found. Trends Databases **7**(1–2), 1–195 (2017). https://doi.org/10.1561/1900000056

Modal Schema Graphs for Graph Databases

Stephan Mennicke[✉]

Technische Universität Braunschweig, Institut für Informationssysteme,
Mühlenpfordtstraße 23, 38106 Braunschweig, Germany
mennicke@ifis.cs.tu-bs.de

Abstract. Although graph databases are conceived schema-less, additional knowledge about the data's structure and/or semantics is beneficial in many graph database management tasks, from efficient storage, over query optimization, up to data integration. Today's commonly used graph data models do not represent primal suspects regarding their lack of schema prior to data population. More than 20 years ago, also semistructured data has been introduced without an a-priori conceptual modeling phase. Neat models, called schema graphs, have been proposed and proven useful, yet heavily relying on the employed data model, which had been rooted labeled graphs. We generalize schema graphs in two respects: (1) Our notions are based on labeled graphs because the root node assumption is invalid in the spirit of modern graph data models. (2) We propose and study modal schema graphs to increase the expressive power of the original model. Modal schema graphs allow for (conditional) structural requirements without an otherwise necessary logical device. Furthermore, we elaborate on the consequences of our expressiveness enhancement with respect to applications and algorithmic complexity.

Keywords: Graph databases · Schema graphs · Modal specifications

1 Introduction

Since the early years, graph databases have been considered as *unstructured* or *semistructured* data collections, having no fixed schema before populating the database [2,5]. This allows for a flexible data integration by adding information at will and availability. The conceptual modeling process has, however, not vanished but is postponed to query formulation time, which has now to cope with issues regarding heterogeneity or even incompleteness [22,23]. Beyond query formulation, meta information about the data stored in a graph database has been considered useful for query decomposition and optimization [13,26], but also for data translation and integration [6].

The lack of schemata in semistructured data got the attention of Buneman et al., proposing *schema graphs* [2,8] to the rescue. They designed schema graphs as meta data for rooted labeled graphs, back then the prevalent graph data

© Springer Nature Switzerland AG 2019
A. H. F. Laender et al. (Eds.): ER 2019, LNCS 11788, pp. 498–512, 2019.
https://doi.org/10.1007/978-3-030-33223-5_41

model [1,7]. Conformance between graph databases and schema graphs forms the basis of object classification and the type of conformance they chose has excellent algorithmic properties. However, crucial to their methodology is the rooted data model, making schema graphs hardly a useful tool for today's graph data models [4,5]. The main obstacle is the existence of root nodes in both, data and schema graph. A node that reaches any other node in the graph via a directed path is called a *root node*. Such a node is only rarely observed in modern graph databases, except for those building on XML [2]. Generalizing the notions of schema graphs and schema graph conformance is, thus, the first goal of this paper (Sect. 3). Buneman et al.'s schema graphs express structural upper bounds, i.e., a schema limits the allowed structure of a database instance but cannot enforce certain key properties [2,8]. Therefore, our second goal is to extend schema graphs in a conservative fashion (Sect. 4) and analyze its consequences w.r.t. expressive power and complexity (Sect. 5).

We contribute *knowledge graph*-ready schema graphs, preserving as many as possible properties from the *schema graphs* presented more than 20 years ago for semistructured data. Furthermore, we directly integrate so-called *key properties* [22,23], that are edges required by a database instance of a given schema, an aspect that was missing in [8]. We employ the well-established theory of *modal specifications* [18] to distinguish allowed from required structure in an integrated schema model. While may and must modalities allow us to formulate quite flexible schema graphs, deciding schema subsumption, i.e., whether one schema is more specific than another one w.r.t. their database instances, becomes intractable [19]. We still identify a prominent subclass of schema graphs with tractable subsumption, namely *deterministic schema graphs* [26], and define the precise semantics of the resulting model.

Of course there are other proposals adding and using schema knowledge for graph databases. Calvanese et al. extend schema graphs of [8] to overcome some limitations, including a form of requirement expressions [9]. They use description logics to complement a single schema graph, also enabling for certain cardinality constraints. They stay, however, in the realm of tree-shaped graph data and spend a lot of effort in extending the labeling alphabet. In contrast, we stay inside a simple yet flexible graphical formalism by introducing a second type of edges to reach the desired expressiveness. Abiteboul et al. highlight that a logical system, like Datalog or description logics, is capable of expressing many more constraints, even those not classifying as pure schema information [2]. Annotative extensions of RDF, e.g., RDF schema [25], may be used to provide meta data, but such annotations do not reflect on the graph data's internal structure. *Data guides* use a summary-based approach [14]. After the database has been populated, they try to derive a summary of the link structure, useful for navigating through the data. Such summaries have recently been exploited as indexing structures for semistructured data [27].

A large corpus of literature and technologies has been forged around the *pattern matching* technology. Akhtar et al. formalize the concept of functional dependencies as well as equality generating dependencies for RDF [3]. At the

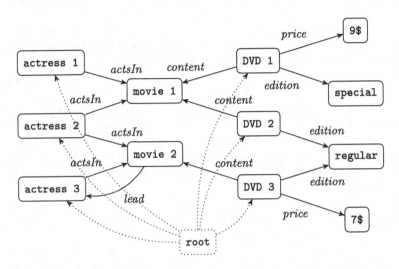

Fig. 1. A movie and DVD product graph database sample

core, they employ graph patterns that are matched against a database, i.e., graph-homomorphic instances are obtained, and then evaluated towards semantic properties like keys or functional dependencies. Also Fan et al. [10,12] created a matching-based method for keys and dependencies, incorporating literals and recursive key constraints. The W3C recommends shapes (graph patterns) and constraints to express the semantics of graph (RDF) data, which has resulted in SHACL [17]. SHACL's validation, as well as the other proposals, have a schema graph pattern that is matched against the database. Besides intractable validation [10,12], this methodology automatically requires every edge present in the schema also to be present in the database. In contrast, schema graphs here and 20 years ago are rather thought of as specifying allowed structures [8] by simply exchanging the direction of validation, now called *conformance*. This means that a graph database is matched against the schema, implementing a natural notion of *allowed structure*. Only some *key properties* are required, which we picture here by means of a modal extension.

2 Graph Data Models

In consideration of the wide variety of graph data models [5,15], we choose *directed edge-labeled graphs*, or simply *labeled graphs*, $G = (V, \Sigma, E)$. V is a finite set of nodes, Σ a finite labeling alphabet, and $E \subseteq V \times \Sigma \times V$ the directed and labeled edge relation of G. We use $v \xrightarrow{a}_G w$ as a shorthand for $(v, a, w) \in E$. A sequence of nodes, $\pi = v_0 v_1 \ldots v_{k-1} v_k \in V^+$ ($k \in \mathbb{N}$), is a *path between* v_0 and v_k if there are $a_1, a_2, \ldots, a_k \in \Sigma$, such that $v_{i-1} \xrightarrow{a_i}_G v_i$ or $v_i \xrightarrow{a_i}_G v_{i-1}$ ($1 \le i \le k$). π is a *directed path from* v_0 *to* v_k if only forwards edges $v_{i-1} \xrightarrow{a_i} v_i$ ($1 \le i \le k$) are used. We say that v_k is *reachable from* v_0 if there is a directed

path from v_0 to v_k. The set of all reachable nodes from v_0 is denoted $\mathcal{R}_G(v_0)$. G is *connected* iff for any two nodes $v, w \in V$, there is a path between v and w.

We call a labeled graph $G = (V, \Sigma, E)$ a *rooted labeled graph* if there is a (root) node $r \in V$ such that $\mathcal{R}_G(r) = V$, i.e., every node in G is reachable from r. Sometimes, a rooted labeled graph is denoted $G = (V, \Sigma, E, r)$, where $r \in V$ is the designated root node of G. By a *(rooted) graph database DB* we understand a (rooted) labeled graph (O_{DB}, Σ, E_{DB}) that collects some objects as the set of nodes $O_{DB} \neq \emptyset$ and relates them via directed and labeled edges. Consider our small graph database sample depicted in Fig. 1. The database objects are movies, actresses, products, or product-related attribute values. Relations range from *actsIn*, a relationship symbol usually relating actresses to movies they acted in, over *content*, which here relates DVD products to its movie contents, up to *price* and *edition*, which associates products (DVDs) with their prices and editions. The dotted graph database part mimics an artificial root node, making the overall graph rooted. Node `root` reaches any other node. We dispense a concrete labeling of the edges from the root node.

3   Schema Graphs: Then and Now

Figure 2 depicts a schema graph for the rooted graph database in Fig. 1. Note that the schema graph possesses a root node, but otherwise may contain cycles, just as rooted graph databases. Database instances are required to exhibit a *similar structure* as the schema graph. Thereby, the schema graph represents a structural upper bound. If we removed the edge, labeled by *content*, between the types DVD and MOVIE, the graph in Fig. 1 would no longer be an instance of the resulting

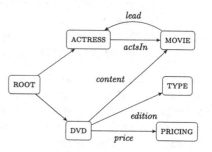

Fig. 2. A rooted schema graph following Abiteboul et al. [2]

schema graph since every DVD node has an edge to some movie node, labeled by *content*. If we removed the edge, labeled by *lead*, between MOVIE and ACTRESS, our graph database would still conform to the schema graph with the side-effect that `actress 3` does not conform to ACTRESS according to this schema.

Schema graphs have been developed in light of tree-shaped graph databases, as apparent in XML document collections. Hence, also *schema graphs* were defined as rooted labeled graphs $S = (T_S, \Pi, E_S, r_S)$, where the elements of T_S are called *types* and Π is a special alphabet containing first-order sentences [8]. These first-order sentences allow a single labeled edge to describe many different actual labels in Σ. For instance, suppose we have an edge $v \xrightarrow{ev(x)} w$ with the predicate label $ev(x)$ that evaluates to `true` whenever an *even number* is given as x. The only restriction, Π must obey, has been to include predicates from a decidable first-order theory [8]. We exclude this extension since the obstacles

of schema graphs migrating from rooted to general graphs are not found in the chosen labeling alphabet.

By design, a schema graph describes the permitted structure but cannot likewise enforce certain substructures [2]. For instance, the schema graph in Fig. 2 allows for linking products to their movie contents, but does not enforce this edge. Conversely, if an edge is not present in the schema graph, it must not exist in the respective database. More precisely, a database object conforms only to a type forbidding a property if itself does not exhibit it. Assessing this notion of *graph database instances* is based on *schema graph conformance*. Buneman et al. define that a graph database DB conforms to schema graph S, denoted $DB \preccurlyeq S$, iff there is a *rooted simulation between DB and S* [8]. A rooted simulation between two rooted labeled graphs $DB = (O_{DB}, \Sigma, E_{DB}, r_{DB})$ and $S = (T_S, \Sigma, E_S, r_S)$ is a binary relation $R \subseteq O_{DB} \times T_S$, such that (i) the roots are related by R, i.e., $(r_{DB}, r_S) \in R$, and (ii) for all $(p, q) \in R$, if $p \xrightarrow{a}_{DB} p'$, then there is a node $q' \in V_S$ with $q \xrightarrow{a}_S q'$ and $(p', q') \in R$. These simulations not only provide upper bounds to the structure of graph database instances, but also come with PTIME algorithms for their evaluation [16]. A rooted simulation between the graph database in Fig. 1 and the schema graph in Fig. 2 is given by

$$
\widehat{R} = \left\{ \begin{array}{l}
(\texttt{root}, \text{ROOT}), (\texttt{actress 1}, \text{ACTRESS}), (\texttt{actress 2}, \text{ACTRESS}), \\
(\texttt{actress 3}, \text{ACTRESS}), (\texttt{movie 1}, \text{MOVIE}), (\texttt{movie 2}, \text{MOVIE}), \\
(\texttt{DVD 1}, \text{DVD}), (\texttt{DVD 2}, \text{DVD}), (\texttt{DVD 3}, \text{DVD}), (\texttt{special}, \text{TYPE}), \\
(\texttt{regular}, \text{TYPE}), (\texttt{7\$}, \text{PRICING}), (\texttt{9\$}, \text{PRICING})
\end{array} \right\}.
$$

Crucial to Buneman et al.'s conformance notion is the existence and placement of root nodes. Without condition (i), the empty simulation (i.e., $R_\emptyset = \emptyset$) would always establish a viable witness for conformance. In the realm of general graph databases we miss designated root nodes and, thus, must be careful when adopting the existing notions. Introducing artificial roots to graph databases or schemas appears infeasible, as for instance, update anomalies are foreseeable: whenever the graph database is subject to change, the root node's incidence must be adjusted accordingly. Fortunately, integrating a small feature of root nodes, namely keeping the graph connected, to the schema-side suffices. This makes our methodology applicable to existing graph databases as we do not impose any change upon them.

Definition 1 (Schema Graph). *A labeled graph* $S = (T_S, \Sigma, E_S)$ *is a* schema graph *if S is a connected graph and $T_S \neq \emptyset$.*

From a formal perspective, types in T_S are chosen arbitrarily, i.e., with no special structure in mind. From a practical point of view, they will follow a *universe of discourse*-kind of argument. Since $T_S \neq \emptyset$, every schema graph S has at least one type, but may have an empty structure. Connectedness of schema graphs will guarantee meaningful (i.e., non-empty) simulations witnessing conformance, even transitively. However, we still have to cope with an important aspect of graph simulations: they are insensitive to leaf nodes. Consider the node 7\$ in Fig. 1, being a leaf node as there are no outgoing edges from 7\$. The desired type

of 7\$ is PRICING, which is verified by the simulation $\widehat{R}$ above. However, every leaf node, especially 7\$, can be simulated by every type of the schema graph, making 7\$ an object of type MOVIE, DVD, or even ROOT. The reason is that 7\$ has no outgoing edges which implies that every type automatically fulfills (ii). What makes 7\$ an object of type PRICING is the incoming edge labeled *price*.

We observe that adopting the reachability characteristic of root nodes from rooted graphs is a crucial requirement when it comes to assessing conformance. To meet the requirement, it suffices to also consider edges going backwards from nodes in the graph database, which excludes situations as described for 7\$. Fortunately, simulations can easily be adapted to also consider edges going backwards from nodes to be simulated, without losing their algorithmic properties [21].

Definition 2 (Schema Graph Conformance). *Let* $S = (T_S, \Sigma, E_S)$ *be a schema graph. A graph database* $DB = (O_{DB}, \Sigma, E_{DB})$ *is an instance of* S, *denoted* $DB \preccurlyeq S$, *iff there is a non-empty dual simulation between* DB *and* S, *that is a binary relation* $R \subseteq O_{DB} \times T_S$ *such that for every* $(p, q) \in R$, *(i)* $p \xrightarrow{a}_{DB} p'$ *implies* $a\ q' \in T_S$ *with* $q \xrightarrow{a}_S q'$ *and* $(p', q') \in R$, *and (ii)* $p' \xrightarrow{a}_{DB} p$ *implies* $a\ q' \in T_S$ *with* $q' \xrightarrow{a}_S q$ *and* $(p', q') \in R$. *We call* R *a* conformance witness *between* DB *and* S.

An empty-structured graph database DB with at least one object trivially conforms to any schema graph. Conversely, every graph database conforms to the *unit schema graph*, that is a schema graph with a single node and a Σ-self loop, as depicted in Fig. 3. Type U simulates every object of a database, indicated by the self-loop labeled by Σ, which is a wildcard for any label $a \in \Sigma$. Hence, the unit schema graph may be a good start when designing a schema for graph data from scratch.

By *schema graph conformance* we have an answer of how to assess whether a graph database is an instance of a given schema pattern. But, based on conformance, how can we use the information for a classification of objects in the database? To this end, we give a similar answer as given by Abiteboul et al.

Fig. 3. The unit schema graph

[2]. An object o of DB is of type $t \in T_S$ (of schema graph S) iff there is a conformance witness R between DB and S with $(o, t) \in R$. The indicated simulation $\widehat{R}$, given above, types all actresses in Fig. 1 by ACTRESS. This approach to classification is, however, not too practical since there may be (exponentially) many conformance witnesses, especially in a big data setting. Having to look through all of them may become quite a cumbersome task. Fortunately, (dual) simulations possess the property of being union-closed [21], entailing a unique maximal dual simulation between a graph database DB and a schema graph S. Thus, this property transfers to conformance witnesses as they are non-empty dual simulations.

Proposition 1 (Proposition 2.1 in [21]). *Let* $DB \preccurlyeq S$. *There is a unique maximal conformance witness* $\widehat{R}$ *between* DB *and* S.

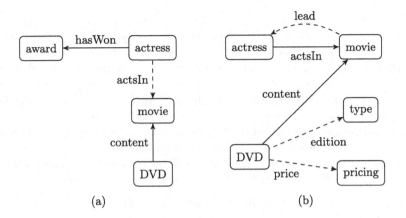

Fig. 4. Two modal schema graphs

The proof of the result demonstrates that the maximal conformance witness $\widehat{R}$ subsumes every other conformance witness R. Hence, in order to get an object classification for database object o, we compute the maximal conformance witness $\widehat{R}$, which can be done in polynomial time, e.g., by HHK [16] or our solution [24], and obtain from $\widehat{R}$ the set of all types $t \in T_S$, o conforms to.

Definition 3 (Object Classification). *Let $DB = (O_{DB}, \Sigma, E_{DB})$ be a graph database instance of the schema graph $S = (T_S, \Sigma, E_S)$, i.e., $DB \preccurlyeq S$. The maximal conformance witness between DB and S, denoted by $\vdash_S^{DB}$, is the object classification induced by S onto DB. We write $o \vdash_S^{DB} t$ if $(o, t) \in \vdash_S^{DB}$.*

Additionally to the structures that are allowed by a schema graph, everything that is not captured is automatically forbidden. Suppose in the graph in Fig. 4(b) we removed all dashed edges. Then our graph database no longer conforms to the resulting schema since for every DVD object, information about PRICING or TYPE is provided. For instance, object DVD 1 cannot be simulated by DVD because the type does not exhibit a *price*-labeled edge. Beyond allowed and forbidden structure, there is another aspect, even Buneman et al. wished to express, that are *key properties* [8]. Key properties are those that are required by the schema in order to assign a certain type to an object in the database. To increase their expressive power, we introduce modalities to schema graphs.

4   Modal Schema Graphs

Abiteboul et al. highlight that schema graphs usually only cover so-called *If* constraints on the data [2]. But certain types also require to have entities described by *key properties*. For instance, representing a book may not require to capture authors or title of the pieces, but certainly the ISBN is crucial for many bibliographic tasks. In light of our DVD movie database example, PRICING or

TYPE may be optional, but the DVDs' *content* is not. So far, schema graphs are not capable of requiring the presence of such properties. Abiteboul et al. sketch *dual schema graphs* [2] capturing a core structure to be exhibited by any graph database instance. Unfortunately dual schema graphs are again rooted graphs, making it impossible to express conditional key properties. Consider the graph depicted in Fig. 4(a) and suppose, we are still interested in the typing of DVD and MOVIE by requiring the *content* edge between these two types. This time, we specialize to those DVD movies, whose actresses have won some award, but only if an actress is listed at all. In the dual schema graph, we also had to enforce the existence of ACTRESS in order to require *hasWon*.

We aim for a more flexible model that allows us to formulate graph requirements altogether with allowed structures in a single model. We achieve the desired flexibility by employing the theory of *modal specifications*, initially introduced by Larsen and Thomsen [18]. They aimed for a system description language that captures the behavior of a variety of implementations [20]. This view is quite comparable to ours since schema graphs can be seen as modal specifications and graph databases as their implementations. Larsen and Thomsen employ a may/must dichotomy, translating to *allowed* and *required* system behavior. We use the same dichotomy in our extended schema graph model to capture allowed and required graph structure.

Definition 4 (Modal Schema Graph (MSG)). $S = (T_S, \Sigma, E_S^\Diamond, E_S^\Box)$ *is a modal schema graph (MSG) iff* $(T_S, \Sigma, E_S^\Diamond)$ *is a schema graph and* $E_S^\Box \subseteq E_S^\Diamond$.

We write $v \xrightarrow{a}_S^\Diamond w$ for $(v, a, w) \in E_S^\Diamond$ and $v \xrightarrow{a}_S^\Box w$ for $(v, a, w) \in E_S^\Box$. We have depicted two MSGs in Fig. 4, where may edges are dashed and must edges are solid edges. The may modality ($\Diamond$) is thought of as expressing the allowed structures, the same way as schema graphs do (cf. Definition 1), while the must modality ($\Box$) encodes required edges. In fact, every schema graph $S = (T_S, \Sigma, E_S)$ is an MSG $(T_S, \Sigma, E_S, \emptyset)$. The requirement that $E_S^\Box \subseteq E_S^\Diamond$ is called *syntactic consistency* and owes to the intuition that required structure must be allowed. Other than syntactic consistency, may and must edges are free to be used throughout the whole graph. Thereby, we achieve a flexible integration of schema graphs and (generalized) dual schema graphs.

Conformance between databases and MSGs must obey the may/must dichotomy. The graph database in Fig. 1 does not conform to Fig. 4(a) since every movie object has an associated actress, but awards have not been captured at all. The database does conform to Fig. 4(b) as every edge in the graph database is allowed and every required edge is also present. If we considered the *lead* as a must edge, then the database in Fig. 1 would still conform to the resulting MSG because of actress 3, movie 2, and DVD 3. The other actresses and movies are untypable by the altered MSG. Hence, while for may edges we follow the principles of Sect. 3, must edges of an MSG are simulated by the graph database, resulting in an alternating-style of dual simulation.

Definition 5 (MSG Conformance). *For an MSG* $S = (T_S, \Sigma, E_S^\Diamond, E_S^\Box)$ *and a graph database* $DB = (O_{DB}, \Sigma, E_{DB})$, *DB is an instance of* S, *denoted* $DB \preccurlyeq_m S$,

iff there is a conformance witness R between DB and $(T_S, \Sigma, E_S^\Diamond)$ such that for all $(p,q) \in R$, (i) $q \xrightarrow{a}{}_S^\Box q'$ implies $\exists p' \in O_{DB} : p \xrightarrow{a}{}_{DB} p' \wedge (p', q') \in R$ and (ii) $q' \xrightarrow{a}{}_S^\Box q$ implies $\exists p' \in O_{DB} : p' \xrightarrow{a}{}_{DB} p \wedge (p', q') \in R$. We call R a modal conformance witness *between* DB and S.

Items (i) and (ii) ensure that whatever structure is required is actually material-ized in a database instance of the given MSG. The may/must dichotomy implies three different aspects, now covered in a simple integrated model: allowed, required, as well as forbidden structure. Database object classification is per-formed using the same principles as given by Definition 3, justified by a similar result as Proposition 1. The following results are direct consequences of Defini-tion 5.

Lemma 1. *Let* $S = (T_S, \Sigma, E_S^\Diamond, E_S^\Box)$ *be an* MSG. *(I)* $(T_S, \Sigma, E_S^\Diamond) \preccurlyeq_m S$ *and (II)* $DB \preccurlyeq_m S$ *implies* $DB \preccurlyeq (T_S, \Sigma, E_S^\Diamond)$.

(I) follows from syntactic consistency by using the identity function on T_S as modal conformance witness. (II) is implied by the fact that a modal conformance witness R is a conformance witness.

5 Expressive Power

So far, we only considered conformance and object classification. Since a single graph database may conform to more than one schema graph, we want to assess when one schema graph is more specific than another. According to Buneman et al., these and other questions may be answered considering the semantics a schema graph. In their case, the set of all graph database instances of the schema S formed their semantics [8], defined for MSG S by

$$[\![S]\!] := \{DB \mid DB \preccurlyeq_m S\}. \tag{1}$$

Schema S_2 is, thus, more general than schema S_1 if $[\![S_1]\!] \subseteq [\![S_2]\!]$. Consequently, S_1 and S_2 are equivalent if $[\![S_1]\!] = [\![S_2]\!]$. This section is dedicated to finding sufficient conditions to characterizing these inclusions for MSGs, in favor of a tractable decision procedure. Therefore, we exploit the concept of conformance ($\preccurlyeq_m$) in a more general context, namely in terms of *refinement* between schemata [8]. MSG conformance naturally extends to refinement between MSGs, which we can employ for (partially) deciding subsumption as well as equivalence. Compared to MSG conformance, now both input models contain must edges. Hence, in $S_1 \preccurlyeq_m S_2$, S_1 must not exceed what is allowed by S_2. Conversely, S_1 cannot forbid what is required by S_2.

Definition 6 (MSG Refinement). *Let* $S_i = (T_i, \Sigma, E_i^\Diamond, E_i^\Box)$ *(i = 1, 2) be* MSGs. S_1 *refines* S_2, *denoted* $S_1 \preccurlyeq_m S_2$, *iff there is a non-empty dual simu-lation* R *between* $(T_1, \Sigma, E_1^\Diamond)$ *and* $(T_2, \Sigma, E_2^\Diamond)$, *such that for* $(p,q) \in R$, *(i) if* $q \xrightarrow{a}{}_2^\Box q'$, *then there is a* $p' \in V_1$ *with* $p \xrightarrow{a}{}_1^\Box p'$ *and* $(p',q') \in R$ *and (ii) if* $q' \xrightarrow{a}{}_2^\Box q$, *then there is a* $p' \in V_1$ *with* $p' \xrightarrow{a}{}_1^\Box p$ *and* $(p',q') \in R$. *We call* R *a* modal refinement witness *between* S_1 *and* S_2.

Note that, except for (i) and (ii), MSG refinement requires conformance between S_1 and S_2, ignoring their must edges (cf. Definition 2). MSG refinement coincides with a dual simulation version of modal refinement [18,20], except for the presence of root nodes. As a consequence, $\preccurlyeq_m$ is not in general a preorder between graphs exhibiting modalities. The reason is that, although the concatenation of (modal) refinement/conformance witnesses R_1 and R_2 is guaranteed to be a dual simulation [21], $R_1 \circ R_2$ may be empty, disqualifying it as a refinement/conformance witness. As we require modal schema graphs to be connected, $R_1 \circ R_2$ is guaranteed to yield a non-empty dual simulation. This is what we prove in the following soundness result for MSGs and their instances.

Lemma 2. *Let S_1, S_2 be MSGs. If $S_1 \preccurlyeq_m S_2$, then $[\![S_1]\!] \subseteq [\![S_2]\!]$.*

Proof. Let $S_i = (T_i, \Sigma, E_i^\Diamond, E_i^\Box)$ $(i = 1, 2)$ and $DB \preccurlyeq_m S_1$ by conformance witness R_1 and $S_1 \preccurlyeq_m S_2$ by refinement witness R_2. We need to show that $R_1 \circ R_2$ is a modal conformance witness between DB and S_2. Since, R_1 and R_2 are dual simulations, $R_1 \circ R_2$ is guaranteed to be a dual simulation. It remains to be shown that (I) it is non-empty and (II) obeys the requirements of Definition 5.

Let us first tackle (II) and pick any $(u, w) \in R_1 \circ R_2$ with $w \xrightarrow{a \ \Box}_{S_2} w'$ ($w' \xrightarrow{a \ \Box}_{S_2} w$, analogously). By construction, there is some $v \in T_1$ with $(u, v) \in R_1$ and $(v, w) \in R_2$. As R_2 is a modal refinement witness, there must be a $v' \in T_1$ with $v \xrightarrow{a \ \Box}_{S_1} v'$ and $(v', w') \in R_2$. As R_1 is a modal conformance witness, there is a $u' \in O_{DB}$ with $u \xrightarrow{a}_{DB} u'$ and $(u', v') \in R_1$. Thus, $(u', w') \in R_1 \circ R_2$.

Towards a contradicition of (I), assume $R_1 \circ R_2 = \emptyset$, which is only possible if for every pair $(u, v) \in R_1$, there is no matching pair $(v, w) \in R_2$. Let $(u, v) \in R_1$. Since $R_2 \neq \emptyset$, there is at least one pair, say $(v_0, w_0) \in R_2$. We show that for every path $\pi = v_0 v_1 \ldots v_k$, there is a $w_k \in T_2$ such that $(v_k, w_k) \in R_2$. Thus, non-existence of w with $(v, w) \in R_2$ implies that S_1 is disconnected, contradicting the assumption that S_1 is an MSG. By induction on the length of π.

Base: For $\pi = v_0$, we have $(v_0, w_0) \in R_2$ by assumption.

Step: Let $\pi = v_0 v_1 \ldots v_n$ be a path between v_0 and v_n. Then $\pi = \pi' \cdot v_n$ with $\pi' = v_0 v_1 \ldots v_{n-1}$. By induction hypothesis, there is a $w_{n-1} \in T_2$ such that $(v_{n-1}, w_{n-1}) \in R_2$. As π is a path, either $v_{n-1} \xrightarrow{a \ \Diamond}_{S_1} v_n$ or $v_n \xrightarrow{a \ \Diamond}_{S_1} v_{n-1}$. Since R_2 is a modal refinement witness, there is a $w_n \in T_2$ with $w_{n-1} \xrightarrow{a \ \Diamond}_{S_2} w_n$ ($w_n \xrightarrow{a \ \Diamond}_{S_2} w_{n-1}$, resp.) and $(v_n, w_n) \in R_2$.

Hence, there is a $w \in T_2$ with $(v, w) \in R_2$, implying $R_1 \circ R_2 \neq \emptyset$. □

Hence, there is a sound schema refinement process as follows. Start with some initial modal schema S_0 and refine it to $S_1, S_2, \ldots, S_k$ $(k \in \mathbb{N})$ with $S_i \preccurlyeq S_{i-1}$ $(1 \leq i \leq k)$ with the guarantee that $[\![S_j]\!] \subseteq [\![S_i]\!]$ $(1 \leq i < j \leq k)$.

Unfortunately, there are MSGs S_1 and S_2 with $[\![S_1]\!] \subseteq [\![S_2]\!]$ but $S_1 \npreccurlyeq_m S_2$. This is a well-known problem inherited from modal refinement. Every refinement notion fixing it would turn the refinement problem into an intractable one [19]. The modal schema graphs depicted in Fig. 5 are adapted and extended versions

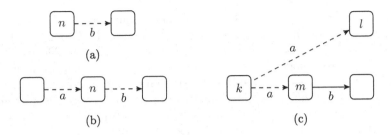

Fig. 5. Completeness counterexample of modal refinement

of the counterexample given by Larsen et al. [19] as the original counterexample cannot cope with the dual simulation aspect of MSG refinement. Let S_1 be a schema graph according to Fig. 5(b) and S_2 to Fig. 5(c). Of course $S_1 \npreceq_m S_2$ since in any refinement witness R must contain (n, m). But m requires b whereas n has only a b-labeled may edge. Nevertheless, it holds that $[\![S_1]\!] \subseteq [\![S_2]\!]$ because databases conforming to S_1, that do not include a b-labeled edge, also conform to S_2 by exploiting the non-determinism in node k. Node l perfectly simulates every node with an incoming a-labeled but missing outgoing b-labeled edge.

Excluding non-determinism as apparent in Fig. 5(c) does, unfortunately, not suffice to evade all non-determinism. Consider now S_1 to be Fig. 5(a), and take S_2 as before. Also $S_1 \npreceq_m S_2$ but again $[\![S_1]\!] \subseteq [\![S_2]\!]$. The reason is that n must be simulated by m (impossible as m requires b), but when it comes to instances (of S_1) that solely consist of isolated nodes, S_2 may switch to node k to simulate isolated nodes. Here, the non-determinism is based on an arbitrary switch between the nodes that ought to simulate other schemata or their instances. Hence, (1) is not the semantics of MSGs up to $\preceq_m$.

We, nevertheless, provide a solution by requiring S_1 and S_2 to be *deterministic*, which excludes the first kind of non-determinism. In order to exclude the second type as well, we will introduce a single entrance type for S_1 and S_2, say x and y, and require the existence of a modal refinement witness R with $(x, y) \in R$. An edge relation $E \subseteq V \times \Sigma \times V$ is *deterministic* iff $v \xrightarrow{a} w_1$ ($w_1 \xrightarrow{a} v$, resp.) and $v \xrightarrow{a} w_2$ ($w_2 \xrightarrow{a} v$, resp.) implies $w_1 = w_2$.

Definition 7 (Deterministic MSG). *A quintuple $S[x] = (T_S, \Sigma, E_S^\Diamond, E_S^\Box, x)$ is a deterministic MSG iff $S = (T_S, \Sigma, E_S^\Diamond, E_S^\Box)$ is an MSG with $E_S^\Diamond$ is deterministic and $x \in T_S$. The set of all objects $o \in O_{DB}$ with $o \vdash_S^{DB} x$ is denoted by $S[x](DB)$. Let $S'[y]$ be another deterministic MSG. $S[x]$ refines $S'[y]$, denoted $S[x] \preceq_m^d S'[y]$, iff $S \preceq_m S'$ by modal refinement witness R with $(x, y) \in R$.*

For deterministic modal schema graphs, we are able to complete the theory of instances. Regarding our counterexamples, we make the fact, that node n types isolated nodes while node m is incapable of doing so, observable. Switching to node k in S_2 is allowed but the set of objects typed by m in a database with only isolated objects is empty.

Lemma 3. *Let $S_1[x], S_2[y]$ be deterministic MSGs. If for every instance $DB \preccurlyeq_m S_1$, $DB \preccurlyeq_m S_2$ and $S_1[x](DB) \subseteq S_2[y](DB)$, then $S_1[x] \preccurlyeq_m^d S_2[y]$.*

Proof. Let $S_1[x] = (T_1, \Sigma, E_1^\Diamond, E_2^\Box, x)$ and $DB_1 = (T_1, \Sigma, E_1^\Diamond)$. $DB_1 \preccurlyeq_m S_1$ (cf. Lemma 1), thus, $DB_1 \preccurlyeq_m S_2$ and $x \in S_2[y](DB_1)$ by assumption. Towards a contradiction, suppose $S_1[x] \npreccurlyeq_m^d S_2[y]$, i.e., there is no modal refinement witness R between S_1 and S_2 with $(x, y) \in R$. Hence, there are paths of minimal length, $\pi_1 = t_0 t_1 t_2 \ldots t_k$ of S_1 and $\pi_2 = u_0 u_1 u_2 \ldots u_k$ of S_2 ($k \geq 0$), such that (I) $t_0 = x$ and $u_0 = y$, (II) $t_{i-1} \xrightarrow{a_i}_{S_1}^\Diamond t_i$ and $u_{i-1} \xrightarrow{a_i}_{S_2}^\Diamond u_i$ ($0 < i \leq k$), but (III) for no $t \in T_1$, either $u_k \xrightarrow{a}_{S_2}^\Box u$ and $t_k \xrightarrow{a}_{S_1}^\Box t$, or $u \xrightarrow{a}_{S_2}^\Box u_k$ and $t \xrightarrow{a}_{S_1}^\Box t_k$. We construct $DB_{\it l}$ from π_1 as the smallest instance of S_1 that contains all the edges (t_{i-1}, a_i, t_i) used in (II). It holds that $DB_{\it l}$ contains the path π_1 with all its nodes, from x to t_k, with $x \in S_1[x](DB_{\it l})$, but neither an incoming a-edge to nor an outgoing a-edge from t_k. Note, $DB_{\it l}$ may contain more edges than the ones in (II) to preserve must structures incident to t_i ($0 \leq i \leq k$).

Because $S_1[x](DB_{\it l}) \subseteq S_2[y](DB_{\it l})$, the maximal modal conformance witness $\widehat{R}$ between $DB_{\it l}$ and $S_2[y]$ contains the element (x, y). Because $S_2[y]$ is deterministic, the only path of S_2, dual simulating π_1, is π_2. But $(t_k, u_k) \notin \widehat{R}$ because u_k requires an incoming/outgoing a-edge not present in $DB_{\it l}$. But then every prefix of π_1 cannot be simulated by a prefix of π_2. Hence, $(x, y) \notin \widehat{R}$ which contradicts the assumption that $S_1[x](DB) \subseteq S_2[y](DB)$ for all $DB \preccurlyeq_m S_1$.

Thus, $S_1[x] \preccurlyeq_m^d S_2[y]$ holds, given that all instances DB of S_1 are instances of S_2 with $S_1[x](DB) \subseteq S_2[y](DB)$. $\square$

Note that the proof only exploits $S_2[y]$ to be deterministic, enabling for an even stronger claim. However, as soon as we assess equivalence of $S_1[x]$ and $S_2[y]$, both need to be deterministic. Lemmas 2 and 3 culminate to the following characterization of modal refinement for deterministic MSGs.

Theorem 1. *Let $S_1[x], S_2[y]$ be deterministic MSGs. $S_1 \preccurlyeq_m^d S_2$ iff for all $DB \preccurlyeq_m S_1$, $DB \preccurlyeq_m S_2$ and $S_1[x](DB) \subseteq S_2[y](DB)$.*

Proof. Many of the claims are already proven by Lemmas 2 and 3. It remains to be shown that $S_1[x](DB) \subseteq S_2[y](DB)$ for all $DB \preccurlyeq_m S_1$ if $S_1[x] \preccurlyeq_m^d S_2[y]$. Let $DB \preccurlyeq_m S_1$ and $o \vdash_{S_1}^{DB} x$. As $S_1[x] \preccurlyeq_m^d S_2[y]$, there is a modal refinement witness R between S_1 and S_2, such that $(x, y) \in R$ (cf. Definition 7). Hence, following the proof of Lemma 2, $\vdash_{S_1}^{DB} \circ R$ is a conformance witness between DB and S_2. Thus, $\vdash_{S_1}^{DB} \circ R \subseteq \vdash_{S_2}^{DB}$ and, therefore, $o \vdash_{S_2}^{DB} y$. $\square$

This result reveals the assumed semantics of graph schemas (cf. (1)) as invalid for (deterministic) modal schema graphs. Additionally to the instances, we have to include the objects typed by the designated type of interest.

Definition 8 (MSG Semantics). *The semantics of deterministic MSGs $S[x]$ is defined by*

$$[\![S[x]]\!]_m := \{(DB, X) \mid DB \preccurlyeq_m S \wedge X = S[x](DB)\}. \tag{2}$$

6 Conclusions

We have revised the notion of *schema graphs* by Buneman et al. [2, 7] for today's exemplars of graph data, e.g., knowledge graphs. We generalized schema graph conformance to not requiring a root node in the graph database, without losing its properties, i.e., conformance checking as well as database object classification in PTIME. We integrated *key properties*, i.e., edges whose existence is required for typing, by means of the must modality of *modal specifications* [18]. Thereby, we do not leave the realm of PTIME conformance and object classification problems.

We found that the original notion of conformance, based on simulations, is not robust to small changes in the graph data model or the schema model. While removing the root node assumption did not entail harm to the theory, we found that adding modalities required a different perspective on the semantics of schema graphs. For deterministic MSGs, we were able to deliver a concise characterization of their semantics. A characterization of the semantics of general MSGs is left for future work.

Although conformance and object classification is in PTIME, it is not immediately clear how the existing algorithms scale with today's knowledge bases. We have some experience in dual simulation matching of patterns against databases for different query tasks, which can be done reasonably fast [24]. But schema graph conformance turns around the game since the database (usually large) fills the position of a query while the schema graph (smaller) provides us with matches. Furthermore, whenever nodes and/or edges are updated, possibly the whole classification must be recomputed [11].

References

1. Abiteboul, S.: Querying semi-structured data. In: Afrati, F., Kolaitis, P. (eds.) ICDT 1997. LNCS, vol. 1186, pp. 1–18. Springer, Heidelberg (1997). https://doi.org/10.1007/3-540-62222-5_33
2. Abiteboul, S., Buneman, P., Suciu, D.: Data on the Web: From Relations to Semistructured Data and XML. Morgan Kaufmann Publishers Inc., San Francisco (2000)
3. Akhtar, W., Cortés-Calabuig, Á., Paredaens, J.: Constraints in RDF. In: Schewe, K.-D., Thalheim, B. (eds.) SDKB 2010. LNCS, vol. 6834, pp. 23–39. Springer, Heidelberg (2011). https://doi.org/10.1007/978-3-642-23441-5_2
4. Angles, R., Arenas, M., Barceló, P., Hogan, A., Reutter, J., Vrgoč, D.: Foundations of modern query languages for graph databases. ACM Comput. Surv. **50**(5), 68:1–68:40 (2017). https://doi.org/10.1145/3104031
5. Angles, R., Gutierrez, C.: Survey of graph database models. ACM Comput. Surv. **40**(1), 1:1–1:3 (2008). https://doi.org/10.1145/1322432.1322433
6. Beeri, C., Milo, T.: Schemas for integration and translation of structured and semi-structured data. In: Beeri, C., Buneman, P. (eds.) ICDT 1999. LNCS, vol. 1540, pp. 296–313. Springer, Heidelberg (1999). https://doi.org/10.1007/3-540-49257-7_19
7. Buneman, P.: Semistructured data. In: Proceedings of the Sixteenth ACM SIGACT-SIGMOD-SIGART Symposium on Principles of Database Systems, PODS 1997, pp. 117–121. ACM, New York (1997). https://doi.org/10.1145/263661.263675

8. Buneman, P., Davidson, S., Fernandez, M., Suciu, D.: Adding structure to unstructured data. In: Afrati, F., Kolaitis, P. (eds.) ICDT 1997. LNCS, vol. 1186, pp. 336–350. Springer, Heidelberg (1997). https://doi.org/10.1007/3-540-62222-5_55

9. Calvanese, D., Giacomo, G.D., Lenzerini, M.: Extending semi-structured data. In: SEBD (1998)

10. Fan, W., Fan, Z., Tian, C., Dong, X.L.: Keys for graphs. Proc. VLDB Endow. **8**(12), 1590–1601 (2015). https://doi.org/10.14778/2824032.2824056

11. Fan, W., Hu, C., Tian, C.: Incremental graph computations: doable and undoable. In: Proceedings of the 2017 ACM International Conference on Management of Data, SIGMOD 2017, pp. 155–169. ACM, New York (2017). https://doi.org/10.1145/3035918.3035944

12. Fan, W., Lu, P.: Dependencies for graphs. In: Proceedings of the 36th ACM SIGMOD-SIGACT-SIGAI Symposium on Principles of Database Systems, PODS 2017, Chicago, IL, USA, 14–19 May 2017, pp. 403–416 (2017). https://doi.org/10.1145/3034786.3056114

13. Fernández, M.F., Suciu, D.: Optimizing regular path expressions using graph schemas. In: ICDE (1997). https://doi.org/10.1109/ICDE.1998.655753

14. Goldman, R., Widom, J.: Dataguides: enabling query formulation and optimization in semistructured databases. In: Proceedings of the 23rd International Conference on Very Large Data Bases, VLDB 1997, pp. 436–445. Morgan Kaufmann Publishers Inc., San Francisco (1997)

15. Gutiérrez, C., Hidders, J., Wood, P.T.: Graph data models. In: Sakr, S., Zomaya, A.Y. (eds.) Encyclopedia of Big Data Technologies, pp. 830–835. Springer, Cham (2019). https://doi.org/10.1007/978-3-319-77525-8_81

16. Henzinger, M., Henzinger, T., Kopke, P.: Computing simulations on finite and infinite graphs. In: FOCS 1995, pp. 453–462. IEEE Computer Society (1995). https://doi.org/10.1109/SFCS.1995.492576

17. Knublauch, H., Kontokostas, D.: Shapes constraint language (SHACL). W3C Recommendation (2017). https://www.w3.org/TR/shacl/

18. Larsen, K.G., Thomsen, B.: A modal process logic. In: Proceedings of the Third Annual Symposium on Logic in Computer Science, pp. 203–210 (1988). https://doi.org/10.1109/LICS.1988.5119

19. Larsen, K.G., Nyman, U., Wąsowski, A.: On modal refinement and consistency. In: Caires, L., Vasconcelos, V.T. (eds.) CONCUR 2007. LNCS, vol. 4703, pp. 105–119. Springer, Heidelberg (2007). https://doi.org/10.1007/978-3-540-74407-8_8

20. Larsen, K.G.: Modal specifications. In: Sifakis, J. (ed.) CAV 1989. LNCS, vol. 407, pp. 232–246. Springer, Heidelberg (1990). https://doi.org/10.1007/3-540-52148-8_19

21. Ma, S., Cao, Y., Fan, W., Huai, J., Wo, T.: Strong simulation: capturing topology in graph pattern matching. ACM Trans. Database Syst. **39**(1), 4:1–4:46 (2014). https://doi.org/10.1145/2528937

22. Mennicke, S., Kalo, J.-C., Balke, W.-T.: Querying graph databases: what do graph patterns mean? In: Mayr, H.C., Guizzardi, G., Ma, H., Pastor, O. (eds.) ER 2017. LNCS, vol. 10650, pp. 134–148. Springer, Cham (2017). https://doi.org/10.1007/978-3-319-69904-2_11

23. Mennicke, S., Kalo, J.C., Balke, W.T.: Using queries as schema-templates for graph databases. Datenbank-Spektrum **18**(2), 89–98 (2018). https://doi.org/10.1007/s13222-018-0286-9

24. Mennicke, S., Kalo, J.C., Nagel, D., Kroll, H., Balke, W.T.: Fast dual simulation processing of graph database queries. In: 35th IEEE International Conference on Data Engineering, ICDE 2019, Macau, China, 8–12 April 2019 (2019)

25. Schreiber, G., Raimond, Y.: RDF 1.1 primer. Technical report, W3C (2014)
26. Tajima, K.: Schemaless semistructured data revisited. In: Tannen, V., Wong, L., Libkin, L., Fan, W., Tan, W.-C., Fourman, M. (eds.) In Search of Elegance in the Theory and Practice of Computation. LNCS, vol. 8000, pp. 466–482. Springer, Heidelberg (2013). https://doi.org/10.1007/978-3-642-41660-6_25
27. Tran, T., Ladwig, G., Rudolph, S.: Managing structured and semistructured RDF data using structure indexes. IEEE Trans. Knowl. Data Eng. **25**(9), 2076–2089 (2013). https://doi.org/10.1109/TKDE.2012.134

A Systematic Approach to Generate Diverse Instantiations for Conceptual Schemas

Loli Burgueño[1,2]([⊠]), Jordi Cabot[3], Robert Clarisó[1], and Martin Gogolla[4]

[1] Universitat Oberta de Catalunya, Barcelona, Spain
{lburguenoc,rclariso}@uoc.edu
[2] Institut List, CEA, Université Paris-Saclay, Paris, France
[3] ICREA, Barcelona, Spain
jordi.cabot@icrea.cat
[4] University of Bremen, Bremen, Germany
gogolla@uni-bremen.de

Abstract. Generating valid instantiations for a conceptual schema is instrumental in ensuring its quality by means of verification, validation or testing. This problem becomes even more challenging when we also require that the computed instantiations exhibit significant differences among them, i.e., they are diverse. In this work, we propose an *automatic* method that guarantees synthesizing a diverse set of instantiations from a conceptual schema by combining model finders, classifying terms and constraint strengthening techniques. This technique has been implemented in the USE tool for UML/OCL.

Keywords: Methodologies and tools for conceptual design · Quality of conceptual models · Integrity constraints

1 Introduction

Verification, validation and testing are different mechanisms to ensure the quality of a conceptual schema. These approaches typically require the same resource: creating one or more instantiations of the conceptual schema. With "instantiation" we refer to an example for an information base of a conceptual schema [16]. These instantiations can be used as *illustrations* to better understand the model, to explain its behavior or to simulate it; as *counterexamples* that describe invalid configurations; and as *test cases* to capture scenarios that should be checked.

A key property of any set of instantiations to be used in a quality assurance process is its *diversity*. That is, the instantiations in the set should cover a broad spectrum of different configurations and scenarios. Otherwise, relevant corner cases might be missed, causing faults and/or wrong conclusions.

This work is partially funded by the H2020 ECSEL Joint Undertaking Project "MegaM@Rt2: MegaModelling at Runtime" (737494) and the Spanish Research Project TIN2016-75944-R.

A. H. F. Laender et al. (Eds.): ER 2019, LNCS 11788, pp. 513–521, 2019.
https://doi.org/10.1007/978-3-030-33223-5_42

Asking a domain expert to create instantiations manually can be very time-consuming and is usually not feasible. Instead, dedicated tools called *model finders* [12,18] can be used to automatically compute (valid) instantiations of a conceptual schema that satisfy all its integrity constraints. Model finders rely on different techniques like constraint solvers, theorem provers or search algorithms to perform this computation [12]. While model finders automate the generation process, they do not guarantee diverse solutions.

One approach that helps model finders generate a diverse output is called *classifying terms* (CT) [14]. Classifying terms are properties that can be used to partition the solution space. Intuitively, a CT is an expression or property defined in such a way that two instantiations yielding different values for the classifying term will be (very) dissimilar. The partitions induced by classifying terms can guide the model finder and direct it to select canonical representatives from each partition, rather than arbitrary instantiations. Thus, a proper choice of classifying terms ensures a good partition and, thus, model diversity. Nevertheless, proposing suitable classifying terms requires domain knowledge. Thus, it is not trivial to automate and requires the participation of a domain expert.

To overcome this issue, this work proposes a method for automatically generating relevant classifying terms for a given conceptual schema. The approach arises from the observation that classifying terms are typically related to the integrity constraints in the schema. Therefore, we propose to *mutate* the schema's integrity constraints in a structured way in order to generate classifying terms. In particular, we extend and adapt the work on *constraint strengthening* [6] to produce these mutants of interest.

Our approach, combining constraint strengthening, classifying terms and model finders, enables the automatic generation of diverse instantiations from a conceptual schema. This result is useful in many areas of conceptual modeling beyond information systems. To describe the method, and without loss of generality, we will consider conceptual schemas expressed as UML class diagrams enriched with OCL constraints to describe integrity constraints.

The rest of the paper is structured as follows. Section 2 discusses the state of the art. Section 3 presents our method for synthesizing classifying terms and Sect. 4 describes its implementation. Section 5 discusses the advantages and shortcomings of this method. Finally, Sect. 6 concludes and discusses the future work.

2   State of the Art

Some works on general purpose satisfiability solvers are focused on *random sampling* [5,7,8]), *i.e.*, finding diverse satisfying assignments to boolean formulas.

In the specific context of model finders, there are many approaches for finding valid instances for a model [12] but only a few consider diversity. Some strategies that have been used are *symmetry breaking* [18], *distance metrics* [9], *abstract graph shapes* [17] or *random restarts* [2]. One of these approaches lets the designer control diversity by defining *classifying terms* [14]: relevant boolean or integer

expressions that partition the set of solutions by exhibiting different results for instantiations that are dissimilar.

Testing methods also rely on model finders to synthesize test cases [1,3]. This process may require *mutating* constraints, selecting edit operators randomly from a predefined catalog. Instead, in this paper we modify constraints in a structured way [6] in order to *strengthen* them. Besides, we explore the (complex) partitions defined by classifying terms instead of simply defining ranges of "meaningful values" for inputs as in [10,15].

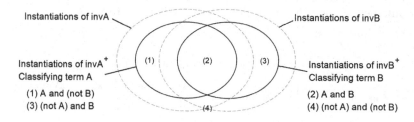

Fig. 1. Diverse instantiations through two Boolean classifying terms

3   Our Generative Method

Our method adapts and combines techniques from two previous works: classifying terms (CT) [14] and the strengthening of integrity constraints [6].

CTs are employed to explore the set of possible correct or incorrect instantiations of a conceptual schema in order to obtain a few diverse instantiations instead of many similar ones. The approach enables the generation of instantiations that satisfy all constraints (positive test cases) as well as instantiations in which some constraints fail (negative test cases). However, until now, CTs had to be manually written by the developer, which limited the usability of the approach. To address this limitation, this work uses the existing integrity constraints in the model as an input and strengthen them (*i.e.*, it mutates them to generate a more restrictive version of the constraint) for obtaining *meaningful* CTs. That is, CTs that generate interesting equivalence classes that can be then taken as input for the generation of diverse instantiations in which border cases become clear. For example, one instantiation where a particular constraint holds and another one where the same constraint fails.

Figure 1 explains the basic idea behind our new approach. As an example, we consider two invariants invA and invB and assume two strengthened versions of them invA+ and invB+ have been identified. By considering the strengthened versions as CTs, one will ideally construct four model equivalence classes and obtain four diverse instantiations that show different behavior with respect to the two CTs. The next sections illustrate each step of this process in more detail using a running example.

3.1 Running Example

As a running example throughout the paper we use the simple conceptual schema depicted in Fig. 2, representing a simplified cloud provisioning model. Different cloud providers offer a number of *CloudServices* to the potential *Customers* who put *Orders* based on their data volume needs. To ensure the integrity of the provisioning, a number of constraints are defined on top of the schema. For instance, we check that orders must be within the Customer budget (constraint orderWithinBudget) or that premium customers have at least one order with a data volume higher or equals to 5. Due to space constraints we only show three invariants below, the rest are available in our Git repository [4].

```
context Customer inv orderWithinBudget:
  self.ord->forAll(o |
    self.budget >= o.dataVol*o.serv.unitPrice)
context cs1,cs2:CloudService inv uniqueProviderMaxDataVol:
  cs1<>cs2 implies
    cs1.provider<>cs2.provider or cs1.maxDataVol<>cs2.maxDataVol
context Customer inv minimumDataVolCompany:
  self.premium implies self.ord->exists(o | o.dataVol>=5)
```

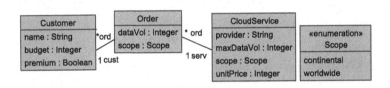

Fig. 2. A simple cloud provisioning schema

3.2 Derivation of Classifying Terms via Constraint Strengthening

Mutation is a technique used in the context of software testing. This process starts from a software artifact, usually a program or function, and systematically introduces small changes to produce new versions of the artifact called *mutants*. These syntactic changes, called *mutation operators*, are intended to mimic frequent developer errors. Then, it is possible to check whether a test suite is capable of detecting that the original artifacts and the mutants do not have the same behavior.

In the context of OCL integrity constraints, strengthening [6] is a method for *structured* mutation. By construction, strengthening guarantees that any mutant it produces is more restrictive than the original OCL constraint, taking into account the semantics of OCL (including OCL's 4-valued logic [13], which considers invalid and undefined values). This is achieved by ensuring that this property holds for each mutation operator.

As an example, below we show sample strengthening candidates (noted using the $^+$ symbol) applied to two expressions including the boolean operator *or* (left)

and the relational operator >= (right). Note that, when the subexpressions are boolean, potential strengthenings may require to strengthen some of its subexpressions. A complete list of candidate strengthenings can be found in [6].

$$[\text{exp1 or exp2}]^+ \;\to\; \begin{array}{l} \text{exp1 } \boxed{\text{and}} \text{ exp2} \\ \text{exp1} \\ \boxed{[\text{exp1}]^+} \text{ or exp2} \end{array} \qquad [\text{exp1} >= \text{exp2}]^+ \;\to\; \begin{array}{l} \text{exp1} > \text{exp2} \\ \text{exp1} = \text{exp2} \\ \text{exp1} > \text{exp2} + 1 \end{array}$$

Strengthening was originally proposed as a way to suggest fixes for integrity constraints that were found to be too lax. Here, we adapt this method to generate classifying terms for a conceptual model. Notice that we are not interested in classifying terms that are more lax than the integrity constraints: if an instantiation does not satisfy an integrity constraint, it will be discarded as invalid. On the other hand, stronger versions of integrity constraints will produce valid instances, which is exactly what we need and the reason why we use invariant strengthening to generate classifying terms.

A first adaptation is that classifying terms are not restricted by a context type like OCL invariants. Thus, we have to rewrite the OCL constraints to provide a meaning for the "self" object via allInstances. For instance, the invariant orderWithinBudget has to be rewritten as:

```
Customer.allInstances->forAll(c |
  c.ord->forAll(o | c.budget >= o.dataVol*o.serv.unitPrice))
```

Once the invariants are rewritten, we apply the strengthenings to obtain the classifying terms. As an example, we show below the resulting classifying term after applying three strengthenings to the three invariants presented above:

```
-- budget: strengthening '>=' -> '='
Customer.allInstances()->forAll(c | c.ord->forAll(o |
  c.budget = o.dataVol*o.serv.unitPrice))
-- uniqueness: strengthening 'or' -> 'and'
CloudService.allInstances()->forAll(cs1,cs2 | cs1<>cs2 implies
  cs1.provider<>cs2.provider and cs1.maxDataVol<>cs2.maxDataVol))
-- minimum: strengthening 'A implies B' -> 'B'
Customer.allInstances()->forAll(c| c.ord->forAll(o | o.dataVol >= 5))
```

3.3   Constructing Diverse Instantiations

As stated before and in [14], a classifying term is a closed OCL query expression that computes a Boolean or an Integer value, i.e., an OCL expression without free variables that, when evaluated in an instantiation, gives a Boolean or an Integer result. Given a collection of classifying terms $CT_1, \ldots, CT_n$ for a conceptual model, the model finder internally operates as follows:

1. Compute an instantiation of the model respecting the stated OCL invariants.
2. Evaluate the classifying terms in the current instantiation (values $v_1, \ldots, v_n$).
3. Internally add a new constraint forbidding that the classifying terms take the values of the found instantiation: $(CT_1 <> v_1)$ or $\ldots$ or $(CT_n <> v_n)$.
4. Repeat the process until no more instantiations can be found.

In the running example, the three constructed Boolean classifying terms `budget`, `uniqueness` and `minimum` will yield eight (2^3) instantiations where in a single instantiation each classifying term is either `false` or `true`. Figure 3 shows two of the eight instantiations and the result of evaluating the three classifying terms in each instantiation.

4   Tool Support

Our method has been implemented inside the USE tool [11]. USE is implemented in Java and provides, among other features: a GUI; packages to load, modify and inspect models and instantiations; and commands to invoke the KodKod relational solver [18] for model finding.

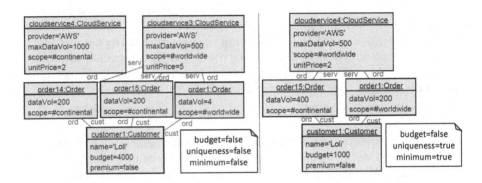

Fig. 3. Two generated instantiations for the Cloud Provisioning example

The *input* of our tool is a UML class diagram annotated with OCL invariants. This model is specified using the textual format employed by USE (`.use`). The *output* is a set of diverse instantiations of the model, which can be visualized as object models within USE. Our implementation is divided into three steps:

1. *Candidate generation:* First, we strengthen each OCL integrity constraint by means of a post-order traversal of its abstract syntax tree (AST). For each boolean expression in the AST, we generate the candidate strenghtenings by combining the strenghtenings of its subexpressions (see Sect. 3.2). The list of candidates for the root of the AST is the list of potential classifying terms for that invariant.

2. *Candidate selection:* Next, we select the subset of candidates to be used as classifying terms to compute instantiations. This choice can be performed in different ways: randomly; using heuristics (*e.g.* choosing the classifying terms that involve the more constrained elements in the model); or with the help of a domain expert (note that choosing classifying terms from a list of candidates requires much less effort than proposing them).

3. *Computation of instantiations:* Finally, we provide the classifying terms to the model finder, which uses them to find representative instantiations in each of the equivalence classes induced by the partition. This process is automated within USE using the command *mv -scrollingAllCT <properties_file>*, which receives as parameters the properties file in which the verification bounds are stated; asks for the classifying terms; and invokes the Kodkod model finder to generate instantiations.

Our running example has been analyzed using this tool implementation, which is available for download from [4].

5 Discussion

Correctness and Completeness. The classifying terms are always added on top of the existing integrity constraints in the schema. Therefore, any solution obtained using classifying terms satisfies all constraints. This guarantees the correctness of any generated instantiation.

Regarding the expressiveness of integrity constraints, our method supports all features of OCL 2.4 except for ordered collections (Sequence, OrderedSet) or recursively defined queries. Without loss of generality, we have focused on the generation of boolean classifying terms but a similar process could be applied for the generation of integer classifying terms.

Performance. Computing the classifying terms adds a performance overhead to the solution generation process, but it is negligible. The classifying term generation time was 151 milliseconds for our running example, which was 1–2 orders of magnitude faster than the time it took to compute a single valid instantiation.

Given that this second task (computing the instantiation) is the bottleneck, any approach aiming to reduce the number of times we need to trigger the generation of a new instantiation to ensure diversity in the result set[1], will significantly reduce the overall computing time.

Heuristics for the Selection of Classifying Terms. The automatic application of our method can generate a very large number of potential classifying terms. Any of them can be used to enforce diverse solutions but a manual exploration of the generated classifying terms quickly reveals some that seem more promising than others (in terms of the degree of diversity they could generate).

The definition of a set of heuristics able to filter the set of classifying terms and propose the *best* ones is left for further work.

Combination Strategies for Classifying Terms. Given two or more classifying terms, we could adapt our approach to change the way in which the equivalent classes are traversed in the solution generation process. For instance, we could focus first on one of the classifying terms and generate diverse examples

---

[1] Most solvers will generate by default very similar results when repetitively prompted for new solutions [5,7,8]. Rather than (potentially unsuccessful) solver-specific tunings, this work proposes a solver-independent solution to achieve diverse results.

only considering that classifying term alone (i.e. emphasizing *local diversity*). Or we could combine all classifying terms and generate solutions that explore equivalent classes taking into account the value of different classifying terms at the same time (i.e. emphasizing *global diversity*).

6   Conclusions

We have presented a new approach to enforce the generation of a diverse set of instantiations from a given schema. Diversity plays an important role in a variety of scenarios such as model exploration, simulation, testing, validation and verification. In our approach, diversity is guaranteed by the systematic generation of classifying terms that partition the solution space of a model into a set of equivalent classes. Such classifying terms are derived from the strengthening of existing integrity constraints in the schema.

In principle, all constraints can be used as "seed" constraints to generate the CTs. Nevertheless, depending on the application scenario, some constraints are potentially more useful than others. For instance, in a model-based testing context, one may want to prioritize constraints over the more restricted parts of the model to maximize the chances of finding errors. Identification of such restricted parts/constraints left as future work. As stated in the previous section, we also plan to work on the definition of strategies to optimally select and combine different CTs and guide the exploration of model solutions for each combination. Again, depending on the goal, a breadth-first strategy may be preferable over a depth-first one (or the other way round). Finally, large case studies must check the usefulness of our proposal and improve its applicability.

References

1. Aichernig, B.K., Salas, P.A.P.: Test case generation by OCL mutation and constraint solving. In: QSIC 2005, pp. 64–71 (2005)
2. Ali, S., Zohaib Iqbal, M., Arcuri, A., Briand, L.C.: Generating test data from OCL constraints with search techniques. IEEE TSE **39**(10), 1376–1402 (2013)
3. Brucker, A.D., Krieger, M.P., Longuet, D., Wolff, B.: A specification-based test case generation method for UML/OCL. In: Dingel, J., Solberg, A. (eds.) MODELS 2010. LNCS, vol. 6627, pp. 334–348. Springer, Heidelberg (2011). https://doi.org/10.1007/978-3-642-21210-9_33
4. Burgueño, L., Clarisó, R., Cabot, J., Gogolla, M.: Constraint mutation source code and examples (2019). http://hdl.handle.net/20.500.12004/1/C/ER/2019/562
5. Chakraborty, S., Fremont, D.J., Meel, K.S., Seshia, S.A., Vardi, M.Y.: On parallel scalable uniform SAT witness generation. In: Baier, C., Tinelli, C. (eds.) TACAS 2015. LNCS, vol. 9035, pp. 304–319. Springer, Heidelberg (2015). https://doi.org/10.1007/978-3-662-46681-0_25
6. Clarisó, R., Cabot, J.: Fixing defects in integrity constraints via constraint mutation. In: QUATIC 2018, pp. 74–82 (2018)
7. Dutra, R., Laeufer, K., Bachrach, J., Sen, K.: Efficient sampling of SAT solutions for testing. In: ICSE 2018, pp. 549–559 (2018)

8. Ermon, S., Gomes, C., Selman, B.: Uniform solution sampling using a constraint solver as an oracle. In: UAI 2012, pp. 255–264 (2012)
9. Ferdjoukh, A., Galinier, F., Bourreau, E., Chateau, A., Nebut, C.: Measurement and generation of diversity and meaningfulness in model driven engineering. Int. J. Adv. Softw. 11(1/2), 131–146 (2018)
10. Fleurey, F., Baudry, B., Muller, P.A., Le Traon, Y.: Qualifying input test data for model transformations. SoSyM 8(2), 185–203 (2007)
11. Gogolla, M., Büttner, F., Richters, M.: USE: a UML-based specification environment for validating UML and OCL. Sci. Comput. Program. 69(1–3), 27–34 (2007)
12. González, C.A., Cabot, J.: Formal verification of static software models in MDE: a systematic review. Inf. Softw. Technol. 56(8), 821–838 (2014)
13. Object Management Group: Object Constraint Language specification (version 2.4). https://www.omg.org/spec/OCL/2.4/
14. Hilken, F., Gogolla, M., Burgueño, L., Vallecillo, A.: Testing models and model transformations using classifying terms. SoSyM 17(3), 885–912 (2018)
15. Jackson, E.K., Simko, G., Sztipanovits, J.: Diversely enumerating system-level architectures. In: EMSOFT 2013, pp. 1–10, September 2013
16. Olivé, A.: Conceptual Modeling of Information Systems. Springer, Heidelberg (2007). https://doi.org/10.1007/978-3-540-39390-0
17. Semeráth, O., Varró, D.: Iterative generation of diverse models for testing specifications of DSL tools. In: FASE 2018, pp. 227–245, April 2018
18. Torlak, E., Jackson, D.: Kodkod: a relational model finder. In: Grumberg, O., Huth, M. (eds.) TACAS 2007. LNCS, vol. 4424, pp. 632–647. Springer, Heidelberg (2007). https://doi.org/10.1007/978-3-540-71209-1_49

Requirements Modeling

Factors Affecting Comprehension of Contribution Links in Goal Models: An Experiment

Sotirios Liaskos[✉] and Wisal Tambosi

School of Information Technology, York University,
4700 Keele Street, Toronto M3J 1P3, Canada
{liaskos,tambosi}@yorku.ca

Abstract. Goal models have long been regarded to be useful instruments for visualizing and analysing decision problems. Key to using goal models for the purpose is the concept of satisfaction contribution between goals. Several proposals have been offered in the literature for representing contributions and performing inferences therewith. Theoretical arguments and demonstrative examples are typically used to support the usefulness and soundness of such proposals. However, the degree to which users of goal models intuitively understand the meaning of a specific contribution representation and use it for making valid inferences constitutes an additional measure of the appropriateness of the representation. We report on an experimental study to compare the intuitiveness of two alternative contribution representation approaches via measuring the degree to which untrained users perform inferences compliant with the semantics defined by the language designers. We further explore the role of individual differences such as cognitive style and attitude and ability with arithmetic in establishing and applying the right semantics. We find significant differences between the representations under comparison as well as effects of various qualities and levels with regards to individual factors. The results inspire further research on the specific matter of contribution links and support the overall soundness and operationalizability of the intuitiveness construct.

Keywords: Conceptual modelling · Goal models · Model comprehension · Experimental study

1 Introduction

For more than two decades, goal models [4,39] have been extensively studied as an instrument for capturing and communicating intentional structures for a variety of purposes within information technology. One of the strengths of such models is their ability to represent alternative ways by which stakeholder goals can be materialized into design solutions [26,27,34]. Using goal models business/systems analysts can reason about and communicate the advantages

© Springer Nature Switzerland AG 2019
A. H. F. Laender et al. (Eds.): ER 2019, LNCS 11788, pp. 525–539, 2019.
https://doi.org/10.1007/978-3-030-33223-5_43

and disadvantages of alternative solutions with respect to their impact to higher level business objectives. Multiple proposals for doing such analysis have been proposed in the literature [3,15,26,27] ([21] for a survey).

To make such analysis possible, goal models employ a concept commonly referred to as *contribution* to represent how satisfaction of one goal affects the satisfaction of another. There is variety with regards to how different goal modelling frameworks treat the representation and meaning of contributions. The traditional approach for representing contributions is through symbolic labels (e.g. "+", "–") [15,20,39] or words ("help","break") [9] expressing the quality (positive or negative) and the size of contribution in high-level terms. The use of numeric values in various ways has also been proposed [3,25,30], whereby, e.g., sign and absolute value are used to represent quality and size of contribution. The approaches vary with regards to both representation and underlying semantics. Theoretical analyses and demonstrations are usually employed to support the soundness and usefulness of each approach. However, an additional indication of the quality of the chosen representation and semantics could be the extent to which untrained users of the model can *intuitively* understand the meaning of the representation and use it to make inferences in a way that complies with the semantics intended by the modelling language designers.

In this paper, we experimentally explore the intuitiveness of two choices for representing contribution links in goal models, one symbolic and one numeric. At the core of the experiment, a series of decision problems modelled in either of the two ways are presented to untrained users who are asked to use the contributions to perform inferences and make decisions. We measure the extent to which their inferences comply with the semantics of each representation. We further explore how individual differences pertaining to cognitive style, attitude and ability with mathematics and mental arithmetic as well as overall working approach taken by the participants affect the degree of success in performing compliant inferences. Among other things, we find that numeric models evoke much more compliant responses, especially among participants who claim to have followed a methodical rather than an intuitive working approach.

The rest of the paper is organized as follows. In Sect. 2 we offer background on goal models, contribution links and their semantics as well as the concept of intuitiveness and individual differences that may affect its manifestation. In Sects. 3 and 4 we describe the experimental design and the results and in Sects. 5 and 6 we review some of the related work and offer concluding remarks.

2   Background

2.1   Goal Models and Contribution Links

The type of goal modelling notation we use in this research is akin to the i^* family of goal modelling notations [4,39]. Two examples can be seen in Fig. 1. The oval- and cloud-shaped nodes represent actor *goals* (states of the world the actor wants to hold in the future), the ovals describing *hard-goals* and the cloud-shaped ones

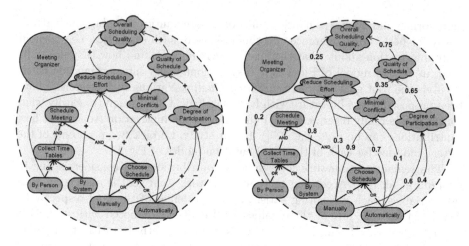

Fig. 1. Goal models with symbolic (left) and numeric (right) contribution links.

soft-goals. As per their standard meaning [39], soft-goals – as opposed to hard-goals – do not have a precise satisfiability criterion. Further, the goal models we study follow a specific structural pattern. Specifically, using *means-ends* and *decomposition* links, hard-goals form a decomposition that shows how different subsets of low-level goals can enable the achievement of the top-level hard-goal. Soft-goals are recipients of *contribution links*, the curved directed lines. Such links can originate from hard-goals or other soft-goals.

A contribution link from goal A to soft-goal B expresses the hypothesis that evidence of satisfaction or denial of goal A has an effect to our belief about the satisfaction or denial of soft-goal B. The exact quality (positive or negative) and level of effect is expressed using a label on top of the contribution link. The literature offers several proposals for what could be used as a label and what it would mean. The original approach [4,15,39] is to use symbols "+", "++", "−" and "−−" denoting respectively various levels of positive and negative contribution. As of iStar 2.0 [9] words are used ("help", "make", "hurt" and "break") in place of symbols. An alternative approach to symbols and words is numbers: a numerical value in the interval [0.0, 1.0] [15,25] or [−100, +100] [3], describes the level of contribution of A to B. Of these various labelling options, the two that are of particular interest here can be seen in Fig. 1. They are henceforth referred to as the *symbolic* and the *numeric* representation (mode).

Even without describing the meaning of the contribution links in any more precision, the models in the figure can already be used for performing useful *inferences.* Focussing on the symbolic model on the left side of Fig. 1, a user who is only minimally informed to the specifics of the notation and has no knowledge of the precise semantics of "+" and "−−", can probably infer that the goal *(Choose Schedule) Automatically* is preferable to goal *(Choose Schedule) Manually* when we are interested in the goal *Reduce Scheduling Effort*. It is easy to see however that more complex inferences are not possible without an appeal to

more formal and precise semantics. Such precise semantics unambiguously define a way for performing inferences. In the absence of such semantics, i.e., without more information about what the labels precisely mean and how they are to be used, in neither model of Fig. 1 is it easy to confidently infer optimal decisions vis-à-vis the root goal *Overall Scheduling Quality*. Various such semantics have been proposed in the literature with both ontological motivation (to clarify what contributions really mean, e.g. [16]) and operational motivation (to suggest how contributions can be used, e.g. [25]). In our study, we pick two proposals of the latter kind, one for each of the representation modes of Fig. 1.

The semantic framework for symbolic contributions we consider is due to Giorgini et al. [15]. According to that framework each goal is associated with two variables, each measuring satisfaction and denial of the goal respectively. The variables take one of three values: Full evidence (denoted with prefix **F**), Partial Evidence (**P**) and No Evidence (**N**) – of, respectively satisfaction (suffix **S**) or denial (**D**). For example, we may have partial evidence of satisfaction and no evidence of denial for one goal (denoted {**PS, ND**}) and partial evidence of denial and full evidence of satisfaction for another goal ({**FS, PD**}); the inconsistency being perfectly acceptable here and actually one of the strengths of the framework. Given a symbolic contribution link as described thus far, a set of rules, seen in Table 1, defines completely what the satisfaction and denial value of the destination of the link is, given the type of the label ("+","++", etc.) and the corresponding satisfaction and denial values of the origin goal. No evidence (**NS** or **ND**) in the origin is propagated as-is independent of label. Multiple incoming links are treated following a precise evidence maximization principle.

Table 1. Symbolic contribution semantics

Label	Effect	Label	Effect	Label	Effect	Label	Effect
++	FS → FS PS → PS PD → PD FD → FD	−−	FS → FD PS → PD PD → PS FD → FS	+	FS → PS PS → PS PD → PD FD → PD	−	FS → PD PS → PD PD → PS FD → PS

While Giorgini et al. offer an equally comprehensive numeric version of their satisfaction propagation framework we here focus on one used (directly or by implication) by Maiden et al. [30] and Liaskos et al. [25], following the same logic as the one followed by the Unified Requirements Notation (URN) [3]. According to this interpretation each goal has a unique satisfaction value in the real interval [0.0, 1.0]. The numeric label on the contribution link represents the share of influence of the satisfaction of the origin goal to the satisfaction of the destination goal. Thus, when a soft-goal is targeted by one or more contribution links, its satisfaction is a linear combination of the satisfaction values of the origin goals

weighted by the labels of the corresponding contribution links, as in:

$$s(g) = \sum_{g' \in O_g} \{s(g') \times w(g', g)\} \tag{1}$$

where g is the soft-goal targeted by the links, O_g the set of goals g' from which the contribution links originate, $w(g', g)$ the numeric weights of those links, and $s(g)$ the satisfaction value of a goal g.

2.2 Intuitiveness and Individual Differences

The intent of a developer of visualized conceptual models like the above box-and-line goal models is to evoke a *mental model* of how the visualization is supposed to be understood and used to make inferences about the domain. Our research question here is whether and to what degree the mental model that is actually evoked within the reader's mind is indeed consistent with the designers' intent, hence promoting "correct" inferences. We use the term *intuitiveness* to furthermore refer to attainment of such consistency with limited or no training. The intuitiveness construct is akin to the concept of *semantic transparency* as per Moody's framework for principled visual design of modeling languages [32]: an intuitive visualized conceptual modelling language is one that allows its users recognize and understand the meaning of the language's constructs based on the visual appearance of the constructs, thus without reference to additional training or explanatory material.

Moreover, when users of a modelling notation are asked to guess the meaning of shapes/symbols and perform inferences therewith, we can hypothesise that *individual differences* in terms of skills, attitudes and styles may affect their choices. One question is whether users attempt to develop a complete and precise theory of how the notation works and make conscious inferences with it or make rough gut-feeling ones based on intuition. A construct that attempts to formalize this distinction is *cognitive style* [1]. According to that construct the approach that decision makers take in solving a judgement problem lies in a *cognitive continuum* [18] between analytical and intuitive cognitive work. While the former describes conscious, controlled, systematic, detail-oriented work towards making an inference, the latter describes quick, approximate, holistic, synthetic and less conscious approach. While Hammond et al. support that cognitive style is largely induced by the task at hand [18], Hayes et al. have shown that decision makers may have a tendency towards one or the other extreme as a personality trait and have developed the CSI (Cognitive Style Index) to measure it [1]. At the same time, simple ability and comfort with mental arithmetic can be a predictor of successful performance of symbol-intensive inferences within a model. Likewise, *math anxiety*, i.e. the presence of feelings of fear, tension, and apprehension with mathematics [19], may affect both how the mathematical/symbolic (e.g. contribution labels) are interpreted and used.

3   Experimental Design

Overview and Research Questions. The goals of our experimental study are to (a) compare the intuitiveness of alternative contribution link representations in the context of assessing optimal decisions within goal models and (b) assess the role of individual differences to the enablement of intuitiveness in the said task. Specifically, the experiment has a confirmatory and an exploratory aspect. We first want to compare the two modes of representation, symbolic (Fig. 1 left, Table 1) vs. numeric (Fig. 1 right, Eq. 1), with regards to their intuitiveness, testing the hypothesis that numeric models are bound to be more intuitive for the purpose of detecting optimal solutions (**RQ1**). The hypothesis is based on the belief that the specific numeric representation utilizes participants' familiarity with numbers and proportions, commonly used in their daily lives. We further want to explore whether individual differences and ways of working, specifically ability and attitude towards math, cognitive style as well as followed approach, affect intuitiveness (**RQ2**). In the absence of earlier experience, no explicit hypotheses are made with regards to RQ2. The experimental design is an extension/revision of an earlier one presented elsewhere [29].

Constructs and Measures. Our central construct is intuitiveness as discussed above. To measure it, we expose experimental participants to a set of models and ask them to perform inferences based on the information in the model. The participants have only basic awareness of the language and the abstract meaning of its constructs but no knowledge of precise semantics. Intuitiveness is measured primarily via *accuracy* of the participant inferences, i.e., the number of inferences that match the ones that the language semantics dictate. Wherever applicable, we also measure *efficiency*, which is the number of accurate (matching) responses divided by the time it took to make the necessary inferences as well as self-reported *confidence* levels of the method followed to make the inferences (*method confidence*) as well as confidence in the inferences themselves (*response confidence*).

With regards to individual difference factors, we administer the 38-point CSI (Cognitive Style Index) [1] to measure cognitive style (*CSI Score*) and the 9-point AMAS (Abbreviated Math Anxiety Scale) [19] to measure math anxiety (*AMAS Level*). We further measure *ability with arithmetic* using a series of custom non-standard exercises in mental arithmetic. We attempted various types and scoring methods for these. The ones that turn out to have some effect, as discussed below, consist of direct multiplication, scored in [0,10] though an exponentially decaying function of the distance between participant response and correct answer, comparisons of two two-number products and comparisons of two linear combinations each containing two terms. Finally the working *approach* that participants followed, between "using their intuition" and "following a specific method" was captured through self-reporting.

Experimental Units. To construct our experimental instruments we first develop a number of goal models. Two (2) sets of models are developed: symbolic and numeric, each containing only the corresponding type of contribution links.

All models consist of one (1) OR-decomposition of hard-goals and an hierarchy of soft-goals to act as criteria for choosing the optimal choice within the OR-decomposition. The soft-goal hierarchy has a unique root goal (such as "Overall Scheduling Quality" of Fig. 1) and the contribution labels are chosen such that one of the alternatives of the OR-decomposition is optimal compared to the others, with respect to the top goal. The optimal is calculated by evaluating the impact of full satisfaction of each of the children of the OR-decomposition to the satisfaction of the root soft-goal when the satisfaction values of all other decomposition children are set to **N** or zero, and then identifying the child that results to the maximum such satisfaction. The exact mechanics depend on the type of model and the corresponding semantics. Consider, for example, the *Choose Schedule* decomposition of Fig. 1. To evaluate the impact of alternative *Manually* in the left model of Fig. 1 we assign it satisfaction values {**FS, ND**} while assuming *Automatically* stays {**NS, ND**}. Similarly, for the numeric model on the right we set $s(Manually) = 1$ and $s(Automatically) = 0$. We then recursively apply the propagation rules of Table 1, or, respectively, Eq. 1 for numeric models, in order to evaluate the satisfaction labels of the higher level goals up to the root soft-goal which is the goal of interest.

Model Sampling. We developed the models used for the instrument by picking a goal structure and populating the contribution links with random contribution labels such that the optimal alternative has a fixed distance from the second optimal one, as measured by the satisfaction each induces to the root soft-goal. This is aimed at allowing sufficient difference between the best and second best to allow for some intuitive detection, but not too obviously.

Calculating the distance from best to second best alternative is straightforward in the case of numeric models: the choice of each alternative will result in a number representing the satisfaction value of the root soft-goal for that alternative; we simply ensure that the largest value is about 0.4 higher than the second largest. For the symbolic models, however, the comparison is less straightforward due to the presence of both satisfaction and denial values. Thus, to allow for comparisons, we aggregate the two values into one. To do so we firstly associate qualitative satisfaction labels **N, P, F** with numeric values 0, 1, 2, respectively. Let then $sat(g)$ and $den(g)$ be the resulting numeric satisfaction and denial values for goal g. The aggregated satisfaction value is then $sat(g) - den(g)$ which is an integer in $[-2, 2]$. For example, the aggregated satisfaction value of a goal g_1 with {**PS, FD**} is $sat(g_1) - den(g_1) = 1 - 2 = -1$ and of a goal g_2 with {**FS, ND**}, $sat(g_2) - den(g_2) = 2 - 0 = 2$. Given this aggregation procedure, we demand that our sample models have a distance of 2 satisfaction levels. For example, a label configuration in which the best alternative makes the root soft-goal {**FS, ND**}, hence aggregated value $2 - 0 = 2$, and the second best makes the root soft-goal {**PS, PD**}, hence aggregated value $1 - 1 = 0$, qualifies as $2 - 0 = 2$. To see why this distance matches the one chosen for the numeric models for a fair comparison, observe first that the maximum distance between alternatives in the symbolic case in terms of aggregated value is 4 ({**FS, ND**} versus {**NS, FD**}). The distance we demanded in symbolic models is 2, thus

half of that space. Observing now that the corresponding maximum distance in numeric models is 1.0, it follows that half-space-size distance would be 0.5. However we end up with 0.4, slightly biasing against numeric models, as for some of our structures we fail to find label configurations yielding 0.5 distance.

Instrument and Tasks. For the experimental instrument we develop a total of six (6) model structures, representing decision problems within three (3) domains: Choosing an Apartment, Choosing a Course, and Choosing a Means of Transportation. Thus, two (2) structures are dedicated to each domain, a smaller one with two alternatives and a larger one with three alternatives. For each of the six structures two sets of labels (henceforth: labelsets) are sampled in either of the two frameworks (symbolic vs. numeric). In all, two sets of (3 domains) × (2 sizes) × (2 labelsets) = 12 distinct goal models are constructed and placed in two separate instruments, the symbolic and the numeric.

Each instrument is then organized as follows. Participants are offered two video presentations introducing them to the concepts of decision alternatives and criteria, as well as goal models and the high-level meaning of either type (depending on instrument) of contribution links. Care is taken so that: (a) the videos are as much as possible identical to each other (e.g. use of same examples and points, about same length, same narrator, same visuals etc.), (b) the videos do not prescribe any exact method for interpreting satisfaction propagation that would allude to specific semantics. Subsequently, participants are sequentially presented with the goal models and are asked to enter which of the two or three alternatives they think is optimal. In the end, they are asked if they used a specific method in making their decision, and what that method is, or whether they used their intuition. The CSI, AMAS questionnaires and math ability test precede the aforementioned tasks. We note that midway in the data collection process, the instrument underwent the following revisions: (a) the math ability test was changed and moved to the end and (b) two questions asking for the participants' confidence in their responses and method followed were added.

Participants. Participation is sought from two sources: (a) undergraduate students of the School of Information Technology, York University, attending a human computer interaction course, and (b) Mechanical Turk (MT) participants with a US college degree. We argue in support of these choices below.

4   Results

Sample. A total of 102 participants are included in the analysis: 27 students (21 males and 6 females) and 75 MT participants (41 males and 34 females). The sample predominantly consists of STEM (Science, Technology, Engineering, Mathematics – 49 total) and Business/Economics (22) students/graduates, but also has a mix of Social Science, Humanities, Arts and other backgrounds (31). Their CSI scores are slightly skewed towards the analytical side – 61 above (analytical) and 41 below (intuitive) population average. Of the AMAS scores, 44 are above (more anxious) and 58 are below (less anxious) population average.

Accuracy Analysis. Accuracy is measured as the raw number (out of 12) of correct (wrt. semantics) choices of optimal alternative. To explore accuracy we first attempt to fit a linear model [38] including representation (numeric vs. symbolic), AMAS Level, CSI Score, and approach as main effects, ignoring interactions for the moment. Most factors seem to offer statistically significant or near-significant results: representation $(F(1, 97) = 72.2, p < 0.001$, Cohen $d = 1.51$ – numeric more accurate than symbolic), AMAS Score $(F(1, 97) = 5.7, p < 0.05, d = 0.33$ – the lower the more the accuracy) and working approach $(F(1, 97) = 5.6, p < 0.05$, min robust $d = 0.39$ – methodical approach more accurate than intuitive approach). The representation effect is very large and the rest of the effects are small to medium by Cohen's d. Thus, those with below average AMAS level (less anxious) score 0.96 more correct questions than those above average. Finally, accuracy is the only measure in which a certain type of mathematical ability tests, described earlier, seem to have a marginally statistically significant effect $(p < 0.025$ tested as a lone factor in a separate model): 2.4 more points (out of the 12) in those arithmetic tests results in 1 more correct response in the decision exercises. A small CSI effect detected presents increased Type I error probability and does not emerge in robust tests; it is, thus, dismissed.

Extending the model with interactions we observe that working approach strongly interacts with representation. Specifically, when participants work methodically (by their declaration), that seems to significantly improve their accuracy (3.4 out of 12 more correct answers) but only in numeric models $(F(1, 91) = 6.7, p < 0.05, d = 1.38)$. Seeing this through a simple effects analysis, whereby we fix approach to a value and explore the effect of representation to accuracy, the representation effect is only present when participants worked methodically – about 4/5 (symbolic group) and 3/4 (numeric group) of the participants.

Efficiency Analysis. Efficiency, operationalized as the ratio of accuracy over total response time, is considered only for the 27 student sample, where response time can be reliably measured; the 75 MT participants are not invigilated thus their exclusive and uninterrupted focus on the experimental tasks cannot be guaranteed. Representation, CSI level, AMAS level and math ability and their interactions are explored. Approach is not considered due to it being highly unbalanced. Representation appears to have a very strong effect to efficiency (Yuen's $t(9.41) = 3.8, p < 0.01$, min robust $d = 0.93$) with a gain of 3.07 correct answers per minute in numeric models versus symbolic ones. However, no other effect or interaction therewith is observed.

Confidence Analysis. Response confidence and method confidence measurements were introduced to the instrument for the last 45 MT participants only and thus the analysis is based on that sample. They are measured on a 7-point "Likert"-style scale and treated as ratio as per normal practice [36]. We again attempt to explain differences in both measures subject to CSI, AMAS, representation mode and approach. In the result, highly analytical respondents have slightly lower *response confidence* $(F(1, 40) = 4.8, p < 0.05, d = 0.42)$

as expected [18]. Representation also appears to have a small ($d = 0.23$) effect to response confidence but with higher Type I error chance ($p < 0.1$). Analysis of *method confidence* does not yield notable effects.

Summary and Explanatory Remarks. The results present substantial evidence that the numeric representation according to the linear model of Eq. 1 leads to more compliant decision-making inferences by untrained users and faster than the qualitative one of Table 1. We can attribute this to the familiarity that users have with numbers and proportions, on which the numeric model is based, and the lack thereof for symbolic labels. However, the effect emerges (strongly) only when the participants say they work methodically, which we interpret as them developing a deeper and more explicit mental model. It follows that in the symbolic case either the evoked method/model is in strong disagreement with the authoritative one, or the latter is correctly guessed but poorly executed. At the same time, the general lack of correlation between arithmetic ability and accuracy, assuming that our custom instruments have any reliability, may indicate that participants in the numeric group do not perform the exact mental calculations as per Eq. 1, which would require to strongly utilize their mental arithmetic skills, but base their success on an evoked heuristic/approximation that works as well. Furthermore, counter to our expectation that AMAS Level would affect only the numeric group it seems to affect both groups, implying the possibility that the requirement for either kind of symbolic inference is akin to a mathematical task, in which, in turn, highly math-anxious individuals tend to perform worse. Finally, we fail to observe any notable effect of cognitive style trait to accuracy, efficiency or even approach taken, indicating that the index might not be useful for studying the phenomena at hand, possibly also indicating exploration of alternative cognitive style constructs [11]. However, the strong effect of self-reported approach taken suggests that cognitive style remains relevant when seen as choice of cognitive strategy inspired by the characteristics of the task at hand [18] rather than a trait.

Validity Threats. We briefly address the most important of construct, internal, external and statistical conclusion validity threats. In terms of *construct validity* our fundamental assumption that intuitiveness can be measured by the alignment between participant-supplied and authoritative inferences can be criticised as avoiding examination of what goes on in participants' minds when confronted with an unknown notation. A possible response is pragmatic: the observed substantial effect on representation accuracy and efficiency is immediately usable even when theoretical clarity is pending: numbers seem to "just" be more intuitive for the particular task. A further criticism can be extended to the ad-hoc development of non-standard math ability tests, which, however, took place in the absence of suitable standard instruments – and are not major effects regardless. Two main threats to *internal validity* revolve around the representation factor. On one hand, the "difficulty" of the symbolic models (distance between first and second optimal) is constructed based on an operation of comparing satisfaction and denial values that may be argued to be arbitrary and off-specification (by [15]). However, in our view, insofar as the two

representations can be used for the same purpose (comparing alternatives) they cannot be considered incomparable .vis-à-vis that purpose. Thus, one still needs to address the question of what ways, other than the ones adopted here, can be considered for fairly constructing absolute preferability distance between satisfaction levels in a two-valued setting. Furthermore, difference in training quality can be argued to work against one of the conditions. Such bias is difficult to measure and control for. We are hoping that our carefully scripted, video-recorded training videos (versus live lectures commonly adopted in similar studies) offer a first line of defence against this threat. Threats to *external validity* concentrate on the choice of participants and models. We first claim that our participants being non-experts and (some of them) students does not harm generalizability. On one hand, there seems to be an implicit desire in the goal modelling community that non-technical stakeholders (users, owners, clients) should be able to use such models. On the other hand, although we could not find research that describes the typical characteristics of either business and systems analysts or their clients, we cannot assume that they are exclusively of a technical background. We, thus, find that our participants constitute a good sample of the population that may be a user of goal models. Furthermore, the choice of models that we used for the instruments brings unavoidable structural, size and domain commitments. Larger models, for example, may be less advantageous for numeric representations, when the method followed does not scale in terms of cognitive effort. Likewise, the tasks we tested them against (picking an optimal alternative) were very particular. Thus, until research with different models is conducted, generalizations should be carefully done for models and tasks of similar characteristics. As a final note on *statistical conclusion* validity, while we pre-hypothesized the effect of representation format, the rest of the factors and interactions thereof were the result of some statistical model exploration. This exploratory attitude aimed at identifying candidate future research directions rather than firmly confirming hypotheses. Thus, except for the effect of representation, the remaining effects continue to be tentative and subject for further confirmation.

5   Related Work

There are several research efforts dedicated towards exploring the effectiveness of common conceptual modeling notations including UML and ER diagrams [8,10,14,35,37] or process models [5,12,13,31]. Much of the research in the area is based on various *understandability* constructs, though there does not seem to be very strong consensus with regards the definition and exact operationalizations of such constructs [22]. The concept of intuitiveness, as we introduce it here as a dimension of understandability, is less frequently considered explicitly, as in work by Jošt et al., for example, where the *intuitive understandability* of various modeling methods are empirically compared [23].

Work focussing on goal models specifically has also emerged. Notable works are by Horkoff and Yu who devise and evaluate an interactive evaluation technique for goal models [20], by Caire et al. [6] who experimentally assess the

success of visualization choices for modelling constructs, by Hadar et al. [17] who compare goal diagrams with use case diagrams on a variety of user tasks and by Carvallo and Franch who studied empirically the development of strategic dependency i^* diagrams by non-technical stakeholders [7].

Compared to these efforts, our research program has been heavily targeted towards a specific construct, i.e., contribution links. In earlier work [28], for example, we attempted an investigation of the qualitative propagation rules of Table 1. Through an experiment of a nature similar to the one described here, we observed, among other things, that positive labels and satisfaction values appear to be more readily understandable than negative labels and denial values. Likewise, we have also compared the various models for quantitative satisfaction propagation including the one used here and three versions of the one proposed by Giorgini et al. [2], to find that there is tendency for participants to follow some models versus others, motivating further research on the subject. Note that in all this work our focus is not the effectiveness of just perceiving information about contributions, which is what, e.g., Moody et al. [33] attempt to improve, but rather understand how contribution is operationally understood and what reasoning it inspires. In a fashion somewhat more similar to that of Moody, Caire et al. [6], i.e., focussing on perception effectiveness, we explored graphical (versus diagrammatic) ways for representing contribution levels and found that simple combinations of pie-graphs and bar-graphs allow for better accuracy [24].

6   Conclusions

We presented an experiment for comparing the intuitiveness of symbolic versus numeric goal models vis-à-vis individual differences and working styles of model users. A number of experimental participants is presented with decision problems formalized in either notation and are asked to identify the optimal alternative, without given much information about the precise meaning of the modelling constructs. Intuitiveness is attained when participant responses accurately match the ones each kind of model prescribes to be correct. We find that numeric models lead participants to more accurate responses when the latter are the result of adopting a specific working method. We further find that mathematics anxiety has a mild negative correlation with performance irrespective of representation. Finally while we fail to observe any notable effect of cognitive style as a trait, we find it to be relevant as a chosen cognitive strategy.

Future work can zero-in on identifying the source of inference errors and inefficiencies through distinguishing between mental model adoption and mental model execution, each being exposed to different sets of biases and influencing factors. For the task, instruments that enhance explanatory analysis need to be devised beyond our black-box technique. Qualitative methods and protocol analysis may prove to be of value. However, rather than just understanding a specialized task within a specific notation, our long-term objective is to develop an empirical perspective and toolset transferable to the study of other important classes of notations, such as business process or entity models.

References

1. Allinson, C.W., Hayes, J.: The cognitive style index: a measure of intuition-analysis for organizational research. J. Manag. Stud. **33**(1), 119–135 (1996)
2. Alothman, N., Zhian, M., Liaskos, S.: User perception of numeric contribution semantics for goal models: an exploratory experiment. In: Mayr, H.C., Guizzardi, G., Ma, H., Pastor, O. (eds.) ER 2017. LNCS, vol. 10650, pp. 451–465. Springer, Cham (2017). https://doi.org/10.1007/978-3-319-69904-2_34
3. Amyot, D., Ghanavati, S., Horkoff, J., Mussbacher, G., Peyton, L., Yu, E.S.K.: Evaluating goal models within the goal-oriented requirement language. Int. J. Intell. Syst. **25**(8), 841–877 (2010)
4. Amyot, D., Mussbacher, G.: User requirements notation: the first ten years, the next ten years. J. Softw. (JSW) **6**(5), 747–768 (2011)
5. Birkmeier, D.Q., Klockner, S., Overhage, S.: An empirical comparison of the usability of BPMN and UML activity diagrams for business users. In: Proceedings of the 18th European Conference on Information Systems (ECIS 2010), pp. 51–62 (2010)
6. Caire, P., Genon, N., Heymans, P., Moody, D.L.: Visual notation design 2.0: towards user comprehensible requirements engineering notations. In: Proceedings of the 21st IEEE International Requirements Engineering Conference (RE 2013), pp. 115–124, July 2013
7. Carvallo, J.P., Franch, X.: An empirical study on the use of i* by non-technical stakeholders: the case of strategic dependency diagrams. Requirements Eng. **24**(1), 1–27 (2018)
8. Cruz-Lemus, J.A., Genero, M., Manso, M.E., Morasca, S., Piattini, M.: Assessing the understandability of UML statechart diagrams with composite states—a family of empirical studies. Empirical Softw. Eng. **14**(6), 685–719 (2009)
9. Dalpiaz, F., Franch, X., Horkoff, J.: iStar 2.0 Language Guide. The Computing Research Repository (CoRR) (2016). arXiv:1605.07767
10. De Lucia, A., Gravino, C., Oliveto, R., Tortora, G.: Data model comprehension an empirical comparison of ER and UML class diagrams. In: Proceedings of the 16th IEEE International Conference on Program Comprehension (ICPC 2008), Amsterdam, The Netherlands, pp. 93–102 (2008)
11. Epstein, S., Pacini, R., Denes-Raj, V., Heier, H.: Individual differences in intuitive-experiential and analytical-rational thinking styles. J. Pers. Soc. Psychol. **71**, 390–405 (1996)
12. Figl, K., Laue, R.: Cognitive complexity in business process modeling. In: Mouratidis, H., Rolland, C. (eds.) CAiSE 2011. LNCS, vol. 6741, pp. 452–466. Springer, Heidelberg (2011). https://doi.org/10.1007/978-3-642-21640-4_34
13. Figl, K., Recker, J., Mendling, J.: A study on the effects of routing symbol design on process model comprehension. Decis. Support Syst. **54**(2), 1104–1118 (2013)
14. Genero, M., Poels, G., Piattini, M.: Defining and validating metrics for assessing the understandability of entity-relationship diagrams. Data Knowl. Eng. **64**(3), 534–557 (2008)
15. Giorgini, P., Mylopoulos, J., Nicchiarelli, E., Sebastiani, R.: Reasoning with goal models. In: Spaccapietra, S., March, S.T., Kambayashi, Y. (eds.) ER 2002. LNCS, vol. 2503, pp. 167–181. Springer, Heidelberg (2002). https://doi.org/10.1007/3-540-45816-6_22
16. Guizzardi, R.S.S., Franch, X., Guizzardi, G., Wieringa, R.: Ontological distinctions between means-end and contribution links in the i* framework. In: Ng, W., Storey, V.C., Trujillo, J.C. (eds.) ER 2013. LNCS, vol. 8217, pp. 463–470. Springer, Heidelberg (2013). https://doi.org/10.1007/978-3-642-41924-9_39

17. Hadar, I., Reinhartz-Berger, I., Kuflik, T., Perini, A., Ricca, F., Susi, A.: Comparing the comprehensibility of requirements models expressed in Use Case and Tropos: results from a family of experiments. Inf. Softw. Technol. **55**(10), 1823–1843 (2013)
18. Hammond, K.R., Hamm, R.M., Grassia, J., Pearson, T.: Direct comparison of the efficacy of intuitive and analytical cognition in expert judgment. IEEE Trans. Syst. Man Cybern. **17**(5), 753–770 (1987)
19. Hopko, D.R., Mahadevan, R., Bare, R.L., Hunt, M.K.: The abbreviated math anxiety scale (AMAS): construction, validity, and reliability. Assessment **10**(2), 178–182 (2003)
20. Horkoff, J., Yu, E.S.K.: Interactive goal model analysis for early requirements engineering. Requirements Eng. **21**(1), 29–61 (2016)
21. Horkoff, J., Yu, E.S.: Comparison and evaluation of goal-oriented satisfaction analysis techniques. Requirements Eng. (REJ) **18**(3), 1–24 (2011)
22. Houy, C., Fettke, P., Loos, P.: Understanding understandability of conceptual models – what are we actually talking about? In: Atzeni, P., Cheung, D., Ram, S. (eds.) ER 2012. LNCS, vol. 7532, pp. 64–77. Springer, Heidelberg (2012). https://doi.org/10.1007/978-3-642-34002-4_5
23. Jošt, G., Huber, J., Heričko, M., Polančič, G.: An empirical investigation of intuitive understandability of process diagrams. Comput. Stand. Interfaces **48**, 90–111 (2016)
24. Liaskos, S., Dundjerovic, T., Gabriel, G.: Comparing alternative goal model visualizations for decision making: an exploratory experiment. In: Proceedings of the 33rd Annual ACM Symposium on Applied Computing (SAC 2018), Pau, France, pp. 1272–1281 (2018)
25. Liaskos, S., Jalman, R., Aranda, J.: On eliciting preference and contribution measures in goal models. In: Proceedings of the 20th International Requirements Engineering Conference (RE 2012), Chicago, IL, pp. 221–230 (2012)
26. Liaskos, S., Khan, S.M., Soutchanski, M., Mylopoulos, J.: Modeling and reasoning with decision-theoretic goals. In: Ng, W., Storey, V.C., Trujillo, J.C. (eds.) ER 2013. LNCS, vol. 8217, pp. 19–32. Springer, Heidelberg (2013). https://doi.org/10.1007/978-3-642-41924-9_3
27. Liaskos, S., McIlraith, S., Sohrabi, S., Mylopoulos, J.: Representing and reasoning about preferences in requirements engineering. Requirements Eng. J. (REJ) **16**, 227–249 (2011)
28. Liaskos, S., Ronse, A., Zhian, M.: Assessing the intuitiveness of qualitative contribution relationships in goal models: an exploratory experiment. In: Proceedings of the 11th ACM/IEEE International Symposium on Empirical Software Engineering and Measurement (ESEM 2017), Toronto, Canada, pp. 466–471 (2017)
29. Liaskos, S., Tambosi, W.: Comparing the comprehensibility of numeric versus symbolic contribution labels in goal models: an experimental design. In: Proceedings of the MODELS 2018 Workshop on Human Factors in Modeling (HuFaMo 2018), Copenhagen, Denmark, pp. 738–745 (2018)
30. Maiden, N.A.M., Pavan, P., Gizikis, A., Clause, O., Kim, H., Zhu, X.: Making decisions with requirements: integrating i* goal modelling and the AHP. In: Proceedings of the 8th International Working Conference on Requirements Engineering: Foundation for Software Quality (REFSQ 2002), Essen, Germany (2002)
31. Mendling, J., Strembeck, M.: Influence factors of understanding business process models. In: Abramowicz, W., Fensel, D. (eds.) BIS 2008. LNBIP, vol. 7, pp. 142–153. Springer, Heidelberg (2008). https://doi.org/10.1007/978-3-540-79396-0_13

32. Moody, D.L.: The "Physics" of notations: toward a scientific basis for constructing visual notations in software engineering. IEEE Trans. Softw. Eng. **35**(6), 756–779 (2009)
33. Moody, D.L., Heymans, P., Matulevičius, R.: Visual syntax does matter: improving the cognitive effectiveness of the i* visual notation. Requirements Eng. **15**(2), 141–175 (2010)
34. Mylopoulos, J., Chung, L., Liao, S., Wang, H., Yu, E.: Exploring alternatives during requirements analysis. IEEE Softw. **18**(1), 92–96 (2001)
35. Purchase, H.C., Welland, R., McGill, M., Colpoys, L.: Comprehension of diagram syntax: an empirical study of entity relationship notations. Int. J. Hum. Comput. Stud. **61**(2), 187–203 (2004)
36. Rosnow, R.L., Rosenthal, R.: Beginning Behavioral Research: A Conceptual Primer, 6th edn. Pearson Prentice Hall, Upper Saddle River (2008)
37. Shoval, P., Frumermann, I.: OO and EER conceptual schemas: a comparison of user comprehension. J. Database Manag. (JDM) **5**(4), 28–38 (1994)
38. Tabachnick, B.G., Fidell, L.S.: Using Multivariate Statistics, 6th edn. Pearson, London (2012)
39. Yu, E.S.K.: Towards modelling and reasoning support for early-phase requirements engineering. In: Proceedings of the 3rd IEEE International Symposium on Requirements Engineering (RE 1997), Annapolis, MD, pp. 226–235 (1997)

iStar-p: A Modelling Language for Requirements Prioritization

Cinthya Flório[1,2] (iD), Maria Lencastre[1] (iD), João Pimentel[3(✉)] (iD),
and João Araujo[4] (iD)

[1] Universidade de Pernambuco, Recife, Brazil
mlpm@ecomp.poli.br
[2] Universidade Federal de Pernambuco, Recife, Brazil
ccf@cin.ufpe.br
[3] Universidade Federal Rural de Pernambuco, Recife, Brazil
joao.hcpimentel@ufrpe.br
[4] Universidade Nova de Lisboa, Lisbon, Portugal
pl91@fct.unl.pt

Abstract. This paper proposes the iStar-p model aiming to provide a visual requirements modelling language with prioritization information. This model extends *i**, a goal-oriented modeling language, by including essential prioritization information, such as prioritization technique, prioritization criteria, the involved stakeholders in the prioritization and their weight, as well as the requirements priority. Early evaluation of the proposal indicates that not only it is easy to be applied and useful, but it also increases the transparency of the prioritization process, by explicitly expressing the factors used to calculate priorities.

Keywords: Requirements engineering · Requirements prioritization · Goal oriented requirements engineering

1 Introduction

Cost, staff limitations, market, and user pressures often constrain software development projects. In this context, requirements prioritization is a fundamental task [7, 8] since it assists in the selection of the essential requirements, by considering criteria like benefits to the business, risks involved, frequency of use, legal requirements, as well as cost, and development time [13, 16].

Studies such as [6, 15], and [2] emphasize the relevance of visual representations of requirements, in addition to textual ones. In [6] the authors also observe that visualization is a form of computing, the goal of which is to arouse consciousness and insight; it transforms data for easier assimilation by an individual's sense of sight. Nevertheless, there is a lack of visual representations targeting at this specific activity of the Requirements Engineering (RE) process, as well as to organize, structure and represent the information that involves the prioritization of requirements [16].

Prioritization of requirements is an often-neglected sub-activity of the analysis and negotiation phase within the RE process. Four preparatory activities can be established to accomplish the requirements prioritization: select stakeholders, determine

A. H. F. Laender et al. (Eds.): ER 2019, LNCS 11788, pp. 540–548, 2019.
https://doi.org/10.1007/978-3-030-33223-5_44

requirements to be prioritized, define prioritization criteria and select the prioritization technique(s) to be applied [13]. The stakeholder's selection is of fundamental importance and should consider a representative of the development team, a project manager, a representative of the user/client and a quality manager. The application of prioritization techniques demands time and availability of stakeholders, as well as dependency information between requirements. However, there is a lack of visual mechanisms to help requirements engineers defining strategies for executing the prioritization [16].

Although the literature presents many modelling languages specific to the domain of RE, [17, 19] and [20], they do not support the representation of specific features of the prioritization of requirements. Characteristics that are not sufficiently available in these languages include prioritization techniques to be adopted, criteria for application, stakeholders, and the weight of stakeholders in the prioritization process. However, some approaches (e.g., [10–12]), have elements and relationships that contribute to the reasoning and analysis of the prioritization of requirements. Nevertheless, [4] observes that many aspects of requirements prioritization are still neglected and treated incompletely or superficially.

The purpose of this work is to provide a visual representation to support requirements prioritization in requirements models. Here we focus on social goal models, e.g., $i*$ models. The objective is to provide support to the strategic planning of requirements prioritization through the provision of visual representation, considering that this can help cognitively in the accomplishment of this activity. The proposal defines the iStar-p, an extension of the $i*$ language [5, 17] developed not only based on interviews with practitioners, but also on a systematic mapping review. Early evaluation of the iStar-p indicates that the proposal is both easy to apply and useful, even though it was considered too time-intensive due to the lack of tool support.

The organization of this paper is described as follows. Section 2 discusses the methodology. Section 3 presents the iStar-p proposal. Section 4 shows evaluation efforts. Section 5 discusses related work. Finally, Sect. 6 presents conclusions and points out directions for future work.

2 Methodology

The first step was to identify the main concepts of the requirements prioritization domain. This was achieved through a systematic mapping review (SMR) on the topic, presented in [3], and through interviews with practitioners [4]. From the 52 concepts identified, seven were deemed essential: requirements identification, requirements priority, prioritization technique, prioritization criteria, stakeholder identification, stakeholders' weight, and the number of stakeholders. In the SMR, it was also observed the lack of mechanisms to support the visual representation of the essential components that are part of the requirements' prioritization process.

The second step was to decide either to create an entirely new language or to extend an existing one. We chose to extend the $i*$ modeling language, as we detected that $i*$ already has some elements that help support the prioritization and that $i*$ current approaches for prioritization specification lack expressiveness [4]. The $i*$ (iStar) language has a broad research community [9]. The iStar 2.0 standard [5] was adopted as

the basis for this proposal. Three concepts of the *i** language, mainly, make it a good starting point for prioritizing requirements: actors, refinements and contribution links.

Therefore, the strategy used for this proposal was the extension of the *i** language aiming to support planning and executing requirements prioritization, called iStar-p. It includes two sub-models: SPlan (sub-model for planning) and SPrio (sub-model for prioritization). These new sub-models comprehend new elements, making *i** more expressive for the context of requirements' prioritization. After the iStar-p model went through the first round of evaluation with practitioners, in a first experiment, a new version of the model was proposed (see Sect. 3). To assess the suitability of the iStar-p model, for usage with different requirements prioritization techniques, we analyzed the most cited and used ones [1].

3   iStar-p: A Model for Requirements Prioritization

The core idea of iStar-p is to include prioritization onto regular *i** models. On the one hand, there is (meta) information about the prioritization process: stakeholders' weights, prioritization technique, and the weight of each prioritization criteria. On the other hand, there are the prioritization values assigned by the stakeholders to each element of the model (i.e., the prioritization itself). SPlan represents the former sub-model (Fig. 1) and, the SPrio represents the latter sub-model (Fig. 2).

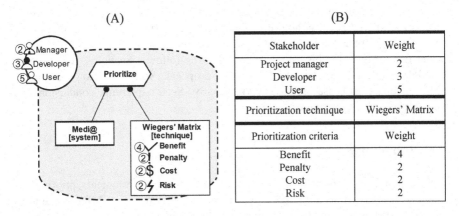

(A)   (B)

Stakeholder	Weight
Project manager	2
Developer	3
User	5
Prioritization technique	Wiegers' Matrix
Prioritization criteria	Weight
Benefit	4
Penalty	2
Cost	2
Risk	2

Fig. 1. Meta information instantiated for Wiegers' Matrix with the SPlan sub-model

Figure 1 shows an example, using the SPlan model, of a prioritization strategy. Figure 1A presents a new kind of actor: Prioritization Team. The icons on top of this actor represent the stakeholders that participate in the prioritization process: project manager, developers, and users. The circle, on top of each of these icons, represent their weights: 2, 3, and 5, respectively. The resource element, filled with a "system" topic, indicates the system (or part of the system) being prioritized (Medi@). The resource, filled with a "technique" topic, indicates the prioritization technique adopted

(Wiegers' Matrix), together with the prioritization criteria to be used (if any). In this example, the criteria are benefit (weight 4), penalty (weight 2), cost (weight 2), and risk (weight 2).

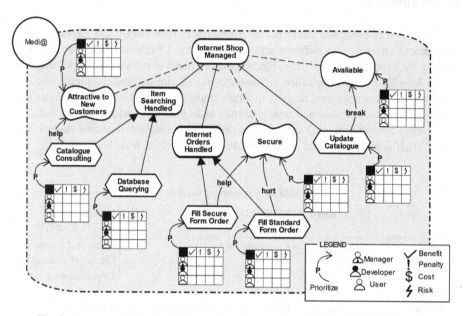

Fig. 2. Empty prioritization elements (matrices) - example of an SPrio sub-model

In Fig. 1B, we display the equivalent text information, as a table, for comparison's sake. Figure 2 shows the Medi@ example with prioritization elements considering the three participants and four criteria, according to the strategy defined in Fig. 1. The prioritization values, assigned to each requirement, are visually displayed as matrices, where rows represent stakeholders and columns represent prioritization criteria (Fig. 2). Thus, each cell in a matrix represents the value assigned by a stakeholder to an element, regarding a particular prioritization criterium. Observe that the participants and criteria, indicated in the matrix, vary according to the project.

In this example, as defined in the SPlan (Fig. 1), the participants are Project manager, Developers, and Users. The criteria are Benefit, Penalty, Development Cost, and Risk. Icons are preferably used instead of text, to prevent bloating the model with too much text. The prioritization element is linked to its respective element through a Prioritizes link, labeled with the letter 'P'.

The iStar-p model can be used both for data gathering and data visualization. In data gathering, participants must receive a model with empty matrices (as shown in Fig. 2), where they should write down the values they assign to each requirement/ criterium pair. For data visualization, a consolidated model with the input of every stakeholder and (possibly) calculated priority values can be used as an input for conflict identification, negotiation, release planning, and so on. For instance, in the matrices of

Fig. 2, a fifth column could be added with averaged priority values calculated based on stakeholders' and criteria's weights.

4   Evaluation

The iStar-p was evaluated using two experiments (Experiment-I and Experiment-II), with practitioners of two different university courses: UPE and UFPE (see Table 1). During the execution phase, the subjects followed these steps: stakeholders' selection, scope definition, criteria selection (planning); and fill the qualities matrices, calculate and rank qualities priorities, analyze qualities impacts on goals and tasks, fill the goal and task matrices, calculate and rank goals and tasks priorities (prioritization itself). For uniformity, all subjects used the same prioritization technique: hundred dollars allocation. This one was selected as it is the most cited ordinal scale technique [1].

Table 1. Experiment summary

	Experiment-I (UPE, Brazil)	Experiment-II (UFPE, Brazil)
Context	Master course in Computer Eng.	Undergrad course on Computer Science
Number of subjects	8 participants	15 participants
Subjects profile	4 Developers, 1 Tester, 1 Interaction Designer (UX), 1 Business Analyst and 1 Not specified	5 Developers 4 Users and 6 Not specified
Previous $i*$ knowledge	No	Yes
Experiment duration	3 h	1 h 50 min
Training	2 classes about: $i*$ Model and Requirements Prioritization	1 Requirements Prioritization class
Prioritization technique	Wiegers Matrix	Hundred Dollar ($100)
Used example	Adapted Media@ system	Adapted Media@ system
iStar-p version	1	2.0 – SPlan and SPrio sub-models

Regarding Ease of Learning, 60% of respondents strongly agreed that the proposal is easy to learn, 20% just agreed, and the remaining 20% were neutral. Thus, most of the respondents stated that the proposal is easy to learn. Moreover, all respondents agreed that the proposal is easy to use (47% just agreed, and 53% strongly agreed). Expressly, most respondents agreed that the use of prioritization matrices within $i*$ models facilitate prioritization: 80% strongly agreed, 13% just agreed, 7% were neutral.

Regarding Transparency, most subjects agreed that the proposal made it clear how the final priority values are obtained: 40% strongly agreed, 47% just agreed, and 13% were neutral. Lastly, most respondents considered the proposal satisfactory: 20% strongly agreed, 73% just agreed, and 7% were neutral. Nonetheless, results regarding fit for use by the industry were less positive: 13% strongly agreed that the proposal is fit for use, 40% just agreed, 40% were neutral, and 7% disagreed. We hypothesize four factors that may have led to this result: (i) the perceived time-effort required to use the proposal with real examples; (ii) the use of $i*$, which is not widely adopted by the industry; (iii) the perceived low importance of prioritization; and (iv) lack of tool support. Full results are available in Table 2. It shows that the majority of the participants agree or fully agree that the proposed model is easy to learn, useful in planning the prioritization, clear in the execution of prioritization, and understanding the meaning of the elements, among other aspects. However, some participants claimed that they would not use the model in a professional environment, because of the consequences that would be generated by the lack of tooling support (such as more time and effort). Participants also reported that it took time and effort to carry out the planning and execution of prioritization.

Table 2. Questionnaire answers with the percentage of each answer

iStar-p model proposal	Experiment I	Experiment II
1. Easy to learn	(A-50%), (D-50%)	(SA-60%), (A-20%), (U-20%)
2. Easy of execute the prioritization	(SA-25%), (A-50%), (U-13%), (D-12%)	(SA-53%), (A-47%)
3. Prioritization matrix along with $i*$ elements facilitate prioritization	(SA-38%), (A-25%), (D-25%), (U-12%)	(SA-80%), (A-13%), (U-7%)
4. Clearness and understandability of the visual elements' representation & scale used	(SA-25%), (A-38%), (U-25%), (D-12%)	(SA-60%), (A-27%), (U-13%)
5. Clarity about how prioritization is executed (transparency)	(SA-25%), (A-38%), (U-25%), (D-12%)	(SA-40%), (A-47%), (U-13%)
6. Usefulness of documenting the prioritization strategy (SPlan sub-model)	(SA-38%), (A-37%), (D-25%)	(SA-47%), (A-33%), (U-20%)
7. Usefulness as a documentation artefact for prioritization	(SA-38%), (A-37%), (U-25%)	(SA-13%), (A-67%), (U-13%)
8. Fidelity of each visual prioritization element representation	(SA-25%), (A-38%), (U-25%), (D-12%)	(SA 47%), (A-33%), (D-20%)
9. Satisfaction with Prioritizing with the model	(SA 25%), (A-50%), (U-13%), (D-12%)	(SA-20%), (A-73%), (U-7%)
10. Potential use in professional environments	(SA-13%), (A-37%), (U-25%), (D-25%)	(SA-13%), (A-40%), (U-40%), (D-7%)

Legend: Strongly agree (SA) - Agree (A) - Undecided (U) - Disagree (D) - Strongly disagree (SD)

Four types of validity threats can be observed: conclusion, internal, construct and external. **Conclusion validity:** We had only 8 participants in Experiment-I and 15 participants in Experiment-II, compromising the statistical pertinence of the results. We plan to perform other experiments with a more significant number of participants, including experts and practitioners. **Internal validity:** The results may be compromised by a fatigue effect as the experiment lasted for almost 2 h; also, each experiment group has used only one prioritization technique and only one example, which may have an impact on the results of the evaluation. **Construct validity:** We defined the experiment with different tasks (e.g., selection of stakeholders, scope definition, criteria selection, rank and analyze qualities, calculate and rank goals and task priorities). This could be confusing for the participants, but we mitigated this threat by providing a tutorial on the relevant topics for the experiment (requirements prioritization concepts, planning, and techniques, and the iStar-p language). Also, giving the tutorial may have caused an evaluation apprehension threat. To mitigate this, we have not informed them about what was being tested. Also, the lack of a control group reduces the value of this empirical evaluation since there is no basis upon which to contrast the results of the treatment group. **External validity:** The participants had little to no prior knowledge in requirements prioritization; this can be used to generalize the results for the acceptance of the approach by non-expert stakeholders.

5   Related Work

There are some approaches that include representations of prioritization elements. [12] proposes the use of AHP with $i*$ models to obtain quantitative indicators of softgoal satisfaction. [10] presents an approach to select alternatives on $i*$ models, based on desired levels of satisfaction of softgoals; so it focuses more specifically on decision making, than on prioritization. Both [12] and [10] can be used together with iStar-p. [12] enables the elicitation of precise values for contribution links, which can aid stakeholders when prioritizing the elements of the model with iStar-p. On the other hand, users can prioritize qualities with iStar-p and use that information when making decisions with the approach of [10]. [11] shows the application of a decision-making technique along with the NFR Framework [18]; this approach is similar to ours, but it is focused on a specific technique, whereas our proposal is technique agnostic; they can be considered complementary since ours is not suitable for pair-wise comparison techniques. [14] provides support for combinatorial optimization in the RE domain; it allows calculating values, to find solutions to constraints, and to perform queries on requirements models; whereas it focuses on processing support for automatic evaluation, our proposal focuses on visual support for manual data gathering and visualization.

6   Conclusion and Future Work

In this paper, we propose the iStar-p, a modelling language that extends $i*$ to support five identified essential elements of requirements prioritization, from [3]. The remaining two, requirements identification (id) and the number of stakeholders, can be generated/calculated automatically through tool support. In this context, $i*$ is a suitable basis, since it can express additional relevant information such as stakeholders' goals, the interplay between its elements, and the effect of alternatives on desired qualities.

Even though we carefully designed the concrete syntax of this proposal, a study of its semiotics is a promising venue to identify further improvement possibilities. Additional mechanisms can also be analyzed to prevent data overload. We have conducted an early empirical evaluation with practitioners and undergrad students. Despite positive results, further evaluation is required not only with more subjects but also in industry settings, to assess the usefulness of the proposal accurately. Finally, the development of a supporting tool could facilitate the adoption of the proposal.

Acknowledgements. This study was financed in part by the Coordenação de Aperfeiçoamento de Pessoal de Nível Superior - Brasil (CAPES) - Finance Code 001, NOVA LINCS UID/CEC/04516/2013, and Fundação de Amparo à Ciência e Tecnologia do Estado de Pernambuco (FACEPE).

References

1. Achimugu, P., Selamat, A., Ibrahim, R., Mahrin, M.: A systematic literature review of software requirements prioritization research. Inf. Softw. Technol. **56**(6), 568–585 (2014)
2. Carod, N., Cechich, A.: Cognitive profiles in understanding and prioritizing requirements: a case study. In: IEEE 5th International Conference on Software Engineering Advances (2010)
3. Cavalcanti, C., Lencastre, M., Fagundes, R., Santos, T., Ferreira, D.: Mechanisms to support requirements prioritization: a systematic mapping review. In: 21st Workshop on Requirements Engineering (2018). https://doi.org/10.17771/pucrio.wer.inf2018-52
4. Cavalcanti, C.: Planejamento e Priorização de Requisitos em Modelos i*. Masters dissertation. University of Pernambuco, Brazil (2017)
5. Dalpiaz, F., Franch, X., Horkoff, J.: iStar 2.0 language guide. arXiv preprint arXiv:1605. 07767 (2016)
6. Gotel, O.C., Marchese, F.T., Morris, S.J.: On requirements visualization. In: 2nd International Workshop on Requirements Engineering Visualization - REV 2007. IEEE (2007)
7. Greer, D.: Requirements prioritisation for incremental and iterative development. In: Requirements Engineering for Sociotechnical Systems, pp. 100–118. IGI Global (2005)
8. Hofmann, H.F., Lehner, F.: Requirements engineering as a success factor in software projects. IEEE Softw. **4**, 58–66 (2001)
9. Horkoff, J., et al.: Taking goal models downstream: a systematic roadmap. In: IEEE RCIS (2014)
10. Horkoff, J., Yu, E.: Finding solutions in goal models: an interactive backward reasoning approach. In: Parsons, J., Saeki, M., Shoval, P., Woo, C., Wand, Y. (eds.) ER 2010. LNCS, vol. 6412, pp. 59–75. Springer, Heidelberg (2010). https://doi.org/10.1007/978-3-642-16373-9_5

11. Kassab, M.: An integrated approach of AHP and NFRs framework. In: 7th IEEE International Conference on Research Challenges in Information Science (2013)
12. Liaskos, S., Jalman, R., Aranda, J.: On eliciting contribution measures in goal models. In: 20th IEEE International Requirements Engineering Conference (2012)
13. Pohl, K.: Requirements Engineering: Fundamentals, Principles, and Techniques. Springer, Heidelberg (2010)
14. Regnell, B., Kuchcinski, K.: A scala embedded DSL for combinatorial optimization in software requirements engineering. In: First Workshop on Domain Specific Languages in Combinatorial Optimization, pp. 19–34 (2013)
15. Savio, D., Poothiyot, A.P.: Extended support for visualizing requirements: filtering and tracing requirements in ReBlock. In: IEEE 5th International Workshop on Requirements Prioritization and Communication (RePriCo), pp. 11–14. IEEE (2014)
16. Thakurta, R.: Understanding requirement prioritization artifacts: a systematic mapping study. Requirements Eng. **22**(4), 491–526 (2017)
17. Yu, E., Giorgini, P., Maiden, N., Mylopoulos, J. (eds.): Social Modeling for Requirements Engineering. MIT Press, Cambridge (2011)
18. Chung, L., Nixon, B.A., Yu, E., Mylopoulos, J.: Non-functional Requirements in Software Engineering, vol. 5. Springer, Heidelberg (2000). https://doi.org/10.1007/978-1-4615-5269-7
19. Van Lamsweerde, A.: Requirements Engineering: From System Goals to UML Models to Software. Wiley, Hoboken (2009)
20. Kaiya, H., Horai, H., Saeki, M.: Agora: attributed goal-oriented requirements analysis method. In: IEEE Joint International Conference on Requirements Engineering (2002)

On the Use of Requirement Patterns to Analyse Request for Proposal Documents

Dolors Costal⊙, Xavier Franch⊙, Lidia López⊙,
Cristina Palomares⊙, and Carme Quer$^{(\boxtimes)}$⊙

Universitat Politècnica Catalunya (UPC-BarcelonaTech), Barcelona, Spain
{dolors, franch, llopez, cpalomares, cquer}@essi.upc.edu

Abstract. Requirements reuse is still today a difficult goal to achieve. One particular context in which requirements reuse may give more benefits than costs is that of call for tenders projects, due to the similarity of the requirements documents (which take the form of requests for proposal documents, RfPs) from one project to another. In this paper, we present an approach aimed at making systematic the assessment of RfPs that technology providers need to conduct in order to decide whether they present a bid or not in a call for tenders project. The approach extends a metamodel we already defined for the former PABRE method, which has a similar goal but from the perspective of the organization that issues the call for tenders. The method is illustrated with an exploratory case study in the field of the railway systems domain.

Keywords: Requirements reuse · Requirement patterns · Call for tenders · Request for Proposals · Bidding process

1 Introduction

Reuse is a cornerstone activity in all facets of engineering, and Requirements Engineering (RE) is not an exception. There are several recent works reporting on approaches to requirements reuse (see [1] for a literature review) and in particular, evidence exists that in industry, reuse practices are not yet commonplace [2].

One of the contexts where requirements reuse may pay off occurs with call for tenders processes articulated around the needs for some technological solution exposed in Request for Proposals (RfPs). Multiple RfPs in a same domain (e.g., railway domain) or for the same type of systems (e.g., business applications) may be similar to each other, which opens the way to requirements reuse. In previous work, we have explored one particular approach to requirements reuse, namely the use of requirement patterns, in order to help customers to efficiently produce new RfPs [3, 4]. Therefore, the focus of this previous work has been on the customer side. In this paper, we want to explore if the adoption of a pattern-based approach to requirements reuse can also be of help to technology providers when processing the RfP.

© Springer Nature Switzerland AG 2019
A. H. F Laender et al. (Eds.): ER 2019, LNCS 11788, pp. 549–557, 2019.
https://doi.org/10.1007/978-3-030-33223-5_45

2 Background

We consider background on requirement patterns and on RfPs. The seminal book by Withall [5] proposed a first exhaustive catalogue of patterns and, since then, other approaches have been proposed [6, 7]. Requirement pattern approaches differ in several respects, see Barros-Justo et al.'s [8]. The most obvious one is the language used to express the requirements, being natural language and use cases the two most popular cases. Other factors that need to be considered are the granularity of the object under reuse, the intended impact in the RE process and the scope.

Regarding RFPs, there are approaches focused on customers and others on providers. Lauesen has approached the customer perspective of call for tenders' processes in several works (e.g., [9]). He has provided some guidelines for the customer, which he reports are not always applied. Our PABRE method [3] was designed for supporting the customer in the preparation of the RfPs. It is based on the creation of pattern catalogues [10, 11] with a well-defined metamodel [12]. The requirements that are part of a RfP are created by instantiating the patterns. On the providers side, Paech et al. [13] report the challenge to deal with large RfPs in a tight period with little or no communication with the customer. They propose a risk-based approach in which different types of risks are sought and identified in new RfPs. The resulting analysis is the input to the RfP evaluation and then it is used to decide about the actions to be taken in the bidding process. From a similar perspective, Breiner et al. [14] propose a 4-phase process to deal with RfPs in IT providers to be tailored in every individual bidding. Both providers approaches are similar in their methodological stand, but they lack of a central repository of knowledge and have little tool support.

In this paper we address the provider perspective to call for tenders processes by applying a pattern-based approach to the assessment of RfPs. We use assets built in the PABRE method and evolve them to include the new relevant information.

3 Research Goal and Research Questions

Our goal is to *evaluate* the benefits of *a pattern-based approach* on *assessing RfPs* from the point of view of *technology providers* in the context of *multiple call for tenders processes in the same domain*. This goal is decomposed into two research questions:

RQ1. What type of information needs to be added to requirement patterns to help technology providers in their assessment of RfPs?

RQ2. Does the use of requirement patterns bring benefits to technology providers when organizing their bidding processes?

4 Patterns in the Railway Domain

As case study for the research questions, we used six RfPs from the railway domain that the Viennese Siemens Mobility department made available for this research in the context of the OpenReq EU project [15]. The RfPs are composed of 17,556 candidate

requirements, classified depending on whether they were considered as a real requirement (DEF) or as merely informative (Prose). For each candidate requirement the document also includes the domain or department of Siemens that is the one that had to do the analysis of the compliance of the requirement. One example of requirement is *"On the body of the half barrier 3 light units are mounted. Lights on the half barrier must be visible at night from at least 20 m under normal visibility conditions"*, while an example of Prose is *"The purpose of the new computerized interlocking system is described in the present Requirements"*.

From the RfPs we constructed 25 patterns of 6 diverse categories. Table 1 summarizes the classification of these patterns and the number of requirements out of the RfPs from which each one has been obtained.

Table 1. Classification of the generated patterns

Type	Category	Pattern	#Reqs
Infrastructure Management	Facility Removal	Remove Facility	3
	Equipment Replacement	Replace Equipment	18
Supporting Systems	Video Surveillance System Installation	Require Video Surveillance System	2
		Establish Video Cameras Location	2
		Establish Video Cameras Mounting	1
		Establish Video Cameras Protection	1
		Establish Monitor Computers	1
		Establish Monitor Location	2
		Establish Monitor Screen	1
		Establish Monitor Display Options	1
		Establish Network Connection Features	2
		Establish Recording Functions	1
	Automatic Block Signaling System Installation	Install Automatic Block Signaling System	10
		Modify Automatic Block Signaling System	16
Non-technical	Training	Make Training Plan	2
		Supply Training Documents	2
		Supply Training Equipment	2
		Establish Trainees	2
		Establish Training Language	1
		Evaluate and Certify Trainees	1
	Warranty	Establish Warranty Period	1
		Provide Assistance	1
		Provide Monitoring Equipment	1
		Remove Defects During Warranty Period	5
		Replace Product During Warranty Period	1

One of the constructed patterns, *Remove Facility*, is depicted in Fig. 1 to present requirement patterns elements. The *Remove Facility* pattern can only take one form (*Facility basic* pattern form). The pattern form has a core part (Fixed part) that expresses its basic linguistic template. It also contains three optional extensions to this core part (Extended parts) to describe the levels of the facility to remove, its size and its

location, respectively. The bold tags enclosed among "%" are representing parameters that would correspond to specific values in the RfPs (for instance, the parameter % typeOfFacility% could be instantiated with the value "Watchman's Post or Family House"). The Domain and Compliance clauses are explained in the next section.

```
Remove Facility
Goal:             Remove a room or an existing building
Pattern form:     Facility basic
Fixed part:       In %railwayLocation% the contractor shall remove a
                     %typeOfFacility%.

Extended parts:
EP1:              Levels of the facility
    Template:     The facility is a %facilityLevels% facility.
    Compliance:   %facilityLevels% is under 9 levels
EP2:              Size of the facility
    Template:     The facility has %units% %unitMeasure%
EP3:              Facility location
    Template:     The facility is identified in the cadastral plot %ca-
                     dastralIdenfication% of the %districtName%
    Compliance:   - The facility is located in a place accessible by road
                  - The facility is situated on a stable ground
Domain:           Installation_Local
```

Fig. 1. Remove Facility requirement pattern

5 RQ1: Pattern Attributes

As result of RQ1, we plan to extend the metamodel of the existing PABRE method [12] with new classes, associations and attributes required. Figure 2 shows the result.

We include in the figure only the relevant excerpt of the PABRE metamodel (e.g., we hide information about classification schemas) over which we include the new elements. Original PABRE classes are filled in salmon color and they show the structure introduced in the previous section: a Requirement Pattern can take one or more Pattern Forms; each Pattern Form is characterized by a Fixed Part and one or more Extended Parts. In the metamodel, an abstract class Pattern Part is introduced for convenience. Dependency allows establishing dependencies between patterns. Glossary Term and Relationship between terms facilitate to deal with synonymy, ambiguity, etc. For the rest, we distinguish:

Information at the organization level (classes in white background). This information needs to be defined only once by the organization:

- Class Domain. The classification of patterns into domains allows selecting the department that will assess every requirement in the RfP. More precisely, every atomic component inside the structure of a pattern, i.e., a part, should be assigned to one domain. We allow this to be made at three different levels: individually at every part, at the level of a pattern form (meaning that all the parts of a pattern form belong to the same domain) and at the level of a pattern (meaning that all the forms of a pattern – and transitively all of its parts– belong to this domain). To model this comfortably, we introduce an abstract class Level. One or more Departments

will participate in the assessment of all requirements of a given Domain. In Fig. 1, we show that the *Remove Facility* pattern has *Installation_Local* as domain.

- Class Assessment Factor. Companies will assess RfPs with respect to factors like cost, effort or risk. Its instances are linked to Value so that the values for every assessment factor can be explicitly defined. For instance, companies can define risk as Assessment Factor, with six possible values (Type1 to Type6) [13].

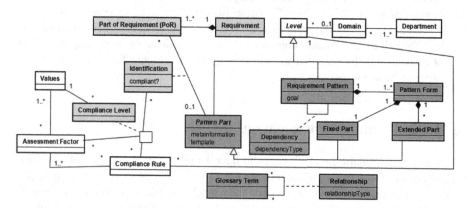

Fig. 2. Extending the PABRE metamodel with information fit for technology providers (Color figure online)

- Class Compliance Rule. Every Pattern Part may have, directly or indirectly, either (through its pattern form or its pattern), one or more Compliance Rules that express a condition to be measured with respect to some Assessment Factors. The purpose of Compliance Rules is to give providers a checklist to decide if every (part of a) requirement appearing in the RfP can be eventually satisfied or not. The class Level is used with the same purpose as in Domain. In Fig. 1, we show three compliance rules attached to two different extended parts, expressing a restriction on the number of levels and two restrictions on the facility location.

Information at the project level (classes in yellow background). This information needs to be defined at every call for tenders project:

- The RfP includes Requirements that can be decomposed into atomic Parts of Requirements (PoR). E.g., *"on cadastral plot 362, cadastral district Acme Acres"* is a PoR about removing a facility that provides its location.
- Association class Identification. These PoR are the ones matching Pattern Parts by giving values to the parameters (not shown in the figure): a PoR may match one Pattern Part, while one Pattern Part can eventually be matched to several PoR. This matching is kept by the Identification association class. For instance, the identification *"The facility is identified in the cadastral plot cadastral plot 362 of the Acme Acres district"* corresponds to the matching of the previous PoR example and the *Facility location* part of the *Remove Facility* pattern

(see Fig. 1). If a PoR does not match any Pattern Part, this means that this PoR is not covered by the current catalogue (i.e., must be handled manually).

- Association class Compliance Level. For every Compliance Rule associated to a Pattern Part identified in a PoR, it is required to propose a Compliance Level in the form of a Value for each of its Assessment Factors. For the previous Identification example the Compliance Rules are: *"The facility is located in a place accessible by road"* and *"The facility is situated on a stable ground"*. These rules can be used to propose the Compliance Level of the identification. As a result of this assessment, the PoR will be labelled as compliant, compliant under conditions or non-compliant. This assessment will be recorded in the compliant? attribute from the Identification association class.

6   RQ2: Preliminary Evaluation

We ran a questionnaire inside Siemens to have a preliminary evaluation of our work. We used the TAM evaluation questionnaire [16]. Specifically, we use a simplified version given that the technology is not fully available. We asked the participants to evaluate their vision on the adoption of the pattern-based approach using two simplified scenarios that focus on the patterns usage. The scenarios presented a RfP for which the respondent company wanted to present a bid and described the steps of the pattern usage proposal with the help of mock ups of an envisaged PABRE system.

Questions can be consulted in the online document that presents the questionnaire[1]. Table 2 presents the results of the evaluation The averages computed should be considered for informal reference purposes only, because the values are given in a Likert scale 1 (strongly agree) to 7 (strongly disagree), therefore in an ordinal scale, not with a ratio. However, they are still useful for intuitive explanations. All questions are positive (i.e., 1 means the most positive answer) except for question 2.2; therefore, in the averages, we have computed the inverse value of its responses (i.e., from N to $7 - N + 1$).

The results show that 3 respondents (E2, E3 and E5) were receptive to the summative Question 6: *"Based on the previous scenarios, and assuming that the PABRE system were available, I would intend to use it"*. Instead, E1 and E4 were reluctant. Respondents with positive attitude were cautious anyway, as clearly stated by E3: *"Although being open-minded, I am not sure whether this approach could work in practice"*. We consider that this position is normal when it comes to considering an emergent, not yet available technology in a mature and complex process.

On the positive side, we can see that the system is perceived as easy-to-use (Question 2), even by E1 and E4. E2 likes the general layout of the solution, while E5 nuances that *"this will depend on the quality of the pattern identification"*. The positive respondents are unanimously positive with respect to relevance (Question 3) and even E1 was neutral at this respect. E3 justifies his/her particularly positive rating *"because it*

---

[1] https://www.upc.edu/gessi/PABRE/OPENREQ-PABRE-Questionnaire.pdf.

can potentially increase productivity". Anyhow, E2 doubts "*[...] that all relevant decisions can be expressed as patterns (due to complexity and efforts)*". This is a valid point that is in line with our general understanding that patterns cannot be realistically expected to embed all possible knowledge in a bidding process. Finally, results demonstrability is also well considered except for E3 (no rationale provided).

On the negative side, respondents were especially concerned with the expected output quality (Question 4). For instance, E2 expresses, "*I think it [the approach] needs human intelligence to solve the task. Wrong results can do harm!*". Concerning the two negative respondents, both of them remarked that the separation of require-ments and prose is considered "*a misleading approach. E.g., a header gives the paragraph the right frame [...]*" (E4). We consider this not a fundamental problem to a pattern-based approach but to the way in which we proposed our process in RQ3. We could then modify the output of the requirements triage in a way that the requirements list keeps the context of every requirement.

Also, E5 made the point that a particular RfP may not fit well with a pattern-based approach, e.g., "*productivity and effectiveness are expected to vary depending on the nature of the requirements document and the quality of the pattern recognition*". The importance of the nature of the requirements document has already been shown in RQ1, where some RfPs were more aligned to the identified patterns than others.

Table 2. Questions to Siemens practitioners to evaluate the pattern-based solution

Criteria		E1	E2	E3	E4	E5	Avg
1. Perceived usefulness		5,00	3,67	3,00	6,00	3,00	4,13
1.1	Productivity	5	4	3	6	3	
1.2	Effectiveness	5	4	3	6	3	
1.3	Useful	5	3	3	6	3	
2. Perceived ease of use		2,33	1,33	6,00	3,33	3,33	3,27
2.1	Understandable	3	2	7	2	2	
2.2	Requires a lot of mental effort	6	7	2	2	4	
2.3	Easy to use	2	1	5	2	4	
3. Relevance		4,00	2,50	3,00	6,00	2,00	3,50
3.1	Pertinent	4	3	3	6	2	
3.2	Relevant	4	2	3	6	2	
4. Output quality		3,00	6,00	7,00	6,00	3,50	6,38
4.1	High quality	3	6	7	6	3	
4.2	No problems with quality	3	6	7	6	4	
5. Result demonstrability		4,33	2,00	6,33	2,67	2,33	3,53
5.1	No difficulty to explain	6	2	6	2	2	
5.2	Communicate consequences	3	2	6	2	2	
5.3	Results apparent	4	2	7	4	3	
6. Behavioral Intention		6	3	2	6	3	4,00
6.1	Intent to use	6	3	2	6	3	

7 Conclusions and Future Work

We have presented a pattern-based approach to support IT providers when assessing RfPs and deciding whether to bid for them or not. The main results are an extension of the PABRE metamodel with the information needed to give support to the provider during the bidding, and the results of a questionnaire to get early feedback from our proposal.

As threat to validity, we have evaluated our approach only in one case (Sect. 6). This case has several characteristics: the (type of) domain, the characteristics of the organization, the size and type of RfP documents and others. Generalizing our results beyond these contextual characteristics requires careful reflection.

Our future work focuses at the automation of the approach. Our intention is to make our approach particularly appealing and more prone to scale in contexts where a considerable number of bidding processes around large RfPs from the same domain take place. The main functionalities that the platform will support are: requirements triage, to classify information from RFPs in order to distinguish the requirements from the document prose; patters identification, that will do the match among requirements and the specific patterns in a catalogue; and decision-making support, intended to help in the decision of compliance of requirements in a RfP. Some components are already available, as the web services to manage the patterns catalogue; others are being developed as the NLP components to pre-process RfPs.

Acknowledgments. This work has been conducted within the Horizon 2020 project OpenReq, supported by the European Union under Grant Nr. 732463. We acknowledge Siemens Mobility (Bierbamer, Obenaus, Sandauer) and Siemens research (Falkner, Schenner) at Wien-Austria for participating in the evaluation (RQ2).

References

1. Irshad, M., Petersen, K., Poulding, S.: A systematic literature review of software requirements reuse approaches. Inf. Softw. Technol. **93**, 223–245 (2018)
2. Palomares, C., Quer, C., Franch, X.: Requirements Reuse and Requirement Patterns: A State of the Practice Survey. Empir. Softw. Eng. **22**(6), 2719–2762 (2017)
3. Renault, S., Méndez-Bonilla, O., Franch, X., Quer, C.: PABRE: pattern-based requirements elicitation. In: RCIS (2009)
4. Franch, X., Quer, C., Renault, S., Guerlain, C., Palomares, C.: Constructing and using software requirement patterns. In: Maalej, W., Thurimella, A. (eds.) Managing Requirements Knowledge, pp. 95–116. Springer, Heidelberg (2013). https://doi.org/10.1007/978-3-642-34419-0_5
5. Withall, S.: Software Requirement Patterns. Microsoft Press, Redmond (2007)
6. Pacheco, C.L., Garcia, I.A., Calvo-Manzano, J.A., Arcilla, M.: A proposed model for reuse of software requirements in requirements catalog. J. Softw.: Evol. Process **27**(1), 1–21 (2015)
7. Barcelos, L.V., Penteaso, R.D.: Elaboration of software requirements documents by means of patterns instantiation. J. Softw. Eng. Res. Dev. **5**, 3 (2017)

8. Barros-Justo, J.L., Benitti, B.V., Cravero-Leal, A.L.: Software patterns and requirements engineering activities in real-world settings: a systematic mapping study. Comput. Stand. Interfaces **58**, 23–42 (2018)

9. Lauesen, S.: COTS Tenders and Integration Requirements. Requir. Eng. J. **11**(2), 111–122 (2006)

10. Palomares, C., Quer, C., Franch, X., Renault, S., Guerlain, C.: A catalogue of functional software requirement patterns for content management systems. In: SAC (2013)

11. Palomares, C., Quer, C., Franch, X., Guerlain, C., Renault, S.: A catalogue of non-technical requirement patterns. In: RePa (2012)

12. Franch, X., Palomares, C., Quer, C., Renault, S., De Lazzer, F.: A metamodel for software requirement patterns. In: Wieringa, R., Persson, A. (eds.) REFSQ 2010. LNCS, vol. 6182, pp. 85–90. Springer, Heidelberg (2010). https://doi.org/10.1007/978-3-642-14192-8_10

13. Paech, B., Heinrich, R., Zorn-Pauli, G., Jung, A., Tadjiky, S.: Answering a request for proposal – challenges and proposed solutions. In: Regnell, B., Damian, D. (eds.) REFSQ 2012. LNCS, vol. 7195, pp. 16–29. Springer, Heidelberg (2012). https://doi.org/10.1007/978-3-642-28714-5_2

14. Breiner, K., Gillmann, M., Kalenborn, A., Müller, C.: Requirements engineering in the bidding stage of software projects – a research preview. In: Fricker, S.A., Schneider, K. (eds.) REFSQ 2015. LNCS, vol. 9013, pp. 270–276. Springer, Cham (2015). https://doi.org/10.1007/978-3-319-16101-3_19

15. Felfernig, A., Stetinger, M., Falkner, A., Atas, M., Franch, X., Palomares, C.: OpenReq: recommender systems in requirements engineering. In: i-Know (2017)

16. Davis, F.F.: Perceived usefulness, perceived ease of use, and user acceptance of information technology. MIS Q. **13**(3), 319–340 (1989)

iStar4RationalAgents: Modeling Requirements of Multi-agent Systems with Rational Agents

Enyo Gonçalves[1,2(✉)], João Araujo[3], and Jaelson Castro[2]

[1] Universidade Federal do Ceará – Campus Quixadá, Quixadá, Brazil
enyo@ufc.br
[2] Universidade Federal de Pernambuco, Recife, Brazil
jbc@cin.ufpe.br
[3] Universidade Nova de Lisboa, Lisbon, Portugal
joao.araujo@fct.unl.pt

Abstract. Multi-agent systems (MAS) involve a wide variety of agents that interact with each other to achieve their goals. Usually, the agents in a MAS can be reactive or proactive, this choice defines the rationale of its elements. Rational Agents is the term used to mention a set of four kinds of reactive and proactive agents. Conceptual models which represent the rational agents' intentionality can be used to design and analyze MAS in a systematic and structured manner. Conceptual modelling can be used to uncover mistakes and gaps in reasoning that are missed or obscured via ad hoc evaluation. However, the modelling of MAS with different rational agents is a non-trivial task, due to the specificity of their domain concepts, also at requirements level. This paper presents an approach to model MAS with rational agents in requirements level using iStar. This is part of a Model-Driven Development approach which has been proposed to support the development of MAS with rational agents involving requirements, architecture, code and test. We extended iStar to support the modelling of main concepts of this domain in a systematic way based on a process to conduct iStar extensions. We modelled a MAS to validate and illustrate the usage of our extension and evaluate the results using a survey with experienced researchers/developers in MAS.

Keywords: Multi-agent system · Rational agents · Modeling · iStar

1 Introduction

Autonomous software based on artificial intelligence (AI) have been widely applied to solve a vast set of problems in companies. In this context, agents are complex entities with behavioral properties, such as autonomy and interaction [7]. Multi-agent system (MAS) is the area of AI that investigates the behavior of a set of autonomous agents, aiming to resolve a problem beyond the capacity of a single agent [7].

A simple agent can act based on reactive or proactive behavior and can be classified according to its internal architecture that determines distinct agency properties, attributes and mental components [11]. Russell and Norvig [11] define four types of agents according to their internal structure: Simple Reflex Agent, Model-Based Reflex Agent, Goal-based Agent and Utility-Based Agent. The type of agent is selected according to

© Springer Nature Switzerland AG 2019
A. H. F. Laender et al. (Eds.): ER 2019, LNCS 11788, pp. 558–566, 2019.
https://doi.org/10.1007/978-3-030-33223-5_46

the environment characteristics and to the subproblem that the agent will resolve. A MAS may encompass multiple types of agents [11].

A model-driven approach has been proposed to model MAS with rational agents. Modelling of the architectural level of MAS with rational agents is supported by MAS-ML 2.0 [3], the code generation is supported by the approach proposed by [9] and the test is supported by the proposal of [12]. Therefore, it is important a proposal of modelling at requirements level to complete the support of the development of MAS with rational agents. The modelling of requirements for a multi-agent system can be preferably an extension of a known and trusted modelling language, such as iStar [14]. We have chosen iStar since it supports the modeling of part of the concepts of MAS with rational agents such as goal, belief, agent, tasks and supports the modeling of organizational concepts as well. This language has a process to conduct iStar extensions (PRISE[1]) which makes it easy the proposal of new iStar extensions.

The aim of this paper is to present an iStar extension to model MAS with rational agents named iStar4RationalAgents. The paper is structured as follows. Section 2 presents the main concepts of MAS. Section 3 presents related work. iStar4RationalAgents is described in Sect. 4. In Sect. 5 shows the modelling of the MAS to support the distance education course of programming people with disabilities. The evaluation of MAS is presented in Sect. 6. Finally, conclusions and future work are discussed in Sect. 7.

2 Background

According to Silva et al. [13], organization is an element that groups agents and sub-organizations. Environment is an element that is the habitat for agents, objects and organizations. Environment has state and behavior. Agent is an autonomous, adaptive and interactive element. MAS-ML defines an agent composed of beliefs, goals, plan and actions. On the other hand, the agent internal structures can be categorized based on proactive and reactive foundations. In this context, four types of internal agent architectures were defined by Russell and Norvig [11].

Simple Reflex Agents. A Simple Reflex (or reactive) Agent [11] selects actions based on the current perception. These perceptions consist of the representation of state aspects that are used by the agent for making decisions. **Model-Based Reflex Agents** have condition-action rules as well. This agent is also able to store its current state in an internal model (beliefs). A function called next function is introduced to map the perceptions and the current internal state into a new internal state used to select the next action. **Goal-Based Agents**. Goal-Based Agents set a specific goal and select the actions that lead to that goal. Planning activity is devoted to find the sequence of actions that is able to achieve the agent's goals [11]. The sequence of actions previously established that leads the agent to reach a goal is a termed plan [13]. Thus, the Goal-Based Agent with planning involves the next function component and also includes the following elements: *Formulate goal function*, which receives the state and

---

[1] http://www.cin.ufpe.br/∼ler/prise.

returns the formulated goal; *Formulate problem function*, which receives the state and the goal and returns the problem; *Planning*, which receives the problem and uses search and/or logic approaches to find a sequence of actions to achieve a goal; and *Action*. **Utility-Based Agents**. Considering the existence of multiple goal states, it is possible to define a measure of how desirable a particular state is. In this case, aiming to optimize the agent performance, the utility function is responsible for mapping a possible state (or group of states) to that measure, according to the current goals [11]. Thus, the utility function is incorporated into the architecture. Also, Utility-Based Agent preserves the same elements as those of a Goal-Based Agent: next function, formulate goal function, formulate problem function, planning and action.

3   Related Work

Our paper is part of an MDD approach to develop MAS with rational agents. In [3], an extension to MAS-ML (Multi-Agent Systems Modeling Language [13]) to model MAS with rational agents in the architectural level is presented. Complementary, an extension was proposed to JADE framework to support the development of rational agents and other MAS entities such as organization, environment and agent roles [9]. In addition, the code generation from MAS-ML models was created by MAS-ML tool to the JADE extended version. Finally, in [12] an agent-based approach was proposed to select test cases and test the performance of rational agent. These works cover a great part of the software development life cycle, but the requirements level is not covered by them. Also, PRISE (**PR**ocess to conduct **iStar** Extensions) has been proposed. It is based on a Systematic Literature Review (SLR) of iStar extensions [2] and interviews and survey with experts [5]. PRISE is supported by a catalogue of iStar extensions [4] and a tool for the creation of PRISE artefacts [6]. This paper presents a new iStar extension that followed the PRISE approach.

4   Extending iStar for Model Rational Agents

We represented the extension in the iStar metamodel and created validation rules. The extension metamodel and validation rules are available[2]. We represented each kind of rational agent and their roles in the metamodel by stereotypes (simple-reflex, model-based-reflex, goal-based and utility-based) associated with Agent and AgentRole metaclasses. MAS-ML agent is represented by an agent without any additional stereotype. Organization, Environment, Planning, Plan and Perception are represented by new metaclasses. Therefore, Belief, a metaclass that was removed in iStar 2.0, was added as an intentional element again. We represented the stereotypes to represent of next-function, formulate-problem, formulate-goal and utility-function and action. The relationship *neededby* was extended to link beliefs and next-function tasks. The Cause/effect was included to connect perception and Action (*Task* metaclass) and connect next-

---

[2] www.cin.ufpe.br/~ler/iStar4rationalagents/metamodel&rules.

function and action (*Task* metaclass). Finally, we created a set of validation rules to analyze the well-formedness of the four kinds of agents and roles.

4.1 Representing the Extension Constructs in the Concrete Syntax

The representations of the extension concepts can be classified into three groups:

1. **Constructs represented by iStar constructs as proposed:** five domain concepts are represented by the iStar constructs. They are used to represent an agent being part of an organization, an agent inhabiting an environment, an organization inhabiting an environment, an agent playing a role in an organization which inhabits an environment and a dependency between an agent and an environment. Furthermore, we extended the *neededby* relationship to connect next-function and beliefs establishing that beliefs are needed by the next-function;

2. **Constructs represented by iStar constructs added with textual markers:** These constructs have a similar meaning of the iStar constructs and specialize them by textual markers. They are four stereotypes (<<simple-reflex>>, <<model-based-reflex>>, <<goal-based >> and <<utility-based>>) applied to agents or agent roles, <<action >> and the specific functions (<<next-function>>, <<formulate-problem>>, <<formulate-goal >> and <<utility-function>>) applied to task. When an action is represented inside the agent roles, it can be defined as a right (an action that can be executed) using the property {type='right'} or a duty (an action that should be executed) using the property {type='duty'}.

3. **Constructs represented by new graphical representations of iStar:** we found the Plan in an existing iStar extension and reused it. Four concepts (Environment, Organization, Perception and Planning) are represented by new symbols. Thus, the new symbols proposed to these four concepts were created using an experiment based on the work of Caire et al. [1]. We performed a five-step experiment with 152 participants. All steps of this experiment are available[3]. Figure 1 presents the final graphical representations of this experiment, used by the extension.

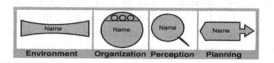

Fig. 1. Symbols related to environment, organization, perception and planning.

4.2 How to Use the Extension

The iStar SD model should be created to represent the MAS concepts. An agent can play a role, inhabit an environment and be part of an organization (Ownership). These relationships are represented by the iStar link participates-in. The dependencies between agents, roles, organizations and environment can be expressed too. Figure 2

---

[3] www.cin.ufpe.br/~ler/iStar4rationalagents/experiment-representations.

shows an agent playing a role (i), an agent being part of an organization (ii), an agent inhabiting an environment (iii), an organization inhabiting an environment (iv), an agent playing a role in an organization which inhabits an environment (v) and a dependency between an agent and an environment. We used simple-reflex agents and roles, these links can be used with all kinds of agents.

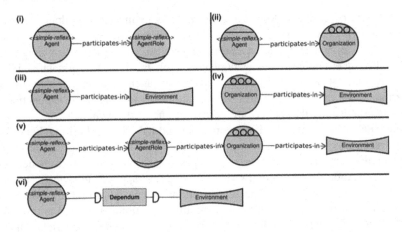

Fig. 2. Generic representations of new constructs in SD model.

Moreover, the SR model should be created to represent the internal details of the agents, roles, organizations and environments involved in the Multiagent System, and representing the relationship between them. The SD model is the starting point to the creation of this model. In our approach, we consider the modelling of the agents' intentional elements as a refinement of their internal elements, similar to the approach used by Mouratidis and Giorgini [10].

The boundaries of the agents should be detailed regarding their intentional elements. The kind of agent defined by MAS-ML is represented by an agent without any stereotype and its boundary is composed of goals, beliefs, plans and actions (i). In the reflex agents (Simple reflex (ii) and Model-based simple reflex (iii)), the perceptions and actions (and next-function in case of model-based reflex agents) should be related by the refinement link with the action as the source. Goals of the goal-based (iv) agents are decomposed on perceptions (which are decomposed on next-function) and planning (which are decomposed into actions). The same to utility-agents (v), but these ones have a utility-function related to the planning by an and-refinement. The beliefs are represented by a *neededby* link connecting a belief and next-function. Figure 3 presents an example of the usage of agents on an SR diagram.

The boundaries of roles related to goal-based and utility agents and kind of agent defined by MAS-ML should represent goals, beliefs and actions related to the role. The boundary of roles of model-based-reflex agents should contain beliefs and actions related to the role and the roles of simple-reflex agents should contain actions related to the role. The actions in roles related to agents should have the information about which of them are mandatory (duty) and which are optional (right). Figure 3 presents an

example of the usage of agents on SR diagram. In addition, environment and organization can be composed of the original iStar nodes and links, an example of environment and organization is presented in Fig. 3.

We created the pistar4rationalagents tool[4] to support the usage of our extension.

5   A MAS Support Programing Courses in Distance Education

We modelled a MOODLE MAS with our extension. The modeling of SD-extended diagram is available[5]. Figure 3 shows part of the SR diagram to MOODLE MAS. The complete version is available[6]. Additionally, the MAS presented in these models were designed at the architectural level, coded, tested and deployed at Brazilian Open University, and Universidade Estadual do Ceará.

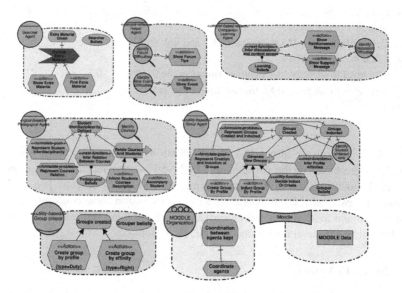

Fig. 3. Agents, agent role, organization and environment in iStar SR model to MOODLE.

6   Evaluation by Experienced Researchers

The purpose of this evaluation is to identify the point of view of the researchers in MAS about our extension by a survey [8]. The universe of this research consists of authors of papers of the last 5 editions of Brazilian events such as WESAAC,

---

[4] https://www.cin.ufpe.br/~ler/piStar4rationalagents/.

[5] www.cin.ufpe.br/~ler/iStar4rationalagents/sdmoodle.

[6] www.cin.ufpe.br/~ler/iStar4rationalagents/srmoodle.

AUTOSOFT and BRACIS. Thus, we contacted 164 researchers from 37 different universities/companies. We received a total of 22 responses from 13 universities and 3 companies. 9 mentioned having advanced knowledge on MAS, 9 intermediate knowledge and 4 emerging. The structure of this survey is available[7]. It was submitted between December 2018 and February 2019. Data of this survey is also available[8].

We compared the perception of the participants about the modelling of the MAS using iStar and the iStar extension. The extension improved the perception of the MAS constructs. We also analyzed the difficulty level perceived by the participants to identify the MAS entities and internal nodes and links. The extension reduced the difficulty level to identify MAS elements in about 50% (see Table 1).

Table 1. Comparative of correct identification and difficult level.

Criteria	Without extension	With extension
1. Correct identification of MAS entities (Agents, agent role, environment and organization)	47.12%	80.1%
2. Correct identification of MAS internal nodes and links (plan, planning, action, next-function...)	20.7%	62%
3. Difficulty level to identify MAS entities (mean -scale 0–10)	6.3	2.9
4. Difficulty level to identify MAS internal nodes and links (mean -scale 0–10)	7.5	3.8

The participants were also asked about the strong points and weaknesses of the approach. A great part of the participants (13/22–59%) recognized that the extension facilitates the identification of MAS entities and their internal elements. The weakness mentioned by two participants was that, with the extension, new concepts are represented in iStar and there is the need to learn and represent these elements in the models. We believe it is a general consequence of all extensions.

6.1 Threats to Validity

According to Kitchenham and Pfleeger [8], there are four validity aspects to consider: Criterion, Construct, Face and Content. **Criterion validity:** We did not find a previous quantitative study for this purpose. Thus, we could not compare this evaluation with previous ones. **Construct validity:** We created the survey with different kind of questions: Likert scale questions, measure effort, yes/no/maybe question, open questions and multiple-choice relation questions. Thus, it could confuse the execution of it by the participants. We mitigated this threat presenting an explanation of the kind of questions at the beginning of the survey. **Face validity:** We tested the survey with a computer science professor with experience in MAS. We can consider this previous

---

[7] https://www.cin.ufpe.br/∼ler/iStar4rationalagents/evaluationsurvey.

[8] www.cin.ufpe.br/∼ler/iStar4rationalagents/data.

evaluation a limitation because of the small number of participants (1). We mitigated this threat, however, by asking him to evaluate again after the corrections of his comments. **Content validity:** We consider the profile of the participants suitable for this evaluation since the majority of the participants (18/22) mentioned having advanced/intermediate expertise in MAS. However, there were not a great number of participants with expertise in modelling ($\sim 50\%$). We tried to mitigate this threat presenting iStar in part of the survey.

7 Conclusions

In this paper, we presented the main results of an approach to model MAS with rational agents in requirements level with an extended version of iStar. We followed PRISE, a process to conduct iStar extensions, during our proposal. We represented the constructs as a set of stereotypes and four new symbols proposed by an experiment similar to the presented by Caire et al. [1]. This approach is supported by piStar4rationalagents tool. We illustrated our proposal by modelling of a MAS with rational agents in a distance education course offered using MOODLE. We modeled a MAS with 5 different kinds of agents, agent roles, organization and environment. Finally, our proposal was evaluated by experienced MAS researchers/developers using a survey. We identified that the extension can ease the identification of these kinds of agents and their elements and can make the interpretation of the diagrams better than using standard iStar. The participants agreed that the proposal of an extension is useful to fill a lack of techniques to represent the MAS with rational agents, the representations of the constructs were considered good and the extension could be useful to model their next MAS.

Acknowledgments. The authors thank CNPq, CAPES, FACEPE and NOVA LINCS UID/CEC/04516/2019.

References

1. Caire, P., Genon, N., Heymans, P., Moody, D.: Visual notation design 2.0: Towards user comprehensible requirements engineering notations. In: RE 2013 (2013)
2. Gonçalves, E., Castro, J., Araujo, J., Heineck, T.: A Systematic Literature Review of iStar extensions. J. Syst. Softw. **137**, 1–33 (2018)
3. Gonçalves, E., et al.: MAS-ML 2.0: supporting the modelling of multi-agent systems with different agent architectures. J. Syst. Softw. **108**, 77–109 (2015)
4. Gonçalves, E., Heineck, T., Araújo, J., Castro, J.: A catalogue of iStar extensions, 21st Workshop on Requirements Engineering (2018)
5. Gonçalves, E., Monteiro, I., de Oliveira, M.A., Castro, J., Araujo, J.: Understanding what is important in iStar extensions proposals: the viewpoint of researchers. Requirements Eng. **24**, 55–84 (2019)
6. Gonçalves, E., Heineck, T., De Oliveira, L., Araujo, J., Castro, J.: PRISE tool: a tool to support the proposal of iStar extensions based on PRISE. In: 22nd Workshop on Requirements Engineering (2019)

7. Jennings, N.R.: Coordination techniques for distributed artificial intelligence. In: Foundations of Distributed Artificial Intelligence, pp. 187–210. Wiley (1996)
8. Kitchenham, B., Pfleeger, S.: Principles of survey research. Softw. Eng. Notes **27**(5), 17–20 (2002)
9. Lopes, Y.S., Cortés, M.I., Gonçalves, E., Oliveira, R.: JAMDER: JADE to multi-agent systems development resource. ADCAIJ **7**, 63 (2018)
10. Mouratidis, H., Giorgini, P.: Secure tropos: a security-oriented extension of the tropos methodology. IJSEKE **17**, 285–309 (2007)
11. Russell, S., Norvig, P.: Artificial Intelligence: A Modern Approach. Prentice Hall, Prentice Hall (2003)
12. Silveira, F.R.V., Campos, G.A.L., Cortes, M.I.: A problem-solving agent to teste rational agents: a case study with reactive agents. In: ICEIS 2014, Lisboa (2014)
13. Silva, V., Lucena, C.: From a conceptual framework for agents and objects to a multi-agent system modelling language. J. Auton. Agents MAS **9**(1–2), 145–189 (2004)
14. Yu, E. Modelling strategic relationships for process reengineering. PhD. Thesis in Computer Science, University of Toronto, Toronto (1995)

Author Index

T0183613

Printed in the United States
By Bookmasters